FLORIDA
Treasures

D1517902

A Reading/Language Arts Program

Program Authors

Dr. Donald R. Bear
University of Nevada, Reno
Reno, Nevada

Dr. Janice A. Dole
University of Utah
Salt Lake City, Utah

Dr. Jana Echevarria
California State University, Long Beach
Long Beach, California

Dr. Douglas Fisher
San Diego State University
San Diego, California

Dr. Vicki Gibson
Longmire Learning Center, Inc.
College Station, Texas

Dr. Jan E. Hasbrouck
Educational Consultant - J.H. Consulting
Seattle, Washington

Dr. Scott G. Paris
University of Michigan
Ann Arbor, Michigan

Dr. Timothy Shanahan
University of Illinois at Chicago
Chicago, Illinois

Dr. Josefina V. Tinajero
University of Texas at El Paso
El Paso, Texas

 Macmillan/McGraw-Hill

Contributors

Time Magazine, Accelerated Reader

learning through listening

Students with print disabilities may be eligible to obtain an accessible, audio version of the pupil edition of this textbook. Please call Recording for the Blind & Dyslexic at I-800-22I-4792 for complete information.

B

The McGraw-Hill Companies

Macmillan McGraw-Hill

Published by Macmillan/McGraw-Hill, of McGraw-Hill Education, a division of The McGraw-Hill Companies, Inc., Two Penn Plaza, New York, New York IOI2I.

Printed in the United States of America

3 4 5 6 7 8 9 07I/043 II I0 09 08

Program Authors

Dr. Donald R. Bear

University of Nevada, Reno
- Author of *Words Their Way* and *Words Their Way with English Learners*
- Director, E.L. Cord Foundation Center for Learning and Literacy

Dr. Douglas Fisher

San Diego State University
- Codirector, Center for the Advancement of Reading, California State University
- Author of *Language Arts Workshop: Purposeful Reading and Writing Instruction* and *Reading for Information in Elementary School*

Dr. Scott G. Paris

University of Michigan, Ann Arbor
- Chair, Graduate Program in Psychology, University of Michigan
- Principal Investigator, CIERA, 1997–2004

Dr. Janice A. Dole

University of Utah
- Investigator, IES Study on Reading Interventions
- National Academy of Sciences, Committee Member: Teacher Preparation Programs, 2005–2007

Dr. Vicki Gibson

- Owner and Director, Longmire Learning Center, Inc. College Station, Texas
- Author of *Differentiating Instruction: Grouping for Success*

Dr. Timothy Shanahan

University of Illinois at Chicago
- Member, National Reading Panel
- President, International Reading Association, 2006
- Chair, National Literacy Panel and National Early Literacy Panel

Dr. Jana Echevarria

California State University, Long Beach
- Author of *Making Content Comprehensible for English Learners: The SIOP Model*
- Principal Researcher, Center for Research on the Educational Achievement and Teaching of English Language Learners

Dr. Jan E. Hasbrouck

Educational Consultant
- Developed oral reading fluency norms for Grades 1–8
- Author of *The Reading Coach: A How-to Manual for Success*

Dr. Josefina V. Tinajero

University of Texas at El Paso
- Past President, NABE and TABE
- Coeditor of *Teaching All the Children: Strategies for Developing Literacy in an Urban Setting* and *Literacy Assessment of Second Language Learners*

Contributing Authors

Dr. Adria F. Klein

Professor Emeritus,
California State University,
San Bernardino

- President, California
  Reading Association, 1995
- Coauthor of *Interactive Writing* and *Interactive Editing*

Dr. Doris Walker-Dalhouse

Minnesota State University,
Moorhead

- Author of articles on multicultural literature and reading instruction in urban schools
- Cochair of the Ethnicity, Race, and Multilingualism Committee, NRC

Dolores B. Malcolm

St. Louis Public Schools
St. Louis, MO

- Past President, International Reading Association
- Member, IRA Urban Diversity Initiatives Commission
- Member, RIF Advisory Board

In memory of our esteemed
colleague and friend,
Dr. Steven A. Stahl

Program Consultants

Dr. Stephanie Al Otaiba

Assistant Professor,
College of Education
Florida State University

Dr. Susan M. Brookhart

Brookhart Enterprises LLC, Helena, MT
Coordinator of Assessment and
Evaluation
Duquesne University, Pittsburgh, PA

Kathy R. Bumgardner

Language Arts Instructional
Specialist
Gaston County Schools, NC

Dr. Connie R. Hebert

National Literacy Consultant
Lesley University
The ReadWrite Place
West Springfield, MA

Dr. Sharon F. O'Neal

Associate Professor,
College of Education
Texas State University–San Marcos

Dinah Zike

Dinah-Might Adventures, L.P.
San Antonio, TX

Florida Program Reviewers

Holly Bagwell
Reading Resource Specialist, K–5
Horizon Elementary
Broward County
Sunrise, FL

Janice Choice
Principal
Pinelock Elementary
Orange County
Orlando, FL

Dr. Lillian Cooper
Principal on Special Assignment
LA/Reading K–5
Miami-Dade County
Miami Springs, FL

Stacey Councill
Teacher, Grade 2
Manatee Elementary
Brevard County
Viera, FL

Michelle D'Intino
Academic Intervention
Specialist
Just Elementary
Hillsborough County
Tampa, FL

DeeAnna Durden
Teacher, Grade 2
Hogan-Spring Glen Elementary
Duval County
Jacksonville, FL

Mary Fischer
Reading Resource Specialist
K–5
Nob Hill Elementary
Broward County
Sunrise, FL

Sherri Goodwin
Reading Resource Teacher
Morgan Woods Elementary
Hillsborough County
Tampa, FL

Elaine Grohol
Elementary Instructional
Specialist
Osceola County
Kissimmee, FL

Deborah Jackson
Teacher, Grade 1
Citrus Elementary
Orange County
Ocoee, FL

Katy Kearson
Reading First Coach, Grades
K–3
Duval County
Jacksonville, FL

Pam LaRiviere
Reading/Curriculum Specialist
Grades K–5
Lehigh Elementary
Lee County
Lehigh Acres, FL

Robin Matthes
Principal
Hillcrest Elementary
Orange County
Orlando, FL

Lois Mautte
AP Schwarzkopf Elementary
Hillsborough County
Lutz, FL

Mary Mickel
Principal
Sabal Palm Elementary
Duval County
Jacksonville, FL

Joy Milner
Reading Specialist
Wesley Chapel Elementary
Pasco County
Wesley Chapel, FL

Carla Mosley
Reading First Coach, Grades K–3
Broward County
Fort Lauderdale, FL

Beth Nichols
Teacher, Kindergarten and First
Grade
Wesley Chapel Elementary
Pasco County
Wesley Chapel, FL

Melinda Ossorio
Reading Resource Specialist, K–5
Watkins Elementary
Broward County
Miramar, FL

Tara Taylor
Assistant Principal
Port Malabar Elementary
Brevard County
Palm Bay, FL

Blanca Villalobos
Teacher, Grade 5
Christina Eve Elementary
Miami-Dade County
Miami, FL

Harriet Waas
Teacher, Grade 4
Pineview Elementary School
Leon County
Tallahassee, FL

Robin White
Reading First Instructional
Specialist
Fulton Holland Educational
Center
Palm Beach County
West Palm Beach, FL

Deborah Wood
Reading Facilitator
Elementary Programs
Brevard County
Viera, FL

RESEARCH **Why It Matters**

Writing

Dr. Adria F. Klein

Writing rubrics that evaluate student writing can be a powerful tool. In order for a rubric to be purposeful, it is important to teach each aspect of the rubric so that the assessment proceeds logically from the instruction. Carefully teaching each component of the rubric will support students in learning to write, peer edit, and evaluate their own writing.

Checklists differ from rubrics in that they are most often answered by a yes-or-no question, help students understand what they are responsible for in the writing process, and should reflect what has been directly taught. Using various peer-review techniques during the writing process helps students build independence in their own work. The use of a checklist gives students guidelines for reviewing and revising their own and others' writing.

Best Practices

Effective writing instruction

- includes checklists to help students understand specific elements of a piece of writing

- helps students use a rubric to identify their efforts and improve their own writing

- sets procedures for peer editing

Professional Development

- **READING, YES! 4–6**
  Video Series: Module 8, *Written Language*

  Online Course: Accredited college course available at **www.macmillanmh.com**

- **TREASURES FOR TEACHERS**
  Video Series: *Writing*

References
- NCTE Beliefs About the Teaching of Writing. By the Writing Study Group of the NCTE Executive Committee, November 2004.
- Spandel, V. (2001). *Creating Writers Through 6—Trait Writing Assessment and Instruction*. NY: Addison, Wesley, Longman.
- Klein, A. F. (1998). "Assessment" in *The Best Practices in Teaching: Reading and Writing in the Elementary Classroom*. Tomkins, G. and Yopp, R. (eds.). NY: Allyn and Bacon.

Theme: Great Ideas

Planning the Unit

Using the Student Book

Wrapping Up the Unit

Additional Lessons and Resources

Main Selections

Unit Assessment

Unit 6 Planner

Theme: Great Ideas

pages 638J–667V

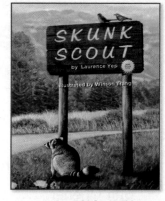

pages 668A–697V

	WEEK 1	WEEK 2
ORAL LANGUAGE • Listening, Speaking, Viewing	**Theme** Fairy Tales **Build Background**	**Theme** Camping Out **Build Background**
WORD STUDY • Vocabulary	**Vocabulary** FCAT *accompany, bridle, consented, delicacies, descended, despair, dismiss, intentions* FCAT Homophones	**Vocabulary** FCAT *bundle, coordination, ease, frustrated, fused, guaranteed, scenery, supervise* FCAT Use a Dictionary: Multiple-Meaning Words
• Phonics/Decoding	**Phonics** Greek Roots	**Phonics** Latin Roots
READING • Comprehension	**Comprehension** **Strategy:** Summarize FCAT **Skill:** Chronological Order	**Comprehension** **Strategy:** Monitor Comprehension FCAT **Skill:** Plot Development
• Fluency	**Fluency** Repeated Reading	**Fluency** Repeated Reading
• Leveled Readers/ELL Readers	**APPROACHING** *Graham the Kind-Hearted* **ON LEVEL** *Daisies in Winter* **BEYOND** *The Three Sisters* **ENGLISH LANGUAGE LEARNERS** *Flowers in Winter*	**APPROACHING** *A Visit to Grand Canyon National Park* **ON LEVEL** *A Visit to Grand Canyon National Park* **BEYOND** *A Visit to Grand Canyon National Park* **ENGLISH LANGUAGE LEARNERS** *The Amazing Grand Canyon*
LANGUAGE ARTS • Writing	**Writing** Eyewitness Account	**Writing** Expository
• Grammar	**Grammar** Adverbs	**Grammar** Adverbs that Compare
• Spelling	**Spelling** Words with Greek Roots	**Spelling** Words with Latin Roots

pages 698A–709V

pages 710A–735V

pages 736A–759V

Review and Assess

WEEK 3

Theme
Improving Lives

Build Background

Vocabulary
elementary, interact, physical, rigid, wheelchair

Context Clues

Phonics
Mythology

Comprehension
Strategy: Monitor Comprehension
Skill: Techniques of Persuasion

Fluency
Repeated Reading

APPROACHING
Everybody's a Star

ON LEVEL
Everybody's a Star

BEYOND
Everybody's a Star

ENGLISH LANGUAGE LEARNERS
The Special Olympics Story

Writing
Research Report

Grammar
Negatives

Spelling
Words from Mythology

WEEK 4

Theme
Balloon Flight

Build Background

Vocabulary
anchored, companion, dense, hydrogen, inflate, launched, particles, scientific
Word Parts: Greek Roots

Phonics
Number Prefixes

Comprehension
Strategy: Monitor Comprehension
Skill: Relevant Facts and Details

Fluency
Repeated Reading

APPROACHING
The Sky's the Limit

ON LEVEL
The Sky's the Limit

BEYOND
The Sky's the Limit

ENGLISH LANGUAGE LEARNERS
The Story of Flight

Writing
Persuasive

Grammar
Prepositions and Prepositional Phrases

Spelling
Number Prefixes

WEEK 5

Theme
Scientists at Work

Build Background

Vocabulary
biology, dormant, erupted, murky, observer, research, scoured, specimens
Word Parts: Latin and Greek Word Parts

Phonics
-able, -ible

Comprehension
Strategy: Summarize
Skill: Chronological Order

Fluency
Repeated Reading

APPROACHING
Searching for Cures

ON LEVEL
Searching for Cures

BEYOND
Searching for Cures

ENGLISH LANGUAGE LEARNERS
Science Finds Cures

Writing
Expository

Grammar
Sentence Combining

Spelling
Words with *-able* and *-ible*

WEEK 6

Sprial Review
Author's Purpose; Relevant Facts and Details; Chronological Order; Context Clues; Greek and Latin Roots; Primary Source

Writing Workshop
Expository

Unit 6 Assessment, 179–212

Comprehension
Chronological Order; Plot Development; Techniques of Persuasion; Relevant Facts and Details

Vocabulary Strategies
Homophones; Dictionary: Multiple-Meaning Words; Context Clues; Word Parts: Greek and Latin Roots

Text Features / Literary Elements / Study Skills
Venn Diagram; Photographs and Captions; Everyday Communications; Simile and Metaphor; Symbolism and Figurative Language

Grammar
Adverbs; Comparisons; Negatives; Prepositions and Prepositional Phrases; Sentence Combining

Writing
Expository

Fluency Assessment

Diagnose and Prescribe
Interpret Assessment Results

Theme: Great Ideas

Literature

Read-Aloud Anthology
Includes Plays for
Readers' Theatre

Student Edition

Leveled Readers

ELL Leveled Readers

**Classroom Library
Trade Books**

Teaching Support

Teacher's Edition

Transparencies

ELL Teacher's Guide

Teacher's Resource Book

**Dinah Zike
Foldables™**

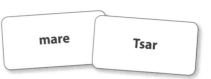

mare   Tsar

Vocabulary Cards

Class Management Tools

**Small Group
How-to Guide**

**Weekly
Contracts**

Rotation Chart

Student Practice

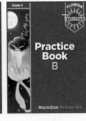

Grade 5
Practice Book A
Macmillan/McGraw-Hill

Grade 5
Practice Book O
Macmillan/McGraw-Hill

Grade 5
Practice Book B
Macmillan/McGraw-Hill

Grade 5
ELL Practice and Assessment
Macmillan/McGraw-Hill

| Approaching Level | On Level | Beyond Level | English Language Learners |

Leveled Practice

Phonics/Spelling PRACTICE BOOK
Annotated Teacher's Edition
Macmillan/McGraw-Hill

Grammar PRACTICE BOOK
Annotated Teacher's Edition
Macmillan/McGraw-Hill

Phonics/Spelling Practice Book　　**Grammar Practice Book**

Home-School Connection
Macmillan/McGraw-Hill

Home-School Connection
- Take-Home Stories
- Homework Activities

WORKSTATION FLIP CHART
Reading Grade 5
Macmillan/McGraw-Hill

WORKSTATION FLIP CHART
Word Study Grade 5
Macmillan/McGraw-Hill

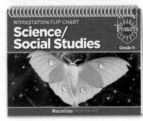

WORKSTATION FLIP CHART
Writing Grade 5
Macmillan/McGraw-Hill

WORKSTATION FLIP CHART
Science/Social Studies Grade 5
Macmillan/McGraw-Hill

Literacy Workstation Activities

FCAT Success!

Time For Kids FCAT Edition with Teacher's Manual

Time For Kids Articles on Transparencies

FCAT Test Prep and Practice

Questions in FCAT Format

Technology

 AUDIO CD
- Listening Library
- Fluency Solutions

 CD ROM
- Vocabulary PuzzleMaker
- Handwriting
- Instructional Navigator Interactive Lesson Planner
- Student Navigator
- Accelerated Reader Quizzes

www.macmillanmh.com
- Author/Illustrator Information
- Research and Inquiry Activities
- Vocabulary and Spelling Activities
- Oral Language Activities
- Computer Literacy
- Leveled Reader Database
- Florida Anchor Papers and Constructed Response Sample Responses

Professional Development

READING, YES!
- Videos
- Online Course

TREASURES FOR TEACHERS
- Videos

READING
Triumphs
AN INTERVENTION PROGRAM

Treasure Chest
FOR ENGLISH LANGUAGE LEARNERS

Also Available

Great Ideas **638E**

Screening, Diagnostic, and Placement Assessments

Screening

Use the Oral Reading Fluency passages on pages 40–51 in our **Screening, Diagnostic, Placement Assessment** book for screening.

Diagnostic Tools for Instructional Placement

For an individually administered Diagnostic, use the Informal Reading Inventory passages on pages 112–119 in our **Screening, Diagnostic, Placement Assessment** book.

For a group administered Placement Test, see pages 229–238 in our **Screening, Diagnostic, Placement Assessment** book.

Use the results from these assessments to determine the instructional levels of your students for differentiated instruction grouping.

Monitoring Progress

Ongoing Informal Assessments

- Daily Quick Check Observations
- Weekly Comprehension Check
- Weekly Fluency Practice Passages

Formal Assessments

- **Weekly Assessment**
- **Fluency Assessment**
- **Running Records**
- **Unit Assessment**
- **Benchmark Assessment**
- **ELL Practice and Assessment**
  Weekly Tests
  Unit Progress Test

Managing and Reporting

  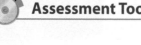 Assessment Online

 Instructional Navigator Interactive Lesson Planner
- All Teacher Edition Pages
- Electronic Lesson Planner
- Student Blackline Masters

Assessment Tool

FCAT Alignment

GRADE 5 UNIT 6 ASSESSED SKILLS	FCAT
COMPREHENSION STRATEGIES AND SKILLS	
• Strategies: Monitor Comprehension, Summarize	◆
• Skills: Chronological Order, Plot Development, Techniques of Persuasion, Relevant Facts and Details	◆
VOCABULARY STRATEGIES	
• Dictionary	◆
• Homophones	
• Context Clues	◆
• Word Parts	◆
TEXT FEATURES AND STUDY SKILLS	
• Venn diagram	◆
• Photographs and captions	◆
• Everyday communications	◆
GRAMMAR, MECHANICS, USAGE	
• Prepositions, prepositional phrases	◆
• Adverbs	◆
• Sentence combining	◆
• Adjectives vs adverbs	◆
• Correcting double negatives	◆
• Punctuation	◆
WRITING	
• Expository	

Unit 6 Opener

Theme Project
LA.5.5.2.1 Listen and speak to gain and share information

Build Background Write this theme statement on the board: *Great ideas may bring surprising results.* Ask: *What are some great ideas you've had for solving a problem? What are some great ideas for a new invention? What are some great ideas that didn't work out as expected?*

Research and Inquiry
Self-Selected Theme Project

Step 1 State the Problem and Identify Needed Information Ask students to think of a great idea to research, come up with their own hypothesis statement, and gather information based on the statement.

Step 2 Identify Resources for Finding Information Explain that students' topics can help them make a research plan and identify resources. Students researching great ideas of the past can examine world history books, public television programs, and Internet sources. Tell students to think creatively—and use multiple sources.

LA.5.6.2
Uses process for collection, processing, presentation of information

Step 3 Find the Information Using the library and a computer, have students find and interpret the sources they identified. They can use text features such as these to locate information within some sources: bold type, captions, headings and subheadings, diagrams, time lines, maps, charts, and illustrations.

LA.5.2.2.1
Locate and use information from text features
LA.5.6.2.1
Apply evaluative criteria

Step 4 Organize the Information Tell students to summarize their findings in the *L* column of their KWL charts. On a separate sheet of paper, have them write details, such as quotes and citations. (For information on citing sources, see the Research Strategy in the Unit 5 opener, page 514H.) Students may organize and write their expository or persuasive presentations using a compare/contrast, cause/effect, problem/solution, chronological order, (sequence) or description text structure.

LA.5.6.1.1
Organize information from multiple sources for performing a task

See the Unit Closer on pages 763K–763L for **Step 5: Create the Presentation** and **Step 6: Review and Evaluate.**

RESEARCH STRATEGIES
Scanning and Skimming

- When you scan a source, you move your eyes quickly over the page, looking for specific key words, phrases, or ideas.
- Scanning can help you tell if a source will answer your research question.
- Skimming takes a little longer. When you skim a source, you find the main ideas.
- Try skimming the first few paragraphs and the last one. That will show if the text gives information you can use.
- Skimming works well with tables, charts, and graphs.
- You may want to skim a source after you scan it.

Cross-Curricular Projects

LANGUAGE ARTS AND LITERATURE ACTIVITY:

FORM A BOOK CLUB LA.5.2.1.8 Explain changes in vocabulary of texts across historical periods

Have students form a book club to research and discuss great ideas in language and literature. Students can

- Look for examples of figurative language in fiction and nonfiction and identify word meanings that have changed over time.
- Look for differences and similarities in literature created in different places or times.
- Identify differences in formal and informal speech.
- Interact with the texts by asking questions, making comments, and marking favorite passages with self-stick notes.

SOCIAL STUDIES ACTIVITY: MAKE A POSTER LA.5.6.4.2 Determine appropriate digital tools for presenting a topic

Have students use electronic resources to research a social studies event. You may wish to assign a particular event, such as the American Civil War. Students can

- Find photographs, illustrations, and other graphics related to the event.
- Compare and contrast visual media for their purpose and effectiveness in portraying the event. Look for different points of view and discuss how visuals impact mood and emotion, influencing the viewer's understanding of the event.
- Present their findings in an oral report to inform—with visuals.

CHARACTER BUILDING–CITIZENSHIP

- While students are creating their posters, discuss how the events that they researched relate to citizenship.
- Point out that citizenship involves many things such as obeying laws, being a good neighbor, protecting the environment, and getting involved in community affairs.

LA.5.5.2.1
Listen and speak to gain and share information

For Technology **research** and **presentation** strategies see the Computer Literacy Lessons on pages 763I–763J.

DISCUSSION AND CONVERSATION GUIDELINES

Group Discussions

Remind students to

- Participate in group and panel discussions, share ideas, and use discussion techniques to reach an agreement. Take turns recording, facilitating, leading, participating, and listening.
- Share ideas, including the effectiveness of the group process, and give others a chance to share theirs.
- Adjust communication styles according to audience, purpose, and situation. Use rules of conversation, such as taking turns without dominating.
- Answer questions with information, details, or opinions.
- Ask questions to get ideas and information. Develop questioning techniques using who, what, when, where, and how.
- Accept and constructively respond to each other's ideas and opinions.

Weekly Theme: Fairy Tales

Week At A Glance

Whole Group

VOCABULARY
dismiss, intentions, despair, bridle, descended, accompany, delicacies, consented

FCAT Dictionary: Homophones

COMPREHENSION
Strategy: Summarize
FCAT Skill: Chronological Order

WRITING
FCAT Expository/Eyewitness Account

FCAT Social Studies
Government and the Citizen

Small Group Options

Differentiated Instruction for Tested Skills

The Golden Mare, the Firebird, and the Magic Ring
by Ruth Sanderson

Main Selection
Genre Fairy Tale

A Real Princess
by Tonya Schaeffer

Vocabulary/ Comprehension

Personal Choices
Learning Through Stories
by Carly Gray

Social Studies Link
Genre Nonfiction Article

Read-Aloud Anthology
• Listening Comprehension
• Readers' Theatre

FCAT Tested FCAT Benchmark

 Tested Skill for the Week

Sunshine State Standard

FCAT FCAT Benchmark

FCAT LEVELED READERS

GR Levels S–X

Genre Fairy Tale

- **Same Theme**
- **Same Vocabulary**
- **Same Comprehension Skills**

Approaching Level

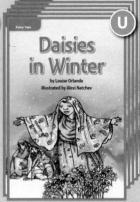

On Level

Beyond Level

English Language Leveled Reader

Sheltered Readers for English Language Learners

ELL Teacher's Guide also available

LEVELED PRACTICE

Practice Book A — Approaching
Practice Book O — On Level
Practice Book B — Beyond
ELL Practice and Assessment — ELL

INTERVENTION PROGRAM

- **Phonics and Decoding**
- **Comprehension**
- **Vocabulary**

Also available, *Reading Triumphs*, Intervention Program

CLASSROOM LIBRARY

Genre Nonfiction

Approaching — On Level — **Beyond**

Trade books to apply Comprehension Skills

FCAT Success!

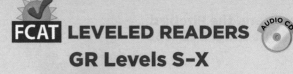

- **FCAT Edition**
- **Content Area Reading**

FCAT Test Preparation and Practice

FCAT Benchmark Assessments

FCAT Unit and Weekly Assessments

HOME-SCHOOL CONNECTION

- Family letters in English, Spanish, and Haitian Creole
- Take-Home Stories

CD ROM
Instructional Navigator
Interactive Lesson Planner

The Golden Mare, the Firebird, and the Magic Ring, 642–659

Integrated ELL Support Every Day

Whole Group

ORAL LANGUAGE
- **Listening**
- **Speaking**
- **Viewing**

WORD STUDY
- **Vocabulary**
- **Phonics/Decoding**

READING
- **Develop Comprehension**

- **Fluency**

LANGUAGE ARTS
- **Writing**

- **Grammar**

- **Spelling**

ASSESSMENT
- **Informal/Formal**

Turn the Page for
Small Group Lesson Plan

Day 1

Listening/Speaking/Viewing

❓ Focus Question What are the features of a fairy tale? Why do you think they are still popular after hundreds of years? LA.5.5.2

Build Background, 638
Read Aloud: "Yeh-Hsien," 639

Vocabulary LA.5.1.6.1

FCAT *dismiss, intentions, despair, bridle, descended, accompany, delicacies, consented,* 640

Practice Book A-O-B, 186

FCAT **Strategy: Dictionary:** Homophones, 641

Read "A Real Princess," 640–641 LA.5.1.6.1

Student Book

Comprehension, 641A–641B

✓ **Strategy:** Summarize
FCAT **Skill:** Chronological Order LA.5.1.7.5
Practice Book A-O-B, 187

Fluency Model Fluency, 639
Partner Reading, 638R LA.5.1.5

FCAT **Writing**

Daily Writing: Write about a goal or quest that could be the center of a fairy tale. Include a brief outline of the story.

Eyewitness Account, 667A

Grammar Daily Language Activities, 667I
✓ Adverbs, 667I
Grammar Practice Book, 161

✓ **Spelling** Pretest, 667G
Spelling Practice Book, 161–162 LA.5.1.4.1

Quick Check Vocabulary, 640
Comprehension, 641B

Differentiated Instruction 667M–667V

Day 2

Listening/Speaking

❓ Focus Question How does the mare help Alexi achieve his goals? LA.5.5.2.1

Vocabulary LA.5.1.6.3
Review Vocabulary Words, 642

Phonics/Decoding LA.5.1.4
Words with Greek Roots, 667E
Practice Book A-O-B, 192

Read *The Golden Mare, the Firebird, and the Magic Ring,* 642–659

Student Book

Comprehension, 642–661

✓ **Strategy:** Summarize
FCAT **Skill:** Chronological Order LA.5.1.7.5
Practice Book A-O-B, 188

Fluency Partner Reading, 638R LA.5.1.5

FCAT **Writing**

Daily Writing: Design a castle for a modern-day fairy tale. Describe how the modern castle would look and then draw it.

Eyewitness Account, 667A

Grammar Daily Language Activities, 667I
Adverbs, 667I
Grammar Practice Book, 162

Spelling Greek Roots, 667G
Spelling Practice Book, 163 LA.5.1.4.1

Quick Check Comprehension: 649, 659
Phonics, 667E

Differentiated Instruction, 667M–667V

Benchmarks

FCAT

Vocabulary	**Comprehension**	**Writing**	**Social Studies**
Vocabulary Words **Dictionary/ Homophones** LA.5.1.6.8 Use homophones to determine meaning	**Strategy:** Summarize **Skill:** Chronological Order LA.5.1.7.5 Identify text structure and explain how it impacts meaning	**Expository/ Eyewitness Account** LA.5.4.2.1 Write in a variety of expository forms	**Government and the Citizen** SS.C.2.2.2.5.1 Extends and refines understanding of personal and civic responsiblity

Turn the Page for **Small Group Options** →

Day 3

Listening/Speaking

?Focus Question Explain the similarities and differences between Alexi's situation in the story and Prince Vincent's situation in "A Real Princess."

Summarize, 661 LA.5.5.2.1

Vocabulary LA.5.1.6.3

Review Words in Context, 667C
FCAT **Strategy:** Dictionary: Homophones, 667D
Practice Book A-O-B, 191
Phonics Decode Multisyllabic Words 667E
LA.5.1.4

Read *The Golden Mare, the Firebird, and the Magic Ring*, 642–659

Student Book

Comprehension

Comprehension Check, 661
FCAT
Skill: Plot Development, 661B

Fluency Repeated Reading, 661A
Partner Reading LA.5.1.5
Practice Book A-O-B, 189

FCAT Writing

Daily Writing: Write a fairy tale in which you replace the royal characters with people in today's society. Use descriptive details.

Writer's Craft: Voice, 667A
Eyewitness Account, 667B LA.5.4.2.1

Grammar Daily Language Activities, 667I
Using *Good* and *Well*, 667J
Grammar Practice Book, 163

Spelling Greek Roots, 667H
Spelling Practice Book, 164 LA.5.1.4.1

Quick Check Fluency, 661A

Differentiated Instruction 667M–667V

Day 4

Listening/Speaking/Viewing

?Focus Question In *The Golden Mare, the Firebird, and the Magic Ring*, what lesson does the Tsar learn? How is this lesson connected to personal or civic responsibilty?
Expand Vocabulary: Fairy Tales, 667F LA.5.5.2

Vocabulary LA.5.1.6

Content Vocabulary: *responsible, civic, moral,* 662
Homophones, 667D
Apply Vocabulary to Writing, 667F

Read "Personal Choices: Learning Through Stories", 662–665

Student Book

Comprehension

Social Studies: Nonfiction Article
FCAT
Text Features: Venn Diagram, 662
Practice Book A-O-B, 190

Fluency Partner Reading, 638R LA.5.1.5

FCAT Writing

Daily Writing: In fairy tales, people are often transformed into animals. Write a brief essay explaining what a character can learn from this.

Writing Trait: Voice, 667B
Eyewitness Account, 667B LA.5.4.2.1

Grammar Daily Language Activities, 667I
Adverbs, 667J
Grammar Practice Book, 164

Spelling Greek Roots, 667H
Spelling Practice Book, 165 LA.5.1.4.1

Quick Check Vocabulary, 667D

Differentiated Instruction 667M–667V

Day 5

Review and Assess

Listening/Speaking/Viewing

?Focus Question What order of events is common to most fairy tales? LA.5.5.2.1
Speaking and Listening Strategies, 667A

Vocabulary LA.5.1.6.1

Spiral Review: Vocabulary Game, 667F

Read Self-Selected Reading, 638R LA.5.2.2.5

Student Book

Comprehension

Connect and Compare, 665
LA.5.2.1.5

Fluency Practice, 661A
Partner Reading, 638R LA.5.1.5

FCAT Writing

Daily Writing: Describe an object you own. What special power could it have in a fairy tale?

Eyewitness Account, 667B LA.5.4.2.1

Grammar Daily Language Activities, 667I
Adverbs, 667J
Grammar Practice Book, 165–166

Spelling Posttest, 667H
Spelling Practice Book, 166 LA.5.1.4.1

FCAT Weekly Assessment, 309–320

Differentiated Instruction 667M–667V

Differentiated Instruction

What do I do in small groups?

Teacher-Led Small Groups

Literacy Workstations

Independent Activities

Focus on Skills

 Skills Focus → Use your **Quick Check** observations to guide additional instruction and practice.

Phonics
Greek Roots

 Vocabulary
Words: descended, bridle, dismiss, despair, delicacies, accompany, intentions, consented
FCAT **Strategy:** Homophones/Recognize Homophones

Comprehension
Strategy: Summarize
FCAT **Skill:** Chronological Order

FCAT **Fluency**

Suggested Lesson Plan

CD ROM
Instructional Navigator
Interactive Lesson Planner

	DAY 1	**DAY 2**
Approaching Level • **Additional Instruction/Practice** • **Tier 2 Instruction**	Fluency, 667N Vocabulary, 667N Comprehension, 667O	Phonics, 667M Vocabulary, 667O Leveled Reader Lesson, 667P • Vocabulary • Comprehension
On Level • **Practice**	Vocabulary, 667Q Leveled Reader Lesson, 667R • Comprehension **ELL** Leveled Reader, 667U–667V	Leveled Reader Lesson, 667R • Comprehension • Vocabulary
Beyond Level • **Extend**	Vocabulary, 667S Leveled Reader Lesson, 667T • Comprehension	Leveled Reader Lesson, 667T • Comprehension • Vocabulary

For intensive intervention see **READING Triumphs**

Small Group Options

Focus on Leveled Readers

Leveled Reader Library

Levels S–X

Apply **FCAT** skills and strategies while reading appropriate leveled books.

Approaching — *Graham the Kind-Hearted* by Lauren Oliver, illustrated by Alexi Natchev (S)

On Level — *Daisies in Winter* by Louise Orlando, illustrated by Alexi Natchev (U)

Beyond — *The Three Sisters* by Louise Orlando, illustrated by Alexi Natchev (X)

ELL — *Flowers in Winter* by Louise Orlando, illustrated by Alexi Natchev

Additional Leveled Reader Resources

LOG ON

Leveled Reader Database

Go to **www.macmillanmh.com**

Search by

- Comprehension Skill
- Content Area
- Genre
- Text Feature
- Guided Reading Level
- Reading Recovery Level
- Lexile Score
- Benchmark Level

Subscription also available.

Day 3

Phonics, 667M
Fluency, 667N
Vocabulary, 667O
Leveled Reader Lesson, 667P
- Comprehension

Fluency, 667Q
Vocabulary, 667Q
Leveled Reader Lesson, 667R
- Comprehension

Fluency, 667S
Vocabulary, 667S
Leveled Reader Lesson, 667T
- Comprehension
ELL Use Graphic Organizers, 667S

Day 4

Phonics, 667M
Leveled Reader Lesson, 667P
- Comprehension
ELL Skill: Chronological Order

Study Skill, 667Q
Leveled Reader Lesson, 667R
- Comprehension

Study Skill, 667S
Leveled Reader Lesson, 667T
- Comprehension

Day 5

Fluency, 667N
Leveled Reader Lesson, 667P
- Make Connections Across Texts

Fluency, 667Q
Leveled Reader Lesson, 667R
- Make Connections Across Texts

Fluency, 667S
Self-Selected Reading, 667T

Managing the Class

What do I do with the rest of my class?

- Teacher-Led Small Groups
- Independent Activities
- Literacy Workstations

Class Management Tools

My To-Do List
✔ Put a check next to the activities you complete.

Reading
☐ Practice fluency
☐ Choose a fairy tale to read

Word Study
☐ Analyze words with Greek roots
☐ Match homophones

Writing
☐ Write an eyewitness account
☐ Write a "Be-Careful-What-You-Wish-For" story

Science
☐ Research an old wives' tale
☐ Discuss any scientific basis for your tale

Social Studies
☐ Compare two Cinderella tales
☐ Discuss why Cinderella tales are so popular

Leveled Readers
☐ Write About It!
☐ Content Connection

Technology
☐ Vocabulary Puzzlemaker
☐ Fluency Solutions
☐ Listening Library
☐ www.macmillanmh.com

Independent Practice
☐ Practice Book, 186–192
☐ Grammar Practice Book, 161–166
☐ Spelling Practice Book, 161–166

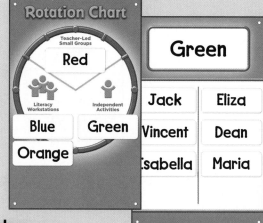

Rotation Chart

Teacher-Led Small Groups

Red

Literacy Workstations — Independent Activities

Blue   Green

Orange

Green

Jack	Eliza
Vincent	Dean
Isabella	Maria

Includes:
- How-to Guide
- Rotation Chart
- Weekly Contracts

Hands-on activities for reinforcing weekly skills

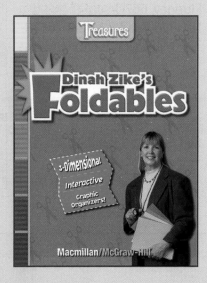

Fish	Frogs
habitat	habitat
food	insects
prey	prey
enemies	enemies

Eight-Tab Foldable

Word	Synonym	Antonym	Prefix or Suffix
normal	typical	unusual	normally

Folded Chart

Independent Activities

FCAT LEVELED READERS

For Repeated Readings and Literacy Activities

Approaching

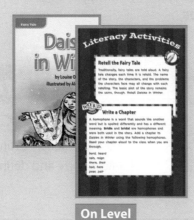
On Level

ELL

Beyond

LEVELED PRACTICE

Skills: Vocabulary, Chronological Order, Fluency, Homophones, Venn Diagrams

Practice Book A
Approaching

Practice Book O
On Level

Practice Book B
Beyond

ELL Practice and Assessment
ELL

Technology

ONLINE INSTRUCTION www.macmillanmh.com

- Meet the Author/Illustrator

- Computer Literacy Lessons

- Research and Inquiry Activities

- Oral Language Activities

- Vocabulary and Spelling Activities

- Leveled Reader Database

LISTENING LIBRARY
Recordings of selections
- Main Selections
- Leveled Readers
- ELL Readers
- Intervention Anthology

FLUENCY SOLUTIONS
Recorded passages for modeling and practicing fluency

VOCABULARY PUZZLEMAKER
Activities providing multiple exposures to vocabulary, spelling, and high-frequency words including crossword puzzles, word searches, and word jumbles

Turn the page for Literacy Workstations.

Managing the Class

Literacy Activities
Collaborative Learning Activities

Reading

Objectives

- Read with a partner for smoothness and understanding
- Practice fluency with Readers Theatre; offer corrective feedback
- Select literature for reading enjoyment
- Keep a personal reading log, reflecting on gains and accomplishments

Word Study

Objectives

- Use a dictionary to find words with Greek roots
- Recognize and define homophones

LA.5.1.5 Read orally with accuracy, appropriate rate, and expression

Reading — Fluency
20 Minutes

- With a partner read aloud the selection on page 189 of your Practice Book.
- Practice reading until you and your partner read the selection quickly and smoothly with "one voice."
- Before you begin you may want to listen to the passage on the audio disc.

Extension
- Listen to another pair and offer corrective feedback.
- **Readers Theatre**: Practice fluency with the play 'Round the World with Nellie Bly.

Things you need:
- Practice Book
- 'Round the World with Nellie Bly, page 207, Read Aloud Anthology

Fluency Solutions
Listening Library

51

LA.5.1.6.11 Use roots and affixes derived from Greek to determine meaning

Word Study — Greek Roots
20 Minutes

- Many English words are based on Greek roots. Some examples of these Greek roots are *auto*, from the Greek word meaning "self, same"; *photo*, from the Greek word meaning "light"; and *tele*, from the Greek word meaning "far away."
- Use a dictionary to find words built on each of these Greek roots. Explain how each English word relates to its Greek root.

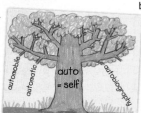

Extension
- Draw a Greek root tree. Write one Greek root and its meaning on the trunk, and then write three to five English words formed from the Greek root on the tree's branches.

Things you need:
- paper and pen or pencil
- markers or crayons
- dictionary

For additional vocabulary and spelling games, go to www.macmillanmh.com

51

LA.5.2.1.9 Select age- and ability- appropriate fiction materials to read

Reading — Independent Reading
20 Minutes

- Read a fairy tale with which you are not familiar. How is this fairy tale different from other fairy tales you have read? How is this fairy tale the same?
- Make a list of things that all fairy tales seem to have in common.

Extension
- Retell the fairy tale you read to a partner. Include as many details as you can remember.
- Have your partner retell a tale to you. Compare lists of the ideas common to all tales to see if you agree.

Things you need:
- library book
- paper and pen or pencil

For more book titles about fairy tales, go to the Author/Illustrator section of www.macmillanmh.com

52

LA.5.1.6.8 Use homophones to determine meanings of words

Word Study — Homophones
20 Minutes

- Write a word on one note card and its homophone on another card. Continue writing words until you have five pairs.
- Combine your cards with a partner's cards. Shuffle. Place the cards facedown in rows and columns.
- Taking turns with your partner, turn over pairs of cards. When you get a match, you must define each of the words to collect the cards. Whoever has the most cards at the end of the game wins.

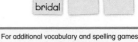

Extension
- Combine your cards with another pair's cards and play the game again.

Things you need:
- note cards
- dictionary
- pen or pencil

For additional vocabulary and spelling games, go to www.macmillanmh.com

Vocabulary PuzzleMaker

52

Literacy Workstations

Writing

Objectives

- Write an eyewitness account
- Write a fairy tale with an interesting beginning that develops a central conflict and has an ending that resolves the conflict

Content Literacy

Objectives

- Write a paragraph based on research
- Compare and contrast fairy tales from different cultures
- Read and research topics to satisfy personal, academic, and social needs

---

LA.5.4.1 Student demonstrates creative writing

Writing — Writing as a Witness
20 Minutes

 Write an eyewitness account of an event that happened or could happen in your neighborhood that would make a good fairy tale.

- Suppose that you are an observer across the street, a reporter, or a crossing guard—anyone who might watch an event or a series of events and be able to describe them. Describe how you watched a modern fairy tale unfold.

Extension

- Read your story to a partner and give each other feedback.
- Make your tale part of a class collection called "Fairy Tales Today."

Things you need:
- paper and pen or pencil

51

LA.5.6.2 Student uses a systematic research process

Science — Science in Fairy Tales
20 Minutes

- "Old wives' tales" are popular sayings or beliefs that often have no basis in fact. For example, one tale says that if you touch a frog you will get warts, though there is no basis in science for this belief.
- Use the Internet or library to research examples of old wives' tales. Choose one and then do research to see if there is any science behind the belief.
- Write a paragraph on your findings.

Extension

- Exchange paragraphs with a partner. Discuss what old beliefs had a basis in science and which did not.

Things you need:
- library or access to the Internet
- paper and pen or pencil

51

LA.5.4.1.1 Write narratives that establish situation and plot

Writing — A Modern Fairy Tale
20 Minutes

- Fairy tales are often about wishes that come true but bring about disaster instead of good fortune. Write a "Be Careful What You Wish For" story in which a character's wish comes true and makes the character regret the wish.
- The character should learn a lesson from the experience. What is the lesson?
- Decide on a sequence of events before you start writing. Also give the narrator a clear voice.

Extension

- Change the ending of your "wish" story. Have the wish bring everything the character hopes for.

Things you need:
- paper and pen or pencil

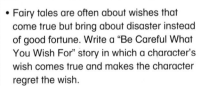
Three Wishes

52

LA.5.6.2 Use process for collection, processing, presentation of information

Social Studies — Fairy Tales and Culture
20 Minutes

- The story of Cinderella is known all over the world in different forms. Research and compare Cinderella tales from two different cultures.
- Use a Venn diagram to show how the tales are alike and how they are different.

Extension

- Make a list of five elements that are common to all the different Cinderella stories you found. Why do you think Cinderella is so popular across cultures? Discuss this with a partner.

Things you need:
- paper and pen or pencil
- library or access to the Internet

Cinderella Around the World

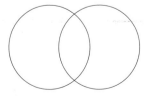 Internet Research and Inquiry Activity
Students can find more facts at www.macmillanmh.com

52

ORAL LANGUAGE
- Build Background
- Read Aloud
- Expand Vocabulary

FCAT VOCABULARY
- Teach Words in Context
- Dictionary: Homophones

COMPREHENSION
- **Strategy:** Summarize
- FCAT **Skill:** Chronological Order

SMALL GROUP OPTIONS
- Differentiated Instruction, pp. 667M–667V

638

Oral Language

Build Background

LA.5.5.2.1
Listen to gain and share information

ACCESS PRIOR KNOWLEDGE

Share the following information:

The brothers Jakob and Wilhelm Grimm spent years interviewing people to collect stories during the 1800s in Germany. Today, Grimms' fairy tales can be read in many languages.

LA.5.5.2.1
Listen and speak to gain and share information

TALK ABOUT FAIRY TALES

Discuss the weekly theme. Ask:

What are your favorite fairy tales, and why do you like them?

 FOCUS QUESTION Have a volunteer read aloud "Talk About It" on **Student Book** page 639 and describe the illustration. Ask:

What are some other creatures in fairy tales?

ENGLISH LANGUAGE LEARNERS

 Access for All

Beginning Name and Repeat Point to items as you describe the picture, and have students point and repeat as they are able: *This is a dragon. A dragon has claws. A dragon has teeth.* Ask, *Are dragons friendly? Are dragons real? How do you know?*

Intermediate Activate Prior Knowledge Help students use vocabulary to describe the dragon: *wild, scary, powerful, magical.* Write names or examples of fairy tales. Ask, *What fairy tales do you know that have dragons or other magical animals? Describe the animals. How are they important in the story?*

Advanced Elaborate Complete the Intermediate task. Model how to use more descriptive and complex sentence structures by restating what students say.

Talk About It

What are the features of a fairy tale? Why do you think fairy tales are still popular after hundreds of years?

LOG ON Find out more about fairy tales at **www.macmillanmh.com**

Fairy Tales

639

Picture Prompt

Look at the picture and write a description of the importance of the colors here. What does red usually mean? Why are the clouds pink?

 **Technology**

For an extended lesson plan and Web site activities for **oral language development**, go to **www.macmillanmh.com**

Read Aloud Read "Yeh-Hsien"

LA.5.2.1.1
Demonstrate knowledge of characteristics of genres

GENRE: Fairy Tale
Review features of a fairy tale:

- a story with imaginary characters and magical elements

- has a plot with conflict between good and bad

Read Aloud pages 120–123

LA.5.1.6.2
Listen to familiar text

LISTENING FOR A PURPOSE

As you read "Yeh-Hsien" in the **Read-Aloud Anthology,** ask students to identify their purpose for listening. Students should be ready to discuss the conflict, and summarize the fairy tale. Choose from among the teaching suggestions.

Fluency Ask students to listen carefully as you read aloud, paying attention to your phrasing, expression, and tone of voice.

LA.5.1.6.2
Listen to and discuss familiar text

RESPOND TO THE FAIRY TALE

Discuss how good triumphs over bad. Ask students to explain how "Yeh-Hsien" resembles or differs from the Cinderella story they know.

Expand Vocabulary

LA.5.1.6
Student develops grade-appropriate vocabulary

Have students choose several words from the selection. Students can use these words to write fairy tales of their own. Encourage students to share their fairy tales with the class. They may wish to analyze events or issues in their tales by role playing short scenes from the tales that involve familiar situations or emotions.

Vocabulary

LA.5.1.6.1
Use new vocabulary taught directly

FCAT

LA.5.1.6.3
Use context clues

TEACH WORDS IN CONTEXT

Use the following routine:

Routine

Define: If you **dismiss** someone from a job, you fire that person.

Example: The manager decided to dismiss the lazy worker.

Ask: What is another way that *dismiss* is used? MULTIPLE MEANING

- **Intentions** are plans to act in a certain way. Michael has intentions to get up early and exercise. Tell about a time when you had good intentions. DESCRIPTION

- **Despair** is lack of all hope. At the end of the eighth inning, the team gave up in despair. How might you go about helping someone in despair? PRIOR KNOWLEDGE

- The straps that fit around a horse's head and guide the horse are called the **bridle.** Mariah longed for a matching saddle and bridle. How does a bridle help control a horse? EXPLANATION

LA.5.1.6.8
Use antonyms to determine meaning

- **Descended** means to have moved from a higher place to a lower one. We descended the stairs to the basement. What is an antonym of *descended*? ANTONYM

LA.5.1.6.8
Use synonyms to determine meaning

- **Accompany** means to go with someone. Tim plans to accompany the girls to the movie. What is a synonym of *accompany*? SYNONYM

- **Delicacies** are rare and delicious foods. Some people think fish eggs and goose liver are delicacies. Name two foods that you consider delicacies. EXAMPLE

- If you **consented** to do something, you gave permission or agreed to it. Rachel's parents consented to let her

Access for All

Vocabulary

dismiss	descended
intentions	accompany
despair	delicacies
bridle	consented

FCAT **Homophones**

Homophones are words that sound the same but have different spellings and meanings. For example, the homophones *bridle* and *bridal* sound alike but have very different meanings.

A Real Princess

by Tonya Schaeffer

Once upon a time there was a prince named Vincent. He was about to turn 30 years old. This was an important age. If he didn't marry a princess by his birthday, the king's advisors would **dismiss** him from the court. They would send the prince away, and he would never be able to become king.

Prince Vincent's **intentions** did not include losing the crown. However, over the years, he had broken the heart of every princess from kingdoms near and far. Now he felt **despair** at finding a real princess to wed. Prince Vincent had lost all hope.

"What will I do?" he asked his mother. "It's not my fault that there are no princesses left."

The queen rolled her eyes. "It's your fault you've treated so many princesses so badly," she snapped back.

640

go on the trip. How is *consented* similar to and different from *allowed*?

COMPARE AND CONTRAST

Quick Check

Do students understand word meanings?

During **Small Group Instruction**

If No → **Approaching Level**
Vocabulary, p. 667N

If Yes → **On Level** Options, pp. 667Q–667R

Beyond Level Options, pp. 667S–667T

ELL   **Access for All**

Personalize and Write
For the word *consented,* write: *The principal consented when the students asked to go on the field trip.* Have students offer examples of situations that require consent. Write the examples in sentence form on the board. Write the word *despair* on the board. Ask students to offer synonyms for the word *despair.* Discuss and list reasons that someone might feel despair.

Just then a young lady approached the castle. Her **bridle** had broken. The harness would not go over her horse's nose.

The girl entered the great hall after she **descended** from the great staircase. She introduced herself as Princess Araya from Zelnorm. When Prince Vincent saw her torn and muddy clothes, he sighed. "This cannot be the princess who will solve my problem," he said to his mother. "In fact, I doubt she's a princess at all," he said.

The queen thought for a moment. "I know how to find out," she said. "However, if it turns out she *is* a princess, you must promise to marry her."

"Done!" Prince Vincent said. He was sure his mother was wrong.

Now the queen had a plan. First, she asked a servant to **accompany** Araya to the dining room. There the princess was fed rare **delicacies** from faraway lands prepared by the royal chef. Then the queen gave orders to get the best room ready.

"I want seven feather-filled mattresses on the bed," she demanded. "Place a small pebble at the bottom of the pile. Only a true princess will be able to feel it."

The next morning the queen asked Araya how she had slept.

"I didn't sleep at all!" Araya said. "I saw a homeless mother and child standing by the castle gate, so I took them two mattresses. When I saw other needy townfolk nearby, I gave away the other mattresses. My father, King Paul, will repay you."

The queen was speechless. Prince Vincent, however, was not. He finally saw the real beauty of Princess Araya and asked her to be his wife. She **consented** to his request, and the two of them became the kindest rulers in all the land.

Reread for **Comprehension**

Summarize

FCAT **Chronological Order** Chronological order refers to the time order or sequence in which **events** or actions occur. A Sequence Chart helps you summarize information by first listing events or actions in the order they take place. Use your Sequence Chart as you reread the selection to help you summarize events chronologically.

Event
↓
↓

641

On Level Practice Book O, page 186

A. Select the correct word from the choices in parentheses. Then write the correct word on the line provided.

1. The princess (descended / described) the stairs to meet the prince in the hall. __descended__

2. No princess was willing to (autograph / accompany) Prince Vincent down the aisle. __accompany__

3. If the prince did not marry, the king would (despair / dismiss) him from the kingdom. __dismiss__

4. Prince Vincent was in (despair / delight), and his future looked hopeless. __despair__

5. The horse's (huntsman / bridle) was broken, and the harness would not fit. __bridle__

6. The queen welcomed the princess as her guest and served her (delicacies / intentions) from different nations. __delicacies__

7. The prince told the queen about his (decorations / intentions) to marry the princess. __intentions__

8. The princess (dismissed / consented) to his proposal, and they lived happily ever after. __consented__

B. Use two vocabulary words to write a sentence for each. Then underline the vocabulary word.

9. The avalanche _descended_ quickly down the mountain.

10. The food festival had many _delicacies_ from all around the world.

Possible responses provided above.

★ **Approaching Practice Book A,** page 186

◆ **Beyond Practice Book B,** page 186

Vocabulary

STRATEGY
DICTIONARY

LA.5.1.6.8
Use homophones to determine meaning

LA.5.1.6.10
Determine meanings of words using a dictionary

Homophones Remind students that homophones are words that sound alike but have different spellings and meanings. For example, *sail* and *sale* are homophones. To confirm the meaning of a homophone, students should use context clues as well as a dictionary.

Display these sentences: *The groom put the bridle and saddle on the horse. The bridal party had a large celebration after the marriage ceremony.*

Have students identify the two words that are homophones. (*bridle* and *bridal*) Have them predict the meanings of the homophones using the context. Then have them look up the words in a dictionary to determine a more precise meaning.

Ask students to look at the last paragraph on page 641 and find homophones for the words *reel, knot, too,* and *inn.* (*real, not, to, two, in*)

LA.5.1.6.3
Use context clues

Read "A Real Princess"

As you read "A Real Princess" with students, ask them to identify clues that reveal the meanings of the highlighted words. Tell students they will read these words again in *The Golden Mare, the Firebird, and the Magic Ring.*

Objectives

- Summarize important ideas, events, and details
- Use academic language: *sequence of events, chronological order*
- Identify chronological order of events in a selection

Materials

- Comprehension Transparencies 26a and 26b
- Graphic Organizer Transparency 26
- Practice Book, p. 187

FCAT Skills Trace

Chronological Order

Introduce	71B
Practice / Apply	641A–B, 642–659, 739A–B, 740–751; Practice Book 187–188, 215–216
Reteach / Review	163B; 283B; 6670–P, R, T; 731B; 7590–P, R, T
Assess	Weekly Tests; Unit 6 Test; Benchmark Tests A, B
Maintain	641A–B, 739A–B; Practice Book 187–188, 215–216

ELL / Access for All

Retell/Model As students reread the selection, have them pause at times and retell what they have read. Ask, *Is this the next important event in the story? Why or why not? Explain your thinking.* Help students as needed.

Reread for
Comprehension

LA.5.1.7
Use strategies to comprehend text

STRATEGY
SUMMARIZE

Remind students that to **summarize** means to state the most important events or ideas in a selection. Students should distinguish between significant (major) details and minor details, as well as relevant and irrelevant information. As a strategy, summarizing can help readers understand what they have read because they have to identify what the selection is about. Then they select the most important ideas, events, and details, and restate them in their own words.

SKILL
CHRONOLOGICAL ORDER

LA.5.2.1.2
Locate and analyze elements of plot structure

EXPLAIN

- The time order in which events in a fiction story take place is called sequence. Understanding the sequence of events in a story helps readers identify and remember key events.

Transparency 26a

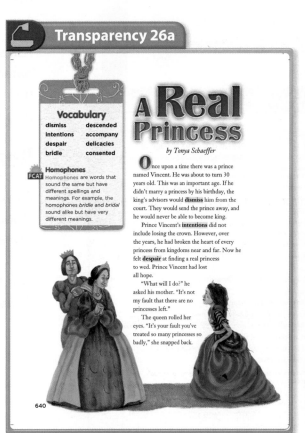

Transparency 26b

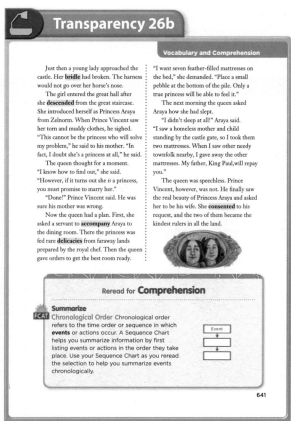

Student Book pages 640–641 available on Comprehension Transparencies 26a and 26b

- The events in a story may be presented in **chronological order,** as they happen in real life. Some narratives unfold in reverse order, from end to beginning. Others interrupt the chronological order and tell events in a sequence that switches from the present to the past and then back to the present again. When authors interrupt the chronological order of events to bring up a past event, they are using a device called flashback.

- Good readers look for clue words such as *once upon a time, over the years, now, just then, when, the next morning,* and *finally* to follow the sequence of events in a story. Placing events in chronological order helps readers remember the story and to understand how the author developed the plot.

LA.5.2.1.2
Locate and analyze elements of plot structure

MODEL

Read the first few paragraphs of "A Real Princess" from **Student Book** page 640.

Think Aloud The story begins with Prince Vincent looking for a princess to marry. However, I notice that this is not the first actual event the author describes in the story. I see that Prince Vincent has dated all of the princesses in the land already and treated them badly.

GUIDED PRACTICE

- Begin the Sequence Chart on **Transparency 26** with the first event in the narrative. (Prince Vincent needs to marry by his thirtieth birthday.)

- Fill in the next item together. Help students identify the chronological order of events in the story.

APPLY

Have students reread the rest of the story and complete the Sequence Chart. Ask students to discuss why the author does not relate story events in strict chronological order.

Transparency 26

The prince needs to marry a princess by his thirtieth birthday, or the court will dismiss him.

↓

Princess Araya, wearing torn and muddy clothes, arrives at the castle. The prince doubts that Araya is a princess. The queen asks the prince whether he will marry Araya if the queen can prove that Araya is a princess. The prince agrees.

↓

Araya is sent to a bed of seven feather mattresses. The queen orders that a pebble be placed under the seventh mattress to test Araya's royal blood. Instead of sleeping, Araya gives the mattresses away to poor people. The prince sees her true worth and agrees to marry her.

Graphic Organizer Transparency 26

FCAT Success!

Test Prep and Practice with Chronological Order, pages 65–96

■ **On Level Practice Book O,** page 187

The sequence of events is the order in which things happen in a story. Determining the **chronological order** of events can help you summarize the action of a story.

Place the correct number for the chronological order of events in the left column next to the event described in the right column.

After Alexi spared the life of the Golden Mare, the horse became devoted to Alexi. Alexi became a huntsman for the Tsar. As his first order of business, Alexi captured the Firebird. Next, he asked Alexi to find Yelena the Fair so she could become his wife. Alexi persuaded Yelena to meet the Tsar. After Yelena discovered the Tsar's intention, she told the Tsar she would not get married without her grandmother's ring. The Golden Mare volunteered to fetch the ring from the lake. Yelena convinced the Tsar that she would turn a pot of water into a fountain of youth for him. The Tsar decided to test the water by having Alexi thrown in. Alexi survived and came out of the water with the ring. The Tsar was convinced that his youth would be restored but he became an infant instead. Since he was too young to rule, Alexi became the Tsar and married Yelena. Alexi released the Firebird and the Golden Mare.

Order	Events from *The Golden Mare, the Firebird, and the Magic Ring*
2	Alexi becomes a huntsman for the Tsar and captures the Firebird.
1	Alexi spares the life of the Golden Mare, and the horse devotes her life to him.
3	Yelena follows Alexi to meet the Tsar.
5	Alexi is thrown into the cauldron of boiling water and survives.
6	Alexi becomes Tsar and releases the Golden Mare.
4	The Golden Mare volunteers to fetch Yelena's magic ring.

★ **Approaching Practice Book A,** page 187

◆ **Beyond Practice Book B,** page 187

Quick Check **Can students identify the chronological order of events?**

During **Small Group Instruction**

If No → **Approaching Level** Comprehension, pp. 6770–677P

If Yes → **On Level** Options, p. 677R

Beyond Level Options, p. 677T

MAIN SELECTION
- *The Golden Mare, the Firebird, and the Magic Ring*

 • **Skill:** Chronological Order

PAIRED SELECTION
- "Personal Choices: Learning Through Stories"

FCAT • **Text Features:** Venn Diagram

SMALL GROUP OPTIONS

- Differentiated Instruction, pp. 667M–667V

Comprehension

LA.5.2.1.1
Demonstrate knowledge of characteristics of genres

GENRE: FAIRY TALE

Have a student read the definition of a Fairy Tale on **Student Book** page 642. As students read the story, they should determine what elements make both the settings and the characters in the fairy tale imaginary.

LA.5.1.7 Use strategies to comprehend text

STRATEGY
SUMMARIZE

Remind students that summarizing fiction means identifying the most important events in a story, and then restating them in their own words.

 SKILL
FCAT **CHRONOLOGICAL ORDER**

LA.5.2.1.2
Analyze elements of plot structure

Remind students that sequence is the order in which story events take place. Putting the events in a story in chronological order can help them understand how the author developed the rising and falling action of the plot.

Comprehension

Genre

Fairy Tales take place long ago, have imaginary characters and settings, and involve good and evil.

Summarize

FCAT Chronological Order
Look for important plot details. As you read, use your Sequence Chart.

Event

Read to Find Out

How does the mare help Alexi achieve his goals?

642

Vocabulary

Vocabulary Words Review the tested vocabulary words: **accompany, bridle, consented, delicacies, descended, despair, dismiss** and **intentions.**

Story Words Students may find these words difficult. Pronounce the words and present the meanings as necessary.

huntsman (p. 644): a person who hunts animals for food

mare (p. 645): a female horse

Tsar (p. 646): a ruler in Russia having great or absolute power or authority

mythical (p. 651): having to do with myths, or ideas and stories that many believe but which aren't true

regal (p. 653): having qualities of a king or other ruler

LA.5.1.6.1 Use new vocabulary taught directly

The Golden Mare, the Firebird, and the Magic Ring

by Ruth Sanderson

Award Winning Selection

643

LA.5.1.7.1 Use prior knowledge to make and confirm predictions

Preview and Predict

Ask students to read the title, preview the illustrations, and make predictions about the story. Have students write about their predictions and anything else they want to know about the story.

Set Purposes

LA.5.1.7.1 Establish purpose for reading

FOCUS QUESTION Discuss the "Read to Find Out" question and how to look for the answer as students read.

Point out the Sequence Chart in the Student Book and on **Practice Book** page 188. Explain that students will use the chart to keep track of events in the story.

LA.5.1.6.2 Read familiar text

Read *The Golden Mare, the Firebird, and the Magic Ring*

Use the questions and Think Alouds for additional instruction to support the comprehension strategy and skill.

Read Together

If your students need support to read the Main Selection, use the prompts to guide comprehension and model how to complete the graphic organizer.

Read Independently

If your students can read the Main Selection independently, have them read and complete the graphic organizer. Remind students to set their purposes for reading and reading rate, and to modify both based on their reading level.

If your students need an alternate selection, choose the **Leveled Readers** that match their instructional level.

Technology

Story available on **Listening Library Audio CD**

On Level Practice Book O, page 188

As you read *The Golden Mare, the Firebird, and the Magic Ring*, fill in the Sequence Chart.

Event

↓

| |

↓

| |

↓

| |

How does the information you wrote in this Sequence Chart help you summarize *The Golden Mare, the Firebird, and the Magic Ring*?

★ **Approaching** Practice Book A, page 188

◆ **Beyond** Practice Book B, page 188

The Golden Mare, the Firebird, and the Magic Ring **643**

Develop Comprehension

1 GENRE: FAIRY TALE

LA.5.2.1.1
Demonstrate
knowledge of
genre forms
with distinct
characteristics
and purposes

What clues in this story help you to identify it as a fairy tale? (Answers may vary, but students should note that the story begins with the words "Once upon a time" and takes place when and where "magical beasts still roamed the earth." The words "Once upon a time" are a popular opening line in many fairy tales, and these stories often contain magical characters and events.)

Have students analyze the elements and style of fairy tales.

2 RECOGNIZE HOMOPHONES

LA.5.1.6.8
Use
homophones
to determine
meaning

Explain that homophones are words that sound alike but have different spellings and meanings. Then ask: What is the difference between the words *herd* and *heard*? Suggest that students use context clues to predict, or guess, the meaning of *herd*. (*Herd* means "a group of animals of one kind, especially large animals feeding or moving together." The word *heard* is the past tense of the verb *hear*, which means "to take in sound through the ear." The meanings of the words are very different, but they are pronounced exactly the same way.)

1   Once upon a time, in a place where magical beasts still roamed the earth, a young man named Alexi left home to seek his fortune and perhaps to find an adventure or two as well.

Alexi was an excellent huntsman, but after traveling for a week he had found neither work nor adventure. One evening, as night **descended** and the moon arose, he made camp at the edge of a glade.

2   A noise of hoofbeats in the forest startled Alexi. Thinking it a herd of deer or some other game, the lad readied his bow. Yet the young hunter did not loose his arrow, for the beast that appeared in the clearing was too

644

ELL
Access for All

Use Illustrations As you read, use the illustrations to check students' understanding of the text in the story and help explain it. After reading the text on pages 644–645, prompt students to describe what is happening in the illustrations: *Tell me about this horse. Tell me about this young man. Who is he? What is the huntsman going to do? What is the mare saying to the huntsman? What does Alexi say he was looking for?* Explain important story information as needed.

wondrous to shoot. It was a golden mare with a silvery-white mane that streamed around her and sparkled in the moonlight.

The Golden Mare stood and gazed at the huntsman, who pointed an arrow at her heart.

"Hold, fair sir, do not shoot," said the mare, to the astonishment of the lad. Alexi lowered his bow and slowly approached the remarkable mare.

"I am at your service for sparing my life," she said. "What is your desire?"

Alexi told the mare he sought work and adventure.

3

4

645

Comprehension

Reader's Purpose: *Story Elements*

Explain/Discuss When reading fiction, a reader's main purpose is to identify the main story elements, including characterization, plot, the character's problem, any conflict the character faces, the rising action that leads to the climax, or turning point in the story, and the resolution of the problem. Another purpose is to evaluate the story elements and determine if a story's characters, setting, and plot are realistic or if they are fantasy.

Apply As students read *The Golden Mare, the Firebird, and the Magic Ring,* have them read for the purpose of identifying the story elements in the fairy tale. Have them evaluate the believability of the characters and the degree to which the plot is believable, or realistic. When students have finished reading, have them discuss what they learned about the story and how reading for a purpose helped them better understand what they read.

LA.5.2.1.2 Locate and analyze character development, rising/falling action, problem/resolution
LA.5.2.1.1 Demonstrate knowledge of genre forms with distinct characteristics and purposes

Develop Comprehension

3 STRATEGY
SUMMARIZE

LA.5.1.7
Student uses strategies to comprehend text

Teacher Think Aloud I know that a summary is a short statement of the most important ideas or events in a passage or story. As a strategy, summarizing the major events can help me identify the problems the characters face, and their attempts to solve them. Let me summarize what has taken place in this story so far. Alexi, a young huntsman, has left his home to seek fortune and adventure. He is walking in the forest when he hears hoofbeats. Thinking it is a herd of deer, he prepares to shoot with his bow and arrow. But he doesn't shoot because he sees something "wondrous." I'll keep reading to find out how the mare helps Alexi. I will also summarize the important events that take place as I read.

4 MAKE PREDICTIONS

LA.5.1.7.1
Use prior knowledge to make and confirm predictions

Making, revising, and confirming predictions makes readers more active by helping them to set a purpose for reading. Rereading and looking for text clues in order to make logical guesses about what might happen can also help you clarify your understanding of the text. What kind of adventure do you think the Golden Mare might provide for Alexi? (Answers will vary but may include the possibility that there are other magical beasts in the forest, and that the Golden Mare will introduce them to Alexi.)

Develop Comprehension

5 CHARACTER

LA.5.2.1.2
Locate and analyze character development

What do the Tsar's actions reveal about his character? (Answers will vary but should include the idea that the Tsar seems to be spoiled and selfish. He is used to getting what he wants. He is annoyed that Alexi will not sell the horse. Even though he is angry at Alexi, he does not want to dismiss him because Alexi may turn out to be a good huntsman.) **Do you think he is a stereotypical fairy tale character? Explain.** (Answers will vary: Students may feel he is not stereotypical because he is not a typical hero or villain.)

6 DRAW CONCLUSIONS

LA.5.2.1.5
Demonstrate understanding and include evidence from the text

Do you think the Tsar might have another reason for hiring Alexi, in addition to his skills as a huntsman? Explain your answer. (Answers may vary but should include the idea that the Tsar may want to try and take Alexi's horse for himself, since he admired it so much.)

"The Tsar of this region could use another huntsman," said the horse. "Tomorrow I will take you to his palace. If he hires you, I promise to serve you well."

The next morning Alexi fashioned a rough **bridle** with a bit of rope, mounted the Golden Mare, and set off for the palace of the Tsar.

The Tsar hired the young man at once, so impressed was he by Alexi's mount. He offered Alexi a princely sum for the mare.

"Thank you, sire," said Alexi, "but I'm afraid she'll allow no rider but me." Annoyed that his offer was declined, the Tsar ordered a saddle and a real bridle put on the horse, but not one of his men could stay on the Golden Mare's back.

5   The Tsar glowered at Alexi, for he usually got what he wanted. "I trust that you will serve me *quite* well," he said coldly, not wanting to **6** **dismiss** him in case he turned out to be a good huntsman.

646

Vocabulary

Read the sentence that contains the word **dismiss.** Have students replace the word in the passage with a word that has the same or nearly the same meaning. (release, discharge)

LA.5.1.6.8 Use synonyms to determine meaning

ELL
Access for All

STRATEGIES FOR EXTRA SUPPORT

Question 7 CHRONOLOGICAL ORDER
Check students' understanding of the expression *lead (someone) to (something)* in Question 7 on page 647. Demonstrate the action, if needed. Say, *Alexi is now a huntsman for the Tsar. How did he get to the Tsar? What events have happened to Alexi since the beginning of the story?* Help students retell each event. Restate what students say in complete sentences. Say, *These events led Alexi to the Tsar.*

In just a few weeks, Alexi became first among the Tsar's huntsmen, **7** for he was a good shot and the Golden Mare was swift at the chase. As luck would have it, there came a day that Alexi spied no game but rode on and on until it began to grow dark. He was about to turn the mare around when he noticed something glowing brightly on the path ahead. It was a golden feather, bright as a flame, and Alexi knew it must be a feather from the great Firebird.

"I will take this prize to the Tsar," said Alexi. "Then perhaps he will look upon me with favor."

The Golden Mare was protective of her kind master. "If you take the Firebird's feather, you will surely learn the meaning of fear," she warned. But so confident was Alexi that he did not heed her words and **8** presented the feather to the Tsar the very next day.

> **FCAT** **Chronological Order**
> What sequence of events in the story leads Alexi to a position as a huntsman with the Tsar?

647

Read

Main Selection   **Student page 647**

Develop Comprehension

7 CHRONOLOGICAL ORDER

FCAT

LA.5.2.1.2 Locate and analyze elements of plot structure

What sequence of events in the story leads Alexi to a position as a huntsman with the Tsar? Add the events to your Sequence Chart in chronological order. (Alexi leaves home to seek his fortune and adventure. In a forest he meets a magical Golden Mare that can speak. Alexi spares her life, and to thank him, the mare takes him to the Tsar. Impressed by the mare, the Tsar hires Alexi as a huntsman.)

8 DRAW CONCLUSIONS

LA.5.2.1.5 Demonstrate understanding of literary selection

Why do you think Alexi does not pay attention to the Golden Mare's warning, even though she has helped him to find a position with the Tsar? (Answers may vary but should include the idea that, even though Alexi has become first among the Tsar's huntsmen, he is still trying to find favor with the Tsar. Alexi thinks that presenting the Tsar with a feather from the Firebird will cause the Tsar to look upon him with favor.)

> Alexi seeks fortune and adventure. He meets a Golden Mare that can speak. The mare takes Alexi to the Tsar. The Tsar is impressed with the mare and hires Alexi as a huntsman.
>
> ↓
>
> [blank box]
>
> ↓
>
> [blank box]

Develop Comprehension

9 **CHRONOLOGICAL ORDER**

LA.5.2.1.2
Locate and
analyze plot
structure

After the Tsar agrees to Alexi's request, what signal words and phrases help you place the sequence of events in chronological order? (Answers should include the words and phrases *At midnight, then, all night,* and *as the first golden rays of dawn lit the sky*.) Use these signal words to relate the events in chronological order. (At midnight the maize was scattered over the field, and Alexi took the saddle off the Golden Mare. Then Alexi hid in a nearby tree. All night they waited. As the first golden rays of dawn lit the sky, the Firebird came flying.) Add your answer to the chart, and underline the signal words that indicate the sequence of events.

> Alexi seeks fortune and adventure. He meets a Golden Mare that can speak. The mare takes Alexi to the Tsar. The Tsar is impressed with the mare and hires Alexi as a huntsman.

> At midnight, maize was scattered over the field, and Alexi took the saddle off the Golden Mare. Then Alexi hid in a nearby tree. All night they waited. As the first golden rays of dawn lit the sky, the Firebird came flying.

Vocabulary

Read the sentence that contains the word **despair**. Ask students to replace *despair* in the sentence with another word or phrase that has the same meaning. (hopelessness, a state of giving up)

LA.5.1.6.8 Use synonyms to determine meaning

As the Tsar greedily took the feather, he saw a way to rid himself of this insolent huntsman, whose horse was a constant reminder of what he could not have.

"You bring me a mere feather!" bellowed the Tsar. "If you are so clever, bring me the whole bird, or I'll have your head brought in on a platter!"

Alexi left the throne room in **despair** and went to the Golden Mare's stall.

"Do not worry," said the Golden Mare. "Ask the Tsar to have a hundred sacks of maize scattered at midnight upon the open field on the hill. I will see to the rest."

The Tsar agreed to Alexi's request, and at midnight his men scattered one hundred sacks of maize on the field. Alexi took the saddle and bridle off the Golden Mare and she wandered loose in the field. Then he hid in the branches of a huge oak tree that

9 stood at the top of the hill. All night they waited.

As the first golden rays of dawn lit the sky, from the eastern edge of the world the Firebird came flying, wings aflame with the reflected light of the sun.

648

649

Develop Comprehension

10 DRAW CONCLUSIONS

LA.5.2.1.5
Demonstrate
understanding
of literary
selection

How do you think Alexi and the Golden Mare will capture the Firebird? (Students should note they plan to use the maize as bait to set a trap for the Firebird. They will probably try to surprise the Firebird while it is feeding on the maize.)

11 MAKE PREDICTIONS

LA.5.1.7.1
Use prior
knowledge
to make
and confirm
predictions

What role do you think the Firebird will play in the story? (Answers will vary but should include the idea that the Firebird is probably a magical creature like the Golden Mare. A hint of its special powers comes when the Golden Mare warns Alexi that he will "learn the meaning of fear" if he takes the feather.)

Have students respond to the selection by confirming or revising their previous predictions and purposes for reading. Have them note any new questions they may have as well.

Quick Check Can students summarize to identify the chronological order of events? If not, see the Extra Support on this page.

Extra Support

Chronological Order

FCAT If students have difficulty, help them to recognize the chronological order of events in the selection by asking them to summarize what has happened in the story so far. Ask questions that prompt them to recognize the event-by-event progress of the story. *What happened when Alexi met the Golden Mare?* (The mare spoke to Alexi and offered to help him.) *Why did the mare take Alexi to meet the Tsar?* (Alexi hoped to become a huntsman for the Tsar.) *Why did the Tsar become annoyed at Alexi when they met?* (He wanted to buy Alexi's mare, but Alexi would not sell it.) Students may wish to make a chain Cause and Effect Chart, showing how one event leads, or causes, another event in the story to occur.

LA.5.2.1.2 Locate and analyze elements of plot structure
LA.5.1.7.8 Use graphic organizers to repair comprehension

Stop here if you wish to read this selection over two days. STOP

Develop Comprehension

12 **STRATEGY**
SUMMARIZE

LA.5.1.7
Use strategies
to comprehend
text

Teacher Think Aloud To keep track of new developments in the story, I will summarize the main events that have occurred since Alexi brought the feather to the Tsar. First, the Tsar said he was angry that Alexi brought him just a feather, and he ordered Alexi to bring him the whole bird. The Golden Mare told Alexi not to worry and to ask the Tsar for a hundred sacks of maize. What happened after that?

(Encourage students to apply the strategy in a Think Aloud.)

LA.5.1.7
Student uses
strategies to
comprehend
text

Student Think Aloud The Tsar's men scattered the maize in a field. Alexi hid in a nearby tree and the mare grazed in the field. When the Firebird came to eat the maize, the Golden Mare moved closer and closer to the Firebird. Then the mare stepped on the bird's tail and pinned it to the ground. Finally, Alexi tied the bird with a rope and put it in a sack.

The mighty bird landed in the field and began to eat the maize. As the Golden Mare grazed nearby, she wandered closer and closer to the Firebird. When the bird was close enough, the mare placed a hoof upon its tail, pinning it to the ground. The Firebird tried in vain to fly away, but the mare held fast. Alexi jumped from the tree, tied the struggling bird securely with rope, and placed it carefully in a sack.

12

650

Language Arts

Cross-Curricular Connection

LITERATURE   LA.5.2.1 Identifies, analyzes, applies knowledge of elements of fiction
LA.5.1.7.6 Identify themes and topics across fiction selections

The Firebird is a popular character in Russian fairy tales. In the best-known tale in which the Firebird appears, a hunter becomes lost in a strange wood where the only living creature is the Firebird, which he snares. In exchange for her life, the magical bird offers the hunter a pledge of help if ever he should call upon her. Discuss the similarities between this tale and *The Golden Mare, the Firebird, and the Magic Ring*. Have students find other tales about the Firebird, perhaps from different countries. After reading, have them compare and contrast characters, story themes, and plots in literature circles. Students should note any patterns or symbolism they find across eras and cultures. Then have them choose a tale and write a critique that identifies main idea, characters, setting, the chronological order of events, conflict, crisis and resolution.

LA.5.2.1.6 Write a critique that identifies main idea, characters, setting, chronological order of events, conflict, crisis and resolution

The Tsar was amazed to see Alexi bearing the mythical Firebird. He ordered a huge, ornate cage built for the magnificent bird. People came from miles around to see the captive Firebird, and all the neighboring tsars were quite jealous of his prize possession. Alexi, however, felt sorry for the bird and wished he had never seen its feather shining in the forest path.

13

651

Develop Comprehension

13 **MONITOR AND CLARIFY: PARAPHRASE**

LA.5.1.7.8 Paraphrase to repair comprehension

When you paraphrase you put all the details the author gives into your own words without adding any of your own ideas. Can you paraphrase the first three sentences on this page? (Answers will vary but should include these main points: The Tsar was very surprised to see Alexi carrying the Firebird. The Tsar had a big, fancy cage built for the bird. People from far away came to see the caged bird. All the other rulers in the area were jealous of the Tsar's bird.)

Remind students to independently self-monitor as they read.

Cross-Curricular Connection

FAIRY TALES IN FILM

Tell students that popular fairy tales are often made into films. For example, the classic fairy tale *Cinderella* has been adapted into many different film versions.

Have students find different film versions of a classic fairy tale. Encourage them to watch several versions of their chosen tale and identify recurring and central themes. Then have them discuss the different filmed versions and compare them with the print version of the tale. Were students able to come to a new understanding about the print version of the tale after watching the films? Finally, have students write a persuasive essay that establishes a controlling idea and supporting arguments about whether the film or print version of the tale is better. Encourage them to include persuasive techniques such as hyperbole, or the use of extreme exaggeration, and words that have emotional appeal.

LA.5.4.3.1 Write persuasive text that establishes a controlling idea and supporting arguments
LA.5.4.3.2 Include persuasive techniques
LA.5.6.3.1 Examine how ideas are presented in a variety of print and non-print media

Develop Comprehension

14 **MAKE PREDICTIONS**

LA.5.1.7.1
Use prior knowledge to make and confirm predictions

Will Alexi be successful in his quest to bring back Yelena to the Tsar? Use information from earlier in the story to help you make your prediction. (Yes, he will be successful. Each of the quests he has undertaken with the Golden Mare, including getting a job with the Tsar at the beginning of the story and capturing the Firebird afterward, is successful.)

15 **MAKE INFERENCES**

LA.5.2.1.5
Demonstrate understanding of literary selection

Why do you think the Golden Mare tells Alexi to ask the Tsar for a brocaded tent, sweetmeats, and delicacies before going to find Yelena the Fair? (Alexi might be able to impress Yelena with these luxurious items and convince her to return with him to the Tsar's palace.)

16 **SYNTHESIZE**

LA.5.2.1.5
Demonstrate understanding and include evidence from the text

What characteristics do Yelena the Fair's boat and the lake on which it sails have in common with other characters or things described in the story? Explain your answer. (There are many references to gold and light in the story. The mare is golden. The Firebird looks like it is on fire when it flies at sunrise. Yelena the Fair sails in a golden boat that Alexi first sees in a "blazing" sunrise. The lake on which Yelena sails is called the Lake of the Sun.)

LA.5.2.1.7
Identify and explain author's use of symbolism

Have students discuss how these characteristics form patterns or symbols and compare them with patterns or symbols used in myths and traditions from other cultures and eras.

Alexi remained the Tsar's best huntsman and brought him much profit. But no matter how well Alexi did, he could not please the Tsar, for the Golden Mare still obeyed Alexi alone.

A few weeks later, the Tsar called Alexi to him.

"Since you seem to have a talent for impossible tasks, I have another one for you," said the Tsar. "In a distant eastern land, Yelena the Fair sails in her golden boat upon the Lake of the Sun. Find her
14 and bring her back to be my bride. It will mean your death if you fail."

With a heavy heart, Alexi went to the Golden Mare, certain that this new task was hopeless. "Ask the Tsar for a brocaded tent
15 and all sorts of sweetmeats and **delicacies**," the mare said, "and I will take you to her."

The Tsar supplied Alexi with a beautiful tent and fine foods, which Alexi packed into saddlebags upon the Golden Mare's broad back.

As they set out, it seemed to Alexi that the mare's feet barely touched the ground, so swiftly did she run. For seven days and nights she ran, through green forests, past waterfalls, up and down mountains, until on the eighth morning she stopped.

16 Silhouetted against the blazing sunrise, the boat of Yelena the Fair sailed upon the Lake of the Sun.

652

Alexi set up the tent and arranged rugs and cushions inside along with the fancy foods he had brought. Then he sat inside and waited for Yelena the Fair. Before long the boat sailed closer and closer to the shore until finally she lowered sail and landed upon the beach. Stepping out lightly, the maiden approached the regal-looking tent and saw the feast that Alexi had laid out.

Yelena and Alexi had a merry time, eating and talking of many things.

"My master the Tsar is rich and powerful, and famous, too," Alexi boasted. "And he has in his possession the legendary Firebird. Perhaps you would accept the Tsar's invitation to be an honored guest at his palace."

Yelena the Fair was so impressed by Alexi's persuasive words and gracious manner that she agreed to **accompany** him. When Alexi lifted the beautiful young maiden upon the Golden Mare's back, he felt a pang of guilt for not mentioning the old Tsar's true **intentions** to make her his wife.

The Tsar was astonished to see Alexi coming through the palace gates with Yelena the Fair.

"My bride!" he exclaimed.

Yelena the Fair was not pleased and quickly realized that Alexi had brought her there under false pretenses. She looked from the old Tsar to the young huntsman who had trapped her.

"I will marry no man," she said to the Tsar, "without my grandmother's wedding ring. It lies under a stone at the bottom of the Lake of the Sun."

"Well," said the Tsar, gesturing impatiently to Alexi, "what are you waiting for? Go at once and fetch the ring!"

When Alexi was alone with the Golden Mare, he said, "I do not wish to fetch Yelena's wedding ring for the Tsar, for then she, too, would be a captive like **18** the Firebird."

653

Comprehension

Make, Confirm, Revise Predictions

Explain To make predictions, good readers use prior knowledge and story clues to make a decision about what will happen next in a story. Sometimes the clues that a reader uses to make predictions are widely separated. For example, there may be information at the beginning of the story, such as a character's actions, and then something several pages later. Remind readers to confirm their predictions as they read. Were they correct? If not, they should revise their predictions. Point out that making, revising, and confirming predictions makes readers more active by helping them to set a purpose for reading. It can also improve their comprehension by helping them to establish patterns in the development of the plot.

Apply As students read, encourage them to make predictions. For example, will the Tsar get what he wants? Have students use clues from the story to help them make and revise their predictions.

LA.5.1.7.1 Use prior knowledge to make and confirm predictions
LA.5.1.7.8 Predict to repair comprehension

Develop Comprehension

17 CHRONOLOGICAL ORDER

FCAT ✓

LA.5.2.1.2 Locate and analyze elements of plot structure

Retell the events that lead to the arrival of Yelena at the Tsar's palace in chronological order. (The Tsar supplies Alexi with a beautiful tent and fine foods. For seven days Alexi travels with the Golden Mare. When they arrive at the Lake of the Sun, they see Yelena's golden boat. After Alexi erects the tent, Yelena comes ashore. She is impressed with Alexi and accompanies him to the Tsar's palace.) **Add answers to the chart.**

18 CHARACTER

LA.5.2.1.2 Locate and analyze character development

In what way does Alexi's character change at this point in the story? How might this change affect the plot? (Answers may vary but should include that, for the first time, Alexi thinks of someone other than himself when he says that he does not want to fetch Yelena's wedding ring. He fears she will be turned into a captive like the Firebird.)

> Alexi seeks fortune and adventure. He meets a Golden Mare that can speak. The mare takes Alexi to the Tsar. The Tsar is impressed with the mare and hires Alexi as a huntsman.

↓

> At midnight, maize was scattered over the field, and Alexi took the saddle off the Golden Mare. Then Alexi hid in a nearby tree. All night they waited. As the first golden rays of dawn lit the sky, the Firebird came flying.

↓

> The Tsar supplies Alexi with a tent and fine foods. For seven days Alexi travels with the Golden Mare. When they arrive at Lake of the Sun, they see Yelena's boat. After Alexi erects the tent, Yelena comes ashore. She is impressed with Alexi's manner and agrees to accompany him to the Tsar's palace.

Develop Comprehension

19 USE ILLUSTRATIONS

Look at the picture on **Student Book** page 654. What clues in the illustration help you to know that the crab, like the Golden Mare, might also be one of the "magical beasts" mentioned at the beginning of the story? How does this event help you to identify the genre of this selection? (Answers should include the fact that the crab has found the ring and is giving it to the Golden Mare. The crab must have been able to understand the Golden Mare's request. Because the crab has magical abilities, this event is characteristic of the fairy tale genre.)

654

Comprehension

Grammar: Demonstrative Pronouns

Explain Tell students that a demonstrative pronoun points to and identifies a noun or pronoun. *This* and *these* refer to things that are nearby either in space or time, while *that* and *those* refer to things that are farther away in space and time.

Discuss Point out the sentence "But what can I do about that?" at the bottom of page 655. Explain that in this sentence, the word *that* is a demonstrative pronoun. It refers to Yelena's previous statement when she tells the Tsar that she cannot marry him because he is too old. The word *that* takes the place of Yelena's statement.

Apply Have students find other examples of demonstrative pronouns as they read the selection. Make sure they do not confuse them with conjunctions.

LA.5.3.4.4 Correct use of demonstrative pronouns

"I will retrieve it then," said the Golden Mare. "Whatever happens, do not worry, for it is a magic ring and can grant its wearer any one wish."

When she reached the Lake of the Sun the mare stamped her hoof three times on the sand. A huge crab crawled out of the water.

"At the bottom of the lake there is a ring under a stone," said the Golden Mare. "Please get it for Yelena the Fair, for she has need of it."

Patiently the Golden Mare waited on the shore while the crab called together all the creatures that crawled on the lake's bottom to search for the ring. After some time he emerged with ring in claw. Delicately the Golden Mare took the ring in her teeth and then fairly flew back to the palace stables, where Alexi awaited.

Alexi presented the ring to the Tsar, who gave it at once to Yelena the Fair.

"You have your ring," he said. "Now let the wedding bells be rung! Let the feast be prepared!"

"Wait," said the shrewd maiden, who saw the remorse in Alexi's eyes. "I cannot marry a man as old as you, for you are surely four times my age."

"But what can I do about that?" asked the Tsar.

"Indeed, you can do something…with my help," said Yelena. **20** "Prepare a cauldron of boiling water, and with my magical power I will turn it into the Water of Youth. If you bathe in it you will become young again."

655

Develop Comprehension

20 MAKE PREDICTIONS

LA.5.1.7.1 Use prior knowledge to make and confirm predictions

Given the events that have taken place so far, whom do you think Yelena will marry? (Answers will vary. Students may suspect that Yelena seems to like Alexi. She was impressed enough with his manners that she agreed to travel with him. She may have been angry with Alexi for deceiving her, but perhaps she forgave him when she saw remorse in his eyes. She might be able to use her magic in some way to marry Alexi.)

Ways to Confirm Meaning

Semantic/Meaning Cues

Explain Tell students that good readers make sure what they read makes sense. One way to do this is by using the context of a word to think of related words that have similar meanings.

Model Have students predict the meaning of *cauldron* on **Student Book** page 655.

Think Aloud I've never seen the word *cauldron* before, but here Yelena the Fair says she wants it filled with boiling water so the Tsar can bathe in it. So a cauldron can hold water. It must also be large enough for a person to fit inside of it. If I replace the word *cauldron* with the word *tub,* the sentence still makes sense.

Apply Encourage students to use context clues and their background knowledge to predict the meaning of other difficult words or phrases such as *emerged* or *shrewd* on page 655 and to tell why and how they used the strategies.

LA.5.1.6.6 Identify "shades of meaning" in related words
LA.5.1.6.3 Use context clues to determine meanings

Develop Comprehension

21 CHRONOLOGICAL ORDER

LA.5.2.1.2
Locate and
analyze
elements of
plot structure

How did the author organize the events in this fairy tale? In what way did the Tsar's jealousy over the huntsman's ownership of the Golden Mare affect the events in the story? (The events of the story are organized in the order that they took place. The Tsar kept giving the huntsman difficult tasks. He hoped the huntsman would fail at one of them so he could own the Golden Mare. This created many problems for the huntsman to overcome.)

22 STRATEGY
SUMMARIZE

LA.5.1.7
Student uses
strategies to
comprehend
text

What are two important events that take place after the Golden Mare returns with the ring that you would include in a summary of the story? Explain why you think they are important.

Student Think Aloud Let's see. I think one of the two most important events that takes place after the Golden Mare returns is Yelena's decision that she cannot marry the Tsar because he is so much older than she is. If she did not feel this way, the cauldron of boiling water would never have been prepared. Another important event is the Tsar's decision to have Alexi test the boiling water. If Alexi had been harmed, the Tsar would never have agreed to jump into the cauldron.

656

The Tsar ordered the cauldron prepared, and soon the water bubbled and steamed.

"Let us first test this miracle," said the Tsar slyly. "You, Alexi, will be the first to enter the pot. Guards, seize him!" The Tsar's men held Alexi fast.

He remembered the Golden Mare's **22** words about the ring and hoped that they were true, for now he knew the meaning of fear.

Yelena the Fair approached the cauldron and passed her hand several times over the boiling water. Silently, she made a wish and dropped the magic ring into the cauldron.

"It is ready," she said.

At the Tsar's signal, the guards flung Alexi into the boiling liquid. **23** He sank below the surface once, twice, and after the third time he rose like a shot and leaped from the cauldron. He was in perfect health and unharmed by the scalding water. No one but Yelena noticed the golden ring on his little finger.

Hoping to be as young and as strong as his huntsman, the Tsar jumped into the cauldron. At the same instant, Alexi made a wish on the magic ring, for he did not desire the Tsar's death.

FCAT Sequence
What key events in the story lead up to the moment when Alexi is flung into the cauldron?

657

Develop Comprehension

23 CHRONOLOGICAL ORDER

FCAT

LA.5.2.1.2 Locate and analyze elements of plot structure

What key events in the story lead up to the moment when Alexi is flung into the boiling water? Use signal words to identify them in chronological order and add them to the Sequence Chart. (Answers may vary but should include the following events: First, the Golden Mare helps Alexi become a huntsman for the Tsar. Then she helps him capture the Firebird and takes him to Yelena the Fair, whom the Tsar wants to marry. The mare goes to fetch Yelena's grandmother's wedding ring. Yelena tells the Tsar he is too old to marry her, but that a cauldron of boiling water will make him young again. Finally, the Tsar wants Alexi to get into the cauldron first.)

> Alexi seeks fortune and adventure. He meets a Golden Mare that can speak. The mare takes Alexi to the Tsar. The Tsar is impressed with the mare and hires Alexi as a huntsman.

> At midnight, maize was scattered over the field, and Alexi took the saddle off the Golden Mare. Then Alexi hid in a nearby tree. All night they waited. As the first golden rays of dawn lit the sky, the Firebird came flying.

> The Tsar supplies Alexi with a tent and fine foods. For seven days Alexi travels with the Golden Mare. When they arrive at Lake of the Sun, they see Yelena's boat. After Alexi erects the tent, Yelena comes ashore. She is impressed with Alexi's manner and agrees to accompany him to the Tsar's palace.

> First, the Golden Mare helps Alexi become a huntsman for the Tsar. Then she helps him capture the Firebird and takes him to Yelena the Fair, whom the Tsar wants to marry. The mare goes to fetch Yelena's grandmother's wedding ring. Yelena tells the Tsar he is too old to marry her, but a boiling cauldron of water will make him young again. Finally, the Tsar wants Alexi to get into the cauldron first.

STRATEGIES FOR EXTRA SUPPORT

Question 23 CHRONOLOGICAL ORDER
Start a word bank of signal words used in sequencing on the board. Help students use them in their retelling of the events in chronological order. Allow students to retell each event as they are able. Encourage students to use gestures to convey meaning. Prompt students through questions if necessary. Restate what they say in complete sentences using more descriptive words and varied vocabulary. As students retell the key events of the story, demonstrate the actions of the characters where appropriate.

Develop Comprehension

24 CHARACTER

LA.5.2.1.2
Locate and
analyze
character
development

How did Alexi's character traits influence his actions in the story? (Alexi was an excellent huntsman—brave and fearless—so he was not afraid to accept the challenges that the Tsar gave him.) **In what way did the changes Alexi goes through during the story affect the events of the plot?** (After Alexi captures the Firebird, he feels sorry for the animal and doesn't think it should be kept in a cage. He also feels a pang of guilt when he deceives Yelena the Fair about the Tsar's intentions. As a result he decides not to fetch her grandmother's ring, and the Golden Mare goes instead.)

25 EVALUATE

LA.5.2.1.5
Demonstrate
understanding
and include
personal
experience

Put yourself in Alexi's place. Would you have attempted to carry out the Tsar's many wishes? Explain your answer. (Accept all answers. Encourage students to include details from the story to support their views as well as a discussion of the story's theme.)

26 CLARIFY WORD MEANINGS

LA.5.1.6
Student uses
multiple
strategies
to develop
vocabulary

Which words or phrases in the selection make it difficult for you to understand what you are reading? What strategies can you use to help you figure them out? (Troublesome words will vary. Students should explain strategies they can use including: reread and look for context clues, read ahead, ask questions, use word parts.)

658

Comprehension

Genre: Fairy Tale

Explain/Discuss A fairy tale is a special kind of folk tale that is often told to children. It often features stereotypical characters—such as a young handsome hero, a beautiful young woman, and an evil villain—as well as magical creatures who have special powers. Fairy tales often have a theme of good vs. evil, and the hero always overcomes the villain. Because the events in fairy tales could never happen in the real world, the plots are not realistic, nor are the characters believable.

Apply Discuss with students the elements of a fairy tale in *The Golden Mare, The Firebird, and the Magic Ring*. Discuss how the characters fit fairy tale stereotypes, what the theme is and how it is expressed through the characters and their actions. Have students compare this fairy tale with others they have read that have similar characters or themes.

LA.5.2.1.1 Demonstrate knowledge of genre forms with distinct characteristics and purposes
LA.5.1.7.6 Identify themes across fiction selections
LA.5.1.7.7 Compare and contrast elements

To everyone's surprise, Alexi reached into the cauldron and lifted out a little baby, smiling and unharmed. The Tsar was indeed young again!

Since the Tsar was now too young to rule, the people made Alexi the Tsar in his place. And Yelena the Fair **consented** to become his bride. So she did marry the Tsar after all. And as for the baby Tsar, he was given a new name and raised as their own child.

As his first official act as Tsar, Alexi ordered the release of the Firebird, for such a bird did not belong in a cage. In a joyful blaze **24** of light it flew to its home in the eastern sky. The Golden Mare ran free once more, but she continued to advise Alexi until the end of his days.

25 **26**

659

Develop Comprehension

LA.5.1.7.1
Use prior knowledge to make and confirm predictions

RETURN TO PREDICTIONS AND PURPOSES

Review students' predictions and purposes. Were they correct? Were they able to place the events in the story in the correct sequence?

LA.5.1.7
Student uses strategies to comprehend text

REVIEW READING STRATEGIES

What questions do you still have about the story, and what strategies could you use to help you answer them? How did identifying the sequence of events in the story help you to identify and remember key events?

PERSONAL RESPONSE

LA.5.2.1.2
Analyze exposition, rising/falling action, problem/resolution

Ask students to discuss the plots of favorite fairy tales. Have them write a short plot synopsis of their favorite fairy tale, using the five main parts of plot as defined on this page.

As an alternative, have students write a paragraph in which they identify the author's purpose and support their position with examples from the story.

Comprehension

Plot: *Exposition, Conflict, Climax, and Resolution*

Explain/Discuss The plot of a story has five main parts. In the beginning, background information, or the exposition, introduces the characters and the situation. The conflict is a problem that causes the events in the story to take place. Complication, or rising action, is what occurs when the main character tries to overcome the conflict. The climax is the turning point in the plot, which somehow resolves, or solves the conflict. The falling action is the resolution of the conflict and the events that follow it. What events make up the rising action of the story? (The Tsar gives Alexi increasingly difficult tasks to complete.) What is the climax of the story? (Just before he is flung into the boiling cauldron, Alexi remembers the words of the Golden Mare.)

Apply Tell students to identify the conflict and resolution of the story in writing, supporting their answers with evidence from the text.

LA.5.2.1.2 Locate and analyze exposition, rising/falling action, problem/resolution

Quick Check **Can students summarize to place the events in the story in chronological order?**

During **Small Group Instruction**

If No → **Approaching Level** Comprehension, pp. 667O–667P

If Yes → **On Level** Options, p. 667R

Beyond Level Options, p. 667T

Author-Illustrator

ONCE UPON A TIME WITH RUTH SANDERSON

Have students read the biography of the author-illustrator.

LA.5.1.7.2 Identify how author's perspective influences text

DISCUSS

- How did a love of horses lead Ruth Sanderson to her career as a writer and illustrator?

- How are Ruth Sanderson's interests shown in the story?

WRITE ABOUT IT

Review with students how Alexi overcomes many obstacles. Discuss how his perseverance was rewarded. Have students write about a time when they overcame an obstacle.

FCAT Author's Purpose

Remind students that there are informative touches to this fairy tale. For instance, it is a celebration of trust and loyalty, and a denunciation of greed and dishonesty.

LA.5.1.7.2 Identify author's purpose

 Technology

Students can find more information about Ruth Sanderson at **www.macmillanmh.com**

Once Upon a Time with Ruth Sanderson

Ruth Sanderson could usually be found reading books about horses in the library where her grandmother worked. This led to her second passion: drawing. On Saturday mornings in the fourth grade, Ruth started a class to teach her friends how to draw. It's no surprise that when Ruth grew up, she went to art school and became a writer and illustrator of children's fantasy and fairy tale books. Ruth is married and has two daughters.

Other books by Ruth Sanderson:
Papa Gatto and *Crystal Mountain*

 Find out more about Ruth Sanderson at **www.macmillanmh.com**

FCAT Author's Purpose
Ruth Sanderson entertains the reader with this fairy tale. What makes the story informative, as well?

660

Author's Craft
Character Development

Explain that one way authors make their characters interesting is by having them change their ideas or behavior. Ruth Sanderson creates a change in Alexi's character. For example, Alexi says:

> I do not wish to fetch Yelena's wedding ring for the Tsar, for then she, too, would be a captive like the Firebird. (p. 653)

Discuss how Alexi changes. Ask what he is like before and after this moment in the story. Stress the contrast of his new outlook and its importance to the plot.

When students reread the story, have them identify Alexi's character traits. Lead students in a discussion about ways Ruth Sanderson makes the changes in Alexi's character believable for readers. Discuss how she expresses her ideas as both the author and the illustrator.

LA.5.2.1.2 Locate and analyze character development

Comprehension Check

Summarize

Use your Sequence Chart to summarize *The Golden Mare, the Firebird, and the Magic Ring*. Keeping track of the order of events can help you better understand the story.

Think and Compare

1. Describe how the story would be different if the author changed the sequence of events. Use story details in your description. **Summarize: Chronological Order**

2. Reread page 653. Why does Alexi feel guilty about persuading Yelena the Fair to visit the Tsar? Use details from the story to explain your answer. **Analyze**

3. If the Golden Mare were to **accompany** you throughout your life, what might you ask her to help you do? Explain. **Synthesize**

4. The Tsar only thinks about himself. How do selfish people create difficult situations? Explain your answer. **Evaluate**

5. Reread "A Real Princess" on pages 640–641. Explain the similarities and differences between Alexi's and Prince Vincent's situations. Use details from both selections in your answer. **Reading/Writing Across Texts**

661

Strategies for Answering Questions

Right There

Model the Right There strategy with question 2.

The answer to this question is directly stated in the selection. The words in the question and the answer are usually the same.

Question 2 Think Aloud: The question directs me to look for the answer on page 653, so this is a clue that the answer is directly stated in the text. When I turn to this page in the story, I find the answer right away, in the middle of the page: "When Alexi lifted the beautiful young maiden upon the Golden Mare's back, he felt a pang of guilt for not mentioning the old Tsar's true intentions to make her his wife."

LA.5.1.7 Student uses strategies to comprehend text

Comprehension Check

 LA.5.1.7 Student uses strategies to comprehend text

SUMMARIZE

Ask students to summarize either orally or in writing the most important events in *The Golden Mare, the Firebird, and the Magic Ring*. Remind them to use their Sequence Charts to help them develop their summaries.

THINK AND COMPARE

Sample answers are given.

LA.5.2.1.2 Locate and analyze plot structure

1. **Chronological Order:** Answers will vary but should show an understanding of the importance of the sequence of events and the fact that any other sequence would not yield the same results.

2. **Analyze:** Alexi feels guilty because he has not told Yelena that the Tsar expects to marry her. USE RIGHT THERE

LA.5.2.1.5 Demonstrate understanding and include personal experience

3. **Text to Self:** Answers will vary, but students will probably point out that they would use the Golden Mare to help them reach certain goals.

4. **Text to World:** Answers will vary but students may mention that selfish people do not help others.

 ### FOCUS QUESTION

LA.5.2.1.5 Demonstrate understanding and include other text/media

5. **Text to Text:** Alexi starts out with nothing, and ends up as Tsar. Vincent had many chances to save his crown, but failed because he did not treat any of the princesses well. In the beginning of "A Real Princess," Vincent thinks mostly of himself. Alexi spares the Golden Mare, but seeks his own fortune and captures the Firebird. They both learn to care more about others.

Objective

- Read accurately with appropriate expression
- Rate: 129–149 WCPM

Materials

- Fluency Transparency 26
- Fluency Solutions Audio CD
- Practice Book, p. 189

LA.5.1.5
Student demonstrates ability to read orally with expression

ELL / Access for All

Echo-Read Work with students to echo-read the concluding paragraph on the transparency. Encourage them to imitate your pauses and the tempo of your reading. As you model the dialogue, point out the word *coldly*, and have students imitate your tone.

 On Level Practice Book O, page 189

I read, I will pay attention to pauses and intonation.

	Once upon a time, a really, really long time ago, there lived
12	a beautiful, kind-hearted girl named Katharine. You would
21	have thought that such a lovely girl would be happy. But she
33	was not. She was sad and terribly lonely.
41	For you see (as is to be expected in a story like this),
54	Katharine's life was filled with sorrow. Her mother died
63	when she was young. Her father brought her to live with her
75	Aunt Mara and cousins Melina and Ursula while he went off
86	to fight for the king. Her father loved Katharine dearly and
97	promised to return for her as soon as possible, but that
108	promise was made many years ago.
114	Over the years Katharine's cousins grew to hate her. They
124	knew that Katharine was kinder and more beautiful than they
134	were. Each day Melina and Ursula were meaner. They
143	ordered her around. Katharine was truly miserable.
150	So what did Katharine do all day? She did everything!
160	Inside she cooked and cleaned. Outside she planted, weeded,
169	and harvested the garden, fed the animals, cleaned the barn,
179	collected the eggs, and milked the cow. 186

Comprehension Check

1. Why was Katharine miserable? **Plot Development** Katharine had a difficult life.
2. Why were Ursula and Melina cruel to Katharine? **Plot Development** They were jealous of her beauty and kindness.

	Words Read	−	Number of Errors	=	Words Correct Score
First Read		−		=	
Second Read		−		=	

⭐ **Approaching Practice Book A,** page 189

◆ **Beyond Practice Book B,** page 189

Fluency
Repeated Reading: *Intonation*

EXPLAIN/MODEL Explain to students that good readers learn to read groups of words together in phrases. Tell them the text on the transparency has been marked with slashes to indicate pauses and stops. A single slash indicates a pause, usually between phrases. A double slash indicates a stop, usually between sentences. Model reading aloud the passage on **Fluency Transparency 26,** having students pay attention to your intonation and pauses.

Transparency 26

The next morning Alexi fashioned a rough bridle with a bit of rope,/ mounted the Golden Mare,/ and set off for the palace of the Tsar.//

The Tsar hired the young man at once,/ so impressed was he by Alexi's mount.// He offered Alexi a princely sum for the mare.//

"Thank you,/ sire,"/ said Alexi,/ "but I'm afraid she'll allow no rider but me."// Annoyed that this offer was declined,/ the Tsar ordered a saddle and a real bridle put on the horse,/ but not one of his men could stay on the Golden Mare's back.//

The Tsar glowered at Alexi,/ for he usually got what he wanted.// "I trust that you will serve me *quite* well,"/ he said coldly,/ not wanting to dismiss him/ in case he turned out to be a good huntsman.//

Fluency Transparency 26 from *The Golden Mare, the Firebird, and the Magic Ring,* page 646

PRACTICE/APPLY Divide students into two groups, and have them alternate reading the sentences in the passage. Listen for phrasing accuracy. Students can also practice fluency using **Practice Book** page 189 or the **Fluency Solutions Audio CD.**

Quick Check   Can students read accurately with appropriate expression?

During **Small Group Instruction**

If No → **Approaching Level** Fluency, p. 667N

If Yes → **On Level** Options, p. 667Q

Beyond Level Options, p. 667S

Comprehension

REVIEW SKILL

PLOT DEVELOPMENT: CHARACTER AND SETTING

LA.5.2.1.2
Analyze plot
structure,
setting, and
character
development

EXPLAIN/MODEL

- The **characters** are the people or animals in a story. Understanding a character's traits can help readers relate to that character's feelings and actions, and how they influence the **plot development** of the story.

- The **plot** is the series of events that take place in a story. Usually the events in a plot unfold in chronological order—from beginning to end. Sometimes one event leads into and causes the event that comes after it. The main character's traits and actions can affect the development of the plot.

- The **setting** of a story is when and where the story takes place. Setting includes the time of year, the date, historical period, place, and situation. Setting can have an important effect on the characters and the plot.

For comprehension practice use Graphic Organizers on pages 40–64 in the **Teacher's Resource Book.**

LA.5.2.1.2
Locate and
analyze plot
structure,
setting, and
character
development

PRACTICE/APPLY

Discuss the characters, plot, and setting of *The Golden Mare, the Firebird, and the Magic Ring.*

- Talk about the problems that Alexi has as a result of the Tsar's character and behavior. In what ways does it affect his own behavior?

- How does the setting of the story influence the events of the plot?

- How does the change in Alexi's character influence the plot development of the story?

Objective

- Review character, plot, and setting as aspects of plot development

FCAT Skills Trace

Plot Development	
Introduce	19A–B
Practice / Apply	20–39, 51A–B, 147A–B, 231A–B, 263A–B, 359A–B, 395A–B, 607A–B, 671A–B; Practice Book 2–3, 9–10, 39–40, 67–68, 76–77, 104–105, 113–114, 178–179, 194–195
Reteach / Review	251B, 441B, 661B Small Group Options
Assess	Weekly Tests; Unit 1–6 Tests
Maintain	51A–B, 147A–B, 231A–B, 263A–B, 359A–B, 395A–B, 607A–B, 671A–B

Informational Text: Social Studies

LA.5.2.1.1 Demonstrate knowledge of characteristics of genres

GENRE: NONFICTION ARTICLE

Have students read the bookmark on **Student Book** page 662. Explain that a nonfiction article

- gives information and facts about people, laces, events, or ideas

- may use graphic organizers, such as charts and Venn diagrams, to highlight major ideas and make information easier to understand.

Text Features: Venn Diagram

LA.5.2.2.1 Use and explain information from text features

EXPLAIN A Venn diagram shows the similarities and differences between two or more sets of things. The similarities are shown in the center section formed by the overlapping ovals, and the differences are shown in the outside sections of the diagram.

APPLY Point out the Venn diagram on page 665. What is being compared? (examples of civic and personal responsibility) Name one example of personal responsibility and one example of civic resposibility (Doing homework and chores at home, keeping promises, and telling the truth are examples of personal responsibility. Voting in elections, helping out neighbors, and participating in school and community events are examples of civic responsibility.)

Social Studies

Genre

Nonfiction Articles give the reader facts about people, places, ideas, or events.

FCAT **Text Feature**

A **Venn Diagram** shows the similarities and differences between two things.

Content Vocabulary
responsible
civic
moral

Personal Choices

Learning Through Stories

by Carly Gray

Suppose you have a choice between keeping a promise to your parents to help them do chores one Saturday and accepting an offer to go roller skating with a friend. How do you choose? What helps us to make good choices?

Some of the world's greatest leaders, teachers, and writers have had important things to say about choices. Many of these thinkers share stories that teach about the challenges of responsibility. When we are **responsible**, we are dependable. We can be counted on to make good decisions.

Responsibility has to do with making good personal choices, as well as choices you make as a member of your community. Personal responsibility happens when people take care of themselves. Taking the opportunity to get a good education is an example of personal responsibility.

Doing your homework without being asked is an example of personal responsibility.

662

Content Vocabulary

Discuss the spelling and meaning for each content vocabulary word for "Personal Choices: Learning Through Stories" on Student Book pages 662–663: *responsible, civic, moral.*

- When someone is **responsible,** he or she can be trusted and is reliable. Why is being a responsible person important?

- **Civic** reponsibility means following rules, obeying laws, and respecting the rights of others in a community. Is voting a civic responsibility? Why or why not?

- A **moral** is a lesson about right and wrong that is taught in a fable. How do morals help people learn responsible ways to act?

LA.5.1.6.1 Use new vocabulary taught directly

Teaching Lessons

Civic responsibility, or being a good citizen, means that people follow rules, obey laws, and respect the rights of others. Civic responsibility is important in your school, community, state, and country. **1**

How do we learn about personal and civic responsibility? One way is by being taught rules by parents, teachers, and other leaders. Another way is through stories. Since the beginning of history, storytellers have used stories to teach children about the ways of a community.

A fable is a kind of story that has a **moral**, or a lesson, at the end. These stories teach children responsible ways to act toward others. The fable about Ant and Grasshopper is a story that teaches about personal responsibility:

The Ant and the Grasshopper

One summer's day, Grasshopper was dancing and singing in the sunshine. Ant was working hard to get an ear of corn to his nest. When Grasshopper saw Ant, he wanted Ant to stop and play with him instead of working so hard. But Ant kept working. He knew winter was coming. **2**

3

What is the difference between how Ant and Grasshopper spend their summers?

663

Make Cultural Connections Write the title *The Ant and the Grasshopper* on the board and give a brief summary of the version you know. Write down the main characters and other key words as you speak. Explain that many cultures have different versions of the story. Encourage students to tell the version they know.

Read the headings with students and check that students understand what each one means. Before reading, help students become familiar with important vocabulary by discussing the text in the center section of the Venn diagram. Point out that two examples share these similarities.

Informational Text

Read "Personal Choices: Learning Through Stories"

Access for All As you read, remind students to apply what they have learned about Venn diagrams. Also have them identify clues to the highlighted words.

1 APPLY

LA.5.2.2.2 Use information from text to answer questions

Why is civic responsibility so important in your school and community? (Answers will vary, but students should note that if no one followed rules or laws, and did not respect the rights of others, then confusion and disorder would result.)

2 MAKE PREDICTIONS

LA.5.1.7.1 Use prior knowledge to make and confirm predictions

Read the first part of the fable about the ant and the grasshopper on page 663. What do you think will happen to the grasshopper when winter comes? (After playing all summer, the grasshopper will most likely not have any food stored for the cold winter months.)

3 DRAW CONCLUSIONS

LA.5.2.1.5 Demonstrate understanding and include evidence from the text

Do you think the grasshopper showed personal responsibility? Why or why not? (No, the grasshopper did not exhibit personal responsibility. Although there is nothing wrong with enjoying the sunshine and warm temperatures of summer, the grasshopper should also have spent some of his time preparing for winter.)

Informational Text

4 **MAKE INFERENCES**

LA.5.2.2.2 Answer questions related to relevant details

In what ways do you think personal responsibility and civic responsibility are related? (Possible answers: Before a person can exhibit examples of civic responsibility, such as voting in elections or participating in community events, he or she must learn the value of personal responsibility, such as keeping promises and telling the truth.)

5 **TEXT FEATURES: VENN DIAGRAM**

LA.5.2.2.1 Use and explain information from text features

According to the Venn diagram on page 665, what two items are examples of both civic and personal responsibility? (Obeying society rules or laws and considering the needs or rights of others are both examples of personal and civic responsibility.)

3

Grasshopper shrugged. "Winter is far off," he thought. The weather was warm, and he was having so much fun. Why should he work? Soon, though, it turned cold. When winter came, Grasshopper had no food. Soon he went begging for Ant to help him. Ant said, "I have food because I planned ahead. Remember this next winter, Grasshopper."

Moral: Know when it is time to work and time to play.

4

What would you do if you were Ant?

Making Good Choices

From personal responsibility comes civic responsibility. Great leaders from the Founding Fathers to famous scientists have talked about the importance of being a good citizen and helpful member of the community. Becoming aware of the rights and responsibilities of citizenship is a good first step. Think about the example of Ant and Grasshopper. How will you show that you are responsible? How will you choose to serve your fellow citizens?

664

On Level Practice Book O, page 190

A **Venn diagram** compares two things. Differences are written in the left and right circles. Similarities are written where the circles overlap.

A. Read the summary of *Cinderella* and fill in the Venn diagram.

Cinderella
Cinderella is a household servant with an evil stepmother, evil stepsisters, and a fairy godmother. She loses a slipper at a ball, and the prince searches the kingdom for the woman to whom it belongs. Cinderella and the prince get married and live happily ever after.

Cinderella — Both — Rhodopis

evil stepmother and stepsisters, prince, fairy godmother, loses slipper at ball | household servants, lost slipper, kingdom is searched, end with marriage and happiness | pharaoh, animal friends, sings and dances, falcon finds the slipper

B. Read the completed Venn diagram and write a summary of *Rhodopis*.

Rhodopis
Rhodopis is a household servant with animal friends for whom she sings and dances. She loses a slipper, and a falcon picks it up and drops it at the pharaoh's throne. The pharaoh then has the kingdom searched for the slipper's owner. Rhodopis and the pharaoh are married and live happily ever after.

★ **Approaching Practice Book A,** page 190

◆ **Beyond Practice Book B,** page 190

Reading a Venn Diagram

In a Venn diagram like the one below, differences are written in the left and right ovals. The similarities are written in the center section.

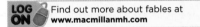

Examples of Personal Responsibility
- Doing homework
- Doing chores at home
- Keeping promises
- Telling the truth

Examples of Both
- Obeying society rules or laws
- Considering the needs or rights of others

Examples of Civic Responsibility
- Voting in elections
- Participating in school and community events
- Helping out neighbors in need

FCAT Connect and Compare

1. Look at the Venn diagram. What are the similarities of both kinds of responsibility? Explain. **Understanding Venn Diagrams**

2. If you wrote a fable, what would the moral of your story be? Why do you think that moral would be an important lesson? **Apply**

3. In *The Golden Mare, the Firebird, and the Magic Ring*, what lesson does the Tsar learn? How is this lesson connected to personal or civic responsibility? **Reading/Writing Across Texts**

 Social Studies Activity

Write your own fable. Then, with a partner, create a Venn diagram comparing and contrasting your fables.

LOG ON Find out more about fables at **www.macmillanmh.com**

665

Informational Text

Connect and Compare

SUGGESTED ANSWERS

FCAT

LA.5.2.2.1 Use and explain information from text features

1. Answers may include: By keeping promises and helping out neighbors in need, people are considering the needs and rights of others in their families and communities.
UNDERSTANDING VENN DIAGRAMS

LA.5.2.1.5 Demonstrate understanding and include personal experience

2. Answers will vary, but students' morals should be related in some way to examples of either personal or civic responsibilities. **APPLY**

FOCUS QUESTION

LA.5.2.1.5 Demonstrate understanding and include other text/media

3. Answers will vary but should include that the Tsar learns a lesson about treating people with respect and keeping his promises.
READING ACROSS TEXTS

Social Studies Activity

Have students make a plan for writing using strategies such as a graphic organizer or online tools. Then have them make a plan for writing that prioritizes ideas and addresses the time needed to complete the task. Students can work with a partner when they have finished their fables.

LA.5.3.1.3 Prewrite by organizing ideas using tools
LA.5.3.1 Use prewriting strategies to formulate a plan

LOG ON **Technology**

Internet Research and Inquiry Activity
Students can find more facts at
www.macmillanmh.com

Connect
Language Arts

Writing

FCAT Voice

LA.5.3.2.1
Elaborate on organized information using word choices appropriate to tone and mood

READ THE STUDENT MODEL

Read the bookmark about voice. Explain that writers choose words that convey tone and mood to readers. In doing so, they also convey their own personalities to readers.

Have students turn to page 644. Point out how these words suggest a formal voice: *roamed the earth* and *seek his fortune*. The narrator's playful personality is evident later: *find an adventure* or *two as well*. Have the class read Natsu Y.'s **eyewitness account** and the callouts. Tell students they will write eyewitness accounts, choosing words that convey their personalities.

Writer's Craft

FCAT Voice

In an eyewitness account, writers describe the events they see and how they feel about what they see. They use words that show **voice**. That way, readers feel as if they were there.

Write an Eyewitness Account

First Steps

by Natsu Y.

I wrote about witnessing my little brother's first steps.

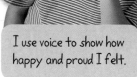

I use voice to show how happy and proud I felt.

→ I witnessed something very important and unexpected the day my little brother, Toshi, turned 11 months old.

We were in the living room after dinner. Toshi was standing up, holding on to the coffee table. He does that well. I sat on the floor a few yards away. Toshi has never walked before. He was never able to balance himself without the coffee table.

"Come on, Toshi! Walk over to me!" I called. I thought he would never do it. I had been calling to him for over a month but he wouldn't move from behind that table.

→ Toshi stared at me, smiling and bouncing. Suddenly, he put his arms straight out and started walking right towards me. I couldn't believe it! One, two, three, four steps, then plop. My little brother had taken his first steps and they were right to me!

666

Features of an Eyewitness Account

In an eyewitness account, the writer describes an important event that he or she has seen or witnessed.

- An eyewitness account tells the writer's feelings and thoughts about the event.

- It includes word choice that conveys the writer's voice.

- It includes vivid details that help readers feel that they witnessed the event, too.

- It has syntactic variety, including simple and complex sentences.

Writing Prompt

People often witness important events.

Think of an important event you have witnessed.

Now write an account of an important event you have witnessed.

FCAT Writer's Checklist

✓ **Focus:** My writing clearly presents an eyewitness account.

✓ **Organization:** My paragraphs include details placed in logical order.

☐ **Support:** I write supporting details in words that show **voice**.

✓ **Conventions:** All words are spelled correctly. I use adverbs correctly.

667

Transparency 101: **Event Chart**
Transparency 102: **Draft**
Transparency 103: **Revision**

Transparency 101

My Brother's First Steps

Event	Sensory Details	Thoughts and Feelings
Toshi stood up.	holding on to the coffee table	he does that well
"Walk over to me!"	calling to him for over a month	
Toshi started walking.	smiling; arms straight out	
One, two, three, four steps	Plop!	right toward me
Toshi took his first steps.		important

Writing Transparency 101

LA.5.3.1.2
Determine purpose and intended audience of writing piece

PREWRITE

Discuss the writing prompt on page 667. Have students share details regarding important events they have witnessed, such as a local team winning a championship or the mayor of the city dedicating a memorial. Help students identify an audience and a purpose for writing.

Display **Transparency 101.** Discuss how Natsu uses a chart to help him plan his account. He records the sequence of events, sensory details, and his thoughts and feelings. Have students work on charts with partners.

LA.5.3.3.1
Evaluate draft for voice

DRAFT

Display **Transparency 102.** Discuss ways to improve the draft. The account is dry and lacks personality. Natsu needs to choose words and add details that better express his personality. He also needs to include his thoughts and feelings about the event.

Before students begin writing, present the explicit lesson on **Voice** on page 667A. Then have students use their charts to write their accounts, focusing on voice and word choice.

LA.5.3.3
Student will revise draft for clarity and effectiveness

REVISE

Display **Transparency 103.** Discuss the revisions. Students can revise their drafts or place them in writing portfolios to work on later. If students choose to revise, have them work with a partner and use the Writer's Checklist on page 667. Have them **proofread/ edit** their writing. For **Publishing Options** see page 667A.

For lessons on **Voice, Denotative and Connotative Language, Adverbs,** and **Spelling** see page 667B, and **5 Day Spelling** and **5 Day Grammar** on pages 667G–667J.

The Golden Mare, the Firebird, and the Magic Ring **667**

ORGANIZATION Voice

Publishing Options

Students can share their accounts orally with the class. See the Speaking and Listening tips below. They can also use their best cursive to write their interviews. (See Teacher's Resource Book pages 168–173 for cursive models and practice.) Then they can work in small groups to create a newsletter or Web site of "leading events of the past ten years: eyewitness accounts."

Speaking and Listening

SPEAKING STRATEGIES

- Speak clearly and naturally.
- Read with expression to show your feelings.
- Look up at your audience often as you read.

LISTENING STRATEGIES

- Listen carefully for details about what the writer saw and felt.
- After the speaker has finished, ask questions about the event.

6-Point Scoring Rubric

Use the rubric on page **763G** to score published writing.

Writing Process

For a complete lesson, see Unit Writing pages **763A–763F.**

LA.5.2.1.7 Examine how language describes people, feelings, and objects

EXPLAIN/MODEL

Explain that voice is especially important in an eyewitness account. Writers describe exactly what they see and feel in highly personal and distinctive ways. Display **Transparency 104.**

Think Aloud The writer describes watching a baby bird hatch from its egg. However, the writing is dull and lacks voice. I don't have any sense of the writer's personality or what she thinks or feels about this event. I don't feel as if I'm witnessing the event, too.

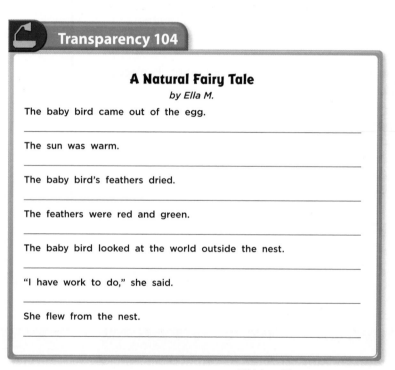

Transparency 104

A Natural Fairy Tale
by Ella M.

The baby bird came out of the egg.

The sun was warm.

The baby bird's feathers dried.

The feathers were red and green.

The baby bird looked at the world outside the nest.

"I have work to do," she said.

She flew from the nest.

Writing Transparency 104

PRACTICE/APPLY

Work with students to rewrite the sentences to show voice. Then have students describe the writers' voices in nonfiction that they have read recently.

As students prepare for and write their accounts, have them focus on voice and word choice.

Writer's Toolbox

LA.5.3.3.1 Evaluate draft for voice; **LA.5.3.3.3** Express ideas vividly through language techniques

SUPPORT

Writing Trait: Voice

Explain/Model Remind students that writers of eyewitness accounts try to involve the readers by using vivid sensory details and language techniques. Have students look at Natsu Y.'s account on page 666. Point out that Natsu includes the visual detail that Toshi is smiling and bouncing. He also includes the sound detail "plop."

Practice/Apply As students draft their accounts, encourage them to include details that appeal to as many senses as possible.

SUPPORT

Denotative and Connotative Language

Explain/Model Explain that language has at least two levels of meaning. Words have definitions that appear in dictionaries. They also have emotional meanings that include feelings and thoughts that readers associate with them. Point out that Natsu uses the word *unexpected*. The denotative meaning is "not looked forward to." The connotative meaning may include feelings of surprise or excitement.

Practice/Apply As students draft their accounts, have them pay attention to the denotative and connotative meanings of words. Remind them that both meanings affect the reader's understanding of voice.

LA.5.3.3.3 Create precision and interest by expressing meanings vividly

Technology

Remind students that they can see how their final, printed copies will look by previewing them onscreen.

LA.5.3.4.4. Edits for correct use of adverbs

CONVENTIONS

Grammar: Adverbs

Explain/Model Explain that adverbs are words that tell how, when, or where an action takes place. Point out that Natsu uses the adverb *suddenly* to describe the action of Toshi's walking.

Practice/Apply Have students skim the passage on page 640 to locate adverbs. For each example, have students note whether it explains how, when, or where an action occurs. As students draft their accounts, remind them to use adverbs to make their writing clear and lively. For a complete lesson on adverbs, including a mechanics lesson on the use of *good* and *well*, see pages 667I–667J.

CONVENTIONS

Spelling: Greek Roots

Point out that Natsu's account is "autobiographical." Suggest that students use their knowledge of Greek roots to define the word *autobiographical*. Remind students to pay attention when they spell words with Greek roots. They can use print or online dictionaries to check spelling in their drafts. For a complete lesson on Greek roots, see pages 667G–667H.

LA.5.3.4.1 Edits for spelling using knowledge of Greek root words

 **FCAT Success!**

Test Prep and Practice with FCAT Writing+, pages 180–230.

Objectives

- Apply knowledge of word meanings and context clues
- Recognize homophones

Materials

- Vocabulary Transparencies 51 and 52
- Practice Book, p. 191

Vocabulary

accompany (p. 653) go along with

consented (p. 659) gave approval or permission

despair (p. 648) loss of hope

delicacies (p. 652) rare or choice kinds of food

intentions (p. 653) purposes; designs; plans

dismiss (p. 646) to fire

descended (p. 644) walked down

bridle (p. 646) part of a harness that fits around a horse's head

ELL
Access for All

Personalize Write, *I accompany my brother to school.* Discuss its meaning. Erase *brother* and *school.* Have students complete the sentence frame and discuss their sentences.

Review
Vocabulary

 FCAT Words in Context

LA.5.1.6.1
Use new vocabulary taught directly and indirectly

EXPLAIN/MODEL

Review the meanings of the vocabulary words. Display **Transparency 51.** Model how to use word meanings and context clues to fill in the first missing word.

Think Aloud I see that the girls are doing something with their father. I also see the words *to the grocery store* at the end of the sentence, so I think they are all probably going to the grocery store. I know that *accompany* means "to go with." When I try *accompany* in the sentence, it makes sense. It is the missing word.

Transparency 51

| accompany | bridle | consented | delicacies |
| descended | despair | dismiss | intentions |

1. The girls were to <u>accompany</u> their father to the grocery store.

2. The mother <u>consented</u> to the boy's attending the birthday party.

3. After losing his job, the man felt a sense of <u>despair</u>.

4. The bride appreciated the exquisite <u>delicacies</u> on the catered menu.

5. Her <u>intentions</u> were to go to college after she graduated from high school.

6. The students hoped that the teacher would <u>dismiss</u> class early.

7. The royal family <u>descended</u> the staircase and made their appearance at the state dinner.

8. The wild horse objected to the <u>bridle</u>.

Vocabulary Transparency 51

PRACTICE/APPLY

 Access for All Instruct students to complete the remaining sentences on their own. Review the students' answers as a class, or instruct students to check their answers with partners.

Antonym Match Put this week's words on cards and have student pairs write antonym cards for each word. Then have pairs swap antonyms. Using the new cards, have the pairs attach the antonym to the original vocabulary word. Discuss different nuances in the antonyms. Check for accuracy.

STRATEGY
DICTIONARY: HOMOPHONES

EXPLAIN/MODEL

LA.5.1.6.8
Use
homophones

Remind students that **homophones** are words that sound alike but are spelled differently. They also have different meanings. If students have trouble figuring out the meaning of a homophone using context clues, they should look it up in a dictionary.

Display **Transparency 52.** Model how to figure out the meanings of the homophones in item 1 using context clues and a dictionary.

Transparency 52

Homophones

1. The seller sold pickles and jams. He stored his goods in the cellar under the kitchen. (A *seller* is a person who sells things. A *cellar* is a room built underground.)

2. The bride and groom changed from their bridal clothes into shirts and jeans. The cowboy put a saddle and bridle on his horse and rode away. (*Bridal* means anything relating to a wedding. A *bridle* is the part of a horse's harness that fits over the head and is used to guide the horse.)

3. During the king's reign, there was peace and prosperity. Unfortunately, the weather was often bad, and there was rain almost daily. (*Reign* is the period of time that a king or queen rules. *Rain* is the water that falls from the sky to Earth.)

4. We threw the ball to our dog. Then he dropped it, and it rolled through the open door. (*Threw* means to have sent something through the air. *Through* means from the beginning to the end of something.)

Vocabulary Strategy Transparency 52

PRACTICE

Have students identify the homophones and determine their meanings in items 2–4 using context clues and a dictionary.

Quick Check

Can students determine word meanings?
Can students recognize homophones?

During **Small Group Instruction**

If No → **Approaching Level** Vocabulary, pp. 667N–667P

If Yes → **On Level** Options, pp. 667Q–667R

Beyond Level Options, pp. 667S–667T

ELL   **Access for All**

Group Work Homophones may be difficult for students because the words may be unfamiliar to them. Have students work in groups to complete the transparency activity so they can help each other. Help them write sentences as needed. Discuss the parts of speech of the words. Help students divide the words into the following categories: *action,* *description,* and *thing.*

FCAT Success!

Test Prep and Practice with vocabulary, pages 6–31.

On Level Practice Book O, page 191

Homophones are words that sound the same but have different spellings and different meanings.

A. Circle the word that makes sense in each sentence.
1. Most fairy tales are stories that you have (herd / **heard**) before.
2. The hero often must race to complete a task in just one (**hour** / our).
3. In some stories, people try to (by / **buy**) happiness with jewels or gold.
4. My baseball team (one / **won**) the game.

B. Write a word from the box next to each word to make pairs of homophones, and write a sentence using one of the homophones in the pair. Possible responses provided.

pear	flower	course	hear

5. here _____ hear _____
Listen, do you hear that noise?

6. coarse _____ course _____
She liked her college history course.

7. pair _____ pear _____
I like to pack a pear in my lunch.

8. flour _____ flower _____
You need flour to bake a cake.

 Approaching Practice Book A, page 191

Beyond Practice Book B, page 191

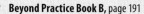

Word Study

Objective

- Decode words with Greek roots

Materials

- Practice Book, p. 192

RESEARCH
Why It Matters

Vocabulary

Etymologies of words are studied by students in the derivational relations stage of spelling. They learn common Greek and Latin roots. Students also learn about cognates and how words in English are related to words in other languages.

Dr. Donald Bear

 Go to
www.macmillanmh.com

■ **On Level Practice Book O,** page 192

Many words are Greek in origin. Word roots are small word parts that usually cannot stand on their own. Knowing the meanings of **Greek roots** can help you define unfamiliar words.

Read the table. Then write the correct word from the box below to complete each sentence.

Greek root	Meaning	Example
astr	star	astronaut
auto	self, same	automatic
photo	light	photogenic
mech	machine	mechanism
graph	thing written	graphic
phon	sound, voice	phonetic

photocopy	astronomer	automobile
biography	mechanic	phonics

1. The vehicle needed a __mechanic__ who knew how its engine worked.
2. We studied sounds and syllables in our __phonics__ class.
3. Ms. Brown made one more __photocopy__ of the worksheet for the new student.
4. The author wrote a __biography__ about Harriet Tubman.
5. Thanks to the __automobile__, we don't have to walk to school.
6. An __astronomer__ looked at the stars through her telescope.

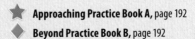 **Approaching Practice Book A,** page 192

◆ **Beyond Practice Book B,** page 192

Phonics

 FCAT Words with Greek Roots

Access for All

LA.5.1.6.11
Use roots and affixes from Greek and Latin

EXPLAIN/MODEL

■ Many English words, especially words related to social studies and science, are made up of word parts, or roots, from the Greek language. Knowing Greek roots can help readers figure out words.

■ Some common Greek roots are *aster,* which means "star"; *auto,* which means "self"; *photo,* which means "light"; *tele,* which means "distance"; *mechan,* which means "machine"; *graph,* which means "write"; and *phon,* which means "sound." Display these roots and their meanings in the classroom.

■ When an affix or another Greek root is added to a Greek root, a new word is formed. For example, *autograph* is made up of the roots *auto* and *graph.* An autograph is a person's signature in that person's handwriting.

Write *mechanic* on the board.

Think Aloud This word has the Greek root *mechan,* which means "machine." The suffix *–ic* means "one who is associated with." When I put the meanings of the Greek root and the suffix together, I get "one who is associated with machines." When I look up *mechanic* in a dictionary, I find that it means "a person who repairs or takes care of machines."

PRACTICE/APPLY

Display the following words. Have students identify the Greek roots: *cosmonaut, telephone, astronomy, photograph, telephoto, automobile, graphic.* Then have them use the meanings of the roots and affixes to predict the meaning of each complex word. They can look up any unknown affixes in a dictionary, then confirm their predictions.

LA.5.1.4.3
Use language structure to read multi-syllabic words

Decode Multisyllabic Words Emphasize to students that many words with Greek roots are multisyllabic. Understanding Greek roots can help students decode such longer words. For practice, see the decodable passages on page 30 of the **Teacher's Resource Book.**

Quick Check Can students decode words with Greek roots?

During **Small Group Instruction**

If No → **Approaching Level** Phonics, p. 667M

If Yes → **On Level** Options, pp. 667Q–667R

Beyond Level Options, pp. 667S–667T

Vocabulary Building
LA.5.1.6 Uses multiple strategies to develop vocabulary

LA.5.1.6.10 Use digital tools

LA.5.2.1.6 Write a book report that identifies main idea, character (s), setting, sequence of events, conflict, crisis and resolution

Oral Language

Expand Vocabulary Write the word *fairy tales* in the center of a word web. Using the selection and print and electronic dictionaries, thesauruses, and encyclopedias, have students find and discuss words that relate to this week's theme.

Vocabulary Building

Homophones A good way to build vocabulary is to learn the meanings of homophones. Write the following word sets on the board. Form two student groups. Ask students in the first group to write clues to the meaning of the word pairs in Set 1. For example, *without a lot of strength; seven days: week/weak*. Students in the second group will do the same for Set 2. Have students exchange papers and identify the correct homophones for each clue.

Set 1: *sea/see, foul/fowl, gate/gait, heel/heal, flew/flu*

Set 2: *creak/creek, sail/sale, read/reed, road/rowed, pause/paws*

LA.5.1.6.8 Use homophones

 ## Apply Vocabulary

Write a Guide Give students the following writing prompt: *Using the vocabulary words, write a how-to parenting guide for Alexi and Yelena. What can they do to prevent the baby Tsar from returning to his old character traits as he grows up?*

Students can also write a book report or review about *The Golden Mare, the Firebird, and the Magic Ring* or another fairy tale using the vocabulary words. Remind them to include the theme, characters, setting, sequence of events, conflict, and resolution, as well as their recommendation to read or not to read.

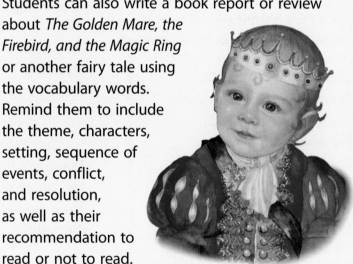

Spiral Review

Vocabulary Game Invite students to sit in a circle. Begin a fairy tale with the line, *Once upon a time, a small girl decided to accompany her father, the king, on a journey to a far-away land.* Ask students to take turns adding to the story. Award one point each time a student incorporates a vocabulary word from this week or from the previous unit into the story. The student with the most points at the end of the story wins.

LA.5.1.6.1 Use new vocabulary

Technology

 Vocabulary PuzzleMaker

 For vocabulary games and practice go to www.macmillanmh.com

5 Day Spelling

LA.5.1.4.1 Understand spelling patterns

Greek Roots

Spelling Words

astronaut	phonics	telegram
telephone	automatic	telephoto
automobile	photograph	autograph
photography	telescope	astronomer
mechanical	mythical	disaster
myth	telegraph	homophone
television	mechanic	

Review correction, discussion, decoration

Challenge videophone, photogenic

Dictation Sentences

1. The <u>astronaut</u> floated in space.
2. The <u>telephone</u> rang loudly.
3. We drove in our <u>automobile</u>.
4. Sam's hobby is <u>photography</u>.
5. It's a <u>mechanical</u> can opener.
6. A goddess appeared in the <u>myth</u>.
7. I watched the game on <u>television</u>.
8. We're learning <u>phonics</u> in school.
9. The <u>automatic</u> door slid open.
10. She smiled for the <u>photograph</u>.
11. I looked through the <u>telescope</u>.
12. **<u>Mythical</u>** stories are fascinating.
13. The <u>telegraph</u> was an invention.
14. A <u>mechanic</u> can fix the car.
15. A <u>telegram</u> announced the news.
16. Sharon used a <u>telephoto</u> lens.
17. I asked for the star's <u>autograph</u>.
18. The <u>astronomer</u> studied the stars.
19. We prevented the <u>disaster</u>.
20. A <u>homophone</u> sounds the same.

Review/Challenge Words

1. The editor made a <u>correction</u>.
2. That was a lively <u>discussion</u>.
3. Flowers are nice for <u>decoration</u>.
4. We spoke through the <u>videophone</u>.
5. Models are very <u>photogenic</u>.

The word in **bold** type is from the main selection.

LA.5.5.2.1 Listen to gain and share information

Day 1 Pretest

ASSESS PRIOR KNOWLEDGE

Using the Dictation Sentences, say the underlined word. Read the sentence aloud and repeat the word. Have students write the words on **Spelling Practice Book** page 161. For a modified list, use the first 12 Spelling Words and the Review Words. For a more challenging list, use Spelling Words 3–20 and the Challenge Words. Students may correct their own tests.

Ask students to cut apart the Spelling Word Cards BLM on **Teacher's Resource Book** page 91 and figure out a way to sort them. They can save the cards for use throughout the week.

Spelling Practice Book, pages 161–162

Fold back the paper along the dotted line. Write the words in the blanks as they are read aloud. When you finish the test, unfold the paper. Use the list at the right to correct any spelling mistakes.

1. _____		1. astronaut
2. _____		2. autograph
3. _____		3. automatic
4. _____		4. automobile
5. _____		5. mythical
6. _____		6. telegraph
7. _____		7. telephone
8. _____		8. telescope
9. _____		9. television
10. _____		10. telegram
11. _____		11. homophone
12. _____		12. phonics
13. _____		13. disaster
14. _____		14. astronomer
15. _____		15. photograph
16. _____		16. photography
17. _____		17. myth
18. _____		18. mechanic
19. _____		19. mechanical
20. _____		20. telephoto
Review Words 21. _____		21. correction
22. _____		22. discussion
23. _____		23. decoration
Challenge Words 24. _____		24. videophone
25. _____		25. photogenic

LA.5.1.6.4 Identify salient features

Day 2 Word Sorts

TEACHER AND STUDENT SORTS

- Write these column headings on the board: *astr/aster, photo, tele, phon, mech, myth*. Tell students they will be sorting the Spelling Words according to these Greek roots.

- Model the sort with the words *phonics* and *disaster*. Place *phonics* in the *phon* column and *disaster* in the *astr/aster* column.

- Using the Word Cards, read a few words aloud and ask volunteers to write the words in the proper columns on the board.

- Have students work in small groups to sort all the Spelling Words and Challenge Words in their word study notebooks. Point out that some words (such as *telephone*) can be sorted into more than one column.

- Check the sort as a class.

Spelling Practice Book, page 163

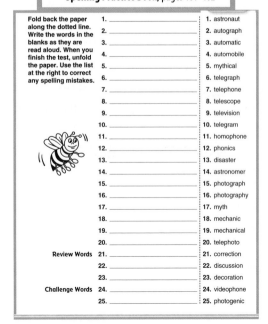

telegram	automatic	homophone	myth
mechanic	disaster	telegraph	astronaut
automobile	telephoto	astronomer	photograph
photography	telescope	autograph	telephone
phonics	mechanical	television	mythical

Sort each spelling word according to the Greek root it contains. Then write the words on the lines below. Some words may be placed into more than one category.

astro
1. astronaut   2. astronomer   3. disaster *(aster)*

auto
1. autograph   2. automatic   3. automobile

photo
1. photograph   2. photography   3. telephoto

tele
1. telegraph   2. telephone   3. telescope
4. television   5. telegram   6. telephoto

phon
1. phonics   2. homophone   3. telephone

mech
1. mechanic   2. mechanical

myth
1. myth   2. mythical

Day 3 — Word Meanings

LA.5.1.6.11 Use roots and affixes from Greek and Latin

DEFINITIONS

- Ask students to return to yesterday's word sort chart. Explain the definitions of the words and use each in a sentence.

- Have students examine the words in each column to figure out the meaning of the Greek root that is common to the words. Students can work in groups and check their answers by looking up the roots in a dictionary.

- Review the Greek roots as a class, and discuss how the Spelling and Challenge Words incorporate these roots in their definitions.

- Since many of the words are nouns, ask students to draw the words or find illustrations in magazines. Display the illustrations next to the Word Cards.

Day 4 — Review and Proofread

LA.5.3.4.1 Edits for spelling

SPIRAL REVIEW

Review words that add the suffix -ion. Write correction, discussion, and decoration on the board. Ask students to identify the root words, and explain how adding -ion changes the meanings of the words.

PROOFREAD AND WRITE

Write these sentences on the board, including the misspelled words. Ask students to proofread, circling the misspelled words and writing them correctly.

1. The astranaut signed autografs at the science fair. (astronaut, autographs)

2. The astraunomer marveled at the quality of the teleskope. (astronomer, telescope)

3. The mechanich said the automobil was beyond repair. (mechanic, automobile)

Day 5 — Assess and Reteach

LA.5.1.6.11 Use roots and affixes from Greek and Latin

POSTTEST

Use the Dictation Sentences on page 667G for the Posttest.

If students have difficulty with any words in the lesson, have them place the words in a list entitled "Spelling Words I Want to Remember" in their word study notebooks.

Challenge student partners to find other words that contain the same Greek roots they studied this week, either in their reading or in other materials. Partners should work together to sort the words according to these Greek roots.

Spelling Practice Book, page 164

telegram	automatic	homophone	myth
mechanic	disaster	telegraph	astronaut
automobile	telephoto	astronomer	photograph
photography	telescope	autograph	telephone
phonics	mechanical	television	mythical

Complete each sentence below with a spelling word.

1. Alexi gazed up at the stars through his __telescope__
2. A __photograph__ of the Tsar would let Yelena the Fair see how old he was.
3. Alexi had no __automobile__, so he had to travel on a horse.
4. The Golden Mare is a __mythical__ creature.
5. The word "fair" is a __homophone__ of "fare" because it sounds the same but is spelled differently.
6. If Alexi hadn't had the ring, it would have been a __disaster__.
7. The Golden Mare told a __myth__ about how the ring was formed.
8. An __astronomer__ taught Alexi how to travel by using the stars.
9. The Tsar designed a __mechanical__ device for hunting birds.
10. The __telephone__ was not yet invented at the time of the story.

Write On!

Use each spelling word in a sentence. Answers will vary.

11. mechanic _____
12. television _____
13. astronaut _____
14. photography _____
15. autograph _____

Spelling Practice Book, page 165

Circle the misspelled words in the passage. Write the words correctly on the lines below.

Andrea turned on the (telivision). There was a program on about a (mithical) bird and a horse. She picked up the (telefone) to call Jill, but no one answered. The (automatick) answering machine clicked on, and Andrea began to leave a message.

"I was doing my (phonics) homework when this show came on!" she exclaimed. "There's a bird on TV that looks just like the one in the (photagraph) you have. Turn on channel eight, if you're home."

1. __television__   2. __mythical__   3. __telephone__
4. __automatic__   5. __phonics__   6. __photograph__

Writing Activity

Write a paragraph about what you would have done if you were Alexi and became Tsar. Use four words from your spelling list.

_____
_____
_____
_____
_____
_____
_____
_____
_____

Spelling Practice Book, page 166

Look at the words in each set below. One word in each set is spelled correctly. Use a pencil to fill in the circle next to the correct word. Before you begin, look at the sample set of words. Sample A has been done for you. Do Sample B by yourself. When you are sure you know what to do, you may go on with the rest of the page.

Sample A:
- Ⓐ kilometer
- Ⓑ killometer
- Ⓒ kilommeter
- Ⓓ killommeter

Sample B:
- Ⓔ phoeton
- Ⓕ foton
- Ⓖ photton
- Ⓗ photon

1. Ⓐ astronat Ⓑ astanaut Ⓒ astronaut Ⓓ astranat
2. Ⓔ autagraph Ⓕ autograph Ⓖ auttograph Ⓗ autograf
3. Ⓐ automattic Ⓑ automatic Ⓒ automatc Ⓓ automattic
4. Ⓔ autommobile Ⓕ autommobil Ⓖ automobil Ⓗ automobile
5. Ⓐ mythical Ⓑ mythiccal Ⓒ mithical Ⓓ mithiccal
6. Ⓔ telegraph Ⓕ tellegraph Ⓖ tellegraph Ⓗ teleggraph
7. Ⓐ tellephone Ⓑ telephone Ⓒ tellephone Ⓓ telephone
8. Ⓔ tellescope Ⓕ telescope Ⓖ telesscope Ⓗ tellesscope
9. Ⓐ tellevision Ⓑ television Ⓒ televission Ⓓ tellevission
10. Ⓔ telegram Ⓕ tellegram Ⓖ telegramm Ⓗ tellegramm
11. Ⓐ homopphone Ⓑ hommophone Ⓒ homophone Ⓓ hommopphone
12. Ⓔ phanics Ⓕ phonix Ⓖ phonnics Ⓗ phonics
13. Ⓐ disaster Ⓑ dissaster Ⓒ disasster Ⓓ dissasster
14. Ⓔ astranomer Ⓕ astronomer Ⓖ astronommer Ⓗ asrtonnomer
15. Ⓐ photograph Ⓑ phottograph Ⓒ photoggraph Ⓓ phottoggraph
16. Ⓔ photography Ⓕ phottography Ⓖ photagraphy Ⓗ photography
17. Ⓐ mytth Ⓑ mith Ⓒ myth Ⓓ myeth
18. Ⓔ machanic Ⓕ mechanic Ⓖ mecanic Ⓗ macanic
19. Ⓐ mechanical Ⓑ mecanical Ⓒ mechanacal Ⓓ mecanacal
20. Ⓔ telephoto Ⓕ tellephoto Ⓖ telefoto Ⓗ tellefoto

Adverbs

Daily Language Activities

Use these activities to reinforce each day's lesson. Write the day's activity on the board, or use **Daily Language Transparency 26.**

DAY 1

Alexi was a good hunter but not the goodest. One day his hunting was going poor, but then he was sudden surprised by the appearance of a beautiful horse. (1: best.; 2: poorly,; 3: suddenly)

DAY 2

They rode swift to the court of the Tsar, who hired Alexi. The Tsar said, "I trust that you will serve me quitely well." (1: swiftly; 2: quite)

DAY 3

Alexi was a very well rider. Riding one day he saw a bright colored feather. The Mare said in a lowly voice, "You should not take the feather." (1: good; 2: brightly; 3: low)

DAY 4

Alexi continued to perform good for the Tsar. He and the Mare worked togetherly to capture the Firebird. (1: well; 2: together)

DAY 5

The Golden Mare clever figured out how to get the magically ring from the bottom of the lake. She asked nice whether the crab would retrieve it. (1: cleverly; 2: magical; 3: nicely)

ELL

Give Examples Write, *How? When? Where?* Underneath write: *They will arrive <u>soon</u>. She went <u>inside</u>. He sings <u>badly</u>.* Explain that the underlined words are adverbs. Adverbs tell how, when, and where. Help students to match the adverb to its corresponding question word.

Day 1 | Introduce the Concept

LA.5.3.4.4. Correct use of adverbs
INTRODUCE ADVERBS

Present the following:

- An **adverb** can be a word that tells more about a verb, an adjective, or another adverb.

- Some adverbs tell the manner, or *how*, an action takes place. For example, *slowly, happily.*

- Some adverbs tell the time, or *when,* an action takes place. For example, *then, now, early.*

- Some adverbs tell the place, or *where,* an action happens. For example, *here, there, inside.*

See Grammar Transparency 126 for modeling and guided practice.

Grammar Practice Book, page 161

- An **adverb** is a word that tells more about a verb, an adjective, or another adverb.
- An adverb can tell *how, when,* or *where* an action takes place.

Underline the adverb in each sentence. On the line, write whether the adverb describes *how, when,* or *where.*

1. Alexi walked slowly through the woods. ___how___
2. The Golden Mare left early to reach the Lake of the Sun. ___when___
3. Angry at the Tsar's words, Alexi trembled inside. ___where___
4. The Golden Mare galloped rapidly through the forest. ___how___
5. The Firebird cried softly in its cage. ___how___
6. He hunted late into the night. ___when___
7. The Tsar treated the Firebird cruelly. ___how___
8. The Firebird flew high into the sky. ___where___
9. Alexi and Yelena the Fair were happily married. ___how___
10. Alexi and the Golden Mare always remained friends. ___when___

Day 2 | Teach the Concept

LA.5.3.4.4. Correct use of adverbs
REVIEW ADVERBS

Review adverbs of manner, time, and place. Point out that adverbs serve as modifiers of adjectives, verbs, or other adverbs.

INTRODUCE ADVERBS BEFORE ADJECTIVES AND OTHER ADVERBS

- An adverb is a word that can describe an adjective.

- An adverb can describe another adverb.

- Adverbs that describe adjectives and other adverbs also tell *how, when,* or *where.*

See Grammar Transparency 127 for modeling and guided practice.

Grammar Practice Book, page 162

- An adverb can describe a verb. It can also describe an adjective or another adverb.

In these sentences, the adverbs describe verbs, adverbs, or adjectives. Underline each adverb. Some sentences contain more than one adverb.

1. The Golden Mare spoke quietly.
2. Yelena the Fair realized that she would be in danger very soon.
3. The Tsar was terribly angry about Alexi's success.
4. The Lake of the Sun shone brilliantly in the morning.
5. The Water of Youth began to boil very quickly.

Complete each sentence with an adverb that describes the underlined word. Choose from the adverbs in the box.

almost	very	completely	finally	quite	rather	too

6. The Tsar acted _____ greedily. more than one answer possible
7. They poured water into the iron pot until it was _____ full.
8. The ship moved _____ gracefully across the water.
9. Alexi stayed awake _____ late that night.
10. Alexi and the Golden Mare _____ defeated the Tsar.

Day 3 — Review and Practice

LA.5.3.4.4. Correct use of adverbs

REVIEW ADVERBS BEFORE ADJECTIVES AND OTHER ADVERBS

Review the way adverbs of time, manner, and place are used in sentences. Adverbs should always appear close to the verbs, adjectives, or other adverbs that they describe.

MECHANICS AND USAGE: USE *GOOD* AND *WELL*

- *Good* is an adjective. It is used to describe nouns.

- *Well* is often an adverb that tells *how*.

- *Well* is an adjective when it means *healthy*.

Day 4 — Review and Proofread

LA.5.3.4.4. Correct use of adverbs

REVIEW ADVERBS

Ask students to explain the three ways in which adverbs are used. Next, invite students to explain the three things that adverbs "tell."

PROOFREAD

Have students identify and correct the following errors.

1. Princess Yelena real wants to avoid marrying the Tsar. (really)

2. She has a well plan. (good)

3. She asks for a vat of very hotly water. She says that her magical power will make the Tsar young again. (hot)

4. Alexi is thrown rough into the water but amazing survives. (roughly, amazingly)

Day 5 — Assess and Reteach

LA.5.3.4.4. Correct use of adverbs

ASSESS

Use the Daily Language Activity and page 165 of the **Grammar Practice Book** for assessment.

RETEACH

Tell students to fold a sheet of paper in half vertically. Ask students to write the corrected Daily Language Activities on the left side of the paper. Have each student work with a partner to underline each adverb in the sentences. On the right side, students should write comments identifying what each adverb describes and what it "tells." If they incorrectly identify an adverb, then review the concept.

Use page 166 of the **Grammar Practice Book** for additional reteaching.

 See Grammar Transparency 128 for modeling and guided practice.

 See Grammar Transparency 129 for modeling and guided practice.

 See Grammar Transparency 130 for modeling and guided practice.

Grammar Practice Book, page 163

- *Good* is an adjective and is used to describe nouns.
- *Well* is an adverb that describes a verb. *Well* tells *how* an action takes place.
- Do not confuse the adjective *good* with the adverb *well*.

Read both sentences in each pair. Circle the letter of the sentence that uses *good* or *well* correctly.

1. a. The Golden Mare was a good friend to Alexi.
   b. The Golden Mare was a well friend to Alexi.
2. a. Yelena the Fair hid her plan good.
   b. Yelena the Fair hid her plan well.
3. a. Alexi ruled good.
   b. Alexi ruled well.
4. a. They played a good trick on the Tsar.
   b. They played a well trick on the Tsar.
5. a. The Tsar did not treat Alexi well.
   b. The Tsar did not treat Alexi good.

Write *well* or *good* to complete each sentence correctly. Then underline the word that *good* or *well* describes.

6. Alexi was a ____good____ ruler to his people.
7. The Tsar thought that if he planned ____well____, he could wed Yelena the Fair.
8. The Tsar would not be a ____good____ husband.
9. Alexi and the Golden Mare worked ____well____ together.
10. The Golden Mare promised to serve Alexi ____well____

Grammar Practice Book, page 164

Read the paragraph below. Rewrite the paragraph correctly on the lines provided.

The Golden Mare was real old when she met Alexi. Because she was amazing, she looked and felt quitely healthy and young. The Golden Mare could gallop quick through the forest as though she were made of wind. Her hooves hard hit the ground when she ran. Alexi could not believe his well fortune when he saw this mysterious creature. He rough rubbed his eyes, expecting the horse to disappear sudden.

The Golden Mare was really old when she met Alexi. Because she was amazing, she looked quite healthy and young. The Golden Mare could gallop quickly through the forest as though she were made of wind. Her hooves hardly hit the ground when she ran. Alexi could not believe his good fortune when he saw this mysterious creature. He roughly rubbed his eyes, expecting the horse to disappear suddenly.

Grammar Practice Book, pages 165–166

A. Rewrite each sentence twice. Each time, add an adverb that tells *when*, *where*, or *how*.

1. The Golden Mare ran.
   more than one answer possible

2. Alexi hunted.
   more than one answer possible

3. Yelena the Fair sailed on the Lake of the Sun.
   more than one answer possible

4. The Tsar gave orders.
   more than one answer possible

5. The Firebird flew.
   more than one answer possible

B. Write *well* or *good* to complete each sentence correctly.

6. The Tsar did not rule ____well____
7. The Golden Mare advised Alexi ____well____
8. The crab was a ____good____ swimmer.
9. The beautiful Firebird flew ____well____ after it had been set free.
10. Yelena the Fair had a ____good____ heart.

End-of-Week Assessment

Administer the Test

 FCAT **Weekly Reading Assessment**
pages 309–320

ASSESSED SKILLS

- Chronological Order
- Vocabulary Words
- Homophones
- Greek Roots
- Adverbs

 Progress Reporter
Macmillan/McGraw-Hill

 CD ROM **Assessment Tool**

Administer the **Weekly Assessment** from the CD-ROM or online.

Weekly Assessment, 309–320

 Fluency

Assess fluency for one group of students per week. Use the Oral Fluency Record Sheet to track the number of words read correctly. Fluency goal for all students:
129–149 words correct per minute (WCPM).

Approaching Level	Weeks 1, 3, 5
On Level	Weeks 2, 4
Beyond Level	Week 6

Fluency Assessment

 **FCAT** **Alternative Assessments**

- **ELL Assessment** pages 162–163

ELL Assessment, 162–163

Diagnose	IF...	Prescribe
		THEN...
VOCABULARY WORDS **VOCABULARY STRATEGY** Homophones Items 1, 2, 3, 4, 5	0–2 items correct …	Reteach skills using the **Additional Lessons** page T6. Reteach skills: Go to **www.macmillanmh.com** **Vocabulary PuzzleMaker** Evaluate for Intervention.
COMPREHENSION Skill: Chronological Order Items 6, 7, 8, 9	0–2 items correct …	Reteach skills using the **Additional Lessons** page T1. Evaluate for Intervention.
SPELLING Greek Roots Items 10, 11, 12	0–1 items correct …	Reteach skills: Go to **www.macmillanmh.com**
GRAMMAR Adverbs Items 13, 14, 15	0–1 items correct …	Reteach skills: **Grammar Practice Book** page 166.
FLUENCY	120–128 WCPM 0–110 WCPM	Fluency Solutions Evaluate for Intervention.

READING
Triumphs
AN INTERVENTION PROGRAM

Also Available

To place students in the Intervention Program, use the **Diagnostic Assessment** in the Intervention Teacher's Edition.

Approaching Level Options

Constructive Feedback

If students fail to understand the relationship between the roots and the meaning of the word, say:

Think about two building blocks. One says astr, *meaning "star." The other says* nomos, *meaning "law." Now, imagine putting the two blocks together to form the word* astronomy, *meaning "science of the laws that govern the stars and planets."*

Repeat as needed with other words with Greek roots.

Additional Resources

Use your observations to help identify students who might benefit from additional instruction. See page T2 for comprehension support and page T5 for vocabulary support. For each skill below, additional lessons are provided. You can use these lessons on consecutive days after teaching the lessons presented within the week.
• Chronological order, T2
• Dictionary: Homphones, T5
• Text Feature: Venn Diagram, T9

Decodable Text

To help students build speed and accuracy with reading multisyllabic words, use additional decodable text on pages 30–31 of the **Teachers' Resource Book.**

Skills Focus ▶ **Phonics**

Objectives　Review words with Greek roots

　　　　　　　Decode multisyllabic words with Greek roots in both familiar and unfamiliar texts

Materials　• math and science books

WORDS WITH GREEK ROOTS

LA. 5.1.6.11 Use roots and affixes derived from Greek to determine meaning

Model/Guided Practice

■ Write the word *asteroid* on the board. Blend the sounds. Explain that the Greek root *aster* (also *astr*), meaning "star," is part of the word *asteroid,* meaning "small planet."

■ Write *astronaut* on the board. *What does* astronaut *mean?*

■ Next practice using word origins to understand the meanings of *autobiography, photodegradable, mechanism,* and student-generated words. Extend the review to point out that some words contain more than one Greek root, as in *photograph.*

MORE MULTISYLLABIC WORDS WITH GREEK ROOTS

LA. 5.1.6.11 Use roots and affixes derived from Greek to determine meaning

■ Write *biography* on the board. Break the word into syllables: *bi/og/ra/phy.* Point out the Greek roots: *bio* means "life" and *graph* means "something written."

■ Have pairs of students decode other words with Greek roots. Write the following words on the board or provide copies of the list. *With your partner, choose a word. Say the word aloud. Identify the Greek root or roots. Use your knowledge of the root(s) to define the word. Check your definition in a dictionary.*

astrodome	photosensitive	phonics
automatic	mechanical	telegraph
graphology	microphone	telescope

WORD FAMILIES: WORDS WITH GREEK ROOTS IN CONTEXT

LA.5.1.4 Student applies grade level phonics

■ Have students search their science and math books for words with Greek roots. Have students identify the roots and their meanings, and then define the words. Tell students to check their definitions against dictionary definitions.

■ Students might have found the following words or terms: *automatic behavior, automatic reflex, automaton, photosynthesis.*

■ To extend the activity, have each student use two or more words with Greek roots and write short paragraphs containing word families of the chosen word. For example, *My mom took the car to the* mechanic. *It was having* mechanical *problems. Somthing was wrong with the electrical* mechanism.

Skills Focus > Fluency

Objective Read with increasing prosody and accuracy at a rate of 129–139 WCPM

Materials • **Approaching Practice Book A,** page 189

MODEL EXPRESSIVE READING

LA.5.1.5 Read orally with accuracy

Model reading the Fluency passage in **Practice Book A,** page 189. Tell students to pay close attention to your pauses and intonation. Then read aloud one sentence at a time, and have students repeat the sentence, first as a class and then one by one. As students read, listen for accuracy.

REPEATED READING

LA.5.1.5 Student demonstrates ability to read orally with accuracy

Have students continue practicing reading the passage aloud as you circulate and provide constructive feedback. During independent reading time, student partners can take turns reading the passage. One partner reads each sentence aloud, and the other repeats it. Remind students to wait until their partners reach end marks before correcting mistakes.

TIMED READING

LA.5.1.5 Read orally with accuracy

Tell students they will do a timed reading of the passage that they have been practicing. With each student:

- Place the passage from Practice Book A, page 189, face down.
- When you say "Go," the student begins reading the passage aloud.
- When you say "Stop," the student stops reading the passage.

As students read, note any miscues. Stop students after one minute. Help them record and graph the number of words they read correctly.

Skills Focus > Vocabulary

Objective Apply vocabulary word meanings

Materials • **Vocabulary Cards** • **Transparencies 26a and 26b**

VOCABULARY WORDS

LA.5.1.6.3 Use context clues to determine meanings of unfamiliar words

Display the **Vocabulary Cards** for this week's words: *dismiss, intentions, despair, bridle, descended, accompany, delicacies, consented.* Help students locate and read the vocabulary words on **Transparencies 26a** and **26b.** Ask students to identify context clues in the story that help them determine the words' meanings. Have students categorize the context clues with labels such as example, synonym, antonym, and so on.

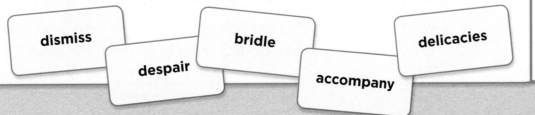

Constructive Feedback

Encourage students to pause according to punctuation. Suggest that students tap their fingers or toes once when they meet commas and semicolons and twice when they meet end marks and colons. Model this practice for students.

★ **Approaching Practice Book A,** page 189

As I read, I will pay attention to pauses and intonation.

	One fine spring day, Graham and his flock of sheep were
11	enjoying the sun. The sheep wandered this way and that
21	over the hillside. As Graham lay in the grass, marveling at
32	his good fortune, he heard a very strange noise.
41	The sound seemed to be coming from a nearby pond. It
52	sounded to Graham as if a woman were choking. Not one to
64	sit by while someone suffered, he rushed to the pond. A
75	beautiful white swan was swimming in circles, trying to
84	remove something caught in her throat. Graham waited for a
94	moment because he didn't want to startle the bird. Then he
105	called softly to the swan.
110	Stretching her long neck uncomfortably, the swan glided
118	over to Graham. The young man and the bird looked into
129	each other's eyes. Graham almost believed he saw tears in
139	the swan's eyes. 142

Comprehension Check

1. What was Graham doing before he went to the pond? **Chronological Order** watching his flock of sheep on the hillside

2. What did Graham notice about the swan? **Plot Development** The swan was beautiful but seemed upset.

	Words Read	−	Number of Errors	=	Words Correct Score
First Read		−		=	
Second Read		−		=	

Small Group

Vocabulary

Review last week's words: (**attraction, discussions, emerged, focused, inquire, sprawled, ventured, unreasonable**) and this week's words (**dismiss, intentions, despair, bridle, descended, accompany, delicacies, consented**). Have students write a sentence for each word.

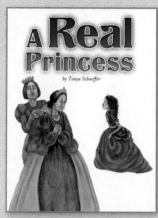

Student Book

ELL

Access for All

Picture Walk Have students use the illustrations from *A Real Princess* to show and describe the chronological order of events. Practice using transition words that help tell the order of events, such as *first, then, next, later,* and *finally.*

Skills Focus > Vocabulary

Objective Review homophones
Materials • **Vocabulary Cards**
• **Student Book** *The Golden Mare, the Firebird, and the Magic Ring*

 FCAT

HOMOPHONES: RECOGNIZE HOMOPHONES

LA.5.1.6.8
Use homophones to determine meaning

Review that homophones are words that sound alike but have different spellings and definitions. Help students identify which of the vocabulary words is a homophone. (bridle) Have students write silly sentences using *bridle* and *bridal* to distinguish the definitions. Challenge them to look through *The Golden Mare, the Firebird, and the Magic Ring* to find as many homophones as they can. (Some homophones on the first two pages are *time/thyme, where/wear, two/too/to, but/butt, for/four, week/weak, night/ knight, made/maid, in/inn, herd/heard, deer/dear, some/sum, mane/main/ Maine, heart/hart, fair/fare, your/you're/yore, you/ewe, so/sew, by/bye/buy, no/ know, not/knot.*) Ask students to repeat the activity with ten homophone sets that they choose from three texts.

Skills Focus > Comprehension

Objective Review chronological order
Materials • **Student Book** *A Real Princess* • **Transparencies 26a and 26b**

STRATEGY
SUMMARIZE

LA.5.1.7 Use strategies to comprehend text

Review with students that summarizing is telling, in the reader's own words, the most important events in a story.

FCAT #### SKILL
CHRONOLOGICAL ORDER

LA.5.2.1.2
Analyze elements of plot structure
LA.5.1.7.5
Identify text structure

■ The chronological order of events is the order of events as they occur in real time. Authors may use words such as *first, second, next, then, later,* and *finally* to indicate chronology.

Explain/Model

Display **Transparencies 26a** and **26b.** Reread the first two paragraphs. Ask a volunteer to underline the first event in the story. Help students distinguish between background information and story events.

Practice/Apply

Reread *A Real Princess* with students and discuss the following questions:

■ What is the prince's first reaction to the princess? What is his final reaction to her? What is the chronological order of events in the queen's test?

Leveled Reader Lesson

Objective Read to apply strategies and skills

Materials • **Leveled Reader** *Graham the Kind-Hearted*

Leveled Reader

PREVIEW AND PREDICT

LA.5.1.7.1
Use prior knowledge to make and confirm predictions

Ask students to preview the cover, table of contents, illustrations, and first two chapters to make predictions about the events in the story. Have students note any questions they have about the story prior to reading.

VOCABULARY WORDS

LA.5.1.6.3
Use context clues

Review vocabulary words as necessary. As you read together, stop to discuss how vocabulary words are used in context.

STRATEGY
SUMMARIZE

LA.5.1.7
Student uses strategies to comprehend text

Remind students that summarizing can help them understand and remember what they read. To summarize, students must identify the most important ideas and events in a story or text and restate them in their own words.

SKILL
CHRONOLOGICAL ORDER

FCAT

LA.5.2.1.2
Locate and analyze elements of plot structure

Remind students to keep track of the chronological order of events.

Think Aloud In the first chapter, the farmer asks Graham to take care of his sheep, but Graham leaves to help a swan in need, and the sheep run away. The same thing happens in the second chapter when the farmer asks Graham to take care of his goats. I see a repeating pattern of events in the story. I'll note them on my chart.

READ AND RESPOND

Tell students to finish reading the first two chapters of the story. Summarize the chronological order of events, and discuss what students think about Graham and the swan.

MAKE CONNECTIONS ACROSS TEXTS

LA.5.1.7.7
Compare and contrast elements in multiple texts

Invite students to compare *Graham the Kind-Hearted* and *The Golden Mare, the Firebird, and the Magic Ring.*

■ How are *Graham the Kind-Hearted* and *The Golden Mare, the Firebird, and the Magic Ring* similar or different? What do you learn about fairy tales based on these stories?

■ How do both of these selections make use of a repeating pattern of events? What effect do these patterns have on the plot?

ELL
Access for All

Visual Sequence Have students draw pictures of the key events in the story. Have them work in pairs to label each picture. As a group, place the pictures in chronological order using the words *first, next* and *finally.*

Student Book

Student Book

Paired Selection

On Level Practice Book O, page 189

As I read, I will pay attention to pauses and intonation.

	Once upon a time, a really, really long time ago, there lived
12	a beautiful, kind-hearted girl named Katharine. You would
21	have thought that such a lovely girl would be happy. But she
33	was not. She was sad and terribly lonely.
41	For you see (as is to be expected in a story like this),
54	Katharine's life was filled with sorrow. Her mother died
63	when she was young. Her father brought her to live with her
75	Aunt Mara and cousins Melina and Ursula while he went off
86	to fight for the king. Her father loved Katharine dearly and
97	promised to return for her as soon as possible, but that
108	promise was made many years ago.
114	Over the years Katharine's cousins grew to hate her. They
124	knew that Katharine was kinder and more beautiful than they
134	were. Each day Melina and Ursula were meaner. They
143	ordered her around. Katharine was truly miserable.
150	So what did Katharine do all day? She did everything!
160	Inside she cooked and cleaned. Outside she planted, weeded,
169	and harvested the garden, fed the animals, cleaned the barn,
179	collected the eggs, and milked the cow. 186

Comprehension Check

1. Why was Katharine miserable? **Plot Development** Katharine had a difficult life.
2. Why were Ursula and Melina cruel to Katharine? **Plot Development** They were jealous of her beauty and kindness.

	Words Read	–	Number of Errors	=	Words Correct Score
First Read		–		=	
Second Read		–		=	

Skills Focus — Vocabulary

Objective	Review vocabulary words
Materials	**Student Book** *The Golden Mare, the Firebird, and the Magic Ring*

VOCABULARY WORDS

LA. 5.1. 6 Student uses multiple strategies to develop vocabulary

Referring to the main selection, tell students to create lists of fairy-tale characters. Then ask students to use the vocabulary words to write small "trailers" that might be used to attract viewers to a movie about each character on their lists. For example: White horses *accompany* Cinderella to the ball. The old woman sees Hansel and Gretel as *delicacies*.

HOMOPHONES: RECOGNIZE HOMOPHONES

FCAT

LA.5.1.6.8 Use homphones to determine meanings of words

Review with students that homophones are words that sound alike but have different spellings and meanings. The words *bridal* and *bridle* are homophones. Write the following words on the board: *main, hart, sum, wood, their, road, grate, maze, sea, threw, hymn, guessed*. Using *The Golden Mare, the Firebird,* and *the Magic Ring*, have students find a homophone for each. Ask students to write sentences that illustrate the meaning of each.

Skills Focus — Study Skill

Objective	Use a Venn diagram
Materials	• **Student Book** *A Real Princess* • **Paired Selection** *Personal Choices: Learning Through Stories* • A version of the fairy tale *The Princess and the Pea*

VENN DIAGRAM

LA. 5.1.7.1 Explain purpose of text features

Use a Venn diagram to compare and contrast *A Real Princess* with *Personal Choices*. Then have students use the diagrams to compare *A Real Princess* with a traditional version of *The Princess and the Pea*.

Skills Focus — Fluency

Objective	Read fluently with good prosody at a rate of 129–149 WCPM
Materials	• **On Level Practice Book O,** p. 189

REPEATED READING

LA.5.1.5 Read orally with appropriate rate

Model reading aloud the Fluency passage on page 189 of **Practice Book O.** Tell students to pay close attention to your pauses and intonation as you read. Then read aloud one sentence at a time, and have students read each sentence back chorally. Listen for accuracy.

Timed Reading Have students read the passage and record their reading rate.

Leveled Reader Lesson

Objective Read to apply strategies and skills

Materials • **Leveled Reader** *Daisies in Winter*

PREVIEW AND PREDICT

LA.5.1.7.1
Use prior knowledge to make and confirm predictions

Have students preview *Daisies in Winter*.

■ What does the title suggest about the story?

■ How does the story begin? What do you think will happen next?

■ Do you have any of your own questions you would like to ask?

SKILL
CHRONOLOGICAL ORDER

FCAT

LA.5.1.7.5
Identify text structure and explain how it impacts meaning

Review: Chronological order is the sequence of story events as they occur in real time. When events are presented in time order, the author often uses clue words, such as *first, then,* or *next*. Sometimes readers must make inferences about events that have been left out of the text. Explain that students will record information about story events in Sequence Charts.

READ AND RESPOND

LA.5.2.2.3
Organize information to show understanding

Read Chapter 1. Pause to discuss the chronological order of events. Ask: What happened to Katharine's mother? Where is her father? How did she come to live with her aunt and cousins? At the end of Chapter 1, begin filling in the Sequence Charts. Have students discuss what they think will happen in Chapter 2 and how they think the story might end.

VOCABULARY WORDS

LA.5.1.6.3
Use context clues to determine meanings

As they read *Daisies in Winter*, ask students to point out the vocabulary words. Discuss how each word is used in context. Ask questions such as: *Why would you accompany someone who promised you delicacies and not someone who consented to dismiss you?* Have students respond in kind.

MAKE CONNECTIONS ACROSS TEXTS

LA.5.1.7.7
Compare and contrast elements in multiple texts

Invite students to recount the chronological orders of events in both *Daisies in Winter* and *The Golden Mare, the Firebird, and the Magic Ring*.

■ How is the chronological order of events in the two books similar? How is it different? How does it help you understand the themes better?

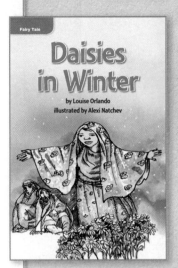

Leveled Reader

ELL
Leveled Reader
Go to pages
667U–667V.

Skills Focus ▶ Vocabulary

Objective   Write fairy tales using vocabulary words

✓ **EXTEND VOCABULARY**

LA.5.1.6.1
Use new vocabulary

Invite students to write short fairy tales, and have them put blanks in place of the vocabulary words. Then have students trade tales and use context clues to fill in the missing words. If time allows have one student begin a tale and another complete it. As an extension they can also rewrite familiar fairy tales, updating them or giving them alternate endings.

A Real Princess
by Tonya Schaeffer

Student Book

Skills Focus ▶ Study Skill

Objective   Understand and use a Venn diagram
Materials   • **Student Book** *A Real Princess*
                • Two other versions of *The Princess and the Pea*

VENN DIAGRAM

LA.5.1.7.1
Explain purpose of text features

Point out that a Venn diagram can be used to compare two or more items. Discuss with students what a Venn diagram comparing three items might look like. Ask what the difficulties would be in making and using it.

Have students construct Venn diagrams to compare *A Real Princess* with another version of *The Princess and the Pea*. Then have students add details from a third version of the story to their Venn diagrams.

ELL   Access for All

Use Graphic Organizers
Ask students to work in pairs and select two fairy tales from the unit to compare using a Venn diagram. Have them compare the characters in both stories using this sentence pattern: _____ and _____ are the same because _____. They are different because _____ .

Skills Focus ▶ Fluency

Objective   Read fluently with good prosody at a rate of 139–149 WCPM
Materials   • **Beyond Practice Book B,** page 189

REPEATED READING

LA.5.1.5
Read orally with appropriate rate

Model reading aloud the Fluency passage on page 189 of **Practice Book B.** Tell students to pay close attention to your intonation and pauses as you read. Then read aloud one sentence at a time, and have students read each sentence back chorally.

During independent reading time, partners can take turns reading the passage they have marked. Remind students to wait until their partners reach end marks before correcting mistakes.

As an extension allow students to record themselves using different intonations. Have them pick the best ones as a group.

◆ **Beyond Practice Book B,** page 189

As I read, I will pay attention to pauses and intonation.

	Once upon a time, in a land far, far away lived a mother with her three
16	daughters and very young son. They lived on a beautiful old farm
28	surrounded by hills and mountains that were covered in wildflowers.
38	The mother loved flowers so much that when her daughters were born
50	she named each sweet child after a flower. Their names were: Rose,
62	Poppy, and Lily. The three girls grew into beautiful young women. They
74	were very smart, just like their mother. They loved to read and knew all
88	about the plants that grew around their home. They were often seen
100	walking the hills collecting flowers to study.
107	Every day, the daughters helped their mother. Rose cared for their
118	herds of sheep and goats. Poppy and Lily worked in the garden. They all
132	baked bread.
134	When the girls finished their chores, they went for walks collecting
145	plants. They drew pictures and took notes about each specimen they
156	found. They also talked, as sisters will on these walks. They talked about
169	their friends, school, flowers, and their dreams.
176	Rose, the eldest sister, loved the hardy plants that covered the cool
188	mountaintop. Her dream was to become an herbalist and discover new
199	medicinal uses for different herbs. 204

Comprehension Check

1. How did the three daughters get their names? **Main Idea and Details**
   They were named after flowers.

2. How did the daughters spend their days? **Plot Development** reading,
   studying, collecting plants; doing chores; and
   taking walks

	Words Read	–	Number of Errors	=	Words Correct Score
First Read		–		=	
Second Read		–		=	

Leveled Reader Lesson

Objective Read to apply strategies and skills

Materials • **Leveled Reader** *The Three Sisters*

PREVIEW AND PREDICT

LA.5.1.7.1
Establish purpose for reading

Have students preview *The Three Sisters,* predict what it is about, and set purposes for reading.

VOCABULARY WORDS

LA.5.1.6.3
Use context clues

Review vocabulary words as necessary. Ask students questions such as, *Which food is considered a delicacy, oysters or fish sticks?* Have them respond in kind.

SKILL
CHRONOLOGICAL ORDER

LA.5.2.1.2
Locate and analyze elements of plot structure

Ask a volunteer to define chronological order and to explain how an author indicates the sequence of events to the reader. Explain that students will read *The Three Sisters* together and that they will use charts to record information about the chronological order of events in the tale.

READ AND RESPOND

As they read, students should identify the chronological order of events and fill in their Sequence Charts. Have them compare charts and note any differences. Can they retell the story using the charts?

Self-Selected Reading

Objective Read independently to identify chronological orders of events and to make connections across texts

Materials • Leveled Readers or trade books at students' reading levels

READ TO IDENTIFY CHRONOLOGICAL ORDER

LA.5.1.7.7
Compare and contrast elements in multiple texts

Invite students to review the beginnings, middles, and ends of *The Three Sisters, A Real Princess,* and *The Golden Mare, the Firebird, and the Magic Ring.* Ask how the chronological order of events in the three fairy tales are similar. Have students summarize their comparisons in Venn diagrams.

Next, invite students to choose books for independent reading. After reading, have students identify the chronological order of events in their stories. Discuss why it is helpful to pay attention to this aspect of a story as they read.

Fairy Tale

The Three Sisters

by Louise Orlando
illustrated by Alexi Natchev

Leveled Reader

Academic Language

Throughout the week the English language learners in your class will need help building their understanding of the academic language used in daily instruction and assessment instruments. The following strategies will help increase their language proficiency and comprehension of content and instructional words.

Oral Language For oral vocabulary development go to www.macmillanmh.com

Strategies to Reinforce Academic Language

- **Use Context** Academic language used by the teacher (see chart below) should be explained in the context of the task during Whole Group. You may use gestures, expressions, and visuals to support meaning.

- **Use Visuals** Use charts, transparencies, and graphic organizers to explain key labels to help students understand classroom language.

- **Model** Demonstrate the task using academic language in order for students to understand instruction.

Academic Language Used in Whole Group Instruction

Content/Theme Words	Skill/Strategy Words	Writing/Grammar Words
conflict (p. 639)	summarize (p. 641A)	eyewitness account (p. 666)
triumphs (p. 639)	chronological order (p. 641A)	adverb (p. 667I)
responsible (p. 662)	text feature (p. 662)	verb (p. 667I)
civic (p. 662)	Venn diagram (p. 662)	adjective (p. 667I)
	similarities (p. 662)	good (p. 667J)
	differences (p. 662)	well (p. 667J)

ELL Leveled Reader Lesson

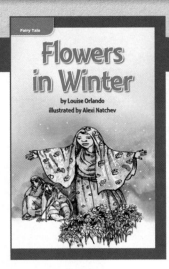

Fairy Tale

Flowers in Winter

by Louise Orlando
illustrated by Alexi Natchev

 Before Reading

DEVELOP ORAL LANGUAGE

 Build Background *Who wants to tell the class a fairy tale?* Prompt the class to help you recall a well-known fairy tale. Use this example to review how characters in fairy tales are either good or evil and how good characters usually prevail.

 Review Vocabulary Write the vocabulary and story support words on the board and discuss their meanings. Model using them in sentences. *My father* consented *to buying me a digital camera. My* intentions *are to take pictures of parks and flowers.*

PREVIEW AND PREDICT

Point to the cover illustration and read the title aloud. *What do you think this story is about? Who are the characters? When does it happen?*

 FCAT Set a Purpose for Reading Show the Sequence Chart and remind students they have used this chart before. Ask them to identify the sequence of events in chronological order and fill in a similar chart.

 During Reading

Choose from among the differentiated strategies to support students' reading at all levels of language acquisition.

Beginning	**Intermediate**	**Advanced**
Shared Reading As you read, model how to identify the main events in sequence and note them in the chart. Check students' comprehension and use vocabulary and support words: *Which month* consented *to Katharine's first request?*	**Read Together** Read through Chapter 1. Ask students to identify and summarize in their charts the events in Katharine's life up to this point. Have them predict what may happen to her next. Then have them continue to read and fill in their charts.	**Independent Reading** Have students read the story. Ask them to identify in sequence the main events that happen. Challenge students to compare and contrast story elements of this story and the story *Space Fruit* from Unit 5.

 After Reading

Remind students to use the vocabulary and story words in their whole group activities. Have them complete the Comprehension Check questions.

Objective

- To apply vocabulary and comprehension skills

Materials

- ELL Leveled Reader

5-Day Planner

DAY 1	• Academic Language
	• Oral Language and Vocabulary Review
DAY 2	• Academic Language
	• ELL Leveled Reader
DAY 3	• Academic Language
	• ELL Leveled Reader
DAY 4	• Academic Language
	• ELL Leveled Reader
DAY 5	• Academic Language
	• ELL Leveled Reader Comprehension Check and Literacy Activities

ELL Teacher's Guide
for students who need additional instruction

Weekly Theme: Camping Out

Week At A Glance

Whole Group

 VOCABULARY
guaranteed, supervise, frustrated, coordination, ease, scenery, bundle, fused

 FCAT Dictionary: Multiple-Meaning Words

COMPREHENSION
Strategy: Monitor Comprehension
FCAT **Skill:** Plot Development

 WRITING
FCAT Expository/How-to

FCAT Science
Processes That Shape the Earth

Small Group Options

 **Differentiated Instruction for Tested Skills**

FCAT Tested FCAT Benchmark

✓ Tested Skill for the Week

✹ Sunshine State Standard

FCAT FCAT Benchmark

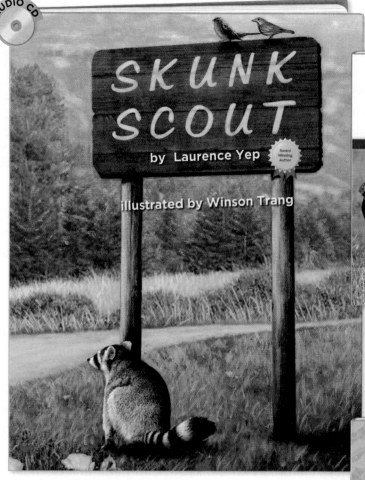

Main Selection
| Genre | Realistic Fiction |

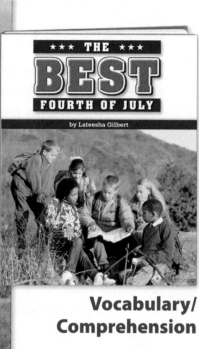

Vocabulary/ Comprehension

 Science Link
| Genre | Nonfiction Article |

Read-Aloud Anthology
• Listening Comprehension
• Readers' Theatre

Resources for Differentiated Instruction

FCAT LEVELED READERS: Science
GR Levels S–X

Genre Realistic Fiction

- Same Theme
- Same Vocabulary
- Same Comprehension Skills

(S)

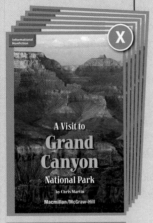

(U)

(X)

A Visit to **Grand Canyon** National Park
by Chris Martin
Macmillan/McGraw-Hill

Approaching Level

On Level

Beyond Level

(U)

The Amazing **Grand Canyon**
by Chris Martin
Macmillan/McGraw-Hill

English Language Leveled Reader

Sheltered Readers for English Language Learners

ELL Teacher's Guide also available

LEVELED PRACTICE

Practice Book A **Practice Book O** **Practice Book B** **ELL Practice and Assessment**

Approaching **On Level** **Beyond** **ELL**

INTERVENTION PROGRAM

- Phonics and Decoding
- Comprehension
- Vocabulary

Also available, *Reading Triumphs*, Intervention Program

CLASSROOM LIBRARY

Genre Biography

  Charlie Pippin

Frindle Andrew Clements

SKUNK SCOUT

Approaching **On Level** **Beyond**

Trade books to apply Comprehension Skills

FCAT Success!

TIME FOR KIDS
FCAT EDITION
INSIDE
• Science Discoveries
• Social Studies Explorations
Macmillan/McGraw-Hill

- FCAT Edition
- Content Area Reading

FCAT Test Preparation and Practice

FCAT Format Benchmark Assessment

FCAT Format Weekly Assessment

FCAT Test Preparation and Practice

FCAT Benchmark Assessments

FCAT Unit and Weekly Assessments

HOME-SCHOOL CONNECTION
- Family letters in English, Spanish, and Haitian Creole

Home-School Connection
Macmillan/McGraw-Hill

- Take-Home Stories

 CD ROM **Instructional** *Navigator* **Interactive Lesson Planner**

Skunk Scout, 672–689

Integrated ELL Support Every Day

Whole Group

ORAL LANGUAGE
- **Listening**
- **Speaking**
- **Viewing**

WORD STUDY
- **Vocabulary**
- **Phonics/Decoding**

READING
- **Develop Comprehension**

- **Fluency**

LANGUAGE ARTS
- **Writing**

- **Grammar**

- **Spelling**

ASSESSMENT
- **Informal/Formal**

Turn the Page for
Small Group Lesson Plan

Day 1

Listening/Speaking/Viewing
❓ Focus Question Have you ever been camping? How is camping out different from living at home? LA.5.5.2
Build Background, 668
Read Aloud: "John Muir, Man of the Mountains," 669

Vocabulary LA.5.1.6.3
✔ FCAT *guaranteed, supervise, frustrated, coordination, ease, scenery, bundle, fused,* 670
Practice Book A-O-B, 193
✔ FCAT **Strategy:** Use a Dictionary: Multiple-Meaning Words, 671

Read "The Best Fourth of July," 670–671 LA.5.1.6.3
Comprehension, 671A–671B
  Strategy: Monitor Comprehension
✔ FCAT **Skill:** Plot Development LA.5.2.1.1
  Practice Book A-O-B, 194

Student Book

Fluency Partner Reading, 668I
Model Fluency, 669 LA.5.1.5
Partner Reading, 668I LA.5.1.5

✔ FCAT **Writing**
Daily Writing: Write a letter to your family or friends about a camping trip that you have taken or would like to take.

How-to Instructions, 697A

Grammar Daily Language Activities, 697I
✔ Adverbs that Compare, 697I
Grammar Practice Book, 167
✔ **Spelling** Pretest: Latin Roots, 697G
Spelling Practice Book, 167–168 LA.5.1.4.1

Quick Check Vocabulary, 670
Comprehension, 671B

Differentiated Instruction 697M–697V

Day 2

Listening/Speaking
❓ Focus Question How does Teddy feel about the camping trip? LA.5.5.2

Vocabulary LA.5.1.6.1
Review Vocabulary Words, 672
Phonics/Decoding LA.5.1.4
Decode Words with Latin Roots, 697E
Practice Book A-O-B, 199

Read *Skunk Scout,* 672–689 LA.5.2.1.2
Comprehension, 672–691
  Strategy: Monitor Comprehension
✔ FCAT **Skill:** Plot Development LA.5.2.1.2
  Practice Book A-O-B, 195

Student Book

Fluency Partner Reading, 668I LA.5.1.5

✔ FCAT **Writing**
Daily Writing: Suppose you are lying in a tent in the woods. Describe the sounds that you would hear as you drift off to sleep.

How-to Instructions, 697A

Grammar Daily Language Activities, 697I
Adverbs that Compare, 697I
Grammar Practice Book, 168
Spelling Latin Roots, 697G
Spelling Practice Book, 169 LA.5.1.4.1

Quick Check Comprehension: 681, 689
Phonics, 697E

Differentiated Instruction 697M–697V

Benchmarks

Turn the Page for
Small Group Options

FCAT

Vocabulary	Comprehension	Writing	Science
Vocabulary Words **Dictionary/Multiple-Meaning Words** LA.5.1.6.9 Determine correct meaning of multiple-meaning words	**Strategy: Monitor Comprehension** **Skill: Plot Development** LA.5.2.1.2 Locate and analyze elements of plot structure	**Expository/How-To Instructions** LA.5.4.2.1 Write in a variety of expository forms	**Process that Shapes the Earth** SC.D.1.2.3.4.2 Understands how geological features result

---

Day 3

Listening/Speaking

❷ Focus Question Compare and contrast the camping experiences that Teddy and Lateesha had. Use details from both selections to support your answer.

Summarize, 691 LA.5.5.2

Vocabulary

Review Words in Context, 697C

FCAT Strategy: Dictionary: Multiple-Meaning Words, 697D

Practice Book A-O-B, 198

Phonics Decode Multisyllabic Words, 697E LA.5.1.4

Read Skunk Scout, 672–689

Student Book

Comprehension

Comprehension Check, 691

FCAT Maintain Skill: Compare and Contrast, 691B

Fluency Repeated Reading, 691A

Partner Reading, 668I

Practice Book A-O-B, 196 LA.5.1.7

FCAT Writing

Daily Writing: You are going on a camping trip for two weeks. Make a list of essential items you would pack. Explain why you need those items.

Writer's Craft: Time-Order Words, 697A
How-to Instructions, 697B LA.5.4.2.1

Grammar Daily Language Activities, 697I
Mechanics and Usage, 697J
Grammar Practice Book, 169

Spelling Latin Roots, 697H
Spelling Practice Book, 170 LA.5.1.4.1

 Fluency, 691A

Differentiated Instruction 697M–697V

Day 4

Listening/Speaking/Viewing

❷ Focus Question Compare and contrast how nature played a role in the events in "An Underwater Park" and Skunk Scout.

Expand Vocabulary: Camping Out, 697F LA.5.5.2

Vocabulary

Content Words: *glaciers, ecosystem, erosion*, 692

Multiple-Meaning Words, 697F

Apply Vocabulary to Writing, 697F

Read "An Underwater Park," 692–695

Student Book

Comprehension

Science: Nonfiction Article

FCAT Text Feature: Photographs and Captions 692

Practice Book A-O-B, 197

Fluency Partner Reading, 668I

FCAT Writing

Daily Writing: You are attending a camp where each camper wants to face a challenge. Describe a challenge you would like to face.

Writing Trait: Word Choice, 697B
How-to Instructions, 697B LA.5.4.2.1

Grammar Daily Language Activities, 697I
Adverbs that Compare, 697J
Grammar Practice Book, 170

Spelling Latin Roots, 697H
Spelling Practice Book, 171 LA.5.1.4.1

 Vocabulary, 697D

Differentiated Instruction 697M–697V

Day 5

Review and Assess

Listening/Speaking/Viewing

❷ Focus Question Would you have made decisions different from the characters in Skunk Scout? Explain.

Speaking and Listening Strategies, 697A

Present How-to Instructions, 697B

Vocabulary

Spiral Review: Vocabulary Game, 697F

Read Self-Selected Reading, 668I LA.5.2.2.5

Comprehension

Connect and Compare, 695 LA.5.2.2.2

Student Book

Fluency Partner Reading, 668I LA.5.1.5

Practice, 691A

FCAT Writing

Daily Writing: Write a job description for a camping buddy in the form of a newspaper ad. Explain skills and personality traits that your camping buddy should have.

How-to Instructions, 697B LA.5.4.2.1

Grammar Daily Language Activities, 697I
Adverbs that Compare, 697J
Grammar Practice Book, 171–172

Spelling Postest, 697H
Spelling Practice Book, 172 LA.5.1.4.1

FCAT Weekly Assessment, 321–332

Differentiated Instruction 697M–697V

Differentiated Instruction

What do I do in small groups?

Teacher-Led Small Groups

Literacy Workstations

Independent Activities

Focus on Skills

Skills Focus → Use your **Quick Check** observations to guide additional instruction and practice.

Phonics
Latin Roots

✔ **Vocabulary**
Words: scenery, guaranteed, coordination, supervise, frustrated, fused, ease, bundle
FCAT ✔ **Strategy:** Dictionary/Multiple-Meaning Words

Comprehension
✔ **Strategy:** Monitor Comprehension
FCAT ✔ **Skill:** Plot Development

FCAT ✔ **Fluency**

Suggested Lesson Plan

Instructional Navigator
Interactive Lesson Planner

	DAY 1	DAY 2
Approaching Level • **Additional Instruction/Practice** • **Tier 2 Instruction**	Fluency, 697N Vocabulary, 697N Comprehension, 697O	Phonics, 697M Vocabulary, 697O Leveled Reader Lesson, 697P • Vocabulary • Comprehension
On Level • **Practice**	Vocabulary, 697Q Leveled Reader Lesson, 697R • Comprehension **ELL** Leveled Reader, 697U–697V	Leveled Reader Lesson, 697R • Comprehension • Vocabulary
Beyond Level • **Extend**	Vocabulary, 697S Leveled Reader Lesson, 697T • Comprehension	Leveled Reader Lesson, 697T • Comprehension • Vocabulary

For intensive intervention see **READING Triumphs**

Small Group Options

Focus on Leveled Readers

Apply **FCAT** skills and strategies while reading appropriate leveled books.

Levels S–X

Approaching On Level Beyond

ELL

Additional Leveled Reader Resources

Leveled Reader Database

Go to www.macmillanmh.com

Search by

- Comprehension Skill
- Content Area
- Genre
- Text Feature

- Guided Reading Level
- Reading Recovery Level
- Lexile Score
- Benchmark Level

Subscription also available.

Focus on Science

Teacher's Annotated Edition

Processes that Shape the Earth

SC.D.1.2.4.5.2 Geological features

Additional Leveled Readers

A Visit to Big Bend National Park

A Visit to Yellowstone National Park

Day 3

Phonics, 697M
Fluency, 697N
Vocabulary, 697O
Leveled Reader Lesson, 697P
- Comprehension

Fluency, 697Q
Vocabulary, 697Q
Leveled Reader Lesson, 697R
- Comprehension

Fluency, 697S
Vocabulary, 697S
Leveled Reader Lesson, 697T
- Comprehension

Day 4

Phonics, 697M
Leveled Reader Lesson, 697P
- Comprehension
ELL Skill: Plot Development

Text Feature, 697Q
Leveled Reader Lesson, 697R
- Comprehension

Text Feature, 697S
Leveled Reader Lesson, 697T
- Comprehension
ELL Prepare an Interview, 697S

Day 5

Fluency, 697N
Leveled Reader Lesson, 697P
- Make Connections Across Texts

Fluency, 697Q
Leveled Reader Lesson, 697R
- Make Connections Across Texts

Fluency, 697S
Self-Selected Reading, 697T

Managing the Class

What do I do with the rest of my class?

Teacher-Led Small Groups

Literacy Workstations

Independent Activities

Class Management Tools

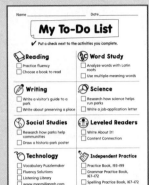

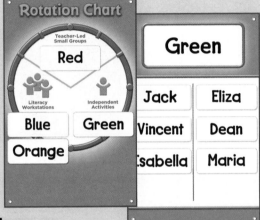

Includes:
- How-to Guide
- Rotation Chart
- Weekly Contracts

FOLDABLES™

Hands-on activities for reinforcing weekly skills

Fish	Frogs
habitat	habitat
food	insects
prey	prey
enemies	enemies

Eight-Tab Foldable

Word	Synonym	Antonym	Prefix or Suffix
normal	typical	unusual	normally

Folded Chart

Independent Activities

 FCAT LEVELED READERS: Science

For Repeated Readings and Literacy Activities

Literacy Activities

Make a Visitor's Guide

Create a one-page handout that you might receive at the Visitor's Center to help you enjoy your visit to Big Bend. The handout might also contain one or more safety tips.

Big Bend Model

Use modeling clay to show elevations at Big Bend. In one large map, show the heights of the river, the desert, the Basin, and the mountains in relation to each other.

Approaching

Literacy Activities

Write a Journal Entry

Imagine that you visited Grand Canyon National Park, stood on the South Rim, and hiked a short distance down into the canyon. Write a journal entry that you might have recorded on that day. Tell what you saw and felt.

Give a Report

You have read about the different forces that formed the Grand Canyon. Choose one of these forces and learn more about it in an encyclopedia. Prepare a brief oral report about it for the class.

On Level

Literacy Activities

Grand Canyon Journal

Pretend that you visited Grand Canyon National Park. You stood on the South Rim, and you hiked into the canyon. Write a short journal entry about something you saw and how you felt. Share your writing with the class.

Give a Report

You read about different forces that formed the Grand Canyon. Work with a partner. Choose one of the forces and draw and label a picture of it. Write a report about how that force changes land.

ELL

Literacy Activities

Yellowstone Brochure

Create a brochure that you might receive at the Visitor's Center to help you enjoy your visit to Yellowstone. Use the cover of the brochure to show one of Yellowstone's most famous sites. Use the middle of the brochure to tell about places to visit. Include some quotations from visitors about the park.

Research Glaciers

Earth science tells us about how the earth formed. Glaciers are one force that helped form Yellowstone National Park. Research how glaciers can carve the land. Then use what you have learned about glaciers might have helped change or create the land there.

Beyond

LEVELED PRACTICE

Skills: Vocabulary, Plot Development, Fluency, Multiple-Meaning Words, Photographs and Captions

Approaching

On Level

Beyond

ELL

Technology

ONLINE INSTRUCTION www.macmillanmh.com

- Meet the Author/Illustrator
- Computer Literacy Lessons
- Research and Inquiry Activities

- Oral Language Activities
- Vocabulary and Spelling Activities
- Leveled Reader Database

 LISTENING LIBRARY

Recordings of selections
- Main Selections
- Leveled Readers
- ELL Readers
- Intervention Anthology

 VOCABULARY PUZZLEMAKER

Activities providing multiple exposures to vocabulary, spelling, and high-frequency words including crossword puzzles, word searches, and word jumbles

 FLUENCY SOLUTIONS

Recorded passages for modeling and practicing fluency

Turn the page for Literacy Workstations.

Managing the Class

Literacy Activities
Collaborative Learning Activities

 Reading

 Word Study

Objectives

- Read aloud for smoothness and clarity; time reading
- Record information from independent reading
- Maintain a personal reading log of accomplishments
- Read independently daily

Objectives

- Use a dictionary to find words with Latin roots
- Locate and use multiple-meaning words

LA.5.1.5 Read orally with accuracy

 Reading — **FLUENCY** — 20 Minutes

- Read silently the passage on page 196 of your Practice Book. Then read the passage aloud, recording your reading on a tape recorder, if possible. Then replay the tape as you follow along in the text. Work with a partner if recording is not possible.
- If you stumbled when reading the passage, read it aloud or record it again. Repeat this process until your reading sounds smooth, without stumbling or hesitation.
- **Time Your Reading**: Listen to the Audio CD.

Extension

- Offer and receive feedback on the reading.

Things you need:
- Practice Book
- tape recorder and tape

Fluency Solutions
Listening Library

53

LA.5.1.6.11 Use roots and affixes derived from Latin to determine meaning

 Word Study — **LATIN ROOTS** — 20 Minutes

- Many English words are based on Latin roots. Some examples of these Latin roots are *aud*, from the Latin word meaning "to hear"; *spect*, from the Latin word meaning "to look or watch"; *port*, from the Latin word meaning "to carry"; and *mit/miss*, from the Latin word meaning "to send."
- Use a dictionary or go online to find words built on each of these Latin roots.
- Write how each English word relates to its Latin root.

Extension

- Choose one Latin root and draw a Latin root tree. Write the Latin root and its meaning on the trunk, and then write the English words formed from the Latin root on the tree's branches.

Things you need:
- paper and pen or pencil
- dictionary or access to the Internet

aud = to hear

For additional vocabulary and spelling games, go to www.macmillanmh.com

53

LA.5.2.2.5 Select age and ability appropriate non-fiction materials to read

Reading — **Independent Reading** — 20 Minutes

- Find a library book or Web site on national parks. Read about a park that you have not seen or visited. When you have finished reading, write down any features that make you want to visit or go camping in the park.

Extension

- Use the Internet or library to search for books on parks around the world that sound interesting to you. List these in your response journal.

National Parks
Yosemite

Things you need:
- paper and pen
- library or access to the Internet

For more books about camping out, go to the Author/Illustrator section at www.macmillanmh.com

54

LA.5.1.6.9 Determine correct meanings of words with multiple meanings

Word Study — **Multiple-Meaning Words** — 20 Minutes

- With a partner scan the dictionary for multiple-meaning words. One of you can scan the entries for the letters from A to M, and the other can scan the entries for the letters from N to Z. Find one multiple-meaning word for each letter of the alphabet. Write the multiple meanings of each word.

Extension

- With a partner choose five of your words and write a sentence to illustrate each meaning of all five words. Underline the words in the sentences.

Things you need:
- paper and pen or pencil
- dictionary

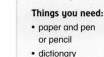

"Which cavity?"

For additional vocabulary and spelling games, go to www.macmillanmh.com

 Vocabulary PuzzleMaker

54

Literacy Workstations

Writing

Objectives

- Write a guide to explain rules for a national park
- Write a personal essay about a place
- Be enthusiastic about writing and learning to write
- Write to communicate ideas and emotions for different audiences

Content Literacy

Objectives

- Research science jobs and write job descriptions
- Research how national parks help communities
- Read and research topics to satisfy personal, academic, and social needs

---

LA.5.4.2.1 Write in a variety of informational forms

Writing — Guide Writing
20 Minutes

- Write a series of short paragraphs for a visitor's guide about how a visitor should behave in a national park. Think about how a visitor should treat nature and historic treasures. Also think about ways for visitors to be kind to fellow visitors. Consider noise, food, drink, animals, picture taking, running, and driving.

Extension

- Draw a poster for young children to explain guidelines for camping out in a national park.

Things you need:
- paper and construction paper
- pen or pencil
- markers or colored pencils

53

LA.5.4.2.2 Record information related to a topic

Science — Parks and Science
20 Minutes

- Brainstorm with a partner how a knowledge of science would be helpful in running a national park.
- Research the ways in which scientists work with national parks. List the different jobs that require science and write a description of each job.

Extension

- Which job would you want at a park? Write a letter to a park explaining why you want to learn that job.

Things you need:
- paper and pen or pencil
- library or access to the Internet

LOG ON Internet Research and Inquiry Activity
Students can find more facts at www.macmillanmh.com

53

LA.5.4.2.1 Write in a variety of expository forms

Writing — Personal Writing
20 Minutes

- Think of a place that should be preserved as your own personal park. The place could be a desert or a wooded area, a farm, a historic area, or a playground.
- Write about the place and explain why you do not want it to be changed.

Extension

- Write a brochure for your personal park. Include a paragraph describing your park. Use bullet points for important features.
- Draw a picture of one of the important features. Provide directions to the park.

Things you need:
- construction paper
- pen or pencil
- colored pencils or markers

54

LA.5.6.2 Use process for collection, processing, presentation of information

Social Studies — Parks and Communities
20 Minutes

- Research the ways in which parks help communities. Include research on national parks dedicated to preserving history.
- Write a list of ways in which parks contribute to the social life of communities.

Extension

- Select a park that focuses on a historical event. Draw a poster encouraging people to visit that park.
- Include information on how to get there, what to see, and what people can learn there.

Things you need:
- paper and pen or pencil
- library or access to the Internet

54

ORAL LANGUAGE
- Build Background
- Read Aloud
- Expand Vocabulary

FCAT VOCABULARY
- Teach Words in Context
- **Dictionary:** Multiple-Meaning Words

COMPREHENSION
- **Strategy:** Monitor Comprehension
- FCAT • **Skill:** Plot Development

SMALL GROUP OPTIONS
- Differentiated Instruction, pp. 697M–697V

Oral Language

Build Background

LA.5.5.2.1
Listen to gain and share information

ACCESS PRIOR KNOWLEDGE

Share the following information:

■ Camping is a popular vacation option for nature-lovers.

■ Hiking, swimming, and fishing are associated with camping.

LA.5.5.2.1
Listen and speak to gain and share information

TALK ABOUT CAMPING OUT

Discuss the weekly theme. Say:

Describe any experience you've had camping out. What did you do?

Access for All

FOCUS QUESTION Ask a volunteer to read "Talk About It" on **Student Book** page 669 and describe the photo.

■ What camping equipment do you see in the photo?

■ What activities do the items suggest?

668

ENGLISH LANGUAGE LEARNERS

Access for All

Beginning Model Have students say what they can about the photo. Point to and name unfamiliar items, such as *tent or lantern.* Describe the photo: *The boy and girl are looking at the sea. They sleep in the tent. They are camping.* Have students repeat. Ask, *Would you like to go camping? Why or why not?*

Intermediate Activate Prior Knowledge Have students describe the photo. Ask, *Have you ever camped out? Where did you go camping? What did you do? What did you see?* For Spanish-speaking students, point out the cognate *-acampar.*

Advanced Elaborate Complete the Intermediate task. As students speak, rephrase what they say and extend their sentences: *So, you went on a three-day camping trip in the mountains.*

Talk About It

Have you ever been camping? How is camping out different from living at home?

LOG ON Find out more about camping out at **www.macmillanmh.com**

CAMPING OUT

669

Picture Prompt

Look at the picture and write a poem about what the children are looking for. Use descriptive details to evoke the surroundings.

 **Technology**

For an extended lesson plan and Web site activities for **oral language development**, go to **www.macmillanmh.com**

Read Aloud Read "John Muir, Man of the Mountains"

LA.5.2.1.1 Demonstrate knowledge of characteristics of genres

GENRE: Biography
Review features of a biography:

■ the true story of a person's life, written by another person

Read Aloud
pages 124–126

LA.5.1.6.2 Listen and discuss familiar text

LISTENING FOR A PURPOSE

Ask students to listen carefully for what John Muir accomplished as you read "John Muir, Man of the Mountains" in the **Read-Aloud Anthology.** They should be prepared to discuss his accomplishments, and their opinions about John Muir. Choose from among the teaching suggestions.

Fluency Ask students to listen carefully as you read aloud, paying attention to your phrasing, expression, and tone of voice.

LA.5.1.6.2 Discuss familiar text

RESPOND TO THE SELECTION

Have students describe John Muir and the setting, and retell the events in the biography in sequence. Remind them to use specific examples from the text.

LA.5.5.2 Student applies listening and speaking strategies

Expand Vocabulary

Have students make up a narrative about a person like John Muir using words from the selection and then tell the story orally to a classmate. Have them make sure that they have established a situation, developed a plot, point of view, and setting with descriptive words and phrases.

Vocabulary

LA.5.1.6.1
Use new vocabulary taught directly

LA.5.1.6.3
Use context clues to determine meaning

TEACH WORDS IN CONTEXT

Use the following routine:

Routine

Define: **Guaranteed** means made sure or certain.

Example: Ed guaranteed cupcakes for the bake sale.

Ask: What is a synonym of *guaranteed*?

SYNONYM

- When you **supervise**, you watch over and direct what is going on. Mr. Logan will supervise students in detention. How are *supervise* and *watch* similar and different? COMPARE AND CONTRAST

- **Frustrated** means to have feelings of discouragement. My mom felt frustrated when our picnic was rained out. What kinds of situations have made you feel frustrated? EXAMPLE

Access for All

- **Coordination** is the ability of parts or things to work together well. Kendra's coordination lets her dance and twirl a baton at the same time. When have you needed good coordination? PRIOR KNOWLEDGE

LA.5.1.6.8
Use antonyms to determine meaning

- **Ease** means to move slowly and carefully. Jim used a shoehorn to ease his heel into the tight boot. What is an antonym of *ease*? ANTONYM

- **Scenery** is the sights of a place or region. We admired the scenery from the train window. Describe scenery that you have seen. DESCRIPTION

- A **bundle** is a group of items held together. Dad prepared a bundle of clothes for hurricane victims. How is a bundle different from a collection? COMPARE AND CONTRAST

Vocabulary

guaranteed	ease
supervise	scenery
frustrated	bundle
coordination	fused

FCAT Dictionary

A word can have many meanings. A **Dictionary** can help you decide which definition is appropriate. For example, *fused* can mean "made into a liquid by heating" or "blended together by melting."

670

- **Fused** means blended or united. Alan fused two pieces of metal using heat. What causes things to be fused together? EXPLANATION

Quick Check   **Do students understand word meanings?**

During **Small Group Instruction**

If No → **Approaching Level**
Vocabulary, p. 697N

If Yes → **On Level** Options, pp. 697Q–697R

Beyond Level Options, pp. 697S–697T

THE ★★★ BEST FOURTH OF JULY

by Lateesha Gilbert

Sunday, July 5

Dear Mom and Dad,

I hope you had a great Fourth of July. You can imagine what a big deal it was here at Camp Freedom. With a name like that, the camp really went all out to celebrate!

For weeks every cabin was working on a Fourth of July skit. Since all the girls in my cabin are super funny, our counselor **guaranteed** the other cabins we would have the funniest skit in camp. At first we were pretty casual about working on it. Then the days went by and no one had come up with a good idea. Our counselor, Jean, started getting worried. Finally, she decided she should **supervise** us and our ideas more closely. She went from cracking jokes with us to being bossy. We all felt **frustrated**. She kept telling us what to do and she would not listen to our ideas. In the end, we did a skit about the founder of the camp, Fannie Freedom. Hardly anyone laughed.

ELL   **Access for All**

Use Vocabulary

For *frustrated*, write: *It's raining. I really want to go outside and play, but I can't. I'm frustrated because I can't do what I want to do.* Discuss the sentences. Write: *I feel frustrated when _____.* Have students use the sentence frame to share their ideas. For the word *supervise*, ask: *What adult supervises you on the playground? Are there younger children that you supervise?*

After the skits we had a cookout, complete with those yummy chocolate, marshmallow, and cracker things. Arranging everything on sticks involved a lot of **coordination**. The ingredients were sticky and hard to manage. I didn't poke my stick all the way through each marshmallow. As I would **ease** the stick into the fire, the marshmallows would fall off. I am surprised the fire didn't go out from all the marshmallows that fell in.

Later that day the counselors took us to the top of Lookaway Mountain. The **scenery** was amazing from up there. The hard part was we had to carry a large **bundle** of blankets tied together with some string. The big surprise at the end of the day was a fireworks display, which lit up the entire sky. On the way back to camp, Jean apologized to us for not listening to our ideas. We told her that we had fun anyway.

By the way, thank you for the package you sent me. Everything was really great. The jelly beans melted and **fused** together, but don't worry. That didn't affect the taste. My bunkmates and I ate them for a late night snack on July Fourth, and everyone agreed they were still delicious!

Love you all,
Lateesha

Reread for **Comprehension**

Monitor Comprehension

FCAT **Plot Development** The events of a story's plot often come about as a result of **actions** taken by the characters. As you read, you make **judgments** about a character's actions. A Judgments Chart helps you monitor your comprehension of how a character's actions affect the plot. Use your Judgments Chart as you reread the selection.

Action	→	Judgment
	→	
	→	
	→	
	→	

671

FCAT **Success!**

Test Prep and Practice with vocabulary, pages 6–31.

On Level Practice Book O, page 193

A. Match the vocabulary word with its definition. Then write the letter of the correct word on the line.

1. ease ___d___   a. joined together
2. scenery ___e___   b. disappointed or kept from doing something
3. bundle ___f___   c. working well together
4. fused ___a___   d. move carefully or slowly
5. guaranteed ___g___   e. landscape
6. supervise ___h___   f. group of things held together
7. frustrated ___b___   g. assured
8. coordination ___c___ h. watch and direct

B. Fill in the paragraph using the eight vocabulary words from section A.

My uncle __guaranteed__ that we would enjoy the __scenery__ of the mountains and lake. But the trip did not start out great. We tried to __ease__ the tent out of the stuffed car, but it wouldn't budge. Next, my older brother became __frustrated__ when he noticed the __bundle__ of hamburgers was __fused__ together. Unfortunately, we did not bring any other food for dinner. We relied on the __coordination__ of all three of us to get the hamburgers separated. While my uncle cooked, he wanted to __supervise__ me as I unpacked the rest of the car. I was about to ask to go home when I saw two baby deer playing with each other. I guess being in nature is worth a frozen dinner and over-stuffed car.

⭐ **Approaching Practice Book A,** page 193
◆ **Beyond Practice Book B,** page 193

Vocabulary

STRATEGY
DICTIONARY

LA.5.1.6.10 Determine meanings of words using a dictionary

Multiple-Meaning Words Remind students that many words have more than one meaning. Point out that when the meaning of a familiar word does not make sense in a sentence, it is probably a multiple-meaning word. Students should look up the word in a dictionary, read all the definitions, and find the one that makes sense in the sentence.

Point out the multiple-meaning word *ease* in the left column of page 671. One familiar meaning is "freedom from trouble or pain," as in the sentence: *Our friends, who worked hard for years, retired and lived a life of ease.* This meaning of *ease* does not make sense in the sentence. Have students look up *ease* in a dictionary and find the meaning that makes sense in the sentence on page 671. (to move slowly and carefully)

LA.5.1.6 Student develops grade-appropriate vocabulary

Read "The Best Fourth of July"

As you read "The Best Fourth of July" with students, ask them to identify clues that reveal the meanings of the highlighted words. Tell students they will read these words again in *Skunk Scout*.

Objectives

- Monitor comprehension
- Use academic language: *make judgments, monitor comprehension, plot development*
- Make judgments about a letter

Materials

- Comprehension Transparencies 27a and 27b
- Graphic Organizer Transparency 27
- Practice Book, p. 194

FCAT Skills Trace

Plot Development	
Introduce	19A–B
Practice / Apply	20–39, 51A–B, 147A–B, 231A–B, 263A–B, 359A–B, 395A–B, 607A–B, 671A–B; Practice Book 2–3, 9–10, 39–40, 67–68, 76–77, 104–105, 113–114, 178–179, 194–195
Reteach / Review	251B, 441B, 661B Small Group Options
Assess	Weekly Tests; Unit 1–6 Tests
Maintain	51A–B, 147A–B, 231A–B, 263A–B, 359A–B, 395A–B, 607A–B, 671A–B

ELL   Access for All

Build Background Prepare students to read the selection by finding out what they know about camping. Introduce words such as *cabin, camp counselor, cookout, bunk, bunkmates.*

Reread for Comprehension

LA.5.1.7 Use strategies to comprehend text

STRATEGY
MONITOR COMPREHENSION

Remind students that good readers **monitor** their **comprehension** as they read. They stop at regular intervals, asking themselves what they have just read. If they have a problem, they use self-correction techniques such as rereading, summarizing, and adjusting their reading rate when necessary. Reading ahead, note-taking, and outlining are other strategies good readers use.

Access for All

FCAT   SKILL
PLOT DEVELOPMENT

Access for All

LA.5.2.1.2 Analyze plot structure and character development

EXPLAIN

Making judgments can help readers follow and understand the **plot development** of a story. Making a judgment means forming an opinion about the value of something, or about whether someone's actions are appropriate. This helps readers analyze character development and how it affects the plot.

To **make judgments** while reading, good readers first notice details about the characters and events in the story. Then they form a

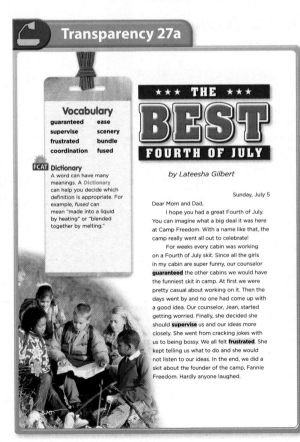
Transparency 27a

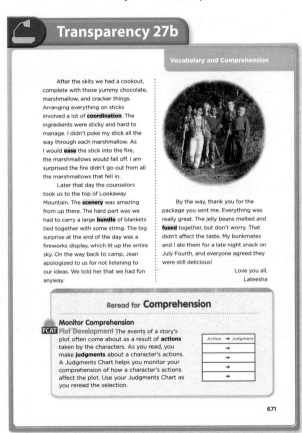
Transparency 27b

Student Book pages 670–671 available on Comprehension Transparencies 27a and 27b

temporary opinion about the character or event based on their own experience, and find evidence in the text to support their judgment.

MODEL

Read the first few paragraphs of "The Best Fourth of July" from **Student Book** page 670.

Think Aloud Lateesha seems to be complaining that she and her friends must pitch in to help the camp celebrate the Fourth of July. She seems to place the blame for her own laziness on her counselor. I can judge from this that Lateesha is not the clearest thinker. She seems to be prejudiced against her counselor, who is just doing her job.

GUIDED PRACTICE

Display **Transparency 27.** Explain that a Judgments Chart can help readers gain a deeper understanding of characters and their motivations. Begin the Judgments Chart with Lateesha's actions. (Lateesha and her cabinmates put off working on their Fourth of July skit, so their counselor Jean takes control of the rehearsals.) Help students judge her action. (Lateesha and her friends are somewhat lazy.)

APPLY

Have students reread the rest of the selection and complete the chart. Remind them that judgments are subjective. Ask students to discuss the pros and cons of passing judgment on characters in a selection.

LA.5.2.1.2
Locate and analyze plot structure and character development

Transparency 27

Action	Judgment
Lateesha and her bunkmates put off writing their Fourth of July skit, so their counselor Jean takes control.	Lateesha and her friends are somewhat lazy.
The bunkmates put on a skit, but no one laughed.	Lateesha and pals resented Jean's ideas.
Lateesha enoys a hike to Lookaway Mountain, but complains that she has to carry heavy gear.	Lateesha is a bit lazy.
Jean apologized for not listening to the girls.	Jean always meant well.

Graphic Organizer Transparency 27

FCAT Success!

Test Prep and Practice with Plot Development, pages 65–96.

■ **On Level Practice Book O,** page 194

When you read a story, you make judgments about the characters and the things they say or do. Making judgments helps you evaluate what you read and understand the **plot development** of a story.

Possible responses provided.
Answer each question below. Then explain your answers.

1. It takes Uncle Curtis three tries to find the exit to Mount Tamalpais. When Uncle Curtis finally makes it to the park, he is given a map of the campgrounds. He "didn't even glance at it but threw it into the backseat." Do you think he made a wise decision when he chose to ignore the map?
   Uncle Curtis made a bad decision because he has shown that he gets lost easily and is not good with directions.

2. Teddy and Bobby wear clothes appropriate for a San Francisco summer—sweatshirts and corduroys. The weather forecast for Mount Tamalpais is hot and humid. Teddy and Bobby decide to pack only sweatshirts and corduroys to take to the camp. What do you think of their clothing decision?
   Teddy and Bobby chose the wrong clothes. The weather at the park is hot and humid, unlike the chilly summer weather in San Francisco.

3. Teddy and Bobby find that the hot dogs and hamburgers, which Teddy had packed in dry ice, are frozen solid. But Uncle Curtis tries to grill the frozen food before it has thawed. Do you think that Teddy's method of packing the meat was successful?
   Teddy's method was unsuccessful because the meat is frozen solid. They will probably throw the hot dogs away because they cannot be cooked.

Quick Check
Can students make judgments about plot development?

During **Small Group Instruction**

If No → **Approaching Level** Comprehension, pp. 697O–697P

If Yes → **On Level** Options, p. 697R

Beyond Level Options, p. 697T

★ **Approaching Practice Book A,** page 194

◆ **Beyond Practice Book B,** page 194

Read

MAIN SELECTION
✓ • *Skunk Scout*
FCAT • **Skill:** Plot Development

PAIRED SELECTION
✓ • "An Underwater Park"
FCAT • **Text Feature:** Photographs and Captions

SMALL GROUP OPTIONS
• Differentiated Instruction, pp. 697M–697V

Comprehension

LA.5.2.1.1 Demonstrate knowledge of characteristics of genres

GENRE: REALISTIC FICTION

Have students read the definition of Realistic Fiction on **Student Book** page 672. As they read, students should look for events that could happen in real life.

LA.5.1.7 Use strategies to comprehend text

**STRATEGY**
MONITOR COMPREHENSION

Remind students that good readers monitor their comprehension as they read. They stop when they have a problem, use self-correction techniques, and decide what they should do to understand what they have read.

SKILL
FCAT
PLOT DEVELOPMENT

LA.5.2.1.2 Analyze elements of plot structure and character development

Remind students that when they make judgments, they form an opinion about an event or a character's actions. This can help them analyze both character and plot development in the story.

Comprehension

Genre
Realistic Fiction has real-life settings, well-developed characters, and realistic problems and solutions.

Monitor Comprehension
FCAT
Plot Development
Use story details to form opinions about the characters and their actions. As you read, use your Judgments Chart.

Action	→	Judgment
	→	
	→	
	→	
	→	

Read to Find Out
How does Teddy feel about the camping trip?

672

⭐ Vocabulary

Vocabulary Words Review the tested vocabulary words: **bundle, coordination, ease, frustrated, fused, guaranteed, scenery,** and **supervise.**

Story Words Students may find these words difficult. Pronounce the words and present the meanings as necessary.

scout (p. 673): a person who is sent out to get information

hawk (p. 674): a bird of prey with a hooked beak, long claws, broad wings, and keen sight

campsite (p. 676): a place where people live outdoors in tents or other shelters

gear (p. 676): equipment needed for some purpose, such as camping

alibis (p. 677): excuses

LA.5.1.6.1 Use new vocabulary taught directly

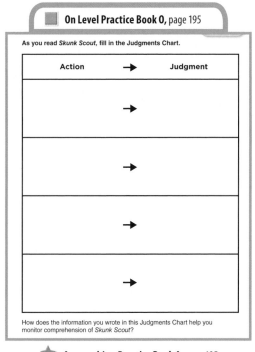

SKUNK SCOUT

by Laurence Yep

illustrated by Winson Trang

Award Winning Author

673

Read Together

If your students need support to read the Main Selection, use the prompts to guide comprehension and model how to complete the graphic organizer.

Read Independently

If your students can read the Main Selection independently, have them read and complete the graphic organizer. Remind students to set their purposes for reading and reading rate, and to modify both based on their reading level.

If your students need an alternate selection, choose the **Leveled Readers** that match their instructional level.

Technology

Story available on **Listening Library Audio CD**

Preview and Predict

LA.5.1.7.1
Use prior knowledge to make and confirm predictions

Ask students to read the title, preview the illustrations, and make predictions about the story. Have students write about their predictions and any questions they have about the story.

LA.5.1.7.1
Establish purpose for reading

Set Purposes

FOCUS QUESTION Discuss the "Read to Find Out" question on **Student Book** page 672. Remind students to look for the answer as they read.

Point out the Judgments Chart in the Student Book and in **Practice Book** page 195. Tell students they will use the chart to keep track of judgments they make as they read the story.

Read *Skunk Scout*

Use the questions and Think Alouds for additional instruction to support the comprehension strategy and skill.

On Level Practice Book O, page 195

As you read *Skunk Scout*, fill in the Judgments Chart.

Action	→	Judgment
	→	
	→	
	→	
	→	

How does the information you wrote in this Judgments Chart help you monitor comprehension of *Skunk Scout*?

★ **Approaching Practice Book A,** page 195

◆ **Beyond Practice Book B,** page 195

Develop Comprehension

1 STRATEGY
MONITOR COMPREHENSION

LA.5.1.7
Use strategies to comprehend text

Teacher Think Aloud *Skunk Scout* is a work of realistic fiction. I can tell from the first paragraph that there will be conflict in this story. Teddy loves city life but he has accepted an invitation to go camping with his uncle and little brother. It sounds like Teddy might have trouble with both Mother Nature and his brother Bobby, which may lead to disagreements. I will want to read this selection carefully before I make judgments about any of the characters. I can stop and check that I understand what is happening by asking myself questions such as *why? what if?* and *how?* before making a judgment.

2 COMPARE CHARACTERS

LA.5.1.7.7
Compare and contrast elements

Uncle Curtis, Bobby, and Teddy react differently to the events that take place on their way to the camp site. Use details from the selection to compare and contrast their reactions. Think about how these contrasts might influence the plot. (Answers should include the idea that Uncle Curtis and Bobby seem much calmer about the whole trip than Teddy does. Teddy gets upset when they keep missing the exit sign on the freeway because Bobby and Uncle Curtis get distracted looking at wildlife from the car. After they miss the exit a second time, Teddy starts issuing orders from the back seat so they will not miss it again.)

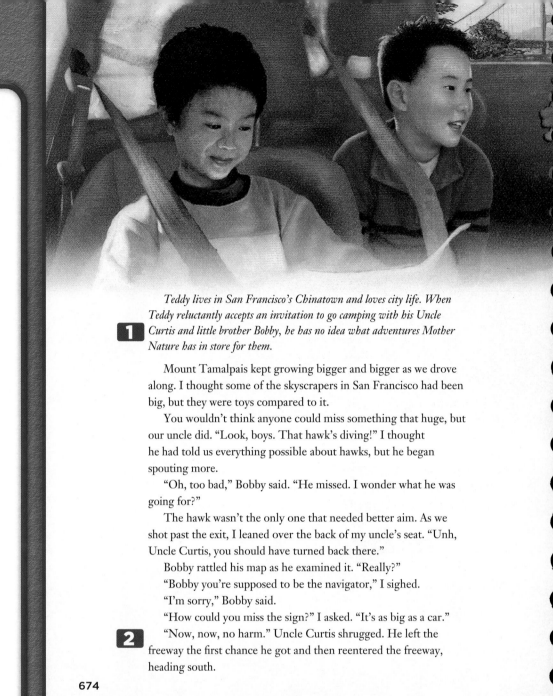

1 *Teddy lives in San Francisco's Chinatown and loves city life. When Teddy reluctantly accepts an invitation to go camping with his Uncle Curtis and little brother Bobby, he has no idea what adventures Mother Nature has in store for them.*

Mount Tamalpais kept growing bigger and bigger as we drove along. I thought some of the skyscrapers in San Francisco had been big, but they were toys compared to it.

You wouldn't think anyone could miss something that huge, but our uncle did. "Look, boys. That hawk's diving!" I thought he had told us everything possible about hawks, but he began spouting more.

"Oh, too bad," Bobby said. "He missed. I wonder what he was going for?"

The hawk wasn't the only one that needed better aim. As we shot past the exit, I leaned over the back of my uncle's seat. "Unh, Uncle Curtis, you should have turned back there."

Bobby rattled his map as he examined it. "Really?"

"Bobby you're supposed to be the navigator," I sighed.

"I'm sorry," Bobby said.

"How could you miss the sign?" I asked. "It's as big as a car."

2 "Now, now, no harm." Uncle Curtis shrugged. He left the freeway the first chance he got and then reentered the freeway, heading south.

674

Comprehension

Plot Structure: *Exposition*

Explain Exposition is a literary technique in which the author gives information about events that have occurred before the beginning of a story. This information can be presented through dialogue, description, or in an introduction before the story begins.

Discuss What information does the exposition to *Skunk Scout* reveal? (Teddy lives in San Francisco's Chinatown and loves city life. He does not really want to go camping.)

Apply Have students suggest other ways the information in the exposition could be presented in the story. For example, Teddy could make his reluctance to go camping made known through a dialogue with Bobby and his uncle.

LA.5.2.1.2 Locate and analyze exposition

Develop Comprehension

FCAT ✓

3 PLOT DEVELOPMENT

LA.5.2.1.2
Locate and
analyze
elements of
plot structure
and character
development

Do you think Teddy's actions in the car are appropriate? Why or why not? What do they reveal about Teddy's character, and his relationship with his uncle and brother? Add your answer to your Judgments Chart. (Answers may vary. Students should note that judgments must be based on evidence from the text. Teddy starts giving everybody orders, claiming they are not paying attention to the directions. In a way this is not appropriate because Teddy is a young boy and Uncle Curtis is in charge of the trip. However, Uncle Curtis and Bobby are both easily distracted. Teddy is getting frustrated by their mistakes, so some students may feel that in this case his actions are appropriate for the situation. Neither Bobby or Uncle Curtis get upset with Teddy, but his attitude may lead to disagreements later in the story.)

Bobby leaned against his shoulder strap. "We'll get it this time."

But just as we got near the correct exit, Uncle Curtis suddenly twisted in his seat. "There's a rabbit!" he cried, pointing.

"Where?" Bobby asked, craning his neck.

As we shot past, I moaned, "We missed it again."

Uncle Curtis glanced into the rearview mirror. "Man, that came up faster than I thought."

I put a hand on his shoulder. "Okay. This time, no hawks. No rabbits. Just exit signs. Okay?"

Uncle Curtis gave a thumbs-up. "Got you."

"And don't you dare say anything except navigation stuff," I warned Bobby. **3**

This time we got off at the right exit. I began to wonder how Uncle Curtis found his own bathroom at home. Maybe Aunt Ethel put up signs.

FCAT **Plot Development**
Do you think Teddy's actions in the car are appropriate? Why or why not?

675

Action →	Judgment
Teddy insists that his uncle and brother pay attention to the map and directions. He seems very bossy. →	Teddy is frustrated by the way Bobby and Uncle Curtis keep missing the exit. He takes appropriate action.

ELL

Access for All

STRATEGIES FOR EXTRA SUPPORT

Question 3 PLOT DEVELOPMENT

Write the words *appropriate* and *inappropriate* on the board and discuss appropriate and inappropriate behavior in school and with adults. Ask, *What happened during the trip? What did Uncle Curtis continue to do? What did Bobby continue to do? What were Teddy's actions? What did Teddy tell Uncle Curtis to do? Do you think Teddy's response was appropriate or inappropriate? Explain your thinking.* Restate what students say in full sentences. As you introduce important vocabulary, write the words on the board.

Read

Develop Comprehension

4 **GENRE: REALISTIC FICTION**

LA.5.2.1.1
Demonstrate knowledge of characteristics of genres

Compare the events in this story with travel experiences that you have had. Do the problems the characters face and their solutions seem realistic? Why or why not? (Answers may vary but should include the idea that people often get lost when they travel to a strange place, or have difficulty reading a map, so the events in the story do seem as if they could happen in real life.)

Discuss the characteristics of realistic fiction with students, and how they apply to *Skunk Scout.*

Vocabulary

Read the sentence that contains the word **scenery**. Have students tell a partner about a time they saw some beautiful scenery, using the word in a sentence.

LA.5.1.6.1 Use new vocabulary

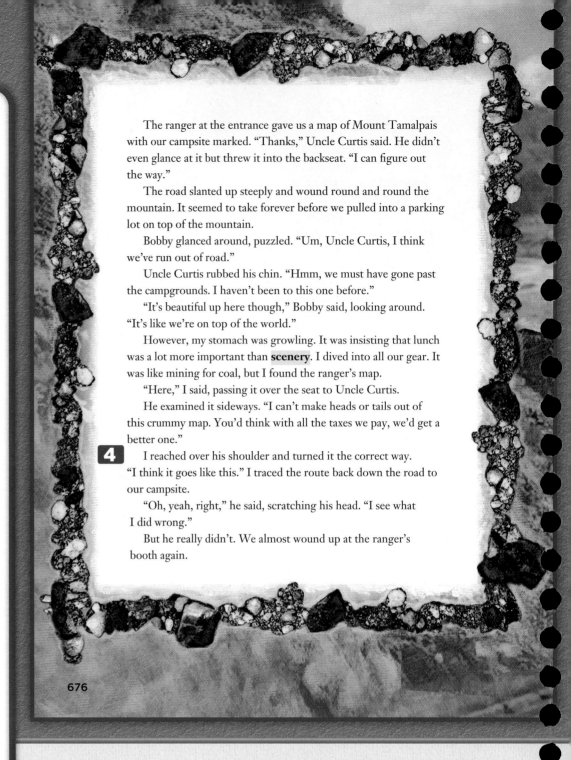

The ranger at the entrance gave us a map of Mount Tamalpais with our campsite marked. "Thanks," Uncle Curtis said. He didn't even glance at it but threw it into the backseat. "I can figure out the way."

The road slanted up steeply and wound round and round the mountain. It seemed to take forever before we pulled into a parking lot on top of the mountain.

Bobby glanced around, puzzled. "Um, Uncle Curtis, I think we've run out of road."

Uncle Curtis rubbed his chin. "Hmm, we must have gone past the campgrounds. I haven't been to this one before."

"It's beautiful up here though," Bobby said, looking around. "It's like we're on top of the world."

However, my stomach was growling. It was insisting that lunch was a lot more important than **scenery**. I dived into all our gear. It was like mining for coal, but I found the ranger's map.

"Here," I said, passing it over the seat to Uncle Curtis.

He examined it sideways. "I can't make heads or tails out of this crummy map. You'd think with all the taxes we pay, we'd get a better one."

4 I reached over his shoulder and turned it the correct way. "I think it goes like this." I traced the route back down the road to our campsite.

"Oh, yeah, right," he said, scratching his head. "I see what I did wrong."

But he really didn't. We almost wound up at the ranger's booth again.

676

Comprehension

Study Skills: *Road Maps*

Explain A map is a flat picture of a part of the earth. A road map shows highways and roads. It usually contains a compass rose, which indicates the cardinal directions *North, South, East* and *West,* as well as labels which identify the names of rivers, cities, and highways.

Discuss Why was it important for Uncle Curtis to hold the map the right way when trying to read it? (He might be going north or east when he thinks he's going south or west.)

Apply Have students write directions to an unfamiliar location in their community using cardinal directions, landmarks, and estimated distances. Then have them create an accompanying map based on their directions.

LA.5.4.2.5 Write directions using cardinal and ordinal directions, landmarks, distances, and create accompanying maps
LA.5.4.2.5 Write directions to unfamiliar locations using landmarks

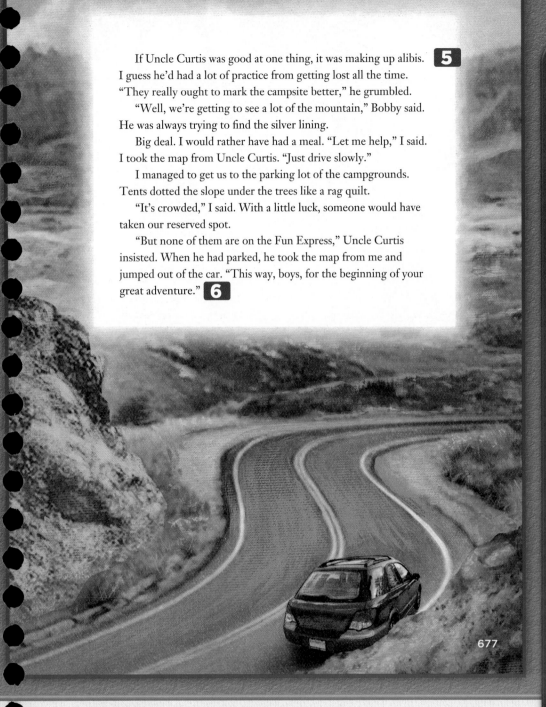

If Uncle Curtis was good at one thing, it was making up alibis. **5**
I guess he'd had a lot of practice from getting lost all the time.
"They really ought to mark the campsite better," he grumbled.

"Well, we're getting to see a lot of the mountain," Bobby said.
He was always trying to find the silver lining.

Big deal. I would rather have had a meal. "Let me help," I said.
I took the map from Uncle Curtis. "Just drive slowly."

I managed to get us to the parking lot of the campgrounds.
Tents dotted the slope under the trees like a rag quilt.

"It's crowded," I said. With a little luck, someone would have
taken our reserved spot.

"But none of them are on the Fun Express," Uncle Curtis
insisted. When he had parked, he took the map from me and
jumped out of the car. "This way, boys, for the beginning of your
great adventure." **6**

677

Develop Comprehension

5 **SYNTHESIZE**

LA.5.2.1.5
Demonstrate
understanding
and include
personal
experience

If you could go on a camping trip,
would you rather travel with Teddy, or
with Bobby and Uncle Curtis? Explain
your answer. (Answers will vary.)

6 **MAKE PREDICTIONS**

LA.5.1.7.8
Predict to
repair compre-
hension

LA.5.1.7.8
Use graphic
organizers to
repair compre-
hension

On the basis of the events that have
taken place so far, including the ones
that took place at the beginning of
the story, do you think the "great
adventure" will be successful? Explain
your answer, citing evidence in the text
on which you based your prediction.
(Answers will vary but should include
the idea that, once Uncle Curtis
observes that the campground is
crowded, he decides to take the boys
on the "Fun Express." This is a clue that
he will try to find a more secluded
campground. Based on his success with
directions so far, students may conclude
that Uncle Curtis will get lost.)

Remind students they can make
predictions using events in the text that
may be widely separated. Rereading
and looking for text clues in order
to make logical guesses about what
might happen can also help them
clarify their understanding of the
text. Suggest that students make a
four-column predictions chart to track
their predictions as they read. The four
columns should be titled: *Story Clues,
What I Know, Prediction, Revision.*

Develop Comprehension

7 MOOD AND TONE

LA.5.2.1.7
Examine how
language
describes
people and
feelings

Teddy complains about everything, but he does so in a humorous way. Give an example of one of Teddy's humorous complaints. Why do you think the author chose to make Teddy's complaints so funny? (Answers will vary but may include that Teddy feels Mother Nature should have tidied up the loose rocks all over the ground for the paying guests. He says "Isn't fun supposed to be less lumpy?" Some students may feel that Teddy's complaints are funny because he doesn't really mean them, and he actually enjoys being with his brother and uncle.)

We followed him up a dirt trail from the parking lot to a patch by some trees. Uncle Curtis stopped. "This is it," he declared, folding the map into neat little squares. "The great outdoors!"

As I kicked at one of the many rocks on the ground, I didn't see what was so great about it. "Isn't fun supposed to **7** be less lumpy?"

My parents are always scolding me about being so messy. However, they should have seen Mother Nature. There were all these pebbles and leaves littering the dirt. I would have tidied up a little, especially for paying guests.

Satisfied, Uncle Curtis surveyed the site. "All this fresh air! It's **guaranteed** to make you feel so tired, you won't notice any rocks."

678

Vocabulary

Read the sentence that contains the word **guaranteed**. Have students describe something that is guaranteed to happen, such as getting wet if you are caught in the rain.

LA.5.1.6.1 Use new vocabulary

Comprehension

Literary Elements: *Mood and Tone*

Explain Remind students that **mood** is the feeling or atmosphere a story creates. Authors carefully select words and craft sentences to create a certain atmosphere. Word choice also plays a part in identifying the author's tone, or his or her attitude toward the characters and events in a story.

Discuss What does the author's choice of words, details, and description reveal about the tone of this story? (The author tells the story in first person, and while his observations are sometimes sarcastic, he does seem to genuinely like his Uncle and little brother.) What kind of mood does the author create through his description of the setting, as well as the words, actions, and feelings of the characters? (Students should suggest that the mood of the story is lighthearted and fun. The author has not placed the characters in any dangerous situations.)

Apply Tell students to watch for changes in the mood and tone of the story as they continue to read.

LA.5.2.1.7 Examine how language describes people, feelings, and objects

I think you could get just as tired breathing bus fumes. However, I kept my mouth shut and helped unload the station wagon. Though it was a very cloudy day, it was still warm and muggy. Almost everyone was in T-shirts and shorts. However, Bobby and I were wearing our usual clothes for a San Francisco summer: sweatshirts and corduroy pants. The corduroy made a flapping sound when the trouser legs rubbed together.

Soon we were both sweating. In San Francisco, the thermostat was set to a sensible sixty degrees or so. Not like this oven. So **8** finally we took off our sweatshirts and tied the sleeves around our waists.

I was glad Grandmother wasn't around. She would have made us keep them on, so we wouldn't catch cold.

As we worked, dust got into everything. It was all over my clothes. It was in my mouth. I felt like I was being buried alive.

It didn't seem to bother Uncle Curtis, though. He was humming happily as he unrolled the army surplus tent. Then he laid out the tent stakes where he wanted them. Finally, he took **9** out an army shovel with a short handle. Unfolding it, he put it together quickly.

"Now I'll demonstrate the fine art of putting up a tent," he said. Kneeling, he used the flat of the shovel blade to hammer the stake into the ground.

679

Develop Comprehension

8 **MONITOR AND CLARIFY: REREAD**

LA.5.1.7.8
Reread to repair comprehension

Why do you think Teddy seems so angry about everything? How can rereading to clarify help you to answer this question? (Answers may vary but after rereading to clarify students should recall that in the introduction, it states that Teddy loves city life and "reluctantly" accepts an invitation to go camping. So even before things started going wrong, Teddy did not want to go along on this trip. No wonder he is so negative about everything that happens.)

Remind students to independently self-monitor their comprehension as they read and to ask themselves open-ended questions to promote better comprehension.

9 **STEPS IN A PROCESS**

LA.5.2.1.2
Analyze elements of plot structure

What signal words does the author use to explain the first steps Uncle Curtis takes as he sets up the tent? (In the fifth and sixth paragraphs on page 679, the words *then, finally,* and *now* all signal the different stages of setting up a tent.)

Develop Comprehension

10 MAKE INFERENCES

LA.5.2.1.5
Demonstrate understanding and include evidence from the text

What kind of relationship do Teddy and Bobby have? Use evidence from the story to explain your answer. (Teddy seems to be jealous of Bobby, and also competitive with him. He sees putting up the tent as an opportunity to prove that he is just as good as his little brother.)

11 PLOT DEVELOPMENT

FCAT ✔

LA.5.2.1.2
Analyze elements of plot structure and character development

Do you think Uncle Curtis's actions are appropriate, or should he have let Bobby continue to try and hammer the stakes into the ground? Explain your answer and then fill in the second box on the chart. (Answers will vary but may include that Uncle Curtis's actions were inappropriate. At first Uncle Curtis seems pleased that Bobby wants to help, but as soon as it appears that Bobby may need some instruction and supervision, he wants Teddy to take over. Part of the experience of camping is learning new things, but Uncle Curtis seems to be impatient.)

Action	→	Judgment
Teddy insists that his uncle and brother pay attention to the map and directions. He seems very bossy.	→	Teddy is frustrated by the way Bobby and Uncle Curtis keep missing the exit. He takes appropriate action.
Uncle Curits becomes impatient when Bobby needs help hammering the stakes into the ground. He asks Teddy to take over.	→	Uncle Curtis's actions are inappropriate. He should have taken the time to show Bobby how to hammer the stakes into the ground properly.

"Me next," Bobby said eagerly.

"You want to try everything, don't you?" Uncle Curtis grinned but he surrendered the shovel.

I knew my little brother, so I stepped back. Bobby thought that energy could always make up for lack of **coordination**. Uncle Curtis, though, made the mistake of staying close to **supervise**. He almost lost a kneecap when Bobby whacked at the tent stake and missed.

"Easy there," Uncle Curtis warned as he stumbled back.

Most of the time I try to get someone else to do all the work.

10 But I saw another chance to prove I was just as good as my little brother.

"Let me have a turn," I said, holding out my hand.

I guess Uncle Curtis figured Bobby could take forever. "Let Teddy do that. You help me get the tent ready."

"But I want to do it," Bobby complained.

Uncle Curtis rubbed his head. "The sooner we set up camp, the **11** sooner I can show you around. Isn't that what's really important?"

Bobby grudgingly handed the shovel to me and helped Uncle Curtis unroll the tent itself.

The ground was a lot harder than it looked. But lifting all those boxes in the store had given me muscles. So I hammered away until I got the stakes in.

It took all three of us to put up the tent. I still thought it leaned a little when we were done.

Uncle Curtis inspected the tent ropes carefully. He acted as though they were the cables holding up the Golden Gate Bridge. Finally, though, he nodded his head in approval. "That looks good."

When we had stowed our gear inside, I said, "I'm hungry. Let's eat."

12 "We've gotten used to eating Spam," Bobby explained.

"When you ride the Fun Express, you dine first class," Uncle Curtis boasted as he went over to the ice chest in the shadow of a big tree. He squatted down and undid the lid's clasps. "I brought hot dogs and hamburgers. I'll make you boys a feast." When he raised the lid, fog rolled out around him.

680

681

Develop Comprehension

 DRAW CONCLUSIONS

LA.5.2.1.5 Demonstrate understanding of literary selection

What do you think Bobby means when he tells Uncle Curtis that he and his brother Teddy have gotten used to eating Spam? (Answers will vary but may include the fact that, in preparation for the camping trip, Bobby and Teddy have been getting used to eating prepackaged foods that can be stored for a long time, such as Spam.)

 Have students respond to the selection by confirming or revising their predictions and purposes for reading. Then have them note any new questions they may have about the selection.

Quick Check   **Are students able to make judgments about characters and events, and the plot development of the story? If not, see the Extra Support on this page.**

Extra Support

Plot Development

FCAT If students are having difficulty, ask them what they know about Uncle Curtis and then have them look for details about this character. Encourage them to begin three-column charts, labeling each column with a character name: Uncle Curtis, Teddy, Bobby. Students can record details about each character in the appropriate column. Tell students to refer to this chart when answering questions or making judgments about what the character says and does, and how the character's actions affect the development of the plot.

LA.5.2.1.2 Locate and analyze elements of plot structure and character development
LA.5.1.7.8 Use graphic organizers to repair comprehension

Stop here if you wish to read this selection over two days. **STOP**

Develop Comprehension

RESEARCH
Why It Matters

Comprehension Research states that predicting what a story will be about has long been valued as an important reading strategy. In fact, predicting is one important component of the very successful teaching strategy of reciprocal teaching. Predicting helps students connect their prior experiences to a new story. Connections like this help make a story more memorable to students.

Janice Dole

LOG ON Go to **www.macmillanmh.com**

682

Cross-Curricular Connection

DRY ICE

Tell students that dry ice is frozen carbon dioxide, the gas we exhale when we breathe. Note that the temperature of dry ice is an extremely cold -109.3°F or -78.5°C. Have students compare these numbers with the temperature of frozen water (32°F or 0°C). Explain that when dry ice melts, it does not turn into a liquid as frozen water does. Instead it sublimates, or turns back into carbon dioxide gas. Dry ice in an ice chest sublimates at a rate of 5 pounds every 24 hours.

Have students make a line graph to chart how many days it would take a 100 pound block of dry ice to sublimate. (5 lbs = 24 hrs; 100 lbs = 480 hrs or 20 days)

LA.5.4.2.2 Organize and record information on graphs
SC.A.1.2.2.5.1 Common materials can be changed and conserved from one state to another by heating and cooling

Bobby and I jumped back. "What's wrong?" my brother asked.

"It's just the dry ice." I laughed. I was enjoying my moment of triumph.

Uncle Curtis fanned his hand over the chest to help blow away some of the fog. "Boy, Teddy, I know this is one batch of meat that's not going to spoil."

White ribbons crept out of the chest and down the sides while Uncle Curtis carefully lifted out a big parcel wrapped in pink butcher paper.

He lost his grin though. "It's like a glacier."

I poked at the package in his hands. It was cold enough to make my body and hands ache. Through the paper, I traced the shape of hot dogs. "They feel like rocks."

Uncle Curtis lifted out the other package and hefted it over his shoulder like a shot put. "The hamburger's like a lump of coal, too."

I wasn't going to let this ruin my achievement. "Let's set them out," I urged. "Part of one of these packages will thaw out and we can have that."

So Uncle Curtis placed both packages out on a rock. "You boys have to get some firewood anyway. Just pick up the dead wood lying around. We're not allowed to chop down any trees."

"Right away," Bobby said, heading out.

"Wait for me, oh, fearless leader," I muttered, and wandered off after Bobby. "Just how much wood do you need to cook food anyway?" I asked the researcher. "I don't think we can carry back **13** a log."

"The books didn't say," Bobby said, "but on television they always seem to use the wood about this thick." He held his fingers apart about six inches.

In the movies, there's always dead wood lying around, but all we could gather were twigs.

683

Develop Comprehension

13 **STRATEGY**
MONITOR COMPREHENSION

LA.5.1.7
Use strategies to comprehend text

Teacher Think Aloud This seems like a good place in the story to stop and see if I understand everything that is taking place. After reading this page, I can ask myself questions and make some inferences about what's going on between Bobby and Teddy. For example, why does Teddy say he's enjoying his moment of triumph after Bobby is scared by all the fog the dry ice creates? I think it may be because Teddy suggested they use dry ice to pack the food. That would make sense. Then, later on, Teddy refers to Bobby as "fearless leader" and "the researcher." Tell me what questions you might ask to understand what Teddy means when he refers to Bobby this way.

(Encourage students to apply the strategy in a Think Aloud.)

LA.5.1.7
Student uses strategies to comprehend text

Student Think Aloud Let's see. Before Teddy calls Bobby "the researcher," he asks him how much wood they need to cook food. I think it's clear that Teddy resents Bobby. But why does he call him "the researcher"? Maybe because Bobby was more excited about the trip than Teddy was. I know when I'm interested in something, I try to find books on the subject. So Bobby may have read books about camping before he and Teddy went on the trip with Uncle Curtis.

Develop Comprehension

14 PLOT DEVELOPMENT

LA.5.2.1.2
Locate and analyze elements of plot structure and character development

Do you think it is appropriate for Uncle Curtis to borrow firewood from other campers nearby? Explain your answer and add it to the chart. (Answers may vary but should include the idea that people should help each other no matter where they are. It is appropriate for Uncle Curtis to ask other campers for some help.)

15 MAKE PREDICTIONS

LA.5.1.7.1
Use prior knowledge to make and confirm predictions

As Teddy goes back to the tent, he hears a rustling in the bushes. What do you think might be making the rustling sound? Explain your answer based on evidence in the text. (Answers will vary but may include a small animal such as a skunk, since a skunk is mentioned in the title of the selection. Teddy observes that the bushes are too small for a large animal like a bear to hide in.)

Action	→	Judgment
Teddy insists that his uncle and brother pay attention to the map and directions. He seems very bossy.	→	Teddy is frustrated by the way Bobby and Uncle Curtis keep missing the exit. He takes appropriate action.
Uncle Curits becomes impatient when Bobby needs help hammering the stakes into the ground. He asks Teddy to take over.	→	Uncle Curtis's actions are inappropriate. He should have taken the time to show Bobby how to hammer the stakes into the ground properly.
Uncle Curtis says nature lovers always share with one another and that this is a code of camping.	→	People should help each other no matter where they are. It is appropriate for Uncle Curtis to ask other campers for help.

Disgusted, I looked at the handful I had. "This isn't even enough for a broom."

Bobby held up his own. "The other campers must have picked the mountain clean."

When we returned, Uncle Curtis stared at the handful of twigs. "That's okay for kindling. But where are the branches?"

"This is all we could find," I confessed helplessly.

Uncle Curtis rubbed the back of his neck. "I was counting on using firewood."

I saw a column of smoke rising a short distance away. "Maybe someone has spare firewood?"

"I'll borrow some. Nature lovers always share with one another. It's the code of camping," Uncle Curtis said. Suddenly he slapped himself. "Ow. Darn mosquitoes."

14 Apparently, there were other creatures besides humans having a meal. "I guess it's time to use my birthday gift," I said.

I went back to the tent. Something rustled in the brush nearby, but the bushes were too small for a bear to hide behind. So I went **15** inside and got the mosquito repellent.

I can't say it did much good. Even as I sprayed my arm, a mosquito flew right through the mist to land on it. "This stuff just makes us tastier to the mosquitoes," I said.

I was hot, sweaty, being eaten alive, and hungry. So hungry that even Spam would have tasted good.

I poked each package in disappointment. "They're still like ice."

Bobby turned the packages over on the rock. They each clonked against the stone. "Darn dry ice." **Frustrated**, he picked up the package and dropped it against the rock. It landed with a loud crack. I thought there was a fifty-fifty chance that either the rock or the meat had broken.

Uncle Curtis grabbed a package under either arm. "We'll defrost the meat as we cook it. What's the menu for today, boys? Hot dogs or hamburgers?"

684

Bobby punched cheerfully at the air. "Hot dogs!" **16**

I guess the dry ice hadn't been such a good idea, after all. Sulking, I jammed my hands in my pockets. "I'll settle for anything that isn't part of the polar ice cap."

Uncle Curtis put the hamburger into the chest and snapped the clasps shut. "You boys bring the buns and mess kits. I'll bring the hot dogs."

685

Ways to Confirm Meaning

Semantic/Meaning Clues

Explain Tell students that when they read, they may come to a word they don't know. Point out that good readers use context clues and prior knowledge, such as their understanding of spelling patterns, to help them predict and clarify meanings.

Model Discuss the meaning of *mess kits* on page 685.

Think Aloud I don't know what a *mess kit* is. Uncle Curtis tells the boys to get it so he can start cooking. I know that a kit is a container used for carrying things. A mess kit must be a set of things that can be used for cooking.

Apply Encourage students to use context clues and their own prior knowledge to figure out the meaning of difficult words and phrases.

LA.5.1.6.3 Use context clues to determine meaning
LA.5.1.4.1 Understand spelling patterns

Develop Comprehension

16 CHARACTER/VISUALIZE

LA.5.2.1.2
Locate and analyze character development

LA.5.2.1.7
Explain author's use of descriptive language

The campers are continuing to encounter difficulties. How do Bobby and Teddy deal with the problems which keep arising? What do their reactions reveal about their characters? How does the descriptive language in the story help you visualize or create a mental image of the characters' actions? (Answers will vary but may include the fact that, of all the characters, Teddy seems less willing to put up with what he encounters in the outdoors. He immediately gets mosquito repellent when Uncle Curtis is bitten, and sulks when the hot dogs appear to be frozen solid. Bobby is more enthusiastic, and appears more willing to accept whatever happens. The author describes Bobby as "punching cheerfully at the air" when he chooses hot dogs for lunch, and Teddy jamming his hands in his pockets, sulking. These descriptions help readers to create a mental image of the characters, and allows them to better understand what is happening in this part of the story.)

LA.5.1.7.7
Compare and contrast elements

Students should contrast the characters' personalities and tell how these contrasts are important to the plot and theme.

Develop Comprehension

17 PLOT DEVELOPMENT

LA.5.2.1.2
Analyze
elements of
plot structure

Was Uncle Curtis right to throw the hot dogs away? Explain your answer and add it to the chart. How do you think this event will affect the plot? (Answers may vary. Some students may say it is possible to eat food that has fallen into a fire because the fire sterilizes the food. But Uncle Curtis says the hot dogs are half raw, too. It is usually not a good idea to eat raw meat. Also, previous cooks had not bothered to clean the grill, so it is hard to know what exactly covered the hot dogs when they fell into the grill. For these reasons it was probably appropriate for Uncle Curtis to throw the hot dogs away, but Teddy may get upset because he is so hungry)

Action		Judgment
Teddy insists that his uncle and brother pay attention to the map and directions. He seems very bossy.	→	Teddy is frustrated by the way Bobby and Uncle Curtis keep missing the exit. He takes appropriate action.
Uncle Curits becomes impatient when Bobby needs help hammering the stakes into the ground. He asks Teddy to take over.	→	Uncle Curtis's actions are inappropriate. He should have taken the time to show Bobby how to hammer the stakes into the ground properly.
Uncle Curtis says nature lovers always share with one another and that this is a code of camping.	→	People should help each other no matter where they are. It is appropriate for Uncle Curtis to ask other campers for help.
It is usually not a good idea to eat raw meat. Also, previous cooks had not bothered to clean the grill.	→	It was appropriate for Uncle Curtis to throw away the hot dogs.

The cooking area was an open space. A row of stoves had been built from stones and metal grills.

Uncle Curtis went over to a table where some campers were eating.

He came back with half a bag of charcoal. "Ten dollars for this," he complained. "Fellow lovers of nature, my eye."

"Well, maybe it's the membership fee to the club," I said.

Uncle Curtis shot me a dirty look as he poured charcoal from the bag into the pit beneath the metal grill. Without lighter fluid, it took a little work and a lot of fanning and blowing before the coals caught.

As the coals slowly turned red, we began to set our stuff out on a nearby picnic table.

The previous cooks had not bothered to clean the grill. Uncle Curtis, though, had brought a spatula. He used it to scrape the metal bars.

In the meantime, we unwrapped the paper. The hot dogs were **fused** together into a lump the size of a football. No matter how hard we tried, we could not break them apart.

"Wait." Bobby proudly opened his borrowed mess kit and took out a fork. When he tried to pry a hot dog off, the tines bent.

We still hadn't freed any hot dogs by the time the coals were ready. By now, Uncle Curtis was too impatient to be careful. Lifting the mass of hot dogs, he set the whole fused lump on the grill. "I'll pry them off as they defrost." Water began dripping onto the coals with loud hisses. As steam rose around the hot dogs, Uncle Curtis straightened the tines of the fork. Carefully he worked at one of the hot dogs. "Almost…almost," he muttered.

With a plop, the hot dog fell through the grill and onto the coals. In no time, it was as black as a stick of charcoal. By the time this had happened to three more hot dogs, I tried to use a stick to **ease** them out of the coals.

Uncle Curtis shoved me back. "They're dirty."

"I don't care," I admitted. "I'm hungry."

17 "And they're half raw, too." He threw them into a trash can.

FCAT Plot Development
Was Uncle Curtis right to throw the hot dogs away?

686

687

Develop Comprehension

18 SUMMARIZE

LA.5.1.7.8 Summarize to repair comprehension

Events on the camping trip seem to be going from bad to worse. What has happened to the campers since they put up the tent? (Answers should include the fact that Uncle Curtis, Bobby, and Teddy have found that their food is frozen solid. They are attacked by mosquitoes, and the mosquito repellent does not work. They can't find enough firewood to cook the food. They have to pay $10 to other campers for some charcoal. They have to clean the grill. The hot dogs fall into the coals, burn, and finally Uncle Curtis throws them away.)

19 SYNTHESIZE

LA.5.2.1.5 Demonstrate understanding and include personal experience

If you were the campers, what would you do differently to make the camping trip more successful? Use ideas and information that you have learned from additional reading and from watching films or TV shows about campers and camping. (Answer will vary but should include student descriptions of information and ideas they have learned about camping from reading both fiction and/or nonfiction reading and from media.)

20 VIEWING ILLUSTRATIONS

LA.5.2.1.4 Identify an author's theme

What is the central theme of the illustration on page 687? How can you tell? (Students should note that the theme is one of disappointment. The boys and their uncle are looking very unhappy and disappointed as the hot dog falls into the fire.)

ELL

Access for All

STRATEGIES FOR EXTRA SUPPORT

Question 18 SUMMARIZE
Have students retell what they have read. For beginning ELL you might provide a retelling frame to help pupils follow. Ask guiding questions to help students identify the most important events: *What do Teddy, Bobby, and Uncle Curtis discover about the food they brought? What do they have trouble finding? Why does Teddy say "there were other creatures besides humans having a meal"?*

Develop Comprehension

21 MAKE PREDICTIONS

LA.5.1.7.1
Use prior knowledge to make and confirm predictions

Based on the events that have already taken place on this camping trip, do you think the campers will have marshmallows for lunch? Why or why not? (Answers will vary but students may say that, based on what has already happened, it is predictable that something else will go wrong and the marshmallows will be ruined.)

22 DRAW CONCLUSIONS

LA.5.2.1.5
Demonstrate understanding of literary selection

What has happened to the marshmallows? How do you know? (The torn bag and the presence of a raccoon licking its sticky paws suggest that the raccoon ripped open the bag and ate the marshmallows.)

23 STRATEGY
MONITOR COMPREHENSION

LA.5.1.7
Student uses strategies to comprehend text

Why do you think the raccoon does not show any fear when Teddy discovers it inside the tent? Do you think it's appropriate for the author to end the story this way? Explain your answer.

Student Think Aloud Teddy thinks the raccoon should be afraid of him because animals are always afraid of people on nature shows. I think because campers are around all the time, the raccoon has simply gotten used to people. It obviously knew it could probably find food in the tent. Since everything else has gone wrong on this camping trip, it seems appropriate for the author to end the story this way.

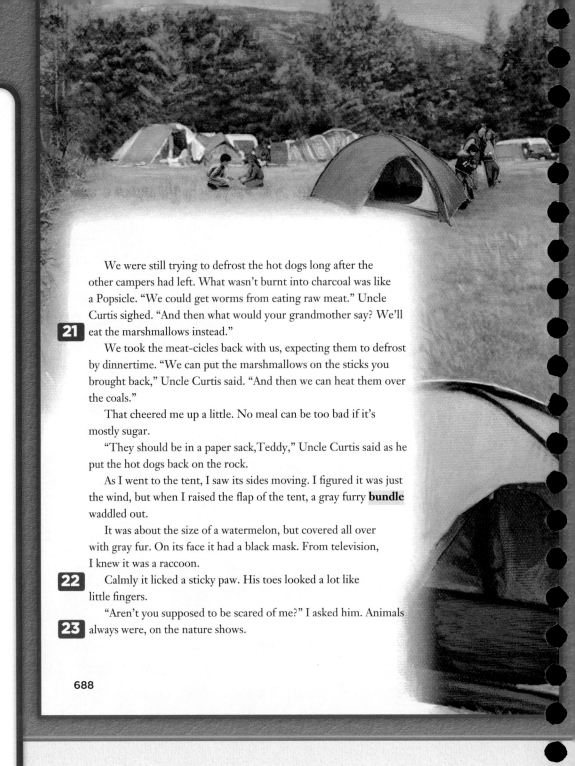

We were still trying to defrost the hot dogs long after the other campers had left. What wasn't burnt into charcoal was like a Popsicle. "We could get worms from eating raw meat." Uncle Curtis sighed. "And then what would your grandmother say? We'll **21** eat the marshmallows instead."

We took the meat-cicles back with us, expecting them to defrost by dinnertime. "We can put the marshmallows on the sticks you brought back," Uncle Curtis said. "And then we can heat them over the coals."

That cheered me up a little. No meal can be too bad if it's mostly sugar.

"They should be in a paper sack, Teddy," Uncle Curtis said as he put the hot dogs back on the rock.

As I went to the tent, I saw its sides moving. I figured it was just the wind, but when I raised the flap of the tent, a gray furry **bundle** waddled out.

It was about the size of a watermelon, but covered all over with gray fur. On its face it had a black mask. From television, I knew it was a raccoon.

22   Calmly it licked a sticky paw. His toes looked a lot like little fingers.

"Aren't you supposed to be scared of me?" I asked him. Animals **23** always were, on the nature shows.

688

I thought I saw him shrug. Then he cleaned the other paw.

"Well, I'm bigger than you," I pointed out to him. "That shoul count for something."

With a sniff, he strolled away into the brush.

I watched him disappear. Then, curious, I raised the flap on the tent.

Inside it was a mess—even worse than my part of our bedroom at home. The sleeping bags had been tumbled about. Worse, the paper bags had been torn open.

Suddenly I understood why the raccoon had licked his paws. The plastic sack with the marshmallows had been split apart. Only a few marshmallows were left. They lay scattered in the dirt. I whirled around. The brush was still shaking in the distance.

"You rotten little pig. I hope you get cavities," I yelled.

689

Develop Comprehension

LA.5.1.7.1
Use prior knowledge to make and confirm predictions

RETURN TO PREDICTIONS AND PURPOSES

Review students' predictions and their purposes for reading. Were their predictions correct? Talk about Teddy's feelings about the camping trip. Discuss any questions students still have about the story now that they have finished reading.

LA.5.1.7
Student uses strategies to comprehend text

REVIEW READING STRATEGIES

- How did making judgments about characters and events help you?

- When will you try using the strategy of rereading to clarify again?

PERSONAL RESPONSE

LA.5.4.1.1
Write narratives that establish plot with rising action, conflict and resolution

Ask students to write a short fiction narrative about two friends who go camping. Encourage them to establish a plot with rising action, a problem or conflict the characters have to solve, and a resolution to the problem at the end of the story.

As an alternative, have students write about a time when they or someone close to them planned an outing where everything went wrong. Suggest that they compare their personal experiences to events in the story, citing specific examples from the text.

Students can also write a paragraph in which they analyze the literary elements in the story and consider the quality of ideas and information the author used.

Quick Check Can students make judgments about characters and events in the story?

During **Small Group Instruction**

If No → **Approaching Level** Comprehension, pp. 697O–697P

If Yes → **On Level** Options, p. 697R

Beyond Level Options, p. 697T

Author and Illustrator

GOING CAMPING WITH LAURENCE YEP AND WINSON TRANG

Have students read the biographies of the author and illustrator.

LA.5.1.7.2 Identify how author's perspective influences text

DISCUSS

- How does Laurence Yep's philosophy of writing about things from a different angle apply to *Skunk Scout*?

- Why do you think Winson Trang focuses on Asian-American subjects as an illustrator?

WRITE ABOUT IT

- Remind students that Teddy and his brother are new at camping. Review how the author reveals this information in the story. Then have students write an adventure they experienced while trying something new.

FCAT ## Author's Purpose

Remind students that a story can be entertaining even though it deals with everday situations. The frozen food that won't thaw and the raccoon that steals campers' food are all events that could happen in real life.

LA.5.1.7.2 Identify author's purpose

 Technology

Students can find more information about Laurence Yep and Winson Trang at
www.macmillanmh.com

Going Camping with Laurence Yep and Winson Trang

Laurence Yep got bit by the writing bug at his California high school. A teacher challenged his entire class to send their essays off to a national magazine. Laurence did, and soon after that he sold his first story. He was paid a penny a word! His advice to young writers: "Writing only requires one step to the side and looking at something from a slightly different angle." Laurence still lives in California with his wife.

Other books by Laurence Yep:
Dragonwings and *Dragon's Gate*

Winson Trang is a book illustrator. He has illustrated many stories, especially those focused on Asian-American subjects. This is the second time he has worked with Laurence Yep. The first book they both worked on was *Child of the Owl*. Winson currently lives in Los Angeles with his wife and son.

FCAT **Author's Purpose**
Because this is realistic fiction, the author's purpose is to entertain. Readers can also expect details that could occur in real life. Identify examples of realism in the story.

LOG ON Find out more about Laurence Yep and Winson Trang at **www.macmillanmh.com**

690

Author's Craft
Point of View

Have students identify the story's narrative point of view (first person, third person, omniscient). Discuss the similarities and differences of each and how point of view affects the text.

Explain that writers can sometimes make a story seem livelier by writing from the narrator's point of view. *Skunk Scout* is told by a first-person narrator, Teddy, who reveals his own opinions about events in the story. For example:

> I thought some of the skyscrapers in San Francisco had been big, but they were toys compared to it. (p. 674)

Ask students to team up with a partner to rewrite one paragraph of the story, changing it from the first-person to the third-person point of view. Have them share how this change alters the story.

LA.5.2.1 Identifies and analyzes elements of fiction

FCAT Comprehension Check

Summarize

Use your Judgments Chart to help you summarize the chapter from *Skunk Scout*. The actions of the two brothers and their uncle while they were camping will help you organize your summary.

Action	→	Judgment
	→	
	→	
	→	
	→	

Think and Compare

1. Describe how your opinions about the characters might change if the story were told by Bobby instead of Teddy. Use story details to explain. **Monitor Comprehension: Plot Development**

2. Reread pages 678–679. What can you tell about Teddy's life at home? Use details from the story in your answer. **Analyze**

3. Would you enjoy going on a camping trip with Uncle Curtis? Explain why or why not. What **gear** would you bring? **Analyze**

4. Do you think it is important to preserve our national parks? Explain your answer. **Evaluate**

5. Reread "The Best Fourth of July" on pages 670–671. Compare and contrast the camping experiences that Teddy and Lateesha had. Use details from both stories to support your answer. **Reading/Writing Across Texts**

691

Strategies for Answering Questions

Author and Me

Model the Author and Me strategy with question 1.

The answer to this question is not stated in the text, but there may be clues. Connect these text clues with what you know to answer the question.

Question 1 Think Aloud: I know that this story is told in the first person point of view. The reader learns about everything that happens on the trip from Teddy. When Uncle Curtis declares, "This is it! The great outdoors!" Teddy thinks to himself that he doesn't see what's so great about it. But Bobby is very enthusiastic about being on the trip with Uncle Curtis. When they get lost, he says "Well, at least we got to see a lot of the mountain." If the story were told from Bobby's point of view, readers might not finish it feeling that the trip was a "disaster."

LA.5.1.7 Student uses strategies to comprehend text

Comprehension Check

FCAT
LA.5.1.7.3 Determine essential message through summarizing

SUMMARIZE

Have students explain the plot and retell the major events in *Skunk Scout* in oral or written form by summarizing the events in the story.

THINK AND COMPARE

Sample answers are given.

FCAT
LA.5.2.1.2 Locate and analyze plot structure and character development

1. **Plot Development:** If Bobby or Uncle Curtis were telling the story, the tone would probably have been more optimistic since they were both more excited than Teddy about the trip. USE AUTHOR AND ME

2. **Analyze:** Students should note that the grandmother is overprotective.

LA.5.2.1.5 Demonstrate understanding and include personal experience

3. **Text to Self:** Students may say they would enjoy accompanying Uncle Curtis because he is enthusiastic. Students may list a tent, canned and frozen foods, and a flashlight as gear they would bring.

4. **Text to World:** Conserving and protecting our natural resources is important to ensure they are still around for future generations to enjoy.

FOCUS QUESTION

LA.5.2.1.5 Demonstrate understanding and include other text/media

5. **Text to Text:** Teddy experienced many problems on his trip with Uncle Curtis because the trip wasn't well planned in advance. Uncle Curtis didn't follow signs. He didn't think about how to cook the food. Lateesha's camping trip turned out much better. They had planned activities including skits and fireworks.

Objective

- Read accurately with appropriate expression
- Rate: 129–149 WCPM

Materials

- Fluency Transparency 27
- Fluency Solutions Audio CD
- Practice Book, p. 196

ELL / Access for All

Echo-Read Discuss the meaning of each paragraph. Have students echo-read the passage with you. Encourage them to imitate your expressiveness and intonation. You can also have them read along with the Fluency Solutions Audio CD. Students who speak tonal languages may need some additional discussion and modeling of intonation in English.

On Level Practice Book O, page 196

As I read, I will pay attention to punctuation and inflection.

	Can you guess what main force created the Grand
9	Canyon? It was the mighty Colorado River.
16	The Colorado is a huge, powerful river. In the spring,
26	melted snow fills the river, and it becomes swift and wild.
37	The river picks up rocks, huge boulders, sand, and pebbles
47	and carries them along. Over millions of years, this gritty
57	river water carved into layer after layer of rock. It carved the
69	deepest canyon of all, the Grand Canyon.
76	One reason the river could carve the rock is that the rock
88	was soft. Soft for rock, that is! Back in time, before there was
101	a Grand Canyon, oceans covered the land.
108	Over millions of years, broken seashells, sand, mud, and
117	clay fell to the bottom of the sea. These small bits of matter
130	that settle on the sea bottom are called sediment. Over
140	millions of years, the sediment turned into rock, called
149	sedimentary rock. And this rock was soft enough for the river
160	to be able to carve a deeper and deeper path through it.
172	But the Colorado River was not the only force to form the
184	Grand Canyon. 186

Comprehension Check

1. How did the Colorado River help form the Grand Canyon? **Main Idea and Details** Gritty river water carved through layers of rock.
2. What is sedimentary rock? **Relevant Facts and Details** a combination of broken seashells, sand, mud, and clay

	Words Read	–	Number of Errors	=	Words Correct Score
First Read		–		=	
Second Read		–		=	

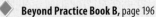

★ **Approaching Practice Book A,** page 196

◆ **Beyond Practice Book B,** page 196

Fluency
Repeated Reading: Punctuation

LA.5.1.5 Student demonstrates ability to read orally with accuracy

EXPLAIN/MODEL Explain to students that good writers use punctuation to make the meaning of a sentence clear to readers. Model reading aloud the entire passage on **Fluency Transparency 27,** with appropriate pauses or inflection to reflect punctuation. Then read one sentence at a time, and have students echo-read each. You may wish to adjust the reading rate based on text difficulty or style.

Teacher Think Aloud I see an exclamation point. It comes at the end of something that Uncle Curtis says. I think it shows how Uncle Curtis feels to be on a camping trip. If I read this aloud, I will say it with enthusiasm.

 Transparency 27

> We followed him up a dirt trail from the parking lot to a patch by some trees. Uncle Curtis stopped. "This is it," he declared, folding the map into neat little squares. "The great outdoors!"
>
> As I kicked at one of the many rocks on the ground, I didn't see what was so great about it. "Isn't fun supposed to be less lumpy?"
>
> My parents are always scolding me about being so messy. However, they should have seen Mother Nature. There were all these pebbles and leaves littering the dirt. I would have tidied up a little, especially for paying guests.
>
> Satisfied, Uncle Curtis surveyed the site. "All this fresh air! It's guaranteed to make you feel so tired you won't notice any rocks."

Fluency Transparency 27 from *Skunk Scout,* page 678

 PRACTICE/APPLY Divide students into two groups. The first group reads the passage a sentence at a time. The second group echo-reads. Then groups switch roles. Students can also practice fluency using **Practice Book** page 196 or the **Fluency Solutions Audio CD.**

Quick Check | **Can students read accurately with appropriate expression?**

During **Small Group Instruction**

If No → **Approaching Level** Fluency, p. 697N

If Yes → **On Level** Options, p. 697Q

Beyond Level Options, p. 697S

Comprehension

REVIEW SKILL
COMPARE CHARACTERS, SETTINGS, EVENTS

LA.5.1.7.7
Compare
and contrast
elements

EXPLAIN/MODEL

- Remind students that readers **compare** when they tell how two or more things are similar. When they **contrast** they identify how they are different.

- To identify similarities between characters and settings in a story, look for words that signal likenesses, such as *both, also, too, just as,* and *like.* Words that signal differences include *but, although, however, nevertheless, on the other hand, in contrast, still, in spite of,* and *even so.*

- Comparing two different settings in a story, and the effect each setting has on the characters as well as the events that take place, can help readers understand a character's feelings and motivations as well as the rising and falling action of the plot.

For comprehension practice use Graphic Organizers on pages 40–64 in the **Teacher's Resource Book.**

PRACTICE/APPLY

Compare the characters, settings and events in *Skunk Scout.*

- Compare and contrast Bobby and Teddy. In what ways are they similar? How are they different? How do the differences in their personalities affect the events of the plot?

- How does the setting change in the story? What effect does this change—from city to country—have on the characters, and the rising action of the plot?

LA.5.1.7.7
Compare
and contrast
elements in
multiple texts

- Have students compare and contrast story elements in another selection with those in *Skunk Scout.*

Objective

- Review compare characters, settings, and events

FCAT Skills Trace

Compare Characters, Settings, Events	
Introduce	329A–B
Practice / Apply	330–347; Practice Book 97–98
Reteach / Review	3550–P, R, T; 691B
Assess	Weekly Test; Unit 3 Test; Benchmark Tests A, B
Maintain	Practice Book 97–98

Informational Text: Science

LA.5.2.1.1
Demonstrate
knowledge of
characteristics
of genres

GENRE: NONFICTION ARTICLE

Have students read the bookmark on **Student Book** page 692. Explain that a nonfiction article

- presents reports about real people, living things, places, situations, or events

- may contain scientific or historical information

- often contains maps, photographs, or interviews that provide additional information

FCAT Text Feature: Photographs and Captions

LA.5.2.2.1
Locate and
explain
information
from text
features

EXPLAIN Photographs and captions help readers understand the content in an informational article. Photographs give readers additional information that helps them to visualize facts and other relevant details that an article contains. Captions should be read carefully. They not only explain what is taking place in the photograph, but they often contain information that is not stated in the text, and can add to a reader's understanding of a topic.

APPLY Point out the photographs and captions on pages 692–695. Have students discuss what these text features add to this article.

Science

Genre

Nonfiction Articles give the reader an account of actual people, places, things, or events.

FCAT Text Feature

Photographs and Captions give visual examples that further explain what the text states.

Content Vocabulary

glaciers

ecosystem

erosion

An Underwater Park

by Tanya Sumanga

Among the greatest treasures of the United States are its national parks. One such park is Biscayne Bay National Park on the southern Florida peninsula. A peninsula is an area of land with water around three sides. The area that is now Biscayne Bay National Park was once a sea bottom. This low, flat peninsula has been changed over time by waves, weather, and shifts of the land.

692

Content Vocabulary   LA.5.1.6.1 Use new vocabulary taught directly

Discuss the spelling and meaning of each content vocabulary word for "An Underwater Park" on Student Book page 693: *glaciers, ecosystem, erosion.*

- **Glaciers** are large masses of ice that move slowly over a land surface. They change the shape of the land as they move. Are there any areas in your community that were formed by glaciers?

- An **ecosystem** is a community of living things within a certain area. Water, algae, air, rocks, soil, fish, and frogs make up the ecosystem of a pond. Can you name another example of an ecosystem?

- **Erosion** is the gradual wearing away of soil and rock by air, water, and glaciers. Do the waves on a beach cause erosion?

◄ Long ago, ice ages changed water and landforms all over the world.

Photographs and Captions
like the ones on this page provide additional information about the park.

▲ Biscayne Bay National Park as seen from the air.

How Biscayne Bay Formed

Glaciers long ago caused many of the changes to Biscayne Bay's landscape. Glaciers are masses of ice that move slowly across land, changing the shape of the land as they move. Glaciers in Florida? It's true. Earth's surface is always changing. Over time the glaciers melted. The water that had once covered parts of Florida returned. All these changes helped create the park as it is today.   **1**

The park has four main ecosystems. An **ecosystem** is a community of living things that interacts with its environment. A mangrove forest along the shore is the park's first ecosystem. Mangroves are tropical trees. The trees and roots slow the water that flows into the bay. They keep the bay's water clean and prevent **erosion**, or wearing away, of the land.   **2** **3**

693

ELL

Access for All

Build Background Find out what students know about Biscayne Bay National Park. Write a few key words on the board in a word wall and explain them through sketches and definitions to build background: *peninsula, glaciers, ecosystem, mangroves, bay, erosion.* Have students each generate one question they have about the park and share them with a partner

For Spanish-speaking students, point out the cognates: *glaciers/glaciars, ecosystem/ecosistema, erosion/erosión.*

Informational Text

Read *"An Underwater Park"*

Access for All As they read, remind students to apply what they have learned about looking for information in photographs and captions. Also have them identify clues to the meanings of the highlighted words. Tell students to adjust their reading rate based on their purpose, the type and difficulty of the text, as well as reading level.

1 ANALYZE

LA.5.2.2.2 Answer questions related to relevant details

What features of Biscayne Bay National Park make it a special place to visit? (The park was once a sea bottom, and even today is a peninsula surrounded by water on three sides. The area has been changed over time by waves, weather, and shifts of the land.)

2 INFER

LA.5.2.2.2 Use information from text to answer questions

How do you think the roots of the mangrove trees help to keep the water in Biscayne Bay clean? (Answers may vary but should include the idea that the roots act as a filter, catching objects such as refuse and other kinds of pollution.)

3 AUTHOR'S PURPOSE

LA.5.1.7.2 Identify author's purpose

Is the author's purpose in "An Underwater Park" to persuade or to inform? How can you tell? (The purpose is to inform because the author gives information about the features of Biscayne Bay National Park, including how it was formed and the ecosystems that can be found there.)

Informational Text

4 CAUSE AND EFFECT

LA.5.1.7.4 Identify cause-and-effect relationships in text

What effect do hurricanes and other tropical storms have on the ecosystems of Biscayne Bay? (Waves generated by these storms can break apart coral reefs. High winds can also empty the shallow bay of water.)

5 TEXT FEATURE: PHOTOGRAPHS AND CAPTIONS

LA.5.2.2.1 Use and explain information from text features

What information does the caption for the picture of the mangrove forest on page 694 give you that is not found in the text? (The forest, like the bay itself, is the result of changes over time.)

Biscayne's many features, like this mangrove forest, are a result of changes over time.

Changes in Biscayne Bay

The second ecosystem is Biscayne Bay itself. A bay is a shallow body of water. Seagrass, a flowering plant that lives underwater in the bay, is food for animals there. Many things can bring changes to this ecosystem, including weather. In 2005 Hurricane Wilma's winds almost emptied the shallow Biscayne Bay. It took 10 hours for the water to return.

The northernmost islands of the Florida Keys are the third ecosystem. The park's largest island, Elliot Key, is the first of the true Florida Keys. It is made up of the remains of coral reefs. A coral reef is made when the skeletons of many small animals called corals join together. If you walk on the island today, you see many different types of coral.

The last ecosystem contained in Biscayne Bay National Park is the third-largest coral reef in the world. Coral reefs have a very mixed population. Over 200 species of fish can be found on Biscayne's reefs. Major weather systems, like hurricanes and tropical storms, can damage coral reefs. Just as these storms can wash away sand from the beaches, the waves can also break apart reefs.

The land and water of Biscayne Bay National Park, like all of Earth, is in a constant state of change. This means that a visitor will always have something new to see.

694

On Level Practice Book O, page 197

Photographs or drawings and their **captions** give more information about the topic of an article.

Look at the drawing and read the caption. Then answer the questions.

Whether camping, hiking, or biking, safety is important.

1. What does the drawing show?
   A young man is on a bicycle in a park setting.

2. What information do you learn from the caption? Relate it to the drawing.
   The caption is about safety while doing outdoor activities. The man on the bicycle is wearing a helmet to illustrate that.

⭐ **Approaching Practice Book A,** page 197

◆ **Beyond Practice Book B,** page 197

6

Like a busy city, the coral reef is full of activity both day and night.

 Connect and Compare

1. Look at the picture above. Why is a coral reef compared to a "busy city"? **Understanding Photographs and Captions**

2. How would you explain to a friend how glaciers have changed the landscape of Biscayne Bay National Park? **Apply**

3. Think about "An Underwater Park" and *Skunk Scout*. Compare and contrast how nature played a role in the events in each selection. **Reading/Writing Across Texts**

 Science Activity

Pick a national park and research interesting facts about the animals, plants, and ecosystems there. Draw a detailed picture and write an informative caption based on your research.

LOG ON Find out more about national parks at www.macmillanmh.com

695

 Research and Inquiry

NATIONAL PARKS

Discuss topics related to national parks, brainstorm a list of topics, and discuss resources students might use to find information. Divide the class into groups and have each research one topic.

When research is complete, have each group create a multimedia presentation for the class using available technologies such as a computer or portable TV and DVD player as well as supporting graphics. As they deliver the presentations, remind them to demonstrate a clear viewpoint, to show an understanding of the topic, to present events or ideas in a logical sequence, and to demonstrate appropriate body language, eye contact, and gestures. Remind them to select language choices for impact.

LA.5.5.2.2 Make formal oral presentations demonstrating appropriate body language, eye contact, and use of gestures
LA.5.5.2.2 Demonstrate appropriate use of supporting graphics and available technologies

Informational Text

Connect and Compare

SUGGESTED ANSWERS

FCAT

LA.5.2.2.1 Use and explain information from text features

1. Sample answer: Just as a city's sidewalks are filled with all different kinds of people, a coral reef is filled with many different kinds of fish.

   UNDERSTANDING PHOTOGRAPHS AND CAPTIONS

2. Answers should include that glaciers change the shape of the land as they slowly move across the landscape. As the glaciers in Florida melted, the water that had once covered part of the state returned. **APPLY**

FOCUS QUESTION

LA.5.2.1.5 Demonstrate understanding and include other text/media

3. In *Skunk Scout,* dry ice changes the food into hard rocks that couldn't be eaten or even cooked properly. In "An Underwater Park" glaciers—frozen water—change the landscape over time. **READING ACROSS TEXTS**

 Science Activity

Have students find photographs of a park's unusual features. Then ask them to describe what makes the features noteworthy. Make sure they include specific content-related vocabulary to describe the ecosystem.

LA.5.6.1.1 Organize information from sources for performing a task
SC.G.1.2.1.5.1 Student knows ways that plants, animals, protists interact

 **Technology**

Internet Research and Inquiry Activity
Students can find facts at
www.macmillanmh.com

Connect
Language Arts

FCAT **WRITING**
- Expository
- Writer's Craft: Time-Order Words

FCAT **WORD STUDY**
- Words in Context
- Multiple-Meaning Words
- Phonics: Latin Roots
- Vocabulary Building

SPELLING
- Latin Roots

GRAMMAR
- Adverbs that Compare

SMALL GROUP OPTIONS
- Differentiated Instruction pp. 697M–697V

Writing

FCAT Time-Order Words

LA.5.3.1.3
Make a plan
for writing
that prioritizes
ideas and
addresses
logical
sequence

READ THE STUDENT MODEL

Read the bookmark. Explain that writers make a story or steps in a process easier to follow by showing a clear order of events or steps. Writers use time-order words to do this.

Have students turn to the last two paragraphs on page 679. Point out that the author shows the steps that Uncle Curtis takes in preparing to set up the tent. Point out the words *Then, Finally,* and *Now.* Then have the class read Michelle Z.'s **instructions** and the callouts. Tell students they will write their own how-to instructions, using time-order words.

Write How-To Instructions

Writer's Craft

FCAT **Time-Order Words**
In giving directions, writers use **time-order words** to show a sequence, such as *first, next, then,* and *finally.* These words help the reader follow the steps in the correct order.

How to Make a Veggie Delight
by Michelle Z.

Plan to make this delicious dish when the campfire coals are hot. First, gather a 12-inch piece of heavy-duty aluminum foil, pre-cut vegetables, water, butter, salt, and pepper.

Next, fold each piece of foil horizontally in half. Press flat and fold the sides shut. Rub the inside of the pocket with butter. Then, fill it with the vegetables until it is about two-thirds full. Sprinkle with salt and pepper and dot with more butter. Next, pour in about a tablespoon of water. Now it's time to cook it. Close the top shut and get an adult to place the pocket on the hot coals. Let it cook for 15 minutes on each side. Finally, enjoy your Veggie Delight!

> I began the directions for making my favorite recipe with a list of required items.

> I used time-order words to guide the process.

696

Features of How-To Instructions

In how-to instructions, the writer tells readers how to make or do something.

- How-to instructions describe each step in order.

- They use sequence words to tell the order of events.

- They use transitions and conjunctions to improve cohesiveness within paragraphs.

- They include details, examples, and graphics to make the explanations clear.

Writing Prompt

People often follow how-to instructions to learn how to make or do something.

Think about something you know how to make or do.

Now write how-to instructions for something you know how to make or do.

FCAT ✎ Writer's Checklist

☑ **Focus:** My writing clearly presents how-to instructions.

☑ **Organization:** My how-to instructions have **time-order words** to show the sequence of steps.

☑ **Support:** I use supporting details to explain each step.

☑ **Conventions:** All words are spelled correctly. I use comparison adverbs such as "more" and "most" correctly.

697

Transparency 105: **How-To Chart**
Transparency 106: **Draft**
Transparency 107: **Revision**

Transparency 105

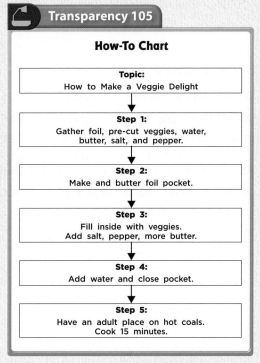

How-To Chart

Topic:
How to Make a Veggie Delight

↓

Step 1:
Gather foil, pre-cut veggies, water, butter, salt, and pepper.

↓

Step 2:
Make and butter foil pocket.

↓

Step 3:
Fill inside with veggies. Add salt, pepper, more butter.

↓

Step 4:
Add water and close pocket.

↓

Step 5:
Have an adult place on hot coals. Cook 15 minutes.

Writing Transparency 105

LA.5.3.1.2 Prewrite by determining purpose and intended audience

PREWRITE

Read the writing prompt on page 697. Have students share things they know how to make or do. Have listeners tell speakers which skills they would be most interested in learning. Help students identify an audience and a purpose for writing.

LA.5.3.1.3 Make a plan for writing that addresses logical sequence

Display **Transparency 105.** Discuss how Michelle uses a chart to help her plan her instructions. She records the sequence of steps in the order that they must be completed. Have students work on charts with partners.

LA.5.3.3.1 Evaluate draft for logical organization

DRAFT

Display **Transparency 106.** Discuss ways to improve the draft. Michelle neglects to use time-order words. She also neglects to use specific words and details to help readers complete the instructions.

Before students begin writing, present the explicit lesson on **Time-Order Words** on page 697A. Then have students use their charts to write their instructions. Remind them to focus on time-order words and word choice.

LA.5.3.3 Student will refine draft

REVISE

Display **Transparency 107.** Discuss the revisions. Students can revise their drafts or place them in writing portfolios to work on later. If students choose to revise, have them work with a partner and use the Writer's Checklist on page 697. Have them **proofread/edit** their writing. For **Publishing Options** see page 697A.

For lessons on **Word Choice, Research, Adverbs that Compare,** and **Spelling** see page 697B, and **5 Day Spelling** and **5 Day Grammar** on pages 697G–697J.

Writer's Craft

SUPPORT **Time-Order Words**

LA.5.3.3.2
Use sequential
organization

Publishing Options

Students can share their instructions orally with the class. See the Speaking and Listening tips below. They can also use their best cursive to write their instructions. (See Teacher's Resource Book pages 168–173 for cursive models and practice.) Then select several easy-to-do student instructions that require little or no outside material, and have small groups follow them in class. Students can report on how easily they were able to follow the instructions.

Speaking and Listening

SPEAKING STRATEGIES

- Practice reading directions.
- Pause before reading a new step.
- Emphasize time-order words.

LISTENING STRATEGIES

- Listen for the topic and each step.
- Restate the directions and ask questions about them.

6-Point Scoring Rubric

Use the rubric on page **763G** to score published writing.

Writing Process

For a complete lesson, see Unit Writing pages **763A–763F**.

EXPLAIN/MODEL

Explain that time-order words are especially important in instructions. Writers must clearly convey the order of steps so that readers can successfully complete the tasks. Display **Transparency 108.**

Think Aloud The writer gives instructions for washing a load of laundry. However, the steps are not in the right order. In fact, if I followed them exactly, I'd have a big mess. Also, the writer does not use time-order words to clarify the order of the steps.

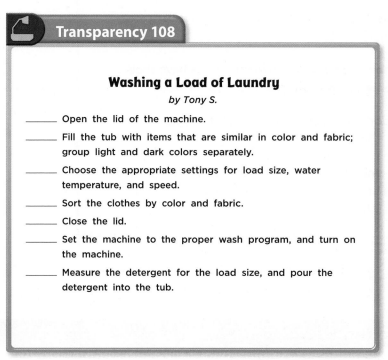

Transparency 108

Washing a Load of Laundry
by Tony S.

_____ Open the lid of the machine.

_____ Fill the tub with items that are similar in color and fabric; group light and dark colors separately.

_____ Choose the appropriate settings for load size, water temperature, and speed.

_____ Sort the clothes by color and fabric.

_____ Close the lid.

_____ Set the machine to the proper wash program, and turn on the machine.

_____ Measure the detergent for the load size, and pour the detergent into the tub.

Writing Transparency 108

PRACTICE/APPLY

Work with students to place the steps in the correct order and to add time-order words. Then have students identify time-order words in instructions that they have read recently.

As students prepare for and write their instructions, have them focus on time-order words and word choice.

Writer's Toolbox

LA.5.3.3.1 Evaluate draft for word choice

SUPPORT

Writing Trait: Word Choice

Explain/Model Tell students that writing that successfully tells how to do something includes strong, specific words and details. Specific words help readers understand what to do. Have students look at Michelle Z.'s instructions on page 696. Point out that Michelle tells readers to get a 12-inch piece of heavy-duty aluminum foil.

Practice/Apply As students draft their instructions, encourage them to focus on strong, specific word choice.

SUPPORT

Research

Explain/Model Point out to students that they may be so familiar with how to complete a particular task that they skip or combine steps. However, to teach someone to do a new task, writers must clearly explain each step. Suggest that students consult reference sources or Internet sites to review the steps in a process. Point out that Michelle may have researched the type of foil that works best over a campfire.

Practice/Apply As students draft their instructions, encourage them to conduct research to provide readers with helpful supporting details.

LA.5.6.2 Student uses a systematic research process

LA.5.3.4.4. Edits for correct use of adverbs

CONVENTIONS

Grammar: Adverbs That Compare

Explain/Model Explain that writers can use adverbs to make comparisons. To compare two actions, writers can use -er or more. To compare more than two actions, writers can use -est or most. Point out that Michelle might want to compare cooking vegetables on the stove with cooking vegetables over a campfire.

Practice/Apply Have students skim the passage on page 670 to locate adverbs that compare. For each example, have students note how many items are being compared. As students draft their instructions, remind them to use adverbs to make comparisons. For a complete lesson on adverbs that compare, including a mechanics lesson on the use of *more* and *most,* see pages 697I–697J.

CONVENTIONS

Spelling: Latin Roots

Point out that Michelle's recipe is portable. Suggest that students use their knowledge of the Latin root to define the word portable. Remind students to pay attention when they spell words with Latin roots. They can use print or online dictionaries to check spelling in their drafts. For a complete lesson on Latin roots, see pages 697G–697H.

LA.5.3.4.1 Edits for spelling using knowledge of Latin root words

Technology

Students can format a list by selecting either the bulleted or numbered feature from the menu on the toolbar.

FCAT Success!

Test Prep and Practice with FCAT Writing+, pages 180–230.

Objectives

- Apply knowledge of word meaning and context clues
- Use dictionaries to figure out multiple-meaning words

Materials

- Vocabulary Transparencies 53 and 54
- Practice Book, p. 198

Vocabulary

coordination (p. 680) ability of things to work well together

ease (p. 686) freedom from pain or trouble

bundle (p. 688) objects or material gathered or bound together

supervise (p. 680) look after and direct work, workers, or a process

scenery (p. 676) the background or natural setting of a place

frustrated (p. 684) felt anger or defeat

guaranteed (p. 678) promised or pledged

fused (p. 686) joined together by melting

ELL · Access for All

Reinforce Vocabulary
Write *Gymnastics takes good coordination.*
Discuss the sentence with students. Erase *gymnastics* and invite students to complete the sentence with other words. Discuss their ideas.

Review
Vocabulary
 FCAT Words in Context

LA.5.1.6 Student uses multiple strategies to develop vocabulary

EXPLAIN/MODEL

Review the meanings of the vocabulary words. Display **Transparency 53.** Read the first sentence out loud. Model how to use word meanings and context clues to fill in the first missing word.

Think Aloud When I read the sentence, I see that something was not planned, so the event was *unorganized.* I think the missing word is probably an antonym for *unorganized.* When I look at the vocabulary words, I see the word *coordination,* and I know it has almost the opposite meaning of *unorganized.* So *coordination* is the correct answer.

> **Transparency 53**
>
> | bundle | coordination | frustrated | fused |
> |---|---|---|---|
> | guaranteed | scenery | supervise | |
>
> 1. We did not plan the <u>coordination</u> of the event properly, so it was unorganized.
> 2. The batter hit the ball with <u>ease</u>, looking effortless.
> 3. Please bring a <u>bundle</u> of sticks for the campfire.
> 4. Since I am group leader, I have to <u>supervise</u> the scouts.
> 5. The wooded <u>scenery</u> gave me a feeling of peace.
> 6. After three failed attempts, we felt <u>frustrated</u>.
> 7. Her hard work <u>guaranteed</u> her success in school.
> 8. The silver and gold were <u>fused</u> together, making the ring look as if it had stripes.

Vocabulary Transparency 53

PRACTICE/APPLY

 Instruct students to complete the remaining sentences on their own.

 Latin and Greek Root Webs Write a root word related to science on a piece of butcher block paper. State the word's meaning and its origins. Then have students create a web of related words on the paper. Have them look through science textbooks for definitions.

LA.5.1.6.9
Determine correct meaning of words with multiple meanings in context

STRATEGY
DICTIONARY: MULTIPLE-MEANING WORDS

EXPLAIN/MODEL

- Multiple-meaning words have more than one meaning. These words may also be different parts of speech.

- Use context clues or a dictionary to determine the meaning of multiple-meaning words. Try each meaning in the sentence to find the one that makes sense.

Display **Transparency 54.** Model how to use the dictionary entry to figure out the meaning of the boldface word in the sentence.

Transparency 54

Multiple-Meaning Words

After the game, we had to **weave** through the crowd to get to our car.

weave (wēv) **1.** *verb* To make something by passing strands or lengths of material over and under one another. *The machine can weave thread into cloth.* **2.** To spin a web or cocoon. *Spiders weave webs.* **3.** To move by turning or twisting. *The fire engine had to weave through traffic to reach the blaze.*

1. The apartment building contained ten **units.**

2. We will **skirt** the mud puddle.

3. The builders will use a large **beam** to support the ceiling.

Vocabulary Strategy Transparency 54

PRACTICE

Have students work in pairs and use a dictionary to find the correct meaning of the boldface word in each sentence.

Quick Check

Can students determine word meanings? Can students choose the correct meaning of a word?

During **Small Group Instruction**

If No → Approaching Level   Vocabulary, pp. 697N–697P

If Yes → On Level   Options, pp. 697Q–697R

Beyond Level   Options, pp. 697S–697T

FCAT Success!

Test Prep and Practice with vocabulary, pages 6–31.

📘 **On Level Practice Book O,** page 198

Words with more than one meaning are **multiple-meaning words.** You can use context clues, or other words in the sentence, to help you figure out the meaning. Sometimes you must use a dictionary to learn the different meanings of the word.

A. Read each sentence. Then circle the letter next to the correct meaning of each underlined word.

1. My first camping trip <u>might</u> have been a disaster, but it turned out great.
   a. physical strength   **b.** expressing possibility or doubt

2. We had to change a flat tire on the way to the campground, but the <u>spare</u> tire worked fine.
   a. extra   b. hold back or avoid

3. After that we set up our tent near some trees and <u>brush</u>.
   a. object with bristles on a handle   **b.** heavy growth of bushes

4. <u>Cavities</u> in the rocks near the river were the perfect place to store our towels while we swam in the lake.
   a. hollow places   b. decayed spots on teeth

5. He still had some <u>change</u> in his pocket.
   a. to become different   **b.** coins

6. As the day came to a <u>close</u>, I was happy to be camping.
   a. end   b. shut

B. Use a dictionary to find two meanings of each multiple-meaning word listed below. Possible responses provided.

7. jam   a. sweet fruit preserve
           b. to press tightly together

8. coat   a. the outer layer (of paint)
           b. heavy jacket or garment

 Approaching Practice Book A, page 198

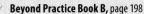 **Beyond Practice Book B,** page 198

Objective
- Decode words with Latin roots

Materials
- Practice Book, p. 199

On Level Practice Book O, page 199

Many words in English have **Latin roots.** You can define unfamiliar words by recognizing a Latin root and using context clues.

Latin Roots	Meaning
aud	to hear
tract	to drag, draw
port	to carry
spect	to look
mit/miss	to send

Read the root chart and write the root of each underlined word in the sentences below. Then use context clues and the meaning of the Latin roots to write a definition of each underlined word.

Possible responses provided.

1. Making a campfire is tricky. First an adult must <u>transport</u> wood to your campsite. __port__ *Transport means* __carry__

2. Then you must <u>inspect</u> the wood to make sure that it is dry. __spect__ *Inspect means* __look at, examine carefully__

3. When an adult lights the fire, you will notice an <u>audible</u> crackle and pop as the wood begins to burn. __aud__ *Audible means* __can be heard__

4. The <u>spectacle</u> of a roaring fire is a wonderful sight. __spect__ *Spectacle means* __display, sight__

5. For some people, the main <u>attraction</u> of a campfire is roasting marshmallows. __tract__ *Attraction means* __draw, quality that draws attention__

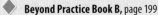

⭐ **Approaching Practice Book A,** page 199

◆ **Beyond Practice Book B,** page 199

Phonics

✓ FCAT Words with Latin Roots

Access for All

LA.5.1.6.11
Use roots and affixes from Greek and Latin

EXPLAIN/MODEL

- Many words in English are made up of word parts from Latin. Latin is an ancient language that was spoken by Romans about 2,000 years ago.

- Some common Latin roots are *aud*, which means "hear"; *spect*, which means "see"; *port*, which means "carry"; *mit/miss*, which means "send"; and *tract*, which means "draw or pull."

- When prefixes and/or suffixes are added to a Latin root, new words are formed. For example, *porter* is made up of the root *port* and the suffix *–er*, which can mean "one who." So *porter* means "a person who carries something."

Write *import* on the board.

Think Aloud I see this word has the Latin root *port,* which means "to carry," and the prefix *im-*, which can mean "in" or "into." When I put the meanings together, I get "carry into." When I look up *import* in a dictionary, I find that one meaning is "to bring merchandise into a country." Knowing the meaning of the Latin root and the prefix helps me understand the word's meaning.

PRACTICE/APPLY

Write the following words on the board and have students identify the Latin roots in each: *portable, export, dismiss, missile, transport, porter, admit, permission, export, report, submit, intermission.* Then have them use their knowledge of prefixes and suffixes to predict the meaning of each word. They can look up any unknown affixes in a dictionary, then confirm their predictions.

LA.5.1.4.3
Use language structure to read multi-syllabic words

Decode Multisyllabic Words Emphasize to students that many words with Latin roots are multisyllabic. Understanding Latin roots can help students decode such longer words. For practice, see the decodable passages on page 31 of the **Teacher's Resource Book.**

> **Quick Check** **Can students decode words with Latin roots?**
>
> During **Small Group Instruction**
>
> **If No** → | Approaching Level | Phonics, p. 697M
>
> **If Yes** → | On Level | Options, pp. 697Q–697R
>
> | Beyond Level | Options, pp. 697S–697T

Vocabulary Building

LA.5.1.6 Student uses multiple strategies to develop vocabulary

LA.5.1.6.10 Determine meanings of words using a thesaurus and digital tools

LA.5.1.6.8 Use homographs to determine meaning

Oral Language

Expand Vocabulary Write *Camping Out* in the center of a word web. Using the selection, print and electronic dictionaries, thesauruses, and encyclopedias, have students brainstorm and discuss words that relate to this week's theme. You may include words such as *forest, tent,* or *campfire.* Write these words in circles that radiate from the center circle of your web. Identify any words that have multiple meanings.

Vocabulary Building

Homographs Homographs are words that have the same spelling, and often the same pronunciation, but have different meanings and origins. Using two or three homographs, tell students to create picture dictionaries. Tell students to draw or cut out pictures that show the definitions of these words. They should write each word at the top of a sheet of paper and then add pictures that show the different meanings of the word.

1. hamper	3. fan	5. yard
2. key	4. file	6. bank

✏️ Apply Vocabulary

Write a Persuasive Paragraph Give students the following writing prompt: *Using the vocabulary words from this week and previous weeks, write a persuasive paragraph about why people should or should not go camping, using a compare-and-contrast structure.* Remind them to use three or more supporting sentences and a concluding sentence. Then have students present their paragraphs orally to the class. Remind them to use the vocabulary words and to make sure that their presentation establishes a clear position, includes relevant evidence to support the position, and addresses potential concerns of the listeners.

LA.5.4.3.1 Write persuasive text that supports arguments for validity of proposed idea with evidence

Spiral Review

Vocabulary Game Create a handout with a center circle surrounded by rows of other circles, as if you are looking at the end of a bundle of sticks. Write vocabulary words from this week and previous weeks in the center circle on each handout. Have students create Word Bundles by writing synonyms and antonyms for the words in the surrounding circles, labeling each. Once a student adds a word to one bundle, he or she should pass the paper to the next student. Tell students to identify any multiple-meaning words as well.

LA.5.1.6.8 Use antonyms and synonyms to determine meaning

Technology

Vocabulary PuzzleMaker

For vocabulary games and practice go to www.macmillanmh.com

5 Day Spelling

LA.5.1.4.1 Understand spelling patterns

Latin Roots

Spelling Words

subtraction	transport	spectacle
transportation	tractor	inspect
missile	spectator	mission
portable	attraction	import
export	dismiss	intermission
committee	inspector	suspect
respect	distract	

Review telescope, astronaut, photograph

Challenge spectacular, protractor

Dictation Sentences

1. We learned <u>subtraction</u> in math class.
2. The bike is my <u>transportation</u>.
3. He worked on the secret <u>missile</u>.
4. I carried the <u>portable</u> radio.
5. Corn is our country's <u>export</u>.
6. A <u>committee</u> chose the book.
7. We will <u>respect</u> the camp rules.
8. Big items are hard to <u>transport</u>.
9. The farmer rode the <u>tractor</u>.
10. The <u>spectator</u> watched the game.
11. Lions are the main <u>attraction</u> at the zoo.
12. The teacher will <u>dismiss</u> the class.
13. The <u>inspector</u> examined the camp.
14. Loud music will <u>distract</u> me.
15. What a <u>spectacle</u> the tent was!
16. Please **inspect** the sleeping bags.
17. Her <u>mission</u> is to finish the job.
18. It's expensive to <u>import</u> goods.
19. He left the theater at <u>intermission</u>.
20. I <u>suspect</u> she is upset with me.

Review/Challenge Words

1. We use the <u>telescope</u> to look at stars.
2. The <u>astronaut</u> landed on the moon.
3. She framed the <u>photograph</u>.
4. The fireworks were <u>spectacular</u>.
5. Draw an angle with your <u>protractor</u>.

The word in **bold** type is from the main selection.

Day 1 Pretest

LA.5.5.2.1 Listen to gain and share information

ASSESS PRIOR KNOWLEDGE

Using the Dictation Sentences, say the underlined word. Read the sentence aloud and repeat the word. Have students write the words on **Spelling Practice Book** page 167. For a modified list, use the first 12 Spelling Words and the Review Words. For a more challenging list, use Spelling Words 3–20 and the Challenge Words. Students may correct their own tests.

Ask students to cut apart the Spelling Word Cards BLM on **Teacher's Resource Book** page 92 and figure out a way to sort them. They can save the cards for use throughout the week.

Day 2 Word Sorts

LA.5.1.6.4 Categorize key vocabulary

TEACHER AND STUDENT SORTS

- Write these column headings on the board: *tract, spect, port, miss/mit*. Explain that students will sort the Spelling Words according to these Latin roots.

- Model the sort with the words *missile* and *tractor*. Place *missile* in the *miss/mit* column and *tractor* in the *tract* column.

- Using the Word Cards, read a few words aloud and ask volunteers to write the words in the proper columns on the board.

- Ask students to copy the chart in their word study notebooks and work in pairs to sort the remaining Spelling and Challenge Words.

- Check the sort as a class.

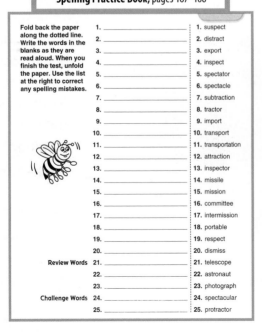

Spelling Practice Book, pages 167–168

Fold back the paper along the dotted line. Write the words in the blanks as they are read aloud. When you finish the test, unfold the paper. Use the list at the right to correct any spelling mistakes.

1. _____ 1. suspect
2. _____ 2. distract
3. _____ 3. export
4. _____ 4. inspect
5. _____ 5. spectator
6. _____ 6. spectacle
7. _____ 7. subtraction
8. _____ 8. tractor
9. _____ 9. import
10. _____ 10. transport
11. _____ 11. transportation
12. _____ 12. attraction
13. _____ 13. inspector
14. _____ 14. missile
15. _____ 15. mission
16. _____ 16. committee
17. _____ 17. intermission
18. _____ 18. portable
19. _____ 19. respect
20. _____ 20. dismiss
Review Words 21. _____ 21. telescope
22. _____ 22. astronaut
23. _____ 23. photograph
Challenge Words 24. _____ 24. spectacular
25. _____ 25. protractor

Spelling Practice Book, page 169

transport	attraction	intermission	portable
spectacle	committee	dismiss	missile
distract	tractor	export	transportation
respect	import	suspect	inspector
spectator	mission	subtraction	inspect

Sort each spelling word according to the Latin root it contains. Then write the words on the lines below.

mit/miss
1. missile   3. committee   5. dismiss
2. mission   4. intermission

port
1. export   3. transport   5. portable
2. import   4. transportation

spect
1. suspect   3. spectator   5. inspector
2. inspect   4. spectacle   6. respect

tract
1. distract   3. tractor
2. subtraction   4. attraction

Day 3 — Word Meanings

LA.5.1.6.11 Use Latin roots to determine meaning

DEFINITIONS

- Ask students to return to yesterday's word sort chart. Explain the definitions of the words and use each in a sentence.

- Have students examine the words in each column to figure out the meaning of the Latin root that is common to the words. Students can work in groups and check their answers by looking up the roots in a dictionary.

- Review the Latin roots as a class, and discuss how the Spelling and Challenge Words incorporate these roots in their definitions.

- Since most words are verbs or nouns, consider having teams compete in a game of charades using the words.

Day 4 — Review and Proofread

LA.5.1.6.11 Use roots and affixes from Greek and Latin

SPIRAL REVIEW

Review words with Greek roots. Write *telescope, astronaut,* and *photograph* on the board. Ask students to identify the Greek root and its definition in each word.

PROOFREAD AND WRITE

Write these sentences on the board, including the misspelled words. Ask students to proofread, circling the misspelled words and correcting them.

1. Inport and exporte merchants depend on the transportashun system. (import, export, transportation)

2. The inspecter was speechless after witnessing the spectecle. (inspector, spectacle)

3. Portoble items are easy to transporte. (portable, transport)

Day 5 — Assess and Reteach

LA.5.1.6.11 Use Latin roots to determine meaning

POSTTEST

Use the Dictation Sentences on page 697G for the Posttest.

If students have difficulty with any words in the lesson, have them place the words in a list entitled "Spelling Words I Want to Remember" in their word study notebooks.

Challenge student partners to look for other words that contain the Latin roots they studied this week, either in their reading or in other materials. Partners should work together to figure out how to sort the words according to these Latin roots and write them in a word study notebook.

Spelling Practice Book, page 170

transport	attraction	intermission	portable
spectacle	committee	dismiss	missile
distract	tractor	export	transportation
respect	import	suspect	inspector
spectator	mission	subtraction	inspect

Definitions

Write the spelling word that has the same, or almost the same, meaning.

1. group of people assigned to one task __committee__
2. person who finds out information or judges something __inspector__
3. a task or project __mission__
4. to send away; a product that is sent from one country to another __export__
5. able to be moved from one place to another __portable__
6. special regard for a person or thing __respect__
7. vehicle used for farming __tractor__
8. the act of removing or taking away __subtraction__
9. a person who witnesses an event __spectator__
10. to shift attention away from something __distract__

Fill in the Blanks

Complete each sentence with a spelling word.

11. I __suspect__ that camping is not much fun in the rain.
12. Cars, buses, trucks, and trains are all forms of __transportation__
13. Some people like to __inspect__ their food before they eat it.
14. I wonder whether other countries __import__ hot dogs from the United States.
15. We left the play during the __intermission__ because we were tired.

Spelling Practice Book, page 171

Circle the misspelled words in the passage. Write the words correctly on the lines below.

My uncle and I went camping for three days. Our car broke down on the first day, so we lost our means of (transportasion) My uncle could only (inspekt) our car—he couldn't fix it. We found an abandoned (tracktor) on the second day, but that didn't work, either. Luckily, I had brought my (portabel) radio with me, so we called for help on the third day. The town put together a (comittee) and went on a (mision) to save us.

1. __transportation__ 2. __inspect__ 3. __tractor__
4. __portable__ 5. __committee__ 6. __mission__

Writing Activity

Write a paragraph about why you would or would not like to go camping. Use four words from your spelling list.

_____
_____
_____
_____
_____
_____
_____
_____
_____
_____
_____
_____

Spelling Practice Book, page 172

Look at the words in each set below. One word in each set is spelled correctly. Use a pencil to fill in the circle next to the correct word. Before you begin, look at the sample set of words. Sample A has been done for you. Do Sample B by yourself. When you are sure you know what to do, you may go on with the rest of the page.

Sample A:
- Ⓐ miccroscope
- Ⓑ mycroscope
- ● microscope
- Ⓓ mykroscope

Sample B:
- Ⓔ eequal
- Ⓕ equal
- Ⓖ equel
- Ⓗ equall

1.
- Ⓐ susppect
- Ⓑ sussppect
- Ⓒ susspect
- Ⓓ suspect

2.
- Ⓔ distract
- Ⓕ disstract
- Ⓖ disttract
- Ⓗ dissttract

3.
- Ⓐ export
- Ⓑ exxport
- Ⓒ expport
- Ⓓ exporrt

4.
- Ⓔ insspect
- Ⓕ innspect
- Ⓖ inspect
- Ⓗ inssspect

5.
- Ⓐ spectater
- Ⓑ spectator
- Ⓒ specktator
- Ⓓ specktater

6.
- Ⓔ specktacle
- Ⓕ spectacle
- Ⓖ specttacle
- Ⓗ spectackle

7.
- Ⓐ subbttraction
- Ⓑ subttraction
- Ⓒ subbtraction
- Ⓓ subtraction

8.
- Ⓔ tractor
- Ⓕ tracter
- Ⓖ tracktor
- Ⓗ trackter

9.
- Ⓐ impport
- Ⓑ immport
- Ⓒ import
- Ⓓ importt

10.
- Ⓔ transsport
- Ⓕ transport
- Ⓖ transpport
- Ⓗ transsportt

11.
- Ⓐ transportashion
- Ⓑ transportation
- Ⓒ transporation
- Ⓓ transporttation

12.
- Ⓔ attraction
- Ⓕ atraction
- Ⓖ attracktion
- Ⓗ attracshion

13.
- Ⓐ insspector
- Ⓑ inspecter
- Ⓒ inspector
- Ⓓ inspecter

14.
- Ⓔ missile
- Ⓕ misile
- Ⓖ missile
- Ⓗ misille

15.
- Ⓐ mishion
- Ⓑ mision
- Ⓒ mission
- Ⓓ misshion

16.
- Ⓔ committee
- Ⓕ comittee
- Ⓖ commitee
- Ⓗ comitee

17.
- Ⓐ intermishion
- Ⓑ intermisshion
- Ⓒ intermision
- Ⓓ intermission

18.
- Ⓔ portble
- Ⓕ portable
- Ⓖ portabel
- Ⓗ portebel

19.
- Ⓐ respeckt
- Ⓑ resspect
- Ⓒ respect
- Ⓓ rispect

20.
- Ⓔ dismiss
- Ⓕ dismiss
- Ⓖ dissmis
- Ⓗ dismis

Daily Language Activities

Use these activities to reinforce each day's lesson. Write the day's activity on the board, or use **Daily Language Transparency 27.**

DAY 1
Uncle Curtis is not a well driver. He drives crazy, mostly because he forgets to read the road signs. (1: good; 2: crazily,)

DAY 2
Teddy studied the map most carefully than Bobby. "Try more harder, Bobby." Bobby said, "I just work more different." (1: more carefully; 2: Try harder; 3: work differently.)

DAY 3
Bobby grumbled, but Uncle Curtis grumbled more loudlier when they missed the turn again. He said, "I'm driving blindlier than a person who can't see." (1: more loudly; 2: more blindly)

DAY 4
Uncle Curtis told Bobby, "Teddy can put up that tent more quicklier than you can." Bobby's hammer swung more closer to his knee than to the tent spike. (1: more quickly; 2: swung closer)

DAY 5
Bobby realized that they should have left home more earlier. Teddy said, "I am starving more desperate than you." (1: earlier; 2: more desperately)

Adverbs That Compare

Day 1 — Introduce the Concept

LA.5.3.4.4. Edits for correct use of adverbs

INTRODUCE ADVERBS THAT COMPARE

Present the following:

- An **adverb** can compare two or more actions.

- Adverbs that compare two actions use *-er* or *more*: *She rides her bicycle faster than I do. Paul moves more quickly than Ed does.*

- Actions that compare three or more actions use *-est* or *most*: *Jim's bike moves the fastest of our three bikes. Paul moves the most quickly of the three boys*

See Grammar Transparency 131 for modeling and guided practice.

Grammar Practice Book, page 167

- An **adverb** can compare two or more actions.
- Add *-er* to most short adverbs to compare two actions.
- Add *-est* to most short adverbs to compare more than two actions.

Read the sentences. Write the correct form of the adverb in parentheses.

1. (hard) Teddy pounded the tent stakes ___harder___ than Bobby did.
2. (near) Of the three, Teddy was the one standing ___nearest___ to the raccoon.
3. (fast) It was Teddy who ran ___fastest___ of all.
4. (soon) Bobby wished that he had spoken up ___sooner___ than he did.
5. (high) The mountain rose ___higher___ than any of San Francisco's skyscrapers.
6. (hard) Of the three of them, Uncle Curtis laughed ___hardest___
7. (fast) Teddy walked ___faster___ than Bobby and Uncle Curtis.
8. (soon) The raccoon arrived ___soonest___ of all.
9. (late) They arrived at the campsite ___later___ than Uncle Curtis expected.
10. (fast) The other campers pitched their tents ___faster___ than Uncle Curtis did.

Day 2 — Teach the Concept

LA.5.3.4.4. Edits for correct use of adverbs

REVIEW ADVERBS THAT COMPARE

Discuss with students how adverbs can be used to compare actions and how they can be recognized.

INTRODUCE COMPARATIVE ADVERBS

- The comparative forms of adverbs are formed in two ways. The form depends on how long the adverb is.

- Add *-er* to most short adverbs to compare two actions. Add *-est* to most short adverbs to compare more than two actions.

- Add *more* or *most* to form comparisons with adverbs that end in *-ly*. Add *more* or *most* to adverbs with two or more syllables. When you use *more* or *most,* do not use the ending *-er* or *-est.*

See Grammar Transparency 132 for modeling and guided practice.

Grammar Practice Book, page 168

- Use *more* or *most* to form comparisons with adverbs that end in *-ly* and with most other adverbs having two or more syllables.
- Use *more* to compare two actions; use *most* to compare more than two.
- When you use *more* or *most,* do not use the ending *-er* or *-est.*

Read the sentences. Write the correct form of the adverb in parentheses.

1. (hungrily) Of them all, it was Teddy who stared at the hotdogs ___most hungrily___
2. (patiently) Bobby waited ___more patiently___ than Teddy did.
3. (quietly) Bobby worked ___most quietly___ of them all.
4. (quickly) Teddy walked ___more quickly___ than Bobby did.
5. (easily) Uncle Curtis got lost ___more easily___ than Teddy did.

Read each sentence. If the adverb is correct, write correct on the line. If it is not correct, rewrite the sentence with the correct form of the adverb.

6. Uncle Curtis grinned happiliest of all.
   ___Uncle Curtis grinned most happily of all.___
7. Bobby learned more quicklier than Teddy.
   ___Bobby learned more quickly than Teddy.___
8. Uncle Curtis ate slowlier than the boys.
   ___Uncle Curtis ate more slowly than the boys.___
9. Teddy treated the map more carefully than did Uncle Curtis.
   ___Correct___
10. Teddy eats more noisily of all.
    ___Teddy eats most noisily of all.___

Day 3 — Review and Practice

LA.5.3.4.4. Edits for correct use of adverbs

REVIEW COMPARATIVE ADVERBS

Review the differences in the ways to make comparisons using adverbs.

MECHANICS AND USAGE: USE *MORE* AND *MOST* WITHOUT *-ER* OR *-EST*

- Use *more* or *most* to form comparisons with adverbs that end in *-ly* or most other adverbs with two or more syllables.

- *More* or *most* almost always appear in front of the adverb.

- Never add *-er* and *more* to the same adverb.

- Never add *-est* and *most* to the same adverb.

 See Grammar Transparency 133 for modeling and guided practice.

Grammar Practice Book, page 169

- Never add *-er* and *more* to the same adverb.
- Never add *-est* and *most* to the same adverb.

Read each sentence. If the sentence uses *more* and *most* correctly, write *correct*. Otherwise, rewrite the sentence correctly using *more* and *most*.

1. The ranger spoke most knowledgeably than Uncle Curtis.
   The ranger spoke more knowledgeably than Uncle Curtis.

2. Teddy unpacked the car more hurriedlier than Bobby did.
   Teddy unpacked the car more hurriedly than Bobby did.

3. Uncle Curtis turned more promptlier the third time they neared the exit.
   Uncle Curtis turned more promptly the third time they neared the exit.

4. Of the three of them, it was Teddy who looked at the raccoon most angrily.
   Correct

5. The experienced campers found the trail more easilier than Uncle Curtis did.
   The experienced campers found the trail more easily than Uncle Curtis did.

6. Bobby asked questions most eagerly than Teddy did.
   Bobby asked questions more eagerly than Teddy did.

7. It was Teddy who unrolled his sleeping bag most roughliest of all.
   It was Teddy who unrolled his sleeping bag most roughly of all.

8. The raccoon found the marshmallows more quickly than did Teddy.
   Correct

Day 4 — Review and Proofread

LA.5.3.4.4. Edits for correct use of adverbs

REVIEW ADVERBS THAT COMPARE

Ask students to explain which adverbs take *-er* or *-est* and which take *more* or *most*. Challenge students to make a list of commonly used adverbs that take the different forms.

PROOFREAD

Have students correct the errors.

1. Bobby searched the forest more thoroughlier than Teddy to find wood for the campfire. (more thoroughly)

2. Teddy returned to the site more sooner than Bobby did. (sooner)

3. Curtis walks the more slower (most slowly) of all my friends.

 See Grammar Transparency 134 for modeling and guided practice.

Grammar Practice Book, page 170

Read the letter below. Rewrite the letter correctly on the lines provided.

Dear Mom and Dad,

I know you think that I'm messy, but I clean more carefullier than Mother Nature does. There are dirt and rocks everywhere in the woods! Since we've been at the campsite, we've been eating most poorly than we do at home. You cook much more expert than Uncle Curtis does. Of all the campers, it's the mosquitoes who seem to be eating happiliest. I hope we come home more sooner rather than late.

Your son,
Teddy

Dear Mom and Dad,

I know you think that I'm messy, but I clean more carefully than Mother Nature does. There are dirt and rocks everywhere in the woods! Since we've been at the campsite, we've been eating more poorly than we do at home. You cook much more expertly than Uncle Curtis does. Of all the campers, it's the mosquitoes that seem to be eating most happily. I hope we come home sooner rather than later.

Your son,
Teddy

Day 5 — Assess and Reteach

LA.5.3.4.4. Edits for correct use of adverbs

ASSESS

Use the Daily Language Activity and page 171 of the **Grammar Practice Book** for assessment.

RETEACH

Have students write down the corrected Daily Language Activities. Ask them to work in pairs to identify the comparative adverbs that appear. Have students underline the adverbs that use the endings *-er* or *-est*. Have them circle the adverbs that require *more* or *most*. Invite pairs to compare their answers with others. If students disagree on an answer, have them present the adverb to the class for a discussion.

Use page 172 of the **Grammar Practice Book** for additional reteaching.

 See Grammar Transparency 135 for modeling and guided practice.

Grammar Practice Book, pages 171–172

A. Choose the sentence in each group that is written incorrectly. Circle the letter of the incorrect sentence.

1. a. Bobby awoke sooner than did Teddy.
   b. Bobby awoke most soonest of all.
   c. Bobby awoke soonest of all.

2. a. Uncle Curtis looked around more eagerly than Teddy.
   b. Uncle Curtis looked around most eagerly of all.
   c. Uncle Curtis looked around more eagerlier than Teddy.

3. a. Bobby works more harder than Teddy does.
   b. Bobby works hardest of all.
   c. Bobby works harder than Teddy does.

4. a. Uncle Curtis eyed the hot dogs more hopefully than Teddy did.
   b. It was Uncle Curtis who eyed the hot dogs most hopefully.
   c. Uncle Curtis eyed the hot dogs most hopefully than Teddy did.

5. a. Teddy missed home more stronglier than Bobby did.
   b. Teddy missed home more strongly than Bobby did.
   c. Of the three campers, Teddy was the one who missed home most strongly.

B. Choose the comparing adverb that best completes the sentence. Circle the letter of your answer.

6. Teddy looked for the marshmallows _____ than he looked for firewood.
   a. eagerly
   b. most eagerly
   c. more eagerly

7. Uncle Curtis snored _____ than Bobby.
   a. most loudly
   b. loudlier
   c. more loudly

8. Bobby searched _____ of all.
   a. more happily
   b. most happily
   c. happily

End-of-Week Assessment

Administer the Test

 ### Weekly Reading Assessment
pages 321–332

ASSESSED SKILLS

- Plot Development
- Vocabulary Words
- Dictionary: Multiple-Meaning Words
- Latin Roots
- Adverbs that Compare

Progress Reporter
Macmillan/McGraw-Hill

Assessment Tool

Administer the **Weekly Assessment** from the CD-ROM or online.

Weekly Assessment, 321–332

 ## Fluency

Assess fluency for one group of students per week. Use the Oral Fluency Record Sheet to track the number of words read correctly. Fluency goal for all students: **129–149 words correct per minute (WCPM).**

Approaching Level	Weeks 1, 3, 5
On Level	Weeks 2, 4
Beyond Level	Week 6

Fluency Assessment

Alternative Assessments

- **ELL Assessment,** pages 166–167

ELL Assessment, 166–167

Diagnose	IF...	Prescribe — THEN...
VOCABULARY WORDS **VOCABULARY STRATEGY** Dictionary: Multiple-Meaning Words Items 1, 2, 3, 4, 5	0–2 items correct ...	Reteach skills using the **Additional Lessons** page T7.  Reteach skills: Go to **www.macmillanmh.com** **Vocabulary PuzzleMaker** Evaluate for Intervention.
COMPREHENSION Skill: Plot Development Items 6, 7, 8, 9	0–2 items correct ...	Reteach skills using the **Additional Lessons** page T2. Evaluate for Intervention.
SPELLING Latin Roots Items 10, 11, 12	0–1 items correct ...	Reteach skills: Go to **www.macmillanmh.com**
GRAMMAR Adverbs that Compare Items 13, 14, 15	0–1 items correct ...	Reteach skills: **Grammar Practice Book** page 172.
FLUENCY	120–128 WCPM 0–110 WCPM	Fluency Solutions Evaluate for Intervention.

READING
Triumphs
AN INTERVENTION PROGRAM

Also Available

To place students in the Intervention Program, use the **Diagnostic Assessment** in the Intervention Teacher's Edition.

Constructive Feedback

To reiterate the relationship between the root and the meaning of the word, say:

Imagine that you need words to describe different acts of carrying. You have the root *port,* meaning "carry." Think about how you might combine this root with other word parts to develop a series of words to describe different acts of carrying. One act of carrying occurs when something is moved from one place to another, or across a distance. You might form the word transport to describe this act.

Repeat as needed.

Additional Resources

Use your observations to help identify students who might benefit from additional instruction. See page T2 for comprehension support and page T5 for vocabulary support. For each skill below, additional lessons are provided. You can use these lessons on consecutive days after teaching the lessons presented within the week.
• Plot Development: Similarities and Differences, T2
• Multiple-Meaning Words, T5
• Text Feature: Interview, T9

Decodable Text

To help students build speed and accuracy with reading multisyllabic words, use additional decodable text on pages 32–33 of the **Teachers' Resource Book.**

Skills Focus ▶ **Phonics**

Objectives	Review words with Latin roots
	Decode multisyllabic words with Latin roots in both familiar and unfamiliar texts
Materials	• **Student Book** *The Best Fourth of July*

WORDS WITH LATIN ROOTS

LA.5.1.6.11
Use Latin roots to determine meaning

Model/Guided Practice

■ Write *audible* on the board. Blend the sounds: /ô də bəl/.

■ Explain that the Latin root *aud,* meaning "hear," is part of the word *audible*, meaning "can be heard."

■ *Let's check another word origin.* Write *audience* on the board. *What does the Latin root* aud *mean? What does the word* audience *mean?*

■ Next write these words to practice using word origins to understand meaning: *audiology, extract, deport, inspect,* and *transmission.*

■ Extend the review to point out that some words contain more than one Latin root, as in *auditorium.*

MORE MULTISYLLABIC WORDS WITH LATIN ROOTS

LA.5.1.6.11
Use Latin roots to determine meaning

■ Write *missionary* on the board. Break the word into syllables: mis/sion/ary. Point out that the Latin root *miss* means "to send." *Missionary* means "person sent out for a special purpose."

■ Have pairs of students work together. Write the following words on the board or provide copies of the list. *With your partner, choose a word. Say it aloud. Identify the Latin root or roots. Use your knowledge of the root(s) to define the word.*

audit	traction	spectacle
audition	tractor	spectacular
auditory	portfolio	spectator
detract	reporter	submissive

ADD TEXT: WORDS WITH LATIN ROOTS IN CONTEXT

■ Review words with Latin roots.

■ Have students search *The Best Fourth of July* for places to add words with Latin roots. For example, students might say that the scenery at the top of Lookaway Mountain was *spectacular* or that Jean wanted campers to *audition* for roles in the skit. Encourage students to add at least one word in each paragraph of the story.

Skills Focus ▶ Fluency

Objective	Read with increasing prosody and accuracy at a rate of 129–139 WCPM
Materials	• **Approaching Practice Book A,** page 196

MODEL EXPRESSIVE READING

LA.5.1.5
Read grade level text with accuracy and expression

Model reading the Fluency passage in **Practice Book A,** page 196. Tell students to pay attention to the punctuation marks and inflections. Then read aloud one sentence at a time, and have students repeat the sentence, first as a class and then one by one. Listen carefully for accuracy.

REPEATED READING

LA.5.1.5
Student demonstrates ability to read orally with accuracy

Have students continue practicing reading the passage aloud as you circulate and provide corrective feedback. During independent reading time, student partners can take turns reading the passage. One partner reads each sentence aloud, and the other repeats it. Remind students to wait until their partners reach end marks before correcting mistakes.

TIMED READING

LA.5.1.5
Student demonstrates ability to read orally with appropriate rate

Tell students they will do a timed reading of the passage that they have been practicing. With each student:

■ Place the passage from **Practice Book A,** page 196, face down.

■ When you say "Go," the student begins reading the passage aloud.

■ When you say "Stop," the student stops reading the passage.

As students read, note any miscues. Stop students after one minute. Help them record and graph the number of words they read correctly.

Skills Focus ▶ Vocabulary

Objective	Apply vocabulary word meanings
Materials	• **Vocabulary Cards** • **Transparencies 27a and 27b**

VOCABULARY WORDS

LA.5.1.6.1
Use new vocabulary

Display the **Vocabulary Cards** for this week's words: *guaranteed, supervise, frustrated, coordination, ease, scenery, bundle, fused.* Help students locate and read these words on **Transparencies 27a** and **27b.** Have students work in small groups to use the words in creating brief skits about being invited to visit Camp Freedom. Groups can perform their skits for the class.

Approaching Level Options

Vocabulary

Review last week's words: **(dismiss, intentions, despair, bridle, descended, accompany, delicacies, consented)** and this week's words **(guaranteed, supervise, frustrated, coordination, ease, scenery, bundle, fused)**. Have students write a sentence for each word.

Student Book

ELL

Access for All

Building Background Ask students what they know about the origin of the Fourth of July holiday. Elicit descriptions of how the holiday is typically celebrated and write the list on the board. Compare this list to the way the Fourth of July is celebrated in the story.

Skills Focus ▶ Vocabulary

Objective Review how to use dictionaries to learn the definitions of multiple-meaning words

Materials
- **Dictionaries**
- **Student Book** *Skunk Scout*

FCAT ✔

DICTIONARY: MULTIPLE-MEANING WORDS

LA.5.1.6.9
Use multiple meanings in context

Have students find the vocabulary words in dictionaries and identify the words with more than one definition. Discuss the multiple meanings of the words, and ask students to write funny sentences for each definition. Challenge students to repeat the activity and find other multiple-meaning words in *Skunk Scout*.

Skills Focus ▶ Comprehension

Objective Review making judgments based on similarities and differences

Materials
- **Student Book** *The Best Fourth of July*

STRATEGY
MONITOR COMPREHENSION

LA.5.1.7
Student uses strategies to comprehend text

Remind students to stop regularly to check that they have understood the material. They can generate questions, summarize certain passages, or reread any confusing sections. Once they are sure they understand the selection, they can go on to make judgments about plot and character.

FCAT ✔

SKILL
PLOT DEVELOPMENT: MAKING JUDGMENTS

LA.5.2.1.2
Analyze elements of plot structure and character development

- Making a judgment means determining whether something is good, worthwhile, believable, or accurate. Remind students that making a judgment about a character's actions can help them analyze both character and plot development.

Explain/Model

Display **Transparencies 27a** and **27b.** Reread the first two paragraphs of *The Best Fourth of July*. Ask volunteers who have attended camps to compare their experiences with Lateesha's experiences and then to form judgments about whether Camp Freedom is a good camp.

Practice/Apply

Ask students to finish reading and to look for answers to these questions.

- Is Lateesha having a good time at Camp Freedom?
- Would you like to spend a summer at Camp Freedom? Why or why not?
- How effective is Jean as a camp counselor?

Leveled Reader Lesson

Objective   Read to apply strategies and skills

Materials
- **Leveled Reader** *A Visit to Grand Canyon National Park*
- **Paired Selection** *An Underwater Park*

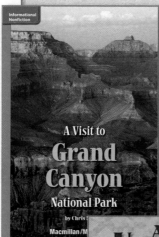

Leveled
Reader

Paired
Selection

PREVIEW AND PREDICT

LA.5.6.1.1
Interpret text
for supporting
predictions
Ask students to look at the cover and preview all visuals and sidebars. Have them skim the table of contents and first two chapters of the book to make predictions about what they will learn about Grand Canyon National Park. Help students note any questions they have prior to reading.

VOCABULARY WORDS

LA.5.1.6.3
Use context
clues
Review vocabulary words as necessary. As you read together, stop to discuss how each word is used in context.

STRATEGY
MONITOR COMPREHENSION

LA.5.1.7
Student uses
strategies to
comprehend
text
Remind students to stop regularly and check that they understand what they're reading. They can generate questions about the text, summarize certain passages, or reread confusing parts of the selection.

SKILL
FCAT
MAKING JUDGMENTS

LA.5.2.2.2
Use
information
from text
to answer
questions
Remind students to make judgments as they read.

Think Aloud When reading nonfiction, I can make judgments about the accuracy and objectivity of the text. The author states that the Grand Canyon is a natural wonder, and like no other place on Earth. The fact that it was formed by natural elements over 2 billion years leads me to agree with this judgment. I will add it to my Judgments Chart.

READ AND RESPOND

LA.5.1.7.7
Compare
and contrast
elements
Tell students to finish reading the first two chapters of the book. Monitor comprehension by asking students compare-and-contrast questions, such as *How are the rock layers of the canyon similar and different?* Discuss whether students think the canyon is a natural wonder.

MAKE CONNECTIONS ACROSS TEXTS

LA.5.1.7.7
Compare
and contrast
elements in
multiple texts
Invite students to compare *A Visit to Grand Canyon National Park* with *An Underwater Park*.

- How are the Grand Canyon and Biscayne Bay similar? Different?

  - Which seems to be the more spectacular place? Why?

ELL   Access for All

Use Description Help students expand their vocabulary by working in groups to describe Grand Canyon National Park. Tell them to use the five senses to organize their descriptions of what it looks, smells, sounds, feels, and tastes like.

Skills Focus ▶ **Vocabulary**

Objective	Review vocabulary words
Materials	• **Dictionaries**
	• **Student Book** *The Best Fourth of July*

✓ VOCABULARY WORDS

LA.5.1.6
Student uses multiple strategies to develop vocabulary

In the style of a hidden word puzzle, prepare a grid with the vocabulary words written horizontally, vertically, and diagonally. Give students a list of the definitions. Have students use the definitions to identify the words and then to find and circle the vocabulary words in the grid.

FCAT ✓ DICTIONARY: MULTIPLE-MEANING WORDS

LA.5.1.6.9
Determine correct meaning of words with multiple meanings

Have students locate the following words in *The Best Fourth of July*: *deal, pretty, fall, part,* and *still*. Then ask students to locate the words in dictionaries and to determine which meanings best fit the context of the selection. Have students write funny sentences that demonstrate each meaning of each word.

Student Book

Skills Focus ▶ **Text Feature**

Objective	Understand the purpose of photographs and captions in nonfiction
Materials	• Photograph with accompanying caption from a magazine or nonfiction book

✓ PHOTOGRAPHS AND CAPTIONS

LA.5.1.7.1
Explain purpose of text features

Have students find a photograph with an accompanying caption in a nonfiction book. Discuss what the caption adds to the reader's understanding of the photograph and whether it adds any additional information to the text on the page.

Skills Focus ▶ **Fluency**

Objective	Read fluently with accuracy and good prosody at a rate of 129–149 WCPM
Materials	• **On Level Practice Book O,** p. 196

REPEATED READING

LA.5.1.5
Student demonstrates ability to read orally with accuracy

Model reading aloud the entire passage on page 196 of **Practice Book O.**

Discuss how to use appropriate pauses and/or inflections to reflect the punctuation used in the passage. Then read one sentence at a time, and have students echo-read each sentence. Listen for accuracy. During independent reading time, partners can take turns modeling and echoing.

Timed Reading   Have students read the passage and record their reading rate.

On Level Practice Book O, page 196

As I read, I will pay attention to punctuation and inflection.

	Can you guess what main force created the Grand
9	Canyon? It was the mighty Colorado River.
16	The Colorado is a huge, powerful river. In the spring,
26	melted snow fills the river, and it becomes swift and wild.
37	The river picks up rocks, huge boulders, sand, and pebbles
47	and carries them along. Over millions of years, this gritty
57	river water carved into layer after layer of rock. It carved the
69	deepest canyon of all, the Grand Canyon.
76	One reason the river could carve the rock is that the rock
88	was soft. Soft for rock, that is! Back in time, before there was
101	a Grand Canyon, oceans covered the land.
108	Over millions of years, broken seashells, sand, mud, and
117	clay fell to the bottom of the sea. These small bits of matter
130	that settle on the sea bottom are called sediment. Over
140	millions of years, the sediment turned into rock, called
149	sedimentary rock. And this rock was soft enough for the river
160	to be able to carve a deeper and deeper path through it.
172	But the Colorado River was not the only force to form the
184	Grand Canyon. 186

Comprehension Check

1. How did the Colorado River help form the Grand Canyon? **Main Idea and Details Gritty river water carved through layers of rock.**
2. What is sedimentary rock? **Relevant Facts and Details a combination of broken seashells, sand, mud, and clay**

	Words Read	–	Number of Errors	=	Words Correct Score
First Read		–		=	
Second Read		–		=	

Leveled Reader Lesson

Objective Read to apply strategies and skills

Materials
- **Leveled Reader** *A Visit to Grand Canyon National Park*
- **Paired Selection** *An Underwater Park*

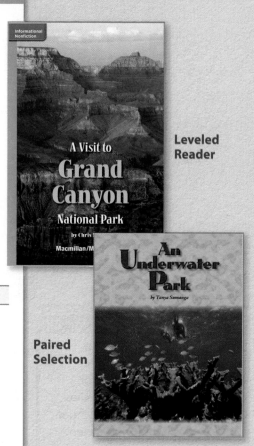

Leveled Reader

PREVIEW AND PREDICT

LA.5.1.7.1
Establish purpose for reading

Have students preview *A Visit to Grand Canyon National Park*.

■ What does the title suggest about the selection?

■ Does Grand Canyon National Park appear to be a place that you would enjoy visiting? Why or why not?

Encourage students to generate their own questions as purposes for reading.

Paired Selection

SKILL
MAKING JUDGMENTS

LA.5.2.2.2
Use information from text to answer questions

Explain that making judgments in nonfiction means forming an opinion about the value, believability, or accuracy of information. Readers can make judgments about the presentation of facts and events to help them understand the text. One way to make judgments is for readers to compare their own knowledge and experiences with what they read. Explain that students will fill in Judgments Charts as they read.

READ AND RESPOND

LA.5.1.7.7
Compare and contrast elements

Read the introduction and Chapter 1. Ask students to paraphrase a selected paragraph. Pause to allow students to compare their own experiences of the Grand Canyon or other places they think qualify as "natural wonders" with the information in the text. At the end of Chapter 1, fill in the Judgments Charts.

VOCABULARY WORDS

LA.5.1.6.3
Use context clues

After they read *A Visit to Grand Canyon National Park*, ask students to point out the vocabulary words. Discuss how each word is used in context. Ask questions such as: *Why were they frustrated when they had to supervise the coordination of the fused bundle?* Have students answer in kind.

MAKE CONNECTIONS ACROSS TEXTS

LA.5.2.2.2
Use information from text to answer questions

Invite students to make judgments based on *A Visit to Grand Canyon National Park* and *An Underwater Park*.

■ Which career would be best for you: park ranger, cartographer, geologist, paleontologist, or marine biologist? Support your judgment with information from *A Visit to Grand Canyon National Park* and *An Underwater Park*.

ELL
Leveled Reader
Go to pages
697U–697V.

Skills Focus — Vocabulary

Objective   Write speeches using vocabulary words

EXTEND VOCABULARY

LA.5.4.3.2
Write persuasive text that includes persuasive techniques

Have students write short speeches that could be used to debate the following question: *Is camping a good family activity?* Students may take either side of the debate. Have them use all of the vocabulary words when developing their persuasive essay. Check to make sure students spell the vocabulary words correctly.

Skills Focus — Text Feature

Objective   Understand the uses and function of photographs and captions in nonfiction

PHOTOGRAPHS AND CAPTIONS

LA.5.1.7.1
Explain purpose of text features

Remind students that photographs and captions in nonfiction text offer visual examples of information in the text, and sometimes add information to the selection that would not be included otherwise.

Have students find a photograph with an accompanying caption in a nonfiction book. Discuss what the caption adds to the reader's understanding of the photograph and whether it adds any additional information to the text on the page.

Skills Focus — Fluency

Objective   Read fluently with accuracy and prosody at a rate of 139–149 WCPM

Materials   • **Beyond Practice Book B,** page 196

REPEATED READING

LA.5.1.5
Read orally with accuracy

Model reading aloud the Fluency passage on page 196 of **Practice Book B.** Tell students to pay close attention to the inflection in your voice as well as to your pronunciation of vocabulary and other difficult words. Then read aloud one sentence at a time and have students echo the reading and intonation. Discuss how proper intonation aids comprehension.

During independent reading time, listen for accuracy as partners take turns reading their marked passage. Remind students to wait until partners reach end marks before correcting mistakes. Encourage students to identify words with Latin roots. As an extension, allow them to record themselves reading and critique each other.

ELL — Access for All

Prepare an Interview

Help students prepare interview questions for members of their families or staff members at school. Review who, what, when, where, and why questions and remind students that open-ended questions yield more information than questions that can be answered with a yes or no.

◆ **Beyond Practice Book B,** page 196

As I read, I will pay attention to punctuation and inflection.

	Yellowstone is in the heart of the American West. Its rivers
11	flow to both the East Coast and the West Coast. The Yellowstone
23	River starts south of the park. It flows to Yellowstone Lake and
35	then out of the park. Later the river joins up with the mighty
48	Missouri River, then the Mississippi, and finally the Gulf of
58	Mexico. Water that flows west out of Yellowstone Park
67	eventually ends up in the Pacific Ocean.
74	To find Yellowstone National Park on a map, look at the place
86	where northwestern Wyoming borders Montana and Idaho. In
94	fact, the park extends just a bit into both of those states.
106	For most people Old Faithful is the symbol of Yellowstone.
116	Old Faithful is a geyser from which heated water and air escape.
128	It gets its name from the fact that it erupts faithfully—
139	approximately every 60 to 120 minutes. It's been doing that for
148	well over 100 years—ever since people started taking notes.
157	When Old Faithful spouts, it's quite a sight! A plume of water
169	more than 100 feet high shoots into the air. 177

Comprehension Check

1. Yellowstone National Park is mostly located in which state? **Main Idea and Details** Wyoming

2. How is the name Old Faithful appropriate? **Relevant Facts and Details** It has been erupting every 60 to 120 minutes for over 100 years.

	Words Read	−	Number of Errors	=	Words Correct Score
First Read		−		=	
Second Read		−		=	

Leveled Reader Lesson

Objective   Read to apply strategies and skills

Materials   • **Leveled Reader** *A Visit to Grand Canyon National Park*

PREVIEW AND PREDICT

LA.5.1.7.1
Establish purpose for reading

Have students preview *A Visit to Grand Canyon National Park,* predict what it is about, and set purposes for reading.

VOCABULARY WORDS

Review vocabulary words as needed. Ask questions such as, *Which activity requires coordination, watching television or playing soccer?*

FCAT

SKILL
MAKING JUDGMENTS

LA.5.2.2.2
Use information from text to answer questions

Ask a volunteer to define the word *judgment* and to explain why it is important to make judgments when reading. Ask how judging whether the treatment of a subject is accurate or inaccurate, objective or biased, can help students monitor their comprehension. Explain that students will read *A Visit to Grand Canyon National Park* together and that they will make judgments and record them in charts as they read.

READ AND RESPOND

LA.5.2.2.3
Organize information to show understanding

As they read, students should identify the criteria they will use to make judgments and fill in their Judgments Charts.

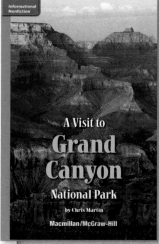

Leveled Reader

Self-Selected Reading

Objective   Read independently to make judgments and to make connections across texts

Materials   • Leveled Readers or trade books at students' reading levels

FCAT **READ TO MAKE JUDGMENTS**

LA.5.2.2.2
Answer questions related to relevant details

LA.5.2.2.5
Select age and ability appropriate non-fiction to read

Invite students to make judgments about *A Visit to Grand Canyon National Park, The Best Fourth of July,* and *An Underwater Park.* Ask students which job they think would best suit them: camp counselor, park ranger, surveyor, climatologist, chemist, naturalist, or marine biologist. Have them explain their choices using details from the texts to support their opinions. Discuss which selection gives the best information about careers in nature. Next, invite students to choose books for independent reading. After reading, have students identify passages in which they formed judgments about characters, people, facts, or events. Ask how making such judgments helped them as they read the selections.

English Language Learners

Academic Language

Throughout the week the English language learners in your class will need help building their understanding of the academic language used in daily instruction and assessment instruments. The following strategies will help increase their language proficiency and comprehension of content and instructional words.

Oral Language For oral vocabulary development go to www.macmillanmh.com

Strategies to Reinforce Academic Language

■ **Use Context** Academic language used by the teacher (see chart below) should be explained in the context of the task during Whole Group. You may use gestures, expressions, and visuals to support meaning.

■ **Use Visuals** Use charts, transparencies, and graphic organizers to explain key labels to help students understand classroom language.

■ **Model** Demonstrate the task using academic language in order for students to understand instruction.

Academic Language Used in Whole Group Instruction

Content/Theme Words	Skill/Strategy Words	Writing/Grammar Words
camping (p. 669)	making judgments (p. 671A)	expository (p. 696)
mountain (p. 676)	monitor comprehension (p. 671A)	how-to instructions (p. 696)
tents (p. 677)	summarize (p. 691)	time-order words (p. 696)
under water (p. 692)	compare and contrast (p. 691B)	adverbs (p. 697I)
glacier (p. 693)	dialogue (p. 692)	compare (p. 697I)
ecosystem (p. 693)		comparative forms (p. 697I)

ELL Reader Lesson

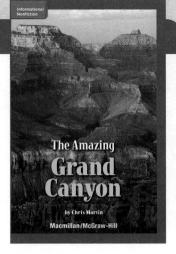

Informational Nonfiction

The Amazing **Grand Canyon**

by Chris Martin

Macmillan/McGraw-Hill

Before Reading

DEVELOP ORAL LANGUAGE

Build Background *Who has gone camping? Where have you camped? If you have never gone camping, would you like to try it?* Point out that when you go camping, you can have fun and learn, too.

Review Vocabulary Write the vocabulary and story support words on the board and discuss their meanings. Model using them in sentences. *On a trail, we wear hiking boots to get around with* ease.

PREVIEW AND PREDICT

Point to the cover illustration and read the title aloud. *What is this photograph of? What will you learn about the Grand Canyon?*

FCAT **Set a Purpose for Reading** Show the Judgments Chart and remind students they have used this chart before. Ask them to do a similar chart to record their opinions and judgments about what they read.

During Reading

Choose from among the differentiated strategies to support students' reading at all levels of language acquisition.

Beginning	Intermediate	Advanced
Shared Reading As you read, model how to make judgments based on what you read and see. Check students' comprehension and use vocabulary and support words.	**Read Together** Read through Chapter 1. Ask students to make judgments about the size of the Grand Canyon. Have students continue to read with a partner and complete their charts.	**Independent Reading** Have students read and make judgments about what they read every day. Then, ask them to fill in their charts. In small groups, have them make a plan to visit the Grand Canyon.

After Reading

Remind students to use the vocabulary and story words in their whole group activities. Have them complete the Comprehension Check questions.

Objective

- To apply vocabulary and comprehension skills

Materials

- ELL Leveled Reader

5-Day Planner

DAY 1	• Academic Language • Oral Language and Vocabulary Review
DAY 2	• Academic Language • ELL Leveled Reader
DAY 3	• Academic Language • ELL Leveled Reader
DAY 4	• Academic Language • ELL Leveled Reader
DAY 5	• Academic Language • ELL Leveled Reader Comprehension Check and Literacy Activities

Grade 5 • ELL TEACHER'S GUIDE

English Language Learners

Macmillan/McGraw-Hill

ELL Teacher's Guide for students who need additional instruction

Student Book Selections

Weekly Theme: Improving Lives

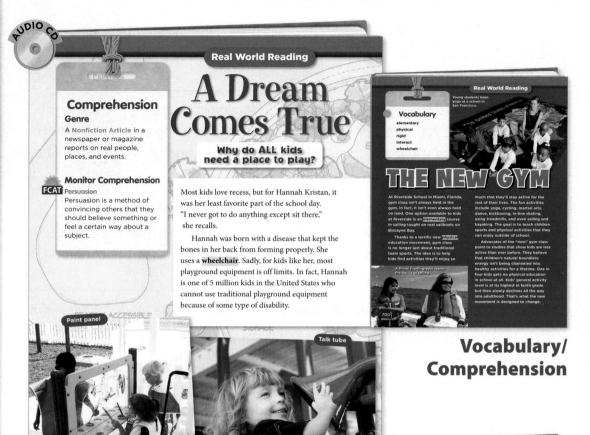

Real World Reading

A Dream Comes True

Why do ALL kids need a place to play?

Most kids love recess, but for Hannah Kristan, it was her least favorite part of the school day. "I never got to do anything except sit there," she recalls.

Hannah was born with a disease that kept the bones in her back from forming properly. She uses a **wheelchair**. Sadly, for kids like her, most playground equipment is off limits. In fact, Hannah is one of 5 million kids in the United States who cannot use traditional playground equipment because of some type of disability.

Comprehension

Genre

A **Nonfiction Article** in a newspaper or magazine reports on real people, places, and events.

Monitor Comprehension

FCAT Persuasion

Persuasion is a method of convincing others that they should believe something or feel a certain way about a subject.

Social Studies Link
Main Selection
Genre Nonfiction Article

Vocabulary/Comprehension

THE NEW GYM

Test Strategy
FCAT Think and Search

Profile of a **Paralympian**

INTERACTIVE **Read-Aloud** ANTHOLOGY with PLAYS
Macmillan/McGraw-Hill

Read-Aloud Anthology
• Listening Comprehension
• Readers' Theatre

Week At A Glance

Whole Group

VOCABULARY
elementary, physical, rigid, interact, wheelchair

FCAT Context Clues

COMPREHENSION
Strategy: Monitor Comprehension
FCAT Skill: Persuasion

FCAT TEST STRATEGY
Think and Search

WRITING
FCAT Expository/Biography

FCAT Social Studies
Government and the Citizen

Small Group Options

Differentiated Instruction for Tested Skills

FCAT Tested FCAT Benchmark
Tested Skill for the Week
Sunshine State Standard
FCAT FCAT Benchmark

698A Unit 6 Week 3

Resources for Differentiated Instruction

FCAT LEVELED READERS: Social Studies

GR Levels S–X

Genre Informational Nonfiction

- **Same Theme**
- **Same Vocabulary**
- **Same Comprehension Skills**

S

U

X

| **Approaching Level** | **On Level** | **Beyond Level** |

U

English Language Leveled Reader

Sheltered Readers for English Language Learners

ELL Teacher's Guide also available

LEVELED PRACTICE

| **Approaching** | **On Level** | **Beyond** | **ELL** |

INTERVENTION PROGRAM

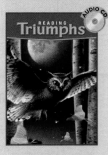 

- **Phonics and Decoding**
- **Comprehension**
- **Vocabulary**

Also available, *Reading Triumphs*, Intervention Program

CLASSROOM LIBRARY

Genre Realistic Fiction

| **Approaching** | **On Level** | **Beyond** |

Trade books to apply Comprehension Skills

FCAT Success!

- **FCAT Edition**
- **Content Area Reading**

FCAT Test Preparation and Practice

FCAT Benchmark Assessments

FCAT Unit and Weekly Assessments

HOME-SCHOOL CONNECTION

- Family letters in English, Spanish, and Haitian Creole
- Take-Home Stories

FLORIDA Suggested Lesson Plan

Integrated ELL Support Every Day

Whole Group

ORAL LANGUAGE
- **Listening**
- **Speaking**
- **Viewing**

WORD STUDY
- **Vocabulary**
- **Phonics/Decoding**

READING
- **Develop Comprehension**

- **Fluency**

LANGUAGE ARTS
- **Writing**

- **Grammar**

- **Spelling**

ASSESSMENT
- **Informal/Formal**

Turn the Page for
Small Group Lesson Plan

Day 1

Listening/Speaking/Viewing

❓ Focus Question How do our physical abilities and health affect the quality of our lives? LA.5.5.2

Build Background, 698
Read Aloud: "The Seeing Stick," 699

Vocabulary LA.5.1.6 .3
☑FCAT *elementary, physical, rigid, interact, wheelchair,* 700
Practice Book A-O-B, 200
☑FCAT **Strategy:** Context Clues, 701

Read "The New Gym," 700–701
Student Book

Comprehension, 701A–701B
☑FCAT **Strategy:** Monitor Comprehension
Skill: Techniques of Persuasion LA.5.1.7.2
Practice Book A-O-B, 201

Fluency Model Fluency, 699
Partner Reading, 698I LA.5.1.5

☑FCAT **Writing**
Daily Writing: What would gym class be like if you could plan it? Write a letter to your principal about the changes you would make.
Generate Questions, 709A

Grammar Daily Language Activities, 709I
☑ Negatives, 709I
Grammar Practice Book, 173

☑ **Spelling** Pretest, 709G
Spelling Practice Book, 173–174 LA.5.1.4.1

Quick Check Vocabulary, 700

Differentiated Instruction 709M–709V

Day 2

Listening/Speaking

❓ Focus Question Why do all kids need a place to play? LA.5.5.2

Vocabulary LA.5.1.6 .3
Review Vocabulary Words, 702

Phonics/Decoding
Words from Mythology, 709E
Practice Book A-O-B, 206

Read *A Dream Comes True,* 702–705
Student Book

Comprehension, 702–705
☑FCAT **Strategy:** Monitor Comprehension
Skill: Techniques of Persuasion LA.5.1.7.2
Practice Book A-O-B, 202

Fluency Partner Reading, 698 I LA.5.1.5

☑FCAT **Writing**
Daily Writing: If you could invent something that could help someone with a disability, what would it be? Write a paragraph about your invention.
Find Information, 709A

Grammar Daily Language Activities, 709I
Negatives, 709I
Grammar Practice Book, 174

Spelling Words from Mythology, 709G
Spelling Practice Book, 175 LA.5.1.4.1

Quick Check Comprehension, 701B
Phonics, 139E

Differentiated Instruction 709M–709V

Benchmarks

FCAT

Vocabulary
Vocabulary Words
Context Clues
LA.5.1.6.3 Use context clues to determine meanings of unfamiliar words

Comprehension
Strategy: Monitor Comprehension
Skill: Techniques of Persuasion LA.5.1.7.2
Identify how author's perspective influences text

Writing
Expository/Biography
LA.5.4.2.1 Write in a variety of informational forms
LA.5.6.2 Uses a process for collection, processing, presentation of information

Social Studies
Government and the Citizen
SS.C.2.2.1.5.1 Understands the importance of participation through community service

Turn the Page for
Small Group Options ➜

Day 3

Listening/Speaking

❓ Focus Question Why do you think "The New Gym" was included in the section along with the other articles about health and fitness? LA.5.5.2.1
Summarize, 705

Vocabulary LA.5.1.6.3
✔ Review Words in Context, 709C
FCAT Strategy: Context Clues, 709D
Practice Book A-O-B, 205

Phonics Decode Multisyllabic Words

Read *A Dream Comes True,* 702–705

Comprehension
Comprehension Check, 705
✔ **FCAT** Maintain Skills: Main Idea and Details, 705A LA.5.1.7.3

Student Book

Fluency Repeated Reading, 705A
Practice Book A-O-B, 203 LA.5.1.5

✔ **FCAT** Writing

Daily Writing: Choose a sport. Write a list of suggestions that would allow this sport to include more disabled athletes.
Organize Information, 709B

Grammar Daily Language Activities, 709I
Correct Double Negatives, 709J
Grammar Practice Book, 175

Spelling Words from Mythology, 709H
Spelling Practice Book, 176 LA.5.1.4.1

 Fluency, 705A

Differentiated Instruction 709M–709V

Day 4

Listening/Speaking/Viewing

❓ Focus Question The author states, "Howitt is committed to changing the world in positive ways." Use details to support this statement. LA.5.5.2
Expand Vocabulary: Improving Lives, 709F

Vocabulary LA.5.1.6.3
Context Clues, 709F
Apply Vocabulary to Writing, 709F

Read "Profile of a Paralympian," 706–707

Test Strategy: Think and Search

Student Book

Research and Study Skills
✔ **FCAT** Everyday Communications, 705B
Practice Book A-O-B, 204

Fluency Partner Reading, 698I LA.5.1.5

✔ **FCAT** Writing

Daily Writing: What is your favorite sport or athletic activity? Write a diary entry about why you like it.
Synthesize and Write, 709B LA.5.4.2.1

Grammar Daily Language Activities, 709I
Negatives, 709J
Grammar Practice Book, 176

Spelling Words from Mythology, 709H
Spelling Practice Book, 177 LA.5.1.4.1

 Vocabulary, 709D

Differentiated Instruction 709M–709V

Day 5
Review and Assess

Listening/Speaking/Viewing

❓ Focus Question Describe how the author of each selection tried to change your mind about an issue. LA.5.5.2.1
Speaking and Listening Strategies, 709A
Presentation of Expository Writing, 709B

✔ Vocabulary LA.5.1.6.3
Spiral Review: Vocabulary Game, 709F

Read Self-Selected Reading, 698I

✔ Comprehension
Strategy: Monitor Comprehension
Skill: Techniques of Persuasion LA.5.1.7.2

Student Book

✔ Fluency Partner Reading, 698I LA.5.1.5

✔ **FCAT** Writing

Daily Writing: Write a short story that begins, "It was almost time for the big game when something surprised us."
Share Information, 709B LA.5.6.2

Grammar Daily Language Activities, 709I
✔ Negatives, 709J
Grammar Practice Book, 177–178

Spelling ✔ Posttest, 709H
Spelling Practice Book, 178 LA.5.1.4.1

✔ **FCAT** Weekly Assessment, 333–344

Differentiated Instruction 709M–709V

Differentiated Instruction

What do I do in small groups?

Teacher-Led Small Groups

Literacy Workstations

Independent Activities

Skills Focus → Use your **Quick Check** observations to guide additional instruction and practice.

Phonics
Mythology

 Vocabulary
Words: wheelchair, interact, physical, elementary, rigid
FCAT **Strategy:** Context Clues/Surrounding Sentences and Paragraphs

Comprehension
 Strategy: Monitor Comprehension
FCAT **Skill:** Techniques of Persuasion

FCAT **Fluency**

Suggested Lesson Plan

CD ROM **Instructional Navigator**
Interactive Lesson Planner

Approaching Level
- **Additional Instruction/Practice**
- **Tier 2 Instruction**

On Level
- **Practice**

Beyond Level
- **Extend**

DAY 1	DAY 2
Fluency, 709N Vocabulary, 709N Comprehension, 709O	Phonics, 709M Vocabulary, 709O Leveled Reader Lesson, 709P • Vocabulary • Comprehension
Vocabulary, 709Q Leveled Reader Lesson, 709R • Comprehension **ELL** Leveled Reader, 709U–709V	Leveled Reader Lesson, 709R • Comprehension • Vocabulary
Vocabulary, 709S Leveled Reader Lesson, 709T • Comprehension	Leveled Reader Lesson, 709T • Comprehension • Vocabulary

For intensive intervention see **READING Triumphs**

Focus on Leveled Readers

Apply FCAT skills and strategies while reading appropriate leveled books.

Levels S–X

 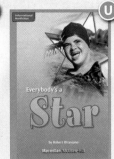 

Approaching | On Level | Beyond

The Special Olympics Story

ELL

Additional Leveled Reader Resources

Leveled Reader Database

Go to **www.macmillanmh.com**

Search by

- Comprehension Skill
- Content Area
- Genre
- Text Feature

- Guided Reading Level
- Reading Recovery Level
- Lexile Score
- Benchmark Level

Subscription also available.

Focus on Social Studies

Teacher's Annotated Edition

Government and the Citizen

SS.C.2.2.1.5.1 Community Service

Additional Leveled Readers

Sports for Everyone!

Uplifted from the Dark

Day 3

Phonics, 709M
Fluency, 709N
Vocabulary, 709O
Leveled Reader Lesson, 709P
- Comprehension

Fluency, 709Q
Vocabulary, 709Q
Leveled Reader Lesson, 709R
- Comprehension

Fluency, 709S
Vocabulary, 709S
Leveled Reader Lesson, 709T
- Comprehension
ELL Meta Language, 709S

Day 4

Phonics, 709M
Leveled Reader Lesson, 709P
- Comprehension
ELL Skill: Techniques of Persuasion

Text Features, 709Q
Leveled Reader Lesson, 709R
- Comprehension

Text Features, 709S
Leveled Reader Lesson, 709T
- Comprehension

Day 5

Fluency, 709N
Leveled Reader Lesson, 709P
- Make Connections Across Texts

Fluency, 709Q
Leveled Reader Lesson, 709R
- Make Connections Across Texts

Fluency, 709S
Self-Selected Reading, 709T

Managing the Class

What do I do with the rest of my class?

Class Management Tools

My To-Do List
Put a check next to the activities you complete.

Reading
- Practice fluency
- Choose a book to read

Word Study
- Research words from mythology
- Define words from context clues

Writing
- Write an explanation
- Write a short essay

Science
- Diagram an invention
- Describe something you'd invent

Social Studies
- Write about improving a design
- Draw your improvement

Leveled Readers
- Write About It!
- Content Connection

Technology
- Vocabulary Puzzlemaker
- Fluency Solutions
- Listening Library
- www.macmillannh.com

Independent Practice
- Practice Book, 200–206
- Grammar Practice Book, 173–178
- Spelling Practice Book, 173–178

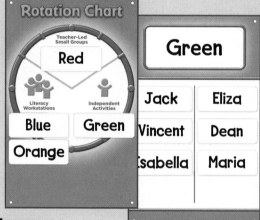

Rotation Chart

Teacher-Led Small Groups — Red

Literacy Workstations — Blue   Independent Activities — Green

Blue   Green

Orange

Green

Jack	Eliza
Vincent	Dean
Isabella	Maria

Includes:
- How-to Guide
- Rotation Chart
- Weekly Contracts

FOLDABLES™

Hands-on activities for reinforcing weekly skills

Fish	Frogs
habitat	habitat
food	insects
prey	prey
enemies	enemies

Eight-Tab Foldable

Word	Synonym	Antonym	Prefix or Suffix
normal	typical	unusual	normally

Folded Chart

Independent Activities

FCAT LEVELED READERS: Social Studies

For Repeated Readings and Literacy Activities

Approaching

On Level

ELL

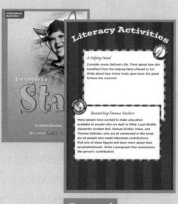
Beyond

LEVELED PRACTICE

Skills: Vocabulary, Techniques of Persuasion, Fluency, Context Clues, Everyday Communications

Approaching

On Level

Beyond

ELL

Technology

ONLINE INSTRUCTION www.macmillanmh.com

- Meet the Author/Illustrator
- Computer Literacy Lessons
- Research and Inquiry Activities

- Oral Language Activities
- Vocabulary and Spelling Activities
- Leveled Reader Database

LISTENING LIBRARY
Recordings of selections
- Main Selections
- Leveled Readers
- ELL Readers
- Intervention Anthology

FLUENCY SOLUTIONS
Recorded passages for modeling and practicing fluency

VOCABULARY PUZZLEMAKER
Activities providing multiple exposures to vocabulary, spelling, and high-frequency words including crossword puzzles, word searches, and word jumbles

Turn the page for Literacy Workstations.

Managing the Class

Literacy Activities

Collaborative Learning Activities

Reading

Objectives

- Read for smoothness; time reading to practice fluency
- Summarize a selected reading
- Select literature daily for reading enjoyment
- Use criteria to choose independent reading materials

Word Study

Objectives

- Research and write about words from mythology
- Use context clues in original sentences

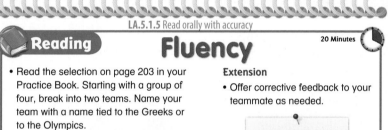

LA.5.1.5 Read orally with accuracy

Reading — Fluency
20 Minutes

- Read the selection on page 203 in your Practice Book. Starting with a group of four, break into two teams. Name your team with a name tied to the Greeks or to the Olympics.
- Make an Olympic torch by rolling paper and taping it. If you read the sentence correctly without stumbling and with proper inflection, pass the reading torch to your partner. If you do stumble, pass it to the other team. The team that has the torch at the end of the selection wins.
- **Time Your Reading:** Listen to the Audio CD.

Extension
- Offer corrective feedback to your teammate as needed.

Things you need:
- Practice Book

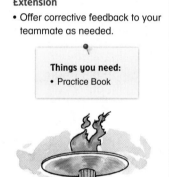

Fluency Solutions
Listening Library

55

LA.5.1.6.10 Determine etymologies using a dictionary or digital tools

Word Study — Words from Mythology
20 Minutes

- Research the origins of the following words from mythology: *atlas, cereal, volcano, titan,* and *echo.*
- On a sheet of paper, write a short description of the origin of the words.

Extension
- Make an illustration of one of the words. Share it with a group.
- Post your words and pictures on a word wall.

Things you need:
- paper and pen or pencil
- dictionary
- markers

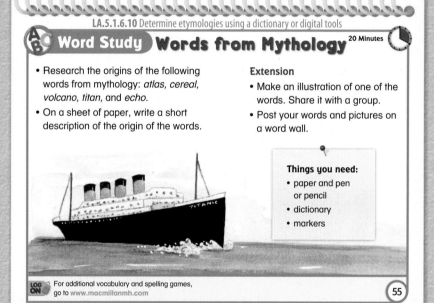

For additional vocabulary and spelling games, go to www.macmillanmh.com

55

LA.5.2.2.5 Select non-fiction materials to read

Reading — INDEPENDENT READING
20 Minutes

- Find a book in the library or an article on the Internet about the Paralympics or other events for the physically challenged.
- Read for three minutes, then mark your place and write a summary of what you learned.

Extension
- In your response journal, tell whether you would like to finish the article or book and why.

Things you need:
- library book or access to the Internet
- paper and pen or pencil

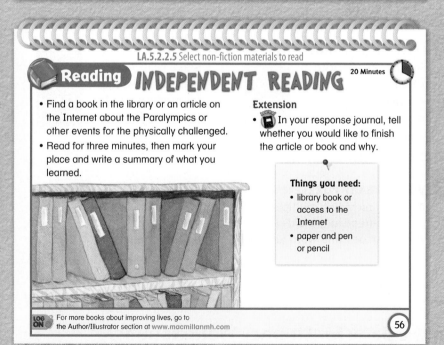

For more books about improving lives, go to the Author/Illustrator section at www.macmillanmh.com

56

LA.5.1.6.3 Use context clues to determine meanings of unfamilar words

Word Study — Context Clues
20 Minutes

- Make a list of six words with which your partner may be unfamiliar. Then write a sentence for each word using context clues to define the word.
- Trade sentences with a partner to see which words you can figure out.

Extension
- Combine your sentences with your partner's sentences. Challenge another team to define the words.

Things you need:
- paper and pen or pencil
- dictionary

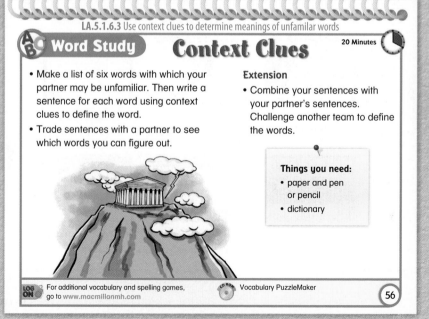

For additional vocabulary and spelling games, go to www.macmillanmh.com

Vocabulary PuzzleMaker

56

Literacy Workstations

Reading   **Word Study**   **Writing**   **Science/Social Studies**

Writing

Objectives

- Write a short editorial
- Write a short personal essay
- Be enthusiastic about writing and learning to write
- Write voluntarily for different purposes

Content Literacy

Objectives

- Research an invention and draw a diagram
- Design an invention based on a need in society

LA.5.4.3 Demonstrates persuasive writing for the purpose of influencing the reader

Writing   **Persuasive Writing**   20 Minutes

- Write about a time when you used an excuse for why you didn't do something that you wanted to do or should have done. The subject could be why you didn't remember to feed your pet, or why you didn't finish your homework, or why you forgot something, for example.

Extension

- Write a short editorial for a local paper persuading people to make resolutions to improve their own lives.

Things you need:
- paper and pen or pencil

> **Resolutions**
> 1. I will feed the dog.
> 2. I will pick up the clothes in my room.
> 3. I will do all of my homework.

55

LA.5.4.2.2 Include visual aids to organize and record information

Science   **Helpful Technology**   20 Minutes

- Read about an invention that has improved people's lives, such as wheelchairs or hearing aids. Make a diagram of the invention and explain how the invention has helped people.

Extension

- Think of a challenge that you would like to conquer, such as having a better sense of direction or being able to jump higher.
- Describe or draw an invention you would like to make to meet that challenge.

Things you need:
- library book or access to the Internet
- paper and colored pencils or markers

55

LA.5.4.2.3 Write expository essays

Writing   **Personal Essay**   20 Minutes

- Write a short essay about a time you overcame a difficult situation. It could be a time when you fell off your bike or skateboard and got up and tried again. It could be a time when you practiced a sports move or a piece of music over and over until you mastered it.
- Explain how you felt when you seemed to be defeated and how you felt when you succeeded.

Extension

- Write about a goal you want to achieve in the next year.
- Explain what the goal is and how you intend to meet that goal.

Things you need:
- paper and pen or pencil

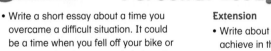

56

LA.5.4.2.1 Write in a variety of expository forms

Social Studies   **Technology and Society**   20 Minutes

- Look around your classroom for examples of furniture or objects that could be better designed and could allow you or your classmates to learn with greater ease or comfort. The object could be a desk, a chair, the board, or a pencil, for example.
- Write your ideas for improvements.

Extension

- Draw your innovation and explain it to a partner.

Things you need:
- pen and paper
- construction paper
- scissors

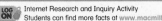

LOG ON Internet Research and Inquiry Activity
Students can find more facts at www.macmillanmh.com

56

Prepare

ORAL LANGUAGE
- Build Background
- Read Aloud
- Expand Vocabulary

FCAT VOCABULARY
- Teach Words in Context
- Context Clues

COMPREHENSION
- **Strategy:** Monitor Comprehension
- **FCAT Skill:** Techniques of Persuasion

SMALL GROUP OPTIONS
- Differentiated Instruction, pp. 709M–709V

Oral Language

Build Background

LA.5.5.2.1
Listen to gain and share information

ACCESS PRIOR KNOWLEDGE

Share the following information:

The Special Olympics helps people with disabilities improve their physical fitness and develop a positive self-image. Over 1 million athletes from more than 160 countries participate.

LA.5.5.2.1
Listen and speak to gain and share information

TALK ABOUT IMPROVING LIVES

Discuss the weekly theme. Ask:

What are some things you or your family have done to help others?

 FOCUS QUESTION Ask a volunteer to read "Talk About It" on **Student Book** page 698 and describe the photo.

- What is happening in the photo?

- How does it relate to the theme?

Talk About It

How do our physical abilities and health affect the quality of our lives?

Find out more about physical fitness at **www.macmillanmh.com**

Improving Lives

698

ENGLISH LANGUAGE LEARNERS

Access for All

Beginning Model Have students say what they can about the photo. Point to unfamiliar items and ask, *What is this?* Model describing the photo in simple sentences: *The men are running. This is a race. The men are in a race.* Help students repeat as they are able.

Intermediate Activate Prior Knowledge Have students discuss their experiences competing. Write the words *physical abilities.* Give examples (*run, throw, catch a ball,* etc.).

Advanced Elaborate Complete the Intermediate task. Write: *self-image.* Discuss how winning or doing well in sports or other activities helps improve a person's self-image.

699

Picture Prompt

Look at the picture and write a biographical sketch about one of the runners. Where was he born? When? What are his accomplishments?

 Technology

For an extended lesson plan and Web site activities for **oral language development,** go to **www.macmillanmh.com**

Read Aloud
Read "The Seeing Stick"

LA.5.2.1.1
Demonstrate knowledge of characteristics of genres

GENRE: Folk Tale
Review features of a folk tale:

- a story based on the customs and traditions of a people or region

- handed down orally from one generation to the next

INTERACTIVE *Read-Aloud* ANTHOLOGY with PLAYS

Read Aloud
pages 127–135

Fables, legends, myths, and tall tales are types of folk tales.

LA.5.5.2
Student applies listening strategies

LISTENING FOR A PURPOSE

As you read "The Seeing Stick" in the **Read-Aloud Anthology**, ask students to listen carefully for the turning point in the story. They should be prepared to discuss the changes that follow. Choose from among the teaching suggestions.

Fluency Ask students to listen carefully as you read aloud, paying attention to your phrasing, expression, and tone of voice.

LA.5.5.2.1
Speak to gain and share information

RESPOND TO THE FOLK TALE

Ask students to retell a family story they've grown up hearing, and to explain what this story reveals about their family.

LA.5.1.6
Student develops grade-appropriate vocabulary

Expand Vocabulary

Ask students to give four or more words heard in "The Seeing Stick" that relate to this week's theme of improving lives. Have students create a mini-crossword puzzle using the words and adding others as necessary, then solve each other's puzzles.

Vocabulary

LA.5.1.6.1 Use new vocabulary taught directly

LA.5.1.6.3 Use context clues to determine meaning

TEACH WORDS IN CONTEXT

Use the following routine:

Routine

Define: **Elementary** means dealing with the beginnings of something.

Example: An elementary course in computers teaches information for beginners.

Ask: What is an antonym for *elementary*?

ANTONYM

- **Physical** means relating to the body. Hard physical work takes a lot of energy. Name an example of physical work. **EXAMPLE**

- **Rigid** means not changing or moving. Our rigid practice schedule did not allow us time to hang out with friends after school. What rules do you think should be rigid? **EXAMPLE**

- **Interact** means to act together with others. Animals in the wild interact with one another. Explain how students in the classroom should interact with one another. **EXPLANATION**

- **Wheelchair** means a chair on wheels that helps a person who cannot walk get from one place to another. Some hospitals insist that every patient use a wheelchair when leaving the building. What experience do you have with a wheelchair? **PRIOR KNOWLEDGE**

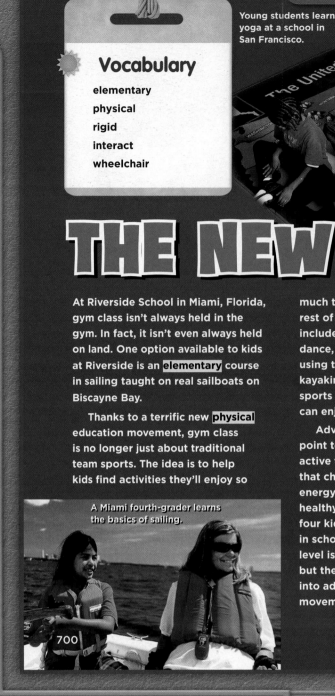

Real World Reading

Young students learn yoga at a school in San Francisco.

Vocabulary

- elementary
- physical
- rigid
- interact
- wheelchair

THE NEW GYM

At Riverside School in Miami, Florida, gym class isn't always held in the gym. In fact, it isn't even always held on land. One option available to kids at Riverside is an **elementary** course in sailing taught on real sailboats on Biscayne Bay.

Thanks to a terrific new **physical** education movement, gym class is no longer just about traditional team sports. The idea is to help kids find activities they'll enjoy so

A Miami fourth-grader learns the basics of sailing.

700

much that they'll stay active for the rest of their lives. The fun activities include yoga, cycling, martial arts, dance, kickboxing, in-line skating, using treadmills, and even sailing and kayaking. The goal is to teach children sports and physical activities that they can enjoy outside of school.

Advocates of the "new" gym class point to studies that show kids are less active than ever before. They believe that children's natural boundless energy isn't being channeled into healthy activities for a lifetime. One in four kids gets no physical education in school at all. Kids' general activity level is at its highest in tenth grade but then slowly declines all the way into adulthood. That's what the new movement is designed to change.

Quick Check **Do students understand word meanings?**

During **Small Group Instruction**

If No → **Approaching Level** Vocabulary, p. 709N

If Yes → **On Level** Options, pp. 709Q–709R

Beyond Level Options, pp. 709S–709T

ELL **Access for All**

Reinforce Vocabulary For *interact,* list the people you interact with at school and explain the interactions. Have students talk about the people they interact with using this sentence frame. *I interact with _____ during _____.* Ask students in groups to list the kinds of interactions and to rate them from the most fun to the least fun and explain their opinions. List other words that have the prefix *inter-*. Discuss their meanings.

Pocket-size GPS guide

Satellite Guidance for the Blind

TIME FOR KIDS

Before leaving her apartment, Carmen Fernandez, a blind woman living in Madrid, Spain, used to carefully memorize her route. If she didn't, she would get lost. But a new device using GPS (Global Positioning Satellite) technology frees her from such a **rigid** routine.

Using the gadget's Braille keypad, she punches in her destination. As she walks, the device calls out directions to her. "Now I can walk home by any route," Fernandez says. "I've learned so much about my own neighborhood."

While the current technology cannot guarantee total accuracy, it already grants a new level of freedom for the visually impaired. It allows them to **interact** more directly with their surroundings and their neighbors. "Soon I'll be giving directions to the taxi driver," says Fernandez.

THE SECOND OLYMPICS

Every two years men and women from around the world come to compete at the Olympic Games. However, this is not the only time a gold medal is up for grabs. After the Olympics come the Paralympics.

The Paralympics are just like the Olympics, but these games are for athletes with physical disabilities. A Paralympic athlete may use a **wheelchair** or get around with the help of a guide dog in everyday life. Athletes who share a particular disability compete to win medals and set world records. Paralympians want others to see them as world-class athletes whose disabilities do not hold them back.

LOG ON Find out more about the Paralympics at www.macmillanmh.com

Canada's team at the 2002 Winter Paralympic Games

701

FCAT **Success!**

Test Prep and Practice with vocabulary, pages 6–31.

On Level Practice Book O, page 200

A. Match the words with their definitions. Then write the letter on the line.

1. rigid ___b___   a. of or relating to the body
2. wheelchair ___d___   b. not yielding or bending
3. interact ___e___   c. simple or basic
4. physical ___a___   d. a chair mounted on wheels
5. elementary ___c___ e. to act on or influence each other

B. Choose the word in parentheses that will complete each sentence. Then write the word on the line.

6. Children should learn (physical, rigid) activities that they will still enjoy when they are adults. ___physical___

7. Sports that allow you to (salute, interact) with the natural environment are exciting. ___interact___

8. The team followed a (rigid, gracious) exercise routine that involved running a mile, 100 push-ups, and jumping rope everyday. ___rigid___

9. A person in a (parasol, wheelchair) can compete in the Paralympics. ___wheelchair___

10. Pete was new to sailing, so he took an (elementary, diverse) sailing class to learn more. ___elementary___

C. Find the vocabulary words in the word search below.

11. j u w o i c s ⟨p h y s i c a l⟩ l k j
12. a k j ⟨e l e m e n t a r y⟩ u e u y p
13. r i g y i u o ⟨w h e e l c h a i r⟩ z
14. a r l ⟨r i g i d⟩ l k j j f i n t e r

★ **Approaching Practice Book A,** page 200
◆ **Beyond Practice Book B,** page 200

Vocabulary

FCAT
LA.5.1.6.3
Use context clues to determine meanings

STRATEGY
CONTEXT CLUES

Context Clues Remind students that context clues are clues within the story or text that help a reader figure out the meaning of an unfamiliar word.

Point out the word *physical* on page 700. Help students identify the context clues in nearby sentences—*sports, activities,* and the names of a variety of sports. Help them see that these activities are all performed by moving the body. Lead them to understand that the meaning of *physical* in this sentence has to do with the body movements needed to perform the sports that are mentioned.

Challenge students to find context clues for the word *device* at the end of the first paragraph on page 701 and use the clues to predict its meaning. (clues: using GPS technology; gadget; meaning: a small machine that does a special job)

Remind students that when they can't use context clues to help them figure out an unfamiliar word, they may need to look it up in a dictionary.

LA.5.1.6.3
Use context clues to determine meanings

Read "The New Gym"

As you read "The New Gym" with students, ask them to identify clues that reveal the meanings of highlighted words. Tell students that they will read these words again in *A Dream Comes True.*

Objectives

- Monitor comprehension
- Use academic language: *techniques of persuasion*
- Evaluate techniques of persuasion

Materials

- Comprehension Transparency 28 (main vocabulary selection)
- Practice Book, p. 201

FCAT Skills Trace

Techniques of Persuasion

Introduce	701A–B
Practice / Apply	702–705; Practice Book 201–202
Reteach / Review	7090–P, R, T
Assess	Weekly Tests; Unit 6 Test

ELL   Access for All

Give Concrete Examples
Write: *1. Everyone is going to a gym these days. 2. Superheroes drink milk. 3. Children who exercise are happier than children who don't exercise. 4. Look and feel great! Exercise for a strong body and mind!* Next to the sentences write: *bandwagon, testimonials, loaded words, glittering generalities.* Explain the persuasive techniques. Then ask students in groups to match each technique to its corresponding sentence. Discuss their decisions.

Reread for
Comprehension

LA.5.1.7 Use strategies to comprehend text

STRATEGY
MONITOR COMPREHENSION

Good readers **monitor their comprehension.** To help them understand the text, they can use self-correction techniques such as rereading, asking questions, summarizing, or adjusting their reading rate.

SKILL
TECHNIQUES OF PERSUASION

LA.5.1.7.2 Identify how author's perspective influences text

EXPLAIN

- One method students can use to monitor information is to identify **techniques of persuasion** that authors use, such as glittering generalities, bandwagon, testimonials, or loaded words.

- Glittering generalities are statements that are broad and vague; they lack detail, or supporting evidence. Bandwagon is the use of persuasive statements that claim that a large number of

Student Book page 700 available on Comprehension Transparency 28

people are doing or buying something, or thinking a certain way. A testimonial is the use of a celebrity to endorse something, and loaded words are those that reflect the listener's value system.

■ As students read a persuasive article, they should evaluate what they read and decide whether the information is valid.

LA.5.1.7.2
Identify how author's perspective influences text

MODEL

Reread "The New Gym" from **Student Book** page 700.

Think Aloud The author cites the statistic that "one in four kids gets no physical education in school at all." How can I check the validity of this information? One thing I could do is use the Internet to access Web sites for the Florida Department of Education as well as the National Department of Education.

GUIDED PRACTICE

■ Begin by writing on the board the following words from "The New Gym": *new, just, traditional, enjoy, advocates, boundless, energy, healthy.* Ask students if they associate positive or negative images with those words. Then ask students how these words influenced their feelings about the new gym idea. Have students name sources they might use to verify the information about physical education and kids.

■ Have students make up examples of persuasion techniques for "The New Gym" using a glittering generality, bandwagon statement, and a testimonial with loaded words.

APPLY

Tell student pairs to rewrite the article "Satellite Guidance for the Blind" on Student Book page 701 by choosing words that will persuade the reader to believe that technology is *interfering* with the lives of people, such as Carmen Fernandez. Ask students to include a list of sources where readers might find information about how technology might actually hinder some people with disabilities.

Quick Check **Can students evaluate techniques of persuasion?**

During **Small Group Instruction**

If No → **Approaching Level** Comprehension, pp. 709O–709P

If Yes → **On Level** Options, p. 709R

Beyond Level Options, p. 709T

RESEARCH
Why It Matters

Comprehension
"Student think alouds ask students to talk out loud about what they are thinking just after they read parts of a text. Thinking aloud shows students how a reader makes sense of a challenging text. It also shows students how expert readers might use different strategies as they process text. Finally, it shows students how to adjust their reading based on how well they understand."

Jan Dole

LOG ON Go to
www.macmillanmh.com

FCAT Success!

Test Prep and Practice with Techniques of Persuasion, pages 32–179.

■ **On Level Practice Book O,** page 201

You encounter techniques of **persuasion** every day. Persuasion is communication meant to convince you that you should believe something, act in a certain way, or participate in something. People trying to persuade you can use a variety of techniques.

Techniques of Persuasion
Testimonial: a statement of support by a noteworthy person
Bandwagon: The product or activity is said to be popular with everyone.
Emotional appeal: Language is used to make a person feel strong emotions.
Repetition: a name being repeated many times
Slogan: a catchy phrase

Match a technique of persuasion to each example.

1. Our wheelchairs are used nationwide by all Paralympians everywhere.
   bandwagon

2. Boundless Playgrounds are fun! Boundless Playgrounds are safe! Boundless Playgrounds make memories! repetition

3. A GPS device in your hands makes your feet "Glad to Walk Positively Anywhere Safely." slogan

4. Hi, I'm proud to use FastBreak Wheelchairs. Because of FastBreak Wheelchairs, I was named one of the top young athletes in the nation.
   testimonial

5. Would you enjoy never going anywhere new, never hearing new sounds, and never meeting new people? Probably not. With GPS, you can be free to walk anywhere, any way, and any time that you want!
   emotional appeal

★ **Approaching Practice Book A,** page 201

◆ **Beyond Practice Book B,** page 201

Read

MAIN SELECTION
- *A Dream Comes True*
- **FCAT** **Skill:** Techniques of Persuasion

TEST PREP
- "Profile of a Paralympian"
- **Test Strategy:** Think and Search

SMALL GROUP OPTIONS

- Differentiated Instruction, pp. 709M–709V

Comprehension

LA.5.2.1.1 Demonstrate knowledge of characteristics of genres

GENRE: NONFICTION ARTICLE

Have students read the definition of a Nonfiction Article on **Student Book** page 702. Students should look for facts and information about real people, places, and events as they read.

LA.5.1.7 Use strategies to comprehend text

STRATEGY
MONITOR COMPREHENSION

Remind students that as they read, they need to stop when they have a problem, use self-correction techniques, and decide what they may need to do in order to understand what they have just read.

FCAT
SKILL
TECHNIQUES OF PERSUASION

LA.5.1.7.2 Identify how author's perspective influences text

Remind students that persuasion means leading others to believe something or to think about a subject in a particular way.

Comprehension

Genre

A **Nonfiction Article** in a newspaper or magazine reports on real people, places, and events.

Monitor Comprehension

FCAT **Persuasion**

Persuasion is a method of convincing others that they should believe something or feel a certain way about a subject.

A Dream Comes True

Why do ALL kids need a place to play?

Most kids love recess, but for Hannah Kristan, it was her least favorite part of the school day. "I never got to do anything except sit there," she recalls.

Hannah was born with a disease that kept the bones in her back from forming properly. She uses a **wheelchair**. Sadly, for kids like her, most playground equipment is off limits. In fact, Hannah is one of 5 million kids in the United States who cannot use traditional playground equipment because of some type of disability.

Paint panel

702

Talk tube

Vocabulary

Vocabulary Words Review the tested vocabulary words: **elementary, physical, rigid, interact,** and **wheelchair.**

Selection Words Students might find these words difficult. Pronounce the words and present the meanings as necessary.

humiliation (p. 704): loss of one's sense of self-respect

isolation (p. 704): the state of being completely separated from others

LA.5.1.6.1 Use new vocabulary taught directly

Hannah Kristan has a great time in this Boundless Playground high-back swing.

Then Hannah heard about Boundless Playgrounds—playgrounds without limits for children with disabilities. The wonderful group behind Boundless Playgrounds helps communities create special playgrounds for children of all abilities. There are swings and sandboxes specially designed for kids with physical disabilities. Kids with vision problems can enjoy the movement of swings and also use musical activities such as chime walls. Since her hometown in Connecticut had nothing like it, Hannah helped raise money for this new kind of playground.

A Boundless Playground is an exciting place for all kids.

703

Read Together

If your students need support to read the Main Selection, use the prompts to guide comprehension and model how to complete the graphic organizer.

Read Independently

If your students can read the Main Selection independently, have them read and complete the graphic organizer. Remind students to adjust their reading rate when reading informational nonfiction.

If your students need an alternate selection, choose the **Leveled Readers** that match their instructional level.

Technology

Story available on **Listening Library Audio CD**

Preview and Predict

LA.5.1.7.1
Use prior knowledge to make and confirm predictions

Ask students to read the title, preview the photographs, and note questions and predictions about the article.

Set Purposes

LA.5.1.7.1
Establish purpose for reading

FOCUS QUESTION Discuss the question about the article. Point out the Opinion and Fact Chart on **Practice Book** page 202. Explain that students will use the chart to record facts and opinions in this article.

Read *A Dream Comes True*

1 | **STRATEGY**
MONITOR COMPREHENSION

LA.5.1.7
Student uses strategies to comprehend text

Teacher Think Aloud I can tell from the first two paragraphs that a problem is presented in the selection, one that the author feels strongly about. I can stop and check that I understand the information in the selection by asking myself questions such as *why? what if?* and *how?* I will also want to read this selection carefully before I come to any conclusions about persuasion techniques the author might be using. How do you think the author will try to persuade readers in this selection?

Student Think Aloud In the middle of the second paragraph, I see that the author uses the word *sadly*. This is a word that has a negative connotation, and it is also a signal word that what follows is the author's opinion. The author thinks it is sad that playgrounds are off-limits to children with disabilities, and will probably try to persuade readers that this should be changed.

Develop Comprehension

2 TECHNIQUES OF PERSUASION

LA.5.1.7.2 Identify how author's perspective influences text

What techniques of persuasion does the author use to convince the reader that Boundless Playgrounds are a good thing? Add one fact and one opinion that the author uses to the chart. (The author includes a testimonial from Matt Cavedon, who designed a swing especially for Boundless Playgrounds and has strong opinions about it. He also has a disability, which makes his opinion carry even more weight.)

3 TEXT FEATURES

LA.5.2.2.1 Locate information from text features

What are two text features of informational nonfiction you can find in this article? (Answers should include photos used as illustrations, as well as quotations from real people and a sidebar with more information.)

4 SYNTHESIZE

LA.5.2.2.2 Use information from text to answer questions

Do you think that the author's opinion—that a Boundless Playground is inviting and fun for all children—is persuasive? Explain your answer. (Answers will vary. The author has supported this opinion with many facts, such as descriptions of equipment, as well as eyewitness accounts of children enjoying the playground, so most will probably agree.) Help students complete the graphic organizer as they read.

Fact	Opinion
Matt Cavedon designed a swing for Boundless Playgrounds	Is this a small thing? Not for her!

Matt Cavedon

NEW EXPERIENCES

Matt Cavedon designed a swing especially for Boundless Playgrounds, but his commitment didn't stop there. In a speech he gave in 2004, Matt, then 15 years old, described an experience he had at the grand opening of a Boundless Playground in Rhode Island:

2 "A girl our age [15 years old] was swinging, laughing, and crying all at once. Her mom explained that it was the girl's first time on a swing! Is this a small thing? Not for her! Not for her mom! Not for the kids without disabilities who came up to her to say congratulations! I wonder how many of those kids had just talked to a person with a disability for the first time. I wonder how many will choose to **interact** with people who have different abilities **3** because of that experience."

704

The inspiration for Boundless Playgrounds was a playground created by Amy Jaffe Barzach. It is named Jonathan's Dream in honor of her son. Jonathan's Dream and many Boundless Playgrounds around the country have a glider swing that can be used by kids who use wheelchairs and their friends. The glider swing at Jonathan's Dream was designed by Matthew Cavedon, who wasn't even 10 years old at the time. Matthew was motivated because he uses a wheelchair himself and wanted to be able to have fun at playgrounds with other kids, regardless of their **physical** abilities or disabilities.

The **elementary** idea behind Boundless Playgrounds is that play is both part of the joy of childhood and an important way for children to learn about the world. Kids who are kept away from playgrounds are denied this enjoyment as well as the learning. Far from being a place of happy excitement, traditional playgrounds are often places of humiliation and isolation for those who can't join in the fun.

Cross-Curricular Connection
Community Playgrounds

When communities build playgrounds, they have to follow regulations in order to provide a safe environment for the children who use them.

Have students apply evaluative criteria and use the library and Internet to find out information about playground safety and regulations. Encourage them to evaluate information by examining several sources. Then have them plan and prepare a persuasive speech about the importance of playground safety. They should use persuasive techniques, such as hyperbole and repetition, and establish and develop a controlling idea. Remind students that when they present their speeches they should demonstrate appropriate eye contact and gestures.

LA.5.6.2.2 Evaluate information by examining several sources of information
LA.5.6.2.1 Apply evaluative criteria to select resources
LA.5.4.3.2 Write persuasive text that includes persuasive techniques
LA. 5.5.2.2 Make formal oral presentations demonstrating appropriate language choices
LA.5.5.2.2 Demonstrate appropriate eye contact and gestures

Amy Barzach and friends at Jonathan's Dream, the playground she designed and named for her son

Contrary to some **rigid** ideas about what a playground for children with special needs should be like, a Boundless Playground is every bit as colorful and challenging as a traditional playground. That's why it is inviting and fun for all children. And for Hannah, Matthew, and other kids like them, a playground like this is also a dream come true.

FCAT

Think and Compare

1. What "dream" has come true for kids in this selection?

2. How does Matt Cavendon persuade his audience that Boundless Playgrounds are worthwhile?

3. According to this article, what do kids miss out on when they can't play at a playground?

4. Why do you think "The New Gym" was included in this section along with the other articles about health and fitness?

705

PERSONAL RESPONSE

Have students respond to the selection by revising or confirming their predictions and noting any additional questions they have after reading.

Comprehension Check

SUMMARIZE

FCAT

LA.5.1.7.3 Determine main idea through summarizing

Have students write a summary of the important information in *A Dream Comes True* and paraphrase the text's main idea.

THINK AND COMPARE

Sample answers are given.

1. **Analyze** Boundless Playgrounds can prevent feelings of humiliation and isolation that children with disabilities experience at other playgrounds where they are unable to use the equipment. The "dream" that has come true is that these children can now enjoy the same playground activities that other children do.

FCAT

LA.5.1.7.2 Identify how author's perspective influences text

2. **Persuasion** Matt Cavedon uses an example to try and persuade his audience that Boundless Playgrounds are worthwhile. He also asks a question that appeals to people's emotions about being accepted by others.

3. **Text to World** Kids miss out on the joy and learning that comes from playing with other children.

LA.5.2.1.5 Demonstrate understanding and include other text/media

4. **Text to Text** Answers will vary. Some students may say that "The New Gym" was included to show that able-bodied children have to focus on improvements in health and fitness just as children with disabilities do.

Cross-Curricular Connection

PERSUASION IN MEDIA

Print and electronic media use persuasive techniques—glittering generalities, bandwagon, and testimonials—as well as bias, propaganda, stereotyping, and exaggeration to persuade readers/viewers to do or think something. Review persuasion techniques. Explain that *bias* means an author favors only one point of view; *propaganda* is information or ideas deliberately spread to influence the thinking of others and is often untrue or unfair. Display print and electronic media examples of persuasion, bias, and propaganda in editorials, articles, and ads in magazines, newspapers, and on television and the Internet. Have students make informed judgments about them, evaluate the messages for effectiveness of organization, presentation, usefulness, and relevance, and discuss their ideas.

LA.5.6.3.1 Recognize differences between logical reasoning and propaganda
LA.5.6.3.1 Examine how ideas are presented in variety of print and non-print media

Objectives

- Read accurately with appropriate expression
- Review Main Idea
- Rate: 129–149 WCPM

Materials

- Fluency Transparency 28
- Fluency Solutions Audio CD
- Practice Book, p. 203

Transparency 28

Advocates of the "new" gym class point to studies that show kids are less active than ever before. They believe that children's natural boundless energy isn't being channeled into healthy activities for a lifetime. One in four kids gets no physical education in school at all. Kids' general activity level is at its highest in tenth grade but then slowly declines all the way into adulthood. That's what the new movement is designed to change.

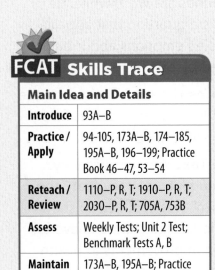

FCAT Skills Trace

Main Idea and Details

Introduce	93A–B
Practice / Apply	94–105, 173A–B, 174–185, 195A–B, 196–199; Practice Book 46–47, 53–54
Reteach / Review	1110–P, R, T; 1910–P, R, T; 2030–P, R, T; 705A, 753B
Assess	Weekly Tests; Unit 2 Test; Benchmark Tests A, B
Maintain	173A–B, 195A–B; Practice Book 46–47, 53–54

LA.5.1.5
Student demonstrates the ability to read orally

Fluency
Repeated Reading: Punctuation

EXPLAIN/MODEL Model reading aloud **Fluency Transparency 28.** Have students echo-read each sentence after you. Point out the punctuation used in the passage. Tell students that, in this selection, apostrophes are used to make a contraction from two words as well as to show possession, and quotation marks are used to indicate a special use of a word.

PRACTICE/APPLY Divide students into two groups. The first group reads the passage a sentence at a time. The second group echo-reads. Then groups switch roles. Pay attention to students' use of the punctuation marks in this passage. For additional practice, have students use **Practice Book** page 203 or the **Fluency Solutions Audio CD.**

Comprehension

REVIEW SKILL
FCAT MAIN IDEA AND DETAILS

LA.5.1.7.3
Determine main idea through inferring and identifying relevant details

EXPLAIN/MODEL

- The main idea of an article is the most important point that an author makes about a topic.

- The rest of the sentences in the article give additional details about the main idea that help to explain or support it.

- The main idea is often stated at the beginning of an article or paragraph. If not, readers must put together details in the text to figure out the unstated main idea.

- Recognizing the main idea can help readers understand and remember an author's most important points, as well as summarize a selection.

PRACTICE/APPLY

- Discuss the main idea of *A Dream Comes True.*

- Discuss the details the author uses in *A Dream Comes True* and how these details support the main idea.

- Have students create an idea web about helping people with disabilities fit in, including the main idea and supporting details.

Research
Study Skills

FCAT Everyday Communications

LA.5.2.2.4
Identify
characteristics
of types of text

LA.5.6.3.1
Recognize
differences
between
logical
reasoning and
propaganda

EXPLAIN

Discuss types of everyday communications and how to use them.

- Businesses or governments gather information on forms. Forms include anything from an order form to a library card application to an income tax form. When you fill out a form, you give information to a business or government agency. To fill out forms correctly, you must read them carefully and follow the directions.

- Consumer materials include things such as warranties, instruction booklets, directions for use, and product information, as well as schedules and maps. Reading these materials carefully helps you use a product correctly and safely, and enables you to get the greatest benefit for your money. You may also use some of these materials for research.

- Ads (a shortened word for "advertisements") try to sell you something. Ads may not be factual or totally honest. Their purpose is to convince you that you need to buy what a company has to sell. Brochures are another kind of ad.

- Newsletters provide information to people who are part of a specific group and are sent to members on a periodic basis.

LA.5.6.1.1
Interpret
informational
text for
performing
a task

MODEL

Display Transparency 6.

Think Aloud I need to help get information for planning the new gym class. I must fill out forms at the library to get a library card. Then I can do some research on gym classes. I must follow directions carefully when I fill out the form.

PRACTICE/APPLY

With an adult's help, have students collect sample forms, brochures, and ads and bring them to class. Then have students look at these samples and find out what kinds of information these materials ask for and what kinds of information the materials provide. Evaluate them for bias, exaggeration, and stereotyping.

Make sure students can identify and apply information contained in directions and forms to complete authentic tasks.

Objective

- Read directions and follow them carefully to fill out forms

Materials

- Study Skills Transparency 6
- Practice Book, p. 204

Transparency 6

APPLYING FOR A LIBRARY CARD

Parkdale Metro Library   No. _____
123 Main St.
Parkdale OH
USA
(555) 555-5555

This application should be written in ink only. Do not write on the line above.

Expires _____

I hereby agree to obey all the rules and regulations of the public library, to pay promptly all fines charged against me for the injury or loss of books, and to report immediately any changes of address.

Mr. Mrs. Miss _____

       First Name   Middle Name   Last Name

Home Address_____

_____

Home Phone_____

_____has my permission to check out library materials from the library. I will assume the responsibility for any overdue fines or charges for damaged/lost materials.

Parent's Signature_____

Date_____

Study Skills Transparency 6

On Level Practice Book O, page 204

You see printed materials every day that provide information about the world around you. **Everyday communications** have many forms.

Study the descriptions below. Then answer the questions.

Consumer materials	Warranty: guarantees a product or its parts for a period of time
	Product instructions: explain how to operate a product
Directions	Maps explain how to get from one place to another.
Advertisements	Help-wanted ad: explains a particular job and how to apply for it
	Store ad: provides information about the store and its merchandise
Brochure	a small booklet that contains information about a place, service, person, or object
Newsletter	a printed report or letter giving information about a special group or organization

1. What might you read if you were looking for a job? **a help-wanted ad**

2. Would you read a brochure or a warranty to learn more about a museum exhibit? **a brochure**

3. A neighborhood club is planning a Fourth of July parade. What would you read to find out when and where the parade begins? **a newsletter**

4. What might you read to learn how to operate your new camera? **product instructions**

5. What would you use to get directions from California to Texas? **a map**

 Approaching Practice Book A, page 204

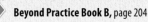 **Beyond Practice Book B,** page 204

Answer Questions

Test Strategy: Think and Search

LA.5.1.7
Student uses strategies to comprehend text

EXPLAIN

Review the steps below to help students use the Think and Search test strategy.

- **Think** about what the question is asking you to find.

- **Search** the text for the information relevant to the question. You may have to look in different parts of the selection.

Have students read the selection on page 706. Use the instruction that follows to help students work through the test questions on page 707. Have students record their answers and make notes on separate sheets of paper.

LA.5.2.1.5
Demonstrate understanding and include evidence from the text

MODEL

Question 1 Read the question and all of the answer choices.

Think Aloud This question is asking me to draw a conclusion about Jennifer Howitt's attitude. I am going to use the Think and Search test strategy for this question. I'll have to think about exactly what the question is asking, as well as Jennifer's attitude. I'm also going to have to think about the four answer choices and decide which one makes sense.

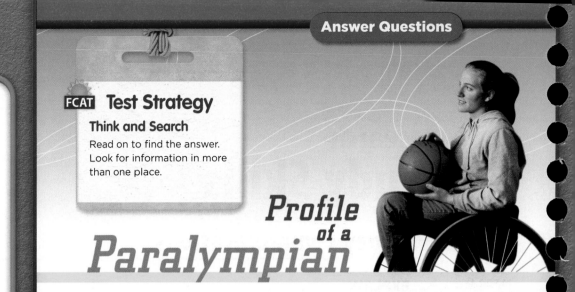

FCAT Test Strategy

Think and Search

Read on to find the answer. Look for information in more than one place.

Profile of a Paralympian

Jennifer Howitt may use a wheelchair, but she isn't sitting out life. Since being paralyzed after breaking her back in a hiking accident at age nine, she has developed into one of the country's top young disabled athletes.

Howitt competed in the 1998 World Athletic Championships in track and field and went to the 2000 Sydney Paralympics as the youngest member of the 12-person U.S. women's wheelchair basketball team. Although the team finished in fifth place, "I was on an emotional high," says Howitt. "It was pretty inspirational. If the entire world can come together to celebrate sport and disability, then it is really possible for us as a planet to work out all our problems." Jennifer's dreams are not limited only to her personal or athletic success.

Since 2001, the Paralympics has been a division of the U.S. Olympic Committee. By working with local as well as national sports organizations, the U.S. Paralympics can encourage Olympic ideals, such as fair play and equality, among the whole of America. This especially includes people with physical disabilities.

Howitt is committed to changing the world in positive ways. She has coached young paraplegic athletes, traveled extensively, and attended Georgetown University in Washington, D.C., where she studied international politics. She hopes "to show young girls with disabilities that they can achieve whatever they want. A disability doesn't get in the way of anything. Maybe you'll have to adapt your goal, but you can always achieve it," Howitt says.

706

Go on ▶

GUIDED PRACTICE

Suggest that students scan the article and search for words or phrases that describe Jennifer Howitt or tell about what she does. Tell students that thinking about these words and phrases will lead them to the correct answer. (Possible words and phrases: isn't sitting out life, developed into, competed, committed, positive ways)

APPLY

Think Aloud I've searched for and found words and phrases about Jennifer. Now I can think about this information, as well as the answer choices. Choice A seems correct, but I'll check the others to make sure. Jennifer is definitely not "sitting out life." The text doesn't mention that she only plays basketball, and choice D clearly doesn't apply to Jennifer. A is the correct answer.

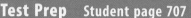
Now answer Numbers 1 through 5. Base your answers on the article "Profile of a Paralympian."

1 Which of the following BEST describes Jennifer's attitude?

(A) inspired

(B) sitting out life

(C) able only to play basketball

(D) unsure about achieving goals

2 What does Jennifer believe about disabilities?

(F) People always need wheelchairs.

(G) People with disabilities live in Washington, D.C.

(H) Disabilities will stop people from moving ahead.

(I) Disabilities should not keep a person from achieving his or her goals.

Tip

Look for information in more than one place.

3 Jennifer has worked to persuade others of her views MAINLY by

(A) going to college.

(B) winning competitions.

(C) sponsoring Paralympians.

(D) being a successful role model herself.

4 Aside from excelling as an athlete, what are some of Jennifer's other achievements? Use details and information from the article in your answer.

5 The author states, "Howitt is committed to changing the world in positive ways." Use details and information from the article to support this statement.

STOP 707

FCAT Success!

Test Prep and Practice with Techniques of Persuasion, pages 32–179.

Technology

Go to www.macmillanmh.com for Sample Responses to questions 4 and 5.

ADDITIONAL GUIDED PRACTICE

Question 2 Read the question and all of the answer choices. Suggest that students *think* about what the question is asking (Jennifer's beliefs about disabilities) and *search* the article for relevant information. (I, the text includes details that support this answer)

Question 3 After reading the question and answer choices, suggest that this question also lends itself to using the Think and Search strategy. Remind students to also think about the answer choices. Emphasize that a fact in an answer choice might be found in the text, but it may not be the best answer to the question. (D, the other choices describe Jennifer but are too narrow to answer the question.)

Questions 4 and 5 Point out the "Read/Think/Explain" icons in the two questions. Tell students that these icons indicate that the questions call for written responses. Question 4 is a short-response item that should take students five minutes to complete. Question 5 is an extended-response item that should take students ten to fifteen minutes to complete.

For both of the written-response items, students should use a combination of the test strategies they have learned to arrive at their answers. Students can use one sheet of paper to plan their responses, and another sheet to write the actual response. Emphasize that students are to use details and information from the article to explain their answers.

See the Constructed Response rubrics on page 763H.

Connect
Language Arts

FCAT WRITING
- Write to a Prompt
- Research and Inquiry

FCAT WORD STUDY
- Words in Context
- Use Context Clues
- Phonics: Words from Mythology
- Vocabulary Building

SPELLING
- Words from Mythology

GRAMMAR
- Negatives

SMALL GROUP OPTIONS
- Differentiated Instruction
  pp. 709M–709V

Write to a Prompt

FCAT Students enjoy different kinds of activities in gym class.

Think of new activities to benefit students in gym class.

Now write to explain why new activities will benefit a gym class.

Expository writing explains, defines, and tells how to do something.

To figure out if a writing prompt asks for expository writing, look for clue words such as explain why or tell what.

Below see how one student concluded a response to the prompt above.

The writer summed up her response to the prompt in the final paragraph.

> The purpose of school is to give our brains and our bodies a workout. Many students find the usual choice of team sports and track and field events boring and uninspiring. Instead of joining the rest of the class, they sit off to the sidelines.
>
> If we added new types of activities such as yoga and aerobics as part of our gym program, more students would be motivated to "get up and GO!" They might start to take the idea of physical fitness more seriously. This could lead to healthful exercise habits that will stay with them for the rest of their lives.

708

FCAT Writing Prompt

EXPLAIN

LA.5.3.1 Use prewriting strategies to generate ideas and formulate a plan

Tell students that often when taking a test, they will be asked to write to a prompt. Explain that a prompt introduces or gives information about a writing topic, then provides instructions about a specific writing assignment related to the information. Explain to students that most prompts will fall under two types of writing or writing modes: expository prompts, which ask the writer to explain something, or narrative prompts, which ask the writer to tell a story.

Before students begin to write to a prompt, they need to find the following information:

- What is the mode or type of writing? Is the prompt expository or narrative?

- What is the purpose for writing? What is the actual assignment? Does the prompt call for a specific form or format?

MODEL

Determine the Writing Mode Read the prompt above the student model aloud, then draw students' attention to the information in the callouts. Review the definition of narrative writing and point out the clue words in the callouts and the specific clue words in the prompt.

Determine the Purpose Ask: *What part of the prompt tells you the purpose for writing?* Point out the second and third sentences. Explain that the second sentence tells students to think about the topic and the third sentence provides the actual assignment.

LA.5.3.1.2 Prewrite by determining purpose and intended audience

Writing Prompt

Respond in writing to the prompt below. Before you write, read the Writing Hints below. Review the hints after you finish writing.

FCAT Student groups often do community service projects to help others.

Think of a community service project you and a group of students could do.

Now write to tell what community service project your group could do.

Writing Hints for Prompts

☑ Carefully read the prompt.

☑ Organize your ideas to plan your writing.

☑ Support your ideas by giving reasons or using more details.

☑ Use negatives and contractions correctly in sentences.

☑ Choose words that help readers understand your ideas.

☑ Review your writing and edit as needed.

709

PRACTICE

LA.5.3.1.1 Generate ideas based upon teacher-directed topics

Have students read the writing prompt on **Student Book** p. 709. Work with students to determine the writing mode and the purpose for writing.

Writing Mode This is an expository prompt. The student is being asked to tell or explain something.

Purpose The student is being asked to think of a community service project that a group of students might do.

APPLY

LA.5.3.1.3 Make a plan for writing that prioritizes ideas

Writing Prompt Have students practice writing from the prompt, simulating a test-taking situation. Distribute to each student a sheet of paper for planning and 3-4 sheets of paper for writing an actual response.

LA.5.3.1.3 Make a plan for writing that addresses time needed to complete task.

Tell students: *After you reread the prompt, you will have 45 minutes to complete your writing. Use one sheet of paper as a planning sheet to organize your thoughts before you begin to draft your response to the prompt. What you write should be written neatly and show that you have planned your response carefully and appropriately.*

SCORING RUBRIC

6 Points	5 Points	4 Points	3 Points	2 Points	1 Point
Focus Writing is on topic and complete. **Organization** Writing is logically organized, with a variety of sentence structure used. **Support** There are ample supporting ideas and word choice is precise. **Conventions** Correct grammar and complete sentences are used.	**Focus** Writing is on topic. **Organization** Writing has a generally successful organizational pattern. **Support** Supporting details are included. Word choice is adequate but may lack precision. **Conventions** Various sentence structures have been used. Punctuation, grammar, and spelling are generally correct.	**Focus** Writing is generally on topic. Some loosely related information is included. **Organization** An organizational pattern is evident, although lapses occur. **Support** Details or ideas are not fully developed. Word choice is adequate. **Conventions** Knowledge of grammar, spelling, and punctuation is evident.	**Focus** Writing is generally on topic, although irrelevant information is included. **Organization** An organizational pattern has been attempted. **Support** Some supporting ideas are not developed. Word choice is limited. **Conventions** Knowledge of grammar, spelling, and punctuation conventions is evident. Many sentences are simple.	**Focus** Writing is somewhat related to the topic but offers few supporting details. **Organization** An organizational pattern is not evident. Word choice is limited and immature. **Support** Few supporting details are offered. **Conventions** Frequent errors occur in grammar, spelling, and punctuation. Most sentences are simple constructions.	**Focus** Writing minimally address the topic. **Organization** No organizational pattern is evident. **Support** Details are irrelevant, and word choice is immature. **Conventions** Frequent errors in grammar, spelling, and punctuation impede communication. Sentence structure is simple at best.

Biography

Publishing Options

To publish their biographies, students should make neat final copies in their best handwriting or type their biographies using computers. Also, they may wish to include drawings or photographs. Additionally, host a Paralympic medal ceremony by asking students to design medals for the subjects of their biographies. Students can use their biographies to make oral presentations of their medals.

Speaking and Listening

SPEAKING STRATEGIES

■ Effectively present the information through verbal and nonverbal communication.

■ Organize the presentation with an introduction, body, and conclusion.

■ Demonstrate a clear viewpoint.

LISTENING STRATEGIES

■ Prepare to listen without interruption.

■ Interpret a speaker's verbal and nonverbal message, purpose, and perspective.

■ Form an opinion on the basis of information presented.

6-Point Scoring Rubric

Use the rubric on page 763G to score published writing.

Writing Process

For a complete lesson, see Unit Writing pages 763A–763F.

GENERATE QUESTIONS

LA.5.3.1.1 Generate ideas based upon teacher-directed topics

Direct students to "The Second Olympics" on **Student Book** page 701. Explain that they will conduct research and write biographies about Paralympians. Remind students that the purpose of expository writing is to inform by giving facts and information. Explain that biographies tell about a person's life and accomplishments.

LA.5.4.2.2 Organize and record information on data tables

Help students brainstorm topics and identify questions to guide them in their research. Draw a spider organizer on the board. Write a topic in the center circle and work with students to fill in the questions for the "legs."

Ask students to research athletes with disabilities who have participated in the Paralympics. Once they have identified an athlete, tell students to research details of the athlete's life.

FIND INFORMATION

LA.5.6.2 Student uses a systematic research process

Remind students that encyclopedias, dictionaries, and other references aren't the only sources of information. Students may use other materials, such as brochures or newsletters, to gather facts for their biographies. Explain that they may find information in their town newspapers, for instance, or in brochures or newsletters of local organizations. Some of these periodicals will also be on the Internet. Students should check periodicals for Web site addresses.

Transparency 109 provides sample note cards that you can use in conjunction with the **Note-Taking** lesson on page 109B.

ORGANIZE INFORMATION

Review the use of outlines with students by using **Transparency 110**, which provides a completed outline that can be used with the **Outlining** lesson on page 109B.

SYNTHESIZE AND WRITE

LA.5.4.2.3 Write informational essays that contain introductory, body and concluding paragraphs

Have students use their outlines to write drafts of their biographies, keeping their purposes and audiences in mind. Remind students to proofread their biographies carefully to look for errors in spelling, punctuation, and grammar. Use **Transparencies 111** and **112** in discussing the revision process.

Writer's Toolbox

Note-Taking

Use **Transparency 109** to review with students how to take notes. Remind students to write a category or main idea at the top of each note card, record the fact or information in their own words, and note the source information. Caution students against plagiarism; suggest that they consult dictionaries or thesauruses to identify alternate word choices and meanings as they summarize and paraphrase. Remind students again to cite the source of each note.

LA.5.4.2.2 Record information related to a topic

Outlining

Discuss with students how to create an outline, using **Transparency 110** as a model. Main ideas are listed under Roman numerals, and supporting details are listed under capital letters. Tell students they will use their note cards to create outlines. Suggest that students use their outlines to experiment with the order in which they present information.

Transparency 110: **Outlining**

LA.5.3.1.3 Prewrite by organizing ideas using tools

Transparency 109

April Holmes – Background

Went high school in Somerdale, New Jersey.

Was a 400-meter champion.

Won several NCAA All-American honors as a sprinter at Norfolk State University.

Lost her leg in a train accident when she was 27.

Source: U.S. Paralympics

April Holmes – Paralympian

Won a silver medal in the 100-meter dash in Lille, France at the International Paralympic World Championships. Set an American record for her class in 14.12 seconds.

Source: U.S. Paralympics

Writing Transparency 109

Research Tips

Evaluating Sources Remind students to ask themselves questions about their sources: *Is this information accurate and current? What are the author's credentials? Will this information help me write my biography? Is this material too difficult for me to read? Do I need to find additional sources?*

LA.5.6.2.1 Apply evaluative criteria to select and use resources

Objectives

- Apply knowledge of word meaning and context clues
- Recognize and use a variety of context clues

Materials

- Vocabulary Transparencies 55 and 56
- Practice Book, p. 205

Vocabulary

elementary (p. 700) introductory; simple, necessary parts to be learned first

physical (p. 700) of or for the body

rigid (p. 701) not bending; stiff; firm

interact (p. 701) act together with others

wheelchair (p. 701) chair on wheels, used especially by people who are sick or unable to walk

ELL　**Access for All**

Reinforce Language
Ask each student to write down one school rule. Write the rules on the board. Classify the rules as *rigid* or *flexible* and discuss why.

Review
Vocabulary
 Words in Context

LA.5.1.6
Student uses multiple strategies to develop vocabulary

EXPLAIN/MODEL

Review the meanings of vocabulary words. Display **Transparency 55.** Model how to use word meanings and context clues to fill in the missing word.

Think Aloud In the first sentence, the speaker does not know much about yoga, so he or she is a beginner. That means that the speaker would probably take a beginning or elementary course. The word *elementary* makes sense in the sentence.

Transparency 55

wheelchair　elementary　rigid　interact　physical

Because I did not know much about yoga, I took the (1) elementary course.

(2) Physical education is my favorite class of the day because I enjoy exercise.

My mom said that the rule about no sleepovers on school nights was (3) rigid and would not change.

The children (4) interact well when they play together.

When my dad broke his leg, he used a (5) wheelchair to get around.

Vocabulary Transparency 55

PRACTICE/APPLY

 Instruct students to complete the remaining sentences on their own. Review the students' answers as a class, or instruct students to check their answers with partners.

 What Would You Do? Have students answer questions stems by choosing the correct vocabulary word from two closely related words. One word should be the vocabulary word and the other a synonym. *Which word would mean something introductory?*

elementary　　firsthand

LA.5.1.6.3
Use context
clues to
determine
word
meanings

STRATEGY
CONTEXT CLUES

EXPLAIN/MODEL

- Tell students that when they read an unfamiliar word, they should not immediately stop reading and look for a dictionary. Writers often provide context clues. Below are tips for finding clues.

- Skip the word and read to the end of the sentence because writers sometimes supply the meanings of, or synonyms for, difficult words.

- Look for clues in nearby sentences.

- Reread the section carefully in case a clue was missed.

 Read the first sentence on **Transparency 56.** Model how to figure out the meaning of the italicized word using the context clue.

 **Transparency 56**

Context Clues

1. He spent several hours *reflecting* on the poem, thinking about what the poet meant by the words.

2. She was unable to see, but her *disability* did not keep her from running in the race.

3. She marked a path to her *destination* on the map.

4. She had dinner *reservations* at 7:00 PM and did not want the restaurant to give her table to someone else.

Vocabulary Strategy Transparency 56

PRACTICE

Have students identify context clues for italicized words in items 2–4. They can check their predictions in a dictionary.

Quick Check
Can students understand word meanings in context?
Can students use context clues to find a word's meaning?

During **Small Group Instruction**

If No → **Approaching Level** Vocabulary, pp. 709N–709P

If Yes → **On Level** Options, pp. 709Q–709R

Beyond Level Options, pp. 709S–709T

ELL Access for All

Model Share your thinking with students as you identify the context clues for the first few sentences on the transparency. Then encourage students to share their thinking for the others. Check that students understand the words and situation described in each sentence.

FCAT Success!

Test Prep and Practice with vocabulary, pages 6-31.

 **On Level Practice Book O,** page 205

You can figure out the meaning of an unfamiliar word by using **context clues**, the words around the unfamiliar word.

Read each sentence. Use context clues to help you define the boldface word. Then write the letter of the best choice on the line.

1. During the game my **opponent** was the best player on the other team.
   An opponent is ___a___.
   a. a competitor   b. an ally   c. a coach

2. The athletes trained at a high **altitude** because it is much more difficult to run in the mountains.
   Altitude is ___b___.
   a. an underwater cave   b. the height above sea level   c. a plateau

3. The winning women's basketball team looked **regal** with their gold medals and flowers on top of the podium.
   Regal means ___c___.
   a. deprived of food   b. serious   c. like royalty

4. Joe was accompanied by his guide dog, who **escorted** him into the gymnasium.
   To be escorted is to be ___b___.
   a. complex   b. guided   c. called

5. For months the team practiced their **maneuvers** until the exercises became natural to them.
   Maneuvers are ___a___.
   a. movements   b. schedules   c. relationships

Approaching Practice Book A, page 205

 Beyond Practice Book B, page 205

Word Study

Objective

- Decode words with roots in mythology

Materials

- Practice Book, p. 206

On Level Practice Book O, page 206

The names of characters from Greek and Roman mythology are origins of many English words. Recognizing **words from mythology** can help you figure out the meanings of unfamiliar words.

A. Match each word to the name from Greek or Roman mythology that best explains each word's origin. Then write the letter of the name on the line.

1. fortune __b__
2. cosmic __f__
3. titanic __h__
4. volcano __j__
5. cereal __i__
6. jovial __a__
7. geology __c__
8. furious __d__
9. January __e__
10. Olympics __g__

a. Jove, the Roman god who controlled the weather
b. Fortuna, the Roman goddess of luck
c. Gaea, the Greek Earth goddess
d. Furies, angry spirits in Greek mythology
e. Janus, the Roman god of beginnings
f. Cosmos, the Greek word for *universe*
g. Mount Olympus, the home of the gods in Greek mythology
h. Titans, Greek giants who had enormous strength
i. Ceres, the Roman goddess of grain
j. Vulcan, the Roman god of fire

B. Use four words from the first column to make two sentences.

11. The geology class will be digging in the earth, looking for the lost fortune of the ancient king.

12. Long ago people believed cosmic forces would cause a volcano to erupt.
Possible responses provided above.

★ **Approaching Practice Book A,** page 206

◆ **Beyond Practice Book B,** page 206

Phonics
Words from Mythology

 Access for All

LA.5.1.4
Student applies grade level phonics

EXPLAIN/MODEL

- English words come from many different sources.

- Mythology, especially from the Greeks and Romans, is one source of words and word parts.

Write the word *titanic* on the board. Write *titan* beside it.

Think Aloud When I read the word *titanic*, I see the word *titan*. I know that the Titans were a family of giants who ruled Earth for awhile in Greek mythology. They were strong and powerful. The word *titanic* must mean "huge" or "powerful." When I look it up in a dictionary, I see that is the definition.

PRACTICE/APPLY

Suggest that students use their dictionaries and encyclopedias to look up the mythological origins of the following words and their meanings. They may also find information on the Internet if they do searches for "words from mythology."

1. jovial	4. gigantic	7. ocean	10. cyclone
2. cosmetic	5. echo	8. fury	11. muse
3. volcano	6. January	9. mentor	12. floral

Students might also work in pairs or small groups to present one or two of the word histories to the class.

LA.5.1.4.3
Use language structure to read multi-syllabic words

Decode Multisyllabic Words Emphasize that understanding words from mythology, many of which are long, can help students decode multisyllabic words. For practice, see the decodable passages on page 32 of the **Teacher's Resource Book.**

Quick Check **Can students decode words from mythology?**

During **Small Group Instruction**

If No → **Approaching Level** Phonics, p. 709M

If Yes → **On Level** Options, pp. 709Q–709R

Beyond Level Options, pp. 709S–709T

Vocabulary Building

LA.5.1.6 Students uses multiple strategies to develop vocabulary

LA.5.1.7.8 Use semantic organizers to repair comprehension

LA.5.4.2.4 Write communications that include date, proper salutation, closing, and signature

Oral Language

Expand Vocabulary Write *Improving Lives* in the center of a word web. To develop vocabulary, have students search for words in newspapers and media for news and current events related to the weekly theme, as well as using print and electronic dictionaries, and encyclopedias. They may include words such as *technology, diversity,* or *understanding* to write in circles that radiate from the center circle of the web.

Vocabulary Building

Context Clues There may be unfamiliar words in *A Dream Comes True* that are not on the vocabulary list. Have students identify words in the text that they were unsure about and work in pairs to find context clues that may help identify the meaning. If no clue exists, they should look up the word in a dictionary.

LA.5.1.6.3 Use context clues to determine word meanings

 Apply Vocabulary

Write a Letter

Give students the following writing prompt:

What has someone done to improve your life? Perhaps a teacher tutored you in math, or a parent or friend offered good advice. Using the vocabulary words, write an informal, friendly letter to the person who improved your life. Explain how the person improved your life and why you are grateful for his or her help. After you have finished writing, discuss the content of the letters you and your classmates wrote with a teacher and other classmates. Remember to include a date, proper salutation, closing and signature in your letter.

Spiral Review

Vocabulary Game Have two teams of students write four context sentences using at least one vocabulary word from this week and at least one word from a previous week in each sentence. If the team uses all the words correctly, they get one point for each word. If not, they get no points. Teams take turns. The team with the most points, wins the game.

LA.5.1.6 Student uses multiple strategies to develop vocabulary

Technology

Vocabulary PuzzleMaker CD–ROM

 For vocabulary games and practice go to www.macmillanmh.com

5 Day Spelling

Spelling Words

clothes	salute	territory
January	fury	terrace
cereal	echo	parasol
mortal	cycle	fortune
lunar	cyclone	furious
atlas	gigantic	gracious
ocean	Olympics	

Review suspect, inspect, mission

Challenge jovial, venerable

Dictation Sentences

1. They wore colorful <u>clothes</u>.
2. <u>January</u> is a cold month.
3. She had <u>cereal</u> for breakfast.
4. All living things are <u>mortal</u>.
5. The <u>lunar</u> eclipse is rare.
6. The <u>atlas</u> contains maps.
7. <u>Ocean</u> water tastes salty.
8. Soldiers <u>salute</u> each other.
9. We tried to calm her <u>fury</u>.
10. Voices <u>echo</u> in the hall.
11. The seasons follow a <u>cycle</u>.
12. We escaped the <u>cyclone</u>'s path.
13. The statue is <u>gigantic</u>.
14. Athletes compete in the <u>Olympics</u>.
15. Flags marked their <u>territory</u>.
16. We ate lunch on the <u>terrace</u>.
17. Her <u>parasol</u> blocked the sun.
18. Nancy inherited a <u>fortune</u>.
19. I was <u>furious</u> after the fight.
20. Paul is <u>gracious</u> to his guests.

Review/Challenge Words

1. She did not <u>suspect</u> that we had planned a surprise.
2. Someone will <u>inspect</u> the house.
3. The <u>mission</u> was accomplished.
4. Melissa is <u>jovial</u> and likable.
5. They are a <u>venerable</u> old family.

LA.5.1.4.1 Understand spelling patterns

Words from Mythology

Day 1 Pretest

LA.5.1.6 Student develops vocabulary

ASSESS PRIOR KNOWLEDGE

Using the Dictation Sentences, say the underlined word. Read the sentence and repeat the word. Have students write the words on **Spelling Practice Book** page 173. For a modified list, use the first 12 Spelling Words and the Review Words. For a more challenging list, use Spelling Words 3–20 and the Challenge Words. Students may correct their own tests.

Ask students to cut apart the Spelling Word Cards BLM on **Teacher's Resource Book** page 93 and figure out a way to sort them. They can save the cards for use throughout the week.

Day 2 Word Sorts

LA.5.1.6.4 Categorize key vocabulary

TEACHER AND STUDENT SORTS

■ Invite pairs to use the Word Cards to sort the Spelling Words and Challenge Words in any way, for example, by parts of speech. They may share their sorts with the class.

■ Write the words *echo* and *January* on the board. Point out that Echo was a nymph in Greek mythology who could only repeat what others said. Janus was the Roman god of beginnings.

■ Challenge groups to research in dictionaries and encyclopedias the origins of four Spelling Words and their connection to mythology or other aspects of Greek or Roman culture.

■ Have students present their findings to the class. Then help students create new word sort categories based on this information.

Spelling Practice Book, pages 173–174

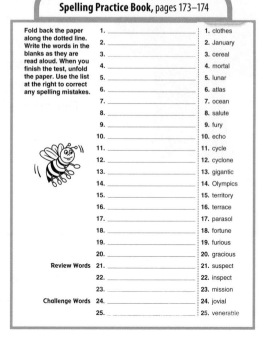

Fold back the paper along the dotted line. Write the words in the blanks as they are read aloud. When you finish the test, unfold the paper. Use the list at the right to correct any spelling mistakes.

1.	1. clothes
2.	2. January
3.	3. cereal
4.	4. mortal
5.	5. lunar
6.	6. atlas
7.	7. ocean
8.	8. salute
9.	9. fury
10.	10. echo
11.	11. cycle
12.	12. cyclone
13.	13. gigantic
14.	14. Olympics
15.	15. territory
16.	16. terrace
17.	17. parasol
18.	18. fortune
19.	19. furious
20.	20. gracious
Review Words 21.	21. suspect
22.	22. inspect
23.	23. mission
Challenge Words 24.	24. jovial
25.	25. venerable

Spelling Practice Book, page 175

territory	cycle	salute	furious
atlas	lunar	gigantic	echo
gracious	Olympics	fortune	ocean
terrace	parasol	mortal	cyclone
clothes	cereal	January	fury

Sort each spelling word according to the number of syllables it contains. Then write the words on the lines below.

One syllable
1. clothes

Two syllables
1. terrace
2. gracious
3. echo
4. ocean
5. atlas
6. mortal
7. fury
8. salute
9. cycle
10. cyclone
11. lunar
12. fortune

Three syllables
1. cereal
2. gigantic
3. parasol
4. furious
5. Olympics

Four syllables
1. territory
2. January

Day 3 — Word Meanings

LA.5.1.6.6 Identify "shades of meaning" in related words

DEFINITIONS

Read each group of related words, or words that share "shades of menaing," below. Ask students to copy the words in their word study notebooks, completing the group by adding a Spelling Word.

1. anger, rage, _____ (fury)

2. area, region, _____ (territory)

3. greet, acknowledge, _____ (salute)

4. enormous, humongous, _____ (gigantic)

5. patio, balcony, _____ (terrace)

Challenge students to come up with other word groups to which they can add Spelling Words, Review Words, or Challenge Words.

Day 4 — Review and Proofread

LA.5.1.6.11 Use Latin roots to determine meaning

SPIRAL REVIEW

Review words with Latin roots. Write *suspect, inspect,* and *mission* on the board. Ask students to identify the Latin root and its definition in each word.

PROOFREAD AND WRITE

Write these sentences on the board, including the misspelled words. Ask students to proofread, circling the misspelled words and correcting them.

1. He located the Atlantic Oshean and Yukon Terratory in the atless. (Ocean, Territory, atlas)

2. A fourius ciclone struck in the middle of Januery. (furious, cyclone, January)

3. The girl was very gratious for her new parasole. (gracious, parasol)

Day 5 — Assess and Reteach

LA.5.3.4.1 Edits for spelling

POSTTEST

Use the Dictation Sentences on page 709G for the Posttest.

If students have difficulty with any words in the lesson, have them copy those words in a list entitled "Spelling Words I Want to Remember" in their word study notebooks.

Have students write a dictionary entry for each word that defines the word and explains its origin.

Spelling Practice Book, page 176

territory	cycle	salute	furious
atlas	lunar	gigantic	echo
gracious	Olympics	fortune	ocean
terrace	parasol	mortal	cyclone
clothes	cereal	January	fury

Complete each sentence below with a spelling word.

1. Hannah helped raise money to build a __gigantic__ playground.
2. Whether you win or lose, it's important to be __gracious__.
3. One famous athlete has his picture on a box of __cereal__.
4. The __Olympics__ are held every four years in a different country.
5. You can look in an __atlas__ to find a map of where the Olympics will be held.
6. The new playground will not cost a __fortune__ to build.
7. You can hear the __echo__ of your own voice if the Olympic stadium is empty.
8. Many athletes train by swimming in the __ocean__ during the warmer months.
9. Putting on __clothes__ can sometimes be challenging for people with disabilities.
10. The new school gym program will begin in __January__.

Write On!

Use each spelling word in a sentence. Answers will vary.

11. parasol
12. cyclone
13. terrace
14. mortal
15. territory

Spelling Practice Book, page 177

Circle the misspelled words in the passage. Write the words correctly on the lines below.

Jake heard his footsteps ecko as he walked into the jigantic stadium. Today he would compete in his first Olimpics. He had been training since Januery. He swam in the osean three times a week and had been watching his diet closely. This morning he had eaten a bowl of sereal and and a piece of toast. The day he had been waiting for had finally come.

1. echo
2. gigantic
3. Olympics
4. January
5. ocean
6. cereal

Writing Activity

Write a paragraph about a time when you helped someone accomplish a goal. Use four words from your spelling list.

Spelling Practice Book, page 178

Look at the words in each set below. One word in each set is spelled correctly. Use a pencil to fill in the circle next to the correct word. Before you begin, look at the sample set of words. Sample A has been done for you. Do Sample B by yourself. When you are sure you know what to do, you may go on with the rest of the page.

Sample A:
- Ⓐ Wednesday
- Ⓑ Wendsday
- Ⓒ Whendsday
- Ⓓ Wensday

Sample B:
- Ⓔ Satturday
- Ⓕ Saturday
- Ⓖ Satterday
- Ⓗ Saterday

1. Ⓐ cerreal Ⓑ sereal Ⓒ cereal Ⓓ cerial
2. Ⓔ terrase Ⓕ terace Ⓖ terrace Ⓗ terase
3. Ⓐ gracious Ⓑ grashious Ⓒ graceious Ⓓ grayshus
4. Ⓔ echoe Ⓕ ecko Ⓖ ecco Ⓗ echo
5. Ⓐ giggantic Ⓑ gigantic Ⓒ jigantic Ⓓ jiggantic

6. Ⓔ ocean Ⓕ ohcean Ⓖ oshun Ⓗ oacean
7. Ⓐ attlas Ⓑ atlass Ⓒ atlas Ⓓ attlass
8. Ⓔ cloathez Ⓕ clothez Ⓖ cloathes Ⓗ clothes
9. Ⓐ territory Ⓑ terrtory Ⓒ teritory Ⓓ teritorry
10. Ⓔ parasol Ⓕ parassol Ⓖ parrasol Ⓗ parasoll

11. Ⓐ moretal Ⓑ mortle Ⓒ mortel Ⓓ mortal
12. Ⓔ fuery Ⓕ fury Ⓖ fuiry Ⓗ furey
13. Ⓐ fuirious Ⓑ fureious Ⓒ furious Ⓓ fuerious
14. Ⓔ January Ⓕ Jannuary Ⓖ Januery Ⓗ Januarry
15. Ⓐ Olympicks Ⓑ Olimpics Ⓒ Ollympics Ⓓ Olympics

16. Ⓔ selute Ⓕ salute Ⓖ sallute Ⓗ sellute
17. Ⓐ cicle Ⓑ scycle Ⓒ cycle Ⓓ scicle
18. Ⓔ cyclone Ⓕ ciclone Ⓖ scyclone Ⓗ siclone
19. Ⓐ loonar Ⓑ luner Ⓒ lunear Ⓓ lunar
20. Ⓔ foretune Ⓕ fortune Ⓖ fourtune Ⓗ fortun

Daily Language Activities

Use these activities to reinforce each day's lesson. Write the day's activity on the board, or use **Daily Language Transparency 28.**

DAY 1
Helium is more lighter than air hot-air balloons use helium to fly. Who is the more successful balloonist. (1: is lighter; 2: air. Hot-air; 3: most successful balloonist?)

DAY 2
is our trip today. We don't know nobody who is going. Mr. rico could not be no more helpful. (1: Is; 2: today?; 3: anybody; 4: Rico could not be any more)

DAY 3
We didnt go to the library to get no books. why dont we go now, (1: didn't; 2: get any; 3: Why don't; 4: now?)

DAY 4
Reading four books isnt no problem for george. He love to read Science books. He even learned about jigantic oshun waves. (1: isn't any; 2: George.; 3: loves; 4 science; 4: gigantic ocean)

DAY 5
Jamie spilled sereal on his cloths. He don't never usually do that. Even if he is only a toddler. (1: cereal; 2: clothes.; 3: doesn't usually; 4: that, even)

ELL
Access for All

Use Students' Ideas
Write: *nobody, no one, never, nothing.* Co-construct with students sentences using the words, and explain that they are negative statements. Next write: *anybody, anyone, ever, anything.* Co-construct with students negative statements using the words. Point out and explain double negatives as they arise. This may differ from the student's primary language.

Negatives

LA.5.3.4 Student will edit for language conventions
INTRODUCE NEGATIVES

Present the following:

Access for All

- A negative is a word or a phrase that means *no.*

- Do not use more than one negative in a spoken or written sentence.

- Negatives include words such as *nobody, nothing, never, no one,* and *nowhere,* as well as *no* and *not.*

- Positives include words such as *any, ever, anything, anybody, anyone,* and *anywhere.*

  See Grammar Transparency 136 for modeling and guided practice.

Grammar Practice Book, page 173

- A **negative** is a word that means "no," such as *not, never, nobody, nowhere,* and the contraction *n't.*
- Do not use two negatives in the same sentence.
- You can fix a sentence with two negatives by removing one of the negatives.

Correct the sentences by removing one of the negatives.
1. Some children never not exercise.
   Some children never exercise.
2. Until now, nobody never learned how to sail.
   Until now, nobody learned how to sail.
3. Yesterday she couldn't give no directions to the taxi driver.
   Yesterday she couldn't give directions to the taxi driver.
4. Athletes don't never give up.   Possible response:
   Athletes never give up. Athletes don't give up.
5. Hannah couldn't play on no playgrounds.
   Hannah couldn't play on playgrounds.
6. Nothing nowhere was written in Braille.
   Nothing was written in Braille.
7. The girl had never played with no other kids.
   The girl had never played with other kids.
8. Matthew never had no fun on the swings.   Possible response:
   Matthew never had fun on the swings.
9. Jennifer never forgets no kind words.
   Jennifer never forgets kind words.
10. She can't not stop trying.
    She can't stop trying.

LA.5.3.4 Student will edit for language conventions
REVIEW NEGATIVES

Discuss how to recognize a negative. Ask what words are negatives, how negatives differ from positives, and how many negatives can be used in a sentence.

INTRODUCE NEGATIVE CONTRACTIONS

A negative contraction is made up of a verb combined with the word *not.* An apostrophe shows where a letter or letters have been left out, as in *are not/aren't, have not/haven't, should not/shouldn't. Will not/won't* is an exception.

Do not use another negative in a sentence that contains a negative contraction.

  See Grammar Transparency 137 for modeling and guided practice.

Grammar Practice Book, page 174

- Correct a sentence with two negatives by changing one negative word to a positive word.

Negative	Positive
no, none	any
never	ever
nothing	anything
nobody	anybody
no one	anyone
nowhere	anywhere

Rewrite each sentence, replacing one of the negative words with a positive word.
1. The kids never have nothing bad to say about gym class.
   The kids never have anything bad to say about gym class.
2. No one never passes up a chance to learn kickboxing.
   No one ever passes up a chance to learn kickboxing.
3. No person nowhere should be without a new GPS device.
   No person anywhere should be without a new GPS device.
4. What if you couldn't find nobody to give you directions?
   What if you couldn't find anybody to give you directions?
5. None of the athletes say nothing negative.
   None of the athletes say anything negative.
6. There weren't no playgrounds where she could play.
   There weren't any playgrounds where she could play.

Day 3 — Review and Practice

LA.5.3.4 Student will edit for language conventions

REVIEW NEGATIVE CONTRACTIONS

Review negative contractions.

MECHANICS AND USAGE: CORRECT DOUBLE NEGATIVES

- Do not use two negatives in the same sentence. This is known as a double negative: *I didn't know nobody. I won't never go.*

- Correct a sentence with two negatives by changing one negative to a positive word or by dropping one negative: *I didn't know anybody. I won't ever go.*

See Grammar Transparency 138 for modeling and guided practice.

Grammar Practice Book, page 175

- A **negative** is a word that means "no," such as *not, never, nobody, nowhere,* and the contraction *n't.*
- Do not use two negatives in the same sentence.
- You can fix a sentence with two negatives by removing one of the negatives.
- You can correct a sentence with two negatives by changing one negative to a positive word.

Read each group of sentences. Cross out the sentence that is incorrect.

1. Exercising inside is never as much fun as exercising outside.
   Exercising inside is not as much fun as exercising outside.
   ~~Exercising inside is not never as much fun as exercising outside.~~

2. None of the kids remain active when they become adults.
   ~~No kids never remains active when they become adults.~~
   No kids remain active when they become adults.

3. ~~Carmen never goes nowhere without it.~~
   Carmen never goes anywhere without it.
   Carmen doesn't go anywhere without it.

4. They don't let anything hold them back.
   ~~They don't let nothing hold them back.~~
   They let nothing hold them back.

Read the sentences. Rewrite each sentence two different ways.

5. She couldn't never play in the sandbox.
   Answers may vary. She could never play in the sandbox. She couldn't ever play in the sandbox.

6. The playgrounds didn't have no signs in Braille.
   Answers may vary. The playgrounds didn't have any signs in Braille. The playgrounds had no signs in Braille.

Day 4 — Review and Proofread

LA.5.3.4 Student will edit for language conventions

REVIEW NEGATIVES

Ask students to explain the differences between negatives and positives. Ask students how to avoid double negatives.

PROOFREAD

Have students correct the following.

1. They didn't know nothing about ballooning. (They didn't know anything about ballooning.)

2. We couldn't do nothing. (We couldn't do anything.)

3. We never did nothing more fun. (We never did anything more fun.)

4. The balloon couldn't be no more beautiful. (The balloon couldn't be more beautiful.)

See Grammar Transparency 139 for modeling and guided practice.

Grammar Practice Book, page 176

Read the paragraph below. Rewrite the paragraph correctly on the lines provided.

Thank you, Sara, and good morning, everyone. There aren't no boring sports headlines today! First, the Paralympics began last night. None of the athletes had no trouble showing spirit. The fans, too, never showed nothing but excitement. During the first basketball game, nobody couldn't get no shot past Jennifer Howitt. She didn't defend the basket with no fancy moves—she just played well. Her team had never won no games before last night. They couldn't not be more proud. The players on the other team weren't never sorry that they lost. These Paralympic athletes are not never sore losers. The positive energy at the game was thrilling! And now back to you, Sara, for the day's weather. Responses may vary.

Thank you, Sara, and good morning, everyone. There are no boring sports headlines today! First, the Paralympics began last night. None of the athletes had any trouble showing spirit. The fans, too, never showed anything but excitement. During the first basketball game, nobody could get a shot past Jennifer Howitt. She didn't defend the basket with any fancy moves—she just played well. Her team had never won any games before last night. They couldn't be more proud. The players on the other team weren't sorry that they lost. These Paralympic athletes are never sore losers. The positive energy at the game was thrilling! And now back to you, Sara, for the day's weather.

Day 5 — Assess and Reteach

LA.5.3.4 Student will edit for language conventions

ASSESS

Use the Daily Language Activity and page 177 of the **Grammar Practice Book** for assessment.

RETEACH

Have students work in pairs to write short stories about a town that has become mysteriously deserted. They should use as many negative words as possible, without using double negatives. Have partners trade stories with another pair. Partners then rewrite the stories using positive words in place of negative words.

Use page 178 of the Grammar Practice Book for additional reteaching.

See Grammar Transparency 140 for modeling and guided practice.

Grammar Practice Book, pages 177–178

If the sentence is correct, write correct on the line. If it is not correct, rewrite it correctly. Possible responses below.

1. The classes aren't never boring.
   The classes are never boring.

2. Why can't we sail nowhere today?
   Why can't we sail anywhere today?

3. Nobody never stays active.
   Nobody stays active.

4. Carmen wouldn't walk around her neighborhood none.
   Carmen wouldn't walk around her neighborhood.

5. I've never eaten no Spanish food.
   I've never eaten Spanish food.

6. The guide dog didn't want treats.
   Correct.

7. Isn't no one going to the playground?
   Isn't anyone going to the playground?

8. Matthew has never said nothing about his wheelchair.
   Matthew has never said anything about his wheelchair.

9. No one should never have to wait until high school to go on a swing.
   No one should have to wait until high school to go on a swing.

10. Jennifer has not never been lazy.
    Jennifer has never been lazy.

End-of-Week Assessment

Administer the Test

Weekly Reading Assessment
pages 333–344

ASSESSED SKILLS

- Techniques of Persuasion
- Vocabulary Words
- Context Clues
- Words from Mythology
- Negatives

Progress Reporter
Macmillan/McGraw-Hill

Assessment Tool

Administer the **Weekly Assessment** from the CD-ROM or online.

Weekly Assessment, 333–344

Fluency

Assess fluency for one group of students per week. Use the Oral Fluency Record Sheet to track the number of words read correctly. Fluency goal for all students: **129–149 words correct per minute (WCPM).**

Approaching Level	Weeks 1, 3, 5
On Level	Weeks 2, 4
Beyond Level	Week 6

Fluency Assessment

Alternative Assessments

- **ELL Assessment,** pages 170–171

ELL Assessment, 170–171

Diagnose		Prescribe
	IF...	**THEN...**
VOCABULARY WORDS **VOCABULARY STRATEGY** Context Clues Items 1, 2, 3, 4	0–2 items correct …	Reteach skills using the **Additional Lessons** page T8. Reteach skills: Go to **www.macmillanmh.com** **Vocabulary PuzzleMaker** Evaluate for Intervention.
COMPREHENSION Skill: Techniques of Persuasion Items 5, 6, 7, 8, 9	0–2 items correct …	Reteach Skills using the **Additional Lessons** page T3. Evaluate for Intervention.
SPELLING Words from Mythology Items 10, 11, 12	0–1 items correct …	Reteach skills: Go to **www.macmillanmh.com**
GRAMMAR Negatives Items 13, 14, 15	0–1 items correct …	Reteach skills: **Grammar Practice Book** page 178.
FLUENCY	120–128 WCPM	Fluency Solutions
	0–110 WCPM	Evaluate for Intervention.

READING
Triumphs
AN INTERVENTION PROGRAM

Also Available

To place students in the Intervention Program, use the **Diagnostic Assessment** in the Intervention Teacher's Edition.

A Dream Comes True

709L

Constructive Feedback

If students fail to understand the relationship between the myth and the word, say:

When the Trojan war ended, Odysseus tried to go home. Unfortunately, because he had angered one of the gods, he spent ten years traveling the world before he finally reached home. Now, English speakers use the word *odyssey* to describe any extended wandering or journey.

Repeat as needed with other words from mythology.

Additional Resources

Use your observations to help identify students who might benefit from additional instruction. See page T2 for comprehension support and page T5 for vocabulary support. For each skill below, additional lessons are provided. You can use these lessons on consecutive days after teaching the lessons presented within the week.
• Persuasion, T2
• Context Clues, T5

Decodable Text

To help students build speed and accuracy with reading multisyllabic words, use additional decodable text on pages 34–35 of the **Teachers' Resource Book.**

Skills Focus ▶ Phonics

Objectives   Review words from mythology

Decode multisyllabic words from mythology in both familiar and unfamiliar texts

Materials   • **Student Book** *The New Gym, Satellite Guidance for the Blind,* and *The Second Olympics*

WORDS FROM MYTHOLOGY

LA.5.1.6.10 Determine etymologies using a dictionary

Model/Guided Practice

■ Write *arachnid* on the board. *Say the word with me:* arachnid.

■ Explain that *arachnid*, which describes spiders, scorpions, mites, and ticks, comes from the Greek myth about Arachne, who brags that she is a better weaver than the goddess Athena. This boast angers Athena, who turns Arachne into a spider, sentencing her to weave forever.

■ *Let's check another origin.* Write *odyssey* on the board. An odyssey *is an "extended wandering or journey." Use a dictionary to learn its mythological origin.* Next use *flora* and *museum* as other words that come from myths.

■ Extend the review to allow students to read a version of the myth about Arachne or another myth.

MULTISYLLABIC WORDS FROM MYTHOLOGY

LA.5.1.4.3 Use language structure to read multi-syllabic words

■ Write *labyrinth* on the board. Break the word into syllables: *lab/y/rinth*. Explain that a labyrinth is a maze. The word comes from the Greek myth in which Daedalus builds a labyrinth for King Minos to house the Minotaur. Blend the syllables: /lab ə rinth/. *Say the word with me:* labyrinth.

■ Have pairs of students decode other longer words from mythology. Write the following words on the board or provide copies of the list. *With your partner, choose a word. Say the word aloud. Consult a dictionary or an encyclopedia to learn the word's mythological origin.*

ambrosia	lunar	nectar
calypso	martial	siren
chronology	mercurial	tantalize
Herculean	narcissism	zephyr

MYTH SEARCH: WORDS FROM MYTHOLOGY IN CONTEXT

LA.5.1.6.10 Determine etymologies using a dictionary.

LA.5.6.4 Student develops technology skills

■ Have students search *The New Gym, Satellite Guidance for the Blind,* and *The Second Olympics* for words from mythology. Have students consult dictionaries or thesauruses to explain the mythological origins of *martial* and *Olympics*.

■ To extend the activity, have each student search a library database or the Internet to locate a myth about Mt. Olympus, or have students write their own myths, incorporating at least five words from mythology.

Skills Focus ▶ Fluency

Objective Read with increasing prosody and accuracy at a rate of 129–139 WCPM

Materials • **Approaching Practice Book A,** page 203

MODEL EXPRESSIVE READING

LA.5.1.5
Student demonstrates ability to read orally with accuracy

Model reading the Fluency passage in **Practice Book A,** page 203. Tell students to pay close attention to your pronunciation of difficult or unfamiliar words. Then read aloud one sentence at a time and have students repeat the sentence, first as a class and then one by one. As students read, listen carefully for accuracy.

REPEATED READING

LA.5.1.5
Student demonstrates ability to read orally

Have students continue to practice reading the passage aloud as you circulate and provide constructive feedback. During independent reading time, student partners can take turns reading the passage. One partner reads each sentence aloud, and the other repeats it. Remind students to wait until their partners reach end marks before correcting mistakes.

TIMED READING

LA.5.1.5
Student demonstrates ability to read orally with appropriate rate

Tell students they will do a timed reading of the passage that they have been practicing. With each student:

- Place the passage from **Practice Book A,** page 203, face down.
- When you say "Go," the student begins reading the passage aloud.
- When you say "Stop," the student stops reading the passage.

As students read, note any miscues. Stop students after one minute. Help them record and graph the number of words they read correctly.

Skills Focus ▶ Vocabulary

Objective Apply vocabulary word meanings

Materials • **Vocabulary Cards** • **Transparency 28**

VOCABULARY WORDS

LA.5.1.6.1
Use new vocabulary

Display the **Vocabulary Cards** for this week's words: *elementary, physical, rigid, interact, wheelchair.* Help students locate and read these words on **Transparency 28.** Review each word's meaning. Invite students to use the vocabulary words to write personal responses to *The New Gym.*

elementary **physical** **rigid** **interact** **wheelchair**

⭐ **Approaching Practice Book A,** page 203

As I read, I will pay attention to pronunciation.

	Growing up, Brian was very shy. He had a hard time
11	interacting with other people.
15	Then Brian got involved in Special Olympics when he
24	was 14. His first event was a swimming race. "And he
34	got a medal," Brian's mom said. "He was a winner for
45	the first time in his life. Suddenly, Brian felt just as good as
58	his brothers. From that moment on, he became a different
68	person. He walked to school with his head held high. He
79	stopped hiding and began to talk. It was a real miracle."
90	Brian's success inspired his mother. She wanted to battle
99	her own disability. On his eighteenth birthday, Brian won his
109	first gold medal. People cheered. Someone began to sing
118	"Happy Birthday" over the loudspeaker. The crowd joined in.
127	Lorraine Loeb stood up from her **wheelchair** to sing
136	along. "It was the first time in 18 years that I stood alone,"
148	she said. 150

Comprehension Check

1. How did Brian change when he got involved with Special Olympics? **Main Idea and Details** He held his head high, stopped hiding, and began to talk.
2. How did Brian's success inspire his mother? **Plot Development** She was inspired to overcome her own disability.

	Words Read	–	Number of Errors	=	Words Correct Score
First Read		–		=	
Second Read		–		=	

Small Group

Vocabulary

Review last week's words: **(guaranteed, supervise, frustrated, coordination, ease, scenery, bundle, fused)** and this week's words **(elementary, physical, rigid, interact, wheelchair)**. Have students write a sentence for each word.

Student Book

ELL

Access for All

Persuasive Techniques Select a typical situation and discuss what you would say in order to borrow something or to invite someone to a party or to ask for an explanation.

Skills Focus

Vocabulary

Objective	Review context clues
Materials	• **Student Book** *A Dream Comes True*

FCAT **CONTEXT CLUES: SURROUNDING SENTENCES AND PARAGRAPHS**

LA.5.1.6.3 Use context clues to figure out meanings of unfamiliar words

Remind students that context clues are clues within the text that help a reader figure out what a word means. Invite students to find context clues for vocabulary words. Then ask students to write their own "context clue" sentences. For example: *Students sat rigid in their chairs as they waited nervously to begin the test.* Identify and discuss the context clues in their sentences. Categorize the clues as synonyms, antonyms, examples, etc.

Skills Focus

Comprehension

Objective	Review how to identify persuasion
Materials	• **Student Book** *The New Gym*
	• **Transparency 28**

STRATEGY
MONITOR COMPREHENSION

LA.5.1.7 Use strategies to comprehend text

Review with students that readers can monitor their comprehension of a selection by summarizing, asking questions, or rereading.

FCAT

SKILL
TECHNIQUES OF PERSUASION

LA.5.1.7.2 Identify how author's perspective influences text

■ Persuasion is a way of convincing others to believe in something or to think about a subject in a particular way.

■ Techniques of persuasion that authors use include glittering generalities, bandwagon, supporting an opinion with facts, using loaded words that appeal to readers' emotions, and presenting quotations from experts or the personal stories of people who support a specific point of view.

Explain/Model

Display **Transparency 28.** Reread the first two paragraphs of *The New Gym.* Ask a volunteer to circle words and phrases that lead him or her to think positively about the new physical education movement.

Practice/Apply

Reread *The New Gym* with students and discuss the following questions:

■ How does the author feel about the new physical education movement? How does the author support this opinion?

■ How do you think the new physical education movement will persuade kids to be more active? Explain.

Leveled Reader Lesson

Objective   Read to apply strategies and skills

Materials   • **Leveled Reader** *Everybody's a Star*

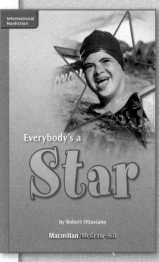

Informational Nonfiction

Everybody's a

Star

by Robert Ottaviano

Macmillan/McGraw-Hill

Leveled Reader

PREVIEW AND PREDICT

LA.5.1.7.1
Establish purpose for reading

Discuss the cover and ask students to preview and skim the photos, table of contents, and first two chapters. Have students make predictions about the selection and the author's opinions about the Special Olympics. Tell students to note any questions they have.

VOCABULARY WORDS

LA.5.1.6.3
Use context clues

Review vocabulary words as necessary. As you read together, stop to discuss how each word is used in context.

STRATEGY
MONITOR COMPREHENSION

LA.5.1.7
Student uses strategies to comprehend text

Remind students to stop regularly and check that they understand what they're reading. If students have trouble, they can generate questions, summarize certain passages, or reread confusing parts of the text.

FCAT

SKILL
TECHNIQUES OF PERSUASION

LA.5.1.7.2
Identify how author's perspective influences text

Remind students to identify the author's purpose for writing and his techniques of persuasion as they read *The Special Olympics Story*.

Think Aloud In the first chapter, I learn that the author believes the Special Olympics are important because the athletic events help people with disabilities improve their health and confidence. The author tells the stories of Tomas Murray and Brian Loeb to support his opinion. I'll record this information on a Fact and Opinion Chart to show that the author persuades readers by using both facts and opinions.

READ AND RESPOND

Tell students to finish reading the introduction and first two chapters. Monitor comprehension by asking students to summarize what they read. Discuss their thoughts about the Special Olympics and the Shriver family.

MAKE CONNECTIONS ACROSS TEXTS

LA.5.1.7.7
Compare and contrast elements in multiple texts

Invite students to compare *The Special Olympics Story* and *A Dream Comes True*.

- How are people with disabilities presented in these selections?

- What do the authors of the two selections want to persuade readers to believe about people with disabilities? Which selection do you find more persuasive? Explain your answer.

ELL   Access for All

Multiple-Meaning Words
Discuss the meaning of the word *star* as applied to an athlete or other celebrity. List the qualities of a star in the sky. Have students compare these qualities to the use of the word *star* as it describes Olympic athletes.

THE NEW GYM

Student Book

Skills Focus ▶ Vocabulary

Objective   Review vocabulary words

Materials   • **Vocabulary Cards**

           • **Student Book** *The New Gym, Satellite Guidance for the Blind,* and *The Second Olympics*

✔ VOCABULARY WORDS

LA.5.1.6
Student uses multiple strategies to develop vocabulary

Organize the class into small groups. Invite a member from one group to choose a Vocabulary Card and to draw a picture on the board that represents the word. For example, a student may draw a picture of a circle below a chair for *wheelchair*. Then invite the other groups to guess the word that the drawing illustrates. The group that correctly guesses the word takes the next turn.

FCAT CONTEXT CLUES: SURROUNDING SENTENCES AND PARAGRAPHS

LA.5.1.6.3
Use context clues

Have students find three vocabulary words in *The New Gym, Satellite Guidance for the Blind,* and *The Second Olympics* and identify the context clues that surround each word.

Skills Focus ▶ Text Features

Objective   Review everyday communications

Materials   • Samples of various forms, advertisements, brochures, and newsletters

✔ EVERYDAY COMMUNICATIONS

Define forms and describe their uses. Define and describe the uses of advertisements, brochures, and newsletters. Display one of each type at a time, and have students identify which type of everyday communication it is.

On Level Practice Book O, page 203

As I read, I will pay attention to punctuation and pronunciation.

     Wheelchair basketball is probably the oldest competitive
7   wheelchair sport. It began after World War II as a way to get
19   disabled veterans active. Now children ages 6 and up are
28   playing wheelchair basketball in gyms everywhere. They
35   play on the same size court and use most of the same rules as
49   their classmates. And they're getting a lot of exercise, too.
59   Only a few rules are adapted in wheelchair basketball.
68   For example, if a player takes more than two pushes of the
80   wheelchair while dribbling, a traveling penalty is called. Even
89   if only the wheel of a player's wheelchair goes out of bounds,
101   the player is out of bounds. A player who lifts out of his or her
116   seat to get a **physical** advantage gets charged with a foul. So
128   does a player whose feet touch the floor.
136   Like wheelchair hockey, each wheelchair basketball player
143   is classified according to his or her ability level.
152   Wheelchair basketball, like wheelchair hockey, takes
158   coordination. Players must use their hands to move their
167   wheelchairs. At the same time, they must be able to handle
178   the ball. 180

Comprehension Check

1. Why does wheelchair basketball take coordination? **Main Idea and Details**
   Players must move their wheelchairs and dribble at the same time.
2. Why are sports adapted for wheelchairs? **Cause and Effect**
   It gives everyone a chance to play.

	Words Read	−	Number of Errors	=	Words Correct Score
First Read		−		=	
Second Read		−		=	

Skills Focus ▶ Fluency

Objective   Read fluently with accuracy at a rate of 129–149 WCPM

Materials   • **On Level Practice Book O,** p. 203

REPEATED READING

LA.5.1.5
Read orally with appropriate rate

Model reading aloud the Fluency passage on page 203 of **Practice Book O.** Emphasize to students that slowly breaking unfamiliar words into syllables helps them pronounce the words correctly. Then read one sentence at a time, and have students read each sentence back chorally. Listen for accuracy.

Timed Reading   Have students read the passage and record their reading rate.

Leveled Reader Lesson

Objective Read to apply strategies and skills

Materials • **Leveled Reader** *Everybody's a Star*

PREVIEW AND PREDICT

LA.5.1.7.1
Use prior knowledge to make and confirm predictions

Have students preview *Everybody's a Star*.

■ What does the title suggest about the selection?

■ What is the author trying to persuade you to believe about adaptive sports?

Encourage students to generate their own questions as purposes for reading.

FCAT

SKILL
TECHNIQUES OF PERSUASION

LA.5.1.7.2
Identify how author's perspective influences text

Review: Authors use persuasion techniques, such as loaded words or glittering generalities, in order to convince readers to agree with an opinion or a point of view. Good readers recognize and evaluate an author's use of these techniques to determine whether the author's opinion is supported by facts.

READ AND RESPOND

Read the first two pages of *Everybody's a Star*. Pause to discuss with students the author's opinion of adaptive sports and the persuasive techniques he uses.

VOCABULARY WORDS

LA.5.1.6.3
Use context clues to determine meanings

After students read *Everybody's a Star*, ask them to point out the vocabulary words. Discuss how each word is used in context. Ask questions such as: *Why would rigid physical exercise not be appropriate for elementary school students?*

MAKE CONNECTIONS ACROSS TEXTS

LA.5.1.7.7
Compare and contrast elements in multiple texts

Invite students to name and evaluate persuasion techniques that the authors use in *Everybody's a Star*, *The New Gym*, and *A Dream Comes True*.

■ How are the techniques similar, and how are they different?

■ Which selection do you find the most persuasive? Explain your answer.

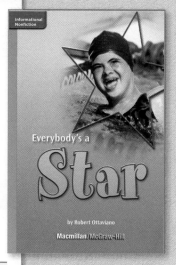

Leveled Reader

ELL
Leveled Reader
Go to pages
709U–709V.

Skills Focus ▶ Vocabulary

Objective   Use vocabulary words in descriptions

EXTEND VOCABULARY

LA.5.1.6.1
Use new vocabulary

Have students design a computer classroom or a gym that could be used by students with various levels of ability. Student designers can draw floor plans and label the equipment they envision and then use the vocabulary words in written descriptions of their plans.

Skills Focus ▶ Text Features

Objective   Analyze types of everyday communication

Materials   • Newspaper or magazine advertisements

EVERYDAY COMMUNICATIONS

LA.5.6.3.1
Examine how ideas are presented in print media

Review ways in which people communicate in any of the week's texts. Discuss with students how the texts might be different if the information were communicated in another manner.

LA.5.2.2.4
Understand characteristics of types of text

LA.5.6.2.2
Examine several sources of information

Challenge students to brainstorm different ways people communicate information. Explore how information is relayed in ads, consumer materials, brochures, newsletters, forms, and directions. Next, distribute advertisements to student groups and have each write a brochure or newspaper article based on the product information in the ad.

Skills Focus ▶ Fluency

Objective   Read fluently with accuracy at a rate of 139–149 WCPM

Materials   • **Beyond Practice Book B,** page 203

REPEATED READING

LA.5.1.5
Student demonstrates ability to read orally

Model reading aloud the Fluency passage on page 203 of **Practice Book B.** Emphasize that breaking unfamiliar words into syllables helps students pronounce the words correctly. Then read one sentence at a time and have students read each sentence back chorally.

LA.5.1.5
Read orally with appropriate rate

As an extension, have students practice reading the passages without any punctuation. Then have them implement the punctuation marks. Finally, allow them to tape both versions to note differences and offer critiques.

ELL   Access for All

Meta Language One way people communicate is through gestures and body language. Give two or three examples of gestures used in the United States to express not knowing, frustration, and approval. An example of approval could be an okay sign, a thumbs-up sign, or a nod of the head.

◆ **Beyond Practice Book B,** page 203

As I read, I will pay attention to pronunciation.

	At the age of two, Anne contracted an eye disease called trachoma.
12	By age five she was nearly blind. Anne's mother died when she was
25	nine. After her father left the family, Anne and her young brother
37	Jimmie were brought to the Tewksbury orphanage. It was a large and
49	dreary building. Jimmie died there, and Anne who was only 10, was
60	left alone in the world.
65	But when Anne, known as Annie, turned 14, things began to get
76	better for her. Annie pleaded to go to school. She wanted to learn.
89	One man listened to her.
94	Impressed by Annie's plea, the Boston philanthropist R.F. Sanborn
102	arranged for her to go to the Perkins Institution, a school for the
115	blind. At the school, Annie befriended Laura Bridgman. Laura had
125	become famous because she was able to communicate even
134	though she was deaf and blind. Many people visited the school to see
147	the remarkable young woman. Annie learned to sign so that the two
159	could **interact**. At first Annie hated the **rigid** rules of the school, but
172	she loved to learn. By the time she finished school, Annie was
184	number one in her class. 189

Comprehension Check

1. What challenges did Annie experience in her early life? **Plot Development**
   She was nearly blind by age 5. Her mother died; her father left the family.

2. How did Annie's life change when she turned 14? **Plot Development**
   Annie got the chance to attend school.

	Words Read	–	Number of Errors	=	Words Correct Score
First Read		–		=	
Second Read		–		=	

Leveled Reader Lesson

Objective	Read to apply strategies and skills
Materials	• **Leveled Reader** *Everybody's a Star*
	• **Student Book** *A Dream Comes True*

Leveled Reader

PREVIEW AND PREDICT

LA.5.1.7.1
Establish purpose for reading

Have students preview *Everybody's a Star* predict what it is about, and set purposes for reading.

VOCABULARY WORDS

LA.5.1.6.3
Use context clues

Review vocabulary words as necessary. Ask students questions such as, *Which is a physical activity, watching a movie or running? How can you interact with someone in a wheelchair?* Have students respond in kind.

FCAT **SKILL**

TECHNIQUES OF PERSUASION

LA.5.1.7.2
Identify how author's perspective influences text

Ask a volunteer to define the term *persuasion* and to explain various techniques authors use to persuade readers of an opinion or a point of view. Explain that students will read *Everybody's a Star* together. Tell students to pay attention to persuasive language in the text.

READ AND RESPOND

Discuss whether the text is informational or persuasive based on the author's purpose. Students should identify different techniques of persuasion in the text.

Self-Selected Reading

Objective	Read independently to analyze techniques of persuasion and make connections across texts
Materials	• Leveled Readers or trade books at students' reading levels

FCAT **READ TO IDENTIFY TECHNIQUES OF PERSUASION**

LA.5.1.7.7
Compare and contrast elements in multiple texts

Invite students to summarize and evaluate *Everybody's a Star* and *A Dream Comes True*. Ask students why they think personal stories are used in these selections. Discuss why personal stories can be more persuasive than facts and numbers. Ask students which of the personal stories in the selections they find most persuasive, and have them explain their answers.

Next, invite students to choose books for independent reading. After reading, have students identify any persuasive techniques used by the authors of their chosen texts. Discuss whether the persuasive techniques were successful and why.

English Language Learners

Academic Language

Throughout the week the English language learners in your class will need help building their understanding of the academic language used in daily instruction and assessment instruments. The following strategies will help increase their language proficiency and comprehension of content and instructional words.

Technology

Oral Language For oral vocabulary development go to www.macmillanmh.com

Strategies to Reinforce Academic Language

- **Use Context** Academic language used by the teacher (see chart below) should be explained in the context of the task during Whole Group. You may use gestures, expressions, and visuals to support meaning.

- **Use Visuals** Use charts, transparencies, and graphic organizers to explain key labels to help students understand classroom language.

- **Model** Demonstrate the task using academic language in order for students to understand instruction.

Academic Language Used in Whole Group Instruction

Content/Theme Words	Skill/Strategy Words	Writing/Grammar Words
Special Olympics (p. 698)	monitor comprehension (p. 701A)	biography (p. 709A)
disabilities (p. 698)	persuasion (p. 701A)	negatives (p. 709I)
physical fitness (p. 698)	convincing (p. 702)	positives (p. 709I)
wheelchair (p. 702)		negative contractions (p. 709I)
abilities (p. 703)		double negatives (p. 709J)
physical (p. 704)		

ELL Leveled Reader Lesson

Informational Nonfiction

The **Special Olympics** Story

by Robert Ottaviano

Macmillan/McGraw-Hill

 ## Before Reading

DEVELOP ORAL LANGUAGE

 LOG ON **Build Background** *What sports do you play or watch? Why do people like sports?* List the sports and discuss reasons people like them.

Review Vocabulary Write the vocabulary and story support words on the board and discuss their meanings. Model using them in sentences. Physical *activities are activities we do with our bodies. In baseball, the players* interact *with each other.*

PREVIEW AND PREDICT

Point to the cover illustration and read the title aloud. *What do you notice about this person? What do you think you will learn in this book?*

 FCAT **Set a Purpose for Reading** Show the Fact and Opinion Chart and remind students they have used it before. Ask them to use a similar chart as they identify facts and opinions in this book.

 ## During Reading

Choose from among the differentiated strategies to support students' reading at all levels of language acquisition.

Beginning	Intermediate	Advanced
Shared Reading As you read, model identifying facts and opinions. Check students' comprehension and use vocabulary and support words: *Give me an example of a rule that is used in* physical *education? Is this a fact or an opinion?*	**Read Together** Read through Chapter 1. Ask students to identify facts and opinions about the Special Olympics. Have them continue to read with a partner, and take turns to identify facts and opinions about the sports and the players described.	**Independent Reading** Have students read the book. As they read, ask them to fill in their charts with a partner, taking turns to identify facts and opinions. Have them discuss how the community can get more involved in promoting sports for people with disabilities.

 ## After Reading

Remind students to use the vocabulary and story words in their whole group activities. Have them complete the Comprehension Check questions.

Objective
- **To apply vocabulary and comprehension skills**

Materials
- **ELL Leveled Reader**

5-Day Planner

DAY 1	• Academic Language
	• Oral Language and Vocabulary Review
DAY 2	• Academic Language
	• ELL Leveled Reader
DAY 3	• Academic Language
	• ELL Leveled Reader
DAY 4	• Academic Language
	• ELL Leveled Reader
DAY 5	• Academic Language
	• ELL Leveled Reader Comprehension Check and Literacy Activities

Grade 5 • ELL TEACHER'S GUIDE

English Language Learners

FLORIDA Treasures

Macmillan/McGraw-Hill

ELL Teacher's Guide for students who need additional instruction

Student Book Selections

Week At A Glance

Whole Group

 VOCABULARY
launched, particles, dense, inflate, anchored, companion, hydrogen, scientific

 FCAT Word Parts: Greek Roots

COMPREHENSION
Strategy: Monitor Comprehension
FCAT Skill: Relevant Facts and Details

WRITING
FCAT Persuasive Essay

FCAT Science
The Nature of Science

Small Group Options

Differentiated Instruction for Tested Skills

 **FCAT** Tested FCAT Benchmark
Tested Skill for the Week
Sunshine State Standard
FCAT FCAT Benchmark

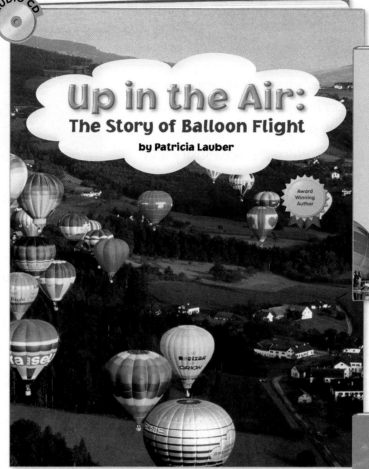

Up in the Air: The Story of Balloon Flight
by Patricia Lauber

 Science Link
Main Selection
Genre Nonfiction

The Science of Hot-Air Balloons
by Enriquez Mera

Vocabulary/ Comprehension

Hot-Air Balloon Haiku
by Rita Bristol

Genre Poetry (Haiku)

Read-Aloud Anthology
• Listening Comprehension
• Readers' Theatre

Resources for **Differentiated Instruction**

FCAT LEVELED READERS: Science
GR Levels S–Y

Genre Informational Nonfiction

- **Same Theme**
- **Same Vocabulary**
- **Same Comprehension Skills**

Approaching Level | **On Level** | **Beyond Level**

English Language Leveled Reader

Sheltered Readers for English Language Learners

ELL Teacher's Guide also available

LEVELED PRACTICE

Approaching | **On Level** | **Beyond** | **ELL**

INTERVENTION PROGRAM

- Phonics and Decoding
- Comprehension
- Vocabulary

Also available, *Reading Triumphs*, Intervention Program

CLASSROOM LIBRARY

Genre Realistic Fiction

Approaching | **On Level** | **Beyond**

Trade books to apply Comprehension Skills

FCAT Success!

- **FCAT Edition**
- **Content Area Reading**

  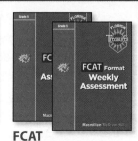

FCAT Test Preparation and Practice

FCAT Benchmark Assessments

FCAT Unit and Weekly Assessments

HOME-SCHOOL CONNECTION

- Family letters in English, Spanish, and Haitian Creole
- Take-Home Stories

FLORIDA Suggested Lesson Plan

CD ROM **Instructional Navigator** Interactive Lesson Planner

Up in the Air: The Story of Balloon Flight, 714–729

Integrated **ELL** Support Every Day

Whole Group

ORAL LANGUAGE
- **Listening**
- **Speaking**
- **Viewing**

WORD STUDY
- **Vocabulary**

- **Phonics/Decoding**

READING
- **Develop Comprehension**

- **Fluency**

LANGUAGE ARTS
- **Writing**

- **Grammar**

- **Spelling**

ASSESSMENT
- **Informal/Formal**

Day 1

Listening/Speaking/Viewing
❓ **Focus Question** Why do you think people still like to go up in hot-air balloons? LA.5.5.2

Build Background, 710
Read Aloud: "The Montgolfier Brothers," 711

Vocabulary LA.5.1.6.1
FCAT *launched, particles, dense, inflate, anchored, companion, hydrogen, scientific,* 712
Practice Book A-O-B, 207
FCAT Strategy: Word Parts: Greek Roots, 713

Read "The Science of Hot-Air Balloons," 712–713 LA.5.1.6.1

Comprehension, 713A–713B
Strategy: Monitor Comprehension
FCAT Skill: Relevant Facts and Details LA.5.1.7.3
Practice Book A-O-B, 208

Fluency Partner Reading, 710I LA.5.1.5
Model Fluency, 711

FCAT Writing
Daily Writing: Suppose you could fly like a bird. Describe the details of your flight including your destination and how you felt.
Persuasive Essay, 735A

Grammar Daily Language Activities, 735I
Prepositions and Prepositional Phrases, 735I
Grammar Practice Book, 179

Spelling Pretest, 735G
Spelling Practice Book, 179–180 LA.5.1.4.1

Quick Check Vocabulary, 712
Comprehension, 713B

Differentiated Instruction 735M–735V

Day 2

Listening/Speaking
❓ **Focus Question** How has the invention of ballooning been useful? LA. 5.5.2.1

Vocabulary LA.5.1.6.3
Review Vocabulary Words, 714

Phonics LA.5.1.4
Number Prefixes, 735E
Practice Book A-O-B, 213

Read *Up in the Air: The Story of Balloon Flight,* 714–729

Comprehension, 714–729
Strategy: Monitor Comprehension
FCAT Skill: Relevant Facts and Details LA.5.1.7.3
Practice Book A-O-B, 209

Fluency Partner Reading, 710I LA.5.1.5

FCAT Writing
Daily Writing: Suppose you are one of the people who helped make balloon flight possible. Write a letter to a friend explaining why your work is important.
Persuasive Essay, 735A

Grammar Daily Language Activities, 735I
Prepositions and Prepositional Phrases, 735I
Grammar Practice Book, 180

Spelling Number Prefixes, 735G
Spelling Practice Book, 181 LA.5.1.4.1

Quick Check Comprehension: 721, 729
Phonics, 735E

Differentiated Instruction 735M–735V

Turn the Page for
Small Group Lesson Plan

Benchmarks

FCAT

Vocabulary	**Comprehension**	**Writing**	**Science**
Vocabulary Words **Word Parts/Greek Roots** LA.5.1.6.11 Use roots and affixes derived from Greek to determine meaning	**Strategy: Monitor Comprehension** **Skill: Relevant Facts and Details** LA.5.1.7.3 Determine main idea through relevant details	**Persuasive/Persuasive Essay** LA.5.4.3 Develop and demonstrate persuasive writing	**The Nature of Science** SC.H.3.2.1 Understand that people invent new tools to solve problems and do work

Turn the Page for **Small Group Options**

Day 3

Listening/Speaking

❓ Focus Question Compare and contrast the different ways hot-air balloons are able to fly. Use details from each story in your answer.

Summarize, 731 LA.5.5.2.1

Vocabulary LA.5.1.6.3

Review Words in Context, 735C
Strategy: Word Parts: Greek Roots, 735D
Practice Book A-O-B, 212
Phonics Decode Multisyllabic Words LA.5.1.4

Read *Up in the Air: The The Story of Balloon Flight,* 714–729

Student Book

Comprehension

✔ Comprehension Check, 731
FCAT **Maintain Skill:** Chronological Order, 731B

Fluency Repeated Reading, 731A
Partner Reading, 710I LA.5.1.5
Practice Book A-O-B, 210

FCAT Writing

Daily Writing: Prepare a dialogue between a mother goose and her young. All are flying in formation and have seen a balloon for the first time.
Writer's Craft: Organize Ideas, 735A LA.5.4.4
Persuasive Essay, 735B

Grammar Daily Language Activities, 735I
Commas with Phrases, Appositives, 735J
Grammar Practice Book, 181

Spelling Number Prefixes, 735H
Spelling Practice Book, 182 LA.5.1.4.1

Quick Check Fluency, 731A

Differentiated Instruction 735M–735V

Day 4

Listening/Speaking/Viewing

❓ Focus Question What is the difference between information in the haiku and the information presented in *Up in the Air: A Balloon's Flight?* LA.5.5.2
Media Literacy, 727
Expand Vocabulary: Balloon Flight, 735F

Vocabulary LA.5.1.6

Greek Roots, 735F
Apply Vocabulary to Writing, 735F

Read "Hot-Air Balloon Haiku," 732–733

Student Book

Comprehension

✔ Poetry: Haiku
FCAT Simile and Metaphor, 732
Practice Book A-O-B, 211

Fluency Partner Reading, 710I LA.5.1.5

FCAT Writing

Daily Writing: Design a postal stamp celebrating balloon flight. Write a note to a friend explaining your design.
Writing Trait: Ideas and Content, 735B
Persuasive Essay, 735B LA.5.4.4

Grammar Daily Language Activities, 735I
Prepositions and Prepositional Phrases, 735J
Grammar Practice Book, 182

Spelling Number Prefixes, 735H
Spelling Practice Book, 183 LA.5.1.4.1

Quick Check Vocabulary, 735D

Differentiated Instruction 735M–735V

Day 5

Review and Assess

Listening/Speaking/Viewing

❓ Focus Question Would you like to learn how to fly a hot-air balloon? What generalizations can you make to explain your answer? LA.5.5.2.1
Speaking and Listening Strategies, 735A
Present Explanatory Essay, 735B

✔ Vocabulary LA.5.1.6

Spiral Review: Vocabulary Game, 735F

Read Self-Selected Reading, 710I LA.5.2.2.5

Student Book

✔ Comprehension

Connect and Compare, 733
LA.5.2.1.5

✔ Fluency Partner Reading, 710I LA.5.1.5
Practice, 731A

FCAT Writing

Daily Writing: If you were traveling in a hot-air balloon near where you live, describe what you would see.
Persuasive Essay, 735B

Grammar Daily Language Activities, 735I
✔ Prepositions and Prepositional Phrases, 735J
Grammar Practice Book, 183–184

✔ **Spelling** Posttest, 735H
Spelling Practice Book, 184 LA.5.1.4.1

FCAT **Weekly Assessment, 345–356**

Differentiated Instruction 735M–735V

Differentiated Instruction

What do I do in small groups?

Teacher-Led Small Groups

Literacy Workstations

Independent Activities

Focus on Skills

 Skills Focus Use your **Quick Check** observations to guide additional instruction and practice.

Phonics
Number Prefixes

 Vocabulary
Words: inflate, launched, hydrogen, anchored, companion, scientific, particles, dense
FCAT **Strategy:** Word Parts/Greek Roots

Comprehension
Strategy: Monitor Comprehension
FCAT **Skill:** Relevant Facts and Details

FCAT **Fluency**

Suggested Lesson Plan

CD ROM **Instructional Navigator** Interactive Lesson Planner

	DAY 1	DAY 2
Approaching Level • **Additional Instruction/Practice** • **Tier 2 Instruction**	Fluency, 735N Vocabulary, 735N Comprehension, 735O	Phonics, 735M Vocabulary, 735O Leveled Reader Lesson, 735P • Vocabulary • Comprehension
On Level • **Practice**	Vocabulary, 735Q Leveled Reader Lesson, 735R • Comprehension **ELL** Leveled Reader, 735U–735V	Leveled Reader Lesson, 735R • Comprehension • Vocabulary
Beyond Level • **Extend**	Vocabulary, 735S Leveled Reader Lesson, 735T • Comprehension	Leveled Reader Lesson, 735T • Comprehension • Vocabulary

For intensive intervention see **READING Triumphs**
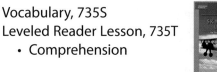

Small Group Options

Focus on Leveled Readers

Apply FCAT skills and strategies while reading appropriate leveled books.

Levels S–Y

Approaching

On Level

Beyond

ELL

Additional Leveled Reader Resources

Leveled Reader Database
Go to **www.macmillanmh.com**

Search by
- Comprehension Skill
- Content Area
- Genre
- Text Feature
- Guided Reading Level
- Reading Recovery Level
- Lexile Score
- Benchmark Level

Subscription also available.

Focus on Science
Teacher's Annotated Edition

Nature of Science
SC.H.3.2.1. Tools solve problems

Additional Leveled Readers
Airships: Sailors of the Skies
Up, Up, and Away: Science in the Sky

Day 3

Phonics, 735M
Fluency, 735N
Vocabulary, 735O
Leveled Reader Lesson, 735P
- Comprehension

Fluency, 735Q
Vocabulary, 735Q
Leveled Reader Lesson, 735R
- Comprehension

Fluency, 735S
Vocabulary, 735S
Leveled Reader Lesson, 735T
- Comprehension

Day 4

Phonics, 735M
Leveled Reader Lesson, 735P
- Comprehension
- **ELL** Skill: Relevant Facts and Details

Literary Elements, 735Q
Leveled Reader Lesson, 735R
- Comprehension

Literary Elements, 735S
Leveled Reader Lesson, 735T
- Comprehension
- **ELL** Use a Frame, 735S

Day 5

Fluency, 735N
Leveled Reader Lesson, 735P
- Make Connections Across Texts

Fluency, 735Q
Leveled Reader Lesson, 735R
- Make Connections Across Texts

Fluency, 735S
Self-Selected Reading, 735T

Managing the Class

What do I do with the rest of my class?

Teacher-Led Small Groups

Literacy Workstations

Independent Activities

Class Management Tools

My To-Do List

✓ Put a check next to the activities you complete.

Reading	Word Study
☐ Practice fluency	☐ Work with number prefixes
☐ Choose a book to read	☐ Use words with Greek roots

Writing	Science
☐ Write an explanation	☐ Research weather balloons
☐ Write a vivid description	☐ Make generalizations about weather balloons

Social Studies	Leveled Readers
☐ Research how hot-air balloons have changed history	☐ Write About It!
☐ Create a time line	☐ Content Connection

Technology	Independent Practice
☐ Vocabulary Puzzlemaker	☐ Practice Book, 207–213
☐ Fluency Solutions	☐ Grammar Practice Book, 179–184
☐ Listening Library	☐ Spelling Practice Book, 179–184
☐ www.macmillanmh.com	

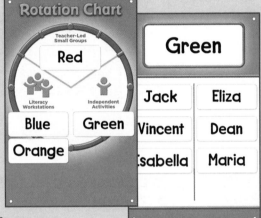

Rotation Chart

Teacher-Led Small Groups — **Red**

Literacy Workstations — Independent Activities

Blue   **Green**

Orange

Green

Jack	Eliza
Vincent	Dean
Isabella	Maria

Includes:
- How-to Guide • Rotation Chart • Weekly Contracts

FOLDABLES™

Hands-on activities for reinforcing weekly skills

Dinah Zike's Foldables

3-Dimensional! Interactive Graphic Organizers!

Macmillan/McGraw-Hill

Fish	Frogs
habitat	habitat
food	insects
prey	prey
enemies	enemies

Eight-Tab Foldable

Word	Synonym	Antonym	Prefix or suffix
normal	typical	unusual	normally

Folded Chart

Independent Activities

FCAT LEVELED READERS: Science

For Repeated Readings and Literacy Activities

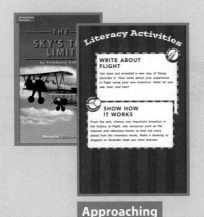

WRITE ABOUT FLIGHT

You have just invented a new way of flying. Describe it. Then write about your experience in flight using your new invention. What do you see, hear, and feel?

SHOW HOW IT WORKS

From the text, choose one important invention in the history of flight. Use resources such as the internet and reference books to find out more about how the invention works. Make a drawing or diagram to illustrate what you have learned.

Approaching

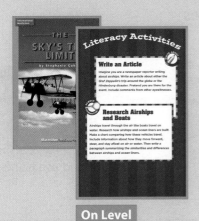

Write an Article

Imagine you are a newspaper reporter writing about airships. Write an article about either the *Graf Zeppelin's* trip around the globe or the Hindenburg disaster. Pretend you are there for the event. Include comments from other eyewitnesses.

Research Airships and Boats

Airships travel through the air like boats travel on water. Research how airships and ocean liners are built. Include information about how they move forward, steer, and stay afloat on air or water. Then write a paragraph summarizing the similarities and differences between airships and ocean liners.

On Level

Write an Article

Work with a partner. Pretend you are newspaper reporters writing about airships. Write a short article about either the *Graf Zeppelin's* trip around the globe or the Hindenburg disaster. Pretend you are there for the event. What are people saying?

Research Airships and Boats

Airships travel through the air like boats travel on water. Work with a partner. Research how airships and ocean liners are built. Make a chart comparing how these vehicles move forward, steer, and stay afloat on air or water. How are they similar? How are they different?

ELL

A Good Scientist

What kind of person makes a good scientist? Write a description of such a person. Tell what qualities the person should have and what strengths might help that person succeed.

Answering Scientific Questions

Scientists ask themselves questions. Then they try to find answers for those questions. What questions do you have about the sky or space? Write two questions. Then tell what kinds of experiments or actions might produce answers to those questions. Use drawings or other graphics if they will make your explanation clearer to others.

Beyond

LEVELED PRACTICE

Skills: Vocabulary, Relevant Facts and Details, Fluency, Greek Roots, Simile and Metaphor

Practice Book A

Approaching

Practice Book O

On Level

Practice Book B

Beyond

ELL Practice and Assessment

ELL

Technology

ONLINE INSTRUCTION www.macmillanmh.com

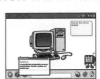

- Meet the Author/Illustrator
- Computer Literacy Lessons
- Research and Inquiry Activities

- Oral Language Activities
- Vocabulary and Spelling Activities
- Leveled Reader Database

LISTENING LIBRARY

Recordings of selections
- Main Selections
- Leveled Readers
- ELL Readers
- Intervention Anthology

FLUENCY SOLUTIONS

Recorded passages for modeling and practicing fluency

VOCABULARY PUZZLEMAKER

Activities providing multiple exposures to vocabulary, spelling, and high-frequency words including crossword puzzles, word searches, and word jumbles

---

Turn the page for Literacy Workstations.

Literacy Activities

Collaborative Learning Activities

Reading

Objectives

- Read a passage for smoothness and clarity
- Time reading to practice fluency
- Summarize passages from a book
- Read independently daily; read as a leisure activity

Word Study

Objectives

- Build and use words with number prefixes
- Build and use words with Greek roots

LA.5.1.5 Read orally with accuracy

Reading — Fluency

20 Minutes

- With a partner read aloud from the fluency passage on page 210 of your Practice Book. Take turns reading the sentences, practicing pronunciation and responses to end punctuation. Read each sentence until you both read smoothly.
- You may want to listen to the pronunciation and responses to end punctuation on the audio disc.

Extension

- Give each other corrective feedback until you both read without stumbling.
- **Time Your Reading:** Listen to the Audio CD.

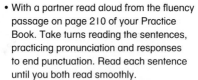

Things you need:
- Practice Book
- paper and pen or pencil
- scissors

Fluency Solutions
Listening Library

57

LA.5.1.4 Student applies grade level phonics

Word Study — Number Prefixes

20 Minutes

- Make a list of number prefixes and their definitions, such as *uni-, bi-, tri-,* and *cent-*.
- Find two words in the dictionary that begin with each prefix on your list. Write each word on one side of a note card and the definition of the word on the other side of the card. Use these flash cards with a partner until both of you know all of the words. Review your partner's cards as well.

Extension

- Create ten nonsense words with number prefixes. For instance, you could say that a "heptatable" is a table with seven sides. Quiz your partner about what each word might mean.

Things you need:
- note cards
- dictionary
- pen or pencil

octo=eight

For additional vocabulary and spelling games, go to www.macmillanmh.com

57

LA.5.2.2.5 Select age and ability appropriate non-fiction

Reading — Independent Reading

20 Minutes

- Find a library book or an Internet article or story that involves a hot-air balloon race. The reading can be fiction, like *Around the World in 80 Days,* or nonfiction or poetry.
- Read several pages and write down on a card everything you remember from what you have read.

Extension

- In your response journal, discuss what other independent reading you would like to do on the subject.

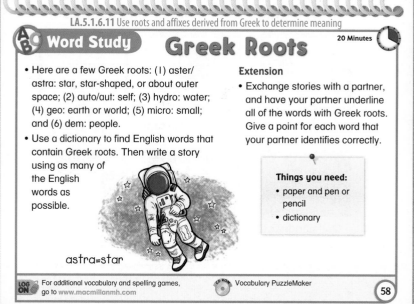

Things you need:
- paper and pen or pencil
- library or access to the Internet

For more books about balloon flight, go to the Author/Illustrator section at **www.macmillanmh.com**

58

LA.5.1.6.11 Use roots and affixes derived from Greek to determine meaning

Word Study — Greek Roots

20 Minutes

- Here are a few Greek roots: (1) aster/astra: star, star-shaped, or about outer space; (2) auto/aut: self; (3) hydro: water; (4) geo: earth or world; (5) micro: small; and (6) dem: people.
- Use a dictionary to find English words that contain Greek roots. Then write a story using as many of the English words as possible.

Extension

- Exchange stories with a partner, and have your partner underline all of the words with Greek roots. Give a point for each word that your partner identifies correctly.

Things you need:
- paper and pen or pencil
- dictionary

astra=star

For additional vocabulary and spelling games, go to www.macmillanmh.com

Vocabulary PuzzleMaker

58

Literacy Workstations

Writing

Objectives
- Write a clear explanation of gravity
- Write a descriptive passage about riding a hot-air balloon

Content Literacy

Objectives
- Make generalizations based on facts
- Write a historical time line based on research
- Read to perform a task

LA.5.4.2 Student demonstrates technical writing

Writing — Writing to Explain
20 Minutes

- Using details and examples from daily life on Earth, write a clear explanation of gravity as you might describe it to a young child.

Extension
- Exchange explanations of gravity with a partner and write any questions about gravity that are not addressed in your partner's explanation. Exchange papers again. Add the answers to each other's questions to your explanations.

Things you need:
- paper and pen or pencil

57

LA.5.4.2.2 Record information related to a topic

Science — BALLOONS AND WEATHER
20 Minutes

- Research the history of how balloons have been used to track weather.
- Make five fact cards on how weather balloons help people forecast and understand weather.

Extension
- What generalizations can you make about weather balloons? Are weather balloons generally helpful? Do scientists usually trust the information provided by weather balloons? Think of more questions that can help you generalize the information.

Things you need:
- paper and pen or pencil
- library books or access to the Internet

57

LA.5.4.1 Student demonstrates creative writing

Writing — DESCRIPTIVE WRITING
20 Minutes

- If you could take a balloon ride above any place on Earth, where would you go? Describe the sensations you might feel as you take off. Describe the colors, the sizes of people and animals, and the buildings and natural formations that you might see.

Extension
- Turn your descriptive writing into a poem. Share it with a partner.

Things you need:
- paper and pen or pencil

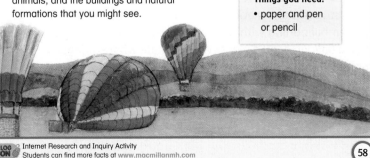

LOG ON — Internet Research and Inquiry Activity
Students can find more facts at www.macmillanmh.com

58

LA.5.4.2.2 Include visial aides to organize and record information

Social Studies — Hot-Air Balloons and History
20 Minutes

- Research how hot-air balloons have changed history. Look at the use of balloons in wars, science, and recreation, for example.
- Find three events or inventions connected to hot-air balloons. Place them on a time line that mentions other historical events of the time.

Extension
- With a partner put your events together on one time line, and share them with another pair.

Things you need:
- paper and pen or pencil
- construction paper
- scissors
- library or access to the Internet

58

BALLOON FLIGHT

710

ORAL LANGUAGE
- Build Background
- Read Aloud
- Expand Vocabulary

 FCAT VOCABULARY
- Teach Words in Context
- **Word Parts:** Greek Roots

COMPREHENSION
- **Strategy:** Monitor Comprehension
- **FCAT** **Skill:** Relevant Facts and Details

SMALL GROUP OPTIONS
- Differentiated Instruction, pp. 735M–735V

Oral Language

Build Background

LA.5.5.2.1
Listen to gain and share information

ACCESS PRIOR KNOWLEDGE

Share the following information:

The Albuquerque International Balloon Fiesta, held annually in New Mexico, is one of the largest hot-air balloon events in the world. At dawn all balloons take to the sky.

LA.5.5.2.1
Listen and speak to gain and share information

TALK ABOUT BALLOON FLIGHT

Discuss the weekly theme. Ask:

Have you ever seen or flown in a hot-air balloon? What do you remember?

 FOCUS QUESTION Ask a volunteer to read "Talk About It" on **Student Book** page 711 and describe the photo.

- What is happening in the photo?

- What are some interesting things you notice about the balloons?

ENGLISH LANGUAGE LEARNERS

 Access for All

Beginning **Model** Have students say what they can about the photo. Make statements about the photo and have students repeat as they are able: *These are hot-air balloons. People are watching the balloons.* Ask, *How many balloons do you see? Would you like to fly in a balloon?*

Intermediate **Discuss** Have students describe the photo. Find out what students know about hot-air ballooning. Have them compare hot-air ballooning with riding on a plane. Ask, *Would you prefer to fly in a balloon or on a plane? Why?* Restate what students say in complete sentences using descriptive language.

Advanced **Generate Questions** Complete the Intermediate task. Ask students to generate questions about hot-air ballooning.

Talk About It

Nowadays people can travel quickly by plane to almost any part of the world. Why do you think people still like to go up in hot-air balloons?

 Find out more about balloon flight at **www.macmillanmh.com**

711

Picture Prompt

Look at the picture and write a descriptive paragraph about the colors you see in this photo. How do they make you feel? Why?

LOG ON Technology

For an extended lesson plan and Web site activities for **oral language development**, go to **www.macmillanmh.com**

Read Aloud
Read "The Montgolfier Brothers"

LA.5.2.1.1
Demonstrate knowledge of characteristics of genres

GENRE: Narrative Nonfiction Review features of narrative nonfiction:

Read Aloud
pages 136–140

- an account of actual people, events, or situations told like a fiction story

- provides facts and other true information

LA.5.1.6.2
Listen to and discuss familiar text

LISTENING FOR A PURPOSE

As you read "The Montgolfier Brothers" in the **Read-Aloud Anthology,** ask students to listen carefully for what the brothers accomplished, and how they accomplished it. Choose from among the teaching suggestions.

Fluency Ask students to listen carefully as you read aloud, paying attention to your phrasing, expression, and tone of voice.

LA.5.1.6.2
Discuss familiar text

RESPOND TO THE SELECTION

Ask students to share what they found most interesting about the Montgolfier brothers, and why they think the brothers experimented with hot-air balloons.

LA.5.1.6
Student develops grade-appropriate vocabulary

Expand Vocabulary

Have students choose four or more words from the selection that relate to this week's theme of balloon flight. Invite students to design their own hot-air balloons and use the words to describe their balloons to the class.

Vocabulary

FCAT
LA.5.1.6.3
Use context clues

TEACH WORDS IN CONTEXT

Use the following routine:

LA.5.1.6.1
Use new vocabulary taught directly

Routine

Define: Something that is **launched** is started in motion or sent off.
Example: A new satellite was launched at the Kennedy Space Center.
Ask: What else can be launched? EXAMPLE

■ **Particles** are small bits or pieces of an element. The nurse removed dirt particles from the child's eye. How are particles different from chunks? COMPARE AND CONTRAST

LA.5.1.6.8
Use antonyms to determine meaning

■ Things that are **dense** are thick or packed closely together. Campers sometimes got lost in the dense woods. What is an antonym for *dense?* ANTONYM

LA.5.1.6.8
Use synonyms to determine meaning

■ **Inflate** means to cause to swell by filling with air or gas. Ned remembered to inflate both bicycle tires. What is a synonym of *inflate?* SYNONYM

■ **Anchored** means held firmly in place.

Access for All

The old sailboat was anchored in the harbor. Why do boats have to be anchored? EXPLANATION

■ **Hydrogen** is a light gas that burns easily. Two hydrogen atoms combined with one oxygen atom forms water. What else do you know about hydrogen? PRIOR KNOWLEDGE

■ **Scientific** means having to do with or used in science. A microscope is an example of scientific equipment. Name something else that is scientific. EXAMPLE

■ A **companion** is a person or animal who keeps somebody company. Jack and Jill were constant companions. What qualities does a good companion have? DESCRIPTION

Vocabulary

launched	anchored
particles	companion
dense	hydrogen
inflate	scientific

FCAT **Word Parts**
Greek Roots help you understand entire word families. The word *hydrogen* has the Greek root *hydr-*. This root means "water." Most words beginning with *hydr-* have something to do with water.

712

Quick Check

Do students understand word meanings?

During **Small Group Instruction**

If No → **Approaching Level**
Vocabulary, p. 735N

If Yes → **On Level** Options, pp. 735Q–735R

Beyond Level Options, pp. 732S–735T

The Science of Hot-Air Balloons

by Enriquez Mera

Since the first hot-air balloon was **launched** in 1783, few things have changed about how they fly. However, some new differences have made ballooning a safer activity enjoyed by many people worldwide.

In the past hot-air balloons were always made out of linen and paper. Today most are made of nylon. Long pieces of nylon, called *gores*, are stitched together to create the balloon. Balloonists use nylon because it is a thin and light material. Also, it cannot be damaged by heat.

ELL   **Access for All**

Draw For *anchored*, draw a hot-air balloon with a line anchoring it to the ground. Say, *The balloon cannot rise. It is anchored.* Draw a picture of a boat that is anchored and ask, *What vehicle is anchored?* Erase the line from the balloon and explain with gestures the word *launch*. Ask, *What vehicles do we launch in space? In the water?* List and draw the vehicles.

Heat is the basic ingredient needed for ballooning. As air becomes hotter, tiny **particles** of matter move faster and faster. As the balloon fills with warmer particles, it begins to rise. This is because the air inside is lighter than the **dense** air surrounding the balloon. It is the warmer air particles that allow the balloon to float above the cooler air.

How the air is heated to **inflate** the hot-air balloon has changed a great deal since the early days of ballooning. Back in 1783 fire from damp straw and wool heated the air as the balloon remained **anchored** to the ground. Usually, a brave man or woman and a **companion** would climb into the basket, cut the line, and soar into the air.

Now balloonists use propane—the same gas used in most outdoor grills—instead of straw. For hot-air balloons, it is piped from a tank to metal tubes. Once there, a small fire heats up the tubes and the propane. When the propane flame is released, it creates hot air that fills the inside of the hot-air balloon.

Besides propane, another gas that could be used is **hydrogen**. Hydrogen is a gas that has no odor, color, or taste and burns very easily. One advantage of hydrogen gas is that it does not need to be heated. However, hydrogen is expensive, so it is mostly used for balloons during **scientific** studies. These are studies designed to gather information that will help scientists.

Whether for science or sport, more people than ever are taking to the air in balloons.

Reread for **Comprehension**

Monitor Comprehension

FCAT **Relevant Facts and Details** A fact is information that can be proven true. Some details state an author's **opinion** and cannot be proven true. Recognizing facts and opinions that are relevant to the main idea can help you understand a selection. Use your Fact and Opinion Chart as you reread the selection to evaluate which facts and opinions are relevant to the main idea.

Fact	Opinion

713

FCAT Success!

Test Prep and Practice with vocabulary, pages 6–31.

On Level Practice Book O, page 207

| launched | particles | dense | inflate |
| anchored | hydrogen | scientific | companion |

A. Choose the word from the list above that best completes each sentence. Then write the word on the line.

1. The hot-air balloon soared through the air because it was not ___anchored___, or held down, to the ground by anything.

2. The balloons soar because the hot-air is light and the air surrounding it is heavy and ___dense___.

3. People in hot-air balloons are ___launched___ into the sky.

4. The large balloons ___inflate___ when they are filled with hot air.

5. The small pieces of matter in air move faster as the air heats. Then the ___particles___ spread out, and the balloon rises.

6. ___Hydrogen___ is a gas that is lighter than air, so it also can be used in hot-air balloons.

7. Some people ride in hot-air balloons to do ___scientific___ experiments.

8. You and a ___companion___ might enjoy sharing a hot-air balloon ride.

B. Label the statements True or False.

9. The science club launched the balloon, and it dug deep into the earth. ___False___

10. You can inflate a balloon with hydrogen or hot air. ___True___

11. The balloon will not move when it is anchored to the ground. ___True___

12. To conduct scientific experiments you must bring a companion. ___False___

 Approaching Practice Book A, page 207

Beyond Practice Book B, page 207

Vocabulary

FCAT **STRATEGY**
WORD PARTS

LA.5.1.6.11 Use roots and affixes derived from Greek to determine meaning of complex words

Greek Roots Remind students that by learning the meanings of Greek roots, they may be able to define some unfamiliar words. However, they may still have to consult a dictionary to verify meanings.

Point to the word *hydrogen* in "The Science of Hot-Air Balloons. It contains the Greek root *hydro,* which means "water." Write these words on the board: *hydrant, hydraulic, hydrophobia.* Ask what root these words share. (hydr, meaning *water*) Point out that these words belong to the same word family because they all contain the Greek root *hydro.* Have students use a dictionary to determine the meaning of the words, as needed.

Read "The Science of Hot-Air Balloons"

LA.5.1.6.3 Use context clues

As you read "The Science of Hot-Air Balloons" with students, ask them to identify context and other clues that reveal the meanings of the highlighted words. Tell students they will read these words again in *Up in the Air.*

Objectives

- Evaluate a nonfiction text
- Use academic language: *fact, opinion*
- Identify fact and opinion
- Identify relevant facts and details

Materials

- Comprehension Transparencies 29a and 29b
- Graphic Organizer Transparency 29
- Practice Book, p. 208

FCAT Skills Trace

Relevant Facts and Details	
Introduce	199A
Practice / Apply	293A–B, 294–305, 451A–B, 452–455, 713A–B, 714–729; Practice Book 83–84, 127–128, 208–209
Reteach / Review	3130–P, R, T; 321A; 4590–P, R, T; 573A; 7350–P, R, T
Assess	Weekly Tests; Units 3, 4, 6 Tests; Benchmark Tests A, B
Maintain	293A–B, 451A–B, 713A–B; Practice Book 83–84, 127–128, 208–209, 691B

ELL   Access for All

Monitor Comprehension

Explain Write on the board: *Fact or Opinion?* Under it write these statements: *Phyllis Reynolds Naylor writes children's books. Many of her books have won awards. Shiloh is the best book that Phyllis Reynolds Naylor has ever written.* Help students identify each statement as a *fact* or *opinion* and explain whether the statement could be checked in an outside source. Co-construct other facts and opinions.

LA.5.1.6.2
Read familiar text

LA.5.1.7
Use strategies to comprehend text

Reread for
Comprehension

STRATEGY
MONITOR COMPREHENSION

Good readers **monitor** their **comprehension** as they read by stopping at regular intervals and asking themselves if they understand what they have just read. If they do not understand something, they use self-correction techniques such as rereading, asking questions, or adjusting their reading rate to help them make sense of the text.

FCAT SKILL
RELEVANT FACTS AND DETAILS

Access for All

EXPLAIN

LA.5.1.7.3
Determine main idea through identifying relevant details

- A **fact** is a statement that can be proven true. An **opinion** represents someone's feelings or beliefs but is not necessarily false. Words and phrases such as *I think, I feel, perhaps,* and *the best* are signals that an author is stating an opinion.

- Good readers distinguish between facts and opinions as a way to evaluate what they read, hear, view, and write. A Fact and Opinion Chart can help readers keep track of facts and opinions.

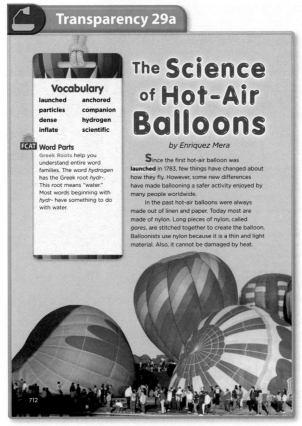

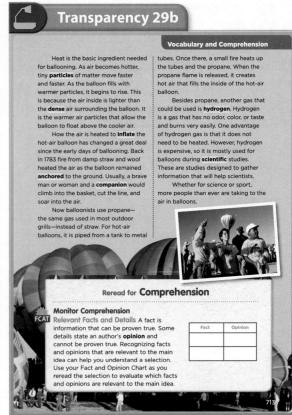

Student Book pages 712–713 available on Comprehension Transparencies 29a and 29b

■ A **relevant detail** is an important piece of information that may be either a fact or an opinion. Identifying relevant facts and details in a text can help you to figure out the main idea. As you read, ask yourself, *Does this information support what the paragraph is all about?* to determine whether a fact or detail is relevant to the main idea.

LA.5.1.7.3 Determine main idea through identifying relevant details

MODEL

Read the first paragraph of "The Science of Hot-Air Balloons" from **Student Book** page 712. Model identifying relevant facts and details for students using the Think Aloud strategy.

Think Aloud The first sentence in this paragraph states a fact that can be checked: the first hot-air balloon was launched in 1783. The information that changes since then have made ballooning a safer activity is the author's opinion, and not a fact that can be checked. However, I think this is a relevant detail that supports the main idea of this nonfiction article, which will explain changes in the sport since it was first introduced.

GUIDED PRACTICE

Display **Transparency 29** to introduce the Fact and Opinion Chart to students. Begin the chart with information from the text. (FACT: The first hot-air balloon was launched in 1783. OPINION: Some changes in ballooning have made it a safer activity.) Have students fill in the rest of the chart as they continue to read.

APPLY

Have students reread the rest of the selection and complete the chart, determining which opinions are still relevant details.

Transparency 29

Fact	Opinion
The first hot air balloon was launched in 1783.	Some changes in ballooning have made it a safer activity

Graphic Organizer Transparency 29

FCAT Success!

Test Prep and Practice with Relevant Facts and Details, pages 32–64

■ **On Level Practice Book O,** page 208

When you read a selection, you look for **facts,** which are statements that can be proven true. Authors may also include their opinions, which may be **relevant details** that support the main idea but cannot be proven true.

Read the pairs of sentences. Tell which sentence is a fact and which is an opinion. Possible responses provided.

1. Today there are no clouds, no storms, and no high winds. It is a perfect day for ballooning.
[F, O]

2. Thousands of people belong to hot-air balloon clubs. Most people from different parts of the world like ballooning.
[F, O]

3. Joseph Montgolfier marveled that hot air rises. He and his brother built the first hot-air balloon. [O, F]

4. Early hot-air balloons flew amazingly high. Early hot-air balloons carried no people.
[O, F]

5. The first public balloon flight was in France. A Frenchman was the best choice to ride in a balloon. [F, O]

Quick Check | **Can students identify relevant facts and details?**

During **Small Group Instruction**

If No → **Approaching Level** Comprehension, pp. 735O–735P

If Yes → **On Level** Options, p. 735R

Beyond Level Options, p. 735T

 Approaching Practice Book A, page 208

◆ **Beyond Practice Book B,** page 208

Read

MAIN SELECTION
- *Up in the Air: The Story of Balloon Flight*
- **FCAT** • **Skill:** Relevant Facts and Details

PAIRED SELECTION
- "Hot-Air Balloon Haiku"
- **FCAT** • **Literary Elements:** Simile and Metaphor

SMALL GROUP OPTIONS
- Differentiated Instruction, pp. 735M–735V

Comprehension

LA.5.2.1.1
Demonstrate knowledge of characteristics of genre

GENRE: NONFICTION

Have students read the definition of Nonfiction on **Student Book** page 714. As they read, students should look for facts about real people, places, events, and situations.

LA.5.1.7
Student uses strategies to comprehend text

STRATEGY
MONITOR COMPREHENSION

Remind students that good readers monitor their comprehension as they read and use self-correction techniques such as rereading, asking questions, or adjusting their reading rate.

SKILL
RELEVANT FACTS AND DETAILS

LA.5.1.7.3
Determine main idea through identifying relevant details

Remind students that a fact is a statement that can be proven true. An opinion is a statement of a person's beliefs. A relevant detail is an important piece of information in a text that may be either a fact or an opinion.

Comprehension

Genre
Nonfiction gives information and facts about real people, places, events, and situations.

Monitor Comprehension
FCAT **Relevant Facts and Details**
As you read, use your Fact and Opinion Chart to help you determine which details support the main idea.

Fact	Opinion

Read to Find Out
How has the invention of ballooning been useful?

714

Vocabulary

Vocabulary Words Review the tested vocabulary words: **anchored, companion, dense, hydrogen, inflate, launched, particles,** and **scientific.**

Selection Words Students may find these words difficult. Pronounce the words and present the meanings as necessary.

altitude (p. 717): the measurement of the distance above Earth's surface

chemist (p. 723): an expert in chemistry, the science that deals with the characteristics of elements

helium (p. 727): a very light, colorless, odorless gas that does not burn

LA.5.1.6.1 Use new vocabulary taught directly

Up in the Air:
The Story of Balloon Flight
by Patricia Lauber

Award Winning Author

715

LA.5.1.7.1
Use prior knowledge to make and confirm predictions

LA.5.1.7.1
Establish purpose for reading

Preview and Predict

Ask students to read the title, preview the illustrations, and make predictions about the selection. Ask: *What features of informational nonfiction can you find?* Have students write about their predictions and anything else they might want to know about the selection.

Set Purposes

FOCUS QUESTION Discuss the "Read to Find Out" question and remind students to look for the answer as they read.

Point out the Generalizations Chart on **Practice Book** page 209. Tell students they will use the chart to keep track of generalizations they make as they read the selection.

Read *Up in the Air: The Story of Balloon Flight*

Use the questions and Think Alouds for additional instruction to support the comprehension strategy and skill.

Read Together	Read Independently
If your students need support to read the Main Selection, use the prompts to guide comprehension and model how to complete the graphic organizer.	If your students can read the Main Selection independently, have them read and complete the graphic organizer. Remind students to set and modify their reading rate based on purposes, difficulty, and type of text.

If your students need an alternate selection, choose the **Leveled Readers** that match their instructional level.

Technology

Story available on **Listening Library Audio CD**

On Level Practice Book O, page 209

As you read *Up in the Air: The Story of Balloon Flight*, fill in the Fact and Opinion Chart.

Fact	Opinion

How does the information you wrote in the Fact and Opinion Chart help you monitor comprehension of *Up in the Air*?

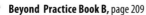

★ **Approaching Practice Book A,** page 209

◆ **Beyond Practice Book B,** page 209

Develop Comprehension

1 STRATEGY
MONITOR COMPREHENSION

LA.5.1.7
Use strategies to comprehend text

Teacher Think Aloud *Up in the Air: The Story of Balloon Flight* is nonfiction. I know that an informational nonfiction selection gives facts and information about a topic, and may contain unfamiliar words . As I read I will stop and check from time to time to see if I understand the important ideas and information in the selection. I'll ask myself questions such as *why? what if?* and *how?* before identifying relevant facts and details that support the main idea.

2 NARRATIVE NONFICTION

LA.5.2.1.1
Demonstrate knowledge of genre forms with distinct characteristics and purposes

How is this nonfiction article different from the kind of nonfiction information you might find in an encyclopedia entry? (Answers will vary but should include the fact that the author uses descriptive, colorful language.)

3 FIGURATIVE LANGUAGE

LA.5.2.1.7
Identify author's use of figurative language and similes

What examples of figurative language does the author use on this spread? (Answers should include personification ["tongues of orange flame"] and simile ["silent as a cloud"].)

716

Saturday promises to be fair, with no high winds, no storms. It's a perfect day for ballooning. Members of the balloonist club turn out early and set to work. Fans blow air into the balloons. Tongues of orange flame shoot out of roaring gas burners, heating air to make the balloons rise. The balloons **inflate** and stand up. Pilots climb into their baskets, the ground crews let go of the ropes, and it's up, up, and away.

A balloon floats along, silent as a cloud, until a pilot turns on the burners to heat air inside and gain altitude. Balloons cannot be steered. They travel only where the winds carry them. By changing altitude, though, a pilot may find a different wind, going in a different direction. A chase crew follows on land to bring balloonists and balloons home at journey's end.

Today thousands of people in many parts of the world belong to balloon clubs. Their sport was invented more than 200 years ago by a handful of people who willingly risked their lives flying the balloons they had built.

1
2
3
4

As the balloons fill with hot air, they stand upright. They are ready to soar away, carrying pilots and passengers in big baskets called gondolas.

717

Develop Comprehension

4 DRAW CONCLUSIONS

LA.5.2.2.2
Use information from text to answer questions

Why do you think the people who bring balloonists home are called the "chase crew"? Is this a good name for them? Why or why not? (Answers may vary but should include the idea that the word *chase* means to run after something in order to catch it. Since balloons cannot be steered, the crew on the ground have to chase after them because they don't know where they will come down. For these reasons the "chase crew" is a good name for the group of people who follow balloonists on land.)

Vocabulary

Read the sentence that contains the word **inflate**. Ask students to replace *inflate* in the passage with a word or phrase that has the opposite meaning. (deflate, contract, lose air)

LA.5.1.6.8 Use antonyms to determine meaning

Develop Comprehension

5 RELEVANT FACTS AND DETAILS

FCAT

LA.5.2.2.2
Answer questions related to explicitly stated main ideas or relevant details

Find one fact and one opinion in the first paragraph on page 719. Explain whether each is relevant to the main idea of the paragraph. Then add this information to the Fact and Opinion Chart. (Answers may vary but should include that the year in which the Montgolfier brothers built and launched the first hot-air balloon is a fact that can be checked. The statement that people have always dreamed of flying like birds is the author's own opinion, but it is still relevant to the main idea of this paragraph: people tried to fly in balloons for hundreds of years.

Fact	Opinion
The Montgolfier brothers launched the world's first hot-air balloon in 1783.	People have always dreamed of soaring like birds

MONTGOLFIER BALLOON. Ascent of a Montgolfier balloon from Paris, c. 1864: engraving from an English newspaper.

718

 Music

Cross–Curricular Connection

MUSIC

Share with students one of the most well-known songs about hot-air balloons, the Fifth Dimension's "Up, Up, and Away." As they listen to the recording, have students think about how the music and lyrics capture the thrill of floating in a giant hot-air balloon. Then invite students to sing along with the recording.

Encourage students to write their own songs about hot-air balloons. Have them write their lyrics on a cutout of a hot-air balloon. Invite students to share their songs with the class.

LA.5.4.1 Student develops creative writing
LA.5.4.1.2 Write a variety of expressive forms

The Story of Ballooning

People have always dreamed of soaring like a bird or floating like a cloud. Over several hundred years a few people thought they knew how to do this. They theorized that a certain kind of big balloon might lift them up. The balloon would be lighter than the air around it, and it would float in air as a boat floats in water. But no one managed to make such a balloon until 1783 when two French brothers built and **launched** the world's first hot-air balloon. Their names were Joseph and Etienne Montgolfier.

5

The World's First Balloon Flight

Hot smoky air rising from a fire had given Joseph Montgolfier an idea. Perhaps such air would make a balloon rise. Using small balloons Joseph found that it did.

6

After many experiments the brothers built a balloon that was about 30 feet across and 38 feet tall. It had a wooden frame at the base and was made of linen backed with paper. On June 5, 1783, near the city of Lyons, France, the Montgolfiers built a huge fire of damp straw and wool. Hot air poured into the base of the balloon. As a small crowd watched in amazement, the balloon stirred, swelled, and finally rose upright.

7

Eight men were holding the balloon down. At a signal they let go. It rose some 6,000 feet into the air and stayed aloft for ten minutes, landing gently in a nearby vineyard. This was the world's first public balloon flight.

The Montgolfiers mistakenly thought smoke, not hot air, made a balloon rise. They used damp fuel to create dense smoke which escaped in flight.

719

Develop Comprehension

6 **WRITING TRAIT: IDEAS AND CONTENT**

LA.5.2.2.2
Answer questions related to main ideas

Is the author's explanation about how balloons float in the air clear? Why or why not? How might the author improve the explanation? (Answers will vary but may include the idea that the author needs to explain how an object can be lighter than air. Some students may suggest that the Montgolfiers' mistaken theory about smoke should be part of the text instead of placed in a caption.)

7 **CHRONOLOGICAL ORDER**

LA.5.1.7.8
Summarize to repair comprehension

Sometimes a small event can inspire a bigger one. Starting with the idea Joseph Montgolfier had, summarize the sequence of events, in chronological order, that led to the world's first balloon flight. (Answers should include the following facts: Joseph Montgolfier saw hot, smoky air rising from a fire; he used small balloons filled with hot air to test the idea of balloon flight; then he and his brother built the first large balloon and launched it in June 1783.)

Develop Comprehension

8 **MONITOR AND CLARIFY:
READ AHEAD**

LA.5.1.7.8
Use strategies
to repair
compre-
hension

Professor Charles uses hydrogen to fill his balloon. Why did the Montgolfier brothers not use this lighter-than-air gas? How might the strategy of Read Ahead help you to answer this question? (Answers may vary, but students should note that hydrogen was a newly discovered gas. The text states that Charles was a professor. He might have been a professor of science, and for this reason could have been one of the first people to know about hydrogen. If students read ahead, they may discover that the Montgolfier brothers might not have known about this new gas.)

LA.5.1.7.8
Make notes
to repair
comprehension

LA.5.1.7.8
Use graphic
organizers
to repair
comprehension

LA.5.1.7.8
Clarify by
checking other
sources

Suggest that students make notes as they read about information they want to know that the text does not provide. They can then transfer the notes onto a K-W-L chart and read ahead to see if their questions are answered. When students have finished the selection, ask them how they can clarify information in the text. (By checking other sources.)

Professor Charles' hydrogen balloon came to a bad end when attacked by pitchforks and dragged through the mud.

720

A Lighter-than-Air Balloon

Meanwhile in Paris, Professor Jacques A. C. Charles had designed a lighter-than-air balloon. He filled his balloon with a newly discovered gas called **hydrogen**, which weighed much less than air.

On August 27, 1783, Professor Charles launched his balloon at 5 P.M. As a crowd watched, it rose 3,000 feet and disappeared into the clouds.

Forty-five minutes later the balloon came down outside a village 15 miles away. The villagers, who had never heard of such a thing as a balloon, thought a monster had fallen out of the sky. As it bounced toward them, they attacked it with pitchforks. When at last the monster lay still, men tied it to a horse's tail and dragged it through the mud to make sure it was dead.

Now there were two ways to send balloons aloft: with hot air and with hydrogen. The fires were messy and dangerous, but hydrogen took a lot of time to make. Nevertheless, most of the early flights were made with hot-air balloons.

8

Professor Jacques A. C. Charles

9

10

FCAT Relevant Facts and Details

The author tells of villagers attacking a balloon as a monster. Are these details relevant to the main idea of the selection? Why or why not?

721

Develop Comprehension

9 **CAUSE AND EFFECT**

LA.5.1.7.4 Identify cause-and-effect relationships in text

Why did the villagers react to Professor Charles' balloon as they did? (Answers should include the idea that people are often afraid of things they don't understand. The villagers had never seen anything like the balloon before. In addition, after falling from the sky, the balloon bounced toward them. For this reason they might have thought it was alive.)

10 **RELEVANT FACTS AND DETAILS**

LA.5.2.2.2 Answer questions related to explicitly stated main ideas or relevant details

The author tells of villagers attacking a balloon as a monster. Are these details relevant to the main idea of the selection? Why or why not? (Yes. Students should note that this event supports the idea that hot-air balloons were still a novelty in 1783, and most people were unfamiliar with them.)

Have students respond to the selection by confirming or revising their predictions and purposes for reading. Suggest that they note any additional questions they may have.

Extra Support

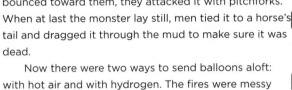

Relevant Facts and Details

FCAT If students are having difficulty distinguishing fact from opinion, and identifying relevant facts and details, have them reread the text on page 721. Point out the information in the first two paragraphs, and ask whether these details are facts. (Yes. This is an historical figure and date that can be checked.) Then ask students if the statement *the fires were messy and dangerous* is a fact or an opinion. (Opinion) Explain that not everyone would think the fires were messy, which is why this statement is an opinion. Help students see that this opinion is a relevant detail because it helps support the main idea: that there were now two ways to send balloons aloft, but one method remained more popular.

LA.5.1.7.8 Use strategies to repair comprehension

Quick Check   **Are students able to identify relevant facts and details as they read? If not, see the Extra Support on this page.**

Stop here if you wish to read this selection over two days.

Develop Comprehension

11 DRAW CONCLUSIONS

LA.5.2.2.2
Answer
questions
related to
relevant
details

Why were a trio of animals the first passengers to go up in a balloon? (Answers may vary but should include the idea that the text implies that balloon flight was dangerous and that people did not know whether it was possible to breathe thousands of feet above the surface of Earth. Animals were the first living things to go up in a balloon so that people could learn more about any risks involved before going up themselves.)

12 MAKE INFERENCES

LA.5.2.2.2
Use
information
from text
to answer
questions

What kind of fuel did the balloon that carried the animals use? How do you know? (Answers should include the fact that the selection says the balloon drifted to Earth after the air in the balloon cooled, so it must have used hot air rather than hydrogen.)

The king and queen of France watched the launching of the first balloon passengers.

722

The First Passenger Balloons

The first passengers to go up in a balloon were a trio of animals—a duck, a rooster, and a lamb. On September 19, 1783, they traveled in a wicker basket, or gondola, attached to a balloon. After a short flight, the air in the balloon cooled and the passengers drifted safely to Earth. Their flight showed that it was possible to breathe while floating a few thousand feet above Earth.

It was now time for humans to risk ballooning. A daring young French chemist was the first. On October 15, 1783, François Pilâtre de Rozier went up 100 feet. He was **anchored** to the ground by a long rope called a tether. His balloon carried a big metal pan under its mouth. A fire in the pan sent hot air into the balloon. The flight was a success. After that de Rozier made many tethered flights to find out how much straw and wool he needed to burn for each hour he stayed in the air.

By November 21, de Rozier was ready to make the first untethered flight. A huge crowd gathered to watch. The giant balloon filled, and at 1:54 P.M., de Rozier and a **companion** were up, up, and away. When the balloon was 200 feet in the air, the pair took off their hats and bowed to those below. Then they sailed off over Paris. The travelers flew for 25 minutes and covered about five miles before landing in a field outside the city.

11

12

13

Spectators watch de Rozier and his companion as they take flight in a hot-air balloon.

723

Develop Comprehension

13 SUMMARIZE

LA.5.1.7.8
Summarize to repair comprehension

Who was responsible for the first five balloon flights, and when did they take place? Identify each flight and explain what made it special. (The Montgolfier brothers were responsible for the first hot-air balloon flight that took place on June 5, 1783. Professor Charles was behind the second flight, which took place on August 27, 1783. It was the first flight to use hydrogen. The next flight, made on September 19, 1783, had three animal passengers and was a hot-air flight. The first human passenger flight, made in a tethered balloon, took place on October 15, 1783. On November 21, 1783, the first free flight made with a passenger took place.)

STRATEGIES FOR EXTRA SUPPORT

Question **13** SUMMARIZE
Write in three columns: *Who Made the Flight? When Did He/They Make It? Why Was the Flight Important?* Tell students to scan pages 719–723 looking for the dates of the five flights and the people who were involved. For each flight have students find the information that explains why the flight was unique or important.

Vocabulary

Read the sentence that contains the word **anchored**. Ask students in what way things can be anchored, and have them answer in a complete sentence. Example: *A tent can be anchored with a stake.*

LA.5.1.6 Student develops vocabulary

Develop Comprehension

14 DRAW CONCLUSIONS

LA.5.2.2.2
Use information from text to answer questions

This section of the article is entitled "Daring Balloonists." What made Pierre Blanchard so daring? (Answers may vary but should include that Blanchard wanted to do things that no one else had done. He made the first balloon flight across the English Channel. He also made the first flight in North America, and conducted scientific experiments while he was up in the air.)

15 STRATEGY
MONITOR COMPREHENSION

LA.5.1.7
Student uses strategies to comprehend text

Teacher Think Aloud The author says that the chief discoveries in balloon flight were made in 1783. But on the same page, she writes that in 1794 Jean-Pierre Blanchard made several experiments in a hot-air balloon at 5,000 feet. Tell me what question you could ask yourself to make sure you understand the point the author is trying to make.

(Encourage students to apply the strategy in a Think Aloud.)

Student Think Aloud Let's see. The author says that daring balloonists would keep setting records, but the chief discoveries were made in 1783. I can ask myself this question: *Does the author mean that distance records were still made after 1783, but the way hot-air balloons worked did not change?* I'll read ahead to see if my question is answered.

Blanchard and Jeffries were saluted by boats near the English and French coasts.

724

Daring Balloonists

Between 1783 and 1785, many men, and some women, went up in balloons. Some went for sport. Others, more daring, wanted to do what no one had done before. Jean-Pierre Blanchard was one of these. Blanchard wanted to cross the English Channel from England to France.

On January 7, 1785, the wind was blowing the right direction over the cliffs of Dover. Blanchard and his American friend John Jefferies filled their balloon with hydrogen, climbed in, and set off for France.

The first half of the trip went smoothly, but then the balloon began leaking gas. The water came closer and closer. To lighten the load, they threw everything overboard—their bags of sand, food and drink, anchors. They were still sinking. Finally they stripped and threw their clothes overboard, saving only their cork life jackets.

The weather changed. The air grew warmer, heating the gas. The balloon rose, and they sailed over the French coast, landing in a forest where they were soon rescued.

On January 9, 1793, Blanchard made the first flight in North America, taking off from Philadelphia and carrying out **scientific** experiments at 5,000 feet. He brought back sealed bottles of air that showed there was less oxygen at that height than at sea level. He also measured his heartbeat and found it was faster. At sea level it beat 84 times a minute; at 5,000 feet it beat 92.

In the years ahead, daring balloonists would keep setting records, but the chief discoveries were made in 1783, when a handful of people who dreamed of flying up, up, and away, made the dream come true.

On June 4, 1784, Marie Thible, an opera singer, became the first woman to make a balloon flight. She sang an aria while floating over Lyons, France.

FCAT Relevant Facts and Details
The author says that all the chief discoveries in balloon flight were made in 1783. Is this a fact or an opinion? How can you tell?

725

Cross-Curricular Connection

SCIENCE ACTIVITY USING BALLOONS

Up in the Air: The Story of Balloon Flight discusses different physical properties of balloons and matter. It might be difficult for students to understand that air is matter since they cannot see it. Do this activity with students to demonstrate that air is matter:

■ Blow up a balloon. Explain to students, while blowing up the balloon, that air is matter because it takes up space and this is why the balloon is getting bigger.

■ Show students what happens when you remove the matter inside the balloon. Stick a pin in the balloon so that it breaks or so that the air leaks out quickly. Have students observe that once the weight of the air was removed from the balloon, the balloon shrunk back to its original size.

LA.5.5.2.1 Listen to gain and share information

Develop Comprehension

16 MAIN IDEA AND DETAILS

LA.5.1.7.3 Determine main idea through inferring

What is the main idea of the section entitled *Daring Balloonists?* Name two details that support this idea. (Answers may vary but should include a statement such as: *Many daring men and women went up in balloons between 1783 and 1785.* Details could include: Pierre Blanchard's first trip was made in 1785 across the English Channel; in 1793 Blanchard made the first free flight in North America; Marie Thible became the first woman to make a balloon flight in 1784.)

17 RELEVANT FACTS AND DETAILS

FCAT

LA.5.2.2.2 Answer questions related to main ideas and relevant details

The author says that all the chief discoveries in balloon flight were made in 1783. Is this a fact or an opinion? How can you tell? (Students should note that since this information contains a date that can be checked, it is a probably a fact.) Is this information relevant to the main idea? Explain. (Students may say that this fact is not relevant to the main idea, which is about the daring men and women who went up in hot air balloons between 1783 and 1785.)

Have students add their answer to their Fact and Opinion Charts.

Fact	Opinion
The Montgolfier brothers launched the world's first hot-air balloon in 1783.	People have always dreamed of soaring like birds
The chief discoveries in ballooning were made in 1783	

Develop Comprehension

18 USE ILLUSTRATIONS

LA.5.2.2.1 Locate information from text features

Look at the picture on page 726. What method is the man in the picture using to inflate the balloon? What kind of balloon is it? (The man in the photo is using a gas heater to warm the air, so this is a hot-air balloon.)

19 USE TEXT FEATURES

LA.5.2.2.1 Locate, explain, and use information from text features

What text features of an informational nonfiction selection can you find in this article? How did they help you understand the information the author presented? (Answers may vary but should include subheadings to organize information and diagrams to explain how a process works. Students may also mention the time line on pages 728–729 from their preview of the selection.)

20 COMPARE AND CONTRAST

LA.5.1.7.7 Compare and contrast elements

SC.A.1.2.2.5.1 Student knows that common materials can be changed from one state to another by heating and cooling

In what way is buoyancy in water and in air similar? (When something is placed in water it takes up space, pushing the water aside. The water pushes back, and this upward force is called buoyancy. It keeps what is placed in the water afloat. When the air inside a balloon is heated, some of the molecules that make up the air are forced out. This makes the air inside lighter than the air outside. The balloon is forced up when the inside air presses against the air outside the balloon.)

A balloonist uses a gas heater to warm the air.

18

726

📘 Comprehension

Grammar: Demonstrative Pronouns

Explain Remind students that a demonstrative pronoun points to and identifies a noun or pronoun. *This* and *these* refer to things that are nearby either in space or time, while *that* and *those* refer to things that are farther away in space and time.

Discuss Point out the sentence "One of these is hydrogen, the lightest gas known" at the bottom of page 727. Explain that in this sentence, the word *these* is a demonstrative pronoun. It refers to the gases that are lighter than air that the author referred to in the previous sentence.

Apply Ask students to read the second-to-last sentence on page 727. Have them find the demonstrative pronoun in the sentence, and the noun that it refers to (*That* is the demonstrative pronoun. It refers to the singular noun *hydrogen*.)

LA.5.3.4.4 Correct use of demonstrative pronouns

Why a Balloon Rises and Floats   **19**

When you place a block of wood in water, it takes up space, pushing some of the water aside. As the wood pushes against the water, the water pushes back. This upward force is called *buoyancy*. Buoyancy is the force that keeps things afloat.

A hot-air balloon rises and floats in an ocean of air for the same reason that the block of wood floats in water. It **20** has buoyancy.

Like all matter, air is made of tiny **particles** called molecules. When air is heated, its molecules spread out and move faster. When the air inside a balloon is heated, some of the molecules inside the balloon are forced out. The air inside becomes thinner, or less **dense**. It weighs less than before, but it takes up the same amount of space. As a result, the air inside the balloon weighs less than an equal amount of outside air. Buoyancy carries the balloon up.

Some gases are lighter than air because the molecules themselves are less dense. One of these is hydrogen, the lightest gas known. However, it is a dangerous gas that can burn and explode. That is why balloonists today use helium, which is slightly heavier but does not burn or explode. Helium is the gas used in party balloons.

The Science Behind Hot-Air Balloons   **22**

21

Air inside weighs less than air outside, so the balloon is carried up by buoyancy.

When air inside a balloon is heated, some of the molecules are forced out.

Air is made of tiny particles called molecules.

727

Develop Comprehension

21 STRATEGY
MONITOR COMPREHENSION

LA.5.1.7
Students uses strategies to comprehend text

What do all the ways of making a balloon float in the air—hydrogen, helium, and hot air—have in common with one another? Explain how you reached your answer.

Student Think Aloud To figure out what hydrogen, helium, and hot air have in common, I can ask myself a question: What makes a balloon float in the air? The text says a hot-air balloon rises and floats in the air because it has buoyancy. When air is heated, air molecules spread out and move faster. Certain gases, like hydrogen and helium, are lighter than air already because their molecules are less dense. So that's what hydrogen, helium, and hot air have in common: their molecules are less dense—or more spread out— than the air around it.

22 **CAUSE AND EFFECT**

LA.5.1.7.4
Identify cause-and-effect relationships in text

Why do balloonists today use helium instead of hydrogen? (Hydrogen is the lightest gas known, but it can also burn and explode. Helium is slightly heavier than hydrogen, but it is much safer.)

Media Literacy

Explain *Up in the Air* gives a lot of information about traveling by balloon. Explain that in many places around the world tourists can take balloon flights to see sights such as the pyramids in Egypt.

Discuss Talk with students how the various media, including print, TV, and radio, might report on a hot-air balloon ride. Ask students which medium might be the most effective in advertising a trip, and to give reasons for their conclusions. Then ask: *What kinds of verbs and adjectives would tempt people to try a balloon trip?*

Apply Have students write and design an advertisement for a trip in a hot-air balloon. Suggest that they use elements of spacing and design to enhance the appearance of the document and add graphics where appropriate.

LA.5.4.1.2 Write a variety of expressive forms
LA.5.3.5.2 Use elements of spacing and design to enhance appearance of document
LA.5.3.5.2 Add graphics where appropriate

Read

Develop Comprehension

23 STRATEGY
WORD PARTS

LA.5.1.6.11 Use roots and affixes derived from Greek and Latin to determine meaning of complex words

What does the word *astronauts* on page 729 mean? The word part *astro* comes from the Greek word *astron*, meaning star, and the word part *naut* comes from the Greek word *nautikos*, meaning sailor. How can using word parts and affixes help you figure out the meaning of a complex word such as *astronaut?* (Answers should include the fact that an astronaut is a person trained to fly in a spacecraft, which is similar to the literal Greek translation, "sailor among the stars.")

24 RELEVANT FACTS AND DETAILS

FCAT

LA.5.2.2.2 Answer questions related to explicitly stated main ideas or relevant details

What is the main idea, or subject matter, of this time line? (Balloons Then and Now.) Name three relevant facts or details from the timeline that support this idea. (Answers will vary.)

Balloons Then and Now

In the centuries since 1783, balloons have found many uses in both war and peace. Many balloonists have competed to soar the highest or to make the longest voyage. Here are a few important events.

1860s: In the Civil War, Union troops, like the French Army before them, used balloons to spy behind enemy lines to see how battles were going.

1900s: The early 1900s brought the dirigible, or blimp. Made of several balloons, it was fitted with motors and propellers that let the pilot steer. A cabin on the underside held more than 100 people on Atlantic crossings.

1875: Three French scientists, exploring the atmosphere, soared to 25,000 feet in a balloon. The men took bottles of oxygen with them, but when the balloon landed only one scientist had survived.

1932: The man who invented a way to travel safely high into the atmosphere was a Swiss named Auguste Piccard, who built a ball-shaped aluminum gondola. Sealed inside with oxygen tanks, he safely reached a height of 54,000 feet.

728

Vocabulary

Semantic Organizers

Explain *Up in the Air* contains many specialized vocabulary words. Using a semantic organizer can help you to remember what a word means by recording its definition, any synonyms or antonyms the word has, and a sentence containing the word.

Discuss Point out the word *transmit* on page 729. Ask: *Are there any context clues that can help you to figure out the meaning of this word? What are some synonyms for* transmit?

Apply Have students create a semantic organizer for *transmit*. They should place the word in a center square, two balloons to the left that contain antonyms or synonyms for the word, a square to the right with the definition, and beneath it a box that contains a sentence using the word.

LA.5.1.7.8 Use semantic organizers to repair comprehension

1961: Brave men kept going higher and higher. Two U.S. Navy officers, Malcolm D. Ross and Victor Prather, Jr., went up 113,740 feet in an open gondola to test space suits for astronauts.

23

Present day: Planes have long been the way to travel by air, but you often see a dirigible carrying a TV crew above a football game or other sports event.

24

1999: Others had crossed the oceans, but Bertrand Piccard (grandson of Auguste) and Brian Jones were the first to balloon non-stop around the world, covering 30,000 miles in 20 days. Their balloon was a cross between a hot-air balloon and a gas balloon.

Every day: Hundreds of small weather balloons explore the atmosphere and transmit their findings to Earth.

729

ELL

Access for All

Read a Time Line Review the time line on pages 728–729 with students. Ask, *What were balloons first used for? What are dirigibles used for today? How high did the French scientists travel in 1875? Did Auguste Piccard travel higher or lower than the French scientists? Who traveled the highest?* Help students answer in complete sentences.

Develop Comprehension

LA.5.1.7.1 Use prior knowledge to make and confirm predictions

RETURN TO PREDICTIONS AND PURPOSES

Review students' predictions and their purposes for reading. Were they correct? Did they find out how the invention of hot-air balloons has been useful? Have students note any additional questions they may have that were not answered in the selection. Ask where they might look to find the answer.

LA.5.1.7 Use strategies to comprehend text

REVIEW READING STRATEGIES

How did identifying relevant facts and details help you to understand the information in the text?

Journal

PERSONAL RESPONSE

LA.5.4.1 Student develops and demonstrates creative writing

Discuss with students what they feel is the most useful purpose for which balloons are used today. Then have them think about whether they would like to go up in a hot-air balloon. Have students write a paragraph on what they think the experience might be like using text descriptions or examples from the text.

Quick Check **Can students identify relevant facts and details?**

During **Small Group Instruction**

If No → **Approaching Level** Comprehension, pp. 735O–735P

If Yes → **On Level** Options, p. 735R

Beyond Level Options, p. 735T

Author

UP, UP, AND AWAY
WITH PATRICIA LAUBER

Discuss the biography of the author.

LA.5.1.7.2
Identify
author's
purpose

DISCUSS

- How does Patricia Lauber's research make the topic of balloon flight more interesting?

- Why does Patricia Lauber enjoy doing research?

Invite students to look back through their Reading journals and reflect on their progress and accomplishments this year. Discuss what they choose to read as a leisure activity.

WRITE ABOUT IT

After discussing the earliest hot-air balloon flights, have students write a paragraph telling what they think it would be like to ride in a hot-air balloon back in 1793.

FCAT Author's Purpose

Tell students that text features usually convey additional information to supplement the text. For example, point to the illustrations and captions on page 727. Discuss how the captions highlight information and the drawings illustrate concepts.

LA.5.1.7.2 Identify author's purpose

LOG ON   Technology

Students can find more information about Patricia Lauber at **www.macmillanmh.com**

Up, Up, and Away
with Patricia Lauber

Patricia Lauber says she was probably born wanting to write but had to wait until she had gone to school to learn a few things. She has been writing happily ever since and has produced about 125 books. Many are about things in the natural world, such as volcanoes, dinosaurs, and planets. Patricia loves doing the research for these books because she is always learning something new. Filled with enthusiasm about a new subject, she shares what she has learned by writing books. Patricia Lauber lives in Connecticut with her husband and their two cats, Beemer and Meetoo.

Another book by Patricia Lauber:
Living with Dinosaurs

LOG ON   Find out more about Patricia Lauber at **www.macmillanmh.com**

FCAT Author's Purpose

This nonfiction piece informs and explains. Identify text features that offer information.

730

Author's Craft
Sensory Images

Explain that images that appeal to readers' senses can make information vivid and lively. Patricia Lauber uses many **sensory images.** For example:

> Tongues of orange flame shoot out of roaring gas burners, heating air to make the balloons rise. (p. 717)

Discuss why Patricia Lauber might use sensory images in a nonfiction article.

Ask students to identify the senses to which each image in the example appeals. Then ask them to find other examples of sensory language in the article and to identify the senses to which they appeal.

LA.5.2.1.7 Identify and explain author's use of descriptive language

FCAT Comprehension Check

Summarize

Making generalizations will help you organize relevant facts and details and summarize them more effectively. Use your Fact and Opinion Chart to help you summarize *Up in the Air*.

Fact	Opinion

Think and Compare

1. Describe a few facts about a modern–day balloon ride. Use details to explain how these facts relate to the main idea of the article. **Monitor Comprehension: Relevant Facts and Details**

2. Reread page 723. Why were animals sent up as the first balloon passengers? Include facts and details from the selection to support your answer. **Analyze**

3. Hot-air balloons transformed life over 200 years ago. Think about a recent **scientific** invention that has affected you. Identify the invention and tell how it has changed your life. **Evaluate**

4. People risked their lives to fly in hot-air balloons. How has their commitment to science contributed to the modern world? **Explain**

5. Reread "The Science of Hot-Air Balloons" on pages 712–713. Compare and contrast the different ways hot-air balloons are able to fly. Use details from each selection in your answer. **Reading/Writing Across Texts**

731

Strategies for Answering Questions

Author and Me

Model the Author and Me strategy with question 2.

The answer is not stated in the text, but there may be clues. Connect these text clues with what you know to answer the question.

Question 2 Think Aloud: On page 723 the author writes that the first passengers to go up in a balloon were a lamb, a duck, and a rooster. After a short flight, they drifted down to Earth, and the people who sent them up saw that they were safe. This proved that it was possible to breathe a few thousand feet above Earth. Although the author does not say so directly, I can infer that the people who conducted the experiment concluded that it was safe for people to go up in balloons, too.

LA.5.1.7 Student uses strategies to comprehend text

Comprehension Check

SUMMARIZE

FCAT
LA.5.1.7.3 Determine main idea through summarizing

Have students summarize orally or in writing the most important information in *Up in the Air:* and paraphrase the text's main idea.

THINK AND COMPARE

Sample answers are given.

FCAT
LA.5.2.2.2 Answer questions related to main idea and relevant details

1. **Relevant Facts and Details:** In a modern-day balloon ride, people ride in a basket, gas burners heat the air to make the balloon rise, the balloon goes where the wind carries it, and crew members follow on land to meet the passengers. The time line also says that people sometimes fly in a dirigible to watch sporting events.

LA.5.2.2.2 Use information from text to answer questions

2. **Analyze:** The first balloon passengers were animals because people were not certain that it would be possible to breathe while floating above Earth. USE AUTHOR AND ME

LA.5.2.1.5 Demonstrate understanding and include personal experience

3. **Text to Self:** Students should explain their answers with examples.

4. **Text to World:** Their commitment to science led to many experiments and to other types of flight. Today, weather balloons are used to explore the atmosphere.

FOCUS QUESTION

LA.5.2.1.5 Demonstrate understanding and include other text/media

5. **Text to Text:** Some balloons fly using hot air to make the balloon lighter than the cold air outside. Balloonists burned straw and wool when they flew the first hot-air balloons. Now they use propane burners. Other balloons are buoyant because they are filled with light gases, either hydrogen or helium.

Objective

- Read accurately with appropriate tempo
- Rate: 129–149 WCPM

Materials

- Fluency Transparency 29
- Fluency Solutions Audio CD
- Practice Book, p. 210

ELL **Access for All**

Echo-Read Ask questions to ensure that students understand the meaning of the passage. Echo-read the passage with students a few times, starting at a slower speed and increasing the speed each time. You can also have students read along with the Fluency Solutions Audio CD.

On Level Practice Book O, page 210

As I read, I will pay attention to tempo and phrasing.

12	It is a beautiful day at the football stadium. Fans fill the
22	seats and wait for the kickoff. Suddenly, a strange shadow
33	appears on the field. People sitting in the upper rows hear
44	a low whirring sound overhead. Floating in the sky is a
47	football-shaped balloon.
57	Most of us have seen them on television during sporting
69	events. They are like silent ships sailing on a sea of sky.
77	These strange-looking balloons are called blimps. They are
82	cousins to the hot-air balloon.
93	Blimps and hot-air balloons are part of a group of flying
101	machines known as lighter-than-air craft. They are filled
108	with gas that weighs less than air.
118	Blimps are also members of the airship family. Just like
127	boats, airships have motors and rudders. The motors give
136	airships speed. The rudders help steer. These additions make
144	airships very different from hot-air balloons. Hot-air balloons
154	have little control over their speed or direction. Airships can
	even fly against the wind. 159

Comprehension Check

1. Compare and contrast blimps and hot-air balloons. **Compare and Contrast** Both are filled with gas that weighs less than air. Blimps have motors and rudders, and hot-air balloons do not.
2. Where do people commonly see blimps? **Main Idea and Details** Most people see blimps at sporting events.

	Words Read	–	Number of Errors	=	Words Correct Score
First Read		–		=	
Second Read		–		=	

⭐ **Approaching Practice Book A,** page 210

◆ **Beyond Practice Book B,** page 210

LA.5.1.5 Student demonstrates ability to read orally with accuracy and appropriate rate

Fluency
Repeated Reading: *Tempo*

EXPLAIN/MODEL Tell students that they will be working on increasing tempo. Model increasing tempo by reading the first two sentences of the passage, first at a slow tempo and then at a faster tempo. Tell students that it is important to pronounce words correctly and not to leave out words as they increase their reading speed. Model reading aloud the two paragraphs on **Fluency Transparency 29.**

Transparency 29

The first passengers to go up in a balloon were a trio of animals—a duck, a rooster, and a lamb. On September 19, 1783, they traveled in a wicker basket, or gondola, attached to a balloon. After a short flight, the air in the balloon cooled and the passengers drifted safely to Earth. Their flight showed that it was possible to breathe while floating a few thousand feet above Earth.

It was now time for humans to risk ballooning. A daring young French chemist was the first. On October 15, 1783, François Pilâtre de Rozier went up 100 feet. He was anchored to the ground by a long rope called a tether. His balloon carried a big metal pan under its mouth. A fire in the pan sent hot air into the balloon. The flight was a success.

Fluency Transparency 29
from *Up in the Air: The Story of Balloon Flight*

PRACTICE/APPLY Have one student read the first sentence at a slow pace. A second student joins in, then a third, until all students are reading together. Continue reading until everyone has been included. Repeat this pattern twice, each time at a slightly faster pace. Students can also practice fluency using **Practice Book** page 210 or the **Fluency Solutions Audio CD.**

Cooperative Learning

Access for All

Quick Check	**Can students read accurately with appropriate tempo?**

During **Small Group Instruction**

If No → **Approaching Level** Fluency, p. 735N

If Yes → **On Level** Options, p. 735Q

Beyond Level Options, p. 735S

Comprehension

REVIEW SKILL
CHRONOLOGICAL ORDER

LA.5.2.2.3
Organize
information
to show
understanding

EXPLAIN/MODEL

- Remind students that sequence refers to the time order of events in an oral or written selection. When an author relates the events in the order that they occurred, whether the selection is a story or a nonfiction account of an historical event, the events are said to be in **chronological order.**

- Sometimes two or more events may happen simultaneously in a story or nonfiction account, or a flashback or flashforward may interrupt the chronological order of events. Signal words such as *first, second, then, meawhile, before,* and *later* often reveal the chronological order of events in a selection. In nonfiction, dates can often be used to determine the chronological order of events.

- Model for students by asking them to look over "The Science of Hot Air Balloons" on page 712 and find sequence words. Discuss the use of these words in the selection.

LA.5.2.2.3
Organize
information
to show
understanding

PRACTICE/APPLY

Discuss the chronological order of events in *Up in the Air: The Story of Balloon Flight.*

- Did Professor Jacques A.C. Charles design his lighter-than-air balloon before, after, or at the same time that the Montgolfier brothers flew their hot-air balloon?

- How does the author let readers know after the introduction that she is about to describe events that happened over 200 years ago?

- Place the following events from the story in chronological order: Marie Thible becomes the first woman to take a balloon flight, a trio of animals go up in a balloon, de Rozier makes the first untethered flight, a crowd of French villagers attacks Professor Charles's balloon.

Objective

- Review the chronological order of events in a selection.

FCAT Skills Trace

Chronological Order

Introduce	71B
Practice / Apply	641A–B, 642–659, 739A–B, 740–751; Practice Book 187–188, 215–216
Reteach / Review	163B; 283B; 6670–P, R, T; 731B; 7590–P, R, T
Assess	Weekly Tests; Unit 6 Test; Benchmark Tests A, B
Maintain	641A–B, 739A–B; Practice Book 187–188, 215–216

Poetry

LA.5.2.1.1
Demonstrate
knowledge of
characteristics
of genres

GENRE: HAIKU

Have students read the bookmark on **Student Book** page 732. Explain that a haiku

- is a three-line poem that contains much descriptive language, often about nature

- often has a set number of syllables in each line—five, seven, five

- often contains figures of speech such as similes and metaphors to give added meaning to a word or expression

 ## Literary Elements:
Simile and Metaphor

LA.5.2.1.7
Explain
author's use
of similes and
metaphors

Literary elements enhance imagery and add emotion to poetry.

- A **simile** and a **metaphor** both make comparisons between two things.

- A simile uses the words *like* or *as* to make the comparison.

- A metaphor compares two things directly without using the words *like* or *as*.

1 **GENRE: HAIKU**

LA.5.2.1.1
Demonstrate
knowledge of
genre forms
with distinct
characteristics
and purposes

How is haiku unlike other forms of poetry you know? (It is very short, does not use full sentences, and offers a snapshot image or idea.)

2 **LITERARY ELEMENT: SIMILE**

 Find another simile in these haikus. ("With petals as white as sheets"; petals are likened to sheets.)

LA.5.2.1.7 Identify author's use of similes

FCAT **Poetry**

Haiku is an unrhymed form of Japanese poetry that is three lines long. The first line has five syllables; the second line, seven syllables; the third line, five syllables.

Literary Elements

A **Simile** is a comparison of two essentially unlike things that uses the words *like* or *as*.
A **Metaphor** is a comparison of two essentially unlike things that does *not* use the words *like* or *as*.

Hot-Air Balloon Haiku

by Rita Bristol

1 Balloon, so high up.
A big, bright, bouncing bubble
Too buoyant to burst.

This is an example of a metaphor.

2 What a strange flower!
With petals as white as sheets.
A bee sleeps within.

732

After students have finished reading, have them interpret the haiku and identify the style and characteristics of this kind of poetry.

As an extension have students write their own haiku about balloons, using these poems as a model. Then students can memorize one or more of the haiku on pages 732–733 and/or their own haiku and recite them for the class.

LA.5.5.2.1 Listen and speak for poetic recitations
LA.5.4.1 Student develops creative writing

What do clouds feel like
Floating above the balloon
As it takes you far? **3**

It floats like freedom
In the hazy August light
Soon, though, it will land.

This is an example
of a simile.

FCAT Connect and Compare

1. Find another example of metaphor in one of the other haiku. **Metaphor**

2. How do these four haiku help readers get a stronger sense of seeing or being in a hot-air balloon? **Analyze**

3. What is the difference between the information in these haiku and the information presented in "Up in the Air"? **Reading/Writing Across Texts**

 LOG ON Find out more about haiku at **www.macmillanmh.com**

733

---

3 DESCRIPTION

LA.5.2.1.7
Examine how language describes objects

What general image of hot-air balloons do these poems convey? (the image of bright, warm weightlessness)

Connect and Compare

FCAT

SUGGESTED ANSWERS

LA.5.2.1.7
Explain author's use of metaphors

1. The metaphor "What a strange flower!" compares a hot-air balloon to the petals of a flower. METAPHOR

LA.5.2.1.7
Examine how language describes feelings and objects

2. Answers will vary. The reader can "see" that the balloon resembles the shape of a flower or a bubble. The simile "floats like freedom" emphasizes that the balloon can move as it pleases, at its own speed and in its own space. The metaphor of a bouncing bubble creates a sense of fun. ANALYZE

FOCUS QUESTION

LA.5.2.1.5
Demonstrate understanding and include other text/media

3. The information in "Up in the Air" explains how balloons work. The haiku describes the speaker's feelings and thoughts about balloon flight rather than the science behind balloons. READING/
WRITING ACROSS TEXTS

On Level Practice Book O, page 211

When you read poetry, you often encounter poetic elements such as **similes** and **metaphors.** Similes and metaphors use language to create striking or unexpected images for the reader. These are figures of speech that compare or associate two things. Similes use *like* or *as* in the comparison. Metaphors do not use *like* or *as*.

Read the poem to answer the following questions.

Balloon Flight Haiku

It floats in the air
Like a bird's loosened feather,
drifting among blue.

The azure ocean
above our very heads
is where it sails high.

Unlike a feather,
it is guided by someone
who chooses its course.

1. What similes can you find in the haiku?
   like a bird's loosened feather; unlike a feather

2. What metaphors can you find in the haiku?
   The azure ocean above our heads; where it sails high

3. What comparisons are made in the haiku? The balloon is compared to a feather; the sky is compared to the ocean; the balloon is compared to a ship.

4. Which comparison is not stated directly? How do you know the comparison is made?
   The balloon is compared to a ship. The metaphors "azure ocean" and "it sails high" imply a ship.

★ **Approaching Practice Book A,** page 211

◆ **Beyond Practice Book B,** page 211

 LOG ON **Technology**

Internet Research and Inquiry Activity Students can find more facts at **www.macmillanmh.com**

Connect
Language Arts

✓ **FCAT WRITING**
- Persuasive
- Writer's Craft: Organize Ideas

✓ **WORD STUDY**
- FCAT Words in Context
- Word Parts: Greek Roots
- **Phonics:** Number Prefixes
- Vocabulary Building

✓ **SPELLING**
- Number Prefixes

✓ **GRAMMAR**
- Prepositions/Prepositional Phrases

SMALL GROUP OPTIONS
- Differentiated Instruction, pp. 735M–735V

Writing

FCAT Organize Ideas

LA.5.1.5.1
Read grade
level text

READ THE STUDENT MODEL

Read the bookmark about organizing ideas. Explain that writers organize ideas in ways that make sense for readers.

Have students skim and scan the subheads in *Up in the Air: The Story of Balloon Flight*. Note the order in which the author presents the topics, and discuss whether this order makes sense for readers. Then have the class read Tamara E.'s **persuasive essay** and the callouts. Tell students they will write persuasive essays of their own, organizing their ideas so their information is presented logically.

Writer's Craft

FCAT Organize Ideas
When writers want to persuade, they decide which arrangement of their ideas will work best to convince the reader. Writers often **organize ideas** in a way that will make their writing more effective.

Write About a Challenge

Facing My Fear
by Tamara E.

Have you ever wanted to try something new but were too afraid? I have always been afraid of heights, but last summer my cousin persuaded me to take a ride in a hot-air balloon. I'm so glad that I did it!

The pilot was nice and the balloons were beautiful! Once I was in the air, I saw the whole town and farms under me. Even now when I walk around, I think of what the view would be like from up high.

I got the best feeling from doing it because I had overcome a fear I had. I think all people should face their fears by trying something new.

> Instead of starting with my own experience, I began my essay with a question.

> I used details to help persuade my readers.

734

Features of a Persuasive Essay

In a persuasive essay, the writer encourages readers to act or to change their thinking.

- A persuasive essay includes a statement of opinion.

- It includes supporting reasons, explanations, or examples.

- The ideas are arranged in a logical order.

- The writer may directly address readers through the use of the second-person pronoun *you*.

Writing Prompt

Many people are faced with trying new activities that challenge them.

Think of an activity you tried that challenged you.

Now write about an activity you tried that challenged you.

FCAT Writer's Checklist

✓ **Focus:** My writing is persuasive and I have a topic I can explain well.

☑ **Organization:** I *organize ideas* to explain my point of view more effectively.

✓ **Support:** I use supporting details to explain my main idea.

✓ **Conventions:** All words are spelled correctly. I use prepositions and prepositional phrases correctly.

735

Transparency 113: **Chart**
Transparency 114: **Draft**
Transparency 115: **Revision**

Transparency 113

Topic	• Facing My Fear
Opinion(s)	• Fearing something can make you not try doing it. • You'll be happy if you can face your fear.
Ideas and Details	• afraid of heights • went on balloon ride • had a great time • wasn't scared
Ideas for Conclusion	• a great feeling • everyone should face their fears

Writing Transparency 113

PREWRITE

LA.5.3.1.2 Prewrite by determining purpose and intended audience

Read and discuss the writing prompt on page 735. Have members of small student groups share challenging activities that they have done. Tell students to explain how the activities were challenging and why others should try them. Help students identify an audience and a purpose for writing.

Display **Transparency 113.** Discuss how Tamara uses a chart to help her plan her essay. Have students work on charts with partners.

DRAFT

LA.5.3.1.3 Make a plan for writing that addresses logical sequence

Display **Transparency 114.** Discuss ways to improve the draft. For example, Tamara might add why hot-air ballooning was challenging for her and why the experience was beneficial.

Before students begin writing, present the explicit lesson on **Organize Ideas** on page 735A. Then have students use their outlines to plan and write their essays. Remind them to focus on ordering their ideas logically.

REVISE

LA.5.3.3 Student will revise draft

Display **Transparency 115.** Discuss the revisions. Tamara adds details and ideas. Students can revise their drafts or place them in writing portfolios to work on later.

If students choose to revise, have them work with a partner and use the Writer's Checklist on page 735. Have them **proofread/edit** their writing. For **Publishing Options,** see page 735A.

For lessons on **Ideas and Content, Using a Thesaurus, Prepositions and Prepositional Phrases,** and **Spelling,** see page 735B, and **5 Day Spelling** and **5 Day Grammar** on pages 735G–735J.

SUPPORT **Organize Ideas**

LA.5.3.3.1
Evaluate draft for logical organization

Publishing Options

Students can share their essays orally with the class. See the Speaking and Listening tips below. They can also use their best cursive to write their essays. (See Teacher's Resource Book pages 168–173 for cursive models and practice.) Then students can bind their essays into a class magazine. Ask the librarian to display the magazine in the school library.

Speaking and Listening

SPEAKING STRATEGIES

- Practice reading your essay to yourself.
- Speak clearly and in a natural tone of voice.
- Make frequent eye contact with the audience.

LISTENING STRATEGIES

- Listen carefully to identify the speaker's opinion.
- Ask questions to gain information not presented.
- Think about whether the speaker's supporting examples are convincing.

6-Point Scoring Rubric

Use the rubric on page **763G** to score published writing.

Writing Process

For a complete lesson, see Unit Writing pages **763A–763F**.

EXPLAIN/MODEL

Explain that writers must sequence their ideas in ways that make the most sense for readers. Good writers work to lead their readers from one idea to the next without confusion. Display **Transparency 116.**

Think Aloud The writer wants people to try new activities as a way to learn about themselves. He gives a supporting example about taking an art class. However, the order of ideas is confusing for readers. Brandon needs to think about rearranging his ideas to make his essay easy for readers to follow.

Transparency 116

Painting My Way Through Life
by Brandon Q.

_4_ The teacher sensed my confusion and came to help me. I told her that I had made a mistake. She said, "There are no mistakes in art, just opportunities."

_2_ I am not an artist. I can't draw. I can't paint. One day in an art class, the teacher gave everyone a silk scarf to paint. I was so worried that I would ruin the fine material.

_1_ Have you ever been afraid to try something new? Maybe you were afraid of embarrassing yourself or looking silly. Trying new activities, however, can help you learn about yourself.

_5_ That art lesson has stayed with me. I'm not afraid to try something new.

_3_ I started to work. Before I knew it I had painted a black line that I didn't want.

Writing Transparency 116

PRACTICE/APPLY

Work with students to rearrange the paragraphs into a logical order. Then, have students note the order of ideas in essays that they have read recently.

As students prepare for and write their essays, have them focus on idea arrangement, ideas and content, and word choice.

Writer's Toolbox

LA.5.4.3.2 Write persuasive text that includes persuasive techniques

SUPPORT

Writing Trait: Ideas and Content

Explain/Model Tell students that the art of persuasion relies on building relationships with readers. One way to build relationships is for writers to share thoughts and feelings with readers. Writers can also reflect on the significance of their topics. Have students look at Tamara E.'s essay on page 734. Point out that Tamara admits to readers that she was afraid of heights, and she tells readers how hot-air ballooning changed her life.

Practice/Apply As students draft their essays, encourage them to strengthen ideas and content by building relationships with readers through thoughts, feelings, and reflection.

CONVENTIONS

LA.5.3.4.4. Edits for correct use of parts of speech

Grammar: Prepositions/ Prepositional Phrases

Explain/Model Explain that a preposition introduces a phrase that ends with a noun or pronoun. The phrase makes a connection between two nouns or pronouns in a sentence. Point out that Tamara uses the prepositional phrase *near her town* to connect the nouns *field* and *town*.

Practice/Apply Have students skim the rest of the essay for other prepositional phrases. Encourage students to use prepositional phrases in their essays. For a complete lesson, including a **mechanics** lesson on commas and prepositional phrases and appositives, see pages 735I–735J.

SUPPORT

Use a Thesaurus

Explain/Model Point out to students that some words create stronger impressions for readers than other words do. Tell students that writers can consult thesauruses to strengthen word choice. Point out that Tamara may have consulted a thesaurus to choose words such as *overcome* or *challenge*.

Practice/Apply As students draft their essays, encourage them consult thesauruses to strengthen word choice.

LA.5.1.6.10 Determine alternate word choices using a thesaurus

CONVENTIONS

Spelling: Number Prefixes

Point out that Tamara might have used binoculars during her balloon ride. Suggest that students use their knowledge of the number prefix *bi-* to define the word *binoculars*. Remind students to pay attention when they spell words with number prefixes. They can use print or online dictionaries to check spelling in their drafts. For a complete lesson on number prefixes, see pages 735G-735H.

LA.5.3.4.1 Edits for spelling

Technology

Students can center the titles of their essays and their names by highlighting the information and clicking the Align Center buttons on their computers.

FCAT Success!

Test Prep and Practice with FCAT Writing+, pages180–230.

Objectives

- Apply knowledge of word meaning and context clues
- Build words from Greek roots

Materials

- Vocabulary Transparencies 57 and 58
- Practice Book, p. 212

Vocabulary

launched (p. 719) something that is set in motion

inflate (p. 717) to cause something to swell by forcing air or gas into it

companion (p. 723) person who goes along with or accompanies another

anchored (p. 723) to be firmly held in place

scientific (p. 725) using the facts and laws of science

particles (p. 727) small units of matter

dense (p. 727) closely packed together; thick

hydrogen (p. 721) colorless, odorless gas

ELL

Categorize Write, *Something that inflates. Something that is launched. Something that is anchored.* Write and draw an example of each. Say, *rocket.* Have students tell you the category or categories under which the word fits. Repeat with other words.

Review
Vocabulary
 FCAT Words in Context

LA.5.1.6.3 Use context clues to determine word meanings

EXPLAIN/MODEL

Review the meanings of vocabulary words. Display **Transparency 57.** Model how to use word meanings and context clues to fill in the missing word in the first example. Use the Think Aloud strategy.

Think Aloud For the balloons to be in the sky, they must have been lifted into the air, or launched. When I put *launched* in the sentence, it makes sense.

Transparency 57

scientific   launched   companion   anchored   inflate
hydrogen   dense   particles

1. The hot-air balloons were <u>launched</u> into the sky.
2. Billy asked me to <u>inflate</u> the balloon.
3. My mom was my traveling <u>companion</u> when I toured Mexico.
4. We <u>anchored</u> the boat and began looking for whales.
5. We used the <u>scientific</u> method to prove that air has weight.
6. The scientist looked at <u>particles</u> under the microscope.
7. The fog was so <u>dense</u> that school was delayed.
8. Water is made of <u>hydrogen</u> and oxygen.

Vocabulary Transparency 57

 PRACTICE/APPLY

Instruct students to complete the remaining sentences on their own. Review the students' answers as a class, or instruct students to check their answers with partners.

 Word Maps Students can work on finding synonyms, antonyms, and examples of the vocabulary words. Ask questions of the class as a group. For example: *dense:* synonym word box: *thick;* antonym word box: *clear;* example word box: *a foggy sky;* non-example word box: *a sunny day.* Post word webs for reference.

STRATEGY
WORD PARTS: GREEK ROOTS

LA.5.1.6.11
Use roots
and affixes
from Greek
to determine
meaning

EXPLAIN/MODEL

Many English words are made up of Greek roots, which are word parts that come from the ancient language Greek. When an affix or another Greek root is added to a Greek root, new words are formed. For example, the word *astronaut* is made up of two Greek roots, *astro,* which means "star," and *naut,* which means "sailor." So *astronaut* literally means "a star sailor."

Display **Transparency 58.** Go over the roots and their meanings. Model how to figure out the meaning of *autograph* in item 1 using the meanings of the Greek roots.

Transparency 58

GREEK ROOTS

auto = self   tele = distance

bio = life   photo = light

logos = study of   pod = foot

graph = write   octo = eight

1. autograph   (self-writing)
2. biology   (study of life)
3. photograph   (something written or recorded by light)
4. octopus   (animal with eight arms)
5. telegraph   (writing sent over distance)
6. biography   (writing about someone's life)

Vocabulary Strategy Transparency 58

PRACTICE

Guide students through items 2–6. Have students use a dictionary to verify meanings.

Quick Check
Can students understand word meanings in context?
Can students use Greek roots to find a word's meaning?

During **Small Group Instruction**

If No → **Approaching Level** Vocabulary, pp. 735N–735P

If Yes → **On Level** Options, pp. 735Q–735R

     Beyond Level Options, pp. 735S–735T

ELL

Make Associations/Visuals Have students write each root and its meaning and sentences with a word containing the root: *path = feelings I feel sympathy for someone who is sick. I feel sad because he is sick.* Encourage students to use color and illustrations in their work.

FCAT **Success!**

Test Prep and Practice with vocabulary, pages 6–31.

On Level Practice Book O, page 212

Many English words have roots that originally came from the ancient Greek language. Knowing what the **Greek root** means will help you figure out the meaning of the word.

Root	Meaning
hydro	water
aster/astro	star
dem	people
graph	write
log/logue	word
pod	foot

Use the chart above to help you choose which word is being described in each item below.

1. The lightest gas, this element is found in water and all organic substances. (helium, hydrogen) __hydrogen__
2. This is a noun that means "a conversation, often in a story." (dialogue, dialect) __dialogue__
3. This object has three "feet." (tricycle, tripod) __tripod__
4. This kind of political system allows the people to vote for their government. (democracy, monarchy) __democracy__
5. This is a form of communication that people use to write in Morse code. (telephone, telegraph) __telegraph__
6. This is the study of the stars and planets. (geology, astronomy) __astronomy__

 Approaching Practice Book A, page 212

Beyond Practice Book B, page 212

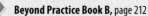

Objective
- Decode words with number prefixes

Materials
- Practice Book, p. 213

ELL / Access for All

Draw and Categorize
Write the words *unicycle*, *bicycle*, and *tricycle* and draw each one. Relate the number of wheels to each prefix. Give other examples of each prefix. Categorize the words by their short *i* and long *i* sounds and practice pronouncing the words alone and in sentences.

On Level Practice Book O, page 213

Prefixes are word parts added to the beginning of other words or word parts. A prefix changes the word's meaning. Some prefixes refer to an amount and are called **number prefixes**.

prefix	number	example
uni-	1	unity
bi-	2	bicycle
tri-	3	triceratops
cent-	100	centennial

A. Choose the best prefix for the boldface word. Then write the complete word on the line.

1. The girl put on her soccer ____**form** before the game.
   uniform

2. Every ____**meter** counts when carefully measuring the length of a board. _centimeter_

3. The ____**cycle** has three wheels. _tricycle_

4. Stephanie was ____**lingual** and knew two languages.
   bilingual

B. Circle the prefix in each word. Then write a definition of the word that is based on the meaning of the prefix.

5. (tri)angle _a shape with three angles_
6. (uni)verse _one system of stars and planets_
7. (bi)sect _to divide into two sections_
8. (centi)pede _an insect with one hundred feet_
9. (tri)pod _an object with three feet_
10. (uni)corn _a mythical one-horned animal_

★ **Approaching Practice Book A,** page 213

◆ **Beyond Practice Book B,** page 213

Phonics

 ## Number Prefixes *uni-, bi-, tri-, cent-*

Access for All

LA.5.1.4.2
Recognize structural analysis

EXPLAIN/MODEL

- Some prefixes stand for numbers.

- The prefix *uni-* means "one," *bi-* means "two," *tri-* means "three," and *cent(i)-* means "hundred."

Write the word *centimeter* on the board. Model how to decode the meaning of the word by using the Think Aloud strategy and prior knowledge of number prefixes.

Think Aloud When I read the word *centimeter,* I see the prefix *cent(i).* I know that *cent* means "hundred." I know that the root *meter* means "to measure." I think the word *centimeter* means "to measure things in units of a hundred."

LA.5.1.6
Student uses multiple strategies to develop vocabulary

PRACTICE/APPLY

Write these words on the board. Ask volunteers to read each word and identify the prefix. Then have students predict the meaning of each word and then look it up in a dictionary.

1. uniform	4. unicorn	7. centipede	10. bicycle
2. bisect	5. bilevel	8. century	11. universe
3. triplet	6. triangle	9. unison	12. triple

Have students invent new words using the number prefixes. Have them present their words and corresponding definitions to the class.

LA.5.1.4.3
Use language structure to read multi-syllabic words

Decode Multisyllabic Words Make sure students don't allow the number of syllables in a word to distract them from recognizing the presence of a number prefix. Examples of longer words with number prefixes include *university* and *binoculars*. For more practice, see the decodable passages on pages 36–37 of the **Teacher's Resource Book.**

Quick Check — **Can students decode words with number prefixes?**

During **Small Group Instruction**

If No → **Approaching Level** Phonics, p. 735M

If Yes → **On Level** Options, pp. 735Q–735R

Beyond Level Options, pp. 735S–735T

Vocabulary Building

LA.5.1.6 Student uses multiple strategies to develop vocabulary

LA.5.1.6.11 Use roots derived from Greek; LA.5.1.6.10 Determine word choices using digital tools

LA.5.1.6 Student develops grade-appropriate vocabulary

Oral Language

Expand Vocabulary Have students write *balloon flight* in the center of a word web like the one below. Using the selection, and print and electronic dictionaries, thesauruses, and the glossary, have students find, brainstorm, and discuss words that relate to this week's theme. Have them identify any words that are formed from Greek roots.

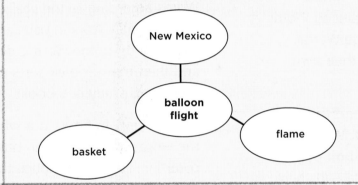

Spiral Review

Vocabulary Game Draw a hot-air balloon on the board. Hand each student a note card or small square of paper. On the paper have students write a vocabulary word from one of the previous weeks and place it in a box or basket. Make two teams. Invite students to draw from the basket one word to define, name the part of speech, and use in a sentence. If a student performs all the tasks correctly, the card can be taped to the board as a sandbag on that team's side of the balloon. The team with the most sandbags wins.

Vocabulary Building

Word Origins Many words in English have come from other languages. Show students how to find the origin, or etymology, of the word *pilot*, using a standard dictionary. Point out that *pilot* comes from the Italian word *pilota,* which originally came from a Greek word that meant "steering oars." Have students find the origins of the following words in the selection using a standard dictionary: *altitude, inflated, tethered, balloon, explode.* Have them report their findings to the class.

LA.5.1.6.10 Determine etymologies using a dictionary

Apply Vocabulary

Write an Explanatory Paragraph Write the following prompt on the board: *Write a paragraph using the vocabulary words in which you explain why balloon flight is important today. Include your own ideas as well as references to the selection to support your ideas. You can also include references to other works, such as TV shows or films. Make sure that your paragraph has a topic sentence and contains introductory, body, and concluding paragraphs.*

LA.5.4.2.3 Write expository essays that contain introductory, body, and concluding paragraphs

5 Day Spelling

Number Prefixes *uni-, bi-, tri-, cent-*

Spelling Words

tripod	bicycle	centipede
triplet	tricycle	centimeter
unicorn	unicycle	century
uniform	triangle	binoculars
unison	bisect	universe
biweekly	trio	university
triple	unify	

Review cereal, terrace, atlas

Challenge bilingual, trilogy

Dictation Sentences

1. A <u>tripod</u> supports the camera.
2. The <u>triplet</u> looks like her sisters.
3. The <u>unicorn</u> is a graceful animal.
4. I wore my school <u>uniform</u>.
5. The group spoke in <u>unison</u>.
6. The magazine comes <u>biweekly</u>.
7. Our city is <u>triple</u> the size of yours.
8. Jackie likes to ride her <u>bicycle</u>.
9. Ted prefers the <u>tricycle</u>.
10. The clown rode a <u>unicycle</u>.
11. The <u>triangle</u> has three sides.
12. To <u>bisect</u> is to divide into two.
13. A **trio** of singers performed.
14. Pep rallies can <u>unify</u> the school.
15. The <u>centipede</u> crawled slowly.
16. Tanya measured a <u>centimeter</u>.
17. A **century** is one hundred years.
18. I looked through the <u>binoculars</u>.
19. Superheroes always save the <u>universe</u>.
20. He attends a state <u>university</u>.

Review/Challenge Words

1. <u>Cereal</u> is my favorite breakfast food.
2. The house has a lovely <u>terrace</u>.
3. I used the <u>atlas</u> for my research.
4. The translator is <u>bilingual</u>.
5. Tolkien wrote a famous <u>trilogy</u>.

Words in **bold** type are from the main selection.

Day 1 — Pretest

ASSESS PRIOR KNOWLEDGE

Using the Dictation Sentences, say the underlined word. Read the sentence aloud and repeat the word. Have students write the words on **Spelling Practice Book** page 179. For a modified list, use the first 12 Spelling Words and the Review Words. For a more challenging list, use Spelling Words 3–20 and the Challenge Words. Students may correct their own tests.

Ask students to cut apart the Spelling Word Cards BLM on **Teacher's Resource Book** page 94 and figure out a way to sort them.

Use Spelling Practice Book page 180 for more practice with this week's spelling words.

For leveled Spelling word lists, go to **www.macmillanmh.com**

Day 2 — Word Sorts

TEACHER AND STUDENT SORTS

- Write the prefixes *uni, bi-, tri-, cent-* on the board as column headings. Review with students how a prefix is added to the front of a root word to make a new word.

- Explain that students will sort the Spelling Words and Challenge Words according to the prefixes. Students may work in pairs and begin by using the Word Cards and then transfer their sorts to their word study notebooks.

- Ask students to figure out what the words in each column have in common. Help them notice that the prefixes indicate numbers in the Latin language. Add the corresponding numbers (1, 2, 3, 100) to the column headings.

- Challenge students to think of other words that begin with the same prefixes.

Spelling Practice Book, pages 179–180

Fold back the paper along the dotted line. Write the words in the blanks as they are read aloud. When you finish the test, unfold the paper. Use the list at the right to correct any spelling mistakes.

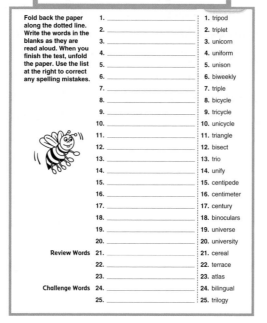

1. _____	1. tripod
2. _____	2. triplet
3. _____	3. unicorn
4. _____	4. uniform
5. _____	5. unison
6. _____	6. biweekly
7. _____	7. triple
8. _____	8. bicycle
9. _____	9. tricycle
10. _____	10. unicycle
11. _____	11. triangle
12. _____	12. bisect
13. _____	13. trio
14. _____	14. unify
15. _____	15. centipede
16. _____	16. centimeter
17. _____	17. century
18. _____	18. binoculars
19. _____	19. universe
20. _____	20. university
Review Words 21. _____	21. cereal
22. _____	22. terrace
23. _____	23. atlas
Challenge Words 24. _____	24. bilingual
25. _____	25. trilogy

Spelling Practice Book, page 181

uniform	unison	bisect	tricycle
trio	tripod	university	unify
universe	biweekly	triangle	bicycle
binoculars	unicycle	centipede	unicorn
triplet	centimeter	triple	century

Sort each spelling word according to its prefix. Then write the words on the lines below.

uni-

1. uniform
2. unicorn
3. unify
4. unison
5. universe
6. unicycle
7. university

bi-

1. bisect
2. biweekly
3. binoculars
4. bicycle

tri-

1. tricycle
2. triplet
3. triple
4. triangle
5. trio
6. tripod

cent-

1. century
2. centipede
3. centimeter

Day 3 — Word Meanings

LA.5.1.6.1 Use new vocabulary that is taught directly

DEFINITIONS

- Review the definitions of the Spelling Words as a class.

- Invite pairs of students to make illustrations for two Spelling Words. Assign words as necessary to make sure all words are covered.

- Have students share their illustrations with the class so the class can guess the words. Illustrations may be displayed with the Word Cards in the classroom.

- Ask partners to use the two vocabulary words in a sentence. The sentence should use each of the words correctly. Pairs may share their sentences with the class once the class has guessed the words correctly.

Day 4 — Review and Proofread

LA.5.3.4.1 Edits for spelling

SPIRAL REVIEW

Review words from mythology. Write *cereal, terrace,* and *atlas* on the board. Ask students to identify the origin of the word and explain how it is related to mythology and Greek or Roman culture.

PROOFREAD AND WRITE

Write these sentences on the board, including the misspelled words. Ask pairs of students to proofread, circling the misspelled words and correcting them.

1. When I was little, I had a trycicle, but now I have a bycicle. (tricycle, bicycle)

2. The univercity has been educating students for over a sentury. (university, century)

3. The centipeid crawled only a centameter. (centipede, centimeter)

Day 5 — Assess and Reteach

LA.5.1.6.7 Use meaning of affixes to determine meaning

POSTTEST

Use the Dictation Sentences on page 735G for the Posttest.

If students have difficulty with any words in the lesson, have them place the words in a list entitled "Spelling Words I Want to Remember" in their word study notebooks.

Challenge student partners to look for more words with the number prefixes they studied this week, either in their reading or in other materials. Partners should work together to sort the words according to the prefixes.

Spelling Practice Book, page 182

uniform	unison	bisect	tricycle
trio	tripod	university	unify
universe	biweekly	triangle	bicycle
binoculars	unicycle	centipede	unicorn
triplet	centimeter	triple	century

Definitions

Write the spelling word that has the same, or almost the same, meaning.

1. a name for three musical performers __trio__
2. a wormlike animal with many pairs of legs __centipede__
3. an imaginary horselike animal with a single, long horn __unicorn__
4. a figure with three sides and three angles __triangle__
5. occurring every two weeks __biweekly__
6. a group or set of three, usually in music __triplet__
7. a mode of transportation that has one wheel __unicycle__
8. to cut into two equal parts __bisect__
9. a unit of length __centimeter__
10. together or at the same time __unison__

Fill in the Blanks

Complete each sentence with a spelling word.

11. Each member of the balloonist club wore a red __uniform__
12. It would be strange to see a grownup riding a __tricycle__
13. Ballooning can bring people closer together and __unify__ an entire state.
14. One man improved the hot-air balloon about a __century__ ago.
15. Ballooning can make you feel like you are exploring the __universe__
16. Using __binoculars__, you can see people below from hundreds of feet in the air.

Spelling Practice Book, page 183

Circle the misspelled words in the passage. Write the words correctly on the lines below.

Jean-Pierre Blanchard and John Jefferies took one of the most daring trips of the century. They practiced biweeklie to make sure that everything went smoothly. The trip was going well until the temperature got colder, and they began to sink. "Help us!" they cried in unison. To make the balloon lighter, Blanchard removed part of his uniform. Using his banoculars, Jefferies could see a small place to land. On the way down, they missed a tree branch by less than a centumeter.

1. __century__
2. __biweekly__
3. __unison__
4. __uniform__
5. __binoculars__
6. __centimeter__

Writing Activity

Write a paragraph about where you would go if you had a chance to ride in a hot-air balloon. Use four words from your spelling list.

Spelling Practice Book, page 184

Look at the words in each set below. One word in each set is spelled correctly. Use a pencil to fill in the circle next to the correct word. Before you begin, look at the sample set of words. Sample A has been done for you. Do Sample B by yourself. When you are sure you know what to do, you may go on with the rest of the page.

Sample A:
- Ⓐ byplane
- Ⓑ biplane
- Ⓒ bipplane
- Ⓓ biplain

Sample B:
- Ⓔ triddent
- Ⓕ triedent
- Ⓖ trident
- Ⓗ trydent

1.
- Ⓐ unnifform
- Ⓑ unniform
- Ⓒ uniiform
- Ⓓ uniform

2.
- Ⓔ biesect
- Ⓕ bissect
- Ⓖ bisect
- Ⓗ bysect

3.
- Ⓐ trycicle
- Ⓑ triscyckle
- Ⓒ tricycle
- Ⓓ tricicle

4.
- Ⓔ triplet
- Ⓕ tripplet
- Ⓖ tripllet
- Ⓗ trippllett

5.
- Ⓐ tripel
- Ⓑ tripple
- Ⓒ triple
- Ⓓ trippel

6.
- Ⓔ uniccorn
- Ⓕ unicorn
- Ⓖ uniccorn
- Ⓗ unnicorn

7.
- Ⓐ unify
- Ⓑ unnify
- Ⓒ unefy
- Ⓓ uniffy

8.
- Ⓔ unisson
- Ⓕ unnison
- Ⓖ unison
- Ⓗ unnisson

9.
- Ⓐ univearse
- Ⓑ univeerse
- Ⓒ univverse
- Ⓓ universe

10.
- Ⓔ unicycle
- Ⓕ unicicle
- Ⓖ uniscycle
- Ⓗ unnicycle

11.
- Ⓐ biweekly
- Ⓑ byweekly
- Ⓒ bieweekly
- Ⓓ biweakly

12.
- Ⓔ bynoculars
- Ⓕ binnoculars
- Ⓖ binoculars
- Ⓗ binocculars

13.
- Ⓐ tryangle
- Ⓑ triangel
- Ⓒ triangle
- Ⓓ trieangle

14.
- Ⓔ bisickle
- Ⓕ biecycle
- Ⓖ bycycle
- Ⓗ bicycle

15.
- Ⓐ trio
- Ⓑ treeo
- Ⓒ trieo
- Ⓓ tryo

16.
- Ⓔ centurry
- Ⓕ centtury
- Ⓖ century
- Ⓗ centturry

17.
- Ⓐ centtipede
- Ⓑ centtipede
- Ⓒ centipeed
- Ⓓ centippede

18.
- Ⓔ centimetter
- Ⓕ centimmeter
- Ⓖ centimeter
- Ⓗ centimmetter

19.
- Ⓐ tripod
- Ⓑ triepod
- Ⓒ trypod
- Ⓓ trippod

20.
- Ⓔ universsity
- Ⓕ universeity
- Ⓖ univversity
- Ⓗ university

Daily Language Activities

Use these activities to reinforce each day's lesson. Write the day's activity on the board or use **Daily Language Transparency 29.**

DAY 1
Balloon flights were common the late 1700s. People watched them from excitement. (1: by the late 1700s *or* in the late 1700s; 2: with *or* for excitement.)

DAY 2
Two hundred years ago, no one had even dreamed for hot-air balloons. A pair scientists figured out how warm air rises. (1: of hot-air; 2: of scientists)

DAY 3
In late eighteenth-century France Professor Charles designed a new kind balloon. In a stroke genius he filled it of hydrogen gas. (1: France,; 2: of balloon; 3: of genius; 4: with hydrogen)

DAY 4
Across the ocean, Jean-Pierre Blanchard rode of a balloon the United States. Down below, he discovered that air of 5,000 feet is different air in sea level. (1: ocean [no comma]; 2: in a balloon in the; 3: below [no comma]; 4: at; 5: from air at sea level.)

DAY 5
In the following years balloonists would keep learning into science. They learned that balloons are like a block to wood water. (1: years,; 2: about *or* from science.; 3: of wood in water.)

ELL   Access for All

Modeled Activities
Prepositions can be difficult for students because some words are often used in two-word verbs and idioms *(over: start over, all over)*. Repeated use of prepositions in modeled writing activities will help students over time to learn their meanings and usage.

Prepositions/Prepositional Phrases

Day 1 — Introduce the Concept

LA.5.3.4.4. Edits for correct use of parts of speech
INTRODUCE PREPOSITIONS

Present the following:

- A preposition is positioned before a noun or pronoun and relates that noun or pronoun to another word in the sentence.

- Prepositions used often are *about, above, across, after, at, behind, by, down, for, from, in, near, of, on, over, to,* and *with.*

See Grammar Transparency 141 for modeling and guided practice.

Grammar Practice Book, page 179

- A **preposition** comes before a noun or pronoun and relates that noun or pronoun to another word in the sentence.
- Common prepositions are *about, above, across, after, at, behind, down, for, from, in, near, of, on, over, to,* and *with.*

Read each sentence. Underline the prepositions. There may be more than one preposition in each sentence.

1. The balloon flew above the village.
2. Jean-Pierre Blanchard floated over the English Channel.
3. A duck, a rooster, and a sheep rode in the basket of the balloon.
4. The balloon rose to a height of one hundred feet.
5. They floated in a new direction.
6. Weather balloons give us information about the atmosphere.
7. Buoyancy keeps balloons in the air.
8. Bertrand Piccard stayed in a balloon for 20 days.
9. The balloon dropped gently from the sky.
10. The balloon landed in a forest behind a field.

Day 2 — Teach the Concept

LA.5.3.4.4. Edits for correct use of parts of speech
REVIEW PREPOSITIONS

Discuss with students how prepositions tie a noun or pronoun to other words in a sentence. Ask students to name as many prepositions as they can.

INTRODUCE PREPOSITIONAL PHRASES

- A prepositional phrase is a group of words that begins with a preposition and ends with a noun or pronoun.

- The object of a prepositional phrase is the noun or pronoun that follows the preposition.

- A prepositional phrase makes a connection between the two nouns or pronouns in a sentence.

See Grammar Transparency 142 for modeling and guided practice.

Grammar Practice Book, page 180

- A **prepositional phrase** is a group of words that begins with a preposition and ends with a noun or pronoun.
- A prepositional phrase makes a connection between two nouns or pronouns in a sentence.
- The **object** of a preposition is the noun or pronoun that follows the preposition.

Underline the preposition in each sentence. Circle the object of the preposition.

1. Jacques Charles learned about (hydrogen.)
2. They waved from the (balloon.)
3. Balloonists cannot be afraid of (heights.)
4. François Pilâtre De Rozier anchored his balloon with a (tether.)
5. The first human passenger flew over (Paris.)

Complete each sentence with a prepositional phrase. *more than one answer possible*

6. The wind was strong __on the day__ that they left.
7. There were 25 members __in the balloon__ club
8. A duck, a rooster, and a sheep rode __in the balloon__
9. __In the field__, the balloonists prepared to launch.
10. The balloons __in the sky__ were a beautiful sight.

Day 3 Review and Practice

LA.5.3.4.4. Edits for correct use of parts of speech

REVIEW PREPOSITIONAL PHRASES

Review prepositional phrases. Provide a preposition and have students use it in a number of prepositional phrases.

MECHANICS AND USAGE: COMMAS WITH PREPOSITIONAL PHRASES AND APPOSITIVES

- Prepositional phrases often begin a sentence. A prepositional phrase that introduces a sentence is also called an introductory phrase. If a prepositional phrase starting a sentence is four or more words, use a comma to set it off from the rest of the sentence. Do not set off a prepositional phrase of three words or less unless the sentence is confusing without it.

- Use a comma to set off an appositive.

 See Grammar Transparency 143 for modeling and guided practice.

Grammar Practice Book, page 181

- A prepositional phrase may come at the beginning of a sentence. A prepositional phrase that begins a sentence is also called an **introductory phrase**.
- If a prepositional phrase that begins a sentence is four or more words, place a comma after the phrase.

Read the following two paragraphs. Place commas where they are needed.

In the year 1783, scientific progress met old-fashioned beliefs. On an otherwise normal day, a group of French villagers got quite a surprise. Down from the sky, a strange creature slowly floated. With pitchforks and other farm tools, the villagers struck the creature. Under this furious attack, the creature finally stopped moving.

To the eighteenth-century villagers, the object from the sky looked like a monster. At the time of the monster's visit, very few people had ever seen a balloon. From his science studies, Professor Jacques A. C. Charles had learned that a newly discovered gas called hydrogen weighed less than air. When he filled a sack with this gas, the sack floated into the air. From the heart of Paris, Charles had released his balloon and then watched as it floated away. In their attack, the villagers destroyed the first hydrogen balloon.

Day 4 Review and Proofread

LA.5.3.4.4. Edits for correct use of parts of speech

REVIEW PREPOSITIONS AND PREPOSITIONAL PHRASES

Ask students to list as many prepositions as they can. Challenge volunteers to create sentences about *Up in the Air* that use prepositional phrases. Ask the class to identify prepositions and prepositional phrases.

PROOFREAD

Have students correct the following:

1. Before the Enlightenment people did not think seriously for science. (Enlightenment,; about *or* of science)

2. In fact, no one knew above the tiny particles air called molecules. (fact no one knew about the tiny particles of air)

3. Inside a balloon, air particles start moving. (balloon air particles)

 See Grammar Transparency 144 for modeling and guided practice.

Grammar Practice Book, page 182

Read the paragraph below. Rewrite the paragraph correctly on the lines provided. Be sure to add commas where needed and to remove incorrect commas. Replace any prepositions that are used incorrectly.

From her balloon perch Cynthia looked at the world laid out beneath her. The trees reached from her as though to tickle the balloon basket as she passed. The lakes and rivers sparkled and winked on the sun. The green above the grass looked brighter than Cynthia had ever thought it could. She gave a sigh to contentment. She wished that she could stay about her balloon, forever.

From her balloon perch, Cynthia looked at the world laid out beneath her. The trees reached for her as though to tickle the balloon basket as she passed. The lakes and rivers sparkled and winked in the sun. The green of the grass looked brighter than Cynthia had ever thought it could. She gave a sigh of contentment. She wished that she could stay in her balloon forever.

Day 5 Assess and Reteach

LA.5.3.4.4. Edits for correct use of parts of speech

ASSESS

Use the Daily Language Activity and page 183 of the **Grammar Practice Book** for assessment.

RETEACH

Have students write the corrected Daily Language Activities on a sheet of paper. Ask them to write on every other line. Next, have students underline the prepositional phrases and circle the objects of the prepositions. Ask students to draw an arrow from each object of a preposition to the noun or pronoun it connects with. If students have trouble, review the concept.

Use page 184 of the **Grammar Practice Book** for additional reteaching.

 See Grammar Transparency 145 for modeling and guided practice.

Grammar Practice Book, pages 183–184

Circle the letter of the preposition that fits best in each sentence.

1. Experiments _____ science led to the discovery of hydrogen gas.
   a. near
   b. in
   c. at

2. The villagers _____ the ground looked up at the balloon.
   a. on
   b. in
   c. after

3. _____ all the balloons in the sky, Carl liked the red and yellow one best.
   a. Of
   b. To
   c. Down

4. Bertrand Piccard flew around the world _____ twenty days.
   a. on
   b. with
   c. in

5. _____ the end of the day, the balloon drifted to the ground.
   a. At
   b. Across
   c. Of

6. A breeze blew the balloons _____ the sky.
   a. with
   b. after
   c. across

7. The first free flight in North America started _____ Philadelphia.
   a. about
   b. near
   c. down

8. Many early balloon flights occurred _____ France.
   a. on
   b. in
   c. under

Administer the Test

 Weekly Reading Assessment
pages 345–356

ASSESSED SKILLS

- Relevant Facts and Details
- Vocabulary Words
- Word Parts: Greek Roots
- Number Prefixes
- Prepositions and Prepositional Phrases

 Assessment Tool

Administer the **Weekly Assessment** from the CD-ROM or online.

Fluency

Assess fluency for one group of students per week. Use the Oral Fluency Record Sheet to track the number of words read correctly. Fluency goal for all students: **129–149 words correct per minute (WCPM).**

Approaching Level	Weeks 1, 3, 5
On Level	Weeks 2, 4
Beyond Level	Week 6

Alternative Assessments

- **ELL Assessment,** pages 174–175

Weekly Assessment, 345–356

Fluency Assessment

ELL Assessment, 174–175

Diagnose		Prescribe
	IF...	**THEN...**
VOCABULARY WORDS **VOCABULARY STRATEGY** Word Parts: Greek Roots Items 1, 2, 3, 4, 5	0–2 items correct …	Reteach skills using the **Additional Lessons,** page T9. **LOG ON** Reteach skills: Go to www.macmillanmh.com **CD ROM** **Vocabulary PuzzleMaker** Evaluate for Intervention.
COMPREHENSION Skill: Relevant Facts and Details Items 6, 7, 8, 9	0–2 items correct …	Reteach skills using the **Additional Lessons,** page T4. Evaluate for Intervention.
SPELLING Number Prefixes Items 10, 11, 12	0–1 items correct …	**LOG ON** Reteach skills: Go to www.macmillanmh.com
GRAMMAR Prepositions and Prepositional Phrases Items 13, 14, 15	0–1 items correct …	Reteach skills: **Grammar Practice Book** page 184.
FLUENCY	120–128 WCPM 0–110 WCPM	**AUDIO CD** Fluency Solutions Evaluate for Intervention.

READING

Triumphs

AN INTERVENTION PROGRAM

Also Available

To place students in the Intervention Program, use the **Diagnostic Assessment** in the Intervention Teacher's Edition.

Up in the Air: The Story of Balloon Flight

Constructive Feedback

If students fail to understand the relationship between the prefix and the meaning of the word, say:

The word *cycle* is used to describe any repeating pattern. It is also used to describe a vehicle whose wheels move in a repeating pattern. A number prefix is added to describe how many wheels a cycle has. A *unicycle* has one wheel. A *bicycle* has two wheels. A *tricycle* has three wheels.

Repeat as needed with other words with number prefixes.

Additional Resources

Use your observations to help identify students who might benefit from additional instruction. See page T2 for comprehension support T5 for vocabulary support. For each skill below, additional lessons are provided. You can use these lessons on consecutive days after teaching the lessons presented within the week.
• Relevant Facts and Details, T2
• Word Parts: Greek Roots, T5

Decodable Text

To help students build speed and accuracy with reading multisyllabic words, use additional decodable text on pages 36–37 of the **Teachers' Resource Book.**

Skills Focus ▶ Phonics

Objectives Review words with number prefixes *uni-, bi-, tri-, cent-*

Decode multisyllabic words with number prefixes in both familiar and unfamiliar texts

Materials • **Student Book** *The Science of Hot-Air Balloons*

WORDS WITH NUMBER PREFIXES

LA.5.1.4
Student applies grade level phonics

LA.5.1.4.2
Recognize structural analysis

Model/Guided Practice

■ Write *universe* on the board. Say the sound that each letter, blend, or digraph stands for. Blend the sounds: /yoo nə vurs/. *Say it with me:* universe.

■ Explain that *universe* contains the number prefix *uni-* meaning "one." The word *universe* means "one whole world, Earth, or cosmos."

■ *Here's another word.* Write *unicycle* on the board. *The prefix* uni- *means "one." The word* unicycle *means "vehicle with one wheel."*

■ Use *unique, unitard,* and *unite* as examples of other words with *uni-*; extend the review to include *bi-, tri-,* and *cent-*.

MORE MULTISYLLABIC WORDS WITH NUMBER PREFIXES

LA.5.1.6.7
Use meaning of base words, affixes to determine meanings of complex words

■ Write *bicentennial* on the board. Break the word into syllables: bi/cen/ten/ni/al. Have students repeat the word. Point out the two number prefixes: *bi-* and *cent-*. Explain that *bicentennial* means "happening every two hundred years."

LA.5.1.4.3
Use language structure to read multi-syllabic words

■ Have pairs of students practice decoding other words with number prefixes. Write the following words on the board or provide copies of the list. *With your partner, choose a word. Say the word aloud. Identify the number prefix and use it to determine the meaning of the word. Check your definition against one in a dictionary.*

bipartisan	triathlon	centenarian
bicoastal	triceps	centigrade
bicolor	tricycle	centigram
bicultural	tripod	centiliter

■ Check each pair for progress and accuracy.

WRITING WITH NUMBERS: WORDS WITH NUMBER PREFIXES IN CONTEXT

LA.5.1.6.7
Use meaning of base words, affixes to determine meanings of complex words

■ Have students search their math and science texts for words with number prefixes. They may find *biceps, billion, binary, bisect, bisector, centigrade, centigram, centiliter, centimeter, triangle, triangular, trillion, triple, union, unit, universe, universal,*

■ Then extend the activity by having students use several words with number prefixes to explain how something works.

Skills Focus ▶ Fluency

Objective	Read with increasing prosody and accuracy at a rate of 129–139 WCPM
Materials	• **Approaching Practice Book A,** page 210

MODEL EXPRESSIVE READING

LA.5.1.5
Read orally with accuracy

Model reading the Fluency passage in **Practice Book A,** page 210. Read aloud one sentence at a time, and have students repeat the sentence, first as a class and then one by one. Increase your tempo as you go along, and listen carefully for accuracy.

REPEATED READING

LA.5.1.5
Student demonstrates ability to read orally with accuracy

Have students continue practicing reading the passage aloud as you circulate and provide corrective feedback. During independent reading time, student partners can take turns reading the passage. One partner reads each sentence aloud, and the other repeats it. Remind students to wait until their partners reach end marks before correcting mistakes.

TIMED READING

LA.5.1.5
Student demonstrates ability to read orally with appropriate rate

Tell students they will do a timed reading of the passage that they have been practicing. With each student:

- Place the passage from **Practice Book A,** page 210, face down.
- When you say "Go," the student begins reading the passage aloud.
- When you say "Stop," the student stops reading the passage.

As students read, note any miscues. Stop students after one minute. Help them record and graph the number of words they read correctly.

Skills Focus ▶ Vocabulary

Objective	Apply vocabulary word meanings
Materials	• **Vocabulary Cards** • **Transparencies 29a and 29b**

VOCABULARY WORDS

LA.5.1.6
Student develops vocabulary

Display the **Vocabulary Cards** for this week's words: *launched, inflate, companion, anchored, scientific, particles, dense, hydrogen.* Help students locate and read the words on **Transparencies 29a** and **29b.** Review each word's meaning. Ask students to use the vocabulary words and context clues to write interesting or humorous sentences about flight.

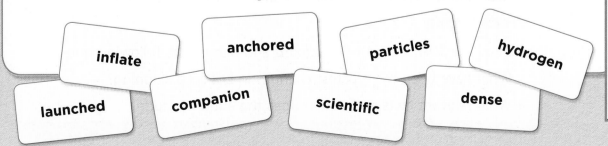

inflate · anchored · particles · hydrogen · launched · companion · scientific · dense

---

Constructive Feedback

Encourage students to time their readings with stop watches. Challenge students to decrease their reading times with successive readings. Model this practice for students.

RESEARCH
Why It Matters

Vocabulary

Vocabulary learning is multifaceted. It is partly about learning words and partly about learning to use context to infer the meanings of words. Practice in interpreting word meanings from rich contexts is worthwhile.

Tim Shanahan

LOG ON Go to www. macmillanmh.com

⭐ **Approaching Practice Book A,** page 210

As I read, I will pay attention to tempo and phrasing.

	Through the ages many stories have been told of people
10	who wanted to fly. One is the ancient Greek myth of
21	Daedalus (DED-ah-lahs) and Icarus. Daedalus was an
28	inventor, and Icarus was his son. Daedalus made wings for
38	them, using feathers held together with wax. When they tried
48	to fly, Daedalus flew and landed safely. But Icarus flew too
59	high. The sun melted the wax in his wings. The wings came
71	apart. He fell into the sea and drowned.
79	Like the characters in that tale, most of the early
89	inventors had the wrong idea. They wanted to imitate
98	birds by using wings to fly. But people aren't built like
109	birds. Their efforts were doomed to fail.
116	Around 400 B.C. Chinese inventors had a different idea.
123	They built the first kites. Kites stayed aloft with the help of
135	wind. They used gliding motion, or smooth, easy movements,
144	which worked better than flapping like birds. 151

Comprehension Check

1. What did early inventors think about flight? **Main Idea and Details** They wanted to imitate birds.

2. How did kites change the way people thought about flight? **Main Idea and Details** Kites made people think about gliding or smooth movements rather than flapping motions.

	Words Read	−	Number of Errors	=	Words Correct Score
First Read		−		=	
Second Read		−		=	

Vocabulary

Review last week's words: **(elementary, physical, rigid, interact, wheelchair)** and this week's words **(launched, particles, dense, inflate, anchored, hydrogen, scientific, companion)**. Have students write a sentence for each word.

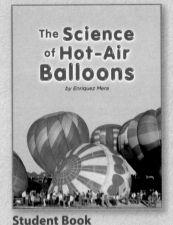

The Science of Hot-Air Balloons
by Enriquez Mera

Student Book

ELL

Access for All

FCAT

Cognates Help Spanish speakers look in a bilingual dictionary for words with the Greek root *hydro*. Explain to them that knowing *hydro* and *hidro* are cognates will help them understand many scientific words in English.

Skills Focus

Vocabulary

Objective Review Greek roots
Materials • **Student Book** *Up in the Air: The Story of Balloon Flight*
• **Dictionaries**

FCAT **WORD PARTS: GREEK ROOTS**

LA.5.1.6.7
Use meaning of base words to determine meanings

- Remind students that identifying the Greek root in a word can help them understand its meaning. Point out the Greek root *hydro* in *hydrogen*, which means "water."

- Ask students to use dictionaries or the glossary to find other words that contain this Greek root *(hydrophobia, hydrotherapy, hydrosphere)*.

- Discuss how these words incorporate the meaning of the root in their definitions. Ask students to write a sentence or paragraph using at least three different words containing the root *hydro*.

Skills Focus

Comprehension

Objective Review relevant facts and details
Materials • **Student Book** *The Science of Hot-Air Balloons*
• **Transparencies 29a and 29b**

STRATEGY
MONITOR COMPREHENSION

LA.5.1.7 Use strategies to comprehend text
Review with students that they can make sure that they understand what they read by summarizing, asking questions, and rereading.

SKILL
RELEVANT FACTS AND DETAILS

LA.5.1.7.3
Determine main idea through identifying relevant details

- Remind students that a fact is a statement that can be proven true. An opinion is a statement of a person's beliefs. A relevant detail is an important piece of information in a text that may be either a fact or an opinion.

- When summarizing, include only relevant facts and details.

Explain/Model

Display **Transparencies 29a** and **29b.** Reread the first two paragraphs of *The Science of Hot-Air Balloons*. Ask a volunteer to circle relevant facts and details and to explain his or her choices.

Practice/Apply

Reread *The Science of Hot-Air Balloons* and discuss the following questions:

- What have been the greatest changes in hot-air ballooning?

- What relevant facts and details does the author include?

Leveled Reader Lesson

Objective Read to apply strategies and skills

Materials • **Leveled Reader** *The Sky's the Limit*

• **Student Book** *The Science of Hot-Air Balloons* and *Up in the Air: The Story of Balloon Flight.*

PREVIEW AND PREDICT

LA.5.1.7.1 Establish purpose for reading
Discuss the cover and ask students to preview the table of contents, illustrations, and first two chapters. Have students make predictions about how technology has changed the way people travel. Set purposes for reading by asking students what they would like to learn as they read.

VOCABULARY WORDS

LA.5.1.6.3 Use context clues
Review vocabulary word meanings as necessary. As you read together, stop to discuss how each word is used in context.

Leveled Reader

STRATEGY
MONITOR COMPREHENSION

LA.5.1.7 Use strategies to comprehend text
Remind students to stop regularly and check that they understand what they're reading. They can generate questions about the text, summarize certain passages, or reread confusing parts.

SKILL
RELEVANT FACTS AND DETAILS

LA.5.1.7.3 Determine main idea through identifying relevant details
Point out that a fact is a statement that can be proven true. An opinion is a statement of a person's beliefs. A relevant detail is an important piece of information in a text that may be either a fact or an opinion.

Think Aloud In chapter one I learn the story about Daedalus and Icarus. However, this information isn't as important to the scientific story of flight as the information about inventors using wind to lift things off the ground. I'll add the information about wind to my Relevant Facts and Details Chart.

READ AND RESPOND

Tell students to finish reading the first two chapters of *The Sky's the Limit.* Discuss students' personal responses to the history of human flight.

MAKE CONNECTIONS ACROSS TEXTS

LA.5.1.7.7 Compare and contrast elements in multiple texts
Invite students to compare *The Sky's the Limit, The Science of Hot-Air Balloons,* and *Up in the Air: The Story of Balloon Flight.*

■ What relevant facts and details do the selections have in common?

■ How do you decide which facts and details are relevant and which are not?

ELL Access for All

Use Affixes Discuss the meaning of the book title. Explain that the picture shows a biplane and that the prefix *bi-* means "two," as it does in the word *bicycle.* Have students list other words with the prefix *bi-*. Use the dictionary to search for words to include in the list.

Paired Selection

Skills Focus

Vocabulary

Objective	Review vocabulary words
Materials	• **Vocabulary Cards**

VOCABULARY WORDS

LA.5.1.6
Student uses multiple strategies to develop vocabulary

Hold up a Vocabulary Card. One student will state the word's part of speech. The next student will provide a definition for the word. The next student will use the word in a sentence. Continue the process with another vocabulary card until all words have been explored and every student has contributed.

FCAT **WORD PARTS: GREEK ROOTS**

LA.5.1.6.7
Use meaning of base words to determine meanings

Have students brainstorm or use dictionaries to list words that contain the Greek roots *hydr(o)* (water) and *heli(o)* (sun). Link the meanings of the Greek roots with the meaning of each word. Then have students use the roots to build word towers.

Skills Focus

Literary Elements

Objective	Analyze and write metaphors and similes
Materials	• **Paired Selection** *Hot-Air Balloon Haiku*

SIMILE AND METAPHOR

LA.5.2.1.3
Demonstrate how figurative language helps communicate meaning in a poem

Have each student choose one of the haiku to recite orally. Discuss the importance and purpose of figurative language, such as similes and metaphors, in the haiku. Have students write two paragraphs about nonfiction topics using similes and metaphors.

Skills Focus

Fluency

Objective	Read fluently with appropriate prosody at a rate of 129–149 WCPM
Materials	• **On Level Practice Book O,** p. 210

REPEATED READING

LA.5.1.5
Student demonstrates ability to read orally with appropriate rate

Model reading aloud the Fluency passage on page 210 of **Practice Book O.** Remind students that moderate speed and appropriate phrasing help listeners understand the passage. Have the class read the passage chorally, and discuss how reading speed can affect a reader's understanding of the passage. Remind students that some foreign words may not follow the rules of English pronunciation.

Timed Reading Have students read the passage and record their reading rate.

On Level Practice Book O, page 210

As I read, I will pay attention to tempo and phrasing.

	It is a beautiful day at the football stadium. Fans fill the
12	seats and wait for the kickoff. Suddenly, a strange shadow
22	appears on the field. People sitting in the upper rows hear
33	a low whirring sound overhead. Floating in the sky is a
44	football-shaped balloon.
47	Most of us have seen them on television during sporting
57	events. They are like silent ships sailing on a sea of sky.
69	These strange-looking balloons are called blimps. They are
77	cousins to the hot-air balloon.
82	Blimps and hot-air balloons are part of a group of flying
93	machines known as lighter-than-air craft. They are filled
101	with gas that weighs less than air.
108	Blimps are also members of the airship family. Just like
118	boats, airships have motors and rudders. The motors give
127	airships speed. The rudders help steer. These additions make
136	airships very different from hot-air balloons. Hot-air balloons
144	have little control over their speed or direction. Airships can
154	even fly against the wind. 159

Comprehension Check

1. Compare and contrast blimps and hot-air balloons. **Compare and Contrast**
Both are filled with gas that weighs less than air. Blimps have motors and rudders, and hot-air balloons do not.
2. Where do people commonly see blimps? **Main Idea and Details**
Most people see blimps at sporting events.

	Words Read	−	Number of Errors	=	Words Correct Score
First Read		−		=	
Second Read		−		=	

Leveled Reader Lesson

Objective Read to apply strategies and skills

Materials
- **Leveled Reader** *The Sky's the Limit*
- **Student Book** *The Science of Hot-Air Balloons*

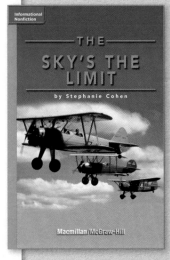

Leveled Reader

PREVIEW AND PREDICT

LA.5.1.7.1
Use prior knowledge to make and confirm predictions

Have students preview *The Sky's the Limit.*

- What does the title suggest about the selection?
- How has the history of flight developed or unfolded?
- What questions of your own would you like to ask?

SKILL
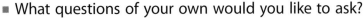
RELEVANT FACTS AND DETAILS

LA.5.1.7.3
Determine main idea through identifying relevant details

Authors use facts and details to support main ideas. A fact is a statement that can be proven true. An opinion is a detail that expresses somebody's personal belief, but may still be relevant because it supports the main idea. When summarizing, readers should include only relevant facts and details. Explain that students will fill in Relevant Facts and Details Charts to help them summarize the selection.

READ AND RESPOND

LA.5.2.2.3
Organize information to show understanding

Read the Introduction and Chapter 1. Pause to allow students to share their own knowledge about kites and balloons. After students have read Chapter 1, have them fill in the Relevant Facts and Details Charts with information from the selection.

VOCABULARY WORDS

LA.5.1.6.3
Use context clues

After students finish reading *The Sky's the Limit*, ask them to point out the vocabulary words. Discuss how each word is used in context. Ask questions such as: *How did dense particles get anchored to the balloon?* Have them respond in kind.

MAKE CONNECTIONS ACROSS TEXTS

LA.5.1.7.7
Compare and contrast elements in multiple texts

Invite students to compare *The Sky's the Limit* with *The Science of Hot-Air Balloons.*

- In *The Science of Hot-Air Balloons*, the author states that today most balloons are made of nylon. Is this fact relevant for a summary? Explain.
- In *The Sky's the Limit,* the author states that Leonardo da Vinci is famous for his art. Is this detail relevant for a summary? Explain.

ELL
Leveled Reader
Go to pages 735U–735V.

Beyond Level Options

Paired Selection

Beyond Practice Book B, page 210

As I read, I will pay attention to tempo and phrasing.

	For thousands of years, people have been fascinated by the sky.
11	At night they looked up to see the moon and stars. In the daytime,
25	people observed the sun and cloud formations. In order to study the sky,
38	early scientists depended on a few simple tools—telescopes, kites,
48	balloons, and thermometers—to make their discoveries.
55	In 1749, Scottish scientist Alexander Wilson flew kites that carried
64	thermometers. The thermometers gave Wilson an idea of air temperatures
74	at different heights. A few years later Benjamin Franklin flew kites to
86	experiment with electricity.
89	Scientists have not been anchored to Earth since the late 1800s. They
100	have sent balloons and rockets into the air to gain knowledge. In 1892
112	the first weather balloons were flown in France. They measured
122	temperature, humidity, and air pressure.
127	Tools in the air also helped scientists learn more about Earth. Soon
139	after the first weather balloons, Swedish scientist Alfred Nobel
148	experimented with rockets. He designed one that flew up and
158	photographed the Earth.
161	Today scientific research takes place in Earth's atmosphere and
170	beyond. With advances in modern technology, scientists can fly into
180	raging storms. Weather balloons can soar high into the air. 190

Comprehension Check

1. Why is it useful that scientists use weather balloons and fly into storms? **Plot Development** Scientist will better understand storms and predict what they might do.
2. How have kites been used as scientific tools? **Relevant Facts and Details** to study air temperatures and to experiment with electricity

	Words Read	−	Number of Errors	=	Words Correct Score
First Read		−		=	
Second Read		−		=	

Skills Focus — Vocabulary

Objective   Write questions and answers

EXTEND VOCABULARY

LA.5.1.6.1
Use new vocabulary

Write a list of questions for the vocabulary words. Each question should provide context clues to the vocabulary word's meaning. For example:

> How would you describe a rocket that has just traveled into the air? It _____. (launched)

> What happens when someone pumps air into a bicycle tire? It _____. (inflates)

Invite students to write their own questions and answers for the vocabulary words.

Skills Focus — Literary Elements

Objective   Use figurative language to write haiku
Materials   • **Paired Selection** *Hot-Air Balloon Haiku*

SIMILE AND METAPHOR

LA.5.2.1.3
Demonstrate how figurative language helps to communicate meaning in a poem

Point out that similes and metaphors are examples of figurative language that compare two unlike objects. Ask students to identify examples of similes and metaphors in *Hot-Air Balloon Haiku*. Ask what information these figures of speech give the reader that facts would not.

Next, have students write their own haikus on subjects of their choice. Challenge students to use similes and metaphors in their poems.

Skills Focus — Fluency

Objective   Read fluently with prosody and accuracy at a rate of 139–149 WCPM
Materials   • **Beyond Practice Book B,** page 210

REPEATED READING

LA.5.1.5
Student demonstrates ability to read orally with appropriate rate

Model reading aloud the Fluency passage on page 210 of **Practice Book B,** using pauses and intonation as necessary for reading at the tempo appropriate for the passage. Then have the class read the passage chorally, copying your tempo.

During independent reading time, listen for accuracy as partners take turns rereading aloud the passage they have marked, focusing on tempo without skipping words. Partners should offer corrective feedback as needed. As an extension, have students take turns reading aloud a passage or report they have written in cursive until they can read it fluently.

Leveled Reader Lesson

Objective   Read to apply strategies and skills

Materials   • **Leveled Reader** *The Sky's the Limit*

PREVIEW AND PREDICT

LA.5.1.7.1
Establish purpose for reading

Have students preview *The Sky's the Limit*, predict what it is about, and set purposes for reading.

VOCABULARY WORDS

LA. 5.1.6.3
Use context clues

Review vocabulary words as necessary. Ask students questions such as, *Which object is usually launched, a rocket or a car?* Have students respond, using two vocabulary words per sentence.

SKILL
RELEVANT FACTS AND DETAILS

LA.5.1.7.3
Determine main idea through identifying relevant details

Authors use facts and details to support main ideas. A fact is a statement that can be proven true. An opinion is a detail that expresses somebody's personal belief, but may still be relevant because it supports the main idea. Explain that students will read *The Sky's the Limit* together and that they will distinguish between relevant facts and details and record them in their Relevant Facts and Details Charts.

READ AND RESPOND

LA.5.2.2.3
Organize information to show understanding

Have students summarize the information and then identify the relevant facts and details in the text as they fill in their charts.

Self-Selected Reading

Objective   Read independently to identify relevant facts and details and to make connections across texts

Materials   • Leveled Readers or trade books at students' reading levels

READ TO IDENTIFY RELEVANT FACTS AND DETAILS

LA.5.1.7.7
Compare and contrast elements in multiple texts

Invite students to identify relevant facts and details in the week's reading selections. Ask students to compare the poems with the nonfiction pieces. Ask how the poems describe flight. Discuss what information the nonfiction pieces offer that the poems do not.

LA.5.2.2.5
Select non-fiction materials to read

Next, invite students to choose non-fiction books to read for enjoyment, based on personal criteria such as favorite authors or recommendations from others. After reading, have them identify relevant facts and details in their texts. Ask a volunteer to explain why it can be helpful to identify relevant facts and details as one reads.

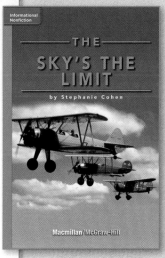

Informational Nonfiction

THE
SKY'S THE
LIMIT
by Stephanie Cohen

Macmillan/McGraw-Hill

Leveled Reader

English Language Learners

Academic Language

Throughout the week the English language learners in your class will need help building their understanding of the academic language used in daily instruction and assessment instruments. The following strategies will help increase their language proficiency and comprehension of content and instructional words.

 **Technology**

Oral Language For oral vocabulary development go to www.macmillanmh.com

Strategies to Reinforce Academic Language

- **Use Context** Academic language used by the teacher (see chart below) should be explained in the context of the task during Whole Group. You may use gestures, expressions, and visuals to support meaning.

- **Use Visuals** Use charts, transparencies, and graphic organizers to explain key labels to help students understand classroom language.

- **Model** Demonstrate the task using academic language in order for students to understand instruction.

Academic Language Used in Whole Group Instruction

Content/Theme Words	Skill/Strategy Words	Writing/Grammar Words
hot-air balloon (p. 710)	monitor comprehension (p. 713A)	persuasive essay (p. 734)
balloon flight (p. 715)	relevant facts and details (p. 713A)	preposition (p. 735I)
floats (p. 717)	Greek roots (p. 713)	prepositional phrase (p. 735I)
invented (p. 728)	summarize (p. 731)	noun (p. 735I)
	haiku (p. 732)	pronoun (p. 735I)
	syllables (p. 732)	object (p. 735I)
	simile and metaphor (p. 732)	introductory phrase (p. 735J)

Leveled Reader Library

ELL Leveled Reader Lesson

Informational Nonfiction

THE STORY OF FLIGHT
by Stephanie Cohen

Macmillan/McGraw-Hill

 Before Reading

DEVELOP ORAL LANGUAGE

LOG ON

Build Background *What flying machines do you know about?* Have students help you make a list of flying machines. Include blimps and hot-air balloons. Elicit how blimps and hot-air balloons are alike and different.

Review Vocabulary Write the vocabulary and story support words on the board and discuss their meanings. Model using them in sentences. *They* launched *the hot-air balloon. At first the balloon was* anchored *to the ground.*

PREVIEW AND PREDICT

Point to the cover illustration and read the title aloud. *What do you call this type of airplane? Do you know how a pilot steers it? Do you think this book will tell you how it's done?*

FCAT

Set a Purpose for Reading Show the Fact and Details Chart and remind students they have used it before. Ask them to fill in a similar chart as they read about the story of flight.

 During Reading

Choose from among the differentiated strategies to support students' reading at all levels of language acquisition.

Beginning	**Intermediate**	**Advanced**
Shared Reading As you read, model how to determine relevant facts based on information from the book. Check students' comprehension and use vocabulary and support words: *What is a fact about airships filled with hydrogen?*	**Read Together** Read through Chapter 1. Ask students to determine relevant facts and details about the design and construction of the first airships and to write them down. Have students continue to read with a partner and complete their charts.	**Independent Reading** Have students read the book. As they read, ask them to determine relevant facts and details about early airships and modern blimps and fill in their charts. Have them write a comparative paragraph about airships and airplanes.

 After Reading

Remind students to use the vocabulary and story words in their whole group activities. Have them complete the Comprehension Check questions.

Objective

• **To apply vocabulary and comprehension skills**

Materials

• **ELL Leveled Reader**

5-Day Planner

DAY 1	• Academic Language • Oral Language and Vocabulary Review
DAY 2	• Academic Language • ELL Leveled Reader
DAY 3	• Academic Language • ELL Leveled Reader
DAY 4	• Academic Language • ELL Leveled Reader
DAY 5	• Academic Language • ELL Leveled Reader Comprehension Check and Literacy Activities

Grade 5 • ELL TEACHER'S GUIDE

English Language Learners

Macmillan/McGraw-Hill

ELL Teacher's Guide
for students who need additional instruction

Student Book Selections

Week At A Glance

Whole Group

VOCABULARY

specimens, erupted, murky, dormant, scoured, biology, research, observer

FCAT Word Parts: Latin and Greek Roots

COMPREHENSION

Strategy: Summarize

FCAT **Skill:** Chronological Order

WRITING

FCAT Expository/Problem-Solving Essay

FCAT Science

The Nature of Science

Small Group Options

Differentiated Instruction for Tested Skills

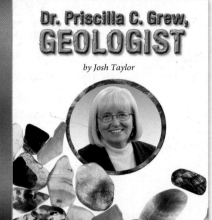

Vocabulary/Comprehension

Hidden Worlds
Looking Through a Scientist's Microscope

by Stephen Kramer
photographs by Dennis Kunkel

 **Science Link**
Main Selection

Genre Nonfiction

Genre Myth

Read-Aloud Anthology
• Listening Comprehension
• Readers' Theatre

FCAT Tested FCAT Benchmark

✓ Tested Skill for the Week

✹ Sunshine State Standard

FCAT FCAT Benchmark

Resources for **Differentiated Instruction**

FCAT LEVELED READERS: Science

GR Levels S–Y

Genre Informational Nonfiction

- **Same Theme**
- **Same Vocabulary**
- **Same Comprehension Skills**

Approaching Level **On Level** **Beyond Level**

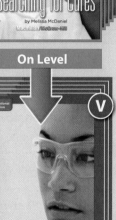

English Language Leveled Reader

Sheltered Readers for English Language Learners

ELL Teacher's Guide also available

LEVELED PRACTICE

Approaching **On Level** **Beyond** **ELL**

INTERVENTION PROGRAM

- Phonics and Decoding
- Comprehension
- Vocabulary

Also available, *Reading Triumphs*, Intervention Program

CLASSROOM LIBRARY

Genre Realistic Fiction

Approaching **On Level** **Beyond**

Trade books to apply Comprehension Skills

FCAT Success!

- **FCAT Edition**
- **Content Area Reading**

FCAT Test Preparation and Practice

FCAT Benchmark Assessments

FCAT Unit and Weekly Assessments

HOME-SCHOOL CONNECTION

- Family letters in English, Spanish, and Haitian Creole
- Take-Home Stories

CD ROM
Instructional Navigator
Interactive Lesson Planner

Hidden Worlds, 740–751

Integrated
ELL Support Every Day

Whole Group

ORAL LANGUAGE

- **Listening**
- **Speaking**
- **Viewing**

WORD STUDY

- **Vocabulary**

- **Phonics/Decoding**

READING

- **Develop Comprehension**

- **Fluency**

LANGUAGE ARTS

- **Writing**

- **Grammar**

- **Spelling**

ASSESSMENT

- **Informal/Formal**

Turn the Page for
Small Group Lesson Plan

Day 1

Listening/Speaking/Viewing

? Focus Question If you could be a scientist, what would you study? What kinds of scientists do the work shown in the photograph on page 736? LA.5.5.2

Build Background, 736
Read Aloud: "The Microscope," 737

Vocabulary LA.5.1.6.1
specimens, erupted, murky, dormant, scoured, biology, research, observer, 738
FCAT
Practice Book A-O-B, 214

Strategy: Word Parts/Greek and Latin Roots, 739
FCAT

Read "Dr. Priscilla C. Grew, Geologist," 738–739
LA.5.1.6.3
Student Book

Comprehension, 739A–739B
Strategy: Summarize
FCAT Skill: Chronological Order LA.5.1.6.11
Practice Book A-O-B, 215

Fluency Model Fluency, 737
Partner Reading, 736I LA.5.1.5

FCAT Writing

Daily Writing: Write an explanation for a child about something in nature (snow, rain, why leaves fall from trees, etc.).
Problem Solving Essay, 759A

Grammar Daily Language Activities, 759I
Sentence Combining, 759I
Grammar Practice Book, 185

Spelling Pretest, 759G
Spelling Practice Book, 185–186 LA.5.1.4.1

Quick Check Vocabulary, 738
Comprehension, 739B

Differentiated Instruction 759M–759V

Day 2

Listening/Speaking

? Focus Question What events influenced Dennis's career in science? LA.5.5.2.1

Vocabulary LA.5.1.6.3
Review Vocabulary Words, 740

Phonics/Decoding LA.5.1.4
Words with *-able, -ible,* 759E
Practice Book A-O-B, 220

Read *Hidden Worlds,* 740–751
Student Book

Comprehension, 740–753
Strategy: Summarize
FCAT Skill: Chronological Order LA.5.1.6.11
Practice Book A-O-B, 216

Fluency Partner Reading, 736I LA.5.1.5

FCAT Writing

Daily Writing: Write a dialogue with another student. Identify a place that you would like to explore, explaining what you hope to discover.

Problem Solving Essay, 759A

Grammar Daily Language Activities, 759I
Sentence Combining, 759I
Grammar Practice Book, 186

Spelling Words with *-able, -ible,* 759G
Spelling Practice Book, 187 LA.5.1.4.1

Quick Check Comprehension, 751
Phonics, 759E

Differentiated Instruction 759M–759V

Benchmarks

FCAT

Vocabulary
Vocabulary Words
Word Parts/Latin and Greek Roots
LA.5.1.6.11 Use roots and affixes derived from Greek and Latin to determine meaning

Comprehension
Strategy: Summarize
Skill: Chronological Order
LA.5.1.7.5 Identify text structure

Writing
Expository/Problem Solving Essay
LA.5.4.2.3 Write expository essays that contain introductory, body, and concluding paragraphs

Science
The Nature of Science
SC.H.3.2.4.5.1 Understand the science process

Turn the Page for
Small Group Options

Day 3

Listening/Speaking

❓Focus Question Compare and contrast Dr. Grew's experiences with Dennis Kunkel's career.

Summarize, 753 LA.5.5.2.1

Vocabulary LA.5.1.6.3

Review Words in Context, 759C

FCAT **Strategy:** Word Parts/Latin and Greek Roots, 759D

Practice Book A-O-B, 219

Phonics Decode Multisyllabic Words, 759E LA.5.1.4

Read Hidden Worlds, 740–751

Student Book

Comprehension

Comprehension Check, 753

FCAT **Skill:** Main Ideas and Details, 753B

Fluency Repeated Reading, 753A

Partner Reading, 736I LA.5.1.5

Practice Book A-O-B, 217

FCAT **Writing**

Daily Writing: Suppose you have discovered a new element. Name the element and describe its properties. Also tell what it can be used for.

Writer's Craft: Beginning, Middle, End, 759A

Problem Solving Essay, 759B LA.5.4.2.3

Grammar Daily Language Activities, 759I

Review Punctuation Marks, 759J

Grammar Practice Book, 187

Spelling Words with -able, -ible, 759H

Spelling Practice Book, 188 LA.5.1.4.1

Quick Check Fluency, 753A

Differentiated Instruction 759M–759V

Day 4

Listening/Speaking/Viewing

❓Focus Question Compare the ways in which the narrator of "Mountain of Fire" and the scientists of Hidden Worlds view the eruption of Mount St. Helens. LA.5.5.2

Expand Vocabulary: Scientists at Work, 759F

Vocabulary LA.5.1.6

Word Families, 759F

Apply Vocabulary to Writing, 759F

Read "Mountain of Fire: A Native American Myth," 754–757

Student Book

Comprehension

Language Arts: Myth

FCAT **Literary Elements:** Symbolism and Figurative Language, 754

Practice Book A-O-B, 218

Fluency Partner Reading, 736I LA.5.1.5

FCAT **Writing**

Daily Writing: Imagine that you are an eyewitness to a volcanic explosion. Describe what you see and hear.

Writing Trait: Organization, 759B

Problem Solving Essay, 759B LA.5.4.2.3

Grammar Daily Language Activities, 759I

Sentence Combining, 759J

Grammar Practice Book, 188

Spelling Words with -able, -ible, 759H

Spelling Practice Book, 189 LA.5.1.4.1

Quick Check Vocabulary, 759D

Differentiated Instruction 759M–759V

Day 5
Review and Assess

Listening/Speaking/Viewing

❓Focus Question What steps do you think you would have to take to become a scientist? LA.5.5.2.1

Speaking and Listening Strategies, 759A

Present Problem and Solution Essay, 759B

Vocabulary LA.5.1.6

Spiral Review: Vocabulary Game, 759F

Read Self-Selected Reading 736I LA.5.2.2.5

Student Book

Comprehension

Connect and Compare, 757 LA.5.2.1.5

Fluency Partner Reading, 736I LA.5.1.5

FCAT **Writing**

Daily Writing: Write a letter to your member of Congress urging support for research into a science issue, such as global warming. Explain why the research is so important.

Problem Solving Essay, 759B LA.5.4.2.3

Grammar Daily Language Activities, 759I

Sentence Combining, 759J

Grammar Practice Book, 189–190

Spelling Posttest, 759H

Spelling Practice Book, 190 LA.5.1.4.1

FCAT **Weekly Assessment, 357–368**

Differentiated Instruction 759M–759V

Differentiated Instruction

What do I do in small groups?

Teacher-Led Small Groups

Literacy Workstations

Independent Activities

Skills Focus → Use your **Quick Check** observations to guide additional instruction and practice.

Phonics
-able, -ible

 Vocabulary
Words: biology, research, specimens, dormant, erupted, scoured, murky, observer

FCAT **Strategy:** Word Parts/Use Latin and Greek Word Parts to Build Word Families

Comprehension
Strategy: Summarize
FCAT **Skill:** Chronological Order

FCAT **Fluency**

Suggested Lesson Plan

 **Instructional Navigator** Interactive Lesson Planner

Approaching Level
- **Additional Instruction/Practice**
- **Tier 2 Instruction**

On Level
- **Practice**

Beyond Level
- **Extend**

DAY 1
Fluency, 759N
Vocabulary, 759N
Comprehension, 759O

Vocabulary, 759Q
Leveled Reader Lesson, 759R
- Comprehension
ELL Leveled Reader, 759U–759V

Vocabulary, 759S
Leveled Reader Lesson, 759T
- Comprehension

DAY 2
Phonics, 759M
Vocabulary, 759O
Leveled Reader Lesson, 759P
- Vocabulary
- Comprehension

Leveled Reader Lesson, 759R
- Comprehension
- Vocabulary

Leveled Reader Lesson, 759T
- Comprehension
- Vocabulary

For intensive intervention see **READING Triumphs**

Small Group Options

Leveled Reader Library

Apply skills and strategies while reading appropriate leveled books.

Levels S–Y

Approaching   **On Level**   **Beyond**

 Science Finds Cures
by Melissa McDaniel

ELL

Additional Leveled Reader Resources

LOG ON   **Leveled Reader Database**

Go to **www.macmillanmh.com**

Search by

- Comprehension Skill
- Content Area
- Genre
- Text Feature
- Guided Reading Level
- Reading Recovery Level
- Lexile Score
- Benchmark Level

Subscription also available.

 Focus on Science

Teacher's Annotated Edition

 Nature of Science

SC.H.3.2.4.5.1 The science process

Additional Leveled Readers

Life on the Deep Sea Floor

Searching for Tomorrow's Energy

Day 3

Phonics, 759M
Fluency, 759N
Vocabulary, 759O
Leveled Reader Lesson, 759P
- Comprehension

Fluency, 759Q
Vocabulary, 759Q
Leveled Reader Lesson, 759R
- Comprehension

Fluency, 759S
Vocabulary, 759S
Leveled Reader Lesson, 759T
- Comprehension

Day 4

Phonics, 759M
Leveled Reader Lesson, 759P
- Comprehension
ELL Skill: Chronological Order

Literary Elements, 759Q
Leveled Reader Lesson, 759R
- Comprehension

Literary Elements, 759S
Leveled Reader Lesson, 759T
- Comprehension
ELL Figurative Language, 759S

Day 5

Fluency, 759N
Leveled Reader Lesson, 759P
- Make Connections Across Texts

Fluency, 759Q
Leveled Reader Lesson, 759R
- Make Connections Across Texts

Fluency, 759S
Self-Selected Reading, 759T

Managing the Class

What do I do with the rest of my class?

Teacher-Led Small Groups

Literacy Workstations

Independent Activities

Class Management Tools

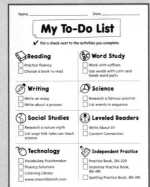

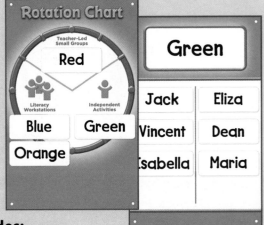

Includes:
- How-to Guide
- Rotation Chart
- Weekly Contracts

FOLDABLES™

Hands-on activities for reinforcing weekly skills

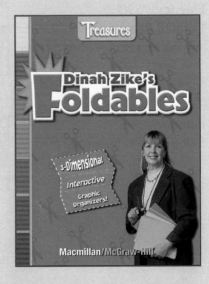

Fish	Frogs
habitat	habitat
food	insects
prey	prey
enemies	enemies

Eight-Tab Foldable

Word	Synonym	Antonym	Prefix or Suffix
normal	typical	unusual	normally

Folded Chart

Independent Activities

 FCAT LEVELED READERS: Science

For Repeated Readings and Literacy Activities

Approaching

On Level

ELL

Beyond

LEVELED PRACTICE

Skills: Vocabulary, Chronological Order, Fluency,
Greek and Latin Roots, Symbolism and Figurative Language

Practice Book A
Approaching

Practice Book O
On Level

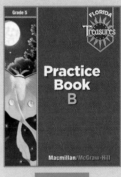
Practice Book B
Beyond

ELL Practice and Assessment
ELL

Technology

ONLINE INSTRUCTION www.macmillanmh.com

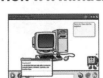

- Meet the Author/Illustrator
- Computer Literacy Lessons
- Research and Inquiry Activities

- Oral Language Activities
- Vocabulary and Spelling Activities
- Leveled Reader Database

 LISTENING LIBRARY
Recordings of selections
- Main Selections
- Leveled Readers
- ELL Readers
- Intervention Anthology

 FLUENCY SOLUTIONS
Recorded passages for modeling and practicing fluency

 VOCABULARY PUZZLEMAKER
Activities providing multiple exposures to vocabulary, spelling, and high-frequency words including crossword puzzles, word searches, and word jumbles

---

Turn the page for Literacy Workstations.

Managing the Class

Literacy Activities

Collaborative Learning Activities

 Reading

 Word Study

Reading — Objectives

- Read with a group and time reading to practice fluency
- Summarize information from a selection
- Read daily as a leisure activity
- Be enthusiastic about reading and learning how to read

Word Study — Objectives

- Spell words with *-able* and *-ible* correctly
- Build and use words with Latin and Greek word parts

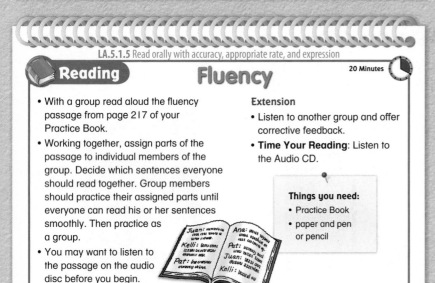

LA.5.1.5 Read orally with accuracy, appropriate rate, and expression

Reading — Fluency 20 Minutes

- With a group read aloud the fluency passage from page 217 of your Practice Book.
- Working together, assign parts of the passage to individual members of the group. Decide which sentences everyone should read together. Group members should practice their assigned parts until everyone can read his or her sentences smoothly. Then practice as a group.
- You may want to listen to the passage on the audio disc before you begin.

Extension

- Listen to another group and offer corrective feedback.
- **Time Your Reading:** Listen to the Audio CD.

Things you need:
- Practice Book
- paper and pen or pencil

Fluency Solutions Listening Library

59

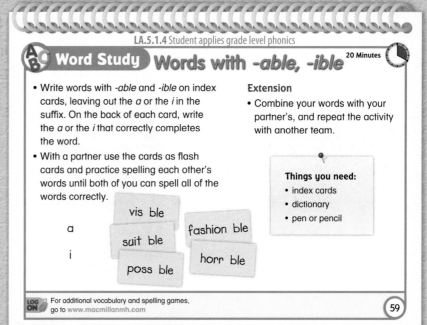

LA.5.1.4 Student applies grade level phonics

Word Study — Words with *-able*, *-ible* 20 Minutes

- Write words with *-able* and *-ible* on index cards, leaving out the *a* or the *i* in the suffix. On the back of each card, write the *a* or the *i* that correctly completes the word.
- With a partner use the cards as flash cards and practice spelling each other's words until both of you can spell all of the words correctly.

a

i

vis ble
suit ble
poss ble
fashion ble
horr ble

Extension

- Combine your words with your partner's, and repeat the activity with another team.

Things you need:
- index cards
- dictionary
- pen or pencil

For additional vocabulary and spelling games, go to www.macmillanmh.com

59

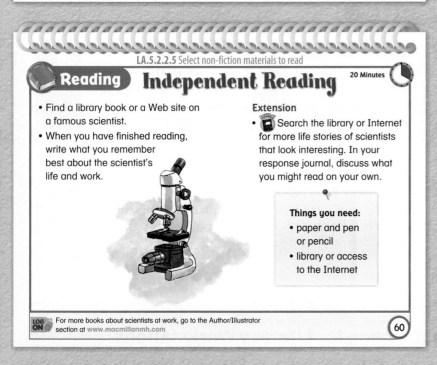

LA.5.2.2.5 Select non-fiction materials to read

Reading — Independent Reading 20 Minutes

- Find a library book or a Web site on a famous scientist.
- When you have finished reading, write what you remember best about the scientist's life and work.

Extension

- Search the library or Internet for more life stories of scientists that look interesting. In your response journal, discuss what you might read on your own.

Things you need:
- paper and pen or pencil
- library or access to the Internet

For more books about scientists at work, go to the Author/Illustrator section at www.macmillanmh.com

60

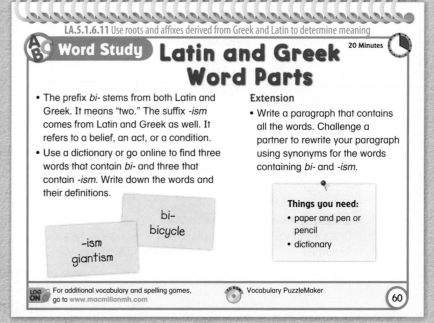

LA.5.1.6.11 Use roots and affixes derived from Greek and Latin to determine meaning

Word Study — Latin and Greek Word Parts 20 Minutes

- The prefix *bi-* stems from both Latin and Greek. It means "two." The suffix *-ism* comes from Latin and Greek as well. It refers to a belief, an act, or a condition.
- Use a dictionary or go online to find three words that contain *bi-* and three that contain *-ism*. Write down the words and their definitions.

bi-
bicycle
-ism
giantism

Extension

- Write a paragraph that contains all the words. Challenge a partner to rewrite your paragraph using synonyms for the words containing *bi-* and *-ism*.

Things you need:
- paper and pen or pencil
- dictionary

For additional vocabulary and spelling games, go to www.macmillanmh.com

Vocabulary PuzzleMaker

60

Literacy Workstations

 **Reading** Grade 5

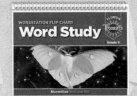 **Word Study** Grade 5

 **Writing** Grade 5

 **Science/Social Studies** Grade 5

Writing

Objectives

- Write an essay to explore a question
- Use research to write fact cards about a process in nature
- Write voluntarily for different purposes

Content Literacy

Objectives

- Write a story based on research
- Write a report based on research
- Read to perform a task

LA.5.4.2.3 Write expository essays

 Writing — Writing to Explore a Question
20 Minutes

- Scientists are always working to discover causes and cures for diseases as well as answer questions about the world around us. Write an essay explaining what you want to know that science has not yet mastered. What mystery about the world do you want uncovered?

Extension

- Read your essay to a partner, and invite the partner to ask questions. Use your partner's questions to help you improve your essay.
- Also, look through your essay for sentences that could be combined.

> **Things you need:**
> - paper and pen or pencil

59

LA.5.4.1 Student develops and demonstrates creative writing

 Science — Scientific Discoveries
20 Minutes

- Research a famous scientist from history, such as Albert Einstein, Marie Curie, or Thomas Edison. Find out about his or her background, education, and discoveries.
- Write a story in which you witness the scientist making one of his or her important discoveries.

Extension

- List the main events of your story out of order. Exchange stories with a partner. Arrange the events in each other's stories in the proper order. If you have trouble, ask your partner for a clue.

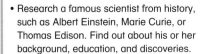
Lives of the GREAT SCIENTISTS

> **Things you need:**
> - paper and pen or pencil
> - library or access to the Internet

59

LA.5.4.1 Student demonstrates creative writing

 Writing — Writing to Explore
20 Minutes

- Think of something that happens in science or nature that you would like to know more about, such as why grass is green or how a garden grows. Use the Internet or the library to research it.
- Make fact cards about the process. Use the cards to write about the process in any genre you wish, such as an essay, a story or myth, a poem, or a letter.

Extension

- Exchange writings with a partner. Discuss how you chose your approach to writing about your subject.

> **Things you need:**
> - paper and pen or pencil
> - library or access to the Internet

LOG ON Internet Research and Inquiry Activity
Students can find more facts at www.macmillanmh.com

60

LA.5.4.2.2 Record information related to a topic

Social Studies — Mythology in Culture
20 Minutes

- In ancient times, when people did not understand something in nature, such as lightning, they would often make up a story to explain the event. Research a myth from long ago that has since been explained by science.
- Write a short report of your findings.

Extension

- With a partner come up with a list of myths or folk tales that people have used to explain complicated science problems.

> **Things you need:**
> - paper and pen or pencil
> - library or access to the Internet

60

ORAL LANGUAGE
- Build Background
- Read Aloud
- Expand Vocabulary

FCAT **VOCABULARY**
- Teach Words in Context
- Word Parts: Greek and Latin Roots

COMPREHENSION
- **Strategy:** Summarize
- **FCAT** **Skill:** Chronological Order

SMALL GROUP OPTIONS
- Differentiated Instruction,
  pp. 759M–759V

Oral Language

Build Background

LA.5.5.2.1
Listen to gain
and share
information

ACCESS PRIOR KNOWLEDGE

Share the following information:

Scientists use a method to solve
problems and make discoveries. They
begin with an observation, ask a
question, form a hypothesis (or theory),
perform an experiment, and then draw
a conclusion.

LA.5.5.2.1
Listen and
speak to gain
and share
information

TALK ABOUT SCIENTISTS AT WORK

Discuss the weekly theme. Ask:

Do you know of any scientists at work
in your community?

 FOCUS QUESTION Have a volunteer
read "Talk About It" on **Student Book**
page 736 and describe the photo. Ask:

What do you think the scientists want
to learn?

SCIENTISTS AT WORK

736

ENGLISH LANGUAGE LEARNERS Access for All

Beginning **Model** Point to and name items in the photo. Have
students point and repeat. *These scientists are paleontologists. They
study fossils.* Have students repeat.

Intermediate **Activate Prior Knowledge** Ask, *What do
paleontologists do?* As students talk, supply vocabulary as needed
and write their ideas: *observe, dig up bones, solve problems, perform
experiments, discover, ask questions.* Ask, *What have you studied in
science class?* For Spanish-speaking students, point out the cognates
scientists/científicos.

Advanced **Elaborate** Complete the Intermediate task. As
students speak, model extending their sentences. *So, you studied
volcanoes and earthquakes in your science class. What did you learn
about them?*

Talk About It

If you could be a scientist, what would you study? What kind of scientists do the work shown in this photograph?

 Find out more about scientists at

www.macmillanmh.com

737

Picture Prompt

Look at the picture and write an essay about how these paleontolgists solved a problem on this dig. What was the problem?

Technology

For an extended lesson plan and Web site activities for **oral language development**, go to **www.macmillanmh.com**

Read Aloud
Read "The Microscope"

LA.5.2.1.1
Demonstrate knowledge of characteristics of genres

GENRE: Poetry
Review features of poetry:

- a composition that often rhymes and has rhythm

LA.5.1.6.2
Listen to and discuss familiar text

LISTENING FOR A PURPOSE

Read Aloud pages 141–143

Ask students to listen carefully for the way the writer uses colorful language to characterize Leeuwenhoek as you read "The Microscope" in the **Read-Aloud Anthology.** Students should be prepared to describe the kind of person Leeuwenhoek was. Choose from among the teaching suggestions.

Fluency Ask students to listen carefully as you read aloud, paying attention to your phrasing, expression, and tone of voice.

LA.5.5.2.1
Listen and speak to gain and share information

RESPOND TO THE SELECTION

Invite students to share their opinions about Leeuwenhoek, and discuss other scientific discoveries they know about that were initially ridiculed.

LA.5.4.1
Student develops creative writing

LA.5.5.2.1
Listen and speak for poetic recitations

Expand Vocabulary

Have students choose four or more words from the selection that relate to this week's theme of scientists at work. Ask students to imagine they are scientists at work, and use the words in a poem about their own scientific discoveries. Invite students to read their poems aloud.

Vocabulary

FCAT
LA.5.1.6.3
Use context
clues

TEACH WORDS IN CONTEXT

LA.5.1.6.1
Use new
vocabulary
taught directly

Use the following routine:

Routine

<u>**Define:**</u> **Specimens** are items or parts typical of a whole group.

<u>**Example:**</u> Jordan collects specimens of different kinds of moths and butterflies.

<u>**Ask:**</u> What is a synonym for *specimens*?

SYNONYMS

LA.5.1.6.8
Use synonyms
to determine
meaning

■ **Erupted** means forced out or burst forth. When volcanoes have erupted, rocks, hot ash, and lava have been thrown into the air. What is a synonym of *erupted*? **SYNONYM**

■ Something that is **murky** is too dark or cloudy to see through clearly. The pond water was murky with algae. What would a murky day look and feel like? **DESCRIPTION**

■ Something that is **dormant** is quiet or not active for a period of time. Some animals, such as chipmunks, remain dormant during the winter. What other things are dormant in winter? **EXAMPLE**

■ **Biology** is the study of living things. Zoology and ecology are two branches of biology. What is a form of life you might study in biology? **EXAMPLE**

■ If something was **scoured,** it was cleaned, cleared, or worn away. The ditch was scoured clear by flooding. How does something become scoured? **EXPLANATION**

Access for All ■ **Research** is a careful study to find and learn facts about a subject. The class did much research in the library for their science reports. In what ways does a person do research? **PRIOR KNOWLEDGE**

Vocabulary

specimens	scoured
erupted	biology
murky	research
dormant	observer

FCAT **Word Parts**
Some words have **Greek** or **Latin Roots**. If you know the meaning of a root, you can figure out a word's definition. For example, *bio-* means "life," so *biology* means "the study of living things."

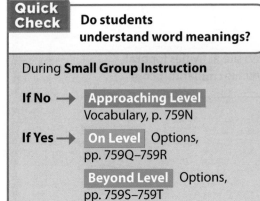

738

■ An **observer** is a person who watches in a close and careful way. She was an observer in the dance class. How is an observer similar to and different from a participant? **COMPARE AND CONTRAST**

Quick Check **Do students understand word meanings?**

During **Small Group Instruction**

If No → **Approaching Level** Vocabulary, p. 759N

If Yes → **On Level** Options, pp. 759Q–759R

Beyond Level Options, pp. 759S–759T

Dr. Priscilla C. Grew, GEOLOGIST

by Josh Taylor

Dr. Priscilla C. Grew is a well-known scientist in the field of geology, the study of Earth's rocks. As a geologist, Dr. Grew looks at a lot of **specimens** to learn how Earth has changed in the past 4.5 billion years.

A good time and place to look for these changes is after a volcano has **erupted**. Afterward, the air becomes dark and **murky** from ash. When the ash settles, it blankets the land. Sometimes a volcano can release hot lava as well. When hot lava spills out, the ground becomes an excellent place to study how new rocks and minerals are formed. This is especially true for the ground near a **dormant** volcano because the area surrounding such a volcano has not changed in a very long time.

ELL   **Access for All**

Give Concrete Examples
For *research,* write: *What do you do when you research a topic?* List students' ideas on the board. Then have students ask and answer the question in pairs. For *biology,* write: *In biology, we study _____.* Ask students to make statements in pairs or as a class using the sentence.

Areas affected by earthquakes are another good place to find a geologist. Early in her career, Dr. Grew helped many people in California lower the chances of getting harmed during major earthquakes. Then Dr. Grew moved to Minnesota where she became the first woman to be named state geologist. She and her team searched all over the state for minerals in the soil. Once they were found, they were **scoured** clean and prepared for studies that Dr. Grew would perform.

After leaving Minnesota, Dr. Grew became the first female director of the University of Nebraska State Museum. Visitors to the museum learn about geology, earth science, and **biology**. They enjoy the displays of rocks and fossils.

During her life and career, Dr. Grew has tried to connect the world of rocks and soil to people's needs. By helping people to be safer during earthquakes and looking for important minerals in the soil, Dr. Grew connects her **research** to the real world. All this makes Dr. Grew more than an **observer**. She is a hands-on scientist who is making a difference.

Dr. Priscilla C. Grew

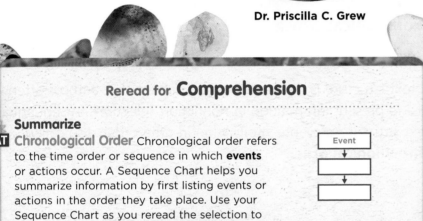

Reread for **Comprehension**

Summarize

FCAT **Chronological Order** Chronological order refers to the time order or sequence in which **events** or actions occur. A Sequence Chart helps you summarize information by first listing events or actions in the order they take place. Use your Sequence Chart as you reread the selection to help you summarize events chronologically.

Event
↓
↓

739

On Level Practice Book O, page 214

| specimens | erupted | murky | dormant |
| biology | scoured | research | observer |

Choose the word that best replaces the underlined word or words. Then write the word on the line.

1. If you are curious about the study of living things, you can make amazing discoveries. ___biology___

2. First you must become someone who watches everything around you. ___observer___

3. Your investigations might take you to a park or even to a lake, where you can study life under the water. ___research___

4. Sometimes a lake will look as though it has no activity, but it is really filled with life. ___dormant___

5. In the water you may find minerals to be cleaned back in the lab. ___scoured___

6. Even if the water is thick and dark, you will probably find something fascinating. ___murky___

7. Take samples of the water so that you can study them under a microscope. ___specimens___

8. You may find evidence that a volcano exploded or evidence of other natural events in your water samples. ___erupted___

⭐ **Approaching Practice Book A,** page 214

◆ **Beyond Practice Book B,** page 214

Vocabulary

STRATEGY
WORD PARTS

LA.5.1.6.11
Use roots and affixes derived from Greek and Latin to determine meaning of complex words

Greek and Latin Roots Remind students that knowing Greek and Latin roots can help them make inferences about the definitions of complex words. They can use a dictionary to find the meanings of roots, prefixes, and suffixes, and to verify word meanings.

Point to the word *biology* on page 739. Write these words on the board: *autobiography, biographical, biologist.* Ask students to use the Greek root *bio* to determine what related meanings these words share. (life, writings about life and the study of life) Point out that all these words belong to the *bio* word family. Knowing the meaning of *bio* can help them figure out the meanings of words that contain it.

LA.5.1.6.3
Use context clues

Read "Dr. Priscilla C. Grew, Geologist"

As you read "Dr. Priscilla C. Grew, Geologist" with students, ask them to identify clues that reveal the meanings of the highlighted words. Tell students they will read these words again in *Hidden Worlds*.

Objectives

- Summarize a biographical sketch
- Use academic language: *chronological order*
- Identify

Materials

- Comprehension Transparencies 30a and 30b
- Graphic Organizer Transparency 30
- Practice Book, p. 215

FCAT Skills Trace

Chronological Order	
Introduce	71B
Practice / Apply	641A–B, 642–659, 739A–B, 740–751; Practice Book 187–188, 215–216
Reteach / Review	163B; 283B; 6670–P, R, T; 731B; 7590–P, R, T
Assess	Weekly Tests; Unit 6 Test; Benchmark Tests A, B
Maintain	641A–B, 739A–B; Practice Book 187–188, 215–216

ELL

Identify Sequence Words
Write the sequence words from the selection on the board: *afterward, when, early, then, once, after, during.* Have students look for the words as they read. Discuss the sentences in which the words appear. Check students' understanding of the sequence words by asking students to tell in their own words the meaning of each sentence.

LA.5.1.6.2
Read familiar text

LA.5.1.7
Student uses strategies to comprehend text

Reread for Comprehension

STRATEGY
SUMMARIZE

A **summary** is a short statement of the most important ideas in a passage or text. Good readers know that summarizing can help them understand what they have read because they have to identify what a passage or selection is about, select the most important ideas, and then restate them in their own words. As a strategy, summarizing can also help readers use skills such as identifying the chronological order of events in a selection.

SKILL
CHRONOLOGICAL ORDER

LA.5.2.2.3
Organize information to show understanding

EXPLAIN

- A text structure is an organizational pattern that authors often use to present information in nonfiction selections. A sequential text structure presents information in time order, also called **chronological order**.

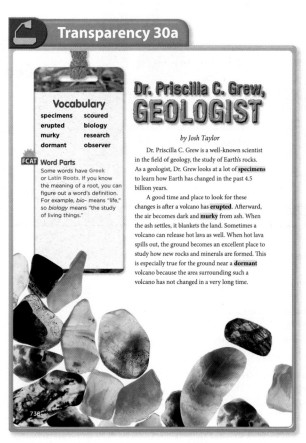

Student Book pages 738–739 available on Comprehension Transparencies 30a and 30b

- Authors use signal words such as *first, next, last, then, afterward, while,* and *during* when they use a chronological order text structure to present information in time order.

- To identify a text structure in which the author puts events in chronological order, readers can ask themselves: *When is the event or step taking place? What words in the text can help me figure out the time order of events? Are there any time phrases, dates, numbered paragraphs, or other clues I can use?*

- Summarizing the order in which events occur in a selection can help readers identify and remember key events.

LA.5.2.2.3
Organize information to show understanding

MODEL

Read the first few paragraphs of "Dr. Priscilla C. Grew, Geologist" from **Student Book** page 738.

Think Aloud The first two paragraphs discuss Dr. Priscilla Grew's work. Dr. Grew studies how Earth has changed in the past 4.5 billion years, and the best place to do this is in an area where a volcano has erupted. I see the clue word *afterward* in the second paragraph, which describes the sequence of events when a volcano erupts. *Afterward, the air becomes dark and murky from ash. When the ash settles, it blankets the land.*

GUIDED PRACTICE

Display **Transparency 30.** Begin the Sequence Chart with the first thing that happens after a volcano has erupted. (The air becomes dark and murky from ash.) Fill in the next item together. Help students identify the chronological order of events in the selection.

APPLY

Have students reread the rest of the selection and complete the Sequence Chart for Dr. Grew's career. Ask students to discuss the importance of Dr. Grew's work.

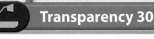
Transparency 30

Event
The air becomes dark and murky from ash.

↓

Event
When the ash settles, it blankets the land.

Graphic Organizer Transparency 30

FCAT Success!

Test Prep and Practice with Chronological Order, pages 65–96.

On Level Practice Book O, page 215

Events in a story or steps in an experiment usually happen in **chronological order**. If you can recognize and follow the sequence, you will better understand what will happen next. Words such as *first, then, next, now,* and *finally* help signal the order in which events or steps occur.

Read the scientific method. Label each step of the scientific method below. Possible responses provided.

Scientific method is specific steps scientists take during an experiment. Scientists try to answer questions they have by performing several tests. By following a specific sequence during different experiments, they are able to determine the answers to their questions.

1. **Initial or First Observation:** Scientists notice something and wonder why.
2. **Gather Information:** Scientists try to find out more.
3. **Hypothesis:** Scientists take their initial observation and create a question that can be tested. A hypothesis should make a prediction of the outcome.
4. **Testing:** Scientists will perform experiments and record data.
5. **Draw a Conclusion:** Using the information from their tests, scientists will compare this data to their hypothesis to see if their prediction is correct or not.

1. Finally I conclude my hypothesis was correct. The birds made a nest to hold their eggs. Draw a Conclusion

2. Then I learned more from a book about birds laying eggs in the spring. Gather Information

3. First I see two blue birds. One is flying from tree to tree. The other is gathering twigs. It is springtime. Initial Observation

4. Next I observe the birds for a week. They choose a large tree branch. The birds gather more twigs and start building a nest. I see three bird eggs. Testing

5. I predict the birds will make a nest to hold their eggs. Hypothesis

 Approaching Practice Book A, page 215

♦ **Beyond Practice Book B,** page 215

Quick Check

Can students identify the chronological order of events?

During **Small Group Instruction**

If No → **Approaching Level** Comprehension, pp. 759O–759P

If Yes → **On Level** Options, p. 759R

Beyond Level Options, p. 759T

Read

MAIN SELECTION

 • *Hidden Worlds*
• **Skill:** Chronological Order

PAIRED SELECTION

• "Mountain of Fire: A Native American Myth"
• **Literary Elements:** Symbolism and Figurative Language

SMALL GROUP OPTIONS

• Differentiated Instruction, pp. 759M–759V

Comprehension

LA.5.2.1.1 Demonstrate knowledge of characteristics of genres

GENRE: NONFICTION

Have students read the definition of Nonfiction on **Student Book** page 740. As they read, students should look for illustrations and any boldfaced words to help them understand the facts and information presented in the text.

LA.5.1.7 Student uses strategies to comprehend text

STRATEGY
SUMMARIZE

Remind students that when they summarize, they identify what the passage or selection is about, select the most important ideas, and then restate the ideas in their own words.

SKILL
CHRONOLOGICAL ORDER

LA.5.2.2.3 Organize information to show understanding

Remind students that a chronological text structure presents information in time order. Good readers look for time phrases and dates that give clues to the order of events as they read.

Comprehension

Genre

Nonfiction gives information and facts about real people, places, events, and situations.

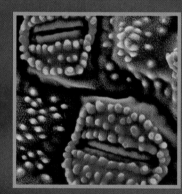

Summarize

Chronological Order
Look for clues that indicate the order of events. As you read, use your Sequence Chart.

Event

Read to Find Out

What events influenced Dennis's career in science?

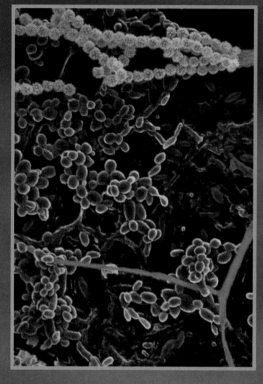

740

Vocabulary

Vocabulary Words Review the tested vocabulary words: **biology, dormant, erupted, murky, observer, research, scoured,** and **specimens.**

Selection Words Students may find these words difficult. Pronounce the words and present the meanings as necessary.

algae (p. 743): simple living organisms made up of one or more cells that contain chlorophyll, usually existing as lower order plants that do not have stems, roots, or leaves

lichens (p. 746): an organism made up of fungi and algae growing together, usually found on tree trunks, on rocks, and on the ground

bacteria (p. 749): tiny one-celled organisms that can be seen only through a microscope

LA.5.1.6.1 Use new vocabulary taught directly

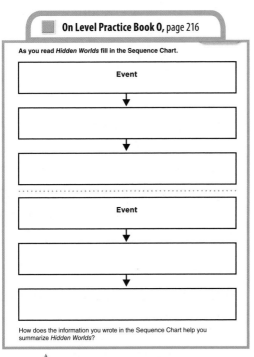

Award Winning Selection

Hidden Worlds

Looking Through a Scientist's Microscope

by Stephen Kramer
photographs by Dennis Kunkel

741

Read Together

If your students need support to read the Main Selection, use the prompts to guide comprehension and model how to complete the graphic organizer.

Read Independently

If your students can read the Main Selection independently, have them read and complete the graphic organizer. Remind them to set a purpose for reading and to adjust their reading rate based on purposes, difficulty, and type of text.

If your students need an alternate selection, choose the **Leveled Readers** that match their instructional level.

Technology

Story available on **Listening Library Audio CD**

LA.5.1.7.1
Use prior knowledge to make and confirm predictions

Preview and Predict

Ask students to read the title, preview the illustrations, and make predictions about the information they might find in the text. Have students write about their predictions and any questions they have before reading the selection.

LA.5.1.7.1
Establish purpose for reading

Set Purposes

FOCUS QUESTION Discuss the "Read to Find Out" question and how to look for the answer as students read.

Point out the Sequence of Events Chart in the Student Book and on **Practice Book** page 216. Tell students they will fill it in as they read.

Read *Hidden Worlds*

Use the questions and Think Alouds for additional instruction to support the comprehension strategy and skill.

On Level Practice Book O, page 216

As you read *Hidden Worlds* fill in the Sequence Chart.

Event

↓

↓

·········

Event

↓

↓

How does the information you wrote in the Sequence Chart help you summarize *Hidden Worlds*?

★ **Approaching** Practice Book A, page 216

◆ **Beyond** Practice Book B, page 216

Develop Comprehension

1 STRATEGY
SUMMARIZE

LA.5.1.7
Use strategies to comprehend text

Teacher Think Aloud I know that a summary is a short statement of the most important ideas in a passage or a text. After previewing the text and reading the first page of *Hidden Worlds,* I see that the information is organized into three separate sections: *Becoming a Scientist, Working as a Scientist,* and *How to Become a Scientist.* These text features can help me identify the main ideas in each section of text. Keeping track of the main ideas will allow me to recognize the most important information the author presents, which I will include when I summarize.

2 DRAW CONCLUSIONS

LA.5.2.2.2
Use information from text to answer questions

How did Dennis's hobbies contribute to his interest in microscopes? (Dennis loved nature and spent a lot of time tending his family's gardens and pets. The microscope helped Dennis take his interest in nature a step further. It allowed him to see the things he wouldn't normally see when he interacted with the animals and plants around him.)

1 Becoming a Scientist

Dennis Kunkel grew up in the Iowa countryside, where cornfields stretched for miles in all directions. Dennis helped tend the flowers and vegetables in the family garden. He went on weekend fishing trips with his parents and his sisters, and he took care of the family pets. Dennis loved nature and being outdoors, but he did not know that someday he would become a scientist.

Then Dennis received a gift that changed his life. "When I was ten years old, my parents gave me a microscope for Christmas," he recalls. "It came with a set of prepared slides—things like insect legs, root hairs, and tiny creatures called protozoans. As soon as I unwrapped the microscope, I forgot about my other presents and tried to figure out how to use it."

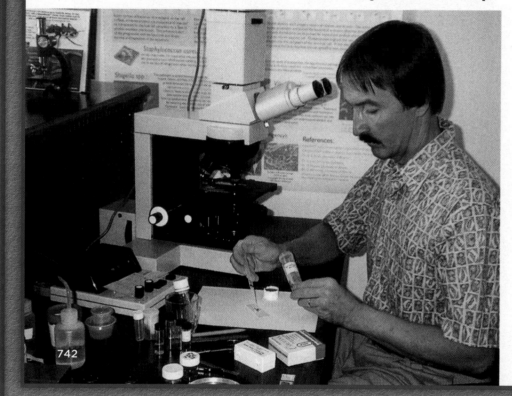

Dennis working at one of his microscopes.

742

When Dennis looked at pond water with his first microscope, he saw these kinds of simple plants. They are green algae. Above: *Volvox*. Right: *Micrasterias*.

The prepared specimens that came with the microscope were dead. Dennis quickly discovered that it was more fun to observe things that were alive and moving, so he began to take collecting trips. One of Dennis's first trips was to a pond about a mile and a half from his house. "I started hiking down there with my little collecting bottles and bringing back water samples to look at under my microscope," he explains. "I couldn't wait to get home from school in the afternoon so I could go to the pond. Before long I was looking at all kinds of fascinating creatures."

4

743

Develop Comprehension

3 **VOCABULARY: LATIN AND GREEK WORD PARTS**

LA.5.1.6.11
Use roots and affixes from Greek and Latin to determine meaning of complex words

Micro- comes from the Greek word *micros,* which means "small." *Scope* comes from the Greek word *skopos,* which means "a spy or watcher." Using this information, what does the word *microscope* mean? What other words can you think of that contain the word parts *micro* or *scope?* How can knowledge of these affixes and their meanings help you to determine the meanings of complex words? (Answers will vary but should include that a microscope is a device that is used to look at things that are too small to be seen with the naked eye. Other words students may suggest that contain the word parts *micro* or *scope* could include *microwave, microphone, microorganism, telescope,* and *periscope.* Students should note that knowledge of these affixes and their meanings can help them to decode unfamiliar words.)

4 **SYNTHESIZE**

LA.5.2.2.2
Use information from text to answer questions

Do you think Dennis Kunkel showed the characteristics of a good scientist as a boy? Explain your answer. (Answers may vary but should include that Dennis is very curious, which is one of the characteristics of a good scientist. He soon realized that it was more interesting to examine things that are alive, and he started making trips to a pond near his house to collect samples.)

Develop Comprehension

5 **CHRONOLOGICAL ORDER**

FCAT

LA.5.2.2.3
Organize information to show understanding

What clue words does the author use to indicate the time order of events in Dennis Kunkel's life? What are those events? Add these events to the Sequence Chart. (Answers should include that the author uses the signal words *after, then,* and *finally* to indicate the sequence of events in Dennis's life. After he graduated from high school, Dennis entered a junior college where he studied biology. Then he transferred to the University of Washington, where he was finally able to work in labs with good microscopes.)

> After high school Dennis went to junior college and worked in a science lab.

↓

> Then Dennis transferred to the University of Washington.

↓

> Finally, he was able to work in labs with good microscopes.

Dennis used his microscope to look at anything he could fit under its lenses. He examined insects, soil samples, and parts of plants. He looked at fur from his pets and seeds from nearby fields. Dennis made drawings of the things he observed, and he spent many hours reading about them.

After Dennis graduated from high school, he enrolled in a junior college in his hometown. A **biology** teacher there encouraged his love of science and microscopes. Dennis often worked in the science lab after school, using microscopes to study the things he collected.

5 Then Dennis transferred to the University of Washington, in Seattle. Finally he could learn and do things he had dreamed about. "I had the chance to work in labs with good microscopes," explains Dennis. "I spent hours speaking with professors and students about science. I had dreamed of exploring and learning about undersea life like Jacques Cousteau, but until I left Iowa I had never even seen the ocean. While I attended the University of Washington, I learned how to scuba dive. It was thrilling to go underwater to observe and collect the plants and animals I wanted to study."

Dennis examines leaves with two young scientists.

FCAT **Chronological Order**
What clue words does the author use to indicate the time order of events in Dennis Kunkel's life? What are those events?

744

Cross-Curricular Connection

MICROSCOPES

Share some facts about microscopes with students.

- A Dutch spectacle maker, Zacharias Janssen, discovered the principle of the compound microscope around 1590.

- In the middle 1600s, a Dutch scientist named Anton Van Leeuwenhoek made microscope lenses that could magnify objects up to 270 times their actual size.

- Electron microscopes, developed in 1931, are microscopes that use a beam of electrons instead of light rays to magnify objects.

Have students research Janssen or Leeuwenhoek using two sources. Have them compare and contrast what they find, write a summary of their findings, and give it as an oral report using any supporting graphics they find in their presentation.

LA.5.5.2.2 Make formal oral presentations demonstrating appropriate use of supporting graphics

Some people are allergic to pollen. Here are several types of pollen that cause watery eyes, runny noses, and sneezing: poplar (orange), alder (dark green), timothy grass (light green), ragweed (spiked yellow), sagebrush (oval yellow), and Scotch broom (plum).

6

In graduate school, Dennis began to use the science department's electron microscopes for his own **research**, studying tiny living things called cyanobacteria. But Dennis also used the microscopes to help other scientists. He helped one of his **7** professors study and classify pollen grains from different kinds of flowers. He helped a fellow graduate student examine wood with an electron microscope to learn about how plant cells deposit minerals and create "hard" wood. He helped other students with their studies of algae, fungi, and flowering plants.

After eight years of graduate work—including thousands of hours of research and work with microscopes—Dennis earned a Ph.D. in botany, the study of plants. Although Dennis was finishing his schooling, he was just beginning a lifetime of scientific learning and discovery.

Dennis worked on research projects at the University of Washington and the University of Hawai'i for about twenty-five years. Now he does much of his work in his home on the island of O'ahu, Hawai'i.

745

Develop Comprehension

6 MAKE INFERENCES

LA.5.2.2.2
Use information from text to answer questions

Why do you think working to study and classify pollen grains from different kinds of flowers would prove to be valuable? (Answers will vary but should include that pollen can cause allergies that result in watery eyes, runny noses, and sneezing. Studying pollen might lead to the development of a medicine that could help people with allergies.)

7 DRAW CONCLUSIONS

LA.5.2.2.2
Use information from text to answer questions

How does helping other scientists benefit Dennis's own research? (Answers may vary, but students should point out that Dennis might learn new information when he helps other scientists who are also studying plants. This information might be helpful in his own research.)

Have students respond to the selection by confirming or revising their predictions and purposes for reading. Suggest that they note any additonal questions they may have as well.

Quick Check

Can students use signal words to identify the chronological order of events? If not, see the **Extra Support** on this page.

Chronological Order

FCAT If students are having difficulty recognizing the text structure of this selection, help by asking them to return to page 742 and summarize the major events in Dennis's life so far, using signal words to put the events in time order. Ask questions to provide prompts for students: *How old was Dennis when he received a microscope, a gift that changed his life?* (Dennis was ten years old when he received a microscope as a Christmas gift.) *What did Dennis do when he graduated from high school?* (After he graduated from high school, Dennis enrolled in junior college.) *What did Dennis do next?* (Then he transferred to the University of Washington.)

LA.5.2.2.3 Organize information to show understanding
LA.5.1.7.8 Summarize to repair comprehension

Stop here if you wish to read this selection over two days.

Develop Comprehension

8 MAIN IDEA AND DETAILS

LA.5.2.2.2
Answer questions related to main ideas and relevant details

How do the section headings in this selection provide clues to help you figure out the main idea? (Answers should include that the headings provide a preview of what the information in that specific section will be about.) **What details support the main idea in this section title?** (Answers may vary but should include the following details: scientists are explorers; they make discoveries by asking questions and trying to answer them; some scientists work in laboratories, and others travel to and work in natural areas.)

9 MAKE INFERENCES

LA.5.2.2.2
Use information from text to answer questions

Why are the places Dennis explores called "hidden worlds"? (Dennis collects specimens from natural areas and uses the microscope to observe the things that are "hidden" to the naked eye.)

10 SYNTHESIZE

LA.5.2.2.2
Use information from text to answer questions

If you were a scientist would you be more interested in working in a laboratory or in natural areas such as mountains, rainforests, and caves? Explain your answer. (Possible answers: Students who are more interested in making observations using microscopes or conducting chemical experiments may prefer working in a laboratory. Students who enjoy being outdoors may prefer working in natural areas. Some students may like to work in both places like Dennis, who collects samples from nature and observes the samples in a laboratory.)

8 Working as a Scientist

Scientists are explorers. They usually make discoveries by asking questions and then trying to answer them. Some scientists find their answers in laboratories, surrounded by equipment and instruments. Others travel to natural areas to find their answers. Dennis's work has taken him to mountains, rainforests, deserts, caves, beaches, and into the sea.

Whenever Dennis goes on field trips, he takes along collecting boxes and bottles. When he returns to the lab, the boxes and bottles are usually full of interesting **specimens**: algae, lichens, mushrooms, seeds, leaves, insects, bark, soil, and flowers. Dennis has explored

9
10 hidden worlds in places ranging from the blast zone of a volcano to the dust balls underneath people's beds!

The aquatic nymph stage of the mayfly. Adult mayflies are slender flying insects found around streams and ponds.

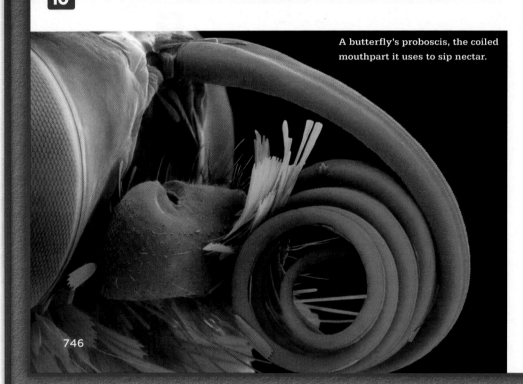

A butterfly's proboscis, the coiled mouthpart it uses to sip nectar.

746

Fluency

Choral Reading

Explain Tell students that they will be doing a choral reading, and that paying close attention to punctuation will help them with proper intonation and expression. Explain to students that when they see a punctuation mark called a colon, it usually means a list of items will follow. In this case the colon introduces a list of specimens that Dennis Kunkel brought back from his scientific travels.

Model Read the two paragraphs on this page, paying particular attention to the punctuation in each paragraph.

Apply Have the class read the passage chorally. First, one student reads a sentence. Then a second student joins in, then a third, and so on, until all students are reading together. When students reach the end of the passage, they should return to the beginning and continue reading until everyone has been included.

LA.5.1.5 Student demonstrates ability to read orally with expression

Dennis and the scientific team collect water samples.

Mount St. Helens

In 1980, a **dormant** volcano called Mount St. Helens **erupted** in Washington State. The blast from the eruption flattened huge forests of tall trees. Floods of boiling mud and water from melting snow **scoured** riverbeds. The countryside was covered with a thick layer of ash for miles around.

Some of the first people allowed to visit the blast zone were biologists, scientists who study living things. They were stunned by the destruction. One of the first things they wanted to know was whether any living things had survived.

A team of scientists from the University of Washington made plans to study the lakes and streams of the blast area. Since Dennis was an expert on algae, the simple plants found in lakes and streams, he was invited to help with the study. The scientists traveled to a camp set up on the north side of Mount St. Helens. Twice a day, a helicopter flew them into the blast zone. All they could see, for miles in every direction, were dead trees blanketed **12** by a heavy layer of ash.

747

Develop Comprehension

11 STRATEGY
SUMMARIZE

LA.5.1.7
Student uses strategies to comprehend text

Teacher Think Aloud I know that Dennis Kunkel went to graduate school. Now we are learning about some of his experiences as a scientist. Summarize the important information the author has presented so far.

(Encourage students to apply the strategy in a Think Aloud.)

Student Think Aloud Like many other scientists, Dennis is an explorer. He makes his discoveries by asking questions and then trying to answer them. In 1980 he went to the blast zone of Mount St. Helens to investigate. He and other scientists wanted to know whether any living things had survived in the blast area.

12 FIGURATIVE LANGUAGE

LA.5.2.1.7
Explain author's use of figurative language

What does the author mean when he writes, "All they could see, for miles in every direction, were dead trees blanketed by a heavy layer of ash"? How does the word *blanketed* help you to picture the scene in your mind? (Answers should include that using the word *blanketed* reinforces the idea that the land was completely covered, the way a bed is covered by a blanket.)

Vocabulary

Read the sentence that contains the word **dormant**. Have students replace the word *dormant* in the passage with a word that has the same meaning. (sleeping, inactive)

LA.5.1.6.8 Use antonyms to determine meaning

Cross-Curricular Connection

CONDUCT A SCIENCE EXPERIMENT

Explain that scientists tested the lakes around Mount St. Helens to see if any life survived the eruption. Students can use a microscope to do their own controlled experiment and test water for signs of life. Have them follow these steps:

- Fill a glass with tap water. Prepare a slide of water and place it under the microscope. Record and describe what you see.

- Place a lettuce leaf in the glass of water and leave it on a windowsill that receives a lot of sun. After three days prepare another slide, recording what you observe.

- Record any observable changes in the water, as well as what you see under the microscope each day for a week. Write up your findings and present them to the class.

Then have students present their findings using sensory details to support their impressions.   **LA.5.6.2** Use a systematic research process

SC.H.1.2.2 The student knows that a successful method to explore the natural world is to observe and record

Develop Comprehension

13 MAKE PREDICTIONS

LA.5.1.7.1 Use prior knowledge to make and confirm predictions

Given that the scientists could see only dead, ash-covered trees for miles in every direction, do you think that they will find any signs of life? Explain your response. (Answers will vary. Some students may note that it would take a microscope and someone with Dennis's skills as a scientist to determine whether life is present. Just because life is not visible to the naked eye doesn't mean it's not there.)

14 GENRE: EXPOSITORY NONFICTION

LA.5.2.2.1 Locate, explain, and use information from text features

LA.5.2.1.1 Demonstrate knowledge of characteristics of genres

Which features of informational text can you find in this selection? How do they help you to understand the information in this nonfiction selection? (Answers may vary but should include that the boldfaced and italicized words alert students to special vocabulary words whose meanings are important for a complete understanding of the text. The subheadings divided the information into sections, each with its own main idea, and the illustrations help students to visualize the scientific information in the text.)

15 CAUSE AND EFFECT

LA.5.1.7.4 Identify cause-and-effect

Why were helicopters unable to land in the blast zone? (Some of the helicopter pilots were afraid that the ash stirred up by the whirling helicopter blades would choke the helicopter engines.)

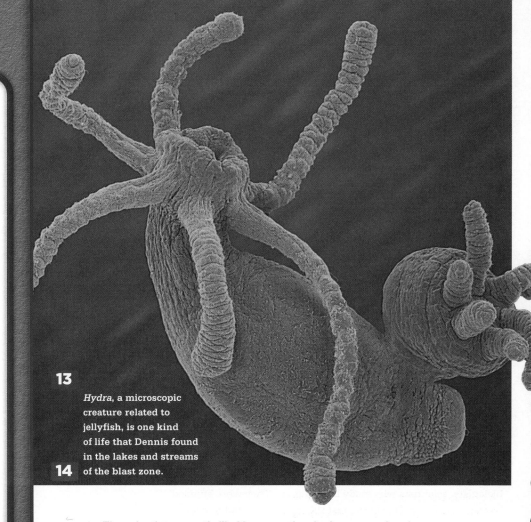

13

Hydra, a microscopic creature related to jellyfish, is one kind of life that Dennis found in the lakes and streams **14** of the blast zone.

The scientists were thrilled because they had never explored the area around an active volcano so soon after this type of eruption. But no one knew when the mountain might erupt again. In fact, no one even knew for sure whether it was safe to land a helicopter in the blast zone. Some pilots thought the ash stirred up by the whirling helicopter blades might choke the engines. **15** So Dennis and the other scientists weren't allowed to land in the study area on the first few trips. They had to collect their water samples while the helicopter was in the air!

748

Ways to Confirm Meaning

Syntactic/Structure

Explain/Model Good readers use the meaning of the sentence, the structure of language, spelling patterns, and illustrations to help them predict the meaning of unfamiliar words. Look at the word *hovered* at the top of page 749. Have students predict its meaning.

Think Aloud I know that *hovered* is a verb because it shows action, and tells what the helicopter is doing. Dennis would have a hard time collecting water samples if the helicopter were moving. The helicopter is also over the lake, so *hovered* cannot be a synonym for *landed*. I think it must mean to stay or remain in the air over a certain spot without moving. A synonym for *hovered* might be *lingered*.

Apply Encourage students to confirm the predicted meaning, and to use grammatical clues to help them predict the meaning of other difficult words such as *hovered* on page 749.

LA.5.1.4.1 Understand spelling patterns; **LA.5.1.4.2** Recognize structural analysis

As Dennis and the team crisscrossed the blast zone in the helicopter, they kept their eyes open for water. When they spotted a lake or pond that had survived the blast, the pilot flew the helicopter into position. As the helicopter hovered over the **murky** gray water, Dennis lowered collecting bottles on ropes. The bottles had triggers so Dennis could open them at different depths. This allowed him to collect some water samples from near the surface **16** and others from deep in the lakes.

The first water samples the scientists collected showed that some of the lakes were completely dead. Nothing had survived the heat, gases, and choking ash of the eruption.

Just a few weeks later, Dennis used microscopes to look at new water samples he had collected from the same lakes. He was **17** amazed to see algae, protozoans, and bacteria living in the water. Within several months, small crustaceans—animals that feed on algae and bacteria—began to reappear in some of the lakes.

Dennis and the other scientists kept careful records of the kinds of living things that returned to the lakes and when they reappeared. They identified the kinds of algae, protozoans, bacteria, and crustaceans they found. Later, Dennis and the team also discovered that frogs and fish were returning to some of these lakes, apparently carried in by surrounding streams. Their studies helped other scientists understand what happens to life in lakes when a nearby volcano erupts—and how living things eventually return to areas where all life was destroyed. **18**

Vorticella,
a single-celled protozoan

> **FCAT** **Chronological Order**
> In the order that they appeared, list the different life forms that developed in the dead lakes near the volcano.

749

Develop Comprehension

16 MAKE INFERENCES

LA.5.2.2.2
Use information from text to answer questions

Why would collecting water at different depths be important in this kind of study? (Answers may vary but should include that while the top of the lake or stream may have been affected by the heat and ash, organisms that live at the bottom of a deep lake might not have been affected.)

17 MONITOR AND CLARIFY: SEEK HELP

LA.5.1.7.8
Clarify by checking other sources

Dennis Kunkel eventually found life in the ponds and lakes of the Mount St. Helens blast zone. What would you do to go about finding out how algae, protozoans, and bacteria suddenly appeared in a dead body of water? (The author does not explain how organisms reappear in a dead pond or lake. To find out students should note that they could ask a science teacher, or consult a reference source such as an encyclopedia or the Internet.)

18 CHRONOLOGICAL ORDER

FCAT

LA.5.2.2.3
Organize information to show understanding

In the order that they appeared, list the different life forms that developed in the dead lakes near the volcano. (First, algae, protozoans, and bacteria reappeared. After a few months, crustaceans reappeared and sometime later frogs and fish returned.)

> After a few weeks, Dennis saw algae, protozoans, and bacteria living in the water.
>
> ↓
>
> Within several months small crustaceans began to reappear.
>
> ↓
>
> Later, Dennis and the team discovered frogs and fish were returning to some of the lakes.

ELL

Access for All

STRATEGIES FOR EXTRA SUPPORT

Question 18 CHRONOLOGICAL ORDER

Write the words *life forms* on the board and give examples: algae, bacteria, fish. Have students identify the sequence words in each paragraph on page 749 starting with the second paragraph ("The first water samples …") and write the words and the life forms in a list: *The first water samples—nothing survived. Just a few weeks later—algae, protozoans, bacteria. Within several months—small crustaceans in some lakes. …* Model this first on the board.

Read

Develop Comprehension

19 MAKE INFERENCES

LA.5.2.2.2
Use information from text to answer questions

What characteristics would make someone a good observer? (Answers will vary but should include someone who is patient and who likes to write or draw.)

20 STRATEGY
SUMMARIZE

LA.5.1.7
Student uses strategies to comprehend text

Dennis suggests that the first thing students should do if they think they might want to be a scientist is to become an observer. Summarize the information in the second paragraph on page 750.

Student Think Aloud Being a careful observer is important if you want to become a good scientist. Make time to observe the natural world around you, and look closely at plants and other interesting objects.

21 CHRONOLOGICAL ORDER

LA.5.2.2.3
Organize information to show understanding

What steps does Dennis Kunkel suggest students should follow after they've learned everything they can about a topic that interests them? (After you've learned everything you can, ask someone to help you with any questions you have. Finally, find a scientist you can talk to and visit.)

Vocabulary

Read the sentence that contains the word **observer**. Ask students what it means to be a good observer and to use the word in their explanation.

LA.5.1.6.1 Use new vocabulary

How to Become a Scientist

Here is Dennis's advice for students who think they might like to become scientists:

Become an **observer**. One of the most important things you can do to become a good scientist and microscopist is practice being a careful observer. Find a comfortable chair and put it in the middle of your garden, yard, or a park. Sit in the chair for ten minutes or thirty minutes or an hour. Watch the insects that fly past or land on the plants. Look at the shapes of leaves and stems and branches. Listen to the sounds of buzzing bees and chirping crickets. See if you can find a sight or smell or sound that surprises you. Use a loupe or magnifying glass to look closely at interesting objects.

Dennis and graduate student examine a South African clawed frog.

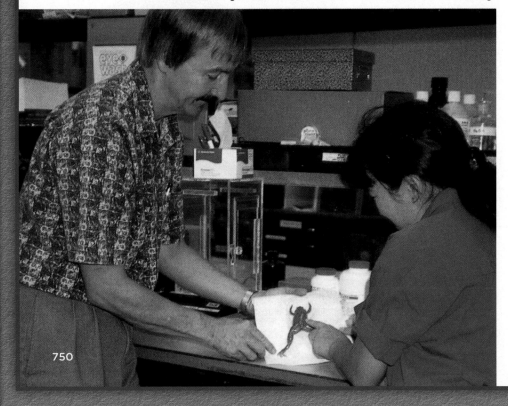

750

ELL

Access for All

STRATEGIES FOR EXTRA SUPPORT

Question 21 CHRONOLOGICAL ORDER
Reread with students the steps on how to become a scientist. Have them retell the steps using the following words: *must, should, can, ought to.* Give examples: *To become a scientist, you* must *become an observer. You* should *ask for help.*

Dennis looking closely at a fern leaf.

Learn everything you can about a topic that interests you. Suppose you'd like to explore flowers by using a microscope. Go to the library and check out some flower books. See what you can find on the Internet. Pick some flowers and carefully take them apart. Use a loupe or a magnifying glass to see how everything fits together. The more you know about flowers from reading about them and observing them, the more you'll understand when you begin looking at them with a loupe or a microscope.

Ask for help from a knowledgeable person. After you've learned everything you can on your own, ask someone else to help with questions you still have. Maybe there's someone at a nearby school or museum who knows about insects, spiders, algae, moss, or something else you'd like to learn about. If you don't have a microscope of your own, maybe a teacher would help you look at some specimens with a school microscope.

Find a scientist to talk to or find a place where scientific research is being done. **21** If you still want to learn more, you may be able to find a scientist to talk to at a nearby college, university, or research station. Write a letter or an e-mail message to the scientist, explaining what you're interested in. Ask if you can schedule a time to visit. Most scientists are happy to talk to students who share their passion for science.

751

Comprehension

Multistep Directions

Explain Remind students that directions are oral or written steps to follow in order to make or do something. Time order words such as *first*, *next*, *then*, and *finally* signal the order of events or steps that need to be taken. Common materials that might contain directions include a basic technical manual, a lab experiment, or pamphlets that tell how to assemble something.

Discuss Review the steps Dennis Kunkel advises students to take if they want to become scientists. Have students look for any signal words Kunkel uses.

Apply Have students prepare a 1 or 2 minute oral presentation in which they summarize Kunkel's multistep directions on how to become a scientist. Suggest that students make notes of Kunkel's most important points, adding signal words where necessary to make the information as clear as possible. Give students time to rehearse and then have volunteers make their presentations to the class. Afterward, have students paraphrase the information in the presentations.

LA.5.4.2.1 Write in a variety of informational forms

Develop Comprehension

LA.5.1.7.8
Use prior knowledge to make and confirm predictions

RETURN TO PREDICTIONS AND PURPOSES

Review the predictions students made, as well as their purposes for reading. Were they correct?

LA.5.1.7
Student uses strategies to comprehend text

REVIEW READING STRATEGIES

How did identifying the chronological order of events help you to understand the information in this selection? Do you have any additional questions? What strategies could you use to answer them?

LA.5.4.2.1
Write in a variety of informational forms

PERSONAL RESPONSE

Have students write a summary of the selection, either individually or with a group or partner. Remind them to use formal paragraph structure and to include the main ideas and and the most significant details.

Students can also write a paragraph in which they identify the author's purpose and support their ideas with examples from the text.

Quick Check Can students identify the chronological order of events in the selection?

During **Small Group Instruction**

If No → **Approaching Level** Comprehension, pp. 759O–759P

If Yes → **On Level** Options, p. 759R

Beyond Level Options, p. 759T

Author and Photographer

**UNDER THE MICROSCOPE
WITH STEPHEN KRAMER AND
DENNIS KUNKEL**

Have students read the biographies of
the author and the photographer.

LA.5.1.7.2
Identify
author's
purpose

DISCUSS

- What is the connection between
  Stephen Kramer's teaching and writing?

- Why are the pictures Dennis Kunkel
  and other scientists have made
  through their microscopes important
  to science?

WRITE ABOUT IT

Discuss how Dennis Kunkel makes
discoveries in his work. What other
careers might involve discoveries?
Invite students to write about a
discovery they have made or would
like to make.

FCAT Author's Purpose

Remind students that information in
a nonfiction article can be conveyed
through graphics. Point out the
photographs of insects, pollen, algae,
and other organisms that reveal details
(such as the proboscis of a butterfly)
unseen by the naked eye.

LA.5.1.7.2 Identify author's purpose

 Technology

Students can find more information
about Stephen Kramer and Dennis
Kunkel at **www.macmillanmh.com**

Under the Microscope with Stephen Kramer and Dennis Kunkel

Stephen Kramer is an author and teacher. When
he is not writing about avalanches or following
Dennis Kunkel into a volcano, he is teaching fifth
graders. Both of his careers focus on a love of
science and teaching. He especially enjoys teaching
children different scientific facts about bats,
rainforests, or machines. Stephen
lives in Vancouver, Washington,
with his wife and their two sons.

Another book by Stephen Kramer:
Tornado

Dennis Kunkel is often found looking at fleas,
bacteria, and blood cells under his microscope. He
has made large contributions to the science world
with what he has witnessed through his lens.
Dennis loves the new information his microscope
unveils because he appreciates the beauty of what
is missed by the naked eye. Dennis's research and
pictures have appeared in magazines, museum
exhibits, and even movies.

 Find out more about Stephen
Kramer and Dennis Kunkel at
www.macmillanmh.com

FCAT Author's Purpose

The author's nonfiction article provides information. How do
the photos illustrate the way a microscope helps scientists?

752

Author's Craft

Photographs and Captions

Explain that **photographs and captions**—like headings,
definitional sidebars, and type styling such as bold and italics—
can add new information and vivid details to informational
nonfiction. Stephen Kramer includes photographs of Dennis
Kunkel's microscope slides as well as captions that
identify the objects on the slides. For example,
page 743 shows a photo of green algae:

Discuss how the photographs and captions help a
reader understand Dennis Kunkel's fascination with microscopes.

Have students examine the photographs, captions, and formatting.
Discuss why Stephen Kramer may have chosen to include each.

LA.5.1.7.1 Explain purpose of text features

 **Comprehension Check**

Summarize

Use your Sequence Chart to summarize important information from *Hidden Worlds: Looking Through a Scientist's Microscope.*

Event
↓
↓

Think and Compare

1. What are the steps Dennis thinks are important in becoming a better scientist? Use selection details in your answer. **Summarize: Chronological Order**

2. Reread page 749. Why did Dennis look for living things after the eruption of Mt. St. Helens? Include facts and details from the selection in your answer. **Analyze**

3. Explain how you would practice becoming a careful **observer**. Include where you would choose to observe and what you might see, smell, hear, and touch. **Evaluate**

4. What effect do scientists like Dennis Kunkel, Albert Einstein, and others, have on the world? Explain your answer. **Analyze**

5. Reread "Dr. Priscilla C. Grew, Geologist" on pages 738–739. Compare and contrast Dr. Grew's experiences with Dennis Kunkel's career. Use details from both selections in your answer. **Reading/Writing Across Texts**

753

 ## Strategies for Answering Questions

Think and Search

Model the Think and Search strategy with question 1.

The answer is found in more than one place in the selection. You need to put different parts of the text together to answer the question.

Question 1 Think Aloud: I know that one of the subheads in this selection is *How to Become a Scientist.* If I look on the page where this subhead appears, I will find part of the answer to this question: *become an observer.* On the following page I can find the rest of the answer: *learn everything you can about a topic that interests you, and ask for help from a knowledgeable person. Finally, find a scientist to talk to, or a place where scientific research is being done.*

LA.5.1.7 Student uses strategies to comprehend text

 ## Comprehension Check

SUMMARIZE

 LA.5.1.7.3 Determine main idea through summarizing

Ask students to do a written or oral summary of *Hidden Worlds* using their completed graphic organizers.

THINK AND COMPARE

Sample answers are given.

LA.5.2.2.3 Organize information to show understanding

1. **Chronological Order:** First, become a good observer. Then learn everything you can about a topic that interests you and ask for help from a knowledgeable person. Finally, find a scientist to talk to, or a place where scientific research is being done. USE THINK AND SEARCH

LA.5.2.1.5 Demonstrate understanding and include evidence from the text

2. **Analyze:** Dennis and other scientists wanted to know if any living things had survived the blast. This would give them information about which life forms were more vulnerable than others.

LA.5.2.1.5 Demonstrate understanding and include personal experience

3. **Text to Self:** Answers will vary, but students should state where and what they would observe, including some of Kunkel's suggestions.

4. **Text to World:** Answers will vary, but should include the idea that scientists help us understand and sometimes improve our world.

FOCUS QUESTION

LA.5.2.1.5 Demonstrate understanding and include other text/media

5. **Text to Text:** Dr. Grew is a geologist. Dr. Kunkel is a botanist. Both scientists have studied volcanoes. Dr. Grew's work has helped people survive earthquakes, while Dr. Kunkel's work helps people understand how plants and other life forms return after a volcanic eruption. Both scientists find answers through research and observation.

Objective

- Read accurately with prosody
- Rate: 129–149 WCPM

Materials

- Fluency Transparency 30
- Fluency Solutions Audio CD
- Practice Book, p. 217

ELL / Access for All

Echo-Read Ask questions about the passage to ensure that students understand it. Echo-read the passage with students. Encourage them to imitate the pauses, intonation, and tempo of your reading. You can also have them read along with the Fluency Solutions Audio CD.

On Level Practice Book O, page 217

As I read, I will pay attention to pauses and intonation.

	The ocean is big. It covers about two-thirds of Earth. The
11	ocean is also deep—very deep. The ocean's average depth is
22	more than 2 miles (3 kilometers). At its deepest it goes down
32	nearly 7 miles (11 kilometers). That's taller than Mount
39	Everest.
40	Think of a place where animals live. You might think of
51	a forest or grassland. But what about the ocean? In fact, the
63	ocean makes up most of Earth's habitat. But to this day, most
75	of the deep ocean has never been explored.
83	For centuries, people thought that the bottom of the deep
93	ocean was lifeless. It is very cold in the deep, dark ocean. No
106	light reaches the bottom. And water is heavy. All that water
117	presses down hard on the sea floor. How could anything live
128	down there?
130	But then scientists began exploring the deep. What they
139	found shocked them. On the deep sea floor, they discovered
149	a world beyond their wildest imagination. It is a strange
159	world teeming with bizarre life. 164

Comprehension Check

1. What is it like at the bottom of the ocean? **Main Idea and Details**
   very cold and dark, water is heavy
2. Why has not much of the deep ocean been explored? **Main Idea and Details**
   It is hard to get to the bottom of the ocean.

	Words Read	−	Number of Errors	=	Words Correct Score
First Read		−		=	
Second Read		−		=	

★ **Approaching Practice Book A,** page 217

◆ **Beyond Practice Book B,** page 217

LA.5.1.5.1 Demonstrate ability to read grade level text

Fluency

Repeated Reading: Pauses and Intonation

EXPLAIN/MODEL Explain to students that good readers learn to read groups of words together in phrases. Explain that the text on **Fluency Transparency 30** has been marked with slashes that indicate pauses and stops. A single slash indicates a pause, usually between phrases and, in this selection, after a colon. A double slash indicates a stop, usually between sentences. Have the class listen carefully to your pauses and intonation as you read.

Transparency 30

Scientists are explorers.// They usually make discoveries by asking questions and then trying to answer them.// Some scientists find their answers in laboratories,/ surrounded by equipment and instruments.// Others travel to natural areas to find their answers.// Dennis's work has taken him to mountains,/ rainforests,/ deserts,/ caves,/ beaches,/ and into the sea.

Whenever Dennis goes on field trips,/ he takes along collecting boxes and bottles.// When he returns to the lab,/ the boxes and bottles are usually full of interesting specimens:/ algae,/ lichens,/ mushrooms,/ seeds,/ leaves,/ insects,/ bark,/ soil,/ and flowers.// Dennis has explored hidden worlds in places ranging from the blast zone of a volcano to the dust balls underneath people's beds!//

Fluency Transparency 30
from *Hidden Worlds,* page 746

PRACTICE/APPLY Have the class do a choral reading. One student reads a sentence. The next student joins in, then a third, until all students are reading together. When students reach the end of the passage, they go back to the beginning until everyone has been included. Students can also practice fluency using **Practice Book** page 217 or the **Fluency Solutions Audio CD.**

Quick Check — Can students read accurately with prosody?

During **Small Group Instruction**

If No → Approaching Level Fluency, p. 759N

If Yes → On Level Options, p. 759Q

Beyond Level Options, p. 759S

Comprehension

 **REVIEW SKILL**
MAIN IDEA AND DETAILS

LA.5.1.7.3
Determine main idea through inferring and identifying relevant details

EXPLAIN/MODEL

■ The **main idea** is the most important point an author makes about a topic. The rest of the sentences in the text usually give **details** that help to support or explain the main idea.

■ To identify the main idea and details that support it, good readers look for a sentence that contains the most important point about a topic. Although it is often found at the beginning of a paragraph or section of text, the sentence that contains the main idea may sometimes be located either in the middle or at the end of a paragraph. A main idea is said to be **explicit** if the author states it directly in the text.

■ Often an author does not directly state the main idea. Then readers must put together details to figure it out. They ask, *What do the sentences tell about, explain, or describe?* Then they use details in the text to state the main idea in their own words. If a main idea is not explicit, or stated directly in the text, it is called an **implicit** main idea.

For comprehension practice use the Graphic Organizers on pages 40–64 in the **Teachers Resource Book.**

LA.5.2.2.2
Answer questions related to main ideas

PRACTICE/APPLY

Identify the main ideas and the details that support them in *Hidden Worlds: Looking Through a Scientist's Microscope.*

■ What is the main idea in the section of text from the selection that covers pages 742–745? How does the heading of this section, "Becoming a Scientist," help you to determine the main idea?

■ What is the main idea in the last section of text, on pages 750–751? Is it an explicit or an implicit main idea? What details on these two pages support the main idea?

■ Identify three details that support the main idea on pages 747–749 of *Hidden Worlds.*

FCAT Skills Trace

Main Idea and Details	
Introduce	93A–B
Practice / Apply	94-107, 173A–B, 174–185, 195A–B, 196–199; Practice Book, 23–24, 46–47, 53–54
Reteach / Review	1110–P, R, T; 1910–P, R, T; 2030–P, R, T; 705A, 753B
Assess	Weekly Tests; Units 1, 2 Tests; Benchmark Tests A, B
Maintain	173A–B, 195A–B; Practice Book 23–24, 46–47, 53–54

Language Arts

LA.5.2.1.1
Demonstrate knowledge of genre forms with distinct characteristics and purposes

GENRE: MYTH

Have students read the bookmark on **Student Book** page 754. Explain that a myth

- presents a story about a culture's beliefs

- is often used to explain events or mysteries in nature, such as the cycle of the seasons

- often features a culture's gods and goddesses, who become characters in the story

- may use symbolism and figurative language to create striking images

Literary Elements:
Symbolism and Figurative Language

LA.5.2.1.7
Explain author's use of symbolism
LA.5.2.1.7
Explain author's use of figurative language

- **Symbolism** is the use of concrete objects to represent ideas or qualities, the way a flag represents a country and all it stands for.

- **Figurative language** is a tool authors use to help the reader visualize or feel what is happening. Some figures of speech include similes and metaphors to describe objects, places, events, or people.

LA.5.2.1.7
Explain author's use of similes and metaphors

- Remind students that a simile compares two unlike objects using *like* or *as*. For example: *The sun looks like a golden ball.* A metaphor compares two unlike things but does not use *like* or *as*. For example: *The sun is a golden ball.*

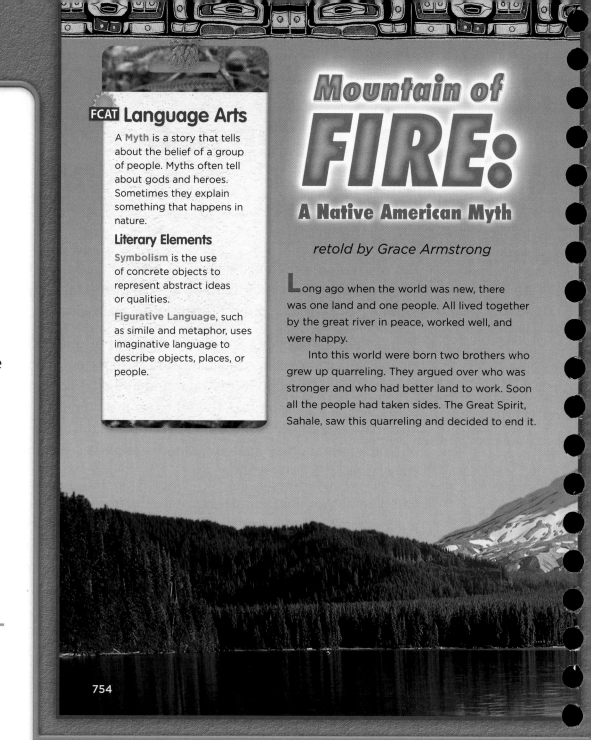

FCAT Language Arts

A **Myth** is a story that tells about the belief of a group of people. Myths often tell about gods and heroes. Sometimes they explain something that happens in nature.

Literary Elements

Symbolism is the use of concrete objects to represent abstract ideas or qualities.

Figurative Language, such as simile and metaphor, uses imaginative language to describe objects, places, or people.

Mountain of FIRE:
A Native American Myth

retold by Grace Armstrong

Long ago when the world was new, there was one land and one people. All lived together by the great river in peace, worked well, and were happy.

Into this world were born two brothers who grew up quarreling. They argued over who was stronger and who had better land to work. Soon all the people had taken sides. The Great Spirit, Sahale, saw this quarreling and decided to end it.

754

> This simile, comparing the voice to thunder, is an example of *figurative language*.

In a voice like low, rumbling **1** thunder, Sahale called the brothers together and gave each one an arrow for his bow. He said, "Wherever your arrow falls, that will be your land, and there you will be a chief." The first brother shot his arrow high in the air, and it landed to the south of the great river. He went there with his people, and they became known as the Multnomahs. The second brother shot his arrow into the air and it landed north of the river. There he went with his people, who became known as the Klickitats.

The brothers lived with their people in peace for some time. As time passed though, envy began to cause quarrels. "The Klickitats have better land," some said. "The Multnomahs have more beautiful land," others cried. Sahale heard this bickering that **2** seemed to grow like a storm and was unhappy with the two tribes. When violence threatened, Sahale stopped it by taking away all fire, even the sun, just as the autumn winds, cold, and snow were beginning.

Only one in all the land still had fire. She was Loo-Wit, an old, wrinkled woman with gray hair and quiet ways. She had stayed apart from all the quarrels. After the people had suffered and seemed to have mended their ways, Sahale asked Loo-Wit if she would like to share her fire with them. "For doing this," he told her, "you may have anything you wish."

755

Read "Mountain of Fire"

Access for All As you read, remind students to apply what they know about figurative language and symbolism.

1 CAUSE AND EFFECT

LA.5.1.7.4 Identify cause-and-effect relationships in text

What was the Great Spirit's motive, or reason, for intervening in the lives of the two brothers? (Sahale was unhappy that the brothers always argued and were dividing the people. He intervened to stop their fighting.)

2 LITERARY ELEMENTS: SYMBOLISM AND FIGURATIVE LANGUAGE

How is a simile used to describe the brothers' bickering? (It is compared to a growing storm.) In what way does the use of this simile help you to visualize how the bickering was becoming stronger, and even dangerous? (Answers may vary but should include the idea that as a storm grows in power, the sky slowly becomes darker and more threatening and the wind picks up. By comparing the brothers' bickering to a growing storm that threatens violence with pummeling rain and lightning and high winds, the author helps readers to visualize the intensity of the brothers' bickering, and how dangerous it was to their people.)

LA.5.2.1.7 Identify author's use of symbolism and similes

ENGLISH LANGUAGE LEARNERS   Access for All

Use Academic Language Discuss myths with which the students are familiar and point out the beliefs, gods or heroes, and the natural event that the myths explain. Write examples of symbolism and figurative language on the board and label them.

As students read, have them pause at times and retell what they have learned about the story. Ask questions to help them and explain the story as needed. At times ask students to predict what will happen next. Help students point out figurative language as they read.

Language Arts

3 ANALYZE

LA.5.2.1.1
Demonstrate
knowledge of
characteristics
of genres

What characteristic of a myth is illustrated when the brothers are turned into mountains? (A myth often attempts to explain nature. This myth explains how two mountains were created.) Now, have students paraphrase this myth.

4 LITERARY ELEMENTS: SYMBOLISM

How does Loo-Wit become a symbol? What does she symbolize? (Loo-Wit becomes a symbol when she and her fire are transformed into a volcano. Through this warning, she symbolizes the need to live together peacefully.)

LA.5.2.1.7
Identify
and explain
author's use of
symbolism

"I wish to be young and beautiful," she said.

"Then that is what you will be," Sahale said.

Sahale led Loo-Wit to a great stone bridge over the river that joined the two lands. The people arrived at the bridge, led by their chiefs, to find the most beautiful woman they had ever seen. She began to give them fire. Loo-Wit kept the fire burning all day until fire was restored to all the people.

This was not to be the end of the quarreling. During this day the two chiefs had both fallen in love with Loo-Wit and wanted her for a wife. Loo-Wit could not choose between them, and once again, fighting erupted.

The two brothers refused to compromise or work on a solution. Because the brothers were unyielding in their positions, Sahale angrily changed the brothers into mountains. The chief of the Klickitats was turned into the mountain known today as Mount Adams. The chief of the Multnomahs was turned into the mountain known today as Mount Hood.

3

The use of the mountains, which are rock hard and immovable, represents the brothers' stubborness and is an example of *symbolism*.

756

On Level Practice Book O, page 218

A myth is a traditional story that explains imaginary events from the past or a traditional world view. Myths describe how a custom, belief, or natural phenomenon came about. **Symbolism** is the use of concrete objects to represent abstract ideas or qualities. **Figurative language** uses imaginative language to describe objects, places, or people.

Read the myth below, then answer the questions.

A long time ago there was one land and one people. Everyone lived together happily and in peace. Then two brothers were born who quarreled over everything. This made the Creator angry. In a voice like low, rumbling thunder, he told the brothers to shoot an arrow into the air. Each brother and his people would live where his arrow landed.

Soon the brothers started quarreling again. Once more the Creator became angry. This time he took away fire from everyone except for one old woman called Loo-Wit. The people stopped quarreling, and the Creator asked Loo-Wit to share her fire. In return, the Creator offered to grant her one wish. She chose to be young and beautiful. When the two brothers saw how beautiful Loo-Wit was, each of them wanted to marry her. Again there was quarreling, which caused the Creator to turn each brother into a mountain and also to make Loo-Wit a mountain.

1. The myth says that the brothers shot their arrows into the air. What does this explain? How the brothers settle in two different places and later, where the mountains are located.

2. What do the mountains symbolize? They symbolize the two brothers and the woman they fought over.

3. Find an example of figurative language in the myth.
"In a voice like low, rumbling thunder"
Possible responses above.

⭐ **Approaching Practice Book A,** page 218

◆ **Beyond Practice Book B,** page 218

Loo-Wit, her heart broken over this, lost her desire to be young and beautiful. Sahale, in his pity, also changed her into a mountain, and placed her between the two brother mountains. She was allowed to keep inside her the fire she had shared with the people.

Because Loo-Wit was beautiful, her mountain was a beautiful cone of dazzling white. Today she is known as Mount St. Helens.

Loo-Wit wants to remind humans to care for Earth and for each other. When she is unhappy, she will awaken as she did in the 1980s.

Once her anger passes, though, the ground heals and plant and animal life have a chance to flourish once again.

 Connect and Compare

1. What do you think of Sahale's decision to turn the quarreling brothers into mountains? What do mountains symbolize? **Symbolism**

2. What elements make this a myth? What would you choose to write a myth about? **Evaluate**

3. Compare the ways in which the narrator of "Mountain of Fire" and the scientists of *Hidden Worlds* view the eruption of Mount St. Helens. What is the value of having different versions of events? **Reading/Writing Across Texts**

LOG ON Find out more about myths at **www.macmillanmh.com**

757

 Connect and Compare

SUGGESTED ANSWERS

LA.5.2.1.7 Identify and explain author's use of symbolism

1. Possible answers: The two brothers deserved this punishment because they could not stop their quarreling. Mountains symbolize the immovable. **SYMBOLISM**

LA.5.2.1.5 Demonstrate understanding and include evidence from the text and personal experience

2. The story explains events in nature and uses the intervention of the Great Spirit to explain the creation of Mount Adams, Mount Hood, and Mount St. Helens. Sample answer: If I had to write a myth, I would choose thunder and how it came to be. **EVALUATE**

 FOCUS QUESTION

LA.5.2.1.5 Demonstrate understanding and include other text/media

3. The authors of *Hidden Worlds* try to explain the eruption of Mount St. Helens scientifically, whereas the narrator of "Mountain of Fire" uses folk beliefs to explain that Mount St. Helens erupted because humans need to remember to take better care of Earth. **READING/WRITING ACROSS TEXTS**

LOG ON **Technology**

Internet Research and Inquiry Activity
Students can find more facts at **www.macmillanmh.com**

FCAT **WRITING**
- Expository
- Writer's Craft: Beginning, Middle, End

WORD STUDY
FCAT
- Words in Context
- Latin and Greek Roots
- **Phonics:** Prefixes -able, -ible
- Vocabulary Building

SPELLING
- Words with -able, -ible

GRAMMAR
- Sentence Combining

SMALL GROUP OPTIONS
- Differentiated Instruction, pp. 759M–759V

Writing

FCAT Beginning, Middle, End

LA.5.2.1.2 Locate and analyze problem/ resolution

READ THE STUDENT MODEL

Read the bookmark and explain that writers organize their writing with clear beginnings, middles, and ends so that readers can follow the ideas or story.

Have students skim and scan the subheads in *Hidden Worlds* on pages 742, 746, and 750. Note how the author structures the article with a clear beginning, middle, and end. Then have the class read Mary A.'s **problem-and-solution essay** and the callouts. Tell students they will write problem-and-solution essays, structuring their essays with clear beginnings, middles, and ends.

Writer's Craft

FCAT Beginning, Middle, End
Using a good **beginning, middle,** and **end** makes an essay about problem-solving easy for readers to understand. State the problem in the beginning, and explain the solution in the middle and end.

Write About Solving A Problem

The Problem of Hole #13

by Mary A.

I explained my problem to readers at the beginning of my essay.

My three best friends and I play miniature golf every Friday night. Hole #13 is an annoying problem for me. Every time, it takes me ten frustrating strokes to finish Hole #13.

My dad suggested I attack the problem in a scientific way. He said I should do research, make observations, and experiment to solve my problem.

I explained how I found a solution with a good middle and end.

First, I did some research. I went to the library and found a book that showed me a better way to putt. Next, I made careful observations. I studied the technique my friends used as they played Hole #13. I saw how they aimed the first shot so that the ball skipped a few inches from the hole. Finally, I experimented on my own and practiced for hours. The next Friday night I used what I had learned. It worked! I improved my score and the problem of Hole #13 was solved.

758

Features of a Problem-and-Solution Essay

In a problem-and-solution essay, the writer explains a problem and the steps taken to solve it.

- A problem-and-solution essay states and explains the main idea or problem in the first paragraph.

- In the middle it describes the sequence of steps taken to solve the problem.

- It uses sequence words, such as *first, then, next, finally,* and *last* to identify the order in which the steps take place.

- It shows a solution at the end. The final sentence wraps things up neatly.

Writing Prompt

People often have to takes steps to solve problems.

Think of a problem you solved and the steps you took to solve it.

Now write about the problem you solved and the steps you took to solve it.

FCAT Writer's Checklist

✓ **Focus:** My writing clearly presents my main idea.

☑ **Organization:** My essay includes a clear beginning, middle, and end.

✓ **Support:** I use supporting details to explain my problem and solution.

✓ **Conventions:** All words are spelled correctly. I combine sentences to improve the flow, and my punctuation is correct.

759

Transparency 117: **Sequence Chart**
Transparency 118: **Draft**
Transparency 119: **Revision**

Transparency 117

| **Problem** |
| I couldn't putt at Hole #13 in miniature golf. |

↓

| **Action** |
| **1.** I looked at the problem in a scientific way. |

↓

| **Action** |
| **2.** I found a library book about putting. |

↓

| **Action** |
| **3.** I watched my friends play Hole #13. |

↓

| **Action** |
| **4.** I experimented and practiced. |

↓

| **Solution** |
| I played the hole and improved my score. |

Writing Transparency 117

PREWRITE

LA.5.3.1.3
Make a plan for writing that addresses logical sequence

Discuss the writing prompt on page 759. Have members of small student groups share problems they faced and how they solved them. Tell listeners to ask speakers questions to help them identify the sequence of the solution steps. Have students set a purpose for writing and identify an audience.

Display **Transparency 117.** Discuss how Mary uses a sequence chart to help her plan her essay. Have students work on charts with partners.

DRAFT

LA.5.3.2.2
Organize information into logical sequence

Display **Transparency 118.** Discuss ways to improve the draft. Suggest that the steps are unclear and that Mary could improve her ending. Before students begin writing, present the explicit lesson on **Beginning, Middle, End** on page 759A. Then have students use their sequence charts to plan and write their essays. Remind them to focus on organization.

REVISE

LA.5.3.3
Student will revise draft for clarity

Display **Transparency 119.** Discuss the revisions. Mary explained the steps more clearly, combined choppy sentences, and improved her ending. Students can revise their drafts or place them in portfolios to work on later.

If students choose to revise, have them work with a partner and use the Writer's Checklist on page 759. Have them **proofread/edit** their writing. For **Publishing Options** see page 759A.

For lessons on **Organization, Outlining, Sentence Combining, and Spelling,** see page 759B, and **5 Day Spelling** and **5 Day Spelling Grammar** on pages 759G–759J.

Publishing Options

Students can share their essays orally with the class. See the Speaking and Listening tips below. They can also use their best cursive to write their interviews. (See Teacher's Resource Book pages 163–173 for cursive models and practice.) Then students can recast their letters in an advice column format in which the problem becomes a question and the solution becomes the columnist's response.

Speaking and Listening

SPEAKING STRATEGIES

- Practice reading your essay before presenting it.
- Speak clearly and with expression.
- Make frequent eye contact with the audience.

LISTENING STRATEGIES

- Listen to understand the problem and solution.
- Look at the speaker.
- Be prepared to evaluate the solution and ask questions.

6-Point Scoring Rubrics

Use the rubric on page **763G** to score published writing.

Writing Process

For a complete lesson, see Unit Writing pages **763A–763F.**

SUPPORT

Beginning, Middle, End

LA.5.3.3.1 Evaluate draft for logical organization

EXPLAIN/MODEL

Explain that writers introduce their topics, expand on them, and then share final thoughts. To do these three things, they must organize their ideas into clear beginnings, middles, and ends. Display **Transparency 120**.

Think Aloud The writer thinks that there are too few bike paths in his town. He plans a sequence of events to solve this problem. However, the writer needs help organizing his ideas into a clear beginning, a middle, and an end.

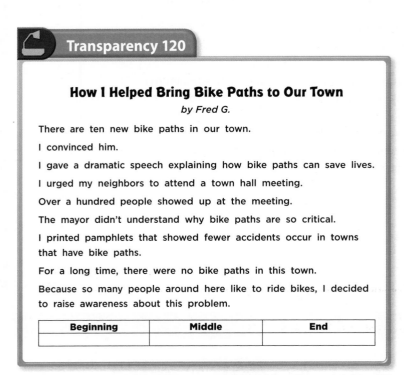

Transparency 120

How I Helped Bring Bike Paths to Our Town
by Fred G.

There are ten new bike paths in our town.

I convinced him.

I gave a dramatic speech explaining how bike paths can save lives.

I urged my neighbors to attend a town hall meeting.

Over a hundred people showed up at the meeting.

The mayor didn't understand why bike paths are so critical.

I printed pamphlets that showed fewer accidents occur in towns that have bike paths.

For a long time, there were no bike paths in this town.

Because so many people around here like to ride bikes, I decided to raise awareness about this problem.

Beginning	Middle	End

Writing Transparency 120

PRACTICE/APPLY

Work with students to place the sentences into the appropriate boxes labeled beginning, middle, or end. Then, have students note the order of ideas in essays that they have read recently.

As students prepare for and write their essays, have them focus on outlining and organizing.

Writer's Toolbox

LA.5.3.3.2 Tighten central idea through use of sequential organization

SUPPORT

Writing Trait: Organization

Explain/Model Tell students that they can group related ideas to make up a section or paragraph of their essays. Suggest that one way to group ideas is to put them in a series, and then move on to discuss each idea separately. Have students look at Mary A.'s essay on page 758. Point out that Mary uses commas to join the three pieces of advice that her father gives her. Then she discusses how she follows each recommendation.

Practice/Apply As students draft their essays, encourage them to organize their ideas succinctly.

LA.5.3.2.2 Combine sentences to enhance clarity

CONVENTIONS

Grammar: Sentence Combining

Explain/Model Explain that writers achieve flow by combining short sentences into longer compound or complex sentences. Point out some of the compound sentences in Mary's third paragraph to illustrate the skill.

Practice/Apply Have students combine series of short sentences into compound and complex sentences. As students write, encourage them to combine short sentences. For a complete lesson on sentence combining, including a **mechanics** lesson on punctuation marks, see pages 759I–759J.

SUPPORT

Outlining

Explain/Model Point out to students that essay writers benefit from planning their ideas before drafting. An outline functions as an idea map that helps writers decide which ideas to include and in what order. Point out that Mary's seqence chart functions as a kind of outline for her essay.

Practice/Apply Before students draft their esays, encourage them build outlines.

LA.5.3.1 Use prewriting strategies to formulate a plan

CONVENTIONS

Spelling: Words with *-able* and *-ible*

Point out that Mary's problem was solvable, that it was able to be solved. Explain that the suffix *-able* is added to the root solve to form an adjective. Remind students to pay attention when they spell words with *-able* and *-ible*. They can use print or online dictionaries to check spelling in their drafts. For a complete lesson on words with *-able* and *-ible*, see pages 759G–759H.

LA.5.1.6.11 Use affixes to determine meaning of complex words

Technology

Remind students that as they edit, they can use the Cut and Paste features to move words or sentences.

FCAT Success!

Test Prep and Practice with FCAT Writing+, pages 180–230.

Objectives

- Apply knowledge of word meaning and context clues
- Build word families from Latin and Greek roots

Materials

- Vocabulary Transparencies 59 and 60
- Practice Book, p. 219

Vocabulary

biology (p. 744) scientific study of living things

dormant (p. 747) sleeping; seeming to sleep

erupted (p. 747) burst forth

murky (p. 747) dark; not clear

observer (p. 750) one who sees or notices

research (p. 745) a careful study to find and learn facts about a subject

scoured (p. 747) clean, cleared, worn away

specimens (p. 746) some of a group or class taken to show what others are like; sample

ELL

Ask Questions Write questions such as the following for each word: *Which two items can be dormant—a plant, a human being, a volcano? When a volcano erupts, which two items come out of it—steam, lava, fire?* Help students answer in full sentences.

Review
Vocabulary
 Words in Context

LA.5.1.6.3
Use context clues to determine word meanings

EXPLAIN/MODEL

Review the meanings of vocabulary words. Display **Transparency 59.** Model how to use word meanings and context clues to fill in the missing word in the first example.

Think Aloud In the first sentence, I see the words *science courses* and *chemistry.* These context clues tell me that the missing word is another kind of science course. I know that *biology* is a kind of science course. *Biology* is the missing word.

Transparency 59

research	erupted	murky	dormant
scoured	biology	observer	specimens

High school offers science courses such as (1) <u>biology</u> and chemistry.

The volcano had been (2) <u>dormant</u> for years, but it (3) <u>erupted</u> with force yesterday.

The (4) <u>murky</u> water made it difficult for us to view the sea life.

One (5) <u>observer</u> told the reporter about the parade.

The students completed (6) <u>research</u> papers on United States history.

The river (7) <u>scoured</u> stream beds of all debris.

We looked at many soil (8) <u>specimens</u> through a microscope.

Vocabulary Transparency 59

 PRACTICE/APPLY

Instruct students to complete the remaining sentences on their own. Review the students' answers as a class, or instruct students to check their answers with partners.

What's Missing? Write a story on a chart, leaving blanks for all this week's vocabulary words. As you read it aloud, have student volunteers provide the correct missing word for each blank until the paragraph is complete. Review answers as a class.

LA.5.1.6.11
Use roots and affixes from Greek and Latin

STRATEGY
WORD PARTS: LATIN AND GREEK ROOTS

EXPLAIN/MODEL

Knowing Greek and Latin roots can help a reader figure out the meanings of unfamiliar words. Many words have the same roots in common and belong to the same word families. For example, words with the Greek root *tele,* meaning "distance" include *television, telephone,* and *telegraph.*

Display **Transparency 60.** Point out the roots and their meanings at the top of the transparency. Have students identify the root *bio* in item 1. Then work with them to use a dictionary to find other words that belong to the same word family as the word *biology* and tell their meanings.

Transparency 60

dict = say   aud = hear

vis = see   bio = life

logos = science of

1. **biology** biography, biosphere, biome

2. **audience** auditory, audition, auditorium, audible

3. **vision** visit, visual, vista, visualize, visible

4. **dictate** dictionary, dictation, dictator, predict, indict

Vocabulary Strategy Transparency 60

PRACTICE

Work with students to find other words that belong to the same word families for items 2–4.

Quick Check
Can students identify correct vocabulary words?
Can students use knowledge of word families?

During **Small Group Instruction**

If No → **Approaching Level** Vocabulary, pp. 759N–759P

If Yes → **On Level** Options, pp. 759Q–759R

Beyond Level Options, pp. 759S–759T

FCAT Success!

Test Prep and Practice with vocabulary, pages 6–31.

On Level Practice Book O, page 219

Many words in English have ancient **Latin or Greek word parts**. Sometimes Latin or Greek word parts create a word family, or a group of words with a common feature or pattern. For example, the Greek root *geo* means "earth." The words *geography, geology, geographer, geode, geometry,* and *geometric* form a word family based on the words' Greek root *geo.*

Origin	Greek	Latin	Greek	Latin	Latin
Word part	bio	dict	tele	man	terr
Meaning	life	speak	far away	hand	earth

Look at the Latin and Greek word parts above. Choose the word in parentheses that best fits with the other two words to form a word family. Then write the word on the line.

1. bionic	biography	(biosphere/bicker)	biosphere
2. dictate	dictation	(dice/dictionary)	dictionary
3. telethon	telephone	(telescope/territory)	telescope
4. manner	maneuver	(manicure/main)	manicure
5. diction	dictator	(decorate/edict)	edict
6. manual	manufacture	(manuscript/mane)	manuscript
7. terrarium	terrestrial	(terrible/terrace)	terrace
8. television	telegram	(telecast/teller)	telecast
9. biology	biologist	(bisect/biographer)	biographer
10. telescopic	telepathy	(telegraph/tale)	telegraph

 Approaching Practice Book A, page 219

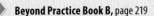 **Beyond Practice Book B,** page 219

Word Study

Objective

- Decode words with *-able, -ible*

Materials

- Practice Book, p. 213

ELL   Access for All

Focus on Meaning
Help students focus on the meaning of words. Write sentences with both words (*agree/agreeable*) using students' names and ideas. Discuss how the suffix changes the meaning of the word and its part of speech. Encourage students to create other sentences using the words *wash/washable*.

On Level Practice Book O, page 220

Some words end with **-able** or **-ible**. When they are added as suffixes they change the word's meaning. Both of these suffixes mean "able to be," "capable of being," "likely to," "worthy of being," "fit for," or "tending to."

A. Think about adding -able or -ible to complete each word. Write the complete word on the line at the right.

1. cap___   capable
2. invis___   invisible
3. poss___   possible
4. us___   usable
5. suit___   suitable
                   Possible responses provided.

B. Add the suffix -able or -ible to create a new word. Write the new word on the line. Then write a sentence containing that word.

6. break   breakable
   That vase is breakable, so put it down!

7. sense   sensible
   Finishing your homework is a sensible idea.

8. convert   convertible
   Her car is a convertible coupe so the top comes down.

9. honor   honorable
   Her decision to donate a hundred books is honorable.

10. collapse   collapsible
    The umbrella folds away because it is collapsible.

★ **Approaching Practice Book A,** page 220

◆ **Beyond Practice Book B,** page 220

Phonics

 Suffixes *–able, –ible*

Access for All

EXPLAIN/MODEL

LA.5.1.4.2 Recognize structural analysis

- The suffixes *-ible* and *-able* can be added to a base word that is a verb or to a root word to make it an adjective. Both suffixes mean "capable of, fit for worthy of." For example, *honor/honorable, ed/edible.*

- When *-ible* or *-able* is added to a base word that ends in a consonant, the *e* is usually dropped—*sense/sensible; use/usable.*

- The suffix *-able* is often added to base words, while *-ible* is often added to word roots. Some exceptions to this generalization are: *collapse/collapsible, sense/sensible, hospit/hospitable.*

Write *likable* on the board.

Think Aloud When I look at this word, I see *lik* and the suffix *-able.* I know that when the suffix *-able* is added to a base word that ends in a consonant and *e,* the final *e* is dropped. Using this information, I can figure out that the base word is *like.* I know that *like* has the long *e* sound because it follows the VCe pattern. When I pronounce the base word and suffix together, I get /līk/ /ə/ /bəl/. When I put the meanings of the base word *like* and the suffix *-able* together, I get "capable of being liked."

PRACTICE/APPLY

LA.5.1.6 Student uses multiple strategies to develop vocabulary

Write the following words on the board: *agreeable, usable, enjoyable, unbelievable, invisible, affordable, bearable, credible, possible.* Have students identify the base word or the word root and the suffix in each and predict what the word means.

LA.5.1.4.3 Use language structure to read multi-syllabic words

Decode Multisyllabic Words Make sure students don't allow the number of syllables to distract them from recognizing the suffix. Examples of longer words with the suffixes *-ible* and *-able* include *unbelievable* and *reprehensible.* For more practice, see the decodable passages on pages 38–39 of the **Teacher's Resource Book.**

Quick Check   Can students decode words with suffixes *-able* and *-ible*?

During **Small Group Instruction**

If No → **Approaching Level** Phonics, p. 759M

If Yes → **On Level** Options, pp. 759Q–759R

Beyond Level Options, pp. 759S–759T

Vocabulary Building

LA.5.1.6 Student uses multiple strategies to develop vocabulary

LA.5.1.6.10 Determine etymologies using digital tools

Oral Language

Expand Vocabulary Have students write *Scientists at Work* in the center of a word web. Have them use the selection and print and electronic sources, such as dictionaries, thesauruses, encyclopedias, newspapers, and technical manuals to find words that relate to this week's theme. They may include words such as *discovery*, *pioneers*, or *laboratory* in circles that radiate from the center of the web. Have students identify words based on Greek and Latin roots.

LA.5.1.6.11 Use roots and affixes from Greek and Latin

Vocabulary Building

Word Families The words *biology* and *microscope* appear in *Hidden Worlds* and are made up of the Greek roots *bios, logos, micro, scope*. Using a dictionary, have students find as many other words as possible that belong to word families with these words. Then have students write context sentences using the words.

LA.5.1.6.1 Use new vocabulary

Apply Vocabulary

Write a Journal Entry or a News Release Have students suppose that they are scientists on the verge of an important discovery. What are they hoping to discover? How will their discovery benefit people? Using the vocabulary words, have them write a journal entry or a news release about their work.

Spiral Review

Vocabulary Game Place word cards for current vocabulary and words from previous weeks in a pile. Have students form teams. The first team draws a card, tells its part of speech and meaning. If the answer is correct, the team must use the word correctly in a sentence. If all criteria are met, the team gets one point. If the responses are incorrect, the card goes back to the bottom of the pile. Then the other team takes a turn. Play continues until all words have been used correctly. The team with the most points at the end wins.

LA.5.1.6 Student uses multiple strategies to develop vocabulary

Technology

Vocabulary PuzzleMaker

For vocabulary games and practice go to www.macmillanmh.com

LA.5.1.4.1 Understand spelling patterns

Words with *-able, -ible*

Spelling Words

enjoyable	possible	capable
breakable	reasonable	sensible
favorable	laughable	unbelievable
likable	comfortable	bearable
usable	convertible	collapsible
respectable	invisible	suitable
affordable	honorable	

Review uniform, bicycle, triangle

Challenge manageable, tangible

Dictation Sentences

1. It was an <u>enjoyable</u> dinner.
2. The glass plates are <u>breakable</u>.
3. Justin earned <u>favorable</u> grades.
4. Mrs. Lee is a <u>likable</u> person.
5. The old bicycle is still <u>usable</u>.
6. Scientists have <u>respectable</u> jobs.
7. They want an <u>affordable</u> car.
8. The experiment is not <u>possible</u>.
9. We paid a <u>reasonable</u> price.
10. The skit is a <u>laughable</u> comedy.
11. This chair is the most <u>comfortable</u>.
12. David drove the <u>convertible</u>.
13. Liz wrote with <u>invisible</u> ink.
14. The king was an <u>honorable</u> man.
15. He is <u>capable</u> of doing the job.
16. That was the most <u>sensible</u> decision.
17. I found an <u>unbelievable</u> deal.
18. Winters are hardly <u>bearable</u>.
19. We folded the <u>collapsible</u> tent.
20. Those are <u>suitable</u> snow shoes.

Review/Challenge Words

1. I wore my band <u>uniform</u>.
2. I'll ride my <u>bicycle</u> to the game.
3. In math class, I drew a <u>triangle</u>.
4. The homework is <u>manageable</u>.
5. The detective needed <u>tangible</u> evidence.

Day 1 Pretest

LA.5.5.2 Student applies listening strategies
ASSESS PRIOR KNOWLEDGE

Use the Dictation Sentences. Say the underlined word, read the sentence aloud, and repeat the word. Have students write the words on **Spelling Practice Book** page 185. For a modified list, use the first 12 Spelling Words and the Review Words. For a more challenging list, use Spelling Words 3–20 and the Challenge Words. Students may correct their own tests.

Ask students to cut apart the Spelling Word Cards BLM on **Teacher's Resource Book** page 95 and figure out a way to sort them. They can save the cards for use throughout the week.

Use Spelling Practice Book page 186 for more practice with this week's spelling words.

For leveled Spelling word lists, go to **www.macmillanmh.com**

Day 2 Word Sorts

LA.5.1.6.4 Identify salient features
TEACHER AND STUDENT SORTS

- Write *-able* and *-ible* on the board as column headings. Explain that students will sort the Spelling Words according to these endings.

- Model sorting the words *usable* and *invisible* on the board. Ask students to use their Word Cards to sort the rest of the Spelling Words. They can then write them in their word study notebooks.

- Have students review the lists to determine whether words change when one of these endings is added. Help them identify the base word or root, and notice that words ending in *e* will drop the *e* before adding the ending. (collapsible, usable, sensible, unbelievable, likable) Mention that *manageable* is an exception to this rule.

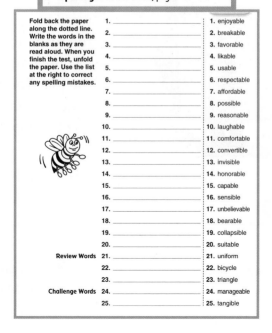

Spelling Practice Book, pages 185–186

Fold back the paper along the dotted line. Write the words in the blanks as they are read aloud. When you finish the test, unfold the paper. Use the list at the right to correct any spelling mistakes.

1. _____	1. enjoyable
2. _____	2. breakable
3. _____	3. favorable
4. _____	4. likable
5. _____	5. usable
6. _____	6. respectable
7. _____	7. affordable
8. _____	8. possible
9. _____	9. reasonable
10. _____	10. laughable
11. _____	11. comfortable
12. _____	12. convertible
13. _____	13. invisible
14. _____	14. honorable
15. _____	15. capable
16. _____	16. sensible
17. _____	17. unbelievable
18. _____	18. bearable
19. _____	19. collapsible
20. _____	20. suitable
Review Words 21. _____	21. uniform
22. _____	22. bicycle
23. _____	23. triangle
Challenge Words 24. _____	24. manageable
25. _____	25. tangible

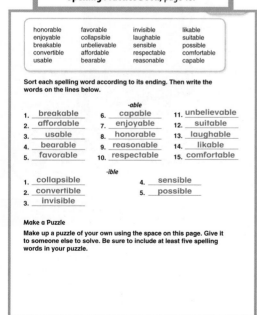

Spelling Practice Book, page 187

honorable	favorable	invisible	likable
enjoyable	collapsible	laughable	suitable
breakable	unbelievable	sensible	possible
convertible	affordable	respectable	comfortable
usable	bearable	reasonable	capable

Sort each spelling word according to its ending. Then write the words on the lines below.

-able

1. breakable
2. affordable
3. usable
4. bearable
5. favorable
6. capable
7. enjoyable
8. honorable
9. reasonable
10. respectable
11. unbelievable
12. suitable
13. laughable
14. likable
15. comfortable

-ible

1. collapsible
2. convertible
3. invisible
4. sensible
5. possible

Make a Puzzle
Make up a puzzle of your own using the space on this page. Give it to someone else to solve. Be sure to include at least five spelling words in your puzzle.

Day 3 Word Meanings

LA.5.1.6 Student develops vocabulary

DEFINITIONS

Read each short definition below. Ask students to copy the definitions into their word study notebooks and guess the Spelling Word that matches each definition.

1. something that is fun (enjoyable)
2. something you cannot see (invisible)
3. amusing or funny (laughable)
4. delicate (breakable)
5. meant to be folded (collapsible)

Invite students to work in small groups and use dictionaries to write other short definitions for Spelling Words, Challenge Words, or Review Words. Groups can exchange papers, and guess the correct words.

Day 4 Review and Proofread

LA.5.1.6.7 Use meaning of affixes to determine meanings

SPIRAL REVIEW

Review words with the number prefixes *uni-*, *bi-*, *tri-*, and *cent-*. Write *uniform, bicycle, triangle,* and *century* on the board. Ask students to identify the prefixes and the numbers they indicate.

PROOFREAD AND WRITE

Write these sentences on the board, including the misspelled words. Ask students to proofread, circling the misspelled words and correcting them.

1. It's unbelieveable how comfortible these shoes are. (unbelievable, comfortable)

2. We spent an enjoyible afternoon riding in the convertable. (enjoyable, convertible)

3. She is capeable of doing a respectible job. (capable, respectable)

Day 5 Assess and Reteach

LA.5.1.6 Student develops grade-appropriate vocabulary

POSTTEST

Use the Dictation Sentences on page 759G for the Posttest.

If students have difficulty with any words in the lesson, have them place the words in a list entitled "Spelling Words I Want to Remember" in their word study notebooks.

Challenge student partners to look for other words ending with *-able* and *-ible*, either in their reading for the week or in other materials. Partners should work together to sort the words according to these endings.

Spelling Practice Book, page 188

honorable	usable	affordable	sensible	suitable
enjoyable	favorable	bearable	respectable	possible
breakable	collapsible	invisible	reasonable	comfortable
convertible	unbelievable	laughable	likable	capable

Sentence Completions

Complete each sentence below with a spelling word.

1. Many tiny creatures are ___invisible___ to the human eye without a microscope.
2. Dennis likes microscopes and thinks that looking through them is ___enjoyable___
3. The scientists had a ___collapsible___ tent that could fold up quickly.
4. Those delicate glass test tubes are ___breakable___, so be careful with them.
5. Dennis is a ___capable___ scientist who can easily do many things.
6. That broken microscope is not ___usable___ and needs to be fixed.
7. She is a ___respectable___ scientist because her work is always well researched.
8. Being a scientist is an ___honorable___ job because it helps future generations.
9. Some colleges are expensive, but others are more ___affordable___
10. We had never seen so much ash before—it was ___unbelievable___ !

Similar Meanings

Write the spelling word that has the same, or almost the same, meaning.

11. cozy ___comfortable___
12. pleasant ___likable___
13. capable of being dealt with ___bearable___
14. practical ___reasonable___
15. having good sense ___sensible___
16. capable of happening ___possible___
17. funny ___laughable___
18. proper ___suitable___

Spelling Practice Book, page 189

Circle the misspelled words in the passage. Write the words correctly on the lines provided.

Welcome to the Hawaii Science College! We do our best to make getting a science degree (affordible) for everyone. You will find the cost of our classes (reasonble) Also, we want your time here as a student to be (enjoyabl) Our teachers are (likeble) people who will help you meet the challenge of college-level homework. With a degree from our school, anything is (possabl)! So let's start the tour. Please let me know whether we can do anything to make your visit here more (comfortibl).

1. ___affordable___ 2. ___reasonable___ 3. ___enjoyable___
4. ___likable___ 5. ___possible___ 6. ___comfortable___

Writing Activity

Write a paragraph about your favorite outdoor activity or school subject. Use four words from your spelling list.

Spelling Practice Book, page 190

Look at the words in each set below. One word in each set is spelled correctly. Use a pencil to fill in the circle next to the correct word. Before you begin, look at the sample set of words. Sample A has been done for you. Do Sample B by yourself. When you are sure you know what to do, you may go on with the rest of the page.

Sample A:
- Ⓐ invinceable
- Ⓑ invinceble
- Ⓒ invincible ●
- Ⓓ invinceible

Sample B:
- Ⓔ dooible
- Ⓕ doible
- Ⓖ doable ●
- Ⓗ dooable

1. Ⓐ collapseable
   Ⓑ collapseible
   Ⓒ collapsible
   Ⓓ collapsable
2. Ⓔ breakable
   Ⓕ breakible
   Ⓖ brakeable
   Ⓗ brakeible
3. Ⓐ affordable
   Ⓑ afordable
   Ⓒ affordible
   Ⓓ afordible
4. Ⓔ usabel
   Ⓕ useible
   Ⓖ usible
   Ⓗ usable
5. Ⓐ bearible
   Ⓑ bearable
   Ⓒ bearible
   Ⓓ bearrible
6. Ⓔ favoreable
   Ⓕ favorible
   Ⓖ favorable
   Ⓗ favoreible
7. Ⓐ capeible
   Ⓑ capeable
   Ⓒ capable
   Ⓓ capible
8. Ⓔ enjoyible
   Ⓕ enjoyyable
   Ⓖ enjoyible
   Ⓗ enjoyable
9. Ⓐ honorible
   Ⓑ honorable
   Ⓒ honorrable
   Ⓓ honorrible
10. Ⓔ convertible
    Ⓕ convertable
    Ⓖ converttible
    Ⓗ converttable
11. Ⓐ invisible
    Ⓑ invisable
    Ⓒ invissible
    Ⓓ invissable
12. Ⓔ reasonnable
    Ⓕ reasonible
    Ⓖ reasonable
    Ⓗ reasonnible
13. Ⓐ respectible
    Ⓑ respectable
    Ⓒ respecttible
    Ⓓ respecttable
14. Ⓔ senseable
    Ⓕ senseable
    Ⓖ sensible
    Ⓗ sensible
15. Ⓐ unbelievible
    Ⓑ unbelieveible
    Ⓒ unbelievable
    Ⓓ unbelievable
16. Ⓔ possible
    Ⓕ possable
    Ⓖ posible
    Ⓗ posable
17. Ⓐ suitible
    Ⓑ suitable
    Ⓒ suiteable
    Ⓓ suiteible
18. Ⓔ laghable
    Ⓕ laghible
    Ⓖ laughible
    Ⓗ laughable
19. Ⓐ likeible
    Ⓑ likable
    Ⓒ likible
    Ⓓ likkable
20. Ⓔ comforttable
    Ⓕ comforttible
    Ⓖ comfortable
    Ⓗ comfortible

Sentence Combining

Daily Language Activities

Use these activities to reinforce each day's lesson. Write the day's activity on the board or use **Daily Language Transparency 30.**

DAY 1
Dennis lived in the countryside. The countryside was beautiful. (Dennis lived in the beautiful countryside.)

DAY 2
Dennis received a microscope. He received it for Christmas. It came with slides. The slides were prepared. (1: Dennis received a microscope for Christmas.; 2: It came with prepared slides.)

DAY 3
Dennis collected samples. The samples were living. He studied them carefully. He studied them under his microscope. (1: Dennis collected living samples.; 2: He studied them carefully under his microscope.)

DAY 4
Dennis collected samples from Washington State. He collected them after a volcano eruption. (After a volcano eruption, Dennis collected samples from Washington State.)

DAY 5
Dennis collected samples from lakes and streams. The lakes and streams were located nearby. (Dennis collected samples from lakes and streams located nearby.)

ELL   Access for All

Combining Sentences
Write this sentence pair: *The boys walked home. They were tired.* Explain how to combine the sentences. Reinforce this skill during writing activities.

LA.5.3.2.2 Combine sentences to enhance clarity

INTRODUCE SENTENCE COMBINING

Present the following:

- A simple sentence expresses one complete thought: *I went to the store.*

- If two simple sentences are about the same subject, they can be combined into a compound sentence: *I went to the store, and I bought some food.*

- Sometimes you can combine two sentences by joining similar ideas: *Working together was a good idea. Working together was fun.* Combine: *Working together was a good idea and fun.*

 See Grammar Transparency 146 for modeling and guided practice.

Grammar Practice Book, page 185

- A **simple sentence** expresses one complete thought.
- If two simple sentences deal with the same subject, they can be combined into a **compound sentence.**
- Sometimes you can combine two sentences by joining similar ideas.

Combine each pair of sentences. Leave out words that repeat or mean the same thing.

1. Dennis went fishing. His dad went fishing.
   Dennis and his dad went fishing.

2. It was fun looking at creatures. The creatures were tiny.
   It was fun looking at tiny creatures.

3. Dennis studied plants. Dennis studied insects.
   Dennis studied plants and insects.

4. Dennis used microscopes. He used them to help other scientists.
   Dennis used microscopes to help other scientists.

5. He observed nature. He observed it every day.
   He observed nature every day.

6. Scientists ask questions. They look for answers.
   Scientists ask questions and look for answers.

7. There was a volcano blast. It was in 1980.
   There was a volcano blast in 1980.

8. They saw dead trees. The trees were covered with ash.
   They saw dead trees covered with ash.

9. Frogs returned to the lakes. Fish returned to the lakes.
   Frogs and fish returned to the lakes.

10. Tell someone that you want to learn. Tell a scientist.
    Tell a scientist that you want to learn.

LA.5.3.2.2 Combine sentences to enhance clarity

REVIEW SENTENCE COMBINING

Discuss with students how to combine sentences by moving a word or a phrase from one sentence to another.

INTRODUCE COMBINING SENTENCES WITH ADJECTIVES, ADVERBS, AND PREPOSITIONAL PHRASES

Present the following:

- *Access for All* — You can combine two sentences that tell about the same noun by adding an adjective to one of the sentences.

- You can combine two sentences that tell about the same action by adding an adverb to one sentence.

- You can also combine two sentences that tell about the same location by adding a prepositional phrase to one sentence.

 See Grammar Transparency 147 for modeling and guided practice.

Grammar Practice Book, page 186

- You can combine two sentences that tell about the same noun by adding an **adjective** to one of the sentences.
- You can combine two sentences that tell about the same action by adding an **adverb** to one sentence.
- You can also combine two sentences that tell about the same location by adding a **prepositional phrase** to one sentence.

Read each pair of sentences. Combine them with an adjective, an adverb, or a prepositional phrase.

1. Dennis walked to a pond. The pond was small.
   Dennis walked to a small pond.

2. He worked in the lab. It was a science lab.
   He worked in a science lab.

3. He went to college. The college was in Seattle.
   He went to college in Seattle.

4. Dennis helped others. He helped them happily.
   Dennis happily helped others.

5. The scientists traveled to a camp. It was a mountain camp.
   The scientists traveled to a mountain camp.

6. Rivers were flooded by mud. They were flooded quickly.
   Rivers were quickly flooded by mud.

7. The helicopter flew over the blast zone. It flew low.
   The helicopter flew low over the blast zone.

8. Dennis found living things. He found them in the lakes.
   Dennis found living things in the lakes.

Day 3 Review and Practice

LA.5.3.2.2 Combine sentences to enhance clarity

REVIEW COMBINING SENTENCES WITH ADJECTIVES, ADVERBS, AND PREPOSITIONAL PHRASES

Review how sentences can be combined by using adjectives, adverbs, and prepositional phrases.

MECHANICS AND USAGE: REVIEW PUNCTUATION MARKS

- Begin every sentence with a capital letter.

- Use the correct end mark for each sentence.

- If a prepositional phrase of four or more words starts a sentence, follow the phrase with a comma. If there is a prepositional phrase of three words or less that would make the sentence confusing to read, insert a comma.

See Grammar Transparency 148 for modeling and guided practice.

Grammar Practice Book, page 187

- Begin every sentence with a capital letter.
- Use the correct end mark, such as a period, question mark, or exclamation point, for each sentence.
- If a prepositional phrase of four or more words starts a sentence, place a comma after the phrase.

Rewrite the sentences. Add capitalization, end punctuation, and commas where they are needed.

1. do you want to study science
   Do you want to study science?
2. at the science lab there are samples to study
   At the science lab, there are samples to study.
3. he grew up in Iowa
   He grew up in Iowa.
4. dennis went to college and became a scientist
   Dennis went to college and became a scientist.
5. near his Hawaii home dennis observes nature
   Near his Hawaii home, Dennis observes nature.
6. dennis dipped bottles into lakes
   Dennis dipped bottles into lakes.
7. in the blast zone everything was covered with ash
   In the blast zone, everything was covered with ash.
8. helicopters flew over the lakes and streams
   Helicopters flew over the lakes and streams.
9. do you know that there is a volcano near Seattle
   Do you know that there is a volcano near Seattle?
10. living things returned to the lake
    Living things returned to the lake.

Day 4 Review and Proofread

LA.5.3.2.2 Combine sentences to enhance clarity

REVIEW COMBINING SENTENCES

Ask students to explain how to combine sentences.

PROOFREAD

Have students combine and punctuate the following sentences.

1. Good scientists are observers. They are careful observers.
   (Good scientists are careful observers.)

2. Scientists also learn about subjects that interest them. Most scientists learn quickly.
   (Scientists also learn quickly about subjects that interest them.)

3. Is there a subject that interests you? Does it really interest you?
   (Is there a subject that really interests you?)

See Grammar Transparency 149 for modeling and guided practice.

Grammar Practice Book, page 188

Read the paragraph below. Rewrite the paragraph, combining short sentences that deal with the same subject and correcting punctuation.

dennis went to school He went to school to become a scientist. scientists study. They study nature Dennis knew that he would like to be a scientist. He knew because he liked to study nature. he learned how to dive. He learned in order to study ocean plants. One day he flew in a helicopter. He flew in one and collected water samples These samples helped scientists learn. They helped scientists learn about how living things survive. do you think science is important Study nature as Dennis did. Go to school like dennis did. Then you can become a scientist, too

Answers may vary.

Dennis went to school to become a scientist.
Scientists study nature. Dennis knew that he would
like to be a scientist because he liked to study nature.
He learned how to dive in order to study ocean plants.
One day he flew in a helicopter and collected water
samples. These samples helped scientists learn about
how living things survive. Do you think science is
important? Study nature and go to school as Dennis
did. Then you can become a scientist, too!

Day 5 Assess and Reteach

LA.5.3.2.2 Combine sentences to enhance clarity

ASSESS

Use the Daily Language Activity and page 189 of the **Grammar Practice Book** for assessment.

RETEACH

On a transparency, prepare a three-column chart. In the first column, copy the uncorrected Daily Language Activities. Ask volunteers to correct the sentences orally. Write their answers in the third column. Ask the class to confirm that each answer is correct. Ask volunteers to explain how they combined the sentences and punctuated them. Write answers in the second column.

Use page 190 of the **Grammar Practice Book** for more reteaching.

See Grammar Transparency 150 for modeling and guided practice.

Grammar Practice Book, pages 189–190

Combine each pair of sentences. Write the new sentence on the line.

1. Dennis cared for pets. They were the family pets.
   Dennis cared for the family pets.
2. He went on trips. He went to collect things.
   He went on trips to collect things.
3. There was a college. It was in his home town.
   There was a college in his home town.
4. She studied plants. They were flowering plants.
   She studied flowering plants.
5. The boxes are full. The bottles are full.
   The boxes and bottles are full.
6. They could see for miles. They could see ash.
   They could see ash for miles.

Rewrite each sentence. Add punctuation and capitals.

7. scientists explore many different places
   Scientists explore many different places.
8. in only a few weeks living things returned to the lakes
   In only a few weeks, living things returned to the lakes.
9. what is your favorite thing to do outside
   What is your favorite thing to do outside?
10. to learn more about science talk to a scientist
    To learn more about science, talk to a scientist.

End-of-Week Assessment

Administer the Test

 Weekly Reading Assessment
pages 357–368

ASSESSED SKILLS

- Chronological Order
- Vocabulary Words
- Word Parts: Latin and Greek Roots
- Words with -*able* and -*ible*
- Sentence Combining

  Assessment Tool

Administer the **Weekly Assessment** from
the CD-ROM or online.

 ## Fluency

Assess fluency for one group of students per week.
Use the Oral Fluency Record Sheet to track the number
of words read correctly. Fluency goals for all students:
129–149 words correct per minute (WCPM).

Approaching Level	Weeks 1, 3, 5
On Level	Weeks 2, 4
Beyond Level	Week 6

Alternative Assessments

- **ELL Assessment,** pages 178–179

**Weekly Assessment,
357–368**

Fluency Assessment

ELL Assessment, 178–179

End-of-Week Assessment

Diagnose		Prescribe
	IF...	**THEN...**
VOCABULARY WORDS **VOCABULARY STRATEGY** Word Parts: Latin and Greek Roots Items 1, 2, 3, 4	0–2 items correct ...	Reteach skills using the **Additional Lessons** page T10. Reteach skills: Go to www.macmillanmh.com **Vocabulary PuzzleMaker** Evaluate for Intervention.
COMPREHENSION Skill: Chronological Order Items 5, 6, 7, 8, 9	0–2 items correct ...	Reteach skills using the **Additional Lessons** page T5. Evaluate for Intervention.
SPELLING Words with *-able* and *-ible* Items 10, 11, 12	0–1 items correct ...	Reteach skills: Go to www.macmillanmh.com
GRAMMAR Sentence Combining Items 13, 14, 15	0–1 items correct ...	Reteach skills: **Grammar Practice Book** page 190.
FLUENCY	120–128 WCPM 0–110 WCPM	Fluency Solutions Evaluate for Intervention.

READING
Triumphs
AN INTERVENTION PROGRAM

Also Available

To place students in the Intervention Program, use the **Diagnostic Assessment** in the Intervention Teacher's Edition.

Constructive Feedback

If students fail to understand the relationship between the suffix, the part of speech, and the meaning of the word, say:

Think about two building blocks. One block says *notice*. *Notice* is a verb that means "pay attention to." The other block says *–able*. The suffix means "capable of, fit for, or worthy of." When you put the two blocks together, you form the word *noticeable*, an adjective meaning "worthy of attention."

Repeat as needed with other words with these suffixes.

Additional Resources

Use your observations to help you identify students who might benefit from additional instruction. See page T2 for comprehension support and page T5 for vocabulary support. For each skill below, additional lessons are provided. You can use these lessons on consecutive days after teaching the lessons presented within the week.
• Chronological Order, T2
• Latin and Greek Word Families, T5

Decodable Text

To help students build speed and accuracy with reading multisyllabic words, use additional decodable text on pages 38–39 of the **Teachers' Resource Book.**

Skills Focus ➤ Phonics

Objective   Review words with *–able, -ible*

Decode multisyllabic words with number prefixes in both familiar and unfamiliar texts

Materials   • **Student Book** *Dr. Priscilla C. Grew, Geologist*

WORDS WITH *-ABLE, -IBLE*

LA.5.1.4.2
Recognize structural analysis

LA.5.1.6.11
Use affixes to determine meanings of complex words

Model/Guided Practice

■ Write *profitable* on the board. *Say it with me:* profitable.

■ Point out that *profitable* contains the suffix *-able*. It means "capable of, fit for, or worthy of." The suffix can be added to a verb or another root word to make an adjective. In this case the suffix is added to *profit*. *Profitable* means "fit for advantage, gain, or benefit." For example, *The bank had a profitable year.*

■ *Let's check another word.* Write *noticeable* on the board. The suffix *-able* is added to *notice* to form the adjective. *Noticeable* means "worthy of attention."

■ Next use *comfort* and *desire* to form adjectives with *-able*, and *extend* the review to include *-ible*.

MORE MULTISYLLABIC WORDS WITH *-ABLE, -IBLE*

LA.5.1.4.3
Use language structure to read multi-syllabic words

■ Write *advisable* on the board. Break the word into syllables: *ad/vis/a/ble*. Point out that the suffix *-able* is added to the word *advise* to form an adjective meaning "worthy of good advice." Then blend the syllables: /ad vīz ə bəl/. *Say the word with me:* advisable.

■ Write the following words on the board or provide copies of the list. Ask students to underline the root word and to define the adjective. Then have them ask partners questions about each word, such as *What character traits do you find admirable?*

admirable	feasible	likeable
adaptable	credible	reasonable
comparable	flexible	regrettable
debatable	horrible	remarkable

WORD DISCOVERY: WORDS WITH *–ABLE, -IBLE* IN CONTEXT

LA.5.1.4
Student applies grade level phonics

■ Have students read *Dr. Priscilla C. Grew, Geologist* with the words listed above in mind. Ask students to use these or other words with *-able* and *-ible* to write sentences that relate to Dr. Grew's activities and accomplishments. For example, *The number of changes to Earth in the past 4.5 billion years is incredible.*

■ To extend the activity, have students use words with these suffixes to write about discoveries they have made.

Skills Focus ▶ Fluency

Objective Read with increasing prosody and accuracy at a rate of 129–139 WCPM

Materials • **Approaching Practice Book A,** page 217

MODEL EXPRESSIVE READING

LA.5.1.5
Read orally with accuracy

Model reading the Fluency passage in **Practice Book A,** page 217. Tell students to pay close attention to your pauses and intonation as you read. Then read aloud one sentence at a time and have students repeat the sentence, first as a class and then one by one.

REPEATED READING

LA.5.1.5
Student demonstrates ability to read orally with accuracy

Have students continue practicing reading the passage aloud as you circulate and provide corrective feedback. During independent reading time, student partners can take turns reading the passage. One partner reads each sentence aloud, and the other repeats it. Remind students to wait until their partners reach end marks before correcting mistakes.

TIMED READING

LA.5.1.5
Student demonstrates ability to read orally with appropriate rate

Tell students they will do a timed reading of the passage that they have been practicing. With each student:

■ Place the passage from **Practice Book A,** page 217, face down.

■ When you say "Go," the student begins reading the passage aloud.

■ When you say "Stop," the student stops reading the passage.

As students read, note any miscues. Stop students after one minute. Help them record and graph the number of words they read correctly.

ELL Access for All

Use Visuals Have students draw a sketch or symbol for each vocabulary word. Discuss how to represent symbolically words such as *biology* that typify a whole category and not just a single concrete object.

Skills Focus ▶ Vocabulary

Objective Apply vocabulary word meanings

Materials • **Vocabulary Cards** • **Transparencies 30a and 30b**

VOCABULARY WORDS

LA.5.1.6.1
Use new vocabulary

Display the **Vocabulary Cards** for this week's words: *specimens, erupted, murky, dormant, biology, scoured, research, observer*. Help students locate and read these words on **Transparencies 30a** and **30b.** Review the meaning of each word. Then hold up one Vocabulary Card at a time and invite students to create silly sentences with each of the words. For a more challenging activity, ask students to build funny stories with each sentence they contribute.

erupted

dormant

murky

scoured

biology

observer

research

⭐ **Approaching Practice Book A, page 217**

As I read, I will pay attention to pauses and intonation.

	Microscopes opened a new door into understanding
7	disease. In 1674 a Dutch scientist named Antoni van
15	Leeuwenhoek (AHN tohnee vahn LAY vun HOOK) looked at
18	a drop of water under a microscope. He observed many
28	"little animals," as he called them, in the water. These little
39	animals are called microbes.
43	Leeuwenhoek was the first person to see microbes. But
52	he didn't know that some microbes cause disease. It took
62	another 200 years before someone figured that out.
69	That person was French chemist Louis Pasteur
76	(LEWee pasTUR). In 1864, he was studying why wine
83	goes bad. He thought it was because of microbes, called
93	bacteria, in the wine. This work led him to believe that
104	bacteria also cause diseases.
108	Pasteur's idea is called the germ theory of disease. Bad
118	bacteria, or germs, get into your body. Then they multiply.
128	This is what makes you sick.
134	A few years later, a German doctor named Robert Koch
144	discovered that different bacteria cause different diseases. 151

Comprehension Check

1. What are microbes and how were they discovered? **Summarize** Microbes are microscopic "animals." Antoni van Leeuwenhoek looked at a drop of water under a microscope.

2. What is the germ theory of disease? **Main Idea and Details** Bad bacteria, called germs, get into the body and multiply. These germs make a person sick.

	Words Read	−	Number of Errors	=	Words Correct Score
First Read		−		=	
Second Read		−		=	

Small Group

Vocabulary

Review last week's words: **(launched, particles, dense, inflate, anchored, hydrogen, scientific, companion)** and this week's words **(specimens, erupted, murky, dormant, biology, scoured, research, observer)**. Have students write a sentence for each word.

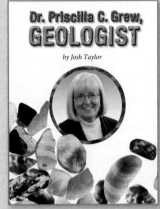

Dr. Priscilla C. Grew, **GEOLOGIST**
by Josh Taylor

Student Book

Skills Focus ▶ **Vocabulary**

Objective Review Greek and Latin roots

Materials • **Vocabulary Cards**

• **Student Book** *Hidden Worlds*

WORD PARTS: GREEK AND LATIN ROOTS

LA.5.1.6.7 Use meaning of base words to determine meanings

Ask students to find all of the vocabulary words in *Hidden Worlds*. Then have them use dictionaries to identify Latin or Greek roots among the vocabulary words. Challenge students to use these roots to build word towers.

Skills Focus ▶ **Comprehension**

Objective Review chronological order

Materials • **Student Book** *Dr. Priscilla C. Grew, Geologist*

STRATEGY
SUMMARIZE

LA.5.1.7 Use strategies to comprehend text

Remind students that when they summarize, they use their own words to tell the most important ideas and details in a passage or text.

SKILL
CHRONOLOGICAL ORDER

LA.5.2.2.3 Organize information to show understanding

LA.5.1.7.5 Identify text structure

■ When authors want to present events or biographical information in time order, or the order in which the events took place, they put the events in chronological order.

■ Good readers look for time phrases, dates, and steps in a process as they read. Clue words include: *first, next, then, finally, before, after,* and so on.

Explain/Model

Display **Transparencies 30a** and **30b.** Reread *Dr. Priscilla C. Grew, Geologist.* Ask a voluteer to circle the states where Dr. Grew lived and worked. Then ask another student whether these locations appear in the text in chronological order.

Practice/Apply

Reread the selection with students, and discuss the following questions:

■ What did Dr. Grew accomplish during her career? Summarize these accomplishments in the order they occurred.

■ How are volcanoes important in studying Earth's changes over time?

Leveled Reader Lesson

Objective Read to apply strategies and skills
Materials • **Leveled Reader** *Searching for Cures*

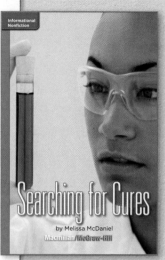

Leveled Reader

PREVIEW AND PREDICT

LA.5.1.7.1 Establish purpose for reading — Discuss the cover and have students preview the table of contents, illustrations, and first two chapters. Ask students to make predictions about ways to fight and prevent diseases. Have students set purposes for reading by asking questions about the book.

VOCABULARY WORDS

LA.5.1.6.3 Use context clues — Review vocabulary word meanings as necessary. As you read together, stop to discuss how each word is used in context.

STRATEGY
SUMMARIZE

LA.5.1.7 Use strategies to comprehend text — Remind students that summarizing means identifying the most important ideas or events in a text and restating them in their own words.

SKILL
FCAT
CHRONOLOGICAL ORDER

LA.5.2.2.3 Organize information to show understanding — Remind students to pay close attention to time-order information as they read *Searching for Cures*.

Think Aloud In the first chapter, I notice dates and phrases related to time, such as "a few years later" and "about the same time." I also notice specific dates: 1300s, 1674, and 1864. I can use this information to complete my Chronological Order Chart and keep track of the time order of events in the selection.

READ AND RESPOND

Tell students to finish reading the first two chapters of the selection. Discuss how students benefit from these scientific discoveries and address any questions they have from reading.

MAKE CONNECTIONS ACROSS TEXTS

LA.5.1.7.7 Compare and contrast elements in multiple texts — Invite students to compare *Searching for Cures*, *Hidden Worlds*, and *Dr. Priscilla C. Grew, Geologist*.

- Which events led Antoni van Leeuwenhoek in *Searching for Cures* and Dennis Kunkel in *Hidden Worlds* to observe pond water under a microscope?

- Compare the chronlogical order of events in Dr. Grew's career with those in Dr. Kunkel's career. How are they similar? How are they different?

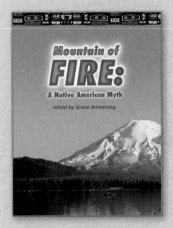

Paired Selection

Skills Focus: Vocabulary

Objective Review vocabulary words

Materials • **Vocabulary Cards**

VOCABULARY WORDS

LA.5.1.6
Student uses multiple strategies to develop vocabulary

Organize the class into small groups. Invite one group to choose a **Vocabulary Card** and act out a definition for the word. The group that correctly guesses the word being demonstrated will choose the next Vocabulary Card and act out its definition.

FCAT

WORD PARTS: GREEK AND LATIN ROOTS

LA.5.1.6.7
Use meaning of base words to determine meanings

LA.5.1.6.11
Use roots to determine meaning of complex words

Write the word *biology* on the board. Have students brainstorm or use dictionaries to list other words that contain the roots *bio* (life) or *-ology* (study of). Link the meanings of the roots with the meaning of each word. Encourage students to find other Greek and Latin roots in the vocabulary word list: *geo, dorm,* and *fin,* for example. Ask students to think of four words for each Greek or Latin root.

Skills Focus: Literary Elements

Objective Identify symbolism, metaphors, and similes

Materials • **Paired Selection** *Mountain of Fire: A Native American Myth*

• Text of a myth from a different culture, such as a Greek myth

SYMBOLISM AND FIGURATIVE LANGUAGE

LA.5.2.1.3
Demonstrate how figurative language communicates meaning in a poem

Discuss the importance and purpose of such literary elements as symbolism, simile, and metaphor in the myth. Review examples of symbolism, metaphor, and simile in *Mountain of Fire: A Native American Myth.* Have students read another myth and identify symbolism, metaphors, and similes in that text.

On Level Practice Book O, page 217

As I read, I will pay attention to pauses and intonation.

	The ocean is big. It covers about two-thirds of Earth. The
11	ocean is also deep—very deep. The ocean's average depth is
22	more than 2 miles (3 kilometers). At its deepest it goes down
32	nearly 7 miles (11 kilometers). That's taller than Mount
39	Everest.
40	Think of a place where animals live. You might think of
51	a forest or grassland. But what about the ocean? In fact, the
63	ocean makes up most of Earth's habitat. But to this day, most
75	of the deep ocean has never been explored.
83	For centuries, people thought that the bottom of the deep
93	ocean was lifeless. It is very cold in the deep, dark ocean. No
106	light reaches the bottom. And water is heavy. All that water
117	presses down hard on the sea floor. How could anything live
128	down there?
130	But then scientists began exploring the deep. What they
139	found shocked them. On the deep sea floor, they discovered
149	a world beyond their wildest imagination. It is a strange
159	world teeming with bizarre life. 164

Comprehension Check

1. What is it like at the bottom of the ocean? **Main Idea and Details**
   very cold and dark, water is heavy
2. Why has not much of the deep ocean been explored? **Main Idea and Details**
   It is hard to get to the bottom of the ocean.

	Words Read	–	Number of Errors	=	Words Correct Score
First Read		–		=	
Second Read		–		=	

Skills Focus: Fluency

Objective Read fluently with prosody at a rate of 129–149 WCPM

Materials • **On Level Practice Book O,** p. 217

REPEATED READING

LA.5.1.5
Read orally with appropriate rate

Model reading aloud the Fluency passage on page 217 of **Practice Book O,** using pauses and intonation as appropriate to reflect phrasing in the passage. Then have the class read the passage chorally, copying your intonation and pauses. Listen for accuracy.

Timed Reading Have students read the passage and record their reading rate.

Leveled Reader Lesson

Objective Read to apply strategies and skills

Materials • **Leveled Reader** *Searching for Cures*

PREVIEW AND PREDICT

LA.5.1.7.1
Use prior knowledge to make and confirm predictions

Have students preview *Searching for Cures*.

■ What does the title suggest about the selection?

■ For what diseases might scientists be searching for cures?

Encourage students to generate their own questions as purposes for reading.

SKILL
CHRONOLOGICAL ORDER

LA.5.2.2.3
Organize information to show understanding

Review: Chronological order is the sequence, or order, in which events occur in time. Explain that students will use Chronological Order Charts to record the sequence of events in *Searching for Cures*.

READ AND RESPOND

Read the Introduction and Chapter 1. Pause to discuss the events that led to the development of Pasteur's germ theory. After students have read Chapter 1, have them fill in their Chronological Order Charts.

VOCABULARY WORDS

LA.5.1.6.3
Use context clues

After they finish reading *Searching for Cures,* ask students to point out the vocabulary words. Discuss how each word is used in context. Ask questions such as: *What specimens of life might you find in a dormant, murky water?* Have students respond in kind.

MAKE CONNECTIONS ACROSS TEXTS

LA.5.1.7.7
Compare and contrast elements in multiple texts

Invite students to think about chronological order in *Searching for Cures* and *Mountain of Fire: A Native American Myth.*

■ Which selection is more specific in conveying chronological order?

■ Explain why you think chronological order might be more important in the selection you chose than in the other selection.

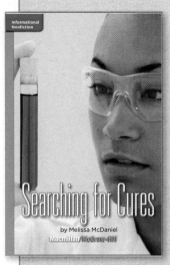

Leveled Reader

ELL
Leveled Reader
Go to pages
759U–759V.

Beyond Level Options

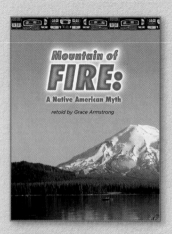

Paired Selection

Figurative Language
Have students work in pairs and look through *Mountain of Fire* for examples of figurative language. Have them locate at least three examples and draw pictures to illustrate the meaning of the language.

Beyond Practice Book B, page 217

As I read, I will pay attention to pauses and intonation.

	Much of the energy people use comes from oil and coal.
11	Oil and coal are fossil fuels. They were made inside the
22	earth from dead plants and animals.
28	Fossil fuels powered many of the advances of the last 200
38	years. They sent trains rumbling down tracks and planes
47	zooming into the sky. They supplied power to run factories.
57	But fossil fuels create a lot of pollution. And sooner or later,
69	they will run out.
73	Scientists are searching for alternatives to replace fossil fuels.
82	Some kinds of alternative energy have been used for thousands
90	of years. Others are only just beginning to be discovered.
102	Fossil fuels helped the modern world grow. But as an
112	energy source, fossil fuels are far from perfect. For one
122	thing, the supply of oil and coal is limited. The oil that is
135	being used now was made many millions of years ago. When
146	this oil is gone, it cannot be replaced. Some observers
156	believe that the world's supply of oil will be gone in 50 years.
168	No big new oil fields have been found since the 1970s.
178	And when new oil fields are found, they contain lower
188	quality oil. The oil is also harder to get at. 198

Comprehension Check

1. How are fossil fuels made? **Main Idea and Details** from dead plants and animals

2. Why are scientists searching for alternatives to replace fossil fuels? **Main Idea and Details** Fossil fuels are limited and cause pollution.

	Words Read	−	Number of Errors	=	Words Correct Score
First Read		−		=	
Second Read		−		=	

Skills Focus ▶ Vocabulary

Objective   Create vocabulary games using vocabulary words

EXTEND VOCABULARY

LA.5.1.6.1
Use new vocabulary

Provide students with three note cards and ask them to write three different clues for vocabulary and content vocabulary words, one per card. For example, for *erupted*, a student might write the following clues:

Clue 1: Pow!!! Bang!!!
Clue 2: The volcano blew its top!
Clue 3: Exploded

Then have students use their cards to play a quiz game with their classmates. Students or teams who guess the correct word get a point. Those with the most points win the game.

Skills Focus ▶ Literary Elements

Objective   Write myths using symbolism and figurative language
Materials   • **Paired Selection** *Mountain of Fire: A Native American Myth*

SYMBOLISM AND FIGURATIVE LANGUAGE

LA.5.2.1.3
Demonstrate how figurative language communicates meaning in a poem

Explain how symbolism and figurative language are tools that help readers understand what the author is saying. Ask students to point out examples of symbolism or figurative language in *Mountain of Fire: A Native American Myth* or any other selection they are reading. Ask students why the author uses figurative language to help tell the story.

Then have students write short myths about natural phenomena of their choice, encouraging them to use symbolism and figurative language.

Skills Focus ▶ Fluency

Objective   Read fluently with accuracy at a rate of 139–149 WCPM
Materials   • **Beyond Practice Book B,** page 217

REPEATED READING

LA.5.1.5
Read orally with appropriate rate

Have volunteers identify technical terms in the passage on page 217 of **Practice Book B** and model the pronunciation of each word. Have students echo you as you read the passage aloud, carefully pronouncing each technical word.

During independent time, listen for accuracy as partners take turns reading the passage they have marked, focusing on the correct pronunciation of scientific vocabulary. Partners should offer corrective feedback.

Leveled Reader Lesson

 Objective   Read to apply strategies and skills

Materials   • **Leveled Reader** *Searching for Cures*

PREVIEW AND PREDICT

Have students preview *Searching for Cures,* predict what it is about, and set purposes for reading.

 ## VOCABULARY WORDS

LA.5.1.6.3
Use context clues to determine meaning

Review vocabulary words as necessary. Ask students questions such as, *Which specimens might someone study in biology--the eggs of a frog or the presidential campaigns of the last decade?* Have them respond in kind, using two vocabulary words.

SKILL
FCAT **CHRONOLOGICAL ORDER**

LA.5.2.2.3
Organize information to show understanding

Ask a volunteer to explain the meaning of chronological order and to give examples of time-order clue words that he or she might find in a selection that uses chronological order as a text structure. Tell students they will read *Searching for Cures* together and that they will record information about chronological order in charts.

READ AND RESPOND

As they read, students should identify time-order clue words and complete their Chronological Order Charts.

Self-Selected Reading

Objective   Read independently to analyze chronological order and make connections across texts

Materials   • Leveled Readers or trade books at students' reading levels

FCAT ## READ TO IDENTIFY CHRONOLOGICAL ORDER

LA.5.1.7.7
Compare and contrast elements in multiple texts

Have students summarize *Mountain of Fire: A Native American Myth, Searching for Cures,* and *Hidden Worlds* to compare the chronological order of events used to explain natural phenomena in the nonfiction pieces with those in a myth. Discuss the kinds of events that are important in each type of writing and how they work together to provide explanations.

Invite students to choose books to read for enjoyment. After reading, have students describe the chronological order of events in their texts. Ask them to identify the signal words that indicate chronological order. Discuss how it helps to identify chronological order as they read.

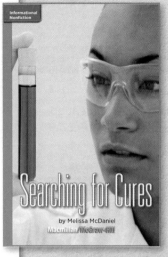

Leveled Reader

RESEARCH
Why It Matters

Comprehension When students are asked to make mental images, the printed text and the mental images together may require students to make a special effort which results in deeper and better understanding of a text. It also seems to be that students who use imagery may be making more active connections between different parts of the text. These connections also improve comprehension.

Jan Dole

LOG ON Go to
www.macmillanmh.com

Academic Language

Throughout the week the English language learners in your class will need help building their understanding of the academic language used in daily instruction and assessment instruments. The following strategies will help increase their language proficiency and comprehension of content and instructional words.

Technology

Oral Language For vocabulary development go to www.macmillanmh.com

Strategies to Reinforce Academic Language

- **Use Context** Academic language used by the teacher (see chart below) should be explained in the context of the task during Whole Group. You may use gestures, expressions, and visuals to support meaning.

- **Use Visuals** Use charts, transparencies, and graphic organizers to explain key labels to help students understand classroom language.

- **Model** Demonstrate the task using academic language in order for students to understand instruction.

Academic Language Used in Whole Group Instruction

Content/Theme Words	Skill/Strategy Words	Writing/Grammar Words
scientists (p. 736)	myth (p. 754)	expository (p. 758)
observation (p. 736)	literary elements (p. 754)	problem-solving essay (p. 758)
hypothesis (p. 736)	symbolism (p. 754)	sentence combining (p. 759I)
experiment (p. 736)	concrete (p. 754)	simple sentence (p. 759I)
conclusion (p. 736)	figurative language (p. 754)	compound sentence (p. 759I)
	simile and metaphor (p. 754)	adjective (p. 759I)
	imaginative language (p. 754)	adverb (p. 759I)
		prepositional phrases (p. 759I)

ELL Leveled Reader Lesson

Informational Nonfiction

Science Finds Cures
by Melissa McDaniel
Macmillan/McGraw-Hill

Before Reading

DEVELOP ORAL LANGUAGE

Build Background *Ask students how scientists find ways to fight and prevent diseases. Have they ever had shots?* Encourage students to use their imaginations and prior knowledge.

Review Vocabulary Write the vocabulary and story support words on the board and discuss their meanings. Model using them in sentences. *I want to* research *a cure for cancer. I will test* cell *specimens, or samples.*

PREVIEW AND PREDICT

Point to the cover illustration and read the title aloud. *What is this scientist doing? Why? What do you think this book will tell you about cures?*

FCAT **Set a Purpose for Reading** Show the Sequence Chart and remind students they have used this chart before. Ask them to identify the sequence of events in chronological order and fill in a similar chart.

During Reading

Choose from among the differentiated strategies below to support students' reading at all stages of language acquisition.

Beginning	Intermediate	Advanced
Shared Reading As you read, model how to identify main events in sequence and list them in the chart. Check students' comprehension. *In the past, why were diseases so infectious?* Model how to use the chart.	**Read Together** Read through Chapter 1. Ask students to identify early explorations of medicine and write them in sequence on their charts. Have students continue to read and identify more recent events. Remind them to list them in chronological order.	**Independent Reading** Have students read the book. Ask them to identify sequentially the main events in the exploration of medical cures and complete their charts. Challenge them to write an fictitious essay in chronolgical order about how they discovered a cure.

After Reading

Remind students to use the vocabulary and story words in their whole group activities. Have them complete the Comprehension Check Questions.

Objective

- **To apply vocabulary and comprehension skills**

Materials

- **ELL Leveled Reader**

5-Day Planner	
DAY 1	• Academic Language
	• Oral Language and Vocabulary Review
DAY 2	• Academic Language
	• ELL Leveled Reader
DAY 3	• Academic Language
	• ELL Leveled Reader
DAY 4	• Academic Language
	• ELL Leveled Reader
DAY 5	• Academic Language
	• ELL Leveled Reader Comprehension Check and Literacy Activities

Grade 5 • ELL TEACHER'S GUIDE

English Language Learners

FLORIDA Treasures

Mars

Macmillan/McGraw-Hill

ELL Teacher's Guide for students who need additional instruction

Show What You Know

FCAT Spiral Review

Show What You Know provides a spiral review of selected skills and strategies through Unit 6. After reading short fiction and nonfiction selections, students take short tests—in FCAT format—that assess reading comprehension in the context of unit skills and strategies.

Have students turn to page 760 in the Student Book and read *The Big, Bad Detective* independently. Distribute **Show What You Know** pages 25–26. Have students complete the assessment. See pages 706–707 if students need a review of test format.

Share Your Thinking

After students have completed the BLM, model your own thinking to show students how they can use test-taking and comprehension, vocabulary, and study skills and strategies to arrive at correct answers.

Question 1 Chronological Order *If the story were told in chronological order, what would happen FIRST?*

Suggest that students search the story to put the answer choices in the order in which they occur. Then tell students to think about how to reorder the answer choices to show chronology (D, Think and Search)

Show What You Know

FCAT Review

- Author's Purpose
- Relevant Facts and Details
- Chronological Order
- Context Clues
- Greek and Latin Roots
- Primary Source

The Big, Bad Detective

Peter Pig thought there was something suspicious about Detective Bibi Lupino. The hair flowing down from her police cap was blond, but the fur on her face was a reddish brown. She claimed to be a bloodhound, but her nose seemed too narrow and pointy. Mostly, though, there was something about the eyes... those quick, darting, almost hungry glances that Detective Lupino made throughout her presentation.

The three pigs had just finished watching a videotape provided by the detective. In it, a grass hut had been blown to pieces by fierce rains and winds. "So you see," Lupino said, "this video proves that the first house was blown down by a freak tropical storm, not..." Lupino covered her mouth to muffle a chuckle. "...a big, bad wolf."

"There!" cried out Paulie Pig. "You see? Now aren't you glad I called the police to report this?"

"But you said the police called you yesterday," said Peter Pig, "not..."

760

LA.5.1.7 Student uses strategies to comprehend text

Review

Apply Test Strategies

Think and Search To use this strategy, **think** about what the question is asking and **search** the selection for the part or parts that will give the correct answer.

Right There To use this test strategy, look for the answer to the question **right there** in the text.

Author and Me To use this test strategy, look at what the **author** tells you, and then think about what **you** already know.

Apply Comprehension Strategies

Review these comprehension strategies, which students have learned about in this and previous units: **Evaluate, Monitor Comprehension, Summarize.** Before they read the passages, remind students that they can choose from the reading strategies they know to help them better understand the passage.

"My dear friends," interrupted Lupino. "The main point is that we get to the truth of the matter."

"What about my twig house?" asked Patsy Pig. "The wolf blew that down, too!"

"Wolf, schmolf," said Lupino. "Take a look at this." Seemingly out of nowhere, Lupino produced an easel and a massive chart with jagged lines across it. "Seismic activity in the area. It was an earthquake that brought the twig house down, not..." Lupino tried to stifle a snicker. "...a big, bad wolf."

"That makes total sense!" squealed Paulie Pig. "Of course it was an earthquake!"

"So you think we should be apologizing to the wolf?" asked Peter. "Maybe send some flowers to say we're sorry for blaming him?"

"Might I make a suggestion?" asked Lupino. "I propose that you invite the wolf over for a nice candlelight dinner, maybe some spare ribs and ham..." Lupino licked her lips. "...burgers. You could settle your differences over a delicious meal."

"That big, bad wolf would just huff and puff and blow out the candles, then gobble us up before salads were served!" said Peter Pig.

"What about this brick house?" asked Patsy Pig. "How do you explain what we heard outside this house that day?"

"Oh, that..." said Detective Lupino. "That was nothing more than an army helicopter flying close to the ground, not..." Lupino struggled to squelch a chortle. "...a big, bad wolf."

"Prove it," Peter Pig said. "I'll bet that if you went outside right now and blew really hard, it would sound nothing like a helicopter."

Detective Lupino's ears perked up. "If that will convince you, then that's what I'll do!" Lupino opened the door and stepped outside. As she closed her eyes and drew in a deep breath, Peter Pig slammed the door shut and locked it.

"What'd you do that for?" asked Paulie Pig.

Peter Pig laughed. "Because no matter what that stupid wolf says or does, he always ends up huffing and puffing!"

761

LA.5.1.7.2
Identify author's purpose

Question 2 Author's Purpose *The author uses dialogue to show the reader that Paulie Pig is*

Suggest that students reread Paulie Pig's dialogue. Point out how easily Paulie is convinced by the wolf's explanations. Tell students to use the dialogue the author provides to draw conclusions about Paulie. (I, Author and Me)

LA.5.1.6.11
Use roots and affixes derived from Greek to determine meaning

Question 3 Word Parts *Which word below has a Greek root that means "shake"?*

Suggest that students write a definition for each word. Alternatively, students might construct quick word webs, noting other words they associate with each answer choice. Then tell students to choose the word that has something to do with shaking. (A, Author and Me)

Question 4 Author's Purpose *The author starts the story by describing Peter's suspicions. Use details from the story to explain what information is revealed in the suspicions and how this relates to the author's purpose in writing the story.*

Students' answers to this extended-response item will vary, but should use a combination of the test strategies to focus on how the author creates light suspense (a sense of danger) and differentiates among the characters. This information engages readers and thus reflects the author's purpose: to entertain. **See the Extended Response Rubric on page 763H.**

Show What You Know BLM, page 25

Student Name _____

Now answer Numbers 1 through 4. Base your answers on the story "The Big, Bad Detective."

1 If the story were told in chronological order, what would happen FIRST?

  A. Lupino shows the pigs a chart.

  B. The three pigs watch a videotape.

  C. Peter Pig has suspicions about the detective.

  D. Paulie Pig receives a phone call from Lupino.

2 The author uses dialogue to show the reader that Paulie Pig is

  F. less polite than the others.

  G. less excited than the others.

  H. more intelligent than the others.

  I. more easily fooled than the others.

3 Which word below has a Greek root that means "shake"?

  A. seismic

  B. tropical

  C. apologize

  D. suspicious

LOG ON Technology

Go to **www.macmillanmh.com** for Sample Responses to question 4.

Have students turn to page 762 in the Student Book and read *National Parks: Our National Treasures* independently. Distribute **Show What You Know** pages 27–28. Have students complete the assessment. See pages 706–707 if students need a review of test format.

Share Your Thinking

After students have completed the assessment, model your own thinking to show students how they can use test-taking and comprehension, vocabulary, and study skills and strategies to arrive at correct answers.

Question 1 Relevant Facts and Details *The National Park Service was created in 1916 by*

Tell students to reread the paragraph about President Ulysses S. Grant. The answer to the prompt is right there in this paragraph. (C, Right There)

LA.5.1.6.11 Use roots and affixes derived from Latin to determine meaning

Question 2 Word Parts *Which word below has a Latin root that means "good"?*

Suggest that students write quick definitions for each word to determine which word has to do with something that is good. (G, Author and Me)

LA.5.6.2.1 Apply evaluative criteria to select resources

Question 3 Text Features: Primary Sources *Which statement comes from a primary source?*

Remind students that a primary source comes directly from someone involved in an event either as a participant or an observer. Primary sources can include quotations, diary entries, and letters. Tell students to search the article to locate each answer choice. Then tell students to think about which answer choice seems most likely to come directly from someone or something

National Parks: *Our National Treasures*

WHERE CAN YOU GO to experience the great outdoors as it was 200 years ago? Fresh air, sparkling lakes, untouched land, and breathtaking scenery are all there for you to enjoy in this country's almost 400 national parks!

Yellowstone National Park

Trappers who had been out West told stories about bubbling mud and steamy springs that gushed hot water and steam. In the East these stories sparked people's interests. Adventurers set out to find the places that inspired such stories. In 1871 a group that included Thomas Moran and William H. Jackson explored the area that would become Yellowstone National Park. Moran was an artist and Jackson was a photographer. They found land formed by a volcano that had erupted more than 640,000 years earlier. Old Faithful and other hot springs amazed the visitors. The stories they had heard seemed to be true!

Moran and Jackson captured the beauty of Yellowstone in paint and on film. Along with Jackson's photographs, Moran's paintings were later used to persuade Congress that Yellowstone needed protection.

762

Review

Apply Test Strategies

Think and Search To use this strategy, **think** about what the question is asking and **search** the selection for the part or parts that will give the correct answer.

Right There To use this test strategy, look for the answer to the question **right there** in the text.

Author and Me To use this test strategy, look at what the **author** tells you, and then think about what **you** already know.

LA.5.1.7 Student uses strategies to comprehend text

President Ulysses S. Grant made Yellowstone the first national park in 1872. This paved the way for the National Park Service, which began in 1916 by an act of Congress.

The Antiquities Act

President Theodore Roosevelt was a great conservationist. More federal land was protected under his administration than under any other president. He said,

The movement for the conservation of wild life and the larger movement for the conservation of all our natural resources are essentially democratic in spirit, purpose, and method.

In 1906 Roosevelt signed the Antiquities Act. This gave the government the power to grant further protection to national parks and other special places because of their beauty or because they are important to history or science. As Stephen T. Mather, the NPS director from 1917 to 1929, said, "The parks do not belong to one state or to one section."

The National Parks and You

When you visit a national park you can do many things. You can see natural waterfalls in Yosemite National Park. You can gaze at the sculpted rock of Grand Canyon National Park. You can learn how animals and plants live together in their natural environment at Joshua Tree National Park. You can explore important events in America's past by visiting Gettysburg National Military Park. At the Clara Barton or Frederick Douglass National Historic Sites, you can learn about people who helped make this country great.

These places, events, and people helped write the American story. By learning about them, you can begin to understand and appreciate your own place in this country's continuing story.

Thomas Moran, *Grand Canyon of the Yellowstone Park*, 1872

Moran became so well known for his watercolors of Yellowstone that people started calling him Thomas "Yellowstone" Moran.

763

involved with the history of the national park system. Note that only one answer is factual, whereas the others are opinions that could be stated at any time. (C, Think and Search)

LA.5.1.7.1 Identify author's purpose

Question 4 Author's Purpose *Why does the author describe Thomas Moran's trip in 1871?*

Remind students that authors include details for different reasons. Tell students to reread the section of text about Yellowstone National Park. Point out that Moran was a painter. Tell students to select the answer choice that supports this detail. (H, Author and Me)

Question 5 Relevant Facts and Details *For what purpose might people visit one of the national parks mentioned in the article? Use relevant facts and details to support your answer.*

Students' answers to this short-response item will vary. Tell students that they could use a combination of test strategies to find and think about relevant facts and details that would support their answer. **See the Short Response Rubric on page 763H.**

Show What You Know, page 27

Student Name _____

Now answer Numbers 1 through 5. Base your answers on the article "National Parks: Our National Treasures."

1 The National Park Service was created in 1916 by

    A. writer Wallace Stegner.
    B. President Ulysses S. Grant.
    C. the United States Congress.
    D. Thomas "Yellowstone" Moran.

2 Which word below has a Latin root that means "good"?

    F. reflect
    G. benefit
    H. explore
    I. photograph

3 Which statement comes from a primary source?

    A. Each park is special, and each park has a story.
    B. Old Faithful and other hot springs amazed the visitors.
    C. The parks do not belong to one state or to one section.
    D. Moran and Jackson captured the beauty of Yellowstone.

LOG ON Technology

Go to **www.macmillanmh.com** for Sample Responses to question 5.

Objectives

- Identify features of a how-to article
- Plan and organize ideas for a how-to article
- Draft and revise expository writing that explains how to do something
- Proofread, publish, and present a how-to article

Materials

- Unit Writing Transparencies 31–36

Features of a How-to Article

- It **explains** or gives information on how to complete a specific task or activity.
- It presents **step-by-step** instructions in **a logical order.**
- It provides **clear details** that are easy to understand and follow.
- It uses **time-order words,** such as *first* or *next,* or **spatial words,** such as *under* or *above.*

Expository: How-to Article

Read Like a Writer

LA.5.5.2.1 Listen to gain and share information

Read aloud the following excerpt from "The Science of Hot-Air Balloons," on **Student Book** pages 712–713. Explain that this is an example of expository writing. It gives information about ballooning and explains steps involved in a balloon launch. Ask students to listen for

- the task or activity that is **explained**
- information presented **step-by-step in a logical order** and **time-order words** or **spatial words**
- **clear details** that are easy to understand

How the air is heated to inflate the hot-air balloon has changed a great deal since the early days of ballooning. Back in 1783 fire from damp straw and wool heated the air as the balloon remained anchored to the ground. Usually, a brave man or woman and a companion would climb into the basket, cut the line, and soar into the air.

Now balloonists use propane—the same gas used in most outdoor grills—instead of straw. For hot-air balloons, it is piped from a tank to metal tubes. Once there, a small fire heats up the tubes and the propane. When the propane flame is released, it creates hot air that fills the inside of the hot-air balloon.

Discuss the Features

LA.5.3.1 Use prewriting strategies

After reading, discuss the following questions with students:

- **What is explained in this excerpt?** (how the air in hot-air balloons was heated in the past and how it is heated now)
- **What time-order and spatial words or phrases are used?** (back in 1783, now; into, inside)

Remind students that a good writer chooses a focus and organizational structure based on purpose, audience, length, and required format. They will often write several drafts, categorizing ideas, organizing them into paragraphs, and blending paragraphs into longer compositions.

Prewrite

LA.5.3.1.3
Make a plan for writing that addresses main idea

Set a Purpose Remind students that one purpose or reason for writing a how-to article is to explain or give information on how to complete a specific task or activity.

Know the Audience Have students think about the audience for their how-to articles, such as friends, family, or classmates. Invite them to consider how much a reader might already know or will need to learn about the task they are explaining.

LA.5.3.1.1
Generate ideas based upon teacher-directed topics

Choose a Topic Tell students that they will be writing an article that explains how to do a specific task. Ask the following questions to help them focus their ideas:

- What do you like to do or make? Consider a game you play, a food you make, or a project you've completed.

- How many steps does it take to do this task?

- What clear details and time-order or spatial words can make your instructions clearer?

Remind students to **focus** and **plan** their writing by choosing a main idea, details, and organizing their information.

Mini Lesson | Organization

LA.5.3.1.3
Prewrite by organizing ideas using strategies and tools

Display **Transparency 31** and point out that together you will follow Alejandro H.'s progress as he develops a how-to article. Point out the following details in Alejandro's sequence chart:

- He presents **step-by-step instructions in a logical order,** listing each step on a separate line.

- He provides **clear details** that are easy to follow.

- He uses **spatial words,** such as *inside* and *on the surface of.*

Ask students to create their own sequence charts to plan their how-to articles.

Organize Ideas Use the transparency to demonstrate how to organize ideas.

Peer Review

Think, Pair, Share Have students think about how to help someone understand the task they are explaining. Then have partners read the list of steps in each other's charts. Invite pairs to point out any steps that are confusing and suggest ways to clarify them.

Flexible Pairing Option Have students choose a partner who is writing about a task that is unfamiliar to them.

Writing Topic

Think about a task or project that you would like to explain to other fifth-graders. Choose one that you think is important or interesting and that you think will appeal to your audience. Write a how-to article that explains how to do this task or project. Remember to use step-by-step instructions that are organized in a logical way.

LA.5.4.2 Develop technical writing that provides information related to real-world tasks

---

Transparency 31

How to Make Frost
Step 1: Place ice cubes in a plastic bag.
Step 2: Use a hammer to break ice into small pieces.
Step 3: Make a layer of ice about three centimeters deep in a can.
Step 4: Put a layer of salt in the can.
Step 5: Fill the can with more layers of ice and salt.
Step 6: Breathe softly on the surface of the can to add more water vapor to the air.
Watch the frost form on the can.

Unit Writing Transparency 31

Draft

Mini Lesson Step-by-Step Instructions

LA.5.3.3.1
Evaluate draft
for logical
organization

Display **Transparency 32** and read it with students. As you discuss Alejandro H.'s draft, point out the following features:

- It is clear from reading this draft that Alejandro chose to **explain** how to make frost to someone unfamiliar with this task.

- Alejandro includes **step-by-step instructions** in a logical order.

- He provides **clear details** that are easy to follow. For example, he explains that the layer of ice in the can needs to be three centimeters deep.

- He uses **time-order words,** such as *first*, *next*, and *then*, and **spatial words**, such as *inside* and *on the surface of*.

Note that Alejandro will have the opportunity to revise and proofread his draft in later stages.

Review Your Sequence Chart Have students review their sequence charts. Tell them to refer to their charts often as they write to help keep their steps in order.

LA.5.3.2.2
Organize
information
into logical
sequence

Write the Draft Help students to remember that the purpose of writing a first draft is to get their ideas on paper. Share the following tips as students begin to write:

- Choose a specific task that you can explain well.

- Picture yourself doing the task. Then write what you see. Give step-by-step instructions in a logical order.

- Include clear details as well as time-order and spatial words to clarify your instructions.

ELL Access for All

Create a Flow Chart
Choose a process with which students are familiar, such as making a sandwich. Assist them in generating a list of steps necessary to complete the task. Write each step on a sentence strip and invite students to create a flow chart by ordering the steps logically. Help students to see how this process is useful when planning their how-to articles.

Transparency 32

How to Make Frost
by Alejandro H.

Have you ever notised the frost that forms on windows in the Winter? Did you know that you can make frost? frost was one form of water. It is made from another form of water called water vapor.

First place ice cubes inside a plastic bag. Use a hammer to break the cubes into small pieces. Next make a layer of ice about three centimeters deep in a can. Then add a thin layer of salt. Repeat layers of ice and salt until the can is full Finally, breathe softly on the surface of the can. The surrounding air must contain water vapor for frost to form, and breathing on the can adds more water vapor to the air.

Watch as frost appears on the can. The frost form when the water vapor freezes on contact with the cold surface of the can.

Unit Writing Transparency 32

Writer's Resources
Use an Internet Search Engine

Tell students that they can use an Internet search engine to start their research. Explain that search engines use a key word or phrase to scan Web sites and return a list of sites with matching information. Explain that some sites offer a feature called *search within a search* in which results can be narrowed by entering secondary key words.

Caution students that not every match will be a useful Web site. Direct them to always check the source of the site to make sure it is a reputable one, instead of just one individual's opinion.

LA.5.6.4 Student develops essential technology skills

Revise

Mini Lesson | Organization

LA.5.3.3.1
Evaluate draft
for word
choice and
logical
organization

Display **Transparency 33** and point out how Alejandro H. revises a good how-to article to make it excellent.

- He strengthens his explanation by adding a list of supplies in the first paragraph. (Organization)

- He inserts a clear detail that is necessary to follow the process in the second paragraph. (Organization)

- He adds spatial words, such as *at the bottom of* and *on top of*, and a time-order word, *now*, to make instructions clearer. (Word Choice)

- He replaces the word *break* with the more vivid word *crush*. (Word Choice)

You may want to note that Alejandro will need to proofread his story to make final corrections.

Guide students to think about the following writing elements as they evaluate and revise their how-to articles. Remind them to use classroom resources to edit their writing.

LA.5.3.3
Student will
refine and
revise draft
for clarity and
effectiveness

Focus Do you explain how to complete a specific task? Do you provide clear details that are easy to follow?

Organization Do you present step-by-step instructions that are organized in a logical way for clarity and effectiveness?

Support Did you include time-order words or spatial words to make your instructions clearer?

Conventions Did you use a dictionary and thesaurus to check your spelling and word choices?

Peer Review

Think, Pair, Share Have partners read their revised drafts to each other, listening for clarity of instructions. Encourage them to point out any confusing statements. Have pairs share with the class an example of one good and one confusing instruction.

Flexible Pairing Option Consider pairing a student whose work needs extensive editing with a student whose work requires minimal editing.

ELL | Access for All

Read with a Peer Pair fluent English speakers with those who are less fluent. Have the pairs read their papers aloud. Encourage students to discuss whether the instructions are clear. Have the fluent-speaking partner restate the instructions in their partner's task to ensure that they make sense. Invite students to use the information from their discussions to make additional revisions to their writing.

Transparency 33

How to Make Frost
by Alejandro H.

Have you ever noticed the frost that forms on windows in the Winter? Did you know that you can make frost? frost was one form of water. It is made from another form of water
_{All you need are ice cubes, a plastic bag, a hammer, an empty coffee can, and salt.}
called water vapor.

First place ice cubes inside a plastic bag. _{and seal tightly} Use a hammer to _{crush} break the cubes into small pieces. Next _{place} make a layer of ice about three centimeters deep _{at the bottom of} in a can. Then add a thin layer of salt. _{on top of the ice} Repeat layers of ice and salt until the can is full Finally, breathe softly on the surface of the can. The surrounding air must contain water vapor for frost to form, and breathing on the can adds more water vapor to the air.

_{Now} Watch as frost appears on the can. The frost form_s when the water vapor freezes on contact with the cold surface of the can.

Speaking and Listening

Have students read their how-to articles aloud. Share these strategies.

Speaking Strategies

- Speak slowly, in a loud, clear voice.
- Use inflection, especially when beginning a new step in the instructions.
- Include gestures to make any demonstration of instructions clearer.

Listening Strategies

- Prepare to listen.
- Listen for each step in the instructions.
- Focus on time-order words and spatial words.

Transparency 34

How to Make Frost

by Alejandro H.

Have you ever noticed the frost that forms on windows in the Winter? Did you know that you can make frost? frost was one form of water. It is made from another form of water called water vapor. All you need are ice cubes, a plastic bag, a hammer, an empty coffee can, and salt.

First, place ice cubes inside a plastic bag. Use a hammer to break the cubes into small pieces. Next, make a layer of ice about three centimeters deep in a can. Then, add a thin layer of salt. Repeat layers of ice and salt until the can is full and seal tightly. Finally, breathe softly on the surface of the can. The surrounding air must contain water vapor for frost to form, and breathing on the can adds more water vapor to the air.

Watch as frost appears on the can. The frost form when the water vapor freezes on contact with the cold surface of the can.

Unit Writing Transparency 34

Proofread/Edit

Mini Lesson | Conventions

LA.5.3.4.3 Edits for correct use of punctuation

LA.5.3.4.4 Edits for correct use of verbs

Display **Transparency 34** to point out examples of Alejandro H.'s proofreading corrections.

- He adds commas after time-order words *first, next,* and *then.*
- He changes *was* to *is* to correct the verb tense.
- He changes *form* to *forms* to make the subject and verb agree.

Have students reread their how-to articles to find and correct mistakes. Remind them to use classroom resources to check spelling, grammar, and punctuation. Review the use of proofreading marks on page 152 of the **Teacher's Resource Book.** Remind students to make sure they have used adverbs correctly.

Peer Review

Think, Pair, Share Invite students to think about and name some prepositions and prepositional phrases. Then have them read a partner's paper and circle examples of both. Invite them to check that these words and phrases are used correctly.

TEACHER CONFERENCE

Use the rubric on page 763G to evaluate student writing and help you formulate questions to foster self-assessment:

- Did you explain how to complete a specific task?
- Did you include step-by-step instructions? Could a reader perform the task based on your explanation?
- What time-order or spatial words did you use?

Publish LA.5.6.4.2 Use appropriate digital tools for publishing

Ask students to write or type a final copy of their how-to articles on a computer. Remind students to use appropriate spacing and to use standard margins. Students can also publish one of the week's writing assignments.

PRESENTATION

Consider asking students to give "how-to" demonstrations, complete with props and supplies. Students can also independently explore opportunities for publication.

Author's Chair Invite students who feel confident about their how-to articles to present them from the Author's Chair.

Raising Scores

READ AND SCORE

Display **Transparency 35** and invite students to follow along as you read the how-to article aloud. Then have students use their student rubric on page 158 of the **Teacher's Resource Book** to assess the writing sample.

Guide students to understand that this how-to article is only a fair writing sample, which would score only a 3, and that they will work together in groups to improve it.

RAISE THE SCORE

Discuss the following shortfalls in the writing sample:

LA.5.3.3.1 Evaluate draft for development of ideas, content, and voice

> **Focus** The writer attempts to explain how to make a glass harmonica, but some details are not stated clearly enough or they are incomplete. (Ideas and Content)
>
> **Organization** An instruction is out of order, making it difficult to understand how to complete the task. (Ideas and Content)
>
> **Support** The article could use more time-order words and spatial words to make the instructions clearer. (Voice)

Now allow students to work in small groups and revise the how-to article to raise the score. Remind them to refer to the student rubric.

SHARE AND COMPARE

Ask groups to share their revised versions with the class, explaining how they improved the writing. Then display **Transparency 36** to show the same how-to article written at an excellent level. Have each group compare this with their revised versions. Remind students that although the two papers vary, they may both be considered excellent. Then have students review the how-to articles they wrote to raise their scores.

Objective

- Revise a how-to article to raise the writing score from a 3 to a 6

CREATE A RUBRIC

Make copies of the blank rubric form on pages 159 and 160 in the **Teacher's Resource Book** and distribute to students. Remind students that an expository writing rubric should assess whether the how-to article presents step-by-step instructions that explain how to complete a specific task; provides clear details that are easy to follow; and uses time-order words and spatial words to make instructions clearer. Students may choose to create simplified rubrics, but their rubrics must have six levels.

Transparency 30

Two Kinds of Wild Weather
by Glenda G.

Which weather condition do you think is scarier, hurricanes or tornados? Hurricanes are fast, with a wind speed of 150–200 miles per hour, but tornados can be even faster, with speeds of up to 300 miles per hour.

While a hurricane can last a week, tornados are usually over in minutes. Yet both weather conditions can leave a trail of destruction. The average width of a hurricane is 300 miles, whereas a tornado is rarely wider than a mile.

Predicting when hurricanes will hit is easier than predicting when tornados will hit. Forecasters can tell whether a hurricane will hit about two days to ten hours in advance. However, forecasters may have only twenty minutes to warn people that a tornado is on the way.

Fortunately, hurricanes don't happen every day. The average number per year is one hundred worldwide. By contrast, there are more than 1,000 tornados in the United States alone.

In conclusion, the hurricane is more predictable, lasts longer, and has a wider range than the tornado. Yet both are scary weather conditions.

Unit Writing Transparency 30

6-Point Writing Rubric

Use this six-point rubric to assess student writing.

SCORING RUBRIC					
6 Points	**5 Points**	**4 Points**	**3 Points**	**2 Points**	**1 Point**
Focus Writing is well focused on the topic and demonstrates a strong sense of command and completeness or wholeness.	**Focus** Writing is focused on the topic and demonstrates a sense of completeness or wholeness.	**Focus** Writing is generally focused on the topic, although some loosely related information may be included.	**Focus** Writing is generally focused on the topic, although irrelevant and extraneous information is included.	**Focus** Writing is somewhat related to the topic, but offers little relevant information.	**Focus** Writing minimally addresses the topic, with little or no relevant information offered.
Organization Writing is logically organized, and includes transitional devices. An interesting variety of sentence structures has been used.	**Organization** Writing has a generally successful organizational pattern. Various sentence structures have been used.	**Organization** An organizational pattern is evident. Lapses in the pattern may occur, however. An effort to vary sentences is evident, but several sentences are of simple construction.	**Organization** An organizational pattern has been attempted, but lapses occur. Some sentence variety appears, but many sentences are of simple construction.	**Organization** An organizational pattern is hardly evident. Most sentences are of simple construction.	**Organization** No organizational pattern is evident. Sentence structure is simple at best.
Support The topic is supported by ample details and ideas. Word choice is intelligent and precise.	**Support** Adequate supporting ideas and details are included. Word choice is adequate but may not be precise.	**Support** Some supporting details and ideas are not fully developed or are not specific. Word choice is generally adequate.	**Support** Some supporting ideas are included, but ideas are not developed. Word choice is limited, predictable, and often vague.	**Support** For the writing related to the topic, few supporting details or examples are offered. Word choice is limited and immature.	**Support** Few if any supporting details appear or are developed; ideas and examples that do appear are irrelevant. Word choice is immature.
Conventions Grammar is correct, as is punctuation and spelling. All sentences are complete, except when fragments are used purposefully.	**Conventions** Punctuation, grammar, and spelling are generally correct. Most sentences are complete, although some fragments appear.	**Conventions** Knowledge of grammar, spelling, and punctuation conventions is evident. Sentence fragments appear.	**Conventions** Although knowledge of grammar, spelling, and punctuation conventions is evident, errors occur. Several sentence fragments appear.	**Conventions** Frequent errors occur in basic grammar, spelling, and punctuation. A number of sentence fragments impede communication.	**Conventions** Frequent errors in grammar, spelling, and punctuation impede communication, as do numerous sentence fragments.

U   Writing that is unscorable or unrelated to the topic or is illegible.

Go to **www.macmillanmh.com** for Anchor Papers for sample expository how-to articles at each writing level.

Constructed Response Rubric

Use these rubrics to assess short and extended responses.

FCAT Reading Short-Response Rubric	
Score	**Description**
2	The student's response demonstrates a thorough understanding of the comprehension skills needed to answer the question. Details and examples are used to support the answer and clearly come from the text.
1	The student's response demonstrates a partial understanding of the comprehension skills needed to answer the question. Some of the support and important details and/or examples are too general or are left out.
0	The student's response demonstrates a complete lack of understanding of the question or the student has left the answer blank.

See Anchor Papers for short response on the **FCAT Anchor Papers** CD-ROM.

FCAT Reading Extended-Response Rubric	
Score	**Description**
4	The student's response demonstrates a thorough understanding of the comprehension skills needed to answer the question. Details and examples are used to support the answer and clearly come from the text.
3	The student's response demonstrates an understanding of the comprehension skills needed to answer the question. Details and examples used as support are not complete or are not text-based.
2	The student's response demonstrates a partial understanding of the comprehension skills needed to answer the question. Some of the support and important details and/or examples are too general or are left out.
1	The student's response is incomplete and does not demonstrate an understanding of the question.
0	The student's response demonstrates a complete lack of understanding of the question or the student has left the answer blank.

See Anchor Papers for extended response on the **FCAT Anchor Papers** CD-ROM.

Unit 6 Computer Literacy

Objectives

- Learn how to create a new slide in a presentation program
- Practice adding multimedia to a slide
- Discuss how to make a quality presentation

Materials

- www.macmillanmh.com
- Presentation program

Vocabulary

presentation a show given for an audience

clip art electronic art that can be inserted into a document

slide a two-dimensional image designed for use on a computer during a presentation

layout the way objects, such as words and graphics, are arranged on a file

LA.5.1.6 Student develops vocabulary

Making a Presentation

ACCESS PRIOR KNOWLEDGE

Discuss with students:

- When would it be helpful to use a presentation program?

- When you present information to other people, what are some different ways to capture their attention?

EXPLAIN LA.5.6.3.2 Use media sources to transmit information

Introduce the lesson vocabulary by writing each word on the board and discussing its definition.

- Tell students that they can create a multimedia **presentation** to share information. Adding **clip art** to a presentation **slide** can make it more interesting. Varying the **layout** of each slide will also improve the presentation.

Students can use their own experiences and knowledge, as well as technology, and other sources, such as technical manuals or how-to books to solve problems when creating a media presentation.

MODEL LA.5.6.4 Student develops technology skills

- Show students how to open a new slide in a presentation program and choose the layout they would like to use.

- Show students how to use the program's clip art library or search for clip art on the Internet.

- Add brief bulleted text to your slide that corresponds with the clip art you selected.

Presentation Techniques

- Explain that information presented on the computer should be kept brief so that it is easy for the audience to read. Use bulleted text whenever possible.

- Multimedia presentations make presentations more enjoyable for the audience. You can use clip art instead of extra text to help illustrate your point.

- Learn from others. Watch other people and see what they do. Then rehearse your own presentation!

LA.5.5.2.1 Listen and speak to gain and share information through formal presentations

GUIDED PRACTICE

Have students connect to www.macmillanmh.com and go to **Computer Literacy Lesson Grade 5 Unit 6.**

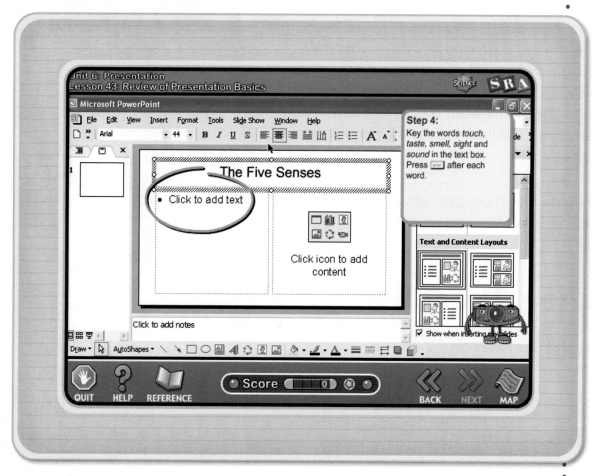

 The online practice lesson is an excerpt from SRA TechKnowledge. For information about the full SRA TechKnowledge program, go to **www.sratechknowledge.com**

Safety Alert

Remind students never to eat or drink around the computers. Spilled food or liquids can permanently damage computers.

Technology in Writing

Remind students that when they are preparing written presentations, technology can help them in all parts of the process—including designing, producing, and presenting their final composition. Using the information from technology and other sources can also help them produce writing that develops and supports independent ideas and contains sources and citations.

LA.5.6.4 Student develops essential technology skills

Leveled Practice

Approaching

Have students create a presentation about themselves with two or three slides. Students can search the Internet or the presentation program library for clip art to insert into their slides.

On Level

Have students create a two or three slide presentation about themselves with clip art and practice presenting in front of a small group of students.

Beyond Level

Have students research a "Great Idea" like an invention and create a presentation with several slides. Students can include clip art or photos from the Internet. Make sure they cite their material correctly.

Theme Project Wrap-Up

Research and Inquiry

After students complete Step 1, Step 2, Step 3, and Step 4 of their project, have them work on the following:

Step 5

LA.5.6.3.2 Use media sources to transmit information

Create the Presentation Have students share what they learned by creating a multimedia presentation on the great idea they researched. Provide students with the information on the Student Checklist so they can check their work. Encourage students to explain and justify their preferences for media choices.

Step 6

Review and Evaluate Use these questions to help you and students evaluate their research and presentation:

A Great Idea All Wrapped Up

Teacher Checklist

Assess the Research Process

Planning the Project

✔ Participated in theme discussion

✔ Identified a great idea to research

✔ Identified and located sources

Doing the Project

✔ Used a hypothesis for research

✔ Evaluated sources, took notes

✔ Skimmed and scanned to locate information

Assess the Presentation

Speaking

✔ Used clear and specific vocabulary

✔ Used vocabulary related to the topic

✔ Addressed audience's questions

Representing

✔ Developed multimedia project

✔ Used text and visuals

✔ Chose visuals that engaged the audience

Assess the Listener

✔ Contributed to discussion after presentation

✔ Expressed personal opinions or ideas

✔ Made at least one positive comment about the work

✔ Interpreted and applied information to new situations and to solving problems

Student Checklist

Research Process

✔ Did you research a great idea?

✔ Did you skim and scan to locate information?

✔ Did you evaluate sources, take notes, and cite sources?

Presenting

Speaking

✔ Did you practice your presentation?

✔ Did you use an organized structure?

✔ Did you include details and examples?

Representing

✔ Did you plan and develop a multimedia presentation?

✔ Did you choose and justify your media choices?

✔ Did you select a wide variety of media?

Use the rubric below to evaluate media presentations.

SCORING RUBRIC FOR THEME PROJECTS			
4 Excellent	**3** Good	**2** Fair	**1** Unsatisfactory
The student • presents the information in a clear and interesting way • uses words and (where relevant) visuals that present important information • may offer sophisticated reflections	**The student** • presents the information in a fairly clear way • uses words and (where relevant) visuals that present relevant information • may offer thoughtful reflections	**The student** • struggles to present the information clearly • may use adequate words and visuals • may offer irrelevant reflections	**The student:** • may not grasp the task • may present sketchy information in a disorganized way • may have extreme difficulty with research

 Home-School Connection

Invite family members, other students, and members of the community to attend students' presentations of their projects.

■ Introduce each guest by name and relationship to students or the community. Videotape the presentations for family members to borrow or to show at the parent/teacher conferences.

■ Before the event, as part of your character building feature, remind students to cooperate so the presentations go smoothly and make the guests feel welcome. Remind listeners and speakers to respect the age, gender, position, and cultural traditions of the audience and each other.

LA.5.5.2.2 Demonstrate appropriate use of supporting graphics

■ Remind speakers to use notes, outlines, and visual aids appropriate to the presentation, to respect the age, gender, position, culture, and interests of the audience, and to show respect for others in verbal and physical communication.

■ Encourage students to demonstrate competence in active listening by interpreting and applying information to new situations and in solving problems.

LA.5.5.2.1 Listen to gain and share information through formal presentations

■ Remind listeners to keep in mind the roles of the communication process, including persuasion, critical analysis, and explanation, as they focus their attention on the speaker and form opinions. Encourage listeners to go beyond information given by a speaker, make inferences, and draw appropriate conclusions.

LA.5.5.2 Student applies speaking strategies

■ Remind speakers to use self-monitoring techniques to assess their effectiveness. They should ask themselves: *Can I discriminate among messages, questions, or responses from the audience and tell how they are different? Can I figure out what the messages, questions, or responses from the audience mean to me as a speaker?*

■ Remind speakers to incorporate peer feedback and teacher suggestions for revisons in content, organization, and delivery as they prepare to give their presentation to another audience.

■ After the presentations are complete, have students work in small groups or alone to write evaluations of the performances and media presentations.

Grade 5
FCAT Format
Unit
Assessment
Macmillan/McGraw-Hill

Administer the Test

UNIT 6 READING ASSESSMENT, pp. 99–114

TESTED SKILLS AND STRATEGIES

COMPREHENSION STRATEGIES AND SKILLS

- Strategies: Monitor Comprehension, Summarize
- Skills: Chronological Order, Plot Development, Techniques of Persuasion, Relevant Facts and Details

VOCABULARY STRATEGIES

- Dictionary
- Multiple-Meaning Words
- Context Clues
- Word Parts

TEXT FEATURES AND STUDY SKILLS

- Venn diagram
- Photographs and captions
- Everyday communications

GRAMMAR, MECHANICS, USAGE

- Prepositions, prepositional phrases
- Adverbs
- Sentence combining
- Adjectives vs adverbs
- Correcting double negatives
- Punctuation

WRITING

- Expository

Use Multiple Assessments for Instructional Planning

To create instructional profiles for your students, look for patterns in the results from any of the following assessments.

Fluency Assessment

Plan appropriate fluency-building activities and practice to help all students achieve the following fluency goal: **129–149 WCMP.**

Grades 1–5
Fluency
Assessment
Macmillan/McGraw-Hill

Running Records

Use the instructional reading level determined by the Running Record calculations for regrouping decisions.

Grades K–6
Running
Records
LEVELS: REBUS–80
Macmillan/McGraw-Hill

Benchmark Assessments

Administer tests three times a year as an additional measure of both student progress and the effectiveness of the instructional program.

Grade 5
FCAT Format
Benchmark
Assessment
Macmillan/McGraw-Hill

CD ROM

Technology

Progress Reporter
Macmillan/McGraw-Hill

- Administer the **Unit Assessment** electronically
- Create alternative tests using the item bank
- Score all tests electronically
- Available on CD-ROM or online.

Analyze the Data

Use information from a variety of informal and formal assessments, as well as your own judgment, to assist in your instructional planning. Students who consistently score at the lowest end of each range should be evaluated for Intervention. Use the **Diagnostic Assessment** in the Intervention Teacher's Edition.

Diagnose		Prescribe
ASSESSMENTS	**IF...**	**THEN...**
UNIT TEST	0–23 questions correct	Reteach tested skills using the **Additional Lessons** (pp. T1–T12).
FLUENCY ASSESSMENT		
Oral Reading Fluency	120–128 WCPM	 Fluency Solutions
	0–119 WCPM	Evaluate for Intervention
RUNNING RECORDS	Level 50 or below	Reteach comprehension skills using the **Additional Lessons** (pp. T1–T5). Provide additional Fluency activities

READING
Triumphs
AN INTERVENTION PROGRAM

Also Available

To place students in the Intervention Program, use the **Diagnostic Assessment** in the Intervention Teacher's Edition.

End-of-Unit Assessment

Glossary

Introduce students to the Glossary by reading through the introduction and looking over the pages with them. Encourage the class to talk about what they see.

Words in a glossary, like words in a dictionary, are listed in **alphabetical order.** Point out the **guide words** at the top of each page that tell the first and last words appearing on that page.

ENTRIES

Point out examples of **main entries,** or entry words, and entries. Read through a sample entry with the class, identifying each part. Have students note the order in which information is given: entry word(s), syllable division, pronunciation respelling, part of speech, definition(s), example sentence(s).

Note if more than one definition is given for a word, the definitions are numbered. Note the format used for a word that is more than one part of speech.

Review the **parts of speech** by identifying each in a sentence:

Inter.	article	n.	conj.	adj.	n.
Wow!	A	dictionary	and	useful	glossary

v.	adv.	pron.	prep.	n.
tell	almost	everything	about	words!

HOMOGRAPHS/HOMOPHONES/HOMONYMS

Point out that some entries are for multiple-meaning words called **homographs.** Homographs have the same spellings but have different origins and meanings, and, in some cases, different pronunciations.

Explain that students should not confuse homographs with **homophones** or **homonyms.** Homophones are words that have the same pronunciation but have different spellings and meanings. Homonyms are words that have the same pronunciation and spelling but have different meanings. Provide students with examples.

PRONUNCIATION KEY

Explain the use of the pronunciation key (either the short key, at the bottom of every other page, or the long key, at the beginning of the Glossary). Demonstrate the difference between primary stress and secondary stress by pronouncing a word with both. Pronounce the words both correctly and incorrectly to give students a clearer understanding of the proper pronunciations.

WORD HISTORY

The Word History feature explains the **etymology** of select words. Explain that *etymology* is the history of a word from its origin to its present form. A word's etymology explains which language it comes from and what changes have occurred in its spelling and/or meaning. Many English words are derivatives of words from other languages, such as Latin or Greek. Derivatives are formed from base or root words.

Glossary
What Is a Glossary?

A glossary can help you find the **meanings** of words in this book that you may not know. The words in the glossary are listed in **alphabetical order**. **Guide words** at the top of each page tell you the first and last words on the page.

Each word is divided into syllables. The way to pronounce the word is given next. You can understand the pronunciation respelling by using the **pronunciation key**. A shorter key appears at the bottom of every other page. When a word has more than one syllable, a dark accent mark (ˈ) shows which syllable is stressed. In some words a light accent mark (ˈ) shows which syllable has a less heavy stress. Sometimes an entry includes a second meaning for the word.

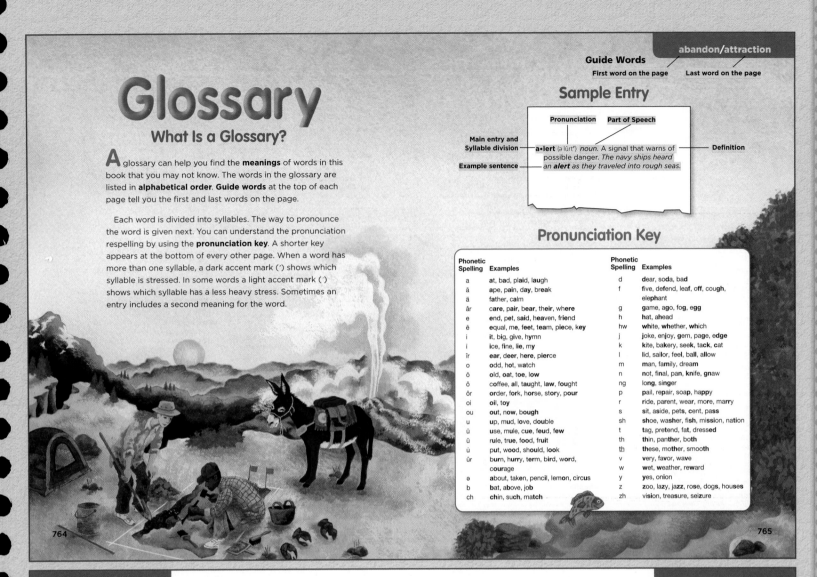

Guide Words
First word on the page   Last word on the page
abandon/attraction

Sample Entry

Pronunciation   Part of Speech

Main entry and Syllable division — **a•lert** (ə lûrtˈ) *noun.* A signal that warns of possible danger. *The navy ships heard an **alert** as they traveled into rough seas.* — Definition

Example sentence

Pronunciation Key

Phonetic Spelling	Examples	Phonetic Spelling	Examples
a	at, bad, plaid, laugh	d	dear, soda, bad
ā	ape, pain, day, break	f	five, defend, leaf, off, cough, elephant
ä	father, calm		
âr	care, pair, bear, their, where	g	game, ago, fog, egg
e	end, pet, said, heaven, friend	h	hat, ahead
ē	equal, me, feet, team, piece, key	hw	white, whether, which
i	it, big, give, hymn	j	joke, enjoy, gem, page, edge
ī	ice, fine, lie, my	k	kite, bakery, seek, tack, cat
îr	ear, deer, here, pierce	l	lid, sailor, feel, ball, allow
o	odd, hot, watch	m	man, family, dream
ō	old, oat, toe, low	n	not, final, pan, knife, gnaw
ô	coffee, all, taught, law, fought	ng	long, singer
ôr	order, fork, horse, story, pour	p	pail, repair, soap, happy
oi	oil, toy	r	ride, parent, wear, more, marry
ou	out, now, bough	s	sit, aside, pets, cent, pass
u	up, mud, love, double	sh	shoe, washer, fish, mission, nation
ū	use, mule, cue, feud, few	t	tag, pretend, fat, dressed
ü	rule, true, food, fruit	th	thin, panther, both
ù	put, wood, should, look	th	these, mother, smooth
ûr	burn, hurry, term, bird, word, courage	v	very, favor, wave
ə	about, taken, pencil, lemon, circus	w	wet, weather, reward
b	bat, above, job	y	yes, onion
ch	chin, such, match	z	zoo, lazy, jazz, rose, dogs, houses
		zh	vision, treasure, seizure

764

765

Aa

a•ban•don (ə banˈdən) *verb.* To leave and not return. *The sailors jumped into the ocean when they were given the order to **abandon** the ship.*

ac•com•pa•ny (ə kumˈpə nē) *verb.* To go together with. *My friend decided to **accompany** me to the store so that I would have someone to talk to.*

ad•just•ed (ə jusˈtid) *verb.* Changed or arranged to fit a need or demand. *We **adjusted** the schedule to include two more singers in the program.*

ad•ver•tise•ment (adˈvər tīzˈmənt, ad vûrˈtis mənt) *noun.* A public notice that tells people about a product, event, or something a person needs. *A successful **advertisement** will convince shoppers to buy a product.*

a•lert (ə lûrtˈ) *noun.* A heightened sense of watchfulness for possible danger. *The navy ship was put on **alert** after an ice storm was reported in the area.*

a•mend•ment (ə mendˈmənt) *noun.* A change in a law caused by voting of government officials or changes to the Constitution. *Women were given the right to vote in all states by an **amendment** to the Constitution.*

a•nat•o•my (ə natˈə mē) *noun.* The structure of an animal or plant or any of its parts. *Medical students study **anatomy** to learn how to treat illnesses in people.*

an•chored (angˈkərd) *verb.* Being held in place by a heavy metal device or object. *The crew is lucky they **anchored** the boat to a rock because the sudden storm would have blown them far from shore.*

ap•pre•ci•a•tion (ə prēˈshē āˈshən) *noun.* A feeling of being thankful. *To show his **appreciation**, Javier gave the boy who found his wallet a small reward.*

a•rous•ing (ə rouzˈing) *verb.* Stirring up or causing excitement. *The opposing team's fans were **arousing** a lot of attention in the bleachers with their cheering.*

ar•roy•o (ə roiˈō) *noun.* A small river or stream. *The **arroyo** had plenty of fish.*

ar•ti•facts (ärˈti fakts) *noun, plural.* Things left over from an earlier time. *Some tools are **artifacts** from a time when they were useful to people.*

as•tron•o•mers (ə stronˈə mərz) *noun, plural.* Students of or experts in astronomy, the science that deals with the planets, starts, and other heavenly bodies. *The **astronomers** measured the distance between the earth and the moon.*

at•mos•phere (atˈmas fîr) *noun.* **1.** The layer of gases that surrounds Earth. *We watched on television as the space shuttle entered the **atmosphere** after its mission to the moon was over.* **2.** A surrounding mood or environment. *Our house has a merry **atmosphere** during the holiday season.*

at•tor•ney (ə tûrˈnē) *noun.* A lawyer; one who helps with legal matters. *Before arguing your case in court, it may be a good idea to hire an **attorney**.*

at•trac•tion (ə trakˈshən) *noun.* A person or thing that draws attention. *The new baby elephant was an **attraction** that drew a lot of people to the zoo.*

---

au•to•graph (ôˈtə graf) *noun.* A person's signature written in that person's own handwriting. *My sister got her favorite singer's **autograph**.*

a•vail•a•ble (ə vāˈlə bəl) *adjective.* Possible to get. *There were five seats **available**.*

Bb

bac•te•ri•a (bak tîrˈē ə) *noun.* One-celled organisms so small they can only be seen through a microscope. *Some good kinds of **bacteria** help us, and some make us ill.*

banned (band) *verb.* Officially forbidden; prohibited. *The school boards **banned** books that contain inaccurate information.*

bed•lam (bedˈlam) *noun.* A place or condition of wild uproar and confusion. *There was **Bedlam** in the hallways when the fire alarm sounded.*

be•hav•ior (bi hāvˈyər) *noun.* A way of acting. *The campers were yelled at by the counselor for their mischievous **behavior**.*

bi•ol•o•gy (bī olˈə jē) *adjective.* Characterized by the study of living things. *The **biology** teacher enjoyed the study of plants.* —*noun.* The study of living things. *Biology is my favorite subject in school.*

blared (blârd) *verb.* Made a loud, harsh sound. *The trumpets **blared** as the Olympic ceremonies began.*

blurt•ed (blûrtˈid) *verb.* Said suddenly or without thinking. *I **blurted** out the answer before the teacher finished the question.*

boy•cott (boiˈkot) *noun.* A planned and organized refusal to have anything to do with a person, group, or nation. *The strikers called for a **boycott** of the company's products.*

bri•dle (brīˈdəl) *noun.* The part of a horse's or donkey's harness that fits over the head and is used to guide or control the animal. *The cowboy fitted the **bridle** over the horse's head before going for a ride.*

brim•ming (brimˈing) *adjective.* Full to the upper edge of a container. *The **brimming** mugs were filled with hot cocoa and whipped cream.*

buf•fet¹ (bufˈit) *verb.* To knock about. *We felt the rough water **buffet** the raft.*

buf•fet² (bəfˈā, bù fāˈ) *noun.* **1.** A piece of furniture with a flat surface for serving food. *Please put the rice on the **buffet** after it has been passed around the table.* **2.** A meal laid out on a table so that guests can serve themselves. *The **buffet** at the wedding featured foods from many countries.*

bul•le•tin board (bù lˈi tin bôrd) *noun.* A board for posting notices, announcements, and pictures. *The teacher uses a **bulletin board** to post class work.*

bun•dle (bunˈdəl) *noun.* A group of things held together. *The deliveryman left a **bundle** of newspapers outside the grocery store.*

bur•dens (bûrˈdənz) *noun, plural.* Things that are carried. *The mule carried the **burdens** down the trail into the canyon.*

Cc

cam•ou•flage (kamˈə fläzhˈ) *noun.* Any disguise, appearance, or behavior that serves to conceal or deceive, such as the protective coloring of an animal. *An octopus uses **camouflage** to change its skin color and blend into its surroundings.*

at; āpe; fär; câre; end; mē; it; īce; pîerce; hot; ōld; sông; fôrk; oil; out; up; ūse; rüle; pùll; tûrn; chin; sing; shop; thin; this; hw in white; zh in treasure.

The symbol ə stands for the unstressed vowel sound in about, taken, pencil, lemon, and circus.

766

767

Glossary

can•celed (kan′səld) *verb.* Did away with, stopped, or called off. *The picnic was **canceled** due to rain.*

ca•pa•ble (kā′pə bəl) *adjective.* Having skill or power; able. *The new planes are **capable** of even greater speed.*

car•ni•vores (kär′nə vôrz′) *noun, plural.* Animals or plants such as sharks, eagles, dogs, and Venus's-flytraps that feed chiefly on flesh. *Lions are **carnivores** who hunt and feed on smaller animals.*

cat•e•go•ries (kat′i gôr′ēz) *noun, plural.* Groups or classes of things. *The menu was divided into three **categories**: snacks, main courses, and desserts.*

cel•e•bra•tion (sel′ə brā′shən) *noun.* The act of honoring with festivities. *Grandma's 100th birthday called for a big **celebration**.*

cha•me•le•on (kə mēl′yən) *noun.* Any of various small, slow-moving lizards that can change the color of their skin to match their surroundings. *The **chameleon** on the tree bark turned brown.*

char•ac•ter•is•tics (kar′ik tə ris′tiks) *noun, plural.* Qualities or features that are typical of or serve to distinguish a person, group, or thing from others. *Courage and bravery are fine **characteristics** to possess.*

chis•eled (chi′zəld) *verb.* Cut or shaped with a sharp metal tool called a chisel. *The numbers were **chiseled** into the stone next to the front doors.*

civ•ic (siv′ik) *adjective.* Of or relating to a citizen or citizenship. *It is the civic duty of each person to vote.*

civ•i•li•za•tion (siv′ə lə zā′shən) *noun.* A society in which agriculture, trade, government, art, and science are highly developed. *The museum had a number of objects that showed how **civilization** has developed over the last 600 years.*

clenched (klencht) *verb.* Grasped or closed tightly. *The boy **clenched** his fist when he saw the bully walking angrily towards him.*

cli•mate (klī′mit) *noun.* 1. *The typical weather conditions of a particular place. Alaska's climate is cold most of the year.* 2. Any place or region considered in terms of its typical weather conditions. *My mom likes a warm **climate** for swimming.*

colo•nel (kûr′nəl) *noun.* One of the ranks of a military officer. *Kevin Andretti was promoted to full **colonel** last month.*

com•bined (kəm bīnd′) *adjective.* Characterized by being joined together or united. *Thanks to the **combined** efforts of the voters in our city, the mayor was reelected.* —*verb.* Joined together; united. *The baker **combined** eggs, butter, sugar, and flour to make cookie dough.*

com•menced (kə menst′) *verb.* Began or started. *When the audience was seated and quiet, the play **commenced**.*

com•pan•ion (kəm pan′yən) *noun.* A person or animal who keeps somebody company. *A dog can be a good **companion** for a lonely person.*

com•pelled (kem peld′) *verb.* Urged, or caused with force. *The rain **compelled** us to postpone our picnic.*

com•pe•ti•tion (kom′pi tish′ən) *noun.* The act of trying to win or gain something from another person or other people. *We're in **competition** with two other teams for the swimming championship.*

com•plex (kəm pleks′) *adjective.* Hard to understand or do. *The math problems were very **complex** because they involved many steps.*

con•sent•ed (kən sen′tid) *verb.* Gave permission or agreed to. *My mom **consented** to my sleeping over at Maria's house for her slumber party.*

con•tact (kon′takt) *noun.* A touching or meeting of persons or things. *My uncle burned his arm when it came in **contact** with the hot stove.*

con•tam•i•na•tion (kən tam′ə nā′shən) *noun.* The process of spoiling or the state of being spoiled; pollution. *Food should be kept covered to prevent **contamination**.*

con•ti•nent (kon′tə nənt) *noun.* One of the seven large land areas on Earth. *I live in the United States, which is on the **continent** of North America.*

co•op•er•a•tion (kō op′ərā′shən) *noun.* Working with another or others for a common purpose. *With **cooperation**, the friends quickly decorated the room for the surprise party.*

co•or•di•na•tion (kō ôr′də nā′shən) *noun.* The ability of parts of the body to work together well. *A gymnast needs good **coordination** when performing on the balance beam.*

cor•ri•dor (kôr′i dər, kor′i dər) *noun.* A long passageway or hallway. *Students walked down the **corridor** to the gymnasium.*

creased (krēst) *adjective.* Characterized by lines or marked by wrinkling. *My teacher would not accept my **creased** book report because it was messy looking.*

cred•it (kred′it) *noun.* **1.** Praise or honor; something owed to a person. *The students who included a visual display with their speeches earned extra **credit**.* **2.** Trust in a person to pay a debt at a later time. *The store gave me **credit** today so I could buy the shirt and pay for it on Friday.*

cross•breed•ing (krôs′brē′ding) *verb.* Breeding different kinds of plants or animals in order to produce hybrids. *The farmer was **crossbreeding** small, sweet peppers with large, tasteless peppers to get large, sweet peppers.*

Dd

dam•ag•es (dam′ij iz) *noun, plural.* Harm that makes things less valuable or useful. ***Damages** to the city totaled in the millions of dollars after the storm.*

dan•gling (dang′ling) *verb.* Hanging loosely. *The diamonds **dangling** from Erin's ears looked pretty in the light.*

de•cen•cy (dē′sən sē) *noun.* Proper behavior, as in speech, actions, and dress. *Mary had the **decency** to admit she made a mistake.*

ded•i•cat•ed (ded′i kā′tid) *verb.* Set apart for a special purpose or use. *The mayor **dedicated** a new museum to the memory of the founders of the city.*

de•fec•tive (di fek′tiv) *adjective.* Having a flaw or weakness; not perfect. *The zipper was **defective** so the coat wouldn't close all the way up.*

del•i•ca•cies (del′i kə sēs) *noun, plural.* Rare or excellent food. *At the food festival there were **delicacies** from around the world.*

at; āpe; fär; câre; end; mē; it; īce; pîerce; hot; ōld; sông; fôrk; oil; out; up; ūse; rüle; pu̇ll; tûrn; **ch**in; sing; shop; thin; **th**is; **hw** in white; **zh** in treasure.

The symbol **ə** stands for the unstressed vowel sound in about, taken, pencil, lemon, and circus.

de•liv•er•ing (di liv′ə ring) *verb.* Taking or carrying something to a particular place or person. *My job is **delivering** groceries to people's homes.*

dense (dens) *adjective.* Packed closely together. *The smoke was very **dense**, making it difficult for firefighters to see.*

de•scend•ed (di sen′did) *verb.* Moved from a higher place to a lower one. *The woman **descended** down the mountain on skis.*

de•spair (di spâr′) *noun.* A complete loss of hope. *The student was filled with **despair** when he couldn't complete his assignment for tomorrow's deadline.*

de•struc•tion (di struk′shən) *noun.* Great damage or ruin. *The tornadoes caused a lot of **destruction** in our neighborhood.*

di•ag•nose (dī′əg nōs′) *verb.* To make a ruling as to the nature of an illness. *The doctor can **diagnose** the patient's illness based on a description of the symptoms.*

dis•as•ters (di zas′tərz) *noun, plural.* Events that cause much suffering, distress, or loss. *Hurricanes are natural **disasters**.*

dis•cus•sions (di skush′ənz) *noun, plural.* Acts of talking about something or exchanging opinions. *There were many **discussions** among the voters about the elections.*

dis•man•tled (dis man′təld) *verb.* Took something apart piece by piece. *The workers dismantled the outdoor stage after the concert.*

dis•miss (dis mis′) *verb.* To take away the job of, or fire. *The manager needed to **dismiss** one of his workers for doing a poor job.*

dis•re•spect•ful (dis′ri spekt′fəl) *adjective.* Having or showing disrespect; rude; impolite. *It is **disrespectful** behavior to make fun of your guests.*

di•verse (di vûrs′, dī vûrs′) *adjective.* Not all the same; varied. *People in my neighborhood come from **diverse** backgrounds.*

dor•mant (dôr′mənt) *adjective.* Temporarily quiet or not active. *Many tourists visited the dormant volcano because the chance of an eruption was low.*

Ee

ease (ēz) *verb.* To move slowly or carefully. *I tried to **ease** the heavy clock off the table without dropping or scratching it.*

ec•o•sys•tem (ek′ō sis′təm, ē′kō sis′təm) *noun.* All the living things within a particular area and their relationship to each other and their physical environment. *The trees, birds, and squirrels help form a forest **ecosystem**.*

ed•u•cate (ej′ə kāt′) *verb.* To teach or train. *It is important to **educate** the students about dangers in the science lab so that no one gets hurt.*

e•lect•ed (i lek′tid) *verb.* Chosen by voting. *The class **elected** a representative to discuss the issue with the principal.*

el•e•gant (el′i gənt) *adjective.* Showing richness and good taste; showing grace and dignity. *The **elegant** dress was trimmed with gold lace.*

el•e•ment•ar•y (el′ə men′tə rē, el′ə men′trē) *adjective.* Dealing with the simple parts or beginnings of something. *We learned **elementary** facts about life cycles by observing how things change as they grow.*

el•e•ments (el′ə mənts) *noun, plural.* Basic parts from which something is made or formed. *A story should have these basic **elements**: a beginning, middle, and end.*

e•merged (i mûrjd′) *verb.* Came into view. *After the giant wave knocked over Pietro, he **emerged** from the water with a piece of seaweed in his mouth.*

en•light•ened (en lī′tənd) *verb.* Gave knowledge or wisdom to; freed from prejudice or ignorance. *The teacher **enlightened** me about new books.*

en•list•ed (en lis′tid) *verb.* Joined the military voluntarily. *Nan's brother **enlisted** in the army after he graduated from high school.*

en•thu•si•asm (en thü′zē az′əm) *noun.* Eager and lively interest. *The audience expressed **enthusiasm** by applauding.*

en•vi•ron•ment (en vī′rən mənt, en vī′ərn mənt) *noun.* The air, water, soil, and all the other things that surround a person, animal, or plant. *Living things need time to get used to changes in an **environment**.*

e•qual•i•ty (i kwol′i tē) *noun.* The quality or condition of being equal. *The Constitution of the United States provides for the **equality** of all Americans under the law.*

e•qua•tor (i kwā′tər) *noun.* An imaginary line encircling the earth halfway between the North and South Poles. *Countries close to the **equator** are the warmest on Earth.*

e•rupt•ed (i rup′tid) *verb.* Forced out or burst forth. *The area was filled with lava after the volcano **erupted**.*

e•vap•o•rates (i vap′ə rāts′) *verb.* To be changed from a liquid or solid into a vapor. *Water **evaporates** when boiled.*

ex•hib•its (eg zib′its) *noun, plural.* Things shown on display. *We went to see the **exhibits** of fossils at the museum.*

ex•pe•di•tion (ek′spi dish′ən) *noun.* A journey with a specific purpose. *The members of the **expedition** had to go back down the mountain because the wind was too strong.*

Ff

fare (fâr) *noun.* The cost of a ride on a bus, train, airplane, ship, or taxi. *My mother paid my **fare** on the bus.*

fire•ball (fīr′bôl′) *noun.* A bright body from space that may trail bright sparks. *The **fireball** shot across the sky and briefly lit up our backyard.*

flick•ered (flik′ərd) *verb.* Shone or burned with an unsteady or wavering light. *The candles **flickered** in the breeze.*

flukes (flüks) *noun, plural.* Chance happenings; unexpected or accidental events, especially lucky ones. *Some discoveries were **flukes** and resulted when scientists were trying to find other things.*

fo•cused (fō′kəst) *verb.* Concentrated or directed attention on. *The basketball player was so **focused** on scoring that he didn't hear the fans roaring.*

for•bid•den (fər bid′ən, fôr bid′ən) *verb.* Ordered not to do something; not allowed. *The children were **forbidden** to play outside after dark.*

frac•tures (frak′chərz) *noun, plural.* Cracks, splits, or breaks, as in a bone. *The boy's leg had multiple **fractures** after the accident.*

fra•grance (frā′grəns) *noun.* A sweet or pleasing smell. *Roses have a strong **fragrance**.*

frig•id (frij′id) *adjective.* Very cold. *The **frigid** water was full of ice and snow.*

at; āpe; fär; câre; end; mē; it; īce; pîerce; hot; ōld; sông; fôrk; oil; out; up; ūse; rüle; pu̇ll; tûrn; **ch**in; sing; shop; thin; **th**is; **hw** in white; **zh** in treasure.

The symbol **ə** stands for the unstressed vowel sound in about, taken, pencil, lemon, and circus.

frus•trat•ed (frus´trā tid) *verb.* Kept from doing something. *Lita was* ***frustrated*** *in trying to light the candle because of the wind.*

func•tion (fungk´shən) *verb.* To work or act; to serve. *Mr. Martinez will* ***function*** *as the principal while Mrs. Arnold is out of town.*

fused (fūzd) *verb.* To blend or unite. *All the crayons in the box were* ***fused*** *together because they were left in the hot sun.*

Gg

gi•gan•tic (jī gan´tik) *adjective.* Like a giant; huge and powerful. *The airplane looked* ***gigantic*** *when I saw it up close.*

gla•cier (glā´shər) *noun.* A large mass of ice moving slowly over some land surface or down a valley. *The* ***glacier*** *formed very slowly over time from a great deal of snow.*

glimpse (glimps) *noun.* A brief look or a passing glance. *I caught a* ***glimpse*** *of the actor as he dashed into the car.*

gnarled (närld) *adjective.* Having many rough, twisted knots. *The worker's hands looked as* ***gnarled*** *as a tree trunk.*

gos•siped (gos´ipt) *verb.* Talked or spread rumors, often unfriendly, about matters related to another person. *Kayla* ***gossiped*** *to her friends about Beth because she was jealous of Beth's good grades.*

gov•er•nor (guv´ər nər) *noun.* The person elected to be the head of a state government in the United States, or of a territory. *The* ***governor*** *of my state will sign the new law.*

grav•i•ty (grav´i tē) *noun.* The force that pulls things toward the center of Earth, causing objects to have weight. *Because of* ***gravity****, a ball thrown in the air will fall back to the ground.*

guar•an•teed (gar´ən tēd´) *verb.* Made sure or certain. *The salesman* ***guaranteed*** *this was the lowest price for a mountain bike.*

gushed (gusht) *verb.* Poured out suddenly and in large amounts. *The quiet fountain suddenly* ***gushed****, surprising the children.*

Hh

hem•i•sphere (hem´ə sfîr´) *noun.* One half of Earth. *The equator divides Earth into the Northern and Southern* ***hemispheres.*** *Earth is also divided into the Western Hemisphere and the Eastern Hemisphere.*

hes•i•ta•tion (hez´i tā´shən) *noun.* A delay due to fear or doubt. *The talented dancers showed no* ***hesitation*** *on stage.*

ho•ri•zon (hə rī´zən) *noun.* The line where the sky and the earth or sea seem to meet. *We watched as the ship seemed to disappear into the* ***horizon****.*

hu•man•i•ty (hū man´i tē, ū man´i tē) *noun.* The quality or condition of being human; human character or nature. *Keeping our air and water clean will help all* ***humanity****.*

hur•ri•canes (hûr´i kānz´, hur´i kānz´) *noun, plural.* Storms with strong winds and heavy rain. ***Hurricanes*** *can rip trees out of the ground.*

hy•brids (hī´bridz) *noun, plural.* The offspring of two animals or plants of different varieties. *Pluots are* ***hybrids*** *that combine the qualities of plums and apricots.*

hy•dro•gen (hī´drə jən) *noun.* A gas that has no odor, color, or taste and burns easily. *Today in class we learned that* ***hydrogen*** *was used in early balloons because it was the lightest element.*

Ii

i•den•ti•ty (ī den´ti tē) *noun.* Who or what a person or place is. *The man at the bank used his driver's license as proof of his* ***identity****.*

im•press (im pres´) *verb.* To have a strong effect on the mind or feelings. *The display of artwork will* ***impress*** *the audience.*

in•dus•try (in´dəs trē) *noun.* Manufacturing plants and other businesses considered as a whole; a particular branch of business, trade, or manufacturing. *The town supports the farm equipment* ***industry****.*

in•ev•i•ta•ble (i nev´i tə bəl) *adjective.* Not able to be avoided; bound to happen. *An* ***inevitable*** *result of closing your eyes is not being able to see.*

in•flate (in flāt´) *verb.* To cause to swell by filling with air or gas. *The air pump at the gas station will* ***inflate*** *the front tires.*

in•ju•ry (in´jə rē) *noun.* Damage or harm done to a person or thing. *Luckily, Roberto's football* ***injury*** *was not serious.*

in•quire (in kwīr´) *verb.* To ask questions or seek information. *I will* ***inquire*** *at the diner about getting a job as a waitress.*

in•still (in stil´) *verb.* To put in or introduce little by little. *Good teachers* ***instill*** *a love of learning in their students.*

in•struct (in strukt´) *verb.* To provide with knowledge, information, or skill; to teach. *The dance teacher will* ***instruct*** *the students in tap, ballet, and jazz.*

in•ten•tions (in ten´shənz) *noun, plural.* Plans to act in a certain way; purposes. *Franklin hated baseball so his* ***intentions*** *for joining the team were unclear.*

in•ter•act (in´tə rakt´) *verb.* To act upon one another. *Band members walked into the audience so they could* ***interact*** *with fans.*

in•va•sion (in vā´zhən) *noun.* The entering of an army into a region to conquer it. *When planning an* ***invasion****, generals must know where the enemy troops are stationed.*

in•ves•ti•ga•tion (in ves´ti gā´shən) *noun.* A careful, thorough examination or search. *The scientist did an* ***investigation*** *to find out which medicine worked better.*

ir•re•sist•i•ble (ir´i zis´tə bəl) *adjective.* Not capable of being resisted or opposed. *On a hot day, a cold drink is so tempting that it is* ***irresistible****.*

is•land (ī´lənd) *noun.* A body of land surrounded by water and smaller than a continent. *We could see the* ***island*** *from the ship.*

Ll

la•bor (lā´bər) *noun.* Hard work; toil. *The construction workers were tired from the backbreaking* ***labor*** *they were hired to do.* —*verb.* To do hard work. *Tired runners* ***labor*** *up the hill at the end of a race.*

land•scape (land´skāp´) *noun.* The stretch of land or scenery viewed from one point or place. *The* ***landscape*** *was filled with tall trees and green pastures.*

Word History

The term **landscape** comes from the Dutch *landschap,* meaning "province, or painting of a land scene." The Dutch word came from the root *land* and the suffix *-schap,* which means "ship."

at; āpe; fär; câre; end; mē; it; īce; pîerce; hot; ōld; sông; fôrk; oil; out; up; ūse; rüle; pu̇ll; tûrn; chin; sing; shop; thin; <u>th</u>is; hw in white; zh in treasure.

The symbol ə stands for the unstressed vowel sound in about, taken, pencil, lemon, and circus.

launched (lôncht) *verb.* Sent off or started in motion. *The science club* ***launched*** *a rocket into the air.*

leg•is•la•ture (lej´is lā´chər) *noun.* A government body having the power to make laws. *People depend on members of the* ***legislature*** *to make laws that are fair.*

lo•ca•tion (lō kā´shən) *noun.* An exact position or place. *The airplane flew by several times before spotting the* ***location*** *of the lost hikers.*

lu•mi•nous (lü´mə nəs) *adjective.* Bright; shining. *The* ***luminous*** *glow coming from the windows made the house look warm.*

lung•ing (lun´jing) *verb.* Making a sudden forward movement. *The pitcher was* ***lunging*** *for the ball when the runner tagged the base.*

Mm

ma•jor (mā´jər) *adjective.* Greater in size, amount, value, importance, or rank. *The Rockies are a* ***major*** *mountain system in America.* —*noun.* An officer in the armed forces. *My uncle is a* ***major*** *in the Army.*

mam•mals (mam´əlz) *noun, plural.* Creatures that are warm-blooded and have a backbone. *Female mammals produce milk to feed their young. Human beings, cattle, bats, and whales are* ***mammals****.*

maze (māz) *noun.* A confusing series of paths or passageways through which people may have a hard time finding their way. *There is a* ***maze*** *in town where people can find their way through tall stalks of corn.*

me•di•a (mē´dē ə) *noun, plural.* Means or form of communication that reaches a large audience. A plural of ***medium****. Television and newspapers are* ***media*** *that influence our daily life.*

mer•chan•dise (mûr´chən dīz´, mûr´chən dīs´) *noun.* Things for sale. *A shipment of new* ***merchandise*** *was delivered to the electronics store last night.*

me•te•or (mē´tē ər) *noun.* A mass of metal or rock that enters Earth's atmosphere from space. *It is rare for a* ***meteor*** *to strike Earth, but it can happen.*

mim•ic•ry (mi mi´krē) *noun.* The close outward resemblance of one kind of animal to another or to an object in its natural environment. *One type of fly uses* ***mimicry*** *to fool animals into thinking it is a wasp.*

mis•chie•vous (mis´chə vəs) *adjective.* Full of mischief, or conduct that is often playful but causes harm. *Cal likes to be* ***mischievous*** *by playing practical jokes.*

mis•sion (mish´ən) *noun.* A special job or task. *My mom sent me on a* ***mission*** *to find my sister's favorite stuffed bear.*

moist•ened (moi´sənd) *verb.* Dampened or made slightly wet. *Ellen* ***moistened*** *the flaps of the envelopes with a damp sponge.*

mor•al (môr´əl) *noun.* The lesson taught by a fable, story, or event. *The* ***moral*** *of the story is, "Always tell the truth."*

mourn•ful (môrn´fəl) *adjective.* Feeling, expressing, or filled with grief or sorrow. *The* ***mournful*** *song on the radio made the listeners feel sad.*

murk•y (mûr´kē) *adjective.* Dark or cloudy. *It was scary sitting in the row boat because there was* ***murky*** *water all around us.*

Nn

nat•u•ral•ist (nach´ər ə list) *noun.* A person who specializes in the study of things in nature, especially plants and animals. *The* ***naturalist*** *spent a lot of time hiking and camping in the woods.*

nav•i•ga•tion (nav´i gā´shən) *noun.* The art or science of figuring out the position and course of boats, ships, and aircraft. *For proper* ***navigation****, pilots rely on equipment to direct them.*

nes•tled (nes´əld) *verb.* Located in a snug and sheltered spot. *Her desk was* ***nestled*** *between piles of books in the back corner of the warehouse.*

no•mads (nō´madz) *noun, plural.* Members of groups or tribes that have no permanent home and move from place to place in search of food or land on which to graze their animals.* ***Nomads*** *may live in deserts.*

Word History

The word **nomad** comes from the Latin word *nomas,* meaning "wanderer." It is related to the Greek word *nomas,* which means "wandering, as in search of pasture."

Oo

ob•ser•va•tions (ob´zər vā´shənz) *noun, plural.* The act, practice, or power of seeing and noticing. *The detective's careful* ***observations*** *helped to solve the crime.*

ob•serv•er (əb zûr´vər) *noun.* A person who watches carefully and with attention. *The nature photographer was a keen* ***observer*** *of flowers and insects.*

or•bit (ôr´bit) *noun.* The path of a heavenly body as it revolves in a closed curve around another heavenly body. *The earth makes a full* ***orbit*** *of the sun in one year.*

or•gan•isms (ôr´gə niz´əmz) *noun, plural.* Living things. Animals, plants, mushrooms, protozoans, and bacteria are all organisms. *The scientist studied* ***organisms*** *that live in ponds.*

o•rig•i•nal (ə rij´ə nəl) *adjective.* Made, done, thought of, or used for the first time. *All of the wood floors in the old house are* ***original****.*

out•cast (out´kast´) *noun.* A person rejected by and driven out of a group. *Jason felt like an* ***outcast*** *when he was thrown off the debating team.*

Pp

parched (pärcht) *adjective.* Dry or thirsty. *The* ***parched*** *land seemed to cry out for rain.*

par•ti•cles (pär´ti kəlz) *noun, plural.* Small bits or pieces of an element. *Tiny* ***particles*** *connect together to make up solid objects.*

pa•tri•ots (pā´trē əts) *noun, plural.* People who love and enthusiastically support their country. *American history views Ben Franklin and John Adams as true* ***patriots****.*

per•ma•nent (pûr´mə nənt) *adjective.* Lasting or intended to last indefinitely without change; enduring. *The concrete will make the goal post* ***permanent****.*

at; āpe; fär; câre; end; mē; it; īce; pîerce; hot; ōld; sông; fôrk; oil; out; up; ūse; rüle; pu̇ll; tûrn; chin; sing; shop; thin; <u>th</u>is; hw in white; zh in treasure.

The symbol ə stands for the unstressed vowel sound in about, taken, pencil, lemon, and circus.

Glossary

per•mis•sion (pər mish′ən) *noun.* Consent or agreement from someone in authority. *I had to get **permission** from my parents before leaving on the school trip.*

phys•i•cal (fiz′i kəl) *adjective.* Having to do with the body. *Doing **physical** activities will help you stay in shape.*

poll•ing (pō′ling) *adjective.* The casting and recording of votes in an election. *Voters go to a **polling** station to cast their votes.*

post•pone (pōst pōn′) *verb.* To put off to a later time. *The officials decided to **postpone** the baseball game until tomorrow because of rain.*

pre•cip•i•ta•tion (pri sip′i tā′shən) *noun.* Any form of water that falls to Earth, such as rain, hail, or snow. *Desert regions get very little **precipitation** each year.*

pred•a•tors (pred′ə tərz) *noun, plural.* Animals that live by preying on, or hunting and eating, other animals. *Lions and wolves are natural **predators** who hunt smaller animals for food.*

pre•oc•cu•pied (prē ăk′yə pīd′) *adjective.* Absorbed in thought; engrossed. *The bride was so **preoccupied** with wedding plans that she forgot her own birthday.*

pres•ence (prez′əns) *noun.* Something felt to be present in a specific place at a given time. *I could sense my mother's **presence** even before I saw her.*

pres•i•den•tial (prez′ə den′shəl) *adjective.* Of or relating to the president. *Two **presidential** candidates will debate.*

pre•vail•ing (pri vā′ling) *adjective.* Most common at a particular time. *The **prevailing** winds made the day cold.*

pre•ven•tion (pri ven′shən) *noun.* The act of preventing, or keeping something from happening. *One tip for fire **prevention** is not playing with matches.*

prey (prā) *noun.* Any animal hunted or killed by another animal for food. *Nature films often show lions hunting their **prey**.*

prog•ress (prog′res) *noun.* A forward movement or gradual betterment. *This century has seen a lot of **progress** in computer science.*

prop•er•ty (prop′ər tē) *noun.* A piece of land. *If you're thinking of building a house, the **property** next to my house is for sale.*

Qq

qual•i•fy (kwol′ə fī′) *verb.* To make fit, as for a certain job or task. *In order to **qualify** for the Olympics, you must be one of the best athletes in the country.*

quest (kwest) *noun.* A search or pursuit. *The explorers went on a **quest** for gold.*

Word History

The word **quest** comes from the Old French word *queste,* which means "search." It goes back to Latin *quaesita,* meaning "thing sought."

Rr

ra•vine (rə vēn′) *noun.* A deep, narrow valley, especially one worn by running water. *As you walk along the edge of the road, be careful not to fall into the **ravine**.*

re•duce (ri dūs′, ri düs′) *verb.* To make less or become smaller in size, number, or degree. *The store should **reduce** its prices.*

re•flect•ed (ri flek′təd) *verb.* Light, sound, images, or heat that is turned, thrown, or bent back at an angle. *The white tents **reflected** the heat from the hot sun onto the sand.*

re•lays (*n.,* rē′lāz; *v.* rē′lāz, ri lāz′) *noun, plural.* Fresh sets or teams, as of workers or animals, prepared to replace or relieve another. *The Pony Express used **relays** to deliver mail across long distances.* —*verb.* Passes along. *When I'm not home, my mother **relays** your messages to me.*

re•luc•tant (ri luk′tənt) *adjective.* Unwilling or hesitant. *My friend wants to try the high dive, but I am **reluctant** to join him because I'm afraid.*

rep•re•sent•a•tive (rep′ri zen′tə tiv) *noun.* A person who is chosen to represent or stand for another or others. *A **representative** from each district was sent to City Hall to vote for the law.*

re•search (ri sûrch′, rē′sûrch′) *noun.* A careful study to find and learn facts about a subject. *Fawn had to do a lot of **research** at the library before she wrote her paper.*

res•er•va•tion (rez′ər vā′shən) *noun.* **1.** Land set aside by a government for a special purpose, such as for Native American tribes to live on. *Native Americans preserved their culture and traditions on the **reservation** where they lived.* **2.** An arrangement to have something kept for another person or persons. *We asked the travel agent to make a plane **reservation** for us.* **3.** Something that causes doubt. *Her serious **reservations** about walking home after dark made sense.*

re•sourc•es (rē′ sôrs′əz, ri sôrs′əz, rē′ zôrs′əz, ri′ zôrs′əz) *noun.* Actual wealth or the means of producing wealth. *Oil is one of our natural **resources**.*

re•spon•si•ble (ri spon′sə bəl) *adjective.* Accountable to someone for the performance of duty or of a certain job or task; faithful to duties; trustworthy; reliable. *The government is **responsible** for upholding the Constitution.*

re•trieve (ri trēv′) *verb.* To get back; recover; regain. *The golfer tried to **retrieve** the golf ball from the lake.*

re•versed (ri vûrst′) *verb.* Moved in the opposite direction from what is usual. *We **reversed** our direction when we realized we were going the wrong way.*

rig•id (rij′id) *adjective.* Not changing; fixed. *Our **rigid** schedule did not allow us to make an unplanned stop at the new park.*

riv•er•bank (riv′ər bangk′) *noun.* The raised ground bordering a river. *The **riverbank** was a very popular place for summer picnics.*

at; āpe; fär; câre; end; mē; it; īce; pîerce; hot; ōld; sông; fôrk; oil; out; up; ūse; rüle; pu̇ll; tûrn; chin; sing; shop; thin; th̲is; hw in white; zh in treasure.

The symbol ə stands for the unstressed vowel sound in about, taken, pencil, lemon, and circus.

ro•bot (rō′bət, rō′bot) *noun.* A machine designed to perform certain human tasks. *The **robot** did a job that was too dangerous for humans to do.*

ro•tat•ed (rō tā′tid) *verb.* Turned around on an axis. *As the wheels **rotated**, the car moved forward.*

Ss

sagged (sagd) *verb.* Drooped down in the middle from weight. *The tent **sagged** from all the rainwater that had collected on top.*

sat•el•lites (sat′ə līts′) *noun, plural.* Artificial objects placed in orbit around another body in space, such as the earth or the moon. *New weather **satellites** track storms forming all around the earth.*

sat•is•fac•to•ry (sat′is fak′tə rē) *adjective.* Good enough to meet a need or desire. *The work done on the house was **satisfactory**, so the owners could move in.*

saun•tered (sôn′tərd) *verb.* Walked in a slow or relaxed way; strolled. *The family **sauntered** through the lush grass in the park.*

scald (skôld) *verb.* To heat to a temperature just below the boiling point. *To **scald** the milk, take it off the heat before it bubbles.*

scen•er•y (sē′nə rē) *noun.* The sights of a place or region. *We admired the beautiful **scenery** while we rode through the mountain range on the train.*

sci•en•tif•ic (sī′ən tif′ik) *adjective.* Having to do with or used in science. *The **scientific** discovery of gravity changed the way people thought about Earth.*

scorch•ing (skôr′ching) *adjective.* Causing intense heat to dry or burn the surface of something. *The **scorching** sun dried up all the plants.*

scoured (skourd) *verb.* Cleaned, cleared, or worn away. *We **scoured** the pan with cleanser until it shone.*

scraw•ny (skrô′nē) *adjective.* Thin, bony, or skinny. *The cat was **scrawny** because she hadn't eaten in days.*

se•clud•ed (si klü′did) *adjective.* Shut off from view. *We found a quiet, **secluded** area in the park for our picnic.*

seg•re•ga•tion (seg′ri gā′shən) *noun.* The practice of separating one racial group, especially African Americans, from the rest of society by making them use different schools and social facilities or making them live in certain areas. ***Segregation** forced African American children to attend schools with poor facilities.*

set•tings (set′ingz) *noun, plural.* The surroundings of something; background; environment. *The gallery showed paintings of cottages in forest **settings**.*

shield (shēld) *noun.* A person or thing that protects against danger, injury, or distress. *I used a magazine as a **shield** against the bright sunlight because I forgot my sunglasses.*

short•age (shôr′tij) *noun.* A small amount or lack of supply. *The storm destroyed many farms, so there was a **shortage** of watermelon.*

shrieks (shrēks) *verb.* Makes loud, shrill cries or sounds. *My little sister **shrieks** when I tickle her.*

site (sīt) *noun.* The position or location of something. *Our house is at a mountain **site** with a beautiful view.*

slumped (slumpt) *verb.* Fell or sunk heavily. *The tired woman **slumped** down in the back seat.*

slurp (slûrp) *verb.* To drink or eat noisily. *It is impolite to **slurp** soup, especially in public.*

sog•gy (sog′ē) *adjective.* Very wet or damp; soaked. *The juicy tomatoes on the sandwich made the bread **soggy**.*

spe•cial•ize (spesh′ə līz) *verb.* To concentrate on a particular product, activity, branch of a profession, or field of study. *These companies **specialize** in making computer software.*

spe•cies (spē′shēz) *noun.* A group of animals or plants that have many characteristics in common. *German shepherds belong to one **species**, and wolves belong to another.*

spec•i•mens (spes′ə mənz) *noun, plural.* Items or parts typical of a group. *The scientist collected **specimens** of some germs that could make people sick.*

spec•tac•u•lar (spek tak′yə lər) *adjective.* Very impressive or unusual. *We watched the **spectacular** fireworks display from our backyard.*

sprawled (sprôld) *verb.* Lay or sat with the body stretched out in an awkward or careless manner. *My brother was so tired from swimming that he **sprawled** out on the blanket and left no room for anyone else.*

spunk (spungk) *noun.* An informal word for courage, spirit, or determination. *The gymnast showed her **spunk** by climbing back up on the balance beam after falling.*

stag•gered (stag′ərd) *verb.* Moved unsteadily or with a swaying motion. *The tired runners **staggered** to the finish line.*

stam•i•na (stam′ə nə) *noun.* The physical ability to withstand fatigue, disease, or hardship; endurance. *A long-distance runner must have **stamina** to finish a race.*

stark (stärk) *adjective.* Bare. *All of the trees had been cut down so the landscape appeared **stark**.*

strands (strandz) *noun, plural.* Things similar to threads. ***Strands** of spaghetti were wrapped around the fork.*

strat•e•gy (strat′i jē) *noun.* A careful plan for achieving a goal. *Our coach used a new **strategy** that confused the best team in the league.*

stunned (stund) *verb.* Shocked or overwhelmed. *Everyone was **stunned** when I won the essay contest because I usually needed help with my writing assignments.*

sub•mit (səb mit′) *verb.* **1.** To give up; to give in to someone's power. *Soldiers may **submit** to the enemy if they are too weak to fight.* **2.** To present. *My teacher asked us to **submit** our reports on Friday.*

at; āpe; fär; câre; end; mē; it; īce; pîerce; hot; ōld; sông; fôrk; oil; out; up; ūse; rüle; pu̇ll; tûrn; chin; sing; shop; thin; th̲is; hw in white; zh in treasure.

The symbol ə stands for the unstressed vowel sound in about, taken, pencil, lemon, and circus.

Glossary

suc•ceed (sək sēd´) *verb.* **1.** To follow in sequence, especially immediately. *The prince was able to* **succeed** *to the throne after the king stepped down.* **2.** To have a good result. *The debating team will* **succeed** *in winning the award.*

suf•frage (suf´rij) *noun.* The right or privilege of voting. *The women who marched at the rally in Washington, D.C., were fighting for* **suffrage.**

su•per•vise (sū´pər vīz´) *verb.* To watch over and direct. *It was a huge responsibility to* **supervise** *all the children swimming in the pool.*

surge (sûrj) *noun.* A large wave or series of waves during a storm. *The storm* **surge** *caused a lot of damage along the coast.*

sur•round•ings (sə roun´dingz) *noun, plural.* The objects, influences, or conditions of a place. *The cabin had beautiful* **surroundings***: flowers, plants, and a nearby lake.*

sur•vive (sər vīv´) *verb.* To live and be active through and after an event. *One must know how to find food and shelter to* **survive** *in the woods.*

sus•pend•ed (sə spen´dəd) *verb.* Held in place as if attached from above. *The spider was* **suspended** *from the roof by a strand of web.*

swag•ger (swa´gər) *noun.* A walk or behavior that is bold, rude, or arrogant. *The star athlete walked into the room with a* **swagger.**

swerved (swûrvd) *verb.* Turned aside suddenly. *The car* **swerved** *to miss the dog crossing the road.*

sym•pa•thy (sim´pə thē) *noun.* The ability to share the feelings of another or others. *I felt great* **sympathy** *for Jim because I knew what it felt like to have my feelings hurt.*

Tt

tech•nol•o•gy (tek nol´ə jē) *noun.* The use of scientific knowledge for practical purposes. *Because of new* **technology***, my computer works much faster.*

tel•e•scope (tel´ə skōp´) *noun.* An instrument for making distant objects, such as stars, appear nearer and larger. *Brad used a* **telescope** *to see the craters on the moon.*

the•o•ry (thē´ə rē) *noun.* An idea that explains a group of facts or an event; something that has not been proven true. *Do you have a* **theory** *that explains why leaves turn color in the fall?*

tilt (tilt) *noun.* A sloping position; angle. *The* **tilt** *of the tray made the cup fall off.*

to•kens (tō´kənz) *noun, plural.* **1.** Pieces that mark movement on a board game. *Andrea moved her* **tokens** *six spaces ahead and won the game.* **2.** Pieces of metal, like coins, used as substitutes for money. *We put* **tokens** *in the machine to play video games at the mall.*

tra•di•tion•al (trə dish´ə nəl) *adjective.* The knowledge, beliefs, or customs that one generation passes to another. *Our* **traditional** *Thanksgiving includes eating turkey and watching television.*

traits (trāts) *noun, plural.* Aspects, qualities, or characteristics that a person or thing possesses. *Bravery and honesty are* **traits** *a person can display.*

trans•formed (trans fôrmd´) *verb.* Changed in shape, form, or appearance. *The builder* **transformed** *the backyard by adding a patio.*

treach•er•ous (trech´ə rəs) *adjective.* Full of danger. *The sharp curves on the* **treacherous** *road caused many traffic accidents.*

treas•ur•er (tre zhə rər) *noun.* The person in charge of the money of a business or a group. *The* **treasurer** *became nervous when he realized money was missing from the company bank account.*

tri•umph (trī´umf) *verb.* To be successful or win. *Everyone is confident that we will* **triumph** *over the problems we are having due to the weather.*

trop•ics (trop´iks) *noun, plural.* A region on Earth lying between the Tropic of Cancer and the Tropic of Capricorn. *Warm seas and sun are often found in the tropics.*

ty•rant (tī´rənt) *noun.* A person who uses power or authority in a cruel or unjust way. *The king was a* **tyrant** *because he punished his subjects unfairly.*

Word History
The word **tyrant** comes from Old French *tiran*, which means "despot." The Old French word came from the Latin word *tyrannus*, which means "ruler or despot." Tyrant can also be traced to the Greek word *tyrannos*, which means "absolute ruler."

Uu

un•con•sti•tu•tion•al (un´kon sti tū´shə nəl) *adjective.* Not in keeping with the constitution of a country, state, or group, especially the Constitution of the United States. *The Supreme Court in this country decides if a law is* **unconstitutional.**

un•en•thu•si•as•ti•cal•ly (un´en thū´zē əs´tik ə lē) *adverb.* Not in an enthusiastic manner; not zealous. *The crowd laughed* **unenthusiastically** *at the comedian's bad jokes.*

un•for•tu•nate (un fôr´chə nit) *adjective.* Unlucky. *It was very* **unfortunate** *that it rained on the day we had tickets to the outdoor concert.*

un•heed•ed (un hē´did) *adjective.* Not paid attention to; disregarded. *The disaster occurred because warnings were* **unheeded.**

un•in•hab•it•ed (un´in hab´i tid) *adjective.* Not lived in. *The* **uninhabited** *house had broken windows and a leaky roof.*

un•pleas•ant (un plez´ənt) *adjective.* Offensive or not pleasing. *There was a very* **unpleasant** *smell near the restaurant's garbage container.*

un•rea•son•a•ble (un rē´zə nə bəl) *adjective.* Not showing or using good sense or judgment. *The teacher was being* **unreasonable** *when he punished the whole class for the bad behavior of one student.*

at; āpe; fär; câre; end; mē; it; īce; pîerce; hot; ōld; sông; fôrk; oil; out; up; ūse; rūle; púll; tûrn; chin; sing; shop; thin; this; hw in white; zh in treasure.

The symbol ə stands for the unstressed vowel sound in about, taken, pencil, lemon, and circus.

780

781

Vv

va•cant (vā´kənt) *adjective.* Not having anyone or anything in it; empty. *If that seat is* **vacant***, you can sit in it.*

va•ri•e•ty (və rī´i tē) *noun.* A number or collection of different things; things of various kinds or parts. *I enjoy eating a wide* **variety** *of fruits and vegetables.*

vast•ness (vast´nis) *noun.* Greatness in size, extent, or number. *The* **vastness** *of the desert made it seem to stretch for miles.*

ven•tured (ven´chərd) *verb.* Went despite risk or danger. *Lucy* **ventured** *out into the storm to look for her dog.*

ver•sions (vûr´zhənz) *noun, plural.* Different or changed forms of an original. *I wrote many* **versions** *of the story before I completed the final draft.*

vet•er•i•nar•i•an (vet´ər ə nâr´ē ən, vet´rə nâr´ē ən) *noun.* A person trained and licensed to give medical or surgical treatment to animals. *I took my dog to the* **veterinarian** *for a checkup.*

vi•brates (vī´brāts) *verb.* Moves back and forth or up and down very fast. *The cell phone* **vibrates** *instead of making a loud ring when someone calls.*

vol•ume (vol´ūm, vol´yəm) *noun.* The amount of space occupied. *Find the* **volume** *of a building block by multiplying its height by its length by its width.*

Ww

wares (wârz) *noun, plural.* Things for sale. *My mother inspects the quality of the* **wares** *at the market before buying anything.*

wheel•chair (hwēl´châr´, wēl´châr´) *noun.* A chair on wheels that is used by someone who cannot walk to get from one place to another. *My grandmother needed to use a* **wheelchair** *after she fell and broke her hip.*

wring (ring) *verb.* To squeeze or twist; to get by force. *I had to* **wring** *out my swimsuit before hanging it in the laundry room.*

Zz

zone (zōn) *noun.* A region or area that has some special quality, condition, or use. *There is a "No Parking"* **zone** *on this street.*

782

Additional Lessons and Resources

CONTENTS

FCAT Comprehension

Objective: Review sequence of events using clue words

LA.5.2.1.2 Locate and analyze elements of plot structure

Chronological Order

Intervention/Remediation

Materials "A Real Princess," Student Book pages 640–641

Review Say: *The time order in which events in a story take place is called* sequence. *Understanding sequence can help you remember key events. The events in a story may be presented in* chronological order, *as they happen in real life. Time-order words such as* then *and* finally *help readers keep track of sequence. In some stories the chronological order is interrupted and events are told in a sequence that switches from the present to the past and then back to the present again. When an author switches to a past event, it is called a* flashback.

Explain Read aloud the first three paragraphs of "A Real Princess" on **Student Book** page 640. Say: *The author disrupts the sequence of events to bring up an event that took place in the past.*

Guided Practice Ask: *What is happening as the story begins? What past event will make it harder for Prince Vincent to find a bride?*

Constructive Feedback

Have students reread the second paragraph on page 640. Ask: *Which sentence tells about a past event? What is a past event that disrupts the sequence called?*

Practice Have students work in pairs. Tell them to scan "A Real Princess" and list clue words that signal the sequence of events.

Constructive Feedback

List the following on the board: *once upon a time, over the years, just then, when, the next morning,* and *finally.* Have students locate these clue words in the story. Ask: *How do the clue words help you follow the sequence of events?*

Chronological Order

Explain Write the following on the board: ___ *Then I got out of bed.* ___ *Finally, I made breakfast.* ___ *My alarm woke me up.*

Guided Practice Ask students to put the events in chronological order by numbering them to show which happened first, next, and last. Ask: *What two time-order words give clues to the sequence of events?*

Practice Have students write in reverse order the events they experienced yesterday. Have them check each other's sequences by reading their lists aloud to partners. Linguistic/Auditory

Flashback

Materials pencil and paper

Explain Tell students they will write a short-short story with a flashback.

Guided Practice/Practice Remind students that authors use flashback to tell about important events that took place before the main action. Have students write short-short stories (sample topic: how they came to like or dislike a food). Tell them to include a flashback. Linguistic

Additional Lessons

FCAT Comprehension

Objective: Making judgments about plot development

LA.5.2.1.2 Analyze plot structure and character development

Plot Development

Intervention/Remediation

Materials "The Best Fourth of July," Student Book pages 670–671

Review Say: *Making a judgment means forming an opinion about the value of something, or about whether someone's actions are appropriate. Making judgments can help readers follow and understand the plot development of a story.*

Explain Read aloud the second paragraph of "The Best Fourth of July" on **Student Book** page 670. Say: *Jean goes all over camp telling everyone that her cabin will perform the best skit. Later, Jean gets nervous and won't listen to the girls' ideas. This action is inappropriate. Jean seems to care more about her campers' winning than about their feelings.*

Guided Practice Explain that sometimes readers have to revise their judgments as they read. Have students read the second paragraph on page 671. Ask: *Who can make a judgment about Jean, based on her apology?*

Constructive Feedback

If students have difficulty making a judgment, ask: *What does Jean acknowledge by apologizing for not listening? Why does Jean apologize?*

Practice Have students read the last paragraph on page 671 and make a judgment about Lateesha's relationship with her parents.

Constructive Feedback

Reread the last paragraph of the story. Ask: *What does the gift package show about Lateesha's parents' feelings toward their daughter? What does Lateesha's thanks and reassurance ("don't worry") suggest about her feelings toward them?*

Plot Development

Explain Write the following on the board: *__ is a great character because __.*

Guided Practice Fill in the blanks with a character of your choice and reasons you have for thinking the character is great. Explain to students that as you followed the development of the plot of the story in which this character appears, you made a judgment about the character. Point out that you gave evidence for your judgment. Ask: *Who can complete the sentence using a different character, with supporting evidence?*

Practice Write the following sentence on the board, and have students complete it: *The main character of __ disappointed me/made me happy because __.* Call on students to fill in the first blank with a story title and the second blank with evidence for their judgments. Auditory

In My Opinion

Materials "Navajo Code Talkers: Five Cinquains," **Student Book** pages 600–601 (From Unit 5)

Explain Tell students that they will listen to a poem read aloud and make a judgment about the speaker.

Guided Practice/Practice Have students work in pairs. Tell students to read aloud the first cinquain on page 600 of their books. Have them make a judgment about the main character (Uncle) and give evidence from the poem to support it. Auditory/Linguistic

Comprehension

Objective: Evaluate techniques of persuasion

LA.5.1.7.2 Identify how author's perspective influences text

Techniques of Persuasion

Intervention/Remediation

Materials "The New Gym," Student Book page 700

Review Say: *Authors may use many techniques—including generalities, bandwagon, testimonials, and loaded words—to persuade readers to agree with them about a topic or issue.*

Explain Read the second paragraph of "The New Gym." Say: *In the first sentence, the writer makes what I suspect may be a generality. When I read further, I see that it is not. The writer supports her statement with facts and details, whereas a generality lacks supporting evidence.*

Guided Practice Say: *Bandwagon is the use of persuasive statements that claim that large numbers of people do or buy something or think a certain way.* Have students find the statement "One in four kids gets no physical education in school at all," in the last paragraph on page 700. Ask: *Is this an example of bandwagon? Explain.*

> **Constructive Feedback**
>
> If students inaccurately evaluate the statement, ask: *Does the writer make a claim about a large group? Can the claim be proved?*

Practice Say: *A testimonial is the use of a celebrity or person of authority to endorse a product.* Have students identify and share an example of the testimonial technique from commercials that they have seen.

> **Constructive Feedback**
>
> Repeat the definition of *testimonial.* Ask: *Was a well-known person featured in your example? Does the person have deep enough knowledge or experience to give accurate information?*

Techniques of Persuasion

Materials two video advertisements

Explain Show one of the video advertisements to the class.

Guided Practice Lead a class discussion in which students identify the technique(s) of persuasion used in the ad. Prompt students by reminding them that such techniques include generalities, bandwagon, testimonials, and "loaded" words (words that reflect the listener's value system). Ask: *Who can describe each technique?*

Practice Have students view the second video advertisement and, without prompting, identify the technique(s) of persuasion that it uses. Visual/Auditory

Advertising Agency

Explain Tell students that they will work in groups to create commercials.

Guided Practice/Practice Organize students in groups. Tell each to identify a food to sell in a commercial. Give groups five minutes to create a short advertising skit, using one or two techniques of persuasion. Have groups perform their commercials. Challenge viewers to identify techniques of persuasion. Kinesthetic/Auditory

Additional Lessons

FCAT ✓ Comprehension

Objective: Identify relevant facts and details

LA.5.1.7.3 Determine main idea through identifying relevant details

Relevant Facts and Details

Intervention/Remediation

Materials "The Science of Hot-Air Balloons," Student Book pages 712–713

Review Say: *A fact can be proven true. An opinion represents someone's feelings or beliefs. A relevant detail is an important piece of information that may be either a fact or an opinion. Both facts and opinions can support the main idea of a selection. However, to add to the understanding of the main idea, they must be relevant to the topic.*

Model Read **Student Book** page 712. Suggest to students that the main idea of the selection is how hot-air balloons work and how they have become safer. Draw students' attention to the third sentence in the second paragraph. Say: *The author provides the name of nylon that is used to make the balloon. While this is an interesting fact, it is not truly relevant to the main idea.*

Guided Practice Ask: *Who can find other facts or opinions that are not relevant to the main idea?*

Constructive Feedback

Read aloud selected sentences and ask: *Is this a fact or an opinion? Does it add to the main idea and so, is it a relevant fact or detail?*

Practice Have students read the rest of the article on page 713. Have students identify statements as relevant to the main idea. You may wish to add details that are related to each topic but not relevant and ask students to assess each statement.

Constructive Feedback

Review selected facts and details from page 713. Ask: *Does this fact help you understand the selection? How is it relevant to the main idea?*

Relevant Facts and Details

Explain Write on the board: *The day was beautiful. It was sunny, with a light wind. The balloonists signalled that they were ready to take off. The crowd cheered as the balloon floated upward. It sailed across the sky like a colorful cloud.* Tell students they will use the information in the paragraph to practice identifying relevant facts and details.

Guided Practice Remind students that relevant facts and details add to an understanding of a main idea. Ask students to identify the main idea of the paragraph. Then have volunteers suggest details, whether statements of fact or opinion, that are not relevant.

Practice Have students describe for partners their weekday afternoon routine. Have partners identify which facts or details are relevant specifically to what the partner does related to schoolwork in the afternoon. Have students switch roles and repeat the exercise. Auditory

Relatively "Miming"

Materials sets of related actions written on strips of paper

Explain Tell students that they will take turns miming and watching a group of actions and choosing which action is not relevant.

Guided Practice/Practice Give each student a strip of paper with instructions for miming a set of actions, one of which is not related. (For example: *Mime using a golf club, swinging a baseball bat, washing your hands, serving a tennis ball.*) Have student pairs take turns miming the actions on their paper and identifying which action is not related tot he others. Kinesthetic/Visual

 **Vocabulary**

Objective: Recognize and correctly use homophones

LA.5.1.6.8 Use homophones to determine meaning

Homophones

Intervention/Remediation

Materials "A Real Princess," pages 640–641; dictionaries

Explain Say: *Homophones are words that sound the same but have different spellings and meanings.*

Model Write the following sentences from the story on the board: *Just then a young lady approached the castle. Her bridle had broken.* Say: *A bridle (b–r–i–d–l–e) goes around a horse's nose to hold the reigns in place. If she is lucky, this young lady may have a bridal (b–r–i–d–a–l) role to play; she may become Prince Vincent's bride.* Write *bridal* on the board so students can compare spellings.

Guided Practice Have students find the word *real* in the second paragraph of the story. Ask: *What does this word mean?* (genuine) Ask: *Who can spell a homophone for* real *that has to do with fishing?* (r–e–e–l)

Constructive Feedback

If students have difficulty, write *reel* on the board. Allow students to use dictionaries to help them answer.

Practice Have students find the word *great*, which appears twice in the second paragraph on page 641. Tell students to identify a homophone for *great* (grate) and use it in a sentence.

Constructive Feedback

If students have difficulty, repeat the definition of *homophones* given in the Explain section. Model how to determine the homophone.

Homophones

Explain Write the following on the board: *I hoped (we'd, weed) go to the beach for vacation. Dad wanted me to (we'd, weed) the garden.*

Guided Practice Ask students to silently identify the correct homophone to complete each sentence. Invite volunteers to circle the correct answers. Ask: *What does* w–e–apostrophe–d *mean?* (we would) *What do you do when you w–e–e–d?* (remove plants that you don't want)

Practice Write on the board a list of homophones such as *dew/do, wood/would, to/too/two,* and *there/their/they're.* Go around the classroom, pointing to each word in turn and having students say a sentence that includes it.
Visual/Auditory

Homophonous Story

Materials paper and pencil

Explain Tell students that they will write stories using homophones.

Guided Practice/Practice Write some homophones on the board; for example, *cheap/cheep, days/daze, road/rode/rowed, fare/fair* and *bare/bear.* Challenge students to write very short stories that include three pairs of homophones.
Visual

FCAT Vocabulary

Objective: Demonstrate understanding of multiple-meaning words

LA.5.1.6.9 Determine correct meaning of words with multiple meanings in context

Multiple-Meaning Words

Intervention/Remediation

Materials "The Best Fourth of July," Student Book pages 670–671; dictionaries

Explain Say: *Many words have more than one meaning. To tell which meaning makes sense in context, first look for context clues. If you are still unsure, use a dictionary.*

Model Read the sentence with the word *cracking* toward the end of page 670. Say: Cracking *has several meanings. "Snapping apart" is the one that I know best. In this sentence, the word* joke *is a context clue that tells me* cracking *does not mean "snapping apart" but "telling."*

Guided Practice Read the last sentence on page 670. Ask: *What does* founder *refer to in this sentence?* (The person who established Camp Freedom) *What is another meaning for the word?* (collapse, go lame, falter)

Constructive Feedback

If students have trouble defining *founder*, have students use dictionaries to give additional definitions.

Practice Have students read the first paragraph on page 671 and identify four multiple-meaning words. (hard, ease, poke, fire) Using context clues, have students write the definitions intended in the story and one additional definition for each word.

Constructive Feedback

If students have trouble giving two definitions for each word, reread the material in the Explain. Then ask: *How can you find a second definition?* (Use a dictionary.)

Multiple-Meaning Words

Materials dictionaries

Explain Write the following on the board: *It takes a <u>smart</u> person to do well on this test. The soap may make your cut <u>smart</u> for a second.*

Guided Practice Read the sentences with students. Have them give two definitions for the word *smart*. (intelligent; sting) Ask: *What context clues tell you what* smart *means in each sentence?* (First sentence: person, test; Second sentence: soap, cut)

Practice Write the word *subject* on the board Have students write two sentences that give context clues to two different meanings of the word. Allow students to use a dictionary if needed. Tell students to trade papers, explain the meanings of *subject* in each other's sentences, and identify the context clues. Visual

Which Is Which?

Materials note cards, markers, dictionaries

Explain Tell students that they will create skits to show two meanings of a multiple-meaning word.

Guided Practice/Practice Assign each student a multiple-meaning word, such as *hide, ring, match,* or *band.* Have students use a dictionary, if needed, to find two meanings for their word. Then, have student pairs write a dialogue using all the word meanings. They should write each word on a note card in marker. Have students act the dialogues out for the class, holding up a note card for each homophone as they use them. Kinesthetic/Auditory

 Vocabulary

Objective: Use context clues to define words

LA.5.1.6.3 Use context clues to determine meanings

Context Clues

Intervention/Remediation

Materials "Satellite Guidance for the Blind," pages 701

Explain Say: *Context clues are clues within a story or text that can help you figure out what a word means.*

Model Read the first paragraph of "Satellite Guidance for the Blind," from page 701. Point out the word *rigid*. Say: *I often find context clues in nearby sentences. The first two sentences in this paragraph help me understand that* rigid *means "not changing or moving." The sentences describe Fernandez's unvarying—that is, rigid—routine before she got a GPS.*

Guided Practice Read aloud the first sentence in the second paragraph of the article. Say: *Suppose you don't know what the word* keypad *means.* Ask: *What context clue could you use to figure out the meaning of* keypad? (punches in)

> **Constructive Feedback**
>
> If students have difficulty identifying the context clue, ask: *What phrase tells how Fernandez uses her keypad?* (punches in her destination, as punching in numbers)

Practice Have students find context clues to the meaning of *route,* which appears twice in the article. Have them use the clues to help partners understand the word's meaning.

> **Constructive Feedback**
>
> If students have difficulty with the Practice, have them reread the first two paragraphs, paying special attention to the first sentence in paragraph 1 and the quote in paragraph 2. Point out the context clues.

Context Clues

Materials science textbook

Explain Write the following on the board: *My parents don't use* pesticides *in our garden. They say* pesticides *kill bugs on plants but are not safe to eat.*

Guided Practice Read the sentences with students. Ask: *Why would a gardener use pesticides?* (To kill bugs) *Why don't the speaker's parents use pesticides in their garden?* (Food plants can be contaminated by pesticides.) Point out that students used context clues to answer questions about pesticides. Ask: *Based on the context, what are pesticides?* (chemical substances used on plants to kill insects)

Practice Write on the board a sentence from the students' science textbook that includes a content-specific word and context clues. Have students use the context clues to write a definition for the content-specific words. Allow them to check word meanings in a dictionary. Visual

Charting Clues

Materials "Jobs in Space," pages 92–93; paper and pencils (From Unit 1)

Explain Tell students that they will make a chart to help them identify unfamiliar words in a selection.

Guided Practice/Practice Ask student pairs to create a table with the following headings: *Word, Sentence with Word, Context Clues, Possible Meaning, New Sentence.* Have students discuss the clues and fill in their charts using the following highlighted words from "Jobs in Space": *mission, zone, maze,* and *function.* Visual/Auditory

FCAT Vocabulary

Objective: Use Greek roots to define unfamiliar words

LA.5.1.6.11 Use roots and affixes derived from Greek to determine meaning

Word Parts: Greek Roots

Intervention/Remediation

Materials "The Science of Hot–Air Balloons," pages 712–713; dictionaries

Explain Say: *Many English words have Greek roots. By learning the meanings of Greek roots, you may be able to define some unfamiliar words.*

Model Point to the word *hydrogen* in "The Science of Hot-Air Balloons." Say: *The Greek root* hydra *means "water." When the gas hydrogen is burned, water is given off. The root describes a property of the gas.*

Guided Practice Write the word *hydropower* on the board. Ask: *What does* hydropower *mean?* (water power) *How is the root reflected in the meaning of the word?*

Constructive Feedback

If students have trouble relating *hydropower* to its root, say: *Most words beginning with* hydr- *have something to do with water.* Then write the following on the board: *hydr = water* Ask: *If* hydr *is water, what is* hydropower? (water power)

Practice Have students write sentences using three words not mentioned previously in this lesson that begin with *hydr-*.

Constructive Feedback

If students have trouble identifying or using words that begin with *hydr-*, allow them to use dictionaries.

Word Parts: Greek Roots

Materials dictionaries

Explain Write the following on the board: *Socrates is my favorite <u>philosopher</u> because his love of knowledge has influenced many people.*

Guided Practice Read the sentence with students. Inform them that the underlined word *philosopher* has the Greek roots *phil* ("love") and *soph* (knowledge). Point out the suffix *-er*, which refers to a person. Ask, *What does a philosopher do?* (studies and shares his or her love of knowledge)

Practice Have students make a word web with *philosopher* at the center and words in the same family in surrounding circles. They should also practice the pronunciations. Allow students to use dictionaries as needed. Visual/Auditory

On the Books

Materials paper, pencils, dictionaries

Explain Tell students that they will make charts showing a family of words with the same Greek root.

Guided Practice/Practice Write on the board the Greek root *biblio* and its meaning, "book." Have students use dictionaries to find English words with the root *biblio*. Tell them to show their findings by making a chart, titled *"Biblio* Words," with columns labeled *Word, Meaning,* and *Example Sentence.* Have students fill in the chart using the words that they identified. Visual

Vocabulary

Objective: Use Greek and Latin roots to define unfamiliar words

LA.5.1.6.11 Use roots and affixes derived from Latin and Greek to determine meaning

Word Parts: Latin and Greek Roots

Intervention/Remediation

Materials "Dr. Priscilla C. Grew, Geologist," pages 738–739; dictionaries

Explain Say: *Knowing Greek and Latin roots can help you figure out the definitions of some English words.*

Model Point to the highlighted word *biology* on page 739. Say: *The Greek root* bio *means "life." Knowing the root helps me figure out that* biology *is the study of life.*

Guided Practice Write the following words on the board: *biography, biologist, biotic.* Ask: *Who can use the root to figure out the meanings of these words?*

Constructive Feedback

If students have trouble using the root *bio* to determine word meanings, write the following on the board: *bio = life* Then ask: *What kind of a book tells about a person's life?* (biography) *What kind of scientist studies living things?* (biologist) *What is another word for a living factor of an ecosystem, such as a plant?* (biotic factor)

Practice Write *granary* on the board. Have students use dictionaries to find the Latin root. Tell them to write a sentence explaining how the root *granum* ("grain") is shown in the word's meaning.

Constructive Feedback

If students have trouble completing the activity, help them locate *granary* in the dictionary. Call on a volunteer to point out the root and its definition.

Word Parts: Latin and Greek Roots

Explain Write the word *geologist* on the board.

Guided Practice Ask: *Who can show me how to divide* geologist *into three word parts?* (geo/log/ist) Tell students that *geo* means "Earth," and *log* means "word" or "study of." Ask: *Who can use the Greek roots to tell the meaning of the English word?* (a scientist who studies Earth)

Practice Write the words *orthodontist* and *psychiatrist* on the board. Tell students that each word names a kind of doctor. Point out the Greek roots *ortho* ("straight") and *psych* ("mind"). Have students use the roots to explain the meanings of the words. Visual

It's Greek to Me

Materials list of words with Greek and Latin roots, note cards, dictionaries

Explain Tell students that they will use dictionaries to identify Greek and Latin roots of assigned words and discuss with partners how the ancient roots relate to the modern definitions.

Guided Practice/Practice Write on the board a list of words containing Greek or Latin roots. These might include *architect, aqueduct, corporation, cosmic, customary,* and *dentist.* Assign students a word or words. They should write the roots and word definitions on note cards, using a dictionary. Then students can compile their cards. Select a student to host and play a game show called "It's Greek to Me" to quiz each other on roots and meanings. The person with the most correct responses wins. Kinesthetic/Auditory

Additional Lessons

Study Skill

Objective: Use Venn diagrams and understand the purpose of photographs and captions

LA.5.2.2.1 Use and explain information from text features

Venn Diagrams, Photographs and Captions

Intervention/Remediation

Materials compare-and-contrast essay or paragraph; pencil and paper

Explain Draw a blank Venn diagram on the board. Say: *A Venn diagram shows the similarities and differences between things. The differences are written in the left and right ovals. The similarities are written in the center section, where the circles overlap.*

Guided Practice/Practice Read the compare-and-contrast essay together as a class. Elicit from students the ideas or facts being compared. Ask: *What is being compared in this paragraph? What similarities or differences are mentioned? What key words signal the comparison?* Help students fill in the Venn diagram on the board with the information from the essay. Invite student partners to draw and fill in their own Venn diagrams with similarities and differences between them.

Constructive Feedback

If students have difficulty, ask: *Did you write the differences in the left and right ovals? Did you write the similarities in the center section?* If students answer affirmatively, review the essay and have students tell two things, ideas, or qualities that are being compared, and explain how they are different and alike. Have students use their responses to revise their Venn diagrams.

Intervention/Remediation

Materials high school, community, or city newspapers; pencil and paper; safety scissors; tape

Explain Remind students: *Photographs and captions can help you understand an article by giving more information about the subject. Photographs visually show what the text explains or describes. Captions provide information about the photographs and may contain additional information not stated in the text..*

Guided Practice/Practice Group students to share newspapers. Have groups locate a captioned photograph in a news or feature article. Ask: *What does the caption tell you about the photograph you are examining?* Have students skim the article, then ask: *How do the photo and caption add to the information presented in the article?* Finally, invite groups to identify another captioned photo and read the article in which it appears. Have them cut out the article, tape it to paper, and write answers to the two questions above.

Constructive Feedback

If students have difficulty linking the captioned photograph to the content of the article, remind them to ask what the photograph shows and locate information on the same topic in the text. Students should be able to use organizational features of text to locate relevant information.

FCAT Study Skill

Everyday Communications

Intervention/Remediation

Materials different types of everyday communications such as a library card application, income tax form, instruction booklet, magazine ad, store brochure, or school newsletter.

Explain Say: *We encounter a lot of paperwork and printed material in the things we do everyday. This material helps us communicate with each other and with institutions like schools, hospitals, and the government.* Discuss the various types of everyday communications: business or government forms, consumer materials, ads, brochures, and newsletters. Display examples of each and explain their purposes to students.

Guided Practice/Practice Assign small groups of students a particular form, application, brochure, ad, newsletter, etc. Ask: *Where do you encounter this type of everyday communication? Why is it important? What information does it ask for? What information does it provide?* Help students fill out as much as they can of the forms and applications. Invite students to bring in or create their own examples of everyday communications.

Constructive Feedback

If students have difficulty understanding everyday communications, review the various types and their functions. Discuss their characteristic features. For example: *An ad usually has images and a catchy slogan.* Help students identify these features.

Additional Lessons

Objectives

- Summarize
- Identify chronological order
- Monitor comprehension
- Analyze plot development

Genre Realistic Fiction

Approaching Level

Summary

Nick has plenty of bright ideas to make life more interesting. He comes up with his greatest idea: He invents a new word. Not everyone thinks this is a good idea. In the end, though, his teacher reveals how she knew he was capable of great things.

FYI for your information

Word etymology is the study of the origin of words. English is largely a composite of many different languages. Words such as *silhouette* and *soufflé* come from French. Spanish gave us the words *rodeo* and *plaza,* among many others. The roots of other words are Greek or Latin in origin. Mrs. Granger explains to Nick that this is the case with the word *pen. Pen* comes from the Latin word for feather, *pinna.* Writing quills, one of the early writing implements, were made from feathers.

Frindle
by Andrew Clements

Before Reading

BUILD BACKGROUND

Brainstorm a list of inventions that students think are important with the class. Ask students:

- What everyday item are you glad someone invented?
- What ideas do you have for an invention?
- Can words and ideas be *invented*? Explain.

PREVIEW AND SET PURPOSES

Have students preview the book's cover and some of the illustrations. Discuss whether the book will be serious or humorous and why students think so. Then have students set a purpose for reading, such as to find out the meaning of the title.

During Reading

LA.5.1.7
Use strategies to comprehend text

APPLY COMPREHENSION SKILLS AND STRATEGIES

Following are suggestions for dividing the reading into manageable sections. For each section, think alouds and discussion questions are provided. Use these to review comprehension strategies and skills taught in this unit.

Chapters 1–4

STRATEGY
SUMMARIZE

Think Aloud Summarizing can help me understand what I am reading. I learn that Nick is a unique person who seems clever. Nick is in the fifth grade and has Mrs. Granger for a teacher. She sounds strict. Nick thinks he can trick her into talking so long that she will forget to give the class homework. However, Mrs. Granger knows what Nick is up to. Instead, she gives him extra homework.

Chronological Order Describe what happened the first day in Mrs. Granger's class. (First, students were given a vocabulary test. Then they received a handout about class procedures. Next, Nick tried to distract Mrs. Granger. Finally, Mrs. Granger gave the class homework, and Nick got an extra assignment.)

Chapters 5–8

STRATEGY
MONITOR COMPREHENSION

Think Aloud Sometimes I slow down the pace of my reading so I can better understand what is taking place in the story. The report that Nick reads about the dictionary has a lot of detailed information. I will slow down and be sure that I understand the ideas in the report before I continue.

Plot Development What do you think about Nick's plan never to use the word *pen* again? How might Nick's behavior affect the plot? (Possible responses: The plan is silly and just meant to annoy Mrs. Granger. Nick's behavior may lead Mrs. Granger to punish Nick or lead to other problems for him.)

Chapters 9–12

STRATEGY
SUMMARIZE

 Think Aloud Summarizing these chapters can help me remember the important events in these chapters. The principal talks to Nick's parents. A newspaper article reports the trouble at school. Nick appears on television. Nick's dad is offered money for use of the word.

Chronological Order What does the reporter receive after her school visit that convinces her to write an article about the new word? (She receives the fifth-grade class picture with all of the kids holding up a "frindle." She notices Nick is identified in the picture.)

STRATEGY
MONITOR COMPREHENSION

 Think Aloud On page 105, I see *engraved*. I can reread the paragraph with the word and look for context clues to check meaning. It says that words were engraved on the pen's barrel, which is metal. I think *engraved* is similar to *carved*.

Plot Development Did Mrs. Granger make the right decision by fighting against the word *frindle*? Explain. (Possible response: Yes, because she helped create interest in the word.)

 ### After Reading

LA.5.2.1.5 Demonstrate understanding of literary selection

LITERATURE CIRCLES

Use page 174 in the **Teacher's Resource Book** to review Listening and Speaking guidelines for a discussion. Use these questions to discuss the book in small groups: *What did you think was the funniest part of the story? How do you know that Nick and Mrs. Granger came to respect one another? Why is it important to follow rules?*

 ### Write About It

Ask students to consider what it may have been like to see the fifth-grade picture taken. Have them write accounts of this experience, describing what they saw and heard. Remind students to check that they use commas to separate introductory words and prepositional phrases.

As an alternative have students write follow-up chapters for *Frindle* that take place after the end of the story.

 Social Studies

Cross-Curricular Connection

Writing Tools

Tell students that as early as 4000 B.C. ancient peoples in the Near East used crude pens that consisted of hollow straws or reeds that supported a short column of liquid. Have students research these and the development of other writing implements such as quill, fountain, and ballpoint pens. Students can present their research in a written or oral format.

Teaching as a Career

What kinds of people become elementary school teachers? How much schooling have they had? What kinds of classes did they have to take? Have interested students answer these and other questions through research or by interviewing several teachers. Remind students that if they collect information by interviewing, they will have to draw conclusions or make generalizations about teachers as a whole. Let students choose a written or oral format for presenting their findings.

Discussion Tips During the discussion of the story elements, or story grammar, of *Frindle*—including character traits, relationships between the setting and the climax—remind students to vary their voice modulation, volume, and pace of speech to emphasize meaning.

Classroom Library

Objectives

- Monitor comprehension
- Analyze plot development
- Summarize
- Identify chronological order

Genre | Realistic Fiction

On Level

Summary

Teddy watches nature programs on television and practices camping skills in his Chinatown apartment, but nothing can prepare him for the outdoors. When his uncle treats Teddy and his younger, know-it-all brother to a camping trip, they encounter many surprises. Perhaps the biggest surprise is the realization that they each have something to contribute.

 for your information

This story is based on camping trips the author took as a young boy. His group sometimes got lost in Golden Gate Park and once hiked from their Mount Tamalpais camp to the ocean. The dry ice incident really happened. It was the author's idea.

Skunk Scout
by Laurence Yep

Before Reading

BUILD BACKGROUND

Brainstorm with students what they know about camping and hiking to create a concept web. Ask students:

- What camping experience have you had or read about?

- How is camping different from your everyday life?

- What tools and equipment do you think make a camping or hiking trip easier?

PREVIEW AND SET PURPOSES

After looking at the cover, have students predict what the book may be about. Then have students set a purpose for reading.

During Reading

LA.5.1.7
Use strategies to comprehend text

APPLY COMPREHENSION SKILLS AND STRATEGIES

Following are suggestions for dividing the reading into manageable sections. For each section, think alouds and discussion questions are provided. Use these to review comprehension strategies and skills taught in this unit.

Chapters 1–4

STRATEGY
MONITOR COMPREHENSION

Think Aloud Words such as *lichee* and *gwoon fun* are unfamiliar. I think these may be foods. As I read I will look for context clues. Learning about these new things helps me learn about the characters' culture and background.

 FCAT

Plot Development Is Teddy's behavior toward his little brother appropriate? Explain. How might this affect the plot development? (No. Just because Bobby does not share his interests is no reason for Teddy to dislike him. His behavior may lead to future disagreements between the brothers.)

Chapters 5–8

STRATEGY
MONITOR COMPREHENSION

Think Aloud I know that I have to call upon my own critical judgment when reading and trying to understand a text. I know that authors of historical fiction often mix facts with their own opinions. Any judgments or conclusions I make must be supported by evidence in the text.

FCAT

Plot Development Do you think the other campers should have charged Uncle Curtis for the charcoal? Explain. (Some students may say that if the other campers paid for the charcoal, it was appropriate for them to charge for it.)

STRATEGY
SUMMARIZE

Think Aloud I'll sum up what I have read so far. In Chapter 9, the meat is still frozen so Uncle Curtis buys food from other campers. Teddy learns that his uncle is not boring and has dreams like anyone else. The boys discover that Grandmother's Lion Salve works great against mosquitoes.

FCAT

Chronological Order List four things that happen after Teddy tells his ghost story. (Bobby gets a little scared. Uncle Curtis tells a scary story. Bobby tells a story about rattlesnakes that makes Teddy nervous. They hear a hissing noise from within their tent.)

Chapters 13–16

STRATEGY
SUMMARIZE

Think Aloud I want to summarize the last chapter. Uncle Curtis talks about being a young boy. He and the boys agree they wouldn't mind camping again as long as they are better prepared. An animal is inside the tent again, but instead of a raccoon, it is a skunk. The skunk sprays Teddy, who thinks of this as one last way Mother Nature is out to get him.

FCAT

Chronological Order How does Teddy help his uncle and brother find their way back to camp? (He sees the trailer with the TV antenna, and he figures it is pointing to a signal tower on a nearby mountain. He figures out the direction they need to follow based on where he remembers the tower to be.)

After Reading

LA.5.2.1.5
Demonstrate understanding of literary selection

LITERATURE CIRCLES

Use page 174 in the **Teacher's Resource Book** to review Listening and Speaking guidelines for a discussion. Use the questions below to discuss the book in small groups.

- What was your favorite part of the book? How does Teddy feel about Uncle Curtis by the end of the book?

- What did the boys accomplish on their camping trip?

Write About It

Have students choose camping activities such as building a campfire, setting up a tent, or protecting food from wild animals. Tell them to research the correct and safe way to do these activities and then write how-to reports to teach others how to do them. Remind students to check their writing to be sure they have used adverbs appropriately.

Science
Cross-Curricular Connection

Spider Diagram

What is the truth about skunks? How and where do they live? When and why do they "spray"? Have students do research to find out all about skunks. Then ask them to present their findings in written or oral reports that include pictures or illustrations.

Social Studies
Cross-Curricular Connection

Campground Map

Have students create campground site maps for fictitious campgrounds. Ask them to use information from the story and include features such as trails, rock outcroppings, creeks, and roads, as well as camping necessities such as picnic tables, cooking pits, bathrooms, and water sources.

Discussion Tips During the discussion of the story elements, or story grammar, of *Skunk Scout*— including character traits, relationships between the setting and the climax—remind students to vary their voice modulation, volume, and pace of speech to emphasize meaning.

Classroom Library

Objectives

- **Monitor comprehension**
- **Analyze plot development**
- **Summarize**
- **Identify chronological order**

Genre	Realistic Fiction

Beyond Level

Summary

Charlie Pippin is an eleven-year-old girl who knows how to make money and get herself into trouble. Always at odds with her father, things become even more tense when she works on a report about the Vietnam War. Her father is a veteran of that war and refuses to talk about it. In the end, Charlie learns to see her father's point of view at the same time she discovers the power of her own voice.

FYI for your information

The Vietnam War is actually a misnomer. The United States never officially declared war on Vietnam. Instead it was a military action that lasted for approximately ten years. The fear was that if communism were allowed to spread from North Vietnam into the south, other countries would fall to communism as well. America's involvement in this action deeply divided the people in this country.

Charlie Pippin
by Candy Dawson Boyd

Before Reading

BUILD BACKGROUND

Explain that the war in Vietnam touched off strong controversy and divided America. Brainstorm with students what they know about the Vietnam War and create a concept web together. Ask students:

- Why do countries go to war? When is war necessary?
- Is there an idea you feel strongly about? What would you do to convince others that you are right?

PREVIEW AND SET PURPOSES

Tell students to look at the front and back covers and speculate about what might be happening in each. Then have students set a purpose for reading, such as to find out who the men are in the newspaper clipping.

During Reading

LA.5.1.7
Use strategies to comprehend text

APPLY COMPREHENSION SKILLS AND STRATEGIES

Following are suggestions for dividing the reading into manageable sections. For each section, think alouds and discussion questions are provided. Use these to review comprehension strategies and skills taught in this unit.

Chapters 1–4

STRATEGY
MONITOR COMPREHENSION

Think Aloud At the beginning, I read more slowly to make sure I understand the problem the characters have. I can always reread what I don't understand. There is a problem between Charlie and her dad. And there might be trouble among Charlie, her teacher, and the principal.

Plot Development Why do you think Mr. Pippin overreacts when the principal calls home? How might this affect the plot? (Possible response: He may be furious with Charlie for breaking a minor rule because the two often have trouble getting along. They may realize their need to understand each other better.)

Chapters 5–8

STRATEGY
SUMMARIZE

Think Aloud I want to summarize what Charlie finds when she looks through Mama Bliss's photographs. She finds pictures of her grandfather in an army uniform and of her father as a baby. She finds a news clipping of a soldier holding an injured soldier and reaching out to another. She realized that the soldier offering comfort is her father.

Chronological Order What happens in the first four chapters of this novel? (Charlie volunteers for a class project to research the Vietnam War. She is caught making origami figures by her teacher, who phones Charlie's father. When Charlie gets home, she finds out her Uncle Ben, a Vietnam veteran, is coming for a visit.)

Chapters 9–12

STRATEGY
MONITOR COMPREHENSION

 Think Aloud When I read dates and numbers, even in fiction, I read them carefully because they might be important. Chris gives many dates and numbers related to wars around the world. I will slow down as I read.

 Plot Development Do you think the statement that people are not naturally peaceful was an appropriate thing for Chris to say after giving his report? (Possible answer: Yes, since he had the facts and figures to defend his statement.)

Chapters 13–16

STRATEGY
MONITOR COMPREHENSION

Think Aloud Mama Bliss says she smells a dead cat on the line. I remember she used this expression back at the beginning of the book on page 32. When I consider the context of this expression in both instances, I can figure out that it means she is suspicious of something.

 Plot Development Do you think it's appropriate for Charlie to go to Washington, D.C., without telling her parents? (Possible response: No, because her parents are still responsible for her.)

After Reading

LA.5.2.1.5
Demonstrate understanding of literary selection

LITERATURE CIRCLES
Use page 174 in the **Teacher's Resource Book** to review Listening and Speaking guidelines for a discussion. Use the questions below to discuss the book in small groups.

- What was the most surprising part of the book?
- How do Charlie and her father overcome their misunderstandings about each other?
- From this book and other things you have read or seen about the Vietnam War, what did you learn about that conflict and people's different reactions to it?

 Write About It
Ask students to think about problems they have had at home, school, or with friends. Have them write essays that explain the problems and tell the steps they took to solve them. Remind students to check their writing to be sure they have not used any double negatives.

 Social Studies

Cross-Curricular Connection

Vietnam Veterans Memorial

The Vietnam Memorial is different from most other military memorials. Students can learn more about the Vietnam Memorial and the artist who created it, Maya Lin. Ask students to find out who the artist is and the process she went through to have her design selected. After viewing photographs of the memorial, have students write their opinions about the structure as a piece of art and as a monument. Discuss with students how facts and opinions are used to shape the opinions of listeners and viewers.

War Debate

Have students take opposing sides in a debate about how war can be prevented, or why it is sometimes necessary. Have them do research to find quotes about war and to read different people's positions on the subject. Remind them that they should research both sides of the issue so that they can effectively respond to their debate opponents. Afterward have students prepare their notes on index cards so that they can speak easily and respond quickly to points made by the opposing side.

 **Classroom Library**

Theme Bibliography

	WEEK 1	WEEK 2
By the Authors and Illustrators	**Sanderson, Ruth.** *The Crystal Mountain.* **Little, Brown, 1999.** The youngest of three sons outwits the fairy thieves who stole his mother's tapestry and marries one of the fairies he has rescued. **APPROACHING**	**Yep, Laurence.** *Dragon's Gate.* **HarperCollins, 1993.** In 1867 a Chinese boy is sent to America to join his father and uncle, who are working to build a tunnel for the transcontinental railroad through the Sierra Nevada Mountains. **BEYOND**

	WEEK 1	WEEK 2
Related to the Theme	**Bryan, Ashley.** *Beautiful Blackbird.* **Atheneum, 2003.** Here is an African tale illustrated with paper collages that tells how all birds are adorned with touches of black paint from the most beautiful bird of all. **APPROACHING**	**George, Kristine O'Connell.** *Toasting Marshmallows: Camping Poems.* **Clarion, 2001.** This collection of poems captures the sights, sounds, smells, and sensations of a family's camping trip. **APPROACHING**
	Kimmel, Eric A. *Three Samurai Cats: A Story From Japan.* **Holiday House, 2003.** Humor, wisdom, and excitement enliven this tale of a feudal lord who gets a samurai cat to rid his castle of a savage rat. **APPROACHING**	**Preller, James.** *The Case of the Marshmallow Monster.* **Scholastic, 2000.** A full moon and a campfire story about a lake creature motivate two friends to find out the real story behind this so-called monster. **APPROACHING**
	San Souci, Robert D. *A Weave of Words: An Armenian Tale.* **Orchard Books, 1998.** A lazy prince learns to read, write, and weave in order to win the affection of his bride-to-be, and finds these skills to be helpful when he confronts an ogre. **ON LEVEL**	**Clements, Andrew.** *A Week in the Woods.* **Simon & Schuster, 2002.** The fifth grade's annual camping trip tests Mark's survival skills and his ability to relate to a teacher who thinks he's a spoiled rich kid. **ON LEVEL**
	Wolkstein, Diane. *Sun Mother Wakes the World: An Australian Creation Story.* **HarperCollins, 2004.** Sun Mother leaves her home in the sky and travels the sleeping Earth as the grass, plants, and trees begin to grow in her footsteps. This is an Aboriginal myth. **ON LEVEL**	**Jacobson, Jennifer.** *Truly Winnie.* **Houghton, 2003.** Going to summer camp for the first time can be worrisome, and Winnie is afraid no one will like her and she won't have a good time. **ON LEVEL**
	Andersen, Hans Christian. *Little Mermaids and Ugly Ducklings: Favorite Fairy Tales.* **Chronicle, 2001.** Here are some of the most beloved fairy tales, such as "Thumbelina," "The Princess and the Pea," and "The Little Mermaid," in a beautiful picture book. **BEYOND**	**Littlefield, Bill.** *The Circus in the Woods.* **Houghton, 2001.** Molly and her family spend most summers at a camp in Vermont. As time goes by Molly discovers a mysterious circus in the woods nearby. **BEYOND**
	Pinkney, Jerry. *Aesop's Fables.* **SeaStar Books, 2000.** Here is a collection of nearly 60 fables, including "Androcles and the Lion" and "The North Wind and the Sun." **BEYOND**	**Pinkwater, Daniel.** *Fat Camp Commandos.* **Scholastic, 2001.** Ralph and Sylvia are angry because they've been sent to a weight-loss camp, so they decide to escape. **BEYOND**

Editors of TIME for *TIME for Kids*, 2005. Facts and figures for 2005.
ON LEVEL

Lauber, Patricia. *Living with Dinosaurs*. Bradbury Press, 1991. This is a re-creation of life among the dinosaurs living in North America 75 million years ago.
APPROACHING

Kramer, Stephen P. *Tornado*. Carolrhoda, 1992. With clear, full-color photos, diagrams, and maps the author shows the destructive capabilities of tornadoes and tsunamis.
ON LEVEL

McBrier, Page. *Beatrice's Goat*. Atheneum, 2001. An impoverished family from Uganda is given an income-producing goat from the Heifer Project, and soon a young girl's dream of attending school is realized.
APPROACHING

Fine, John Christopher. *Free Spirits in the Sky*. Atheneum, 1994. Provides information about the history of hot air ballooning and an account of an early morning flight.
APPROACHING

Ray, Deborah Kogan. *The Flower Hunter: William Bartram, America's First Naturalist*. Farrar, Straus, & Giroux, 2004. Young Billy Bartram eventually becomes his father's assistant and learns about the plants in colonial America.
APPROACHING

Kulling, Monica. *Eleanor Everywhere: The Life of Eleanor Roosevelt*. Random House, 1999. Eleanor Roosevelt was the wife of Franklin Roosevelt and an activist for peace who devoted her life to helping others.
APPROACHING

Karr, Kathleen. *Spy in the Sky*. Hyperion, 1997. When Thaddeus lands his huge balloon in South Carolina at the beginning of the Civil War, Ridley joins him and the two set out to find a way to help the North.
APPROACHING

Swinburne, Stephen R. *The Woods Scientist*. Houghton, 2002. The scientist Sue Morse is a devoted nature lover who shares her knowledge of some of the creatures that inhabit woodlands in the United States.
APPROACHING

Choldenko, Gennifer. *Al Capone Does My Shirts*. Putnam, 2004. The year is 1932 and 12-year-old Moose moves to Alcatraz where his father has just taken a job. He sometimes feels like an inmate when he has to help care for his autistic sister.
ON LEVEL

Paulsen, Gary. *Full of Hot Air: Launching, Floating High, and Landing*. Delacorte, 1993. A humorous commentary on ballooning from taking off to touching down.
ON LEVEL

Jackson, Donna M. *The Wildlife Detectives: How Forensic Scientists Fight Crimes Against Nature*. Houghton, 2000. Scientists at the National Fish and Wildlife Forensics Laboratory in Oregon analyze clues to apprehend people responsible for crimes against animals.
ON LEVEL

Ditchfield, Christin. *Serving Your Community*. Children's Press, 2004. Discusses people who give their time and effort to help others in their community.
ON LEVEL

Van Leeuwen, Jean. *The Amazing Air Balloon*. Dial, 2003. In 1784, 13-year-old Edward Warren, who had a passion for flying, was the first person in America to ascend in a hot air balloon. This is a fictionalized account based on real-life events.
ON LEVEL

Lassieur, Allison. *Marie Curie: A Scientific Pioneer*. Franklin Watts, 2003. Here is a biography of the Polish scientist who was awarded the 1903 Nobel Prize for her discovery of radium.
ON LEVEL

Wheatley, K. L. *Kids Keeping Kids Safe*. Leading Edge Publishing, 1998. Good personal safety habits are the focus in a non-frightening approach.
BEYOND

Warner, Gertrude Chandler. *The Mystery of the Hot Air Balloon*. Whitman, 1995. Benny wants adventure so he helps to uncover a plan that would prevent ballooning from coming to his town.
BEYOND

Byrd, Robert. *Leonardo, Beautiful Dreamer*. Dutton, 2003. The ink and watercolor paintings and the lively text bring Da Vinci's work to life by focusing on paintings like the *Mona Lisa* and discussing his scientific interests.
BEYOND

King-Smith, Dick. *Mysterious Miss Slade*. Crown, 2000. When Patsy and her brother befriend their neighbor they help change her life.
BEYOND

Wirth, Dick. *Ballooning: The Complete Guide to Riding the Winds*. Random House, 1991 Here is the story of 200 years of flight including how balloons are made, the sport of hot air ballooning, and the people who started it all.
BEYOND

Giblin, James Cross. *The Mystery of the Mammoth Bones and How It Was Solved*. HarperCollins, 1999. Charles Peale painstakingly unearths evidence when unknown bones are found on a New York State farm in 1801.
BEYOND

Theme Bibliography

Selection Honors, Prizes, and Awards

The Golden Mare, the Firebird, and the Magic Ring

Unit 6, p. 642
by *Ruth Sanderson*

Texas Bluebonnet Award (2003)

Author/Illustrator: *Ruth Sanderson,* Irma and James H. Black Award for Excellence in Children's Literature (1991) and the Indiana Young Hoosier Book Award (1995) for *The Enchanted Wood*

Skunk Scout

Unit 6, p. 672
by *Laurence Yep*

Author: *Laurence Yep,* Newbery Honor Award (1994) for Dragon's Gate and (1976) for *Dragonwings*; Georgia Children's Book Award (2000) for *The Imp That Ate My Homework*; Children's Book Council Notable Trade Book (1998) for *The Dragon Prince*

Up in the Air: The Story of Balloon Flight

Unit 6, p. 714
by *Patricia Lauber*

Author: *Patricia Lauber,* The Washington Post/Children's Book Guild Award (1983) for her overall contribution to children's literature; New York Academy of Sciences Children's Science Book Award (1983) and Newbery Honor Award (1987) for *Volcano: The Eruption and Healing of Mount St. Helens*; Orbis Pictus Award for Outstanding Nonfiction for Children (1990) for *The News About Dinosaurs* and (1991) for *Seeing Earth from Space*; Oppenheim Toy Portofolio Gold Best Book Award (2004) for *The True-Or-False Book of Dogs*; Kerlan Award for her contribution to children's literature (2000)

Unit 1

Week		Vocabulary	Spelling			
1	**Miss Alaineus** *What's the Buzz About the Geography Bee? Nadia Gomez Sees the Light Car Wash Chronicles Nadia and her Science Project*	slumped soggy capable categories strands gigantic credit luminous	batch rough stump jut tough	nick shrug **tenth** **stuff** laugh	guess sense damp cot fling	gush dove lead notch scan
			Review Words: past		dock	plum
			Challenge Words: cinch		blond	
2	**Davy Crockett Saves the World** *Sluefoot Sue: An American Legend Johnny Appleseed: An American Legend Old Stormalong: An American Legend Who is Johnny Appleseed?*	original wring advertisement commenced fireball impress elected sauntered	folks aim prey yolk greed	greet grind growth **heap** coach	**oak** **paid** paste plead **shave**	theme bride tow spice type
			Review Words: tenth		damp	stuff
			Challenge Words: decay		lifetime	
3	**Forests of the World** **Approaching, On Level, Beyond:** *Amazing Plants* **English Language Learners:** *Plants*	quest settings reduce buffet major	amuse bamboo brood crooks tuna	doom few view hoof hooks	hue bruise booth lose duty	handbook prove mute plume union
			Review Words: coach		theme	bride
			Challenge Words: strewn		accuse	
4	**Ultimate Field Trip 5: Blasting Off to Space Academy** **Approaching, On Level, Beyond:** *How Airplanes Fly: Force and Motion at Work* **English Language Learners:** *How Airplanes Fly*	mission disasters environment zone gravity maze adjusted function	**force** scorn sword swore source	**aboard** course coarse chart barge	harsh marsh starch heart scarce	squares swear flare fare thorn
			Review Words: brood		prove	hoof
			Challenge Words: uproar		gorge	
5	**Pipiolo and the Roof Dogs** *It's Fun When Sam Listens The Wag Brigade Rusty to the Rescue! Mai and Fred*	variety transformed celebration moistened fragrance cooperation canceled theory	squirm dreary nerve squirt verse	surf lurk swerve stern spurts	lurch blurt thirst spur engineer	jeer sneer **clear** fare **year** yearns
			Review Words: aboard		barge	scarce
			Challenge Words: smear		rehearse	

Unit 2

Week		Vocabulary	Spelling			
1	**Shiloh** *The Habits of Rabbits* *The Elephant in the Room* *Black Bear's Backyard* *Elephants in Africa*	injury mournful sympathy delivering slurp shrieks decency bulletin board	**afternoon** background cornfield **cornmeal** earthworm **Review Words:** **Challenge Words:**	**flagpole** **footstep** mountaintop overcome pillowcase blurt first-class	rooftop cardboard ice-skating ninety-one vice president jeer briefcase	all right field trip armchair cheerleader eggshell thirst
2	**Rattlers!** **Approaching, On Level, Beyond:** *Alien: The Brown Tree Snake Story* **English Language Learners:** *The Brown Tree Snake*	species survive alert vibrates surroundings prey predators lunging	abilities countries batches difficulties eddies **Review Words:** **Challenge Words:**	**fangs** identities lashes liberties notches flagpole mangoes	possibilities **rattlers** **reptiles** rodeos **surroundings** vice president sinews	taxes losses potatoes zeroes beliefs ninety-one
3	**Maya Lin, Architect of Memory** **Approaching, On Level, Beyond:** *The Erie Canal: Low Bridge, Everybody Down* **English Language Learners:** *The Erie Canal*	dedicated equality artifacts exhibits site	amusing applied complicated deserved dripping **Review Words:** **Challenge Words:**	easing envied fascinated forbidding gnarled difficulties adoring	injured jogging qualified raking regretted notches diaries	relied renewing skimmed threatening referred rodeos
4	**The Night of San Juan** *Nothing Is Impossible* *Where We Belong* *All or Nothing* *The Family Farm*	forbidden reluctant gossiped irresistible elegant blared mischievous hesitation	bawl **brought** **cautious** **counter** coil **Review Words:** **Challenge Words:**	foul **foundation** **fountain** joint **mouthful** relied buoyant	dawdle sprawls sprouts **turmoil** stout forbidding renown	hoist clause turquoise douse scrawny easing
5	**Black Cowboy Wild Horses** *Nat Love: A Man of the Old and New West* *Alice Greenough: A New Woman of the Old West* *William F. Cody: Showman of the Old West* *Cowgirl Alice Greenough*	vastness enthusiasm horizon ravine presence swerved flickered suspended	absent valley pigment blizzard empire **Review Words:** **Challenge Words:**	mutter goggles fifteen **gallop** dentist sprawls clammy	jogger kennel summon champion **mustang** sprouts hammock	flatter fragment hollow **vulture** culture mouthful

Key Spelling words in bold appear in the selection.

Go to **www.macmillanmh.com** for **Leveled Spelling Lists**.

Unit 3

Word List

Week		Vocabulary	Spelling			
1	**Sleds on Boston Common** **Approaching, On Level, Beyond:** *The Shot Heard Around the World* **English Language Learners:** *The American Revolution Begins!*	navigation instruct swagger patriots tyrant stark governor spunk	**tyrant** profile smoky minus **local** Review Words: Challenge Words:	equal linen legal loser decent valley fatigue	humor closet comet punish vacant fifteen fugitive	recent student shiver cavern panic culture
2	**When Esther Morris Headed West** **Approaching, On Level, Beyond:** *The Story of African American Voting Rights* **English Language Learners:** *African Americans Win the Vote*	representative colonel attorney qualify postpone submit legislature satisfactory	**ideas** poet riot video piano Review Words: Challenge Words:	diary radio fluid genuine rodeo recent situation	meteor cruel casual meander diameter closet variety	fuel patriot ruin diet trial minus
3	**Beyond the Horizon** **Approaching, On Level, Beyond:** *How We Use Energy* **English Language Learners:** *Using Energy*	humanity inevitable unheeded enlightened prevailing	orphan complain hilltop concrete instant Review Words: Challenge Words:	reckless handsome fairground grassland landlord ideas mischief	pilgrim district address improve although piano laughter	partner footprint dolphin cockpit fiddler fuel
4	**My Great-Grandmother's Gourd** **Approaching, On Level, Beyond:** *Dynamic Earth* **English Language Learners:** *Our Changing Earth*	brimming gushed landscape scorching parched scrawny gnarled progress	**python** **scorching** **season** dozen motion Review Words: Challenge Words:	phony active canvas expert embrace partner superb	coastal reserve govern flurry copper footprint bleachers	appoint **beside** cocoon restore observe dolphin
5	**Zathura** *Return to Planet Weird Me, Robot? The Terrariums The Prize*	robot defective meteor rotated staggered reversed dangling tokens	director **shatter** soldier governor error Review Words: Challenge Words:	commander peddler professor pillar splendor appoint **refrigerator**	scissors vapor scholar sugar equator season remainder	labor founder crater **saucer** gentler canvas

Go to www.macmillanmh.com for **Leveled Spelling Lists**.

T23

Unit 4

Week		Vocabulary	Spelling			
1	**Goin' Someplace Special** *The Way It Should Be* *Gramma's Garden* *Sandy's Song* *Dreaming of a Garden*	scald permission autograph fare blurted clenched chiseled spectacular	angle heron lengthen marvel woolen	listen bushel signal nozzle practical	barrel captain frighten slogan mountain	**pretzel** fable global sandal **chuckle**
			Review Words: scissors		pillar	governor
			Challenge Words: dungeon		salmon	
2	**Carlos and the Skunk** **Approaching, On Level, Beyond:** *Survival Instincts: Insects* **English Language Learners:** *How Insects Stay Safe*	glimpse secluded behavior arroyo arousing stunned nestled unpleasant	allow **arousing** boundary bestow grownup	coward **doubting** rowdy **encounter** power	shower trousers grouchy applause lawyer	August laundry caution flawless faucet
			Review Words: angle		mountain	sandal
			Challenge Words: southern		roughness	
3	**Getting Out the Vote** **Approaching, On Level, Beyond:** *Political Debates: Lincoln Versus Douglas* **English Language Learners:** *Lincoln and Douglas Speak*	compelled presidential disrespectful unenthusias- tically succeed preoccupied	excuse contest content refuse protest	conduct subject extract permits insert	desert rebel combat conflict research	compact contract entrance present minute
			Review Words: doubting		allow	caution
			Challenge Words: effect		affect	
4	**Hurricanes** **Approaching, On Level, Beyond:** *Earthquake* **English Language Learners:** *Earthquake*	damages property available contact atmosphere destruction hurricanes surge	future creature searcher feature fracture	gesture legislature pressure measure mixture	**moisture** nature pasture pleasure azure	stretcher treasure rancher butcher lecture
			Review Words: contest		desert	entrance
			Challenge Words: miniature		disclosure	
5	**The Catch of the Day** *Coyote and the Rock* *Brer Rabbit and the Gizzard Eater* *How Thor Got His Hammer* *Brer Rabbit's Ride*	riverbank wares treasurer merchandise educate burdens appreciation unfortunate	ambulance appearance assistance attendance brilliance	dependence substance disturbance **balance** hesitance	ignorance importance performance persistence radiance	resistance reluctance absence residence distance
			Review Words: creature		measure	rancher
			Challenge Words: vigilance		inference	

T24

Key Spelling words in bold appear in the selection.

LOG ON Go to **www.macmillanmh.com** for **Leveled Spelling Lists**.

Unit 5

Word List

Week		Vocabulary	Spelling			
1	**Spirit of Endurance** **Approaching, On Level, Beyond:** *Science in the Snow* **English Language Learners:** *Science at the North and South Poles*	frigid treacherous triumph uninhabited expedition labor dismantled abandon	agent baggage budge challenge damage	plunge **jigsaw** jolt journal judgment	jumble knowledge lodge luggage margin	legend ranger **ridge** surge dodge
			Review Words: assistance	importance	absence	
			Challenge Words: oxygen	surgeon		
2	**Weslandia** *Food Fight* *Fruit From Space* *Land of the Peppertoes* *Space Fruit*	shortage bedlam outcast reflected strategy civilization traditional complex	suite sweet pier peer currant	current **manner** manor pole poll	stationary stationery **waist** waste peal	peel presents presence council counsel
			Review Words: journal	budge	ranger	
			Challenge Words: kernel	colonel		
3	**A Historic Journey** *The Adamsons: Living with Animals* *Animal Observers* *Rachel Carson: Nature's Champion* *Animal Watchers*	instill combined naturalist vacant diverse	disapprove discomfort dishonest dismount disobey	mistaken mistrust misunderstand incorrect preview	preheats inexpensive injustice indefinite disable	discolor disconnect misjudge prejudge prewash
			Review Words: presence	stationary	current	
			Challenge Words: prehistoric	misbehave		
4	**The Unbreakable Code** **Approaching, On Level, Beyond:** *On the Homefront: Life During World War II* **English Language Learners:** *Life At Home During World War II*	corridor reservation enlisted invasion shield location sagged creased	**bottomless** ceaseless **darkness** effortless emptiness	fearless fierceness fondness foolishness forgiveness	fullness hopeless gladness meaningless harmless	motionless needless **stillness** sadness weakness
			Review Words: dishonest	mistaken	preheats	
			Challenge Words: weightlessness	thoughtlessness		
5	**The Gri Gri Tree** *Dan's Whale* *Into the Depths of the Sea* *The Gold at Sunset Cove* *Down in the Sea*	ventured emerged unreasonable attraction inquire discussions sprawled focused	concentrate concentration confuse confusion correct	correction decorate decoration elect **election**	estimate estimation exhaust exhaustion impress	impression locate location discuss **discussion**
			Review Words: hopeless	fearless	forgiveness	
			Challenge Words: conclude	conclusion		

Go to www.macmillanmh.com for **Leveled Spelling Lists**.

T25

Unit 6

Week	Vocabulary	Spelling			
1 **The Golden Mare, the Firebird, and the Magic Ring** *Graham the Kind-Hearted* *Daisies in Winter* *The Three Sisters* *Flowers in Winter*	dismiss intentions despair bridle descended accompany delicacies consented	astronaut autograph automatic automobile **mythical**	telegraph telephone telescope television telegram	homophone phonics disaster astronomer photograph	photography myth mechanic mechanical telephoto
		Review Words: correction		discussion	decoration
		Challenge Words: videophone		photogenic	
2 **Skunk Scout** **Approaching, On Level, Beyond:** *A Visit to Grand Canyon National Park* **English Language Learners:** *The Amazing Grand Canyon*	guaranteed supervise frustrated coordination ease scenery bundle fused	suspect distract export **inspect** spectator	spectacle subtraction tractor import transport	transportation attraction inspector missile mission	committee intermission portable respect dismiss
		Review Words: telescope		astronaut	photograph
		Challenge Words: spectacular		protractor	
3 **A Dream Comes True** **Approaching, On Level, Beyond:** *Everybody's a Star* **English Language Learners:** *The Special Olympics Story*	elementary physical rigid interact wheelchair	cereal terrace gracious echo gigantic	ocean atlas clothes territory parasol	mortal fury furious January Olympics	salute cycle cyclone lunar fortune
		Review Words: suspect		inspect	mission
		Challenge Words: jovial		venerable	
4 **Up in the Air: The Story of Balloon Flight** **Approaching, On Level, Beyond:** *The Sky's the Limit* **English Language Learners:** *The Story of Flight*	launched particles dense inflate anchored companion hydrogen scientific	uniform bisect tricycle triplet triple	unicorn unify unison universe unicycle	biweekly binoculars triangle bicycle **trio**	**century** centipede centimeter tripod university
		Review Words: cereal		terrace	atlas
		Challenge Words: bilingual		trilogy	
5 **Hidden Worlds** **Approaching, On Level, Beyond:** *Searching for Cures* **English Language Learners:** *Science Finds Cures*	specimens erupted murky dormant scoured biology research observer	collapsible breakable affordable usable bearable	favorable capable enjoyable honorable convertible	invisible reasonable respectable sensible unbelievable	possible suitable laughable likable comfortable
		Review Words: uniform		bicycle	triangle
		Challenge Words: manageable		tangible	

Key Spelling words in bold appear in the selection.

Go to **www.macmillanmh.com** for **Leveled Spelling Lists**.

Bb

Dd

Gg

Jj

Ll

Key 5.1 = Grade 5, Book 1

Mm

Nn

Oo

Pp

Key 5.1 = Grade 5, Book 1

Qq

Rr

Read Alouds, 17, 49, 79, 91, 113, 145, 171, 193, 205, 229, 261, 291, 315, 327, 357, 393, 421, 449, 461, 483, 515, 543, 567, 579, 605, 639, 669, 699, 711, 737

Readers' Theater, 460I, 501, 604I

Reading and responding. *See* Literary Response: reading and responding.

Reading independently, 16R, 21, 47M, 47N, 47Q, 47S, 48I, 53, 77M, 77N, 77Q, 77S, 78I, 83, 89M, 89N, 89Q, 89S, 91, 95, 111M, 111N, 111Q, 111S, 112I, 117, 139M, 139N, 139Q, 139S, 144R, 149, 169M, 169N, 169Q, 169S, 170I, 175, 191M, 191N, 191Q, 191S, 192I, 197, 203M, 203N, 203Q, 203S, 204I, 209, 227M, 228N, 227Q, 227S, 228I, 233, 255M, 255Q, 255S, 260R, 265, 289M, 289N, 289Q, 289S, 290I, 295, 313M, 313N, 313Q, 313S, 314I, 319, 325M, 325Q, 325S, 326I, 331, 355M, 355N, 355Q, 355S, 356I, 361, 387M, 387N, 387Q, 387S, 392R, 397, 419M, 419N, 419Q, 419S, 420I, 425, 447M, 447N, 447Q, 447S, 448I, 453, 459M, 459N, 459Q, 459S, 460I, 465, 481M, 481N, 481Q, 481S, 482I, 487, 509M, 509N, 509Q, 509S, 514R, 519, 541M, 541N, 541Q, 541S, 542I, 547, 565M, 565N, 565Q, 565S, 566I, 571, 577M, 577N, 577Q, 577S, 578I, 583, 603M, 603N, 603Q, 603S, 604I, 609, 633M, 633N, 633Q, 633S, 638R, 643, 667M, 667N, 667Q, 667S, 668I, 673, 697M, 697N, 697Q, 697S, 698I, 703, 709M, 709Q, 709S, 710I, 715, 735M, 735N, 735Q, 735S, 736I, 741, 759M, 759N, 759Q, 759S

Reading Process. *See* Comprehension skills; Comprehension strategies; Fluency; Phonics/Word analysis; Vocabulary development.

Reading rate. *See* Monitor and Clarify: reading rate.

Reading together, 21, 53, 83, 95, 117, 149, 175, 197, 209, 233, 265, 295, 319, 331, 361, 397, 425, 453, 465, 487, 519, 547, 571, 583, 609, 643, 673, 703, 715, 741

Realistic fiction. *See* Genre: reading fiction.

Reference and Research. *See* Computer Literacy; Informational text; Research and Inquiry; Study skills; Text features; Theme projects; Vocabulary development.

Relevant facts and details. *See* Comprehension skills: relevant facts and details.

Repetition, 252, 253, 279, 504

Reread for comprehension, 19A–19B, 51A–51B, 81A–81B, 93A–93B, 115A–115B, 147A–147B, 173A–173B, 195A–195B, 207A–207B, 231A–231B, 263A–263B, 293A–293B, 317A–317B, 329A–329B, 359A–359B, 395A–395B, 423A–423B, 451A–451B, 463A–463B, 485A–485B, 517A–517B, 545A–545B, 569A–569B, 581A–581B, 607A–607B, 641A–641B, 671A–671B, 701A–701B, 713A–713B, 739A–739B

Research and Inquiry, 16H, 16I, 16S, 45, 48J, 62, 66, 68, 78J, 89A, 89B, 90J, 137, 144H, 144I, 144S, 167, 170J, 192J, 203A, 203B, 204J, 225, 228J, 260H, 260I, 290J, 311, 314J, 325A, 325B, 326J, 353, 356J, 392H, 392I, 392S, 417, 420J, 445, 448J, 459A, 459B, 460J, 473, 514H, 514I, 514S, 539, 542J, 566J, 573B, 577A, 577B, 578J, 595, 631, 638H, 638I, 695, 709A, 709B. *See also* **Cultural Perspectives; Cross-Curricular connections.**

bibliographies, 513C, 514H

citing and evaluating sources, 16H, 89B, 203B, 321B, 325B, 459B, 513E, 577B, 709B

drawing conclusions, 144H

finding information, 16H, 16I, 16S, 45, 48J, 62, 66, 68, 78J, 89A, 90J, 137, 144H, 144I, 144S, 167, 170J, 192J, 203A, 203B, 204J, 225, 228J, 260H, 260I, 290J, 311, 314J, 325A, 325B, 326J, 353, 356J, 392H, 392I, 392S, 417, 420J, 445, 448J, 459A, 459B, 460J, 473, 514H, 514I, 514S, 539, 542J, 566J, 573B, 577A, 577B, 578J, 595, 631, 638H, 638I, 695, 709A, 709B

formulating questions, 16H, 16I, 45, 89A, 137, 144H, 144I, 203A, 225, 260H, 260I, 325A, 392H, 392I, 417, 445, 459A, 514H, 514I, 539, 573B, 577A, 638H, 638I, 709A

identifying resources, 16H, 89A, 144H, 203A, 260H, 325A, 392H, 459A, 514H, 577A, 638H, 709A

narrowing focus of research, 16H, 16I, 45, 89A, 137, 144H, 144I, 203A, 225, 260H, 260I, 325A, 392H, 392I, 417, 445, 459A, 514H, 514I, 539, 573B, 577A, 638H, 638I, 709A

note taking and outlining, 89A, 89B, 203A, 203B, 325A, 325B, 459A, 459B, 577A, 577B, 709A, 709B

organizing information, 16H, 89A, 89B, 144H, 203A, 203B, 260H, 321A, 321B, 325A, 325B, 325P, 392H, 417, 459A, 459B, 514H, 539, 577A, 577B, 638H, 709A, 709B

paraphrasing, 89B, 203B, 577B

plagiarism, 514H

quoting material, 321B

self-selected theme projects, 16H, 143K–143L, 144H, 259K–259L, 260H, 391K–391L, 392H, 513K–513L, 514H, 637K–637L, 638H, 763K–763L

skimming and scanning, 89B, 321B, 325A, 325Q, 325S, 459A, 577B, 638H

strategies, 16H, 144H, 260H, 392H, 514H, 638H

using key words and questions, 16H, 75, 144H, 260H, 321A, 392H, 514H, 573A, 638H

using print and electronic primary and secondary resources, 16H, 16I, 45, 62, 66, 68, 85B, 89A, 137, 144H, 144I,

Key 5.1 = Grade 5, Book 1

Tt

Key 5.1 = Grade 5, Book 1

Ww

Key 5.1 = Grade 5, Book 1

Acknowledgments

(Continued from Copyright page.)

"Miss Alaineus" by Debra Frasier. Copyright © 2000 by Debra Frasier. Reprinted by permission of Harcourt, Inc.

"My Great-Grandmother's Gourd" by Cristina Kessler, illustrations by Walter Lyon Krudop. Text copyright © 2000 by Cristina Kessler. Illustrations copyright © 2000 by Walter Lyon Krudop. Reprinted by permission of Orchard Books, A Grolier Company.

"The Night of San Juan" is from SALSA STORIES by Lulu Delacre. Copyright © 2000 by Lulu Delacre. Reprinted by permission of Scholastic Press, a division of Scholastic Inc.

"Paul Revere's Ride" by Henry Wadsworth Longfellow is from OUR NATION. Copyright © 2003 by Macmillan/McGraw-Hill.

"Pipiolo and the Roof Dogs" by Brian Meunier, illustrations by Perky Edgerton. Text copyright © 2003 by Brian Meunier. Illustrations copyright © 2003 by Perky Edgerton. Reprinted by permission of Dutton Children's Books, a division of Penguin Young Readers Group.

"Rattlers!" by Ellen Lambeth (sidebar by John Cancalosi) is from RANGER RICK. Copyright © 1998 by the National Wildlife Federation. Reprinted by permission of the National Wildlife Federation.

"Shiloh" is from SHILOH by Phyllis Reynolds Naylor. Copyright © 2000 by Phyllis Reynolds Naylor. Reprinted by permission of Aladdin Paperbacks, an imprint of Simon & Schuster Children's Publishing Division.

"Skunk Scout" is from SKUNK SCOUT by Laurence Yep. Copyright © 2003 by Laurence Yep. Reprinted by permission of Hyperion Books for Children.

"Sleds on Boston Common" by Louise Borden, illustrations by Robert Andrew Parker. Text copyright © 2000 by Louise Borden. Illustrations copyright © 2000 by Robert Andrew Parker. Reprinted by permission of Margaret K. McElderry Books, an imprint of Simon & Schuster Children's Publishing Division.

"Spirit of Endurance" by Jennifer Armstrong, illustrations by William Maughan. Text copyright © 2000 by Jennifer Armstrong. Illustrations copyright © 2000 by William Maughan. Reprinted by permission of Crown Publishing, a division of Random House Inc.

"Suffrage for Women" is from OUR NATION. Copyright © 2003 by Macmillan/McGraw-Hill.

"Suspense" is from THE BIG SKY by Pat Mora. Copyright © 1998 by Pat Mora. Reprinted by permission of Scholastic Press, a division of Scholastic, Inc.

"Through My Eyes" is from THROUGH MY EYES by Ruby Bridges. Copyright © 1999 by Ruby Bridges. Reprinted by permission of Scholastic Press, a division of Scholastic, Inc.

"Ultimate Field Trip 5: Blasting Off to Space Academy" is from ULTIMATE FIELD TRIP 5: BLASTING OFF TO SPACE ACADEMY by Susan E. Goodman. Text copyright © 2001 by Susan E. Goodman. Illustrations copyright © 2001 by Michael J. Doolittle. U.S. Space Camp and U.S. Space Academy are registered trademarks of the U.S. Space Rocket Center. Reprinted by permission of Atheneum Books for Young Readers, an imprint of Simon & Schuster Children's Publishing Division.

"The Unbreakable Code" by Sara Hoagland Hunter, illustrations by Julia Miner. Text copyright © 1996 by Sara Hoagland Hunter. Illustrations copyright © 1996 by Julia Miner. Reprinted by permission of Rising Moon Books for Young Readers from Northland Publishing.

"Weslandia" by Paul Fleischman, illustrations by Kevin Hawkes. Text copyright © 1999 by Paul Fleischman. Illustrations copyright © 1999 by Kevin Hawkes. Reprinted by permission of Candlewick Press.

"When Esther Morris Headed West" by Connie Nordhielm Wooldridge, illustrations by Jacqueline Rogers. Text copyright © 2001 by Connie Nordhielm Wooldridge. Illustrations copyright © 2001 by Jacqueline Rogers. Reprinted by permission of Holiday House.

"Zathura" by Chris Van Allsburg. Copyright © 2002 by Chris Van Allsburg. Reprinted by permission of Houghton Mifflin Company.

ILLUSTRATIONS
Cover Illustration: Leland Klanderman

20-41: Debra Frasier. 50-51: Jeff Crosby. 52-69: Rosalyn Schanzer. 75: Owen Smith. 95: Susan E. Goodman. 108-109: David Gordon. 111: John Hovell. 116-133: Perky Edgerton. 140-141: Barbara Spurll. 148-163: Joel Spector. 169: Erika LeBarre. 178: Richard Orr. 186-187: Siede Preis/Getty Images. 188-189: Mercedes McDonald. 208-221: Edel Rodriguez. 232-251: Jerry Pinkney. 252-253: Jeff Slemons. 256-257: Guy Porfirio. 263: John Hovell. 265-283: Robert Andrew Parker. 284-286: Greg Newbold. 287: John Burgoyne. 289: Neal Armstrong. 294-307: Jacqueline Rogers. 330-349: Walter Lyon Krudop. 351: Argosy. 358: Tyson Mangelsdorf. 360-383: Chris Van Allsburg. 388-389: Guy Porfirio. 394: Rick Powell. 396-413: Jerry Pinkney. 419: John Hovell. 422-423: Loretta Krupinski. 424-441: Jeanne Arnold. 478-479: Susan Swan. 484-485: Mark Weber. 486-505: Wendy Born Hollander. 507: John Kurtz. 510-511: Debby Fisher. 518-519,. 526, 528-532: William Maughan. 533: Kailey LeFaiver. 534-535: William Maughan. 541: Erika LeBarre. 544-545: John Parra. 546-561: Kevin Hawkes. 562-563 Argosy. 565: Erika LeBarre. 571: Rick Nease for TFK. 582-599: Julia Miner. 603: (bg)Julia Miner (tr)Kevin Hawkes. 606: Donna Perrone. 608-627: Marla Baggetta. 634-635: Joel Spector. 640-641: Rebecca Walsh. 642-661: Ruth Sanderson. 663-664: Rex Barron. 672-690: Winson Trang. 702-705: Courtesy of Boundless Playgrounds. 727: Sharon and Joel Harris. 732-733: Tom Foty. 735: Erika LeBarre. 764-765: Wendy Born Hollander. 784-785: Wilson Swain.

PHOTOGRAPHY
All photographs are by Macmillan/McGraw-Hill except where noted below

16-17: Stefan Zaklin/epa/Corbis. 18: (tcr) Royalty-free/CORBIS; (bl) SW Productions/Photodisc/Getty. 19: Tony Freeman/PhotoEdit. 40: Courtesy Debra Frasier. 42-43: David Chasey/Getty Images. 43: (cr) Bettmann/CORBIS; (br) Bettmann/CORBIS. 44: Bettmann/CORBIS. 45: Stockbyte/PunchStock. 46: Thinkstock/Getty. 47: SW Productions/Getty. 48-49: Joe Sohm/Alamy. 49: Arthur Tilley/PictureQuest. 50-51: C Squared Studios/Getty. 70: Courtesy Rosalyn Schanzer. 72: (t) Royalty-free/CORBIS; (cr) Frank Zullo/Photo Researchers, Inc. 73: (tr) The Granger Collection, New York; (bl) Thinkstock/PunchStock. 74: Royalty-Free/CORBIS. 75: The Granger Collection, New York. 76: Scott T. Baxter/Photodisc/Getty. 77: Tom Carter/PhotoEdit. 78-79: Photo 24/Brand X/Getty. 80: Thomas Pakenham. 81: (tl) Goodshot/Punchstock; (l) Courtesy Ohio Department of Natural Resources; (2) John Serrao/Photo Researchers; (3) Dan Tenaglia; (4), (5) Courtesy Time for Kids. 82: (bl) CORBIS/Punchstock. 82-83: (t) Stuart Franklin/Magnum. 83: David Lorenz Winston/Brand X. 84: Stuart Franklin/Magnum. 85: (tl) Rick Nease for TFK; (tr) Ryan McVay/Photodisc/Getty; (bl) CORBIS/Punchstock. 86: David McNew/Getty. 88: SW Productions/Brand X. 89: (tr) C Squared Studios/Getty; (bl) Photodisc/Getty; (br) Dian Lofton for TFK. 90-91: REUTERS/Stringer USA. 92: Photodisc/Getty. 92-93: (t) Ian McKinnell/Getty. 94: (cl) Michael J. Doolittle/Image Works. 94-95: StockTrek/Getty. 95: Bettmann/CORBIS. 96: Michael J. Doolittle/Image Works. 96-97: StockTrek/Getty. 97-98: Michael J. Doolittle/Image Works. 98-99: StockTrek/Getty. 99-100: Michael J. Doolittle/Image Works. 100-101: StockTrek/Getty. 101: Michael J. Doolittle/Image Works. 102: (c) CORBIS SYGMA/CORBIS; (l) Michael J. Doolittle/Image Works. 102-103: StockTrek/Getty. 103: Michael J. Doolittle/Image Works. 104: Michael J. Doolittle/Image Works 104-105: StockTrek/Getty 105: (t) Michael J. Doolittle/Image Works; (b) NASA/AP. 106: (tr) Michael J. Doolittle/Image Works; (inset) Courtesy Susan E. Goodman. 106-107: StockTrek/Getty. 110: MedioImages/Getty. 112-113: Tom Kidd/Alamy. 113: Photodisc/Getty. 114: Alley Cat Productions/Brand X/Getty. 115: American Images/Getty. 132: Courtesy Brian Meunier. 134: Carrie McLean Museum/Alaska Stock Images. 135: (tr) Bettmann/CORBIS; (l) Tracy Morgan/Getty; (2) Yann Arthus-Bertrand/CORBIS; (3) David Ward/DK Images. 136: Jack Sauer/AP. 137: Peter Skinner/Photo Researchers. 138: Royalty-free/CORBIS. 139: GK & Vikki Hart/Photodisc/Getty. 142: Associated Press. 142-143: Sylvain Grandadam/Getty Images. 144-145: REUTERS/HO Old. 146-147: Chas & Elizabeth Schwartz Trust/Animals Animals. 147: Eric and David Hosking/CORBIS. 162: Courtesy Simon & Schuster. 164: zefa/Masterfile. 164-165: Jack Hollingsworth/Photos.com. 165: RaeAnn Meyer/Struve Labs. 166: Joe Munroe/Getty. 166-167: Jack Hollingsworth/Photos.com. 168: Tom L. Geoff/Digital Vision/Getty. 170-171: Claus Meyer/Getty Images. 172: Joe McDonald/CORBIS. 173: OSF/Fogden, M./Animals Animals. 174-175: Tom McHugh/Photo Researchers. 176: Paul Chesley/Getty. 177: (tl) Will Crocker/Getty; (br) Lee Kline. 178: Breck P. Kent/Animals Animals. 179: (t) Joe McDonald/Animals Animals; (br) John Cancalosi/DRK. 180: John Cancalosi. 181: David Boag/Alamy. 182: (t) David A. Northcott/DRK; (br) Deborah Allen. 183: (tr) Stephen Cooper/Getty; (bl) Zigmund Leszczynski/

783

The publisher gratefully acknowledges permission to reprint the following copyrighted material:

"Snakebite" from RATTLESNAKE DANCE: TRUE TALES, MYSTERIES, AND RATTLESNAKE CEREMONIES by Jennifer Owings Dewey. Copyright © 1997 by Jennifer Owings Dewey. Used by permission of Caroline House.

Photo Credits:

All photographs are by Macmillan/McGraw-Hill (MMH) and Ken Karp for MMH except as noted below:

691B: Photodisc. 753B: LWA-Dann Tardif/CORBIS. 763C: Ryan McVay/Getty Images. 763F: ©LWA-Dann Tardif/CORBIS. 763L: Poster: (tl) Photolink/Getty Images; (tc) Siede Preis/Getty Images; (tr) Roy

Acknowledgments

Animals Animals. 184-185: Gary McVicker/Index Stock. 185: John Cancalosi. 186: (tl) Courtesy Ellen Lambeth; (c) Breck P. Kent/Animals Animals. 188-189: Siede Preis/Getty. 190: Paul Edmondson/Getty. 191: IT Stock/PunchStock. 192-193: Izzy Schwartz/Photodisc/Getty. 194: AP. 195: (tl) UPI/NewsCom; (l) McDaniel Woolf/Photodisc/Getty; (2), (3) Royalty-Free/CORBIS; (4) Creatas/Punchstock; (5) Adalberto Rios Szalay/Sexto Sol/Photodisc/Punchstock. 196: AP. 197: (tl) AP; (br) J. Scott Applewhite/AP. 198-200: AP. 202: Comstock. 203: Dian Lofton for TFK. 204-205: Bob Krist/CORBIS. 205: Jeremy Hoare/Life File/Getty. 206-207: Theo Allofs/CORBIS. 220: Courtesy Scholastic, Inc. 222-223: J. Lightfoot/Getty. 224: Cartesia/PhotoDisc Imaging/Getty Images. 224-225: J. Lightfoot/Getty. 225: Wolfgang Kaehler/CORBIS. 226: Richard Hutchings/PhotoEdit. 227: Buddy Mays/CORBIS. 228-229: Jeff Vanuga/CORBIS. 229: C Squared Studios/Getty. 230-231: Lake County Museum/CORBIS. 231: Dallas Historical Society, Texas, USA/Bridgeman. 250: (tl) Courtesy Julius Lester; (tcr)Courtesy Simon & Schuster. 254: Richard Hutchings/PhotoEdit. 255: Guy Grenier/Masterfile. 256: Hot Ideas/Index Stock. 257: William Gottlieb/CORBIS. 258: Classic PIO/Fotosearch. 259: H. Armstrong Roberts/Robertstock. 260-261: SuperStock, Inc./SuperStock. 262: (tr) C Squared Studios/Getty; (inset) Courtesy the Rhode Island Historical Society. 264-265: Kevin Fleming/CORBIS. 282: Courtesy Simon & Schuster. 283: Kevin Fleming/CORBIS. 288: Dynamic Graphic Group/IT Stock Free/Alamy. 290-291: Associated Press. 292-293: WorldTravelPhoto.com/Alamy. 293: Jeff Greenberg/Image Works. 306: (tl) Terri Jepson; (tcr) Courtesy Holiday House. 308: (cr) Museum of London/Topham-HIP/Image Works; (tcr) Wisconsin Historical Society, Image ID: 9320; (bl) Museum of London/Topham-HIP/Image Works. 309: Hulton-Deutsch Collection/CORBIS. 310: Bettmann/CORBIS. 311: (tl) Museum of London/Topham-HIP/Image Works; (tc) Bettmann/CORBIS. 312: BananaStock/PictureQuest. 313: (tr) Photodisc/Getty; (inset) Library of Congress. 314-316: Digital Vision. 317: (tl) The Jackson Citizen Patriot; (l) Photodisc/Getty; (2) Creatas; (3-5) Digital Vision. 318-319: Jeff Hunter/Getty. 319: Paul McErlane/Reuters/NewsCom. 320-321: Joseph Van Os/Getty. 322: John Coutlakis/Asheville Citizen Times. 324: Photodisc/Getty. 325: (bl) Burke/Triolo Productions/Brand X/Alamy; (b) Dian Lofton for TFK; (br) Tracy Montana/PhotoLink/Getty. 326-327: Joel Sartore/National Geographic. 327: Robert Glusic/Getty. 328: Yva Momatiuk/John Eastcott/Minden. 328-329: Craig C. Sheumaker/Panoramic Images. 348: (tcl) Courtesy Cristina Kessler; (cr) Courtesy Walter Lyon Krudop. 350: Ludovic Maisant/CORBIS. 350-351: Kaz Chiba/Getty. 351: Galen Rowell/CORBIS. 352: (tr) Charles Bowman/Getty; (bcl) Walter Bibikow/Index Stock. 353: Photowood/CORBIS. 354: Bob Daemmrich/Image Works. 355: Ross Anania/Getty. 356-357: Rick Fischer/Masterfile. 357: Photodisc/Getty. 382: Courtesy Houghton Mifflin. 384: Andre Jenny/Alamy. 385: Toshiyuki Aizawa/Reuters. 386: SW Productions/Brand X/Getty. 387: Stockbyte/Getty Images. 389: Getty. 390: Tony Freeman/PhotoEdit. 392-393: Bettmann/CORBIS. 412: (tcl) Courtesy Simon & Schuster; (cr) Alan X. Orling. 414: (bc) C Squared Studios/Getty; (inset) Reproduced by permission of the Norman Rockwell Family Agency, Inc.; Collection of the Norman Rockwell Museum at Stockbridge, Massachusetts. 415-416: AP. 417: Steven Senne/AP. 418: Amos Morgan/Photodisc/Getty. 420-421: J. Sneesby/B. Wilkins/Getty. 421: Getty. 440: Courtesy Northland Publishing. 442-443: Leszczynski, Zigmund/Animals Animals. 443: Gloria H. Chomica/Masterfile. 444: Frans Lanting/Minden. 444-445: Steve Bloom/Alamy. 445: (tc) Dwight Kuhn; (tcr) zefa/Masterfile. 446: Getty. 447: Martin Ruegner/ImageState/Alamy. 448-449: AP. 450: The Granger Collection. 451: (bl) AP; (tr) The Granger Collection. 452-453: AP. 453: Erich Hartmann/Magnum. 454-455: AP. 456: (t) Chris Mello/Lonely Planet; (bcl) Digital Vision/Punchstock. 458: Amos Morgan/Photodisc/Getty. 459: (r, b) Dian Lofton for TFK; (cl) Tracy Montana/PhotoLink/Getty. 460-461: Pete Turner/Getty Images. 462-463: Reuters America LLC. 463: James Leynse/CORBIS. 464-465: Weatherstock/Omni-Photo Communications. 466-467: Kjell B. Sandved/Visuals Unlimited. 468-469:Greg Lovett/Palm Beach Post (Image digitally altered by MMH). 470-471: Science VU/NOAA/NASA/Visuals Unlimited. 472-473: David Lane/Palm Beach Post. 474: Nancy P. Alexander. 476: Courtesy Seymour Simon. 476-477: StockTrek/Getty. 480: Tom & Dee Ann McCarthy/CORBIS. 481: Getty. 482-483: Tim Davis/CORBIS. 483: Greg Kuchik/Getty. 504: Courtesy Angela Shelf Medearis. 506: Robert Falls/Bruce Coleman. 508:

Medioimages/Alamy. 509: Ellen Senisi/Image Works. 510: Stock Montage/Getty. 511: Schenectady Museum; Hall of Electrical History Foundation/CORBIS. 512: (t to b) Charles H. Phillips/Time Life Pictures/Getty; Michael Freeman/CORBIS; Bettmann/CORBIS; Schenectady Museum; Hall of Electrical History Foundation/CORBIS; Bettmann/CORBIS; Stock Montage/Getty; Yevgeny Khaldei/CORBIS. 514-515: Hinrich Baesemann/UNEP/Peter Arnold. 515: Photolink/Getty. 516-517: Royalty-Free/CORBIS. 517: Digital Vision/PictureQuest. 520-533: Scott Polar Research Institute. 534: (tcr) Emma Dodge Hanson; (bcl) Courtesy William Maughan. 536-539: Digital Vision/Punchstock. 540: Ariel Skelley/CORBIS. 542-543: Viesti Associates. 543: C Squared Studios/Getty. 562: USDA. 562-563: Kyodo News. 564: Image Source/Getty. 566-567: Flip Nicklin/Minden. 568: Mark A. Philbrick/Brigham Young University. 569: (tl) Joe Andrews; (bcr) AP. 570: David Bowers. 571: (paintings) Courtesy Independence National Historical Park; (frames) Image Farm. 572: (tr) Jeremy Woodhouse/Masterfile; (bl) Missouri Historical Society. 573: Jose Azel/Aurora. 574: (t) Royalty-Free/CORBIS; (tcl) NASA/Science Photo Library/Photo Researchers; (bcr) CORBIS. 576: Ryan McVay/Photodisc/Punchstock. 577: (tr, b, bc) Dian Lofton for TFK; (br) Tracy Montana/PhotoLink/Getty. 578-579: CORBIS. 579: CMCD/Getty. 580-581: J. Speer/Tama News-Herald. 598: Courtesy Northland Publishing. 600-601: (bl) Official US Marine Corps Photo USMC/National Archives; (l to r) Christie's Images/CORBIS. 601: (tr) Saunder, Defense Dept Photo (Marine Corps)/National Archives. 602: Ryan McVay/Photodisc/Getty. 604-605: David Fleetham/Getty Images. 626: (tcr) Ed Scott; (cl) Courtesy Marla Baggeta. 628-629: Kelvin Aitken/AGE. 630: Paul Sutherland Photography. 630-631: Stuart Westmorland/CORBIS. 631: Flip Nicklin/Minden. 632: Jim Arbogast/Getty. 633: Georgette Douwma/Getty. 636: W.A. Sharman; Milepost 92 1/2/CORBIS. 638-639: David Sanger/Alamy 639: Andrew Ward/LifeFile/Getty. 642: Thinkstock Images/Jupiter Images. 660: Courtesy Ruth Sanderson. 666: Digital Vision/Getty. 667: Pete Saloutos/CORBIS. 668-669: Thinkstock/PunchStock. 670: Martin Fox/Index Stock. 690: (tcl) Joanne Ryder; (br) Courtesy Winson Trang. 692, 693: FL Stock/Alamy. 694: Doug Perrine/SeaPics.com. 695: NPS Photo by John Brooks. 696: Ryan McVay/Photodisc/Getty. 697: Hein Heuvel/Zefa/Masterfile. 698-699: Petrus Karagjias. 700: (tr) Elena Dorfman; (tr) Andrew Kaufman/Contact. 701: AP. 702: Courtesy Boundless Playgrounds. 703: (t) James Keyser/Time-Life/Getty; (b) Courtesy Boundless Playgrounds. 704: AP. 705: Dwight Carter. 706: Jeaneen Lund. 708: Photodisc/Getty. 709: (l, b) Dian Lofton for TFK; (br) Tracy Montana/PhotoLink/Getty. 710-711: Andrea Booher/Getty. 711: PhotoLink/Getty. 712-713: Fast Track/Getty. 713: Myrleen Ferguson Cate/PhotoEdit. 714-715: K. Oster/Zefa/Masterfile. 716-717: George D. Lepp/CORBIS. 718: Granger. 719: San Diego Aerospace Museum. 720: Bettmann/CORBIS. 721: CORBIS. 722: French School,(18th century) / Musee d'Art et d'Histoire, Meudon, France, Lauros/Giraudon/Bridgeman. 723: De Frene (18th century)/Bibliotheque Nationale, Paris, France, Lauros/Giraudon/Bridgeman. 724-725: Bettmann/CORBIS. 726: Jay Syverson/CORBIS. 728: (tcl) Bettmann/CORBIS; (tr) Hulton-Deutsch/CORBIS; (bl) Getty; (bcl) Bettmann/CORBIS. 728-729: Getty. 729: (tl) AP; (tr) Tony Ruta/Index Stock; (bl) Fabrice Coffrini/Keystone/AP; (bcr) David Parker/Photo Researchers. 730: (bkgd) K. Oster/Zefa/Masterfile; (tcr) Russell Frost; (br) Kevin R. Morris/CORBIS. 730-731: Photodisc/Getty. 731: K. Oster/Zefa/Masterfile. 734: Bob Daemmrich/PhotoEdit. 735: PhotoLink/Getty Images. 736-737: Annie Griffiths Belt/CORBIS. 738-739: Royalty-Free/CORBIS. 739: Hasselbalch Imaging. 740-750: Dennis Kunkel Microscopy. 751: Stephen Kramer. 752: (tcr) Joshua Kramer; (bcl) Courtesy Dennis Kunkel; (bl) Dennis Kunkel Microscopy. 752-753: Photodisc/Getty. 753: Dennis Kunkel Microscopy. 754-755: (bkgd) David Muench/CORBIS; (t) Christie's Images/CORBIS. 756-157: (bkgd) Gary Braasch/CORBIS; (t) Christie's Images/CORBIS. 758: Amos Morgan/Photodisc/Getty. 759: Steve Skjold/Alamy. 761: (cl) C Squared Studios/Getty; (inset) Grand Canyon of the Yellowstone Park (oil on canvas),Moran, Thomas (1837-1926)/Private Collection/www.bridgeman.co.uk. 762: Digital Vision. 766: ASAP Ltd/Index Stock. 768: Rolf Bruderer/CORBIS. 769: Geostock/Getty. 771: BananaStock/Alamy. 772: Sarkis Images/Alamy. 774: PhotoLink/Getty. 775: Royalty-free/CORBIS. 777: Digital Vision. 778: (tr) photolibrary.com.pty ltd./Index Stock; (bl) Image Source/CORBIS. 780: Foodcollection.com/Alamy. 781: Royalty-Free/CORBIS. 782: PhotoLink/Getty. 786-787: Robert Glusic/Getty Images.

Correlations to the
Sunshine State Standards

- **FCAT Reading Assessed Benchmarks**

- **FCAT Writing + Assessed Benchmarks**

- **Reading and Language Arts**

- **Science**

- **Social Studies**

- **Mathematics**

FCAT Reading
Assessed Benchmarks

The chart below correlates the FCAT Reading Assessed Benchmarks with the new Grade 5 Sunshine State Standards.

FCAT READING ASSESSED BENCHMARKS GRADES 3–5	GRADE 5 SUNSHINE STATE STANDARDS
LA.A.1.2.3 Uses simple strategies to determine meaning and increase vocabulary for reading, including the use of prefixes, suffixes, root words, multiple meanings, antonyms, synonyms, and word relationships.	**LA.5.1.6.3** - use context clues to determine meanings of unfamiliar words **LA.5.1.6.7** - use meaning of familiar base words and affixes to determine meanings of unfamiliar complex words **LA.5.1.6.8** - use knowledge of antonyms, synonyms, homophones, and homographs to determine meanings of words **LA.5.1.6.9** - determine the correct meaning of words with multiple meanings in context
LA.A.2.2.1 Reads text and determines the main idea or essential message, identifies relevant supporting details and facts, and arranges events in chronological order.	**LA.5.1.7.3** - determine the main idea or essential message in grade-level text through inferring, paraphrasing, summarizing, and identifying relevant details **LA.5.2.2.2** - use information from the text to answer questions related to explicitly stated main ideas or relevant details
LA.A.2.2.2 Identifies the author's purpose in a simple text. (Includes LA.A.2.2.3 Recognizes when a text is primarily intended to persuade.)	**LA.5.1.7.2** - identify the author's purpose (e.g., to persuade, inform, entertain, explain) and how an author's perspective influences text
LA.A.2.2.7 Recognizes the use of comparison and contrast in a text.	**L.A.5.1.7.5** - identify the text structure an author uses (e.g., comparison/contrast, cause/effect, and sequence of events) and explain how it impacts meaning in text
LA.A.2.2.8 Selects and uses a variety of appropriate reference materials, including multiple representations of information such as maps, charts, and photos, to gather information for research projects. (Includes LA.A.2.2.5 Reads and organizes information for a variety of purposes, including making a report, conducting interviews, taking a test, and performing an authentic task.)	**LA.5.1.7.1** - explain the purpose of text features (e.g., format, graphics, diagrams, illustrations, charts, and maps), use prior knowledge to make and confirm predictions, and establish a purpose for reading **LA.5.2.2** identifies, analyzes, and applies knowledge of the elements of a variety of nonfiction, informational, and expository texts to demonstrate an understanding of the information presented. **LA.5.2.2.1** - locate, explain, and use information from text features (e.g., tables of contents, glossary, index, transition words/phrases, headings, subheadings, charts, graphs, illustrations) **LA.5.6.1.1** - The student will read and interpret informational text and organize the information (e.g., use outlines, timelines, and graphic organizers) from multiple sources for a variety of purposes (e.g., multi-step directions, problem solving, performing a task, supporting opinions, predictions, and conclusions).
LA.E.1.2.2 Understands the development of plot and how conflicts are resolved in a story.	**LA.5.2.1.2.** - locate and analyze the elements of plot structure, including exposition, setting, character development, rising/falling action, problem/resolution, and theme in a variety of fiction
LA.E.1.2.3 Knows the similarities and differences among the characters, settings, and events presented in various texts.	**LA.5.1.7.7** - compare and contrast elements in multiple texts (e.g., settings, characters, problems)
LA.E.2.2.1 Recognizes cause-and-effect relationships in literary texts. (Applies to fiction, nonfiction, poetry, and drama.)	**LA.5.1.7.4** - identify cause-and-effect relationships in text

FCAT Writing +
Assessed Benchmarks

The chart below correlates the FCAT Writing + Assessed Benchmarks with the new Grade 5 Sunshine State Standards.

FCAT ASSESSED WRITING BENCHMARKS GRADES 3 – 5	GRADE 5 SUNSHINE STATE STANDARDS FOR WRITING
LA.B.1.2.1 The student prepares for writing by recording thoughts, focusing on central idea, grouping related ideas, and identifying the purpose for writing.	**LA.5.3.2.1** using a pre-writing plan to focus on the main idea with ample development of supporting details, elaborating on organized information using descriptive language, supporting details, and word choices appropriate to the selected tone and mood; **L.A.5.3.1** The student will use prewriting strategies to generate ideas and formulate a plan.
LA.B.1.2.2 The student drafts and revises writing in cursive that focuses on the topic; has a logical organization pattern, including a beginning, middle, conclusion, and transitional devices; has ample development of supporting ideas; demonstrates a completeness of wholeness; demonstrates a command of language, including precision in word choice; generally has correct verb and noun forms; with few exceptions, has sentences that are complete, except when fragments are used purposefully; uses a variety of sentence structures; and generally follows the conventions of punctuation, capitalization, and spelling.	**L.A.5.3.2** The student will write a draft appropriate to the topic, audience, and purpose. **L.A.5.3.3** The student will revise and refine the draft for clarity and effectiveness.
LA.B.1.2.3 Student produces final documents that have been edited for correct spelling; correct use of punctuation, including commas in a series, dates, and addresses, and beginning and ending quotation marks; correct capitalization of proper nouns…correct usage of subject/verb agreement, verb and noun forms, and sentence structure…	**LA.5.3.4** The student will edit and correct the draft for standard language conventions. **LA.5.3.4.1** spelling, using spelling rules, orthographic patterns, generalizations, knowledge of root words, prefixes, suffixes, and knowledge of Greek and Latin root words and using a dictionary, thesaurus, or other resources as necessary **LA.5.3.4.2** capitalization including literary titles, nationalities, ethnicities, languages, religions, geographic names and places **LA.5.3.4.3** punctuation, including commas in clauses, hyphens, and in cited sources including quotations for exact words from sources **LA.5.3.4.4** the four basic parts of speech (nouns, verbs, adjectives, adverbs), and subjective, objective, and demonstrative pronouns and singular and plural possessives of nouns **LA.5.3.4.5** subject/verb and noun/pronouns agreement in simple and compound sentences **LA.5.3.5** The student will write a final product for the intended audience.

Reading and Language Arts Sunshine State Standards Grade 5

Each standard is coded in the following manner

LA.	5.	1.	1.	1.
Subject	Grade	Strand	Standard	Benchmark

KEY	TE = Teacher's Edition	LR = Leveled Readers	TFK FCAT = Time for Kids FCAT Edition	FCAT Test Prep = FCAT Test Prep and Practice

GRADE 5: READING PROCESS		Macmillan/McGraw-Hill FLORIDA TREASURES
Phonics/Word Analysis **LA.5.1.4**	**Standard:** The student demonstrates knowledge of the alphabetic principle and applies grade level phonics skills to read text.	
LA.5.1.4.1	understand spelling patterns;	**TE:** 47E, 47G-47H, 47M, 77E, 77G-77H, 77M, 89E, 89G-89H, 89M, 111E, 111G-111H, 111M, 139E 139G-139H, 139M, 169G-169H, 170I, 216, 227B, 227E, 227G-227H, 227M, 255B, 313G-313H, 313M, 325G-325H, 325M, 355E, 355G-355H, 355M, 356I, 387E, 387G-387H, 387M, 392R, 419B, 419E, 419G-419H, 419M, 420I, 447G, 459G, 460I, 481E, 481G-481H, 481M, 509B, 509G-509H, 541E, 541G, 541H, 541M, 550, 667G, 685, 697G, 709G, 735G, 748 759G
LA.5.1.4.2	recognize structural analysis; and	**TE:** 34, 51, 68, 77D, 77F, 77O, 77Q, 139C, 144Q, 144R, 169B, 169E, 169G-169H, 169M, 185, 191B, 191E, 191G-191H, 191M, 192I, 195, 203D, 203E, 203F, 203G-203H, 203M, 203O, 203Q, 203S, 204I, 207, 216, 227C, 227D, 227F, 227O, 227Q, 228I, 260Q, 260R, 263, 274, 277Q, 277S, 289D, 289E, 289F, 289G, 289M, 289O, 289Q, 289S, 313E, 313I, 313M, 314I, 317, 325B, 325D, 325F, 325G-325H, 325M, 325N, 325O, 325Q, 325S, 355E, 355G, 355H, 355M, 387E, 387H, 387M, 451, 459D, 459F, 459O, 459Q, 459S, 460I, 481E, 481G-481H, 481M, 482I, 509B, 509E, 509G-509H, 509M, 509Q, 514R, 517, 527, 541D, 541F, 541O, 541Q, 541S, 545, 564D, 566I, 577B, 577E, 577G-577H, 577M, 578I, 603B, 603E, 603G-603H, 603M, 604I, 633B, 633D, 633E, 633G-633H, 633M, 658, 667E, 667G-667H, 697E, 697G-697H, 710I, 728, 735B, 735E, 735G-735H, 735M, 735Q, 736I, 743, 748, 759B, 759E, 759F, 759G-759H, 759M
LA.5.1.4.3	use language structure to read multi-syllabic words in text.	**TE:** 47E, 47M, 56, 77E, 77M, 89E, 89M, 111E, 111M, 139C, 139E, 139M, 144R, 159, 169E, 169G-169H, 169M, 191E, 191M, 203E, 203M, 207, 227E, 227M, 255E, 255G-255H, 255M, 260R, 271, 289B, 289E, 289G-289H, 289M, 290I, 313B, 313E, 313G-313H, 313M, 314I, 325E, 325G-325H, 325M, 326I, 355B, 355E, 355G-355H, 355M, 356I, 387B, 387E, 387G-387H, 387M, 392R, 419E, 419M, 447B, 447E, 447G-447H, 447M, 448I, 459B, 459E, 459G-459H, 459M, 481E, 481G-481H, 481M, 499, 509E, 509G-509H, 509M, 524, 541E, 541M, 550, 565E, 565M, 577E, 577M, 603E, 633M, 667E, 697M, 709E, 709M, 735E, 748, 759E, 759M

Key 5.1 = Grade 5, Unit 1

Fluency LA.5.1.5	Standard: The student demonstrates the ability to read grade level text orally with accuracy, appropriate rate, and expression.	
LA.5.1.5.1	demonstrate the ability to read grade level text; and	TE: 41A, 47N, 47O, 47S, 71A, 77N, 77Q, 77S, 78I, 85A, 89N, 89Q, 89S, 107A, 111N, 133A, 139N, 163A, 169N, 169Q, 169S, 170I, 187A, 191N, 191Q, 191S, 199A, 203N, 203Q, 203S, 204I, 221A, 227N, 227Q, 227S, 228I, 242, 251A, 255N, 255Q 255S, 260R, 276, 283A, 289N, 289Q, 289S, 290I, 307A, 313N, 313Q, 313S, 314I, 315, 321A, 325N, 325Q, 325S, 326I, 349A, 355N, 355Q, 355S, 356I, 383A, 387N, 387Q, 387S, 392R, 413A, 419N, 419Q, 419S, 420, 420I, 421, 441A, 447N, 447Q, 447S, 448I, 455A, 459N, 459Q, 459S, 460I, 477A, 481N, 481Q, 481S, 482I, 483, 501, 505A, 509N, 509Q, 509S, 514R, 515, 535A, 541N, 541Q, 541S, 542I, 561A, 565N, 565Q, 565S, 566I, 573A, 577N, 577Q, 577S, 578I, 587, 599A, 603N, 603Q, 603S, 604I, 627A, 633N, 633Q, 633S, 638R, 661A, 667N, 667Q, 667S, 668I, 691A, 697N, 697Q, 697S, 698I, 705A, 709N, 709Q, 709S, 710I, 731A, 734, 735N, 735Q, 735S, 736I, 746, 753A, 759N, 759Q, 759S
LA.5.1.5.2	adjust reading rate based on purpose, text difficulty, form, and style.	TE: 21, 41A, 47N, 47O, 47S, 48I, 53, 65, 71A, 77N, 77Q, 77S, 78I, 83, 85A, 89N, 89Q, 89S, 95, 107A, 111N, 111Q, 112I, 117, 133A, 139N, 139Q, 139S, 149, 163A, 169N, 169Q, 169S, 170I, 175, 177, 187A, 191N, 191Q, 191S, 197, 199A, 203N, 203Q, 203S, 204I, 209, 221A, 227N, 227Q, 227S, 228I, 233, 242, 251A, 255N, 255Q 255S, 260R, 265, 276, 283A, 289N, 289Q, 289S, 290I, 295,307A, 313N, 313Q, 313S, 314I, 319, 321A, 325N, 325Q, 325S, 326I, 331, 349A, 355N, 355Q, 355S, 356I, 361, 383A, 387N, 387Q, 387S, 392R, 397, 409, 413A, 419N, 419Q, 419S, 420I, 425, 441A, 447N, 447Q, 447S, 448I, 453, 455A, 459N, 459Q, 459S, 460I, 465, 477A, 481N, 481Q, 481S, 482I, 487, 501, 505A, 509N, 509Q, 509S, 514R, 519, 535A, 541N, 541Q, 541S, 542I, 547, 561A, 565N, 565Q, 565S, 566I, 570, 573A, 577N, 577Q, 577S, 578I, 583, 587, 599A, 603N, 603Q, 603S, 604I, 609, 627A, 633N, 633Q, 633S, 638R, 643, 661A, 667N, 667Q, 667S, 668I, 671, 673, 691A, 697N, 697Q, 697S, 698I, 701, 703, 705A, 709N, 709Q, 709S, 710I, 713A, 714, 715, 731A, 735N, 735Q, 735S, 736I, 741, 746, 753A, 759N, 759Q, 759S
Vocabulary Development LA.5.1.6	Standard: The student uses multiple strategies to develop grade appropriate vocabulary.	
LA.5.1.6.1	use new vocabulary that is introduced and taught directly;	TE: 17, 18-19, 20, 47C, 47F, 47N, 47O, 47P 47Q, 47R, 47S, 47T, 47V, 49, 50-51, 52, 77C, 77F, 77N, 77O, 77P, 77Q, 77R, 77S, 77T, 77V, 79, 80-81, 82, 84, 89C, 89F, 89N, 89O, 89P, 89Q, 89R, 89S, 89T, 89V, 91, 92-93, 94, 111C, 111F, 111N, 111O, 111P, 111Q, 111R, 111S, 111T, 111V, 113, 114-115, 116, 122, 125, 134, 139C, 139F, 139N, 139O, 139P, 139Q, 139R, 139S, 139T, 139V, 143I, 146-147, 148, 157, 159, 164, 169C, 169F, 169H, 169N, 169O, 169P, 169Q, 169R, 169S, 169T, 169V, 171, 172-173, 174, 178, 182, 191C, 191F, 191N, 191O, 191P, 191Q, 191R, 191S, 191T, 191V, 193, 194-195, 196, 203C, 203F, 203N, 203O, 203P, 203Q, 203R, 203S, 203T, 203V, 206-207, 208, 211, 214, 222, 223, 227C, 227F, 227N, 227O, 227Q, 227P, 227Q, 227R, 227S, 227T, 227V, 229, 230-231, 234, 255C, 255F, 255N, 255O, 255P, 255Q, 255R, 255S, 255T, 255V, 259I, 261, 262-263, 264, 278, 289C, 289F, 289N, 289O, 289P, 289Q, 289R, 289S, 289T, 289V, 291, 292-293, 294, 298, 308, 313C, 313F, 313N, 313O, 313P, 313Q, 313R, 313S, 313T, 313V, 315, 316-317, 318, 325C, 325F, 325N, 325O, 325P, 325Q, 325R, 325S, 325T, 325V, 327, 328-329, 335, 350, 355C, 355F, 355N, 355O, 355P, 355Q, 355R, 355S 355T, 355V, 357, 358-359, 360, 387C, 387F, 387N, 387O, 387P, 387Q, 387R, 387S, 387T, 387V, 391I, 393, 394-395, 396, 404,

410, 414, 419C, 419F, 419N, 419O, 419P, 419Q, 419R, 419S, 419T, 419V, 421, 422-423, 424, 442, 447C, 447F, 447N, 447O, 447P, 447Q, 447R, 447S, 447T, 447V, 459, 450-451, 452, 459C, 459F, 459N, 459O, 459P, 459Q, 459R, 459S, 459T, 459V, 461, 462-463, 464, 476, 481C, 481F, 481N, 481O, 481P, 481Q, 481R, 481S, 481T, 481V, 483, 484-485, 506, 509C, 509F, 509N, 509O, 509P, 509Q, 509R, 509S, 509T, 509V, 513I, 515, 516-517, 518, 536, 541C, 541F, 541N, 541O, 541P, 541Q, 541R, 541S, 541T, 541V, 543, 544-545, 546, 562, 565C, 565F, 565N, 565O, 565P, 565Q, 565R, 565S, 565T, 565V, 567, 568-569, 570, 577C, 577F, 577N, 577O, 577P, 577Q, 577R, 577S, 577T, 577V, 579, 580-581, 582, 589, 592, 603C, 603F, 603N, 603O, 603P, 603Q, 603R, 603S, 603T, 603V, 605, 606-607, 608, 615, 619, 628, 633C, 633F, 633N, 633O, 633P, 633Q, 633R, 633S, 633T, 633V, 637I, 639, 640-641, 642, 667C, 667F, 667N, 667O, 667P, 667Q, 667R, 667S, 667T, 667V, 670-671, 672, 676, 678, 697C, 697F, 697N, 697O, 697P, 697Q, 697R, 697S, 697T, 697V, 699, 700-701, 702, 709C, 709F, 709N, 709O, 709P, 709Q, 709R, 709S, 709T, 709V, 711, 712-713, 714, 735C, 735F, 735H, 735N, 735O, 735P, 735Q, 735R, 735S, 735T, 735V, 737, 738-739, 740, 750, 759C, 759F, 759N, 759O, 759P, 759Q, 759R, 759S, 759T, 759V, 673I

LA.5.1.6.2	listen to, read, and discuss familiar and conceptually challenging text;	**TE:** 16R, 17, 18-19, 20-41, 42- 45, 47P, 47R, 47T, 47V, 48I, 49, 50-51, 52-71, 72-75, 77P, 77R, 77T, 77V, 78I, 79, 80-81, 82-85, 89P, 89R, 89T, 89V, 90I, 91, 92-93, 94-107, 108-109, 111D, 111P, 111R, 111T, 111V, 112I, 113, 114-115M 116-133, 134-137, 139P, 139R, 139T, 139V, 144R, 145, 146-147, 148-163, 164-167, 169P, 169R, 169T, 169V, 170I, 171, 172-187, 188-189, 191P, 191R, 191T, 191V, 192I, 193, 194-195, 196-199, 203P, 203R, 203T, 203V, 204I, 205, 206-207, 208-221, 222-225, 227P, 227R, 227T, 227V, 228I, 229, 230-231, 232-251, 255P, 255R, 255T, 255V, 260R, 261, 262-263, 263A, 264-283, 284-287, 289P, 289R, 289T, 289V, 290I, 291, 292-293, 293A, 294-307, 308-311, 313P, 313R, 313T, 313V, 314I, 315, 316-317, 317A, 318-321, 325P, 325R, 325T, 325V, 326I, 327, 328-329, 330-349, 350-353, 355P, 355R, 355T, 355V, 356I, 357, 358-359, 360-383, 387P, 387R, 387T, 387V, 392R, 392I, 393, 394-395, 396-413, 414-417, 419P, 419R, 419T, 419V, 420I, 421, 422-423, 424-441, 442-445, 447P, 447R, 447T, 447V, 448I, 449, 450-451, 451A, 452-455, 459P, 459R, 459T, 459V, 460I, 461, 462-463, 464-477, 478-479, 481P, 481R, 481T, 481V, 482I, 483, 484-485, 486-505, 506-507, 509P, 509R, 509T, 509V, 514R, 515, 516-517, 518-535, 536-539, 541P, 541R, 541T, 541V, 542I, 543, 544-545, 546-561, 562-563, 565P, 565R, 565T, 565V, 566I, 567, 568-569, 570-573, 577P, 577R, 577T, 577V, 578I, 579, 580-581, 582-599, 600-601, 603P, 603T, 603V, 604I, 605, 606-607, 608-627, 628-631, 633P, 633R, 633T, 633V, 638R, 639, 640-641, 642-661, 662-665, 667P, 667R, 667T, 667V, 668I, 669, 670-671, 672-691, 692-695, 697P, 697R, 697T, 697V, 698I, 699, 700-701, 702-705, 709P, 709R, 709T, 709V, 710I, 711, 712-713, 713A, 714-731, 735P, 735R, 735T, 735V, 736I, 737, 738-739, 739A, 740-753, 754-757, 759P, 759R, 759T, 759V; 5.1: T13-T20; 5.2: T11-T18; 5.3: T11-18; 5.4: T12-T19; 5.5: T13-T20; 5.6: T13-T20
LA.5.1.6.3	use context clues to determine meanings of unfamiliar words;	**TE:** 18-19, 23, 24, 26, 47C, 47D, 47F, 47N, 47O, 47P, 47Q, 47R, 47S, 47T, 47V, 50-51, 56, 77C, 77F, 77N, 77P, 77Q, 77R, 77S, 77T, 77V, 80-81, 89C, 89F, 89N, 89P, 89Q, 89R, 89T, 89V, 90I, 92-93, 101, 111C, 111D, 111F, 111N, 111O, 111P, 111Q, 111R, 111S, 111T, 111V, 114-115, 139C, 139F, 139N, 139P, 139Q, 139R, 139S, 139T, 139V, 142, 146-147, 159, 160, 169C, 169F, 169N, 169P, 169Q, 169R, 169S, 169T, 169V, 170I, 172-173, 179, 182, 191C, 191D, 191F,

		191N, 191O, 191P, 191Q, 191R, 191S, 191T, 191V, 194-195, 203C, 203F, 203N, 203P, 203Q, 203R, 203S, 203T, 203V, 206-207, 227C, 227F, 227H, 227N, 227P, 227Q, 227R, 227S, 227T, 227V, 230-231, 255C, 255F, 255N, 255P, 255Q, 255R, 255S, 255T, 255V, 257, 262-263, 271, 272, 289C, 289F, 289N, 289P, 289Q, 289R, 289S, 289T, 289V, 292-293, 313C, 313F, 313H, 313N, 313P, 313Q, 313R, 313S, 313T, 313V, 316-317, 325C, 325F, 325N, 325P, 325Q, 325R, 325S, 325T, 325V, 328, 336, 350, 355C, 355F, 355N, 355P, 355Q, 355R, 355S 355T, 355V, 358-359, 387C, 387F, 387N, 387P, 387Q, 387R, 387S, 387T, 387V, 388, 394-395, 419C, 419F, 419N, 419P, 419Q, 419R, 419S, 419T, 419V, 420I, 422-423, 429, 431, 438, 447C, 447D, 447F, 447N, 447O, 447P, 447Q, 447R, 447S, 447T, 447V, 450-451, 459C, 459F, 459N, 459P, 459Q, 459R, 459S, 459T, 459V, 462-463, 470, 481C, 481F, 481N, 481P, 481Q, 481R, 481S, 481T, 481V, 484-485, 509C, 509F, 509N, 509P, 509Q, 509R, 509S, 509T, 509V, 511, 516-517, 524, 541C, 541F, 541N, 541P, 541Q, 541R, 541S, 541T, 541V, 550, 544-545, 565C, 565F, 565N, 565P, 565Q, 565R, 565S, 565T, 565V, 568-569, 577C, 577F, 577N, 577P, 577Q, 577R, 577S, 577T, 577V, 578I, 580-581, 591, 603C, 603D, 603F, 603N, 603O, 603P, 603Q, 603R, 603S, 603T, 603V, 606-607, 633C, 633F, 633N, 633P, 633Q, 633R, 633S, 633T, 633V, 634, 640-641, 655, 667C, 667F, 667N, 667P, 667Q, 667R, 667S, 667T, 667V, 670-671, 685, 697C, 697F, 697N, 697P, 697Q, 697R, 697S, 697T, 697V, 698I, 700-701, 709C, 709D, 709F, 709N, 709O, 709P, 709Q, 709R, 709S, 709T, 709V, 712-713, 735C, 735F, 735N, 735P, 735Q, 735R, 735S, 735T, 735V, 738-739, 759C, 759F, 759N, 759P, 759Q, 759R, 759S, 759T, 759V; 5.1: T6, T9; 5.2: T5; 5.4: T6; 5.5: T9; 5.6: T7; **TFK FCAT:** Issue 1, 2, 3, 4, 5, 6, 7, 8, 9, 10, 11, 12, 13, 14, 15; **FCAT Test Prep:** 6–31
LA.5.1.6.4	categorize key vocabulary and identify salient features;	**TE:** 17, 19, 47D, 47F, 47H, 49, 51, 77D, 77F, 77N, 79, 81, 89D, 89F, 91, 93, 111D, 111F, 111H 113, 115, 139C, 139D, 139F, 145, 147, 169D, 169F, 169G, 171, 173, 191D, 191F, 191H, 193, 195, 203D, 203F, 205, 207, 227D, 227F, 227N, 229, 231, 255C, 255D, 255F, 255G, 255H, 255M, 261, 263, 289D, 289F, 289G, 291, 293, 313D, 313F, 315, 317, 325D, 325F, 325Q, 327, 329, 355D, 355F, 355O, 357, 359, 387D, 387F, 387O, 393, 395, 419D, 419F, 419G-419H, 421, 423, 447D, 447F, 447G-447H, 449, 451, 459D, 459F, 461, 463, 474, 476, 481D, 481F, 481G-481H, 483, 485, 499, 509D , 509F, 509G-509H, 515, 517, 541D, 541F, 543, 545, 565D, 565F, 567, 569, 577C, 577D, 577F, 579, 581, 591, 603D, 603F, 605, 607, 633D, 633F, 633N, 639, 641, 650, 667D, 667F, 669, 671, 697D, 697F, 699, 701, 709D, 709F, 709G, 711, 713, 735D 735F, 737, 739, 759, 759D, 759F, 759G
LA.5.1.6.5	relate new vocabulary to familiar words;	**TE:** 17, 18, 19, 47D, 47F, 47H, 47N, 47O, 47Q, 49, 50, 59, 63, 77F, 79, 80, 89F, 91, 92, 97, 99, 111F, 111N, 112I, 113, 114, 115, 119, 120, 125, 139C, 139D, 139F, 139O, 139Q, 145, 146, 168, 169F, 169M, 171, 172, 191F, 191N, 193, 194, 203F, 203N, 205, 206, 227F, 229, 230, 237, 255F, 255N, 261, 262, 271, 289F, 289H, 291, 292, 312F, 313C, 313F, 313H, 315, 316, 325F, 326I, 327, 328, 355D, 355F, 355O, 356I, 357, 358, 359, 373, 374, 387D, 387F, 387N, 387S, 393, 394, 419F, 421, 422, 447F, 449, 450, 459F, 461, 462, 481F, 482I, 483, 484, 488, 509F, 509H, 509O, 515, 516, 541F, 543, 544, 545, 565F, 567, 568, 573B, 577C, 577F, 577Q, 579, 580, 603F, 605, 633F, 633N, 639, 640, 667F, 669, 670, 697F, 699, 700, 709F, 711, 712, 735F, 737, 738, 759F; 5.1: T10; 5.3: T7

LA.5.1.6.6	identify "shades of meaning" in related words (e.g., blaring, loud);	**TE:** 19, 25, 33, 47D, 47F, 47O, 59, 111B, 111N, 112I, 115, 120, 139D, 139F, 139O, 139Q, 168–169, 169A–169B, 276, 326I, 329, 341, 355B, 355D, 355F, 355O, 355Q, 355S, 356I, 359, 374, 376, 387D, 387F, 387O, 387Q, 387S, 545, 569, 573B, 577F, 577O, 577S, 633F, 655, 667B, 709H; 5.1: T10; 5.3: T7
LA.5.1.6.7	use meaning of familiar base words and affixes to determine meanings of unfamiliar complex words;	**TE:** 34, 48I, 51, 68, 77D, 77F, 77O, 77Q, 144Q, 144R, 167I, 169B, 169E, 169G-169H, 169M, 185, 192I, 195, 203D, 203E, 203G-203H, 203M, 203O, 203Q, 204I, 207, 216, 227C, 227D, 227F, 227O, 277Q, 257, 263, 289D, 289F, 289O, 289Q, 289S, 314I, 317, 325D, 325F, 325N, 325O, 325Q, 325S, 387H, 389, 448I, 451, 459D, 459F, 459N, 459O, 459Q, 459T, 460I, 481E, 481G-481H, 481M, 482I, 509B, 509E, 509G-509H, 509M, 514Q, 514R, 517, 527, 541D, 541F, 541O, 517Q, 545, 565D, 566I, 577E, 577G–577H, 577M, 578I, 603B, 603C, 603E, 603G-603H, 603M, 604I, 633B, 633D, 633E, 633G-633H, 633M, 658, 710I, 728, 735B, 735E, 735G-735H, 735M, 735O, 735Q, 736I, 743, 759B, 759E, 759G-759H, 759M, 759O; 5.1: T7; 5.2: T6, T7; 5.3: T4, T6; 5.4: T7; 5.5: T6; **TFK FCAT:** Issue 9, 13
LA.5.1.6.8	use knowledge of antonyms, synonyms, homophones, and homographs to determine meanings of words;	**TE:** 19, 47D, 47F, 47H, 47N, 47O, 47Q, 63, 78I, 80, 81, 89D, 89F, 89O, 89Q, 92, 97, 99, 111C, 112I, 115, 119, 120, 125, 139D, 139F, 139O, 139Q, 141, 146, 160, 168, 169Q, 191F, 191N, 194, 203R, 206, 228I, 230, 231, 237, 244, 255D, 255F, 255O, 255R, 262, 278, 292, 303, 313C, 316, 326I, 328, 338, 355F, 355H, 356I, 359, 356I, 358, 373, 374, 387D, 387F, 387O, 387Q, 387S, 392R, 394, 401, 419C, 419D, 419F, 419Q, 422, 428, 433, 447H, 448I, 450, 459B, 459E, 459G-459H, 459M, 467, 481H, 482I, 484, 485, 488, 509I, 509J, 516, 521, 542I, 544, 545, 552, 565B, 565E, 565G-565H, 565M, 566I, 568, 569, 573B, 577C, 577D, 577F, 577O, 577Q, 580, 606, 636, 638R, 640, 641, 644, 646, 648, 667D, 667F, 667O, 667Q, 670, 687F, 697, 712, 717, 738, 747; 5.1: T10; 5.2: T8; 5.5: T8; **TFK FCAT:** Issue 5, 6, 10, 15
LA.5.1.6.9	determine the correct meaning of words with multiple meanings in context;	**TE:** 23, 47F, 77F, 111F, 160, 419O, 460I, 463, 468, 481C, 481D, 481F, 481O, 481Q, 510, 668I, 671, 697D, 697F, 697O, 697Q; 5.4: T8; 5.6: T6; **TFK FCAT:** Issue 1
LA.5.1.6.10	determine meanings of words, pronunciation, parts of speech, etymologies, and alternate word choices by using a dictionary, thesaurus, and digital tools; and	**TE:** 16R, 23, 47D, 47F, 48I, 77D, 77F, 77O, 81, 89D, 89F, 89O, 89Q, 111F, 112I, 115, 139D, 139F, 139O, 139Q, 147, 156, 169D, 169F, 169O, 169Q, 191F, 227F, 255F, 260R, 290I, 293, 302, 313D, 313F, 313O, 313Q, 313S, 326I, 329, 355D, 355F, 355O, 355Q, 387F, 387S, 419F, 419S, 431, 438, 447F, 460I, 463, 468, 481D, 481F, 509F, 517, 541D, 542I, 545, 552, 565D, 565F, 565O, 569, 573, 573B, 577A, 577D, 577F, 577O, 577Q, 577S, 603F, 633B, 633F, 641, 667D, 667F, 671, 697D, 697F, 698I, 709M, 735B, 735F, 759F; 5.1: T10; 5.2: T; 5.3: T5, T7; 5.5: T7, T12
LA.5.1.6.11	use meaning of familiar roots and affixes derived from Greek and Latin to determine meanings of unfamiliar complex words.	**TE:** 96, 111F, 260R, 274, 527, 565D, 565F, 604I, 607, 612, 633C, 633D, 633F, 633O, 633Q, 633S, 638R, 667B, 667E, 667G–667H, 667M, 668I, 697B, 697E, 697G-697H, 697M, 709G-709H, 710I, 713, 728, 735D, 735F, 735O, 735Q, 736I, 739, 743, 759B, 759D, 759F, 759M, 759O, 759Q, 761, 762; 5.5: T10, 5.6: T8, T9
Reading Comprehension LA.5.1.7	**Standard:** The student uses a variety of strategies to comprehend grade level text.	
LA.5.1.7.1	explain the purpose of text features (e.g., format, graphics, diagrams, illustrations, charts, and maps), use prior knowledge to make and confirm predictions, and establish a purpose for reading;	**TE:** 17, 21, 24, 29, 31, 35, 39, 47P, 47Q, 47R, 47S, 47T, 47V, 48, 53, 61, 62, 65, 66, 69, 77P, 77R, 77T, 77V, 83, 85, 89P, 89R, 89T, 89V, 95, 96, 97, 98, 99, 102, 105, 107, 111P, 111R, 111T, 111V, 113, 117, 121, 125, 131, 134, 135-137, 139P, 139Q, 139R, 139S, 139T, 139V, 149, 157, 161, 164, 165, 166,

Key 5.1 = Grade 5, Unit 1

		169P, 169Q, 169R, 169S, 169T, 169V, 171, 175, 177, 179, 181, 183, 185, 186, 191P, 191R, 191T, 191V, 193, 197, 199, 203P, 203R, 203T, 203V, 205, 209, 213, 219, 224, 227P, 227R, 227S, 227T, 227V, 229, 233, 234, 243, 244, 248, 249, 255P, 255R, 255T, 255V, 265, 281, 289P, 289R, 289T, 289V, 295, 305, 313P, 313Q, 313R, 313T, 313V, 319, 321, 325P, 325R, 325T, 325V, 327, 331, 335, 355Q, 355S, 355T, 337, 340, 343, 347, 350, 351, 355P, 355Q, 355R, 355S, 355T, 355V, 361, 367, 375, 381, 387P, 387Q, 387R, 387S, 387T, 387V, 393, 397, 399, 411, 414, 415, 417, 419P, 419R, 419T, 419V, 425, 429, 433, 439, 442-445, 447P, 447R, 447T, 447V, 453, 455, 455B, 459P, 459Q, 459R, 459S, 459T, 459V, 465, 475, 481, 481P, 481R, 481T, 481V, 487, 492, 495, 499, 500, 503, 506, 507, 509P, 509R, 509T, 509V, 512, 519, 533, 541P, 541R, 541T, 541V, 547, 555, 557, 559, 562-563, 565P, 565R, 565T, 565V, 571-572, 573, 575, 577P, 577R, 577T, 577V, 583, 597, 603P, 603R, 603T, 603V, 605, 609, 618, 625, 628-631, 633P, 633Q, 633R, 633S, 633T, 633V, 643, 645, 649, 653, 655, 659, 663, 667P, 667Q, 667R, 667S, 667T, 667V, 673, 684, 688, 689, 697P, 697Q, 697R, 697S, 697T, 697V, 703, 705, 709P, 709R, 709T, 709V, 715, 729, 735P, 735R, 735T, 735V, 741, 747, 748, 751, 752, 759P, 759R, 759T, 759V, 763; 5.1: T13, T15, T17; 5.2: T11, T13, T15; 5.3: T11, T13, T15; 5.4: T12, T14, T16; 5.5: T13, T15, T17; 5.6: T12, T14, T16
LA.5.1.7.2	identify the author's purpose (e.g., to persuade, inform, entertain, explain) and how an author's perspective influences text;	**TE:** 40, 70, 101, 102, 106, 132, 162, 166, 186, 187, 187B, 220, 250, 282, 285, 297, 306, 317A-317B, 318-321, 325Q, 325P, 325R, 325T, 348, 382, 412, 423A–423B, 424–439, 440, 441, 447Q, 447P, 447R, 447T, 454, 472, 476, 477B, 482I, 485A–485B, 486–503, 504, 505, 509Q, 509P, 509R, 509T, 524, 534, 535B, 550, 557, 560, 561B, 581A–581B, 582–597, 598, 599, 599B, 603Q, 603P, 603R, 603T, 611, 616, 621, 626, 627B, 635, 636, 637, 660, 690, 693, 701A-701B, 702-705, 709Q, 709P, 709R, 709T, 730, 752, 761, 763; 5.4: T2, T12, T14; 5.5: T4, T13, T16, T17; 5.6: T3; **TFK FCAT:** Issue 7, 13 **FCAT Test Prep:** 32–179
LA.5.1.7.3	determine the main idea or essential message in grade-level text through inferring, paraphrasing, summarizing, and identifying relevant details;	**TE:** 40, 41, 41B, 62, 71, 85, 93A–93B, 94–105,, 107, 107B, 111Q, 111P, 111R, 111T, 111V, 120, 122, 129, 155, 163, 165, 166, 173A–173B, 174–185, 187, 191Q, 191P, 191R, 191T, 191V, 195A-195B 196–197, 199, 199A, 203Q, 203P, 203R, 203T, 203V, 208-219, 221, 249, 251, 258, 260H, 274, 277, 283, 293A-293B, 294-305, 307, 313Q, 313P, 313T, 313R, 313V, 321A, 325Q, 325S, 325T, 327, 329A, 330, 332, 334, 349, 349B, 352, 383, 390, 413, 413B, 430, 436, 441, 451A-451B, 452-455, 459Q, 459P, 459R, 459T, 459V, 477, 485B, 512, 513, 535, 545A-545B, 546-559, 561, 565Q, 565P, 565R, 565V, 573, 573A, 574, 588, 589, 592, 594, 599, 599B, 607A, 614, 621, 623, 635, 651, 661, 691, 705, 705A, 713A-713B, 714-729, 731, 735Q, 735P, 735R, 735T, 735V, 753, 753B; 5.1: T4, T14, T16, T18; 5.2: T2; 5.3: T2; 5.4: T3; 5.5: T2; 5.6: T4; **TFK FCAT:** Issue 1, 2, 4, 6, 8, 10, 11 **FCAT Test Prep:** 32–64
LA.5.1.7.4	identify cause-and-effect relationships in text;	**TE:** 68, 107B, 115A–115B, 116–131, 133, 139Q, 139P, 139R, 139T, 159, 183, 221B, 223, 244, 257, 269, 303, 307B, 309, 346, 455A, 528, 569A–569B, 570–573, 575, 577Q, 577P, 577R, 577T, 694, 721, 727, 748, 755; 5.1: T5; 5.5: T3, T14, T15, T18; **TFK FCAT:** Issue 5, 9, 12; **FCAT Test Prep:** 97–124

LA.5.1.7.5	identify the text structure an author uses (e.g., comparison/contrast, cause/effect, sequence of events) and explain how it impacts meaning in text;	**TE:** 71B, 81A–81B, 82–85, 85A, 89O, 89P, 89R, 89T, 89V, 107B, 115A-115B, 116-131, 133, 139O, 139P, 139R, 139T, 139V, 163B, 176, 179, 183, 221B, 283B, 307B, 329A-329B, 330-345, 347, 349, 355O, 355P, 355R, 355T, 355V, 383B, 391, 455A, 463A-463B, 464-473, 475, 477, 481O, 481P, 481R, 481T, 481V, 501, 517A, 517B, 518, 521, 523, 526, 527, 528, 530, 532, 535, 537, 569A-569B, 570-573, 577O, 577P, 577R, 577T, 577V, 641A-641B, 642-661, 667O, 667P, 667R, 667T, 667V, 691B, 731B, 739A-739B, 740-753, 759O, 759P, 759R, 759T, 759V, 760; **5.1:** T3, T5, T13, T15, T17-T18; **5.3:** T3; **5.4:** T4, T13, T14, T15, T16, T17; **5.5:** T1, T3; **TFK FCAT:** Issue 3, 14, 15 **FCAT Test Prep:** 125–152
LA.5.1.7.6	identify themes or topics across a variety of fiction and non-fiction selections;	**TE:** 16H, 16-17, 41B, 47R, 48-49, 78-79, 89R, 90-91, 112-113, 129, 143K-143L, 144H, 144-145, 169P, 170-171, 192-193, 204-205, 228-229, 231, 250, 259K-259L, 260H, 260-261, 290-291, 314-315, 326-327, 356-357, 391K-391L, 392H, 392-393, 420-421, 448-449, 460-461, 482-483, 491, 498, 513K-513L, 514H, 514-515, 530, 542-543, 545A-545B, 546-561, 565, 566-567, 578-579, 599B, 604-605, 618, 637K-637L, 638H, 638-639, 650, 658, 668-669, 698-699, 710-711, 736-737, 763K-763L
LA.5.1.7.7	compare and contrast elements in multiple texts (e.g., setting, characters, problems); and	**TE:** 16H, 16I, 41, 45, 47O, 47P, 47R, 47T, 71, 75, 77O, 77P, 77R, 77T, 81A–81B, 82–85, 85A, 87, 89O, 89P, 89R, 89T, 89V, 107, 109, 111O, 111P, 111R, 111T, 130, 133, 136, 137, 139O, 139P, 139R, 139T, 141, 142, 143K, 144H, 144I, 163, 167, 169O, 169P, 169R, 169T, 170J, 187, 189, 191O, 191P, 191R, 191T, 199, 201, 203O, 203P, 204J, 203R, 203T, 221S, 218, 221, 225, 227O, 227P, 227R, 227T, 231, 248, 251, 253, 255O, 255P, 255R, 255T, 259K, 260H, 260I, 283, 287, 289O, 289P, 289R, 289T, 297, 307, 309, 311, 313O, 313P, 313R, 313T, 321, 323, 325O, 325P, 325R, 325T, 329A-329B, 330-347, 349, 355O, 355P, 355R, 355T, 355V, 383B, 349, 353, 355O, 355P, 355R, 355T, 380, 383, 383B, 385, 387O, 387P, 387R, 387T, 389, 391K, 392H, 392I, 402, 413, 417, 419O, 419P, 419R, 419T, 441, 444, 445, 447O, 447P, 447R, 447T, 455, 457, 459O, 459P, 459R, 459T, 464, 477, 478, 479, 481O, 481P, 481R, 481T, 494, 501, 505, 507, 509O, 509P, 509R, 509T, 511, 513, 513K, 514H, 514I, 532, 535, 538, 539, 541O, 541P, 541R, 541T, 561, 563, 565O, 565P, 565R, 565T, 573, 575, 577O, 577P, 577R, 577T, 587, 599, 601, 602, 603O, 603P, 603R, 603T, 627, 631, 633O, 633P, 633R, 633T, 637K, 638H, 638I, 658, 661, 665, 667O, 667P, 667R, 667T, 674, 691, 691B, 695, 697O, 697P, 697R, 697T, 705, 707O, 709P, 709R, 709T, 726, 731, 733, 735O, 735P, 735R, 735T, 753, 757, 759O, 759P, 759R, 759T, 763K; **5.1:** T3, T13, T15, T17-T18; **5.3:** T3, T12, T13, T14, T15, T16 **TFK FCAT:** Issue 3, 14, 15; **FCAT Test Prep:** 125–152
LA.5.1.7.8	use strategies to repair comprehension of grade-appropriate text when self-monitoring indicates confusion, including but not limited to rereading, checking context clues, predicting, note-making, summarizing, using graphic and semantic organizers, questioning, and clarifying by checking other sources.	**TE:** 21, 25, 26, 28, 31, 32, 33, 41, 47P, 47R, 53, 57, 58, 61, 62, 69, 71, 73, 77P, 77R, 83, 84, 85, 89P, 89R, 93A–93B, 94, 96, 101, 104, 105, 107, 110, 111O, 111P, 111R, 111T, 115A–115B, 116, 117, 118, 122, 123, 124, 126, 129, 131, 133, 139P, 139R, 142, 147A–147B, 148, 149, 154, 155, 163, 169M, 169P, 169R, 173A–173B, 174, 175, 176, 178, 184, 186, 187, 191P, 191R, 191T, 195A–195B, 196, 197, 198, 199, 203, 203P, 203R, 207A-207B, 208, 209, 213, 217, 221, 227P, 227R, 231A-231B, 232, 232, 233, 234, 235, 239, 241, 243, 246, 249, 251, 255P, 255R, 255S, 265, 267, 268, 272, 273, 281, 283, 289P, 289R, 289T, 289V, 295, 299, 300, 301, 305, 307, 313O, 313P, 313R, 313V, 319, 321, 321B, 324A, 325O, 325P, 325R, 325S, 325V, 331, 339,

Key 5.1 = Grade 5, Unit 1

340, 341, 343, 344, 345, 347, 349, 351, 355P, 355R, 355V, 361, 370, 371, 376, 378, 379, 381, 383, 387P, 387R, 387T, 387V, 388, 397, 398, 399, 401, 403, 406, 407, 408, 409, 411, 413, 419P, 419R, 425, 427, 428, 430, 433, 437, 439, 441, 447P, 447R, 453, 455, 459P, 459R, 465, 466, 468, 469, 470, 471, 472, 473, 474, 475, 477, 481P, 481R, 487, 491, 492, 495, 496, 503, 505, 505B, 509P, 509R, 517A–517B, 518, 519, 525, 529, 535, 541P, 541R, 547, 550, 553, 558, 561, 565P, 565R, 571, 573, 577P, 577R, 581A–581B, 582, 583, 595, 599, 603P, 603R, 607A–607B, 608, 609, 627, 633P, 633R, 634, 643, 649, 651, 653, 655, 661, 667P, 667R, 671A–671B, 673, 677, 679, 681, 687, 691, 697P, 697R, 703, 705, 709F, 709P, 709R, 709S, 713A–713B, 715, 719, 720, 721, 723, 745, 728, 729, 731, 735P, 735R, 741, 749, 751, 753, 756, 759P, 759R; **5.1:** T14, T16, T18; **5.2:** T11, T12, T13, T14, T16; **5.5:** T13, T14, T16, T17, T18; **5.6:** T12, T13, T15, T16

GRADE 5: LITERARY ANALYSIS	Macmillan/McGraw-Hill **FLORIDA TREASURES**
Fiction **LA.5.2.1**	**Standard:** The student identifies, analyzes, and applies knowledge of the elements of a variety of fiction and literary texts to develop a thoughtful response to a literary selection.	
LA.5.2.1.1	demonstrate knowledge of the characteristics of various genres (e.g., poetry, fiction, short story, dramatic literature) as forms with distinct characteristics and purposes;	**TE:** 16, 20, 31, 40, 42, 49, 52, 56, 62, 63, 72, 79, 82, 91, 94, 108, 113, 116, 118, 132, 134, 148, 152, 159, 164, 171, 174, 188, 189, 196, 205, 208, 217, 218, 232, 333, 245, 252, 261, 264, 279, 284, 291, 294, 297, 308, 315, 318, 325T, 327, 330, 350, 357, 360, 369, 378, 384, 393, 396, 405, 414, 4190, 424, 429, 442, 452, 464, 478, 483, 486, 491, 493, 498, 501, 502, 506, 515, 518, 529, 543, 546, 558, 562, 567, 570, 582, 600, 608, 628, 639, 642, 644, 645, 658, 662, 669, 672, 676, 684, 692, 699, 702, 711, 714, 716, 732, 737, 740, 748, 754, 756; **5.2:** T1
LA.5.2.1.2	locate and analyze the elements of plot structure, including exposition, setting, character development, rising/falling action, problem/resolution, and theme in a variety of fiction;	**TE:** 19A–19B, 20–39, 41, 41B, 470, 47P, 47R, 47T, 51A–51B, 52–69, 71, 770, 77P, 77R, 77T, 119, 122, 124, 127, 128, 132, 133B, 140, 147A–147B, 148–161, 162, 163, 1690, 169P, 169R, 169T, 207A–207B, 208–219, 221, 2270, 227P, 227R, 227T, 231A–231B, 232–249, 251, 251B, 2550, 255P, 255R, 255T, 256, 263A–263B, 264–281, 282, 283, 285, 286, 2890, 289P, 289R, 289T, 289V, 298, 329A–329B, 330–347, 349, 3550, 355P, 355R, 355T, 359A–359B, 360–381, 383, 383B, 385, 3870, 387P, 387R, 387T, 389, 391A, 395A–395B, 396–411, 412, 413, 4190, 419P, 419R, 419T, 426, 427, 431, 434, 439, 441B, 443, 490, 498, 505B, 509T, 510, 511, 517A–517B, 518–533, 535, 5410, 541P, 541R, 541T, 545A–545B, 546–559, 561, 5650, 565P, 565R, 565T, 584, 587, 599B, 607A–607B, 608–625, 626, 627, 6330, 633P, 633R, 633T, 641A, 641B, 642, 645, 646, 647, 648, 653, 656, 657, 658, 659, 660, 661, 661B, 6670, 667P, 667T, 671A–671B, 672–689, 691, 6970, 697P, 697R, 697T, 758, 760; **5.1:** T1, T2; **5.2:** T1, T3, T11, T12, T13, T14, T15, T16; **5.3:** T1, T11, T12, T13, T14, T15, T16; **5.4:** T1; **5.5:** T1, T2, T5; **5.6:** T2, T12, T13, T14, T15, T16, T17; **FCAT Test Prep:** 65–96
LA.5.2.1.3	demonstrate how rhythm and repetition as well as descriptive and figurative language help to communicate meaning in a poem;	**TE:** 79, 108, 1110, 111S, 252, 253, 2550, 255S, 284, 286, 287, 2890, 289S, 478, 479, 4810, 481S, 600-601, 6030, 603S, 632, 7350, 735S, 7590, 759S
LA.5.2.1.4	identify an author's theme, and use details from the text to explain how the author developed that theme;	**TE:** 41B, 129, 130, 274, 277, 346, 349, 349B, 404, 413B, 436, 483, 545A–545B, 546, 549, 553, 556, 559, 599B, 561, 5650, 565P, 565R, 565T, 565V, 587, 599B, 635, 687; **5.5:** T2

LA.5.2.1.5	demonstrate an understanding of a literary selection, and depending on the selection, include evidence from the text, personal experience, and comparison to other text/media;	**TE:** 34, 38, 39, 41, 45, 65, 66, 69, 71, 75, 85, 87, 105, 107, 109, 111P, 130, 131, 133, 137, 151, 160, 161, 163, 167, 171, 185, 187, 189, 199, 201, 205, 217, 219, 221, 225, 234, 237, 239, 243, 245, 246, 248, 249, 251, 251B, 253, 270, 275, 281, 283, 287, 289O, 289P, 289R, 289T, 289V, 305, 307, 311, 313P, 313R, 313T, 321, 325P, 325R, 325T, 329A, 333, 338, 340, 342, 347, 349, 353, 355P, 355R, 355T, 369, 373, 379, 381, 383, 385, 387P, 387R, 387T, 393, 399, 402, 407, 411, 413, 416, 417, 419P, 419R, 447R, 447T, 421, 424, 427, 431, 432, 435, 436, 437, 439, 441, 445, 447, 455, 457, 459P, 459R, 475, 477, 479, 480, 481P, 488, 493, 494, 497, 500, 501, 503, 505, 507, 509P, 509R, 509T, 533, 535, 539, 558, 559, 561, 563, 573, 575, 586, 587, 589, 590, 591, 592, 595, 597, 599, 601, 613 615, 619, 621, 622, 623, 624, 625, 627, 631, 646, 649, 652, 658, 659, 661, 663, 665, 677, 680, 681, 687, 688, 689, 691, 695, 705, 707, 729, 731, 733, 751, 753, 757; 5.2: T12, T14, T16
LA.5.2.1.6	write a book report, review, or critique that identifies the main idea, character(s), setting, sequence of events, conflict, crisis, and resolution;	**TE:** 254, 513K, 528, 559, 566I, 650, 667F
LA.5.2.1.7	identify and explain an author's use of descriptive, idiomatic, and figurative language (e.g., personification, similes, metaphors, symbolism), and examine how it is used to describe people, feelings, and objects;	**TE:** 25, 27, 33, 60, 64, 68, 70, 118, 121, 131, 146, 147, 152, 153, 155, 156, 162, 169F, 169O, 188, 189, 191Q, 191S, 198, 213, 220, 235, 237, 238, 240, 248, 249, 250, 251, 279, 284, 285, 287, 306, 336, 338, 340, 343, 348, 367, 404, 410, 440, 479, 487, 479, 504, 506, 509R, 520, 521, 526, 527, 534, 560, 564, 565B, 584, 587, 598, 600-601, 603Q, 603S, 611, 614, 615, 633A-633B, 652, 678, 685, 716, 730, 732, 733, 747, 754, 755, 756, 757, 759S
LA.5.2.1.8	explain changes in the vocabulary and language patterns of literary texts written across historical periods; and	**TE:** 269, 289T, 405, 431, 478, 545, 565F, 565Q, 638H, 655
LA.5.2.1.9	use interest and recommendations of other to select a balance of age- and ability-appropriate fiction materials to read (e.g., novels, historical fiction, mythology, poetry) to expand the core foundation of knowledge necessary to function as a fully literate member of a shared culture.	**TE:** 47T, 77T, 131, 139T, 169T, 227T, 255T, 228I, 325T, 355T, 356I, 377, 387T, 418T, 447T, 482I, 509T, 513K, 542I, 565T, 566I, 603T, 633T, 637T, 638R, 667T, 697T, 710I; 5.2: T11-T12, T13-1T14, T15-T16, T17-T18; 5.3: T11, T13, T15; 5.6: T12-T13, T14-T15, T16-T17, T18-T19
Non-Fiction LA.5.2.2	**Standard:** The student identifies, analyzes, and applies knowledge of the elements of a variety of non-fiction, informational, and expository texts to demonstrate an understanding of the information presented.	
LA.5.2.2.1	locate, explain, and use information from text features (e.g., table of contents, glossary, index, transition words/phrases, headings, subheadings, charts, graphs, illustrations);	**TE:** 42, 43, 44, 72, 73, 74, 85, 96, 98 99, 102, 105, 107, 135-137, 139P, 139Q, 139S, 143, 144H, 164, 165, 169Q, 169S, 177, 179, 181, 183, 186, 222, 223, 224, 225, 227S, 258, 260H, 289T, 308, 309, 310, 311, 313Q, 313S, 350, 351, 353, 355Q, 355S, 384, 385, 387S, 390, 414, 415, 417, 419Q, 419S, 442, 443, 444, 445, 447Q, 447S, 459, 459A, 507, 509Q, 509S, 512, 522, 533, 536, 537, 538, 539, 562-563, 563, 571, 572, 575, 628, 629, 630, 631, 633Q, 633S, 636, 638H, 664, 665, 692, 694, 695, 704, 726, 740, 748, 762; 5.1: T11, T12; 5.2: T9, T10; 5.3: T9, T10; 5.4: T10, T11; 5.6: T10 **TFK FCAT:** Issue 1, 2, 3, 4, 5, 6, 7, 8, 9, 10, 11, 12, 13, 14, 15; **FCAT Test Prep:** 153–179
LA.5.2.2.2	use information from the text to answer questions related to explicitly stated main ideas or relevant details;	**TE:** 43, 44, 45, 73, 74, 75, 85, 93A–93B, 94–105, 107, 107B, 111O, 111P, 111R, 111T, 111V, 113, 135, 145, 167, 173A–173B, 174–185, 187, 191O, 191P, 191R, 191T, 191V, 195A-195B 196–197, 199, 199A, 203O, 203P, 203R, 203T, 203V, 223, 225, 249, 251, 293A-293B, 294-305, 307, 310, 313O, 313P, 313T, 313R, 313V, 321, 321A, 325A, 325P, 351, 352, 355P, 415, 416, 443, 445, 451A-451B, 452-453, 455, 459O, 459P, 459T, 459R, 459V, 464, 467, 470, 471, 472, 507, 521, 525, 529, 531, 537, 539, 563, 573, 573A, 575, 577A, 629, 630, 663, 664, 693, 397A,

Key 5.1 = Grade 5, Unit 1

LA.5.2.2.3	organize information to show understanding (i.e., representing main ideas within text through charting, mapping, paraphrasing, or summarizing);	**TE:** 16H, 45, 84, 85, 93A,-93B, 95, 98, 99, 103, 104, 105, 107, 144H, 173A-173B, 174-185, 187, 196, 198, 199, 199A, 223, 231A-231B, 233, 236, 238, 240, 245, 247, 251, 260H, 293A-293B, 296, 299, 302, 307, 311, 320, 321, 392H, 455, 463A-463B, 465, 466, 468, 473, 474, 477, 514H, 519, 523, 526, 528, 532, 535, 572, 573, 577A-577B, 599, 603P, 627, 638H, 705, 706, 713A-713B, 715, 728, 731, 739A-739B, 740-751, 753, 753B
LA.5.2.2.4	identify the characteristics of a variety of types of text (e.g., reference, newspapers, practical/functional texts); and	**TE:** 42, 72, 82, 94, 101, 102, 113, 134, 145, 164, 171, 174, 177, 179, 180, 183, 186, 193, 196, 222-225, 229, 232, 244, 248, 308, 318, 325T, 350, 384, 414, 416, 421, 442, 444, 449, 452, 459A, 461, 464, 470, 518, 536, 562, 570, 579, 582, 628, 662, 692, 702, 705B, 706, 709S, 714, 740; 5.1: T13, T15, T17; 5.4: T12, T14, T16; 5.5: T13, T15, T17; 5.6: T11, T13, T15, T17
LA.5.2.2.5	use interest and recommendations of others to select a balance of age and ability appropriate non-fiction materials to read (e.g., biographies and topical areas, such as animals, science, history) to continue building a core foundation of knowledge.	**TE:** 16H, 16I, 16R, 48I, 78I, 85A, 90I, 111T, 112I, 127, 144H, 144I, 144R, 170I, 191T, 192I, 199A, 203T, 204I, 227T, 255T, 260H, 260I, 260R, 289T, 290I, 314I, 325T, 326I, 355T, 392H, 392I, 392R, 420I, 448I, 460I, 513H, 513I, 514R, 578I, 603T, 604I, 668I, 697T, 698I, 701I, 736I, 763H, 763I; 5.1: T13-14, T15-16, T17-T18, T19-T20; 5.2: T17-T18; 5.3: T17-T18; 5.4: T12-T13, T14-15, T16-T17, T18-T19; 5.5: T13-T14, T15-T16, T17-T18, T19-T20; 5.6: T18-T19

GRADE 5: WRITING PROCESS	**Macmillan/McGraw-Hill FLORIDA TREASURES**
Pre-Writing LA.5.3.1 **Standard:** The student will use prewriting strategies to generate ideas and formulate a plan.	
LA.5.3.1.1	generating ideas from multiple sources (e.g., text, brainstorming, graphic organizer, drawing, writer's notebook, group discussion, printed material) based upon teacher-directed topics and personal interests;	**TE:** 16H, 16S, 17, 18H, 18I, 39, 45, 47, 48J, 49, 69, 75, 77, 78J, 79, 83, 88, 87, 90J, 91, 105, 109, 111, 112J, 113, 131, 137, 139, 143A-143B, 143G, 144S, 144H, 144I, 145, 167, 169, 170J, 171, 189, 191, 192J, 193, 203, 204J, 205, 225, 227, 228J, 229, 253, 255, 259A-259B, 259G, 260S, 260H, 260I, 261, 287, 289, 290J, 291, 311, 313, 314J, 315, 325, 325A, 326J, 327, 353, 355, 356J, 357, 385, 387, 391A-391B, 391G, 392S, 392H, 392I, 393, 417, 419, 420J, 421, 445, 447, 448J, 449, 459, 460J, 461, 479, 481, 482J, 483, 507, 509, 513A-513B, 513G, 514S, 514H, 514I, 515, 539, 541, 542J, 543, 563, 565, 566J, 567, 577, 578J, 579, 601, 603, 604J, 605, 631, 633, 637A-637B, 637G, 638S, 638H, 638I, 639, 665, 667, 668J, 669, 695, 697, 698J, 699, 708, 709, 710J, 711, 733, 735, 737, 736J, 757, 759, 763A-763B **FCAT Test Prep:** 181-192, 193-204
LA.5.3.1.2	determining the purpose (e.g., to entertain, to inform, to communicate, to persuade) and intended audience of a writing piece; and	**TE:** 46-47, 76-77, 88-89, 110-111, 138-139, 143A-143B, 144H, 168-169, 190-191, 202-203, 226-227, 254-255, 259A-259B, 260H, 288-289, 312-313, 324-325, 325A, 329H, 354-355, 386-387, 391A-391B, 418-419, 446-447, 447B, 458-459, 480-481, 508-509, 513A-513B, 514H, 540-541, 564-565, 576-577, 602-603, 632-633, 637A-637B, 638H, 666-667, 696-697, 708-709, 709A, 734-735, 758-759, 763A-763B; **FCAT Test Prep:** 181-192, 193-204
LA.5.3.1.3	organizing ideas using strategies and tools (e.g., technology, graphic organizer, KWL chart, log) to make a plan for writing that prioritizes ideas and addresses main idea, logical sequence, and the time needed to complete the task.	**TE:** 46-47, 47A-47B, 77, 77B, 89, 89A-89B, 111, 139, 143B, 143C, 144H, 169, 191, 191B, 203, 203B, 227, 255, 259A-259B, 289, 289B, 313, 313B, 325, 355, 391, 391B, 387, 391B, 392H, 419, 447, 459, 459A, 481, 509, 513A-513B, 513C, 540, 541, 565, 577, 577B, 603, 633, 637A-637B, 638H, 665, 667, 696, 697, 709, 709A, 735 759, 759B, 763A-763B

Drafting LA.5.3.2	Standard: The student will write a draft appropriate to the topic, audience, and purpose.	
LA.5.3.2.1	using a pre-writing plan to focus on the main idea with ample development of supporting details, elaborating on organized information using descriptive language, supporting details, and word choices appropriate to the selected tone and mood;	TE: 46-47, 47A-47B, 76-77, 77A, 88-89, 110-111, 111A, 138, 143B, 143C, 168, 169, 169A, 190, 191, 191A, 203, 226, 227, 227A, 254, 255A, 259C, 288-289, 289A, 313A, 313B, 324, 325A, 354-355, 355A, 386-387, 387A-387B, 391C, 418, 419, 419A, 446-447, 447A, 480, 481, 481A, 500, 509, 509A, 513A, 513C, 513D, 565B, 577A, 577B, 603, 637C, 666-667, 696-697; FCAT Test Prep: 181-192, 193-204
LA.5.3.2.2	organizing information into a logical sequence and combining or deleting sentences to enhance clarity; and	TE: 46-47, 47A, 47B, 77B, 89B, 111B, 138-139, 139A, 143C-143B, 143C-143D, 143F, 191B, 203A-203B, 227A, 254, 255A, 255B, 259B, 288, 289B, 325A-325B, 391A-391B, 391C-391D, 481B, 513A-513B, 513D, 577A-577B, 603A-603B, 637C-637D, 666, 667, 696-697, 697B, 709B, 758, 759B, 759I, 759J, 763A-763B, 763C-763D, 763F
LA.5.3.2.3	creating interesting leads by studying the leads of professional authors and experimenting with various types of leads (e.g., an astonishing fact, a dramatic scene).	TE: 169A, 255B, 391C, 418-419, 419A-419B, 473, 513A-513B, 513C-513D
Revising LA.5.3.3	Standard: The student will revise and refine the draft for clarity and effectiveness.	
LA.5.3.3.1	evaluating the draft for development of ideas and content, logical organization, voice, point of view, word choice, and sentence variation;	TE: 47, 88-89, 110, 111B, 138, 139B, 143D, 143F, 168-169, 169B, 191, 191B, 202, 226, 227, 227B, 254, 255B, 259A-259B, 259C, 259F, 289, 289B, 312, 313A, 313B, 324, 355, 387B, 391A, 391D, 419, 447B, 459A, 480, 481, 481B, 509, 509A-509B, 541, 513A, 513D, 513F, 541B, 602, 603, 603B, 633, 637A, 637D, 637F, 667, 667A, 667B, 697, 697B, 735A, 759, 759A, 763A, 763C, 763D, 763F; FCAT Test Prep: 205-216
LA.5.3.3.2	creating clarity and logic by deleting extraneous or repetitious information and tightening plot or central idea through the use of sequential organization, appropriate transitional phrases, and introductory phrases and clauses that vary rhythm and sentence structure;	TE: 138-139, 139A, 139B, 143D, 143F, 227A, 259F, 289, 289B, 387, 391D, 481B, 513A, 513D, 513E, 541, 602-603, 603A-603B, 637D, 763C, 763D, 763E, 763F, 759B
LA.5.3.3.3	creating precision and interest by expressing ideas vividly through varied language techniques (e.g., foreshadowing, imagery, simile, metaphor, sensory language, connotation, denotation) and modifying word choices using resources and reference materials (e.g., dictionary, thesaurus); and	TE: 169F, 191B, 255B, 259D, 289B, 355A-355B, 391C-391D, 513F, 633A, 637D, 667B
LA.5.3.3.4	applying appropriate tools or strategies to evaluate and refine the draft (e.g., peer review, checklists, rubrics).	TE: 47, 77, 89, 111, 139, 143B, 143D, 143E, 143F, 169, 191, 227, 255, 259B, 259D, 259E, 259F, 289, 313, 325, 355, 387, 391B, 391D, 391E, 391F, 419, 447, 459, 481, 509, 513B, 513D, 513E, 513F, 541, 565, 577, 603, 633, 637B, 637D, 637E, 637F, 667, 697, 709, 735, 759, 763B, 763D, 763E, 763F
Editing for Language Conventions LA.5.3.4	Standard: The student will edit and correct the draft for standard language conventions.	
LA.5.3.4.1	spelling, using spelling rules, orthographic patterns, generalizations, knowledge of root words, prefixes, suffixes, and knowledge of Greek and Latin root words and using a dictionary, thesaurus, or other resources as necessary;	TE: 47B, 47G-47H, 77B, 77G-77H, 89A-89B, 89G-89H, 109B, 111B, 111G-111H, 139B, 139G-139H, 143E, 169B, 169G-169H, 191B, 191G-191H, 192I, 203B, 203G-203H, 203I-203J, 227B, 227F, 227G-227H, 255B, 255G-255H, 259E, 289B, 289G-289H, 313B, 313G-313H, 325B, 325G-325H, 355B, 355G-355H, 387B, 387G-387H, 391D-391E, 419B, 419G-419H, 447B, 447G-447H, 459B, 459G-459H, 481B, 481G-481H, 509B, 509G-509H, 513E, 541B, 541G-541H, 565B, 565G-565H, 577B, 577G-577H, 603B, 603G-603H, 633B, 633G-633H, 637E, 667B, 667G-667H, 697B, 697G-697H, 709B, 706G-709H, 735B, 735G-735H, 759B, 759G-759H; FCAT Test Prep: 217-223, 224-230
LA.5.3.4.2	capitalization, including literary titles, nationalities, ethnicities, languages, religions, geographic names and places;	TE: 47I-47J, 110, 111J, 143E, 169B, 169I-169J, 227B, 255J, 313B, 313J, 355B, 355J, 391E, 471, 513C, 513E, 541B, 541I-541J, 577J, 759J; 5.1: T14 FCAT Test Prep: 217-223, 224-230

Key 5.1 = Grade 5, Unit 1

LA.5.3.4.3	punctuation, including commas in clauses, hyphens, and in cited sources, including quotations for exact words from sources;	**TE:** 47B, 47I–47J, 77B, 77J, 89A-89B, 89I–89J, 111B, 111I–111J, 139B, 139I–139J, 143E, 169B, 191B, 191J, 227B, 227I–227J, 255B, 255I–255J, 259E, 313B, 313J, 325J, 355B, 355J, 387J, 391D, 391E, 481J, 509B, 509J, 513C, 513E, 541B, 565J, 577J, 735J, 759J, 763E FCAT Test Prep: 217-223, 224-230
LA.5.3.4.4	the four basic parts of speech (nouns, verbs, adjectives, adverbs), and subjective, objective, and demonstrative pronouns and singular and plural possessives of nouns; and	**TE:** 77I, 169I-169J, 191B, 191I–191J, 203I–203J, 227B, 227I–227J, 255B, 255I–255J, 259E, 289B, 289I–289J 313B, 313I–313J, 325I–325J, 355B, 355I–355J, 387B, 387I–387J, 391E, 419D, 419I–419J, 447B, 447I–447J, 459I–459J, 477J, 481B, 481I–481J, 509I–509J, 513E, 541B, 541I–541J, 565B, 565I–565J, 577I–577J, 603B, 603I–603J, 633B, 633I–633J, 637E, 652, 667I–667J, 697B, 697I–697J, 726, 735B, 735I–735J, 763E **FCAT Test Prep:** 217-223, 224-230
LA.5.3.4.5	subject/verb and noun/pronoun agreement in simple and compound sentences.	**TE:** 47B, 47I–47J, 77B, 77I–77J, 89A-89B, 89I–89J, 111B, 111I–111J, 139B, 139I–139J, 143E, 289B, 289I–289J, 355B, 355I, 419B, 419I-419J, 459I-459J, 513E, 759B, 759I–759J, 763E FCAT Test Prep: 217-223, 224-230

Publishing **LA.5.3.5**	**Standard:** The student will write a final product for the intended audience	
LA.5.3.5.1	prepare writing using technology in a format appropriate to audience and purpose (e.g., manuscript, multimedia);	**TE:** 47A, 77A, 89A, 111A, 111B, 139A, 143E, 169A, 191A, 191F, 203A, 227A, 255A, 259E, 259I, 259J, 289A, 313A, 325A, 355A, 355B, 387A, 391E, 419A, 447A, 459A, 473, 481A, 509A, 509B, 513E, 541A, 565A, 577A, 603A, 633A, 637E, 637I-637J, 667A, 667B, 697A, 709A, 735A, 759A, 763E, 763I, 763J
LA.5.3.5.2	use elements of spacing and design to enhance the appearance of the document and add graphics where appropriate; and	**TE:** 143E, 169A, 217, 259E, 259I-259J, 289B, 313B, 391E, 447B, 509B, 513E, 513I-513J, 577A, 602, 633B, 637E, 637I-637J, 697A, 727, 763E, 763I-763J
LA.5.3.5.3	share the writing with the intended audience.	**TE:** 47A, 77A, 89A, 111A, 139A, 143E, 169A, 191A, 203A, 227A, 255A, 259E, 289A, 313A, 325A, 355A, 387A, 391E, 419A, 447A, 459A, 481A, 509A, 541A, 565A, 577A, 603A, 633A, 637E, 667A, 697A, 709A, 735A, 759A, 763E

GRADE 5: WRITING APPLICATIONS	**Macmillan/McGraw-Hill** **FLORIDA TREASURES**

Creative **LA.5.4.1**	**Standard:** The student develops and demonstrates creative writing.	
LA.5.4.1.1	write narratives that establish a situation and plot with rising action, conflict, and resolution; and	**TE:** 17, 48J, 75, 203, 227F, 260S, 288-289B, 290J, 326J, 327, 356J, 387F, 391C, 391A-391E, 419I-419J, 420J, 447I-447J, 448J, 458-459, 459I-459J, 481I-481J, 509J, 542J, 578J, 604J, 633F, 638S, 659, 667, 689, 735B; 5.3: T12; 5.6: T13
LA.5.4.1.2	write a variety of expressive forms (e.g., fiction, short story, autobiography, science fiction, haiku) that employ figurative language (e.g., simile, metaphor, onomatopoeia, personification, hyperbole), rhythm, dialogue, characterization, plot, and/or appropriate format.	**TE:** 16S, 46-47, 47A, 47C, 47F, 48J, 49, 77F, 90J, 113, 131, 138-139, 139H, 143A-143G, 143K-143L, 145, 157, 171, 191C, 205, 219, 220, 227F, 243, 245, 250, 252, 255F, 261, 288-289, 289F, 290J, 290, 291, 306, 312-313, 354-355, 355N, 356J, 379, 387F, 392S, 420J, 439, 459F, 460J, 475, 478, 481B, 482J, 483,504, 509F, 514S, 534, 542J, 543, 557, 564-565, 565B, 566J, 577N, 597, 602, 603Q, 603S, 604J, 625, 632-633, 633B, 689, 727; 5.1: T16; 5.5: T14, T16; 5.6: T13

Informative **LA.5.4.2**	**Standard:** The student develops and demonstrates technical writing that provides information related to real-world tasks.	
LA.5.4.2.1	write in a variety of informational/expository forms (e.g., summaries, procedures, instructions, experiments, rubrics, how-to manuals, assembly instructions);	**TE:** 16H, 45, 76-77, 77Q, 79, 89A, 90I, 111M, 129, 143A-143G, 144H, 144I, 169F, 170J, 182, 185, 191F, 192J, 193, 202-203, 203A, 217, 225, 226-227, 227A, 228J, 229, 254-255, 255A, 259A-259G, 259K-259L, 261, 311, 314J, 326J, 353, 355F, 356J, 379, 391K, 392S, 393, 400, 418-419, 419A, 420J, 421, 430,

		439, 446-447, 447A, 449, 460J, 461, 473, 475, 476, 480-481, 481A, 482J, 503, 508, 509, 513A-513G, 514S, 540-541, 541A, 566J, 576-577, 577A, 578J, 602-603, 625, 637A-637G, 666-667, 667A, 668J, 696-697, 698J, 705B, 708-709, 751, 758-759, 763A-763G; 5.3: T14, T16; 5.4: T13, T15, T17; 5.5: T18; 5.6: T17
LA.5.4.2.2	record information (e.g., observations, notes, lists, charts, map labels, legends) related to a topic, including visual aids to organize and record information on charts, data tables, maps and graphs, as appropriate;	TE: 16H, 48I, 48J, 78I, 78J, 89A-89B, 90J, 109B, 112J, 137, 144S, 203A-203B, 204J, 225, 228J, 259K-259L, 260H, 260S, 290I, 290J, 311, 314J, 325A, 326J, 391K, 392H, 392S, 417, 420J, 430, 446-447, 447A-447B, 448J, 460J, 467, 476, 514S, 541S, 551, 577A, 578J, 604J, 631, 668J, 682, 698J, 709A, 709B, 710J, 736J; 5.3: T9; 5.4: T17
LA.5.4.2.3	write informational/expository essays that state a thesis with a narrow focus, contain introductory, body, and concluding paragraphs;	TE: 16S, 76-77, 78J, 90J, 185, 192J, 203A, 204J, 225, 226-227, 259A-259G, 284, 386-387, 392I, 400, 439, 445, 447F, 455, 459A, 481F, 514S, 542J, 573, 576-577, 578J, 603B, 637A-637G, 637K, 698J, 735F, 736J, 758-759, 759A; 5.2: T14
LA.5.4.2.4	write a variety of communications (e.g., friendly letters, thank-you notes, formal letters, messages, invitations) that have a clearly stated purpose and that include the date, proper salutation, body, closing and signature; and	TE: 48J, 91, 110-111, 111A-111B, 111F, 112J, 112-113, 113A, 113B, 143L, 144S, 170J, 190-191, 191A-191B, 204J, 219, 259E, 259L, 260S, 314J, 325F, 356J, 391I, 391L, 419F, 513L, 577F, 626, 637L, 709F, 735F, 763L, 5.1: T14, T18; 5.2: T12, T14, T16
LA.5.4.2.5	write directions to unfamiliar locations using cardinal and ordinal directions, landmarks, and distances, and create an accompanying map.	TE: 192J, 430, 558, 676, 696-697, 697A-697B, 763A-763G; 5.6: T15
Persuasive **LA.5.4.3**	**Standard:** The student develops and demonstrates persuasive writing that is used for the purpose of influencing the reader.	
LA.5.4.3.1	establish and develop a controlling idea and supporting arguments for the validity of the proposed idea with detailed evidence; and	TE: 70, 105, 106, 122, 139F, 168-169, 199, 205, 228J, 249, 259A-259G, 313F, 324-325, 347, 439, 503, 592, 651, 697F, 704; 5.2: T14
LA.5.4.3.2	includes persuasive techniques (e.g., word choice, repetition, emotional appeal, hyperbole).	TE: 70, 77F, 77S, 122, 168-169, 169A-169B, 205, 259A-259G, 324-325, 355F, 651, 697S, 704, 735B
GRADE 5: COMMUNICATION		**Macmillan/McGraw-Hill** **FLORIDA TREASURES**
Penmanship **LA.5.5.1**	**Standard:** The student engages in the writing process and writes to communicate ideas and experiences.	
LA.5.5.1.1	The student will demonstrate fluent and legible cursive writing skills.	TE: 169A, 191A, 203A, 227A, 289A, 419A, 447A, 481A, 509A, 603A, 633A, 673E, 667A, 697A, 709A, 759A
Listening and Speaking **LA.5.5.2**	**Standard:** The student effectively applies listening and speaking strategies.	
LA.5.5.2.1	listen and speak to gain and share information for a variety of purposes, including personal interviews, dramatic and poetic recitations, and formal presentations; and	TE: 16H, 16I, 16, 17, 35, 40, 45, 47A, 47C, 48, 49, 66, 70, 77A, 78, 79, 89A 90, 91, 111A, 111F, 112, 113, 129, 130, 139A, 139F, 143A, 143B, 143D, 143E, 143F, 143K–143L, 144H, 144I, 144, 145, 169A, 169G, 170, 171, 191A, 191G, 192, 193, 203A, 204, 205, 219, 227A, 227G, 228, 229, 255A, 255T, 259A, 259B, 259D, 259E, 259K–259L, 260H, 260I, 260, 261, 289A, 290I, 290J, 290, 291, 297, 313A, 313G, 314I, 314J, 314, 315, 325A, 325V, 326J, 326, 327, 341, 355A, 355F, 355G, 355V, 356J, 356, 357, 387V, 391A, 391E, 391K–391L 392H, 392I, 392, 393, 419A, 419G, 420, 421, 447A, 447G, 448J, 448, 449, 459A, 460, 461, 474, 475, 481A, 481G, 482, 483, 491, 509A-509B, 509D, 509F, 509G, 513A, 513B, 513D, 513E, 513F, 513K–513L, 514H, 514I, 514, 515, 520, 541A, 541S, 542, 543, 565A, 566, 567, 577A, 578, 579, 603A, 604, 605, 633A, 637A, 637B, 637C, 637F, 637E, 637K–637L, 638H, 638I, 638, 639, 667A, 668, 669, 697A, 697G, 698, 699, 709A, 710, 711, 725, 732, 735A, 736, 737, 759A, 763A, 763D, 763E, 763K–763L; 5.3: T16

Key 5.1 = Grade 5, Unit 1

LA.5.5.2.2	make formal oral presentations for a variety of purposes and occasions, demonstrating appropriate language choices, body language, eye contact and the use of gestures, the use of supporting graphics (charts, illustrations, images, props), and available technologies.	**TE:** 16I, 47A, 47T, 66, 68, 77A, 77T, 89A, 89T, 111A, 139A, 139F, 143E, 143K–143L, 144I, 169A, 191A, 203A, 225, 227A, 248, 255A, 259E, 259K–259L, 260I, 261, 268, 289A, 313A, 325A 335, 341, 355A, 387A, 387R, 391E, 391K–391L 392I, 419A, 447A, 459A, 474, 481A, 509A, 513E, 513K–513L, 514I, 525, 530, 531, 541A, 559, 565A, 577A, 595, 603A, 633A, 637, 637E, 637K–637L, 638I, 667A, 695, 697A, 704, 709A, 735A, 744, 759A, 763E, 763K–763L; 5.3: T16

GRADE 5: INFORMATION AND MEDIA LITERACY	**Macmillan/McGraw-Hill** **FLORIDA TREASURES**

Informational Text **LA.5.6.1**	**Standard:** The student comprehends the wide array of informational text that is part of our day to day experiences.

LA.5.6.1.1	The student will read and interpret informational text and organize the information (e.g., use outlines, timelines, and graphic organizers) from multiple sources for a variety of purposes (e.g., multi-step directions, problem solving, performing a task, supporting opinions, predictions, and conclusions).	**TE:** 16H, 89A-89B, 122, 137, 143I-143J, 143K-143L, 144H, 144I, 203A-203B, 225, 227P, 259K-259L, 260H, 311, 325A-325B, 326J, 356J, 391K-391L, 392H, 392S, 438, 455B, 459A-459B, 467, 474, 481F, 513A-513G, 513K, 514H, 530, 577A-577B, 637K, 638, 638H, 695, 697P, 705B, 709A-709B, 763K; 5.2: T10; 5.4: T11

Research Process **LA.5.6.2**	**Standard:** The student uses a systematic process for the collection, processing, and presentation of information.

LA.5.6.2.1	select a topic for inquiry, formulate a search plan, and apply evaluative criteria (e.g., usefulness, validity, currentness, objectivity) to select and use appropriate resources;	**TE:** 16H, 16I, 45, 62, 66, 68, 85B, 89A-89B, 89S, 137, 144H, 144I, 167, 180, 199B, 203A-203B, 203S, 211, 217, 225, 259K-259L, 260H, 260I, 290J, 311, 314J, 325A-325B, 326I, 333, 335, 341, 356J, 379, 387B, 392H, 392I, 402, 417, 455, 459A-459B, 513B, 514H, 514I, 530, 541F, 566J, 590, 592, 618, 638H, 638I, 704, 709A-709B, 762; 5.3: T14; 5.4: T15; 5.5: T18
LA.5.6.2.2	read and record information systematically, evaluating the validity and reliability of information in text by examining several sources of information;	**TE:** 16H, 16S, 89A-89B, 109B, 127, 144H, 183, 203A-203B, 203Q, 203S, 260H, 260I, 297, 321B, 325A-325B, 325H, 387B, 392H, 417, 419B, 445, 459A-459B, 507, 513B, 514H, 530, 541Q, 577B, 631, 638H, 697, 704, 709A-709B
LA.5.6.2.3	write an informational report that includes a focused topic, appropriate facts, relevant details, a logical sequence, and a concluding statement; and	**TE:** 62, 68, 78J, 170J, 225, 259K-259L, 268, 270, 311 314J, 335, 391K-391L, 445, 513A-513G, 530, 539, 637B, 637K, 709A, 763K; 5.3: T14; 5.5: T18
LA.5.6.2.4	record basic bibliographic data and present quotes using ethical practices (e.g., avoids plagiarism).	**TE:** 109B, 143I-143J, 143K, 217, 259K-259L, 260H, 321B, 325B, 387B, 391K, 513A-513B, 513C, 637K, 709A

Media Literacy **LA.5.6.3**	**Standard:** The student develops and demonstrates an understanding of media literacy as a life skill that is integral to informed decision making.

LA.5.6.3.1	examine how ideas are presented in a variety of print and nonprint media and recognize differences between logical reasoning and propaganda; and	**TE:** 16I, 38, 59, 66, 89S, 129, 144I, 157, 244, 260I, 302, 376, 392I, 417, 469, 514I, 522, 638I, 651, 705, 705B, 709S
LA.5.6.3.2	use a variety of reliable media sources to gather information effectively and to transmit information to specific audiences.	**TE:** 16H, 16I, 59, 68, 75, 77Q, 89S, 130, 137, 143K, 144H, 144I, 167, 203A, 203Q, 203S, 227Q, 244, 259K-259L, 260H, 260I, 314J, 325B, 326I, 353, 356J, 392H, 392I, 419B, 439, 489, 514H, 514I, 530, 541F, 553, 565Q, 565S, 623, 638H, 638I, 763C, 763I-763J, 763K

Technology **LA.5.6.4**	**Standard:** The student develops the essential technology skills for using and understanding conventional and current tools, materials and processes.

LA.5.6.4.1	select and use appropriate available technologies to enhance communication and achieve a purpose (e.g., video, presentations); and	**TE:** 72, 77Q, 89S, 129, 130, 143I-143J, 143K-143L, 169B, 199B, 203Q, 203S, 227B, 259I-259J, 259K-259L, 289B, 313B, 353, 391I-391J, 391K-391L, 402, 419B, 447B, 464, 481B, 509B, 513I-513J, 513K-513L, 530, 565B, 565Q, 565S, 623, 624, 631, 637I-637J, 637K-637L, 667B, 697B, 763C, 763I-763J, 763K-763L
LA.5.6.4.2	determine and use the appropriate digital tools (e.g., word processing, multimedia authoring, web tools, graphic organizers) for publishing and presenting a topic.	**TE:** 47B, 77B, 85B,129, 143K-143L, 144I, 169B, 203A, 259C, 259I-259J, 259K-259L, 260I, 289B, 313B, 355B, 353, 387B, 391K-391L, 447B, 513K-513L, 530, 541B, 631, 633B, 637K-637L, 638H, 667B, 697B, 763E, 763K-763L

Science
Sunshine State Standards
Grade 5

Each Grade Level Expectation has been assigned a unique identification code. The numbering system used builds upon the already existing numbering system for the strands, standards, and benchmarks that make up the Sunshine State Standards.

SC.	A.	1.	1.	1.	5.	1
Science	Strand	Standard	Level 1: PreK–2 2: 3–5	Benchmark	Grade	Grade Level Expectation Number (GLE)

KEY	TE = Teacher's Edition	LR = Leveled Readers	TFK FCAT = Time for Kids FCAT Edition	FCAT Test Prep = FCAT Test Prep and Practice

STRAND A: THE NATURE OF MATTER		Macmillan/McGraw-Hill FLORIDA TREASURES
Standard 1: The student understands that all matter has observable, measurable properties.		
Benchmark SC.A.1.2.1	The student determines that the properties of materials (e.g., density and volume) can be compared and measured (e.g., using rulers, balances, and thermometers).	TE: 42-45
GLE SC.A.1.2.1.5.1	uses metric tools to determine the density and volume of materials	
Benchmark SC.A.1.2.4	The student knows that different materials are made by physically combining substances and that different objects can be made by combining different materials.	
GLE SC.A.1.2.4.5.1	knows that different materials can be physically combined to produce different substances.	TFK FCAT: Issue 15

STRAND B: ENERGY		Macmillan/McGraw-Hill FLORIDA TREASURES
Standard 1: The student recognizes that energy may be changed in form with varying efficiency		
Benchmark SC.B.1.2.1	The student knows how to trace the flow of energy in a system (e.g., as in an ecosystem).	
GLE SC.B.1.2.1.5.1	knows how to trace the flow of energy in a system (for example, electricity in a circuit to produce heat, light, sound, or magnetic fields).	LR: 5.3 Week 3: *How We Use Energy*
Benchmark SC.B.1.2.2	The student recognizes various forms of energy (e.g., heat, light, and electricity).	
GLE SC.B.1.2.2.5.1	knows that energy can be described as stored energy (potential) or energy of motion (kinetic).	LR: 5.3 Week 3: *How We Use Energy*
Standard 2: The student understands the interaction of matter and energy.		
Benchmark SC.B.2.2.3	The student knows that the limited supply of usable energy sources (e.g., fuels such as coal or oil) places great significance on the development of renewable energy sources	
GLE SC.B.2.2.3.5.1	knows that the limited supply of usable energy sources (for example, fuels such as coal or oil) places great significance on the development of renewable energy sources.	TE: 318-321

STRAND C: FORCE AND MOTION		Macmillan/McGraw-Hill FLORIDA TREASURES
Standard 2: The student understands that the types of force that act on an object and the effect of that force can be described, measured, and predicted.		
Benchmark SC.C.2.2.2	The student knows that an object may move in a straight line at a constant speed, speed up, slow down, or change direction dependent on net force acting on the object.	

Key 5.1 = Grade 5, Unit 1

GLE SC.C.2.2.2.5.1	knows that objects do not change their motion unless acted upon by an outside force.	**LR:** 5.1 Week 3: *How Airplanes Fly: Forces and Motion at Work*
GLE SC.C.2.2.2.5.2	understands how friction affects an object in motion.	**LR:** 5.1 Week 3: *How Airplanes Fly: Forces and Motion at Work*
Benchmark SC.C.2.2.4	The student knows that the motion of an object is determined by the overall effect of all of the forces acting on the object.	
GLE SC.C.2.2.4.5.1	knows that motion in space is different from motion on Earth due to changes in gravitational force and friction.	**TE:** 94-107, 379; **LR:** 5.1 Week 3: *How Airplanes Fly: Forces and Motion at Work*
GLE SC.C.2.2.4.5.2	understands how inertia, gravity, friction, mass, and force affect motion.	**TE:** 94-107, 379; **LR:** 5.1 Week 3: *How Airplanes Fly: Forces and Motion at Work;* **TFK FCAT:** Issue 1

STRAND D: PROCESSES THAT SHAPE THE EARTH | Macmillan/McGraw-Hill FLORIDA TREASURES

Standard 1: The student recognizes that processes in the lithosphere, atmosphere, hydrosphere, and biosphere interact to shape the Earth.

Benchmark SC.D.1.2.1	The student knows that larger rocks can be broken down into smaller rocks, which in turn can be broken down to combine with organic material to form soil.	
GLE SC.D.1.2.1.5.1	knows that rocks are constantly being formed and worn away.	**TE:** 192J, 350-353; 5.6 Week 2: *A Visit to Grand Canyon National Park*
Benchmark SC.D.1.2.4	The student knows that the surface of the Earth is in a continuous state of change as waves, weather, and shifts of the land constantly change and produce many new features.	
GLE SC.D.1.2.4.5.1	understands how eroded materials are transported and deposited over time in new areas to form new features (for example, deltas, beaches, dunes).	**TE:** 350-353, 692-695; **LR:** 5.3 Week 4: *Our Changing Earth,* 5.6 Week 2: *A Visit to Grand Canyon National Park*
GLE SC.D.1.2.4.5.2	understands that geological features result from the movement of the crust of the Earth (for example, mountains, volcanic islands).	**TE:** 350-353, 692-695; **LR:** 5.3 Week 4: *Our Changing Earth,* 5.6 Week 2: *A Visit to Grand Canyon National Park*
Benchmark SC.D.1.2.5	The student knows that some changes in the Earth's surface are due to slow processes and some changes are due to rapid processes.	
GLE SC.D.1.2.5.5.1	understands how the surface of the Earth is shaped by both slow processes (for example, weathering, erosion, deposition) and rapid, cataclysmic events (for example, earthquakes, tsunamis, volcanoes).	**TE:** 460J, 464-477; **LR:** 5.4 Week 4: *Earthquakes,* 5.6 Week 2: *A Visit to Grand Canyon National Park*

Standard 2: The student understands the need for protection of the natural systems on Earth.

Benchmark SC.D.2.2.1	The student knows that reusing, recycling, and reducing the use of natural resources improve and protect the quality of life.	
GLE SC.D.2.2.1.5.1	extends and refines knowledge of ways people can reuse, recycle, and reduce the use of resources to improve and protect the quality of life.	**TFK FCAT:** Issue 6, 15

STRAND E: EARTH AND SPACE | Macmillan/McGraw-Hill FLORIDA TREASURES

Standard 1: The student understands the interaction and organization in the Solar System and the universe and how this affects life on Earth.

Benchmark SC.E.1.2.1	The student knows that the tilt of the Earth on its own axis as it rotates and revolves around the Sun causes changes in season, length of day, and energy available.	
GLE SC.E.1.2.1.5.2	knows that the angle that the rays of the Sun strike the surface of the Earth determines the amount of energy received and thus the season of the year.	**TE:** 222-225
Benchmark SC.E.1.2.2	The student knows that the combination of the Earth's movement and the Moon's own orbit around the Earth results in the appearance of cyclical phases of the Moon.	
GLE SC.E.1.2.2.5.1	knows the relative positions of the Moon, Earth, and Sun during each of the phases of the Moon.	**TFK FCAT:** Issue 6

STRAND F: PROCESSES OF LIFE | Macmillan/McGraw-Hill FLORIDA TREASURES

Standard 1: The student describes patterns of structure and function in living things.

Benchmark SC.F.1.2.1	The student knows that the human body is made of systems with structures and functions that are related.	
GLE SC.F.1.2.1.5.1	understands how body systems interact (for example, how bones and muscles work together for movement).	**TFK FCAT:** Issue 1

Standard 2: The student understands the process and importance of genetic diversity.

Benchmark SC.F.2.2.1	The student knows that many characteristics of an organism are inherited from the parents of the organism, but that other characteristics are learned from an individual's interactions with the environment.	

| GLE SC.F.2.2.1.5.1 | knows that many characteristics of an organism are inherited from the genetic ancestors of the organism (for example, eye color, flower color). | TFK FCAT: Issue 11 |
| GLE SC.F.2.2.1.5.2 | knows that some characteristics result from the organism's interactions with the environment (for example, flamingos eat a certain crustacean that causes their feathers to be pink). | TFK FCAT: Issue 11 |

STRAND G: HOW LIVING THINGS INTERACT WITH THEIR ENVIRONMENT		Macmillan/McGraw-Hill FLORIDA TREASURES
Standard 1: The student understands the competitive, interdependent, cyclic nature of living things in the environment.		
Benchmark SC.G.1.2.1	The student knows ways that plants, animals, and protists interact.	TE: 604J
GLE SC.G.1.2.1.5.1	understands the various roles of single-celled organisms in the environment.	TE: 536-539; LR: 5.5 Week 1: *Science in the Snow*
GLE SC.G.1.2.1.5.2	knows ways in which protists interact with plants and animals in the environment.	TE: 536-539; LR: 5.5 Week 1: *Science in the Snow* TFK FCAT: Issue 1
Benchmark SC.G.1.2.2	The student knows that living things compete in a climatic region with other living things and that structural adaptations make them fit for an environment.	TE: 78J, 112J, 314S, 420J
GLE SC.G.1.2.2.5.1	understands how changes in the environment affect organisms (for example, some organisms move in, others move out; some organisms survive and reproduce, others die).	TE: 174-187, 420J; LR: 5.2 Week 2: *Alien: The Brown Tree Snake Story* TFK FCAT: Issue 6, 14
Benchmark SC.G.1.2.3	The student knows that green plants use carbon dioxide, water, and sunlight energy to turn minerals and nutrients into food for growth, maintenance, and reproduction.	TE: 542J
GLE SC.G.1.2.3.5.1	knows that green plants use carbon dioxide, water, and sunlight energy to turn minerals and nutrients into food for growth, maintenance, and reproduction.	LR: 5.1 Week 3: *Amazing Plants*
Standard 2: The student understands the consequences of using limited natural resources.		
Benchmark SC.G.2.2.1	The student knows that all living things must compete for Earth's limited resources; organisms best adapted to compete for the available resources will be successful and pass their adaptations (traits) to their offspring.	
GLE SC.G.2.2.1.5.1	knows that adaptations to their environment may increase the survival of a species.	TE: 134-137, 174-187, 182, 442-445, 628-631; LR: 5.4 Week 2: *Survival Instincts: Insects* TFK FCAT: Issue 4
Benchmark SC.G.2.2.3	The student understands that changes in the habitat of an organism may be beneficial or harmful.	
GLE SC.G.2.2.3.5.1	understands patterns of interdependency in ecological systems.	TE: 170J, 228J, 326J, 668J
GLE SC.G.2.2.3.5.2	understands that what benefits one organism may be harmful to other organisms.	
GLE SC.G.2.2.3.5.3	understands that changes in an ecological system usually affect the whole system.	TE: 668J

STRAND H: THE NATURE OF SCIENCE		Macmillan/McGraw-Hill FLORIDA TREASURES
Standard 1: The student uses the scientific processes and habits of mind to solve problems.		
Benchmark SC.H.1.2.2	The student knows that a successful method to explore the natural world is to observe and record, and then analyze and communicate the results.	TE: 482J, 542J, 566J
GLE SC.H.1.2.2.5.1	understands that scientists use different kinds of investigations (for example, observations of events in nature, controlled experiments) depending on the questions they are trying to answer.	TE: 62, 72-75, 570-573, 578J, 710J, 736J TFK FCAT: Issue 4
GLE SC.H.1.2.2.5.2	understands the importance of accuracy in conducting measurements, and uses estimation when exact measurements are not possible.	TE: 72-75, 100 TFK FCAT: Issue 4
Benchmark SC.H.1.2.4	The student knows that to compare and contrast observations and results is an essential skill in science.	
GLE SC.H.1.2.4.5.1	uses strategies to review, compare and contrast, and critique scientific investigations.	TE: 467
GLE SC.H.1.2.4.5.2	knows that an experiment must be repeated many times and yield consistent results before the results are accepted.	TE: 448J
Benchmark SC.H.1.2.5	The student knows that a model of something is different from the real thing, but can be used to learn something about the real thing.	
GLE SC.H.1.2.5.5.1	uses sketches and diagrams to propose scientific solutions to problems.	TE: 356J, 698J

Key 5.1 = Grade 5, Unit 1

Standard 3: The student understands that science, technology, and society are interwoven and interdependent.

Benchmark SC.H.3.2.1	The student understands that people, alone or in groups, invent new tools to solve problems and do work that affects aspects of life outside of science.	
GLE SC.H.3.2.1.5.1	knows areas in which technology has improved human lives (for example, transportation, communication, nutrition, sanitation, health care, entertainment).	**TE:** 48J, 335, 384-385 **TFK FCAT:** Issue 12 **LR:** 5.6 Week 4: *The Sky's the Limit*
GLE SC.H.3.2.1.5.2	knows that new inventions often lead to other new inventions and ways of doing things.	**TE:** 384-385, 392S, 714-731 **TFK FCAT:** Issue 12
Benchmark SC.H.3.2.2	The student knows that data are collected and interpreted in order to explain an event or concept.	**TE:** 260S, 578J
Benchmark SC.H.3.2.3	The student knows that before a group of people build something or try something new, they should determine how it may affect other people.	
GLE SC.H.3.2.3.5.1	understands how a solution to one scientific problem can create another problem.	**TFK FCAT:** Issue 6
Benchmark SC.H.3.2.4	The student knows that, through the use of science processes and knowledge, people can solve problems, make decisions, and form new ideas.	
GLE SC.H.3.2.4.5.1	extends and refines knowledge of ways that, through the use of science processes and knowledge, people can solve problems, make decisions, and form new ideas.	**TE:** 16I, 740-753; **LR:** 5.6 Week 5: *Searching for Cures*

Social Studies
Sunshine State Standards
Grade 5

Each Grade Level Expectation has been assigned a unique identification code. The numbering system used builds upon the already existing numbering system for the strands, standards, and benchmarks that make up the Sunshine State Standards.

SS.	A.	1.	1.	1.	5.	1
Social Studies	Strand	Standard	Level 1: PreK–2 2: 3–5	Benchmark	Grade	Grade Level Expectation Number (GLE)

KEY	TE = Teacher's Edition	LR = Leveled Readers	TFK FCAT = Time for Kids FCAT Edition	FCAT Test Prep = FCAT Test Prep and Practice

STRAND A: TIME, CONTINUITY, AND CHANGE (HISTORY)		Macmillan/McGraw-Hill FLORIDA TREASURES
Standard 1: The student understands historical chronology and the historical perspective.		
Benchmark SS.A.1.2.1	The student understands how individuals, ideas, decisions, and events can influence history.	
GLE SS.A.1.2.1.5.1	extends and refines understanding of the effects of individuals, ideas, and decisions on historical events (for example, in the United States).	**TE:** 16S, 192J, 196-199, 311, 228J, 578J; **LR:** 5.2 Week 3: *The Erie Canal: Low Bridge, Everybody Down!* **TFK FCAT:** Issue 9
Standard 4: The student understands United States history to 1880.		
GLE SS.A.4.2.1.5.2	understands selected geographic, economic, political, and cultural factors that characterized early exploration of the Americas (for example, impact on Native Americans, war between colonial powers, the institution of slavery).	**TE:** 228J
GLE SS.A.4.2.2.5.1	knows significant events in the colonization of North America, including but not limited to the Jamestown and Plymouth settlements, and the formation of the thirteen original colonies.	**TE:** 623 **TFK FCAT:** Issue 9
GLE SS.A.4.2.2.5.2	understands selected aspects of everyday life in Colonial America (for example, impact of religions, types of work, use of land, leisure activities, relations with Native Americans, slavery).	**TE:** 270
Benchmark SS.A.4.2.3	The student knows significant social and political events that led to and characterized the American Revolution.	
GLE SS.A.4.2.3.5.1	understands reasons Americans and those who led them went to war to win independence from England.	**TE:** 260S, 264-283; **LR:** 5. 3 Week 1: *The Shot Heard Around the World*
GLE SS.A.4.2.3.5.2	knows significant events between 1756 and 1776 that led to the outbreak of the American Revolution (for example, the French and Indian War, the Stamp Act, the Boston Tea Party).	**TE:** 264-283; **LR:** 5. 3 Week 1: *The Shot Heard Around the World*
GLE SS.A.4.2.3.5.3	knows selected aspects of the major military campaigns of the Revolutionary War .	**TE:** 264-283; **LR:** 5. 3 Week 1: *The Shot Heard Around the World*
GLE SS.A.4.2.3.5.4	knows reasons why the colonies were able to defeat the British.	**TE:** 264-283; **LR:** 5. 3 Week 1: *The Shot Heard Around the World*
Benchmark SS.A.4.2.5	The student understands geographic, economic, and technological features of the growth and change that occurred in America from 1801 to 1861.	**LR:** 5.2 Week 3: *The Erie Canal: Low Bridge, Everybody Down!*
GLE SS.A.4.2.6.5.1	understands selected economic and philosophical differences between the North and the South prior to the Civil War, including but not limited to the institution of slavery.	**LR:** 5.4 Week 3: *Political Debates: Lincoln vs. Douglas;* **TFK FCAT:** Issue 7
GLE SS.A.4.2.6.5.3	knows causes, selected key events, and effects of the Civil War (for example, major battles, the Emancipation Proclamation, General Lee's surrender at Appomattox Courthouse).	**TE:** 578J
GLE SS.A.4.2.6.5.4	understands selected aspects of Reconstruction policies and ways they influenced the South after the Civil War.	**LR:** 5.3 Week 2: *The Story of African American Voting Rights*
Standard 5: The student understands the United States history from 1880 to the present day.		

Key 5.1 = Grade 5, Unit 1

GLE SS.A.5.2.6.5.2	understands selected causes, key events, people, and effects of World War II (for example, major battles such as the D-Day invasion, the dropping of the atomic bombs on Japan, reasons for the Allied victory, the Holocaust).	**TE:** 600-601; **LR:** 5.5 Week 4: *On the Homefront: Life During World War II*
GLE SS.A.5.2.7.5.1	knows selected economic, political, and social transformations which have taken place in the United States since World War II (for example, Civil Rights movement, role of women, Hispanic immigration, impact of new technologies, exploration of space).	**TE:** 164-167, 414-417; **LR:** 5.3 Week 2: *The Story of African American Voting Rights*

STRAND B: PEOPLE, PLACES, AND ENVIRONMENTS (GEOGRAPHY)		**Macmillan/McGraw-Hill FLORIDA TREASURES**
Standard 1: The student understands the world in spatial terms.		
Benchmark SS.B.1.2.1	The students uses maps, globes, charts, graphs, and other geographic tools including map keys and symbols to gather and interpret data and to draw conclusions about physical patterns.	**TE:** 127 , 514S
GLE SS.B.1.2.1.5.1	extends and refines use of maps, globes, charts, graphs, and other geographic tools including map keys and symbols to gather and interpret data and to draw conclusions about physical patterns (for example, in the United States).	**TE:** 127 , 514S
Standard 2: The student understands the interactions of people and the physical environment.		
Benchmark SS.B.2.2.2	The student understands how the physical environment supports and constrains human activities.	**TE:** 48J, 232-251, 252-253, 326J, 460J, 566J, 604J
GLE SS.B.2.2.2.5.1	understands ways the physical environment supports and constrains human activities in the United States.	**TE:** 232-251, 252-253, 460J

STRAND C: GOVERNMENT AND THE CITIZEN (CIVICS AND GOVERNMENT)		**Macmillan/McGraw-Hill FLORIDA TREASURES**
Standard 1: The student understands the structure, functions, and purposes of government and how the principles and values of American democracy are reflected in American constitutional government.		
GLE SS.C.1.2.2.5.1	knows the names of his or her representatives at the national level (for example, president, members of Congress).	**TE:** 448J
Standard 2: The student understands the role of the citizen in American democracy.		
Benchmark SS.C.2.2.1	The student understands the importance of participation through community service, civic improvement, and political activities.	
GLE SS.C.2.2.2.5.1	extends and refines understanding of ways personal and civic responsibility are important.	**TE:** 90J, 662-665, 702-705; **LR:** 5.6 Week 3: *Everybody's a Star*
GLE SS.C.2.2.3.5.1	knows that a citizen is a legally recognized member of the United States who has certain rights and privileges and certain responsibilities (for example, privileges such as the right to vote and hold public office and responsibilities such as respecting the law, voting, paying taxes, serving on juries).	**TE:** 290J, 452-455; **LR:** 5.4 Week 3: *Political Debates: Lincoln vs. Douglas*
GLE SS.C.2.2.4.5.1	knows examples of the extension of the privileges and responsibilities of citizenship.	**TE:** 290J
Benchmark SS.C.2.2.5	The student knows what constitutes personal, political, and economic rights and why they are important and knows examples of contemporary issues regarding rights.	**TE:** 392S; **LR:** 5.3 Week 2: *The Story of African American Voting Rights*
GLE SS.C.2.2.5.5.1	knows what constitutes personal, political, and economic rights and why they are important (for example, right to vote, assemble, lobby, own property and business).	**TE:** 294-307, 308-311; **LR:** 5.3 Week 2: *The Story of African American Voting Rights*
GLE SS.C.2.2.5.2	knows examples of contemporary issues regarding rights (for example, freedom from discrimination in housing, employment).	**TE:** 294-307, 308-311; **LR:** 5.3 Week 2: *The Story of African American Voting Rights*

STRAND D: PRODUCTION, DISTRIBUTION, AND CONSUMPTION (ECONOMICS)		
Standard 1: The student understands how scarcity requires individuals and institutions to make choices about how to use resources.		
Benchmark SS.D.1.2.1	The student understands that all decisions involve opportunity costs and that making effective decisions involves considering the costs and the benefits associated with alternative choices.	**TE:** 460J
GLE SS.D.1.2.1.5.1	knows examples from United States history that demonstrate an understanding that all decisions involve opportunity costs and that making effective decisions involves considering the costs and the benefits associated with alternative choices.	**TFK FCAT:** Issue 8
Benchmark SS.D.1.2.3	The student understands the basic concept of credit.	
GLE SS.D.1.2.3.5.1	understands the basic concept of credit.	**TFK FCAT:** Issue 13
Benchmark SS.D.2.2.1	The student understands economic specialization and how specialization generally affects costs, amount of goods and services produced, and interdependence.	
GLE SS.D.2.2.1.5.1	understands economic specialization and how specialization generally affects costs, amount of goods and services produced, and interdependence.	**TFK FCAT:** Issue 8

Mathematics
Sunshine State Standards
Grade 5

Each Grade Level Expectation has been assigned a unique identification code. The numbering system used builds upon the already existing numbering system for the strands, standards, and benchmarks that make up the Sunshine State Standards.

MA.	A.	1.	1.	1.	5.	1
Math	Strand	Standard	Level 1: PreK–2 2: 3–5	Benchmark	Grade	Grade Level Expectation Number (GLE)

KEY	TE = Teacher's Edition	LR = Leveled Readers	TFK FCAT = Time for Kids FCAT Edition	FCAT Test Prep = FCAT Test Prep and Practice

STRAND A: NUMBER SENSE, CONCEPTS, AND OPERATIONS		Macmillan/McGraw-Hill FLORIDA TREASURES
Standard 3: The student understands the effects of operations on numbers and the relationship among these operations, selects appropriate operations, and computes for problem solving.		
GLE MA.A.3.2.2.5.1	uses problem-solving strategies to determine the operation(s) needed to solve one- and two-step problems involving addition, subtraction, multiplication, and division of whole numbers, and addition, subtraction, and multiplication of decimals and fractions.	TE: 150
GLE MA.A.3.2.3.5.1	solves real-world problems involving addition, subtraction, multiplication, and division of whole numbers, and addition, subtraction, and multiplication of decimals, fractions, and mixed numbers using an appropriate method (for example, mental math, pencil and paper, calculator).	TE: 100, 150, 303, 308, 310, 311, 414, 415, 417, 438

STRAND B: MEASUREMENT		Macmillan/McGraw-Hill FLORIDA TREASURES
Standard 1: The student measures quantities in the real world and uses the measures to solve problems.		
GLE MA.B.1.2.1.5.3	knows varied units of time that include centuries and seconds.	TE: 308, 310, 311, 414, 415, 417, 512, 513
GLE MA.B.1.2.2.5.3	uses schedules, calendars, and elapsed time to solve real-world problems.	TE: 533
Standard 2: The student compares, contrasts, and converts within systems of measurement (both standard/nonstandard and metric/customary).		

STRAND E: DATA ANALYSIS AND PROBABILITY		Macmillan/McGraw-Hill FLORIDA TREASURES
Standard 1: The student understands and uses the tools of data analysis for managing information.		
GLE MA.E.1.2.1.5.1	knows which types of graphs are appropriate for different kinds of data (for example, bar graphs, line, or circle graphs).	TE: 628-631
GLE MA.E.1.2.1.5.3	chooses reasonable titles, labels, scales and intervals for organizing data on graphs.	TE: 682
GLE MA.E.1.2.1.5.4	generates questions, collects responses, and displays data on a graph.	TE: 682
GLE MA.E.1.2.1.5.6	analyzes and explains orally or in writing the implications of graphed data.	TE: 628-631
GLE MA.E.1.2.3.5.3	uses computer applications to construct labeled graphs.	TE: 513I, 513J

Key 5.1 = Grade 5, Unit 1